Anglo-Saxon Women
and the Church
SHARING A COMMON FATE

This study of literature by clerics who were writing to, for, or about Anglo-Saxon women in the eighth and early ninth centuries suggests that the position of women had already declined sharply before the Conquest – a claim at variance with the traditional scholarly view, which is that the undermining of women's status took place in the years following the Norman invasion. Pope Gregory's letter to Augustine and Theodore's Penitential implicitly convey the early church's view of women as subordinate to men; Aldhelm's *De Virginitate*, the Boniface correspondence, Bede's *History*, the early Lives of Cuthbert and Wilfrid, and Rudolph of Fulda's Life of the missionary nun Leoba all reflect conceptions of womanhood that had hardened into established commonplace by the later middle ages. In support of her claim, Stephanie Hollis also examines the indigenous position of women prior to the conversion of the Anglo-Saxons to Christianity, and considers reasons for the early church's concessions in respect of women. Emblematic of developments in the conversion period, the establishment and eventual suppression of abbess-ruled double monasteries form a special focus of this study.

STEPHANIE HOLLIS is Senior Lecturer in Early English, University of Auckland, New Zealand.

Anglo-Saxon Women and the Church

SHARING A COMMON FATE

Stephanie Hollis

THE BOYDELL PRESS

First published 1992 by The Boydell Press, Woodbridge

The Boydell Press is an imprint of Boydell & Brewer Ltd
PO Box 9, Woodbridge, Suffolk IP12 3DF
and of Boydell & Brewer Inc.
PO Box 41026, Rochester, NY 14604, USA

ISBN 0 85115 317 8

British Library Cataloguing-in-Publication Data
Hollis, Stephanie
  Anglo-Saxon Women and the Church : Sharing
  a Common Fate
  I. Title
  942.01082
  ISBN 0–85115–317–8

    Library of Congress Cataloging-in-Publication Data
Hollis, Stephanie.
  Anglo-Saxon women and the church : sharing a common fate /
Stephanie Hollis.
    p.   cm.
  Includes bibliographical references and index.
  ISBN 0–85115–317–8
  1. Women in Christianity – History. 2. Women – England –
History. 3. English literature – Old English, ca. 450–1100 – History
and criticism.   I. Title.
BV639.W7H58   1992
274.2′03′082 – dc20   92–26212

The paper used in this publication meets the minimum requirements
of American National Standard for Information Sciences –
Permanence of Paper for Printed Library Materials, ANSI Z39.48–1984

Printed in Great Britain by
St Edmundsbury Press Ltd, Bury St Edmunds, Suffolk

Contents

Acknowledgements

Abbreviations

Note on the Presentation of Texts

Introduction   1

1   The Conversionary Dynamic: More Laws for Times Like These   15

2   "Some Special Irregularities of Marriage": *Theodore's Penitential*   46
    and the Case of St Æthelthryth

3   Aldhelm's *De Virginitate*: Soldiers of Christ and Brides of the Lamb   75

4   Confessors and Spiritual Mentors: Hagiographic Ideals and the   113
    Boniface Circle

5   The Advice of Women and Eddius's *Life of Wilfrid*   151

6   A Beautiful Friendship Ruined: Bede's Revisionist Writing of   179
    Ælffled in the *Life of Cuthbert*

7   Queen Converters and the Conversion of the Queen: Bede's   208
    Ecclesiastical History and the Royal Marriage

8   Rewriting Female Lives: Hild of Whitby and Monastic Women in   243
    Bede's *Ecclesiastical History*

9   Rudolph of Fulda's *Life of Leoba*: An Elegy for the Double   271
    Monastery

List of Works Cited   301

Index   315

For Michael: *thæs ofereode, thysses swa mæg.*

Acknowledgements

My thanks are due to Paul Hayward for making available his unpublished dissertation on the Kenelm Legend, and, more generally, for his willingness to share his research interests; his enthusiasm and knowledge have been invaluable. I am grateful, too, to my colleague, Valerie Flint, for her encouragement and support. Above all, I am indebted to Michael Wright for bringing to bear his considerable technical expertise on the preparation of the manuscript and for shouldering most of the burdens of our joint domestic and professional life during the years that this book was in progress. Without his generous and patient support, it could not have been completed. For the assistance he has given in every possible way, I am grateful beyond expression.

Abbreviations

AB	*Analecta Bollandiana*
ASC	*Anglo-Saxon Chronicle*
ASE	*Anglo-Saxon England*
ASPR	*The Anglo-Saxon Poetic Records*
Bib ags Prosa	Bibliothek der angelsäcsischen Prosa
BJRL	*Bulletin of the John Rylands Library*
C&M	Colgrave and Mynors, ed. and trans., *Bede's Ecclesiastical History*
Carm Eccles	Aldhelm, *Carmina Ecclesiastica*
CCCM	Corpus Christianorum Continuatio Mediaevalis
CCSL	Corpus Christianorum Series Latina
DAI	*Dissertation Abstracts International*
EETS	Early English Text Society
	ES: Extra Series; OS: Original Series
EHD	*English Historical Documents*
EconHR	*Economic History Review*
EHR	*English Historical Review*
ELH	*English Literary History*
Epist	Aldhelm, *Epistolae*
FS	*Frühmittelalterliche Studien*
HBS	Henry Bradshaw Society
HDE	Simeon, *Historia Ecclesiae Dunhelmensis*
HE	Bede's *Historia Ecclesiastica*
H&S	Haddan and Stubbs, ed., *Councils and Ecclesiastical Documents*
HTR	*Harvard Theological Review*
JEH	*Journal of Ecclesiastical History*
JMH	*Journal of Medieval History*
L&H	Lapidge and Herren, trans., *Aldhelm: The Prose Works*
MÆ	*Medium Ævum*
MGH	*Monumenta Germaniae Historica*
	AA: *Auctores antiquissimi; Capit Reg Franc: Capitularia Regum Francorum; Conc: Concilia; ES: Epistolae Selectae; SRM: Scriptores rerum Merovingicarum; SS: Scriptores; SRG: Scriptores rerum Germanicarum*
MR	*Mercian Register*
P&P	*Past and Present*
PBA	*Proceedings of the British Academy*

PL	*Patrologia Latina*
RB	*Revue bénédictine*
RES	*Review of English Studies*
RHS	Royal Historical Society
RS	Rolls Series
TRHS	*Transactions of the Royal Historical Society*

Note on the Presentation of Texts

As considerations of length outrule quotations from the original accompanied by translation, I have assumed that the convenience of most readers of this book will be served by presenting the works discussed in the form of translation. In chapter 8, where the discussion rests upon relatively detailed attention to the text, some relevant passages of Latin and Old English are quoted in the notes, and, in the notes to chapter 2, a few canons of *Theodore's Penitential* are quoted from the original, by way of acknowledging the problematic nature of the terminology employed by penitentials; but, for the most part, I have assumed that readers who wish to see the original wording of a text under discussion will prefer to consult a complete edition.

When the edition cited contains a translation, the editor's translation has usually been adopted. For the two prose Lives of Cuthbert, Eddius's Life of Wilfrid, Felix's Life of Guthlac and the Whitby Life of Gregory the Great, I quote from Colgrave's translations. Translations of Bede's *History* are mostly taken from the edition of Colgrave and Mynors (Oxford, 1969); occasionally, if the meaning has not been sacrificed, I quote from the much more idiomatic translation of L. Sherley-Price, *Bede: A History of the English Church and People*, rev. edn. by R.E. Latham (Harmondsworth, 1984). Translations of *Theodore's Penitential* are taken from J.T. McNeill and H.M. Gamer, *Medieval Handbooks of Penance* (New York, 1938). For the Lives of Leoba and Boniface, and the *Hodoeporicon* of Willibald, I quote from the translation of C.H. Talbot, *The Anglo-Saxon Missionaries in Germany* (London, 1954). For *De Virginitate*, I have relied on the translation of M. Lapidge and M. Herren, *Aldhelm: The Prose Works* (Cambridge, 1979). Translations of the Boniface correspondence are either from E. Kylie, *The English Correspondence of Saint Boniface* (London, 1911), or from E. Emerton, *The Letters of Saint Boniface* (New York, 1940); other, more idiomatic, translations are occasionally quoted. I regret that I have not had the benefit of C.E. Fell, *Letters and Letter-writers in Anglo-Saxon England* (forthcoming).

Translations of Old English poetry generally follow S.A.J. Bradley, *Anglo-Saxon Poetry* (London, 1982); occasionally, the phrasing of T.A. Shippey, *Poems of Wisdom and Learning* (Cambridge, 1976), or of M. Swanton, *Beowulf* (Manchester, 1978), is preferred. Translations of Old Icelandic are from U. Dronke, *The Poetic Edda* (Oxford, 1969).

Indebtedness to these, and to other published translations, which include S. Allott, *Alcuin of York* (York, 1974), S. Keynes and M. Lapidge, *Alfred the Great* (Harmondsworth, 1983), M. Lapidge and J.L. Rosier, *Aldhelm: The Poetic Works* (Cambridge, 1985), is acknowledged in the notes.

OE *eth* and *thorn* appear throughout as "th." For convenience of reference, I give line numbers for Old English poetry as they appear in *Anglo-Saxon Poetic Records* (*ASPR*), edited by G.P. Krapp and E.V.K. Dobbie.

Introduction

The following chapters discuss literature by clerics who were writing to, for or about Anglo-Saxon women in the 8th and early 9th centuries, both in England and at the continental mission. In giving prominence to relations between bishops and noblewomen, particularly royal abbesses and queens, I follow the direction given by the surviving literature; I hope, however, to suggest that the literature is broadly indicative of the position of women in the early church and churchmen's attitudes to women generally. In sum, although the eminence of abbesses was greater and their involvement in public affairs was more consider-able than it was to be from the reign of Alfred onwards, the literature reveals an increase in the prestige and authority of male ecclesiastics and a reduction in the status of women, particularly monastic women, and this parallels the overall tendency of canon law. I hope also to suggest that the literature of the conver-sion period is of wider significance because it is both an index of and a contribu-tion to the social emplacement of the conceptions of women that missionaries brought with them. But before I outline the following chapters' development of that point, a brief indication of my indebtedness to some other studies of Anglo-Saxon women may be of use.

Over the last three decades or so, studies of women in the middle ages (mostly concentrating on the period 1200–1500) have tended, overwhelmingly, to hold churchmen and their teachings responsible for the depressed position of medieval women. Few would now venture to argue that the church improved the lot of women. Much less would anyone now be found to agree with Wright that the clergy "laboured to destroy, or at least to diminish, the old patriarchal spirit, and to emancipate the female sex from the too great authority of fathers and husbands,"[1] although there is a residual inclination to entertain the position that monasticism enhanced the lives of women; as Eckenstein (in 1896) viewed it, "the right to self-development and social responsibility which the woman of today so persistently asks for is in many ways analogous to the right which the convent secured to womankind a thousand years ago."[2] Dorothy Stenton was not the first to have been struck by the contrast between "master-ful and independent Anglo-Saxon ladies" and the "legally dependent but still masterful" women of the 12th and 13th centuries. Her study, *The English Woman in History*, which appeared in 1957, offered the first fully developed and

---

[1] T. Wright, *Womankind in Western Europe* (London, 1869); quoted C. Fell, et al., *Women in Anglo-Saxon England and the Impact of 1066*, paperback edn. (Oxford, 1986), p. 13.

[2] L. Eckenstein, *Women Under Monasticism* (Cambridge, 1896), p. ix. Eckenstein, consistently, regarded the dissolution of the monasteries as having significantly increased the subjection of women by depriving them of their only non-domestic sphere of activity, but she is among those who see a sharp decline in English women's prestige in the Anglo-Norman period; see esp. pp. 80, 198–213.

substantiated argument in support of the view that the position of women in England underwent a radical change for the worse in the period immediately following the Norman Conquest. Stenton, too, blamed the church for the sudden decline that she believed had taken place, but she was unusual in recognizing that the effect of the church's teachings on women depended on the social structure within which it operated. She was also willing to allow a distinction between the church's official attitude to women and the stance adopted by individual churchmen in their personal relations. She concluded:

> The evidence which has survived from Anglo-Saxon England indicates that women were more nearly the equal companions of their husbands and brothers than at any other period before the modern age. In the higher ranges of society this rough and ready partnership was ended by the Norman Conquest, which introduced into England a military society relegating women to a position honourable but essentially unimportant. With all allowance for the efforts of individual churchmen to help individual women, it must be confessed that the teaching of the medieval Church reinforced the subjection which feudal law imposed on all wives.[3]

The present study, though attempting to hold to its original intention of giving full value to the affection and esteem in which individual churchmen held particular monastic women, as well as to documentary intimations that the history of women under Christianity has not consisted of unrelieved repression, has not succeeded in redressing the balance. On the contrary, it finds pervasive indications of conflict between women and churchmen and of clerical disesteem. But it may nevertheless be true that churchmen and their teaching were not in any simple sense the architects of medieval women's misfortunes. I have tried (perhaps insufficiently) to refrain from evaluating the overall impact of the conversion on the position of women as a whole. Not only is there little direct evidence of the church's interactions with non-aristocratic women, but all deductions concerning the nature of pre-conversion (and hence pre-literate) Anglo-Saxon society are inevitably contentious. I am, nevertheless, viewing the conversion of England as a process of cultural negotiation, and accept that the relatively high social status of Anglo-Saxon noblewomen represents the continuity of indigenous custom. All the same, it seems probable that, just as the

---

[3] D.M. Stenton, *The English Woman in History* (London, 1957), p. 28. That the legal position of Anglo-Saxon women compared favourably with their Anglo-Norman counterparts had been argued by F. Buckstaff, "Married Women's Property in Anglo-Saxon and Anglo-Norman Law and the Origin of the Common Law Dower," *Annals of the American Academy of Political and Social Science* 4 (1893), 233–64. Studies observing the relative legal independence of Anglo-Saxon women which appeared prior to Dorothy Stenton's include: E. Young, "The Anglo-Saxon Family Law," in *Essays in Anglo-Saxon Law*, ed. H. Adams (Boston, 1876), pp. 121–82; H.D. Hazeltine, *Zur Geschichte der Eheschliessung nach angelsächsischen Recht* (Berlin, 1905). B. Bandel, "The English Chroniclers' Attitude toward Women," *Journal of the History of Ideas* 16 (1955), 113–18, discussed the contrast in terms of political opportunities. F.M. Stenton brought to light an important new range of evidence in "The Historical Bearing of Place-Name Studies: The Place of Women in Anglo-Saxon Society," *TRHS* 4th ser. 25 (1943), 1–13, and he emphasized the power of individual royal women and the high status of women generally in *Anglo-Saxon England* (Oxford, 1943). So also did D. Whitelock, *The Beginnings of English Society* (Harmondsworth, 1952).

development of military feudalism in the 11th century assisted the implementation of those aspects of the church's teachings on women that reinforced their subjection, so the misogyny that the church inherited from the early Fathers found points of contact with the unconverted societies with which missionaries came into contact, and that it achieved social effectiveness by virtue of its fusion with existing inequalities.

Dietrich, in a bibliographical essay surveying studies of Anglo-Saxon women prior to 1979, expressed qualified agreement with Dorothy Stenton:

> If a well-born English woman of the late medieval or early modern period had looked back on her Anglo-Saxon ancestor she would not have seen a "Golden Age" for women as this essay might at times have implied: but she probably would have seen there much to envy. Certainly living conditions would have been a trifle more 'rustic'; but she would have seen her Anglo-Saxon counterparts possessing rights, exercising alternatives and wielding power that she could barely attain in the best of circumstances.[4]

At the time Dietrich wrote, few had argued against the view that Anglo-Saxon women enjoyed a relatively favourable and influential position in their society, although prejudicial treatment and omission of evidence in some studies, Dietrich noted, significantly diminished the impression of power and independence that the Stentons and others had claimed for them.[5] Above all, the prestige and influence of monastic women in the Anglo-Saxon period has long

---

[4] S.C. Dietrich, "An Introduction to Women in Anglo-Saxon Society (c 600–1066)," in *The Women of England from Anglo-Saxon Times to the Present*, ed. B. Kanner (Hamden, Conn., 1979), pp. 32–56. D.M. Stenton, pp. 28–29, 75–76, 348, had posited that the "rough equality" between men and women that obtained at all levels of Anglo-Saxon society continued among the peasant classes, while upper class women became increasingly subject to their husbands as feudal lords. J. Scammell reached opposite conclusions regarding peasant women, in "Freedom and Marriage in Medieval England," *EconHR* 27 (1974), 532–7; "Wife-Rents and Merchet," *EconHR* 2nd ser. 29 (1976), 487–90. Cf. E. Searle, "Freedom and Marriage in Medieval England: An Alternative Hypothesis," *EconHR* 29 (1976), 482–6. R. Hill, "Marriage in Seventh-Century England," in *Saints, Scholars, and Heroes*, ed. M.H. King and W.M. Stevens (Collegeville, Minn., 1979), I, 67–75, argued that legislators regarded women as chattels, and that parents, valuing daughters only for the bride-price, maintained an artificial scarcity by infanticide; see also C.J. Clover, "The Politics of Scarcity: Notes on the Sex Ratio in Early Scandinavia," in *New Readings on Women in Old English Literature*, ed. H. Damico and A.H. Olsen (Bloomington, 1990), pp. 100–36. Demographic imbalance, whether or not artificially created (e.g., neither Hill nor Clover calculates the effects of child-bearing), seems more likely to have enhanced than to have diminished women's status, and legislation concerning the bride-price can be read as signifying that the bride-price was an index of women's social value, rather than their status as mere chattels.

[5] Dietrich is particularly critical of D.P. Kirby, *The Making of Early England* (New York, 1968), and J.T. Rosenthal, *Angles, Angels, and Conquerors: 400–1154* (New York, 1973), because they ignore evidence of the power of royal women and monastic women's contribution to the growth of the church. She also considers that, although R.I. Page, *Life in Anglo-Saxon England* (London, 1970), explicitly endorses the view that Anglo-Saxon women enjoyed "considerable freedom in law and practice," he misrepresents their social involvement by confining them to a separate chapter of his study. Fell, 1986, pp. 7–14, who outlines 19th century trends, notes that one of the first commentators on the social position of Anglo-Saxon women, S. Turner, *History of the Anglo-Saxons* (London, 1799–1805), argued that they were accorded "honour, consequence and independence," and that J. Thrupp, *The Anglo-Saxon Home* (London, 1862), who rejected Turner's conclusions, advanced no evidence for his own, diametrically opposed, point of view.

been emphasized. Talbot, for instance, observed: "Never, perhaps, has there been such an age in which religious women exercised such great power."[6]

Christine Fell, whose study of Anglo-Saxon women first appeared in 1984 (*Women in Anglo-Saxon England and the Impact of 1066*), also concurs with Dorothy Stenton in regarding the Norman Conquest as a critical watershed in the history of women. Like Stenton, she presents the centuries before the Conquest as a single and largely undifferentiated period, sharply distinguished from the 12th and later centuries with respect to attitudes to women. She also accepts Stenton's view that the development of military feudalism combined with ecclesiastical doctrine to trigger a sharp decline, and adds, by way of further explanation, developments within the church itself: "The impact of the Norman Conquest," she observes, "is almost instantly followed by the impact of the Gregorian reform, when theological concept hardens into canon law, and canon law acquires control of much legislation concerning women." Professor Fell goes to the heart of the matter in pointing out that the essential question about the patristic "theories on the inferiority of women" that loom so large in most accounts of the position of women in the period 1200–1500 is whether or not they were socially actualized; she does not believe that they were socially actualized in pre-Conquest England. Dietrich, somewhat similarly, postulated that "the patristic view of the evil of women" gained increasing ascendancy from the 12th century, and observed: "Why those attitudes changed and in what way, if any, that change in attitude was related to the decline in actual authority and position of women in the church (i.e., the relationship between the theoretical and the actual) are subjects that require further study."[7] The implicit reasons for the non-actualization of patristic theories on the inferiority of women that Fell advances are the strong position traditionally held by Anglo-Saxon women and the absence of repressive prejudice on the part of Anglo-Saxon churchmen. She writes:

> What is important is not whether such theories existed, or even how often they were repeated, it is the extent of their actual application within society as a whole, both secular and ecclesiastical. Throughout the Anglo-Saxon period they seem to have little practical effect. On the contrary, in the first enthusiasm for Christianity we not only see men and women engaging as equals in the challenge of a new religion and way of life, we see also women specifically asked to take a full and controlling part. No women could have been asked to take on so powerful a role as the early abbesses unless they were used to handling power, but Christianity is certainly not at this stage cramping their range of activity and responsibility. We see traces of anti-female propaganda in letters or homilies from the pens of clergy and in the penitentials, but these seem to have been ineffectual in practice.[8]

---

[6] *The Anglo-Saxon Missionaries in Germany* (London, 1954), pp. xii–xiii. The political influence of royal abbesses and the importance of their contribution to the church is generally accepted, following F.M. Stenton: see *Anglo-Saxon England*, 3rd edn. (Oxford, 1971), esp. pp. 324–9.

[7] Dietrich, p. 38.

[8] Fell, 1986, pp. 13–14. The assumption that abbesses' rule of the double monasteries is indicative of the power customarily wielded in society by upper class women is a long-standing

In effect, Professor Fell regards the pre-Conquest church as socially extraneous, although significant in so far as it offered opportunities for the cultivation of scholarship and provided (through the establishment of double monasteries) an additional sphere for the exercise of power by women who were accustomed to wielding it. Consistently, then, she does not draw much upon the specifically ecclesiastical sources that make up the bulk of the surviving documentation; in particular, she barely refers to *Theodore's Penitential* (or any other forms of ecclesiastical regulation) because she does not consider that *Theodore's Penitential* sheds light on the actualities of Anglo-Saxon society. Mayr-Harting also cast doubt on the implementation of ecclesiastical regulation: "Whether Anglo-Saxon women, who were accorded a high status in society and were often formidable personalities in their own right, always submitted to the male-drafted rules and codes which constitute our evidence, we cannot say," he remarked.[9]

Fell's study was closely followed (in 1986) by Jane Chance's *Woman as Hero in Old English Literature*. Chance essentially inverts the "attractive and indeed assertive picture" of Anglo-Saxon women presented by Fell and others. She concludes that "Anglo-Saxon society demanded passivity, rather than leadership and initiative, from most of its women. Those exceptions who became political, social or religious leaders and models did so only through great wisdom and chastity, virtues which – according to the metaphors used throughout the literature – were themselves considered heroic."[10] This divergence of views springs in part from the material employed as evidence. Whereas Fell draws on an impressive range of literary and non-literary sources, Chance concentrates primarily on the vernacular poetry; to substantiate some of her claims – as, for instance, the assertion that "even women agreed they should forgo sovereignty over men" – she draws on 12th century chronicles.[11] Whereas Fell regards the position of women throughout the pre-Conquest period as substantially un-altered but distinguishes between early and late sources of evidence, Chance

one; see esp. G.F. Browne, *The Importance of Women in Anglo-Saxon Times, and Other Addresses* (London, 1919), p. 11.

[9] H. Mayr-Harting, *The Coming of Christianity to Anglo-Saxon England* (London, 1972), p. 240.

[10] J. Chance, *Woman as Hero in Old English Literature* (Syracuse, NJ, 1986), p. 111. Literary surveys which confine themselves to vernacular poetic representations, especially those which have appeared since 1975, are generally more apt to give a less favourable impression of the position of Anglo-Saxon women than do historical studies: see esp. A. Renoir, "A Reading Context for *The Wife's Lament*," in *Anglo-Saxon Poetry: Essays in Appreciation for John C. McGalliard*, ed. L.E. Nicholson and D.W. Frese (Notre Dame, 1975), pp. 224–51; E.T. Hansen, "Women in Old English Poetry Reconsidered," *Michigan Academician* 9 (1976), 109–17; B.W. Kliman, "Women in Early English Literature: 'Beowulf' to the 'Ancrene Wisse,' " *Nottingham Medieval Studies* 21 (1977), 32–49; A.L. Klinck, "Female Characterization in Old English Poetry and the Growth of Psychological Realism: *Genesis B* and *Christ I*," *Neophilologus* 63 (1979), 597–610. (E.W. Williams, however, added a further dimension to the view that Anglo-Saxon women enjoyed a freedom unknown until recent times; see "What's So New about the Sexual Revolution? Some Comments on Anglo-Saxon Attitudes towards Sexuality in Women Based on Four Exeter Book Riddles," *Texas Quarterly*, 18 [1975], 46–55.) Some of the more recent of the essays ed. Damico and Olsen, 1990, however, evince a deliberate intention to reverse this trend, and "question the uncritical acceptance of Anglo-Saxon women as passive victims" (p. 16); see, e.g., A. Renoir, "Eve's I.Q. Rating: Two Sexist Views of *Genesis B*," pp. 262–72.

[11] See Chance, pp. 60–4; at pp. 53–64, she touches upon evidence other than vernacular poetry, including Bede's *History*, OE *Martyrology*, and Ælfric's *Lives of Saints*.

regards the pre-Conquest period as homogeneous, if not atemporal; the verna-cular poetry from which she draws conclusions about Anglo-Saxon society as a whole is commonly dated to the 9th and 10th centuries, with the exception of *Beowulf*, which some scholars would place as early as the late 7th century and others as late as the early 11th.[12] On the influentiality of the church, Fell and Chance are diametrically opposed. Whereas Fell's portrayal of the favourable social position of Anglo-Saxon women rests upon the argument that patristic conceptions had no real effect on social actualities, Chance assumes a society thoroughly penetrated by them: "There were thus two archetypes of women that ordered the Anglo-Saxon social world," she writes, "two social roles of women, typified by the biblical contrast between Ave/Eva. . . . Anglo-Saxon woman modeled herself upon the ideal exemplar of the Virgin Mary, the epi-tome of both secular and ecclesiastical perfection." Chance, then, does not regard representations of women in doctrinal poems such as *Christ I* and *Genesis B* as polemical models that constitute a pressure towards conformity but pres-ents them as universally accepted social ideals, which she holds to be embodied even in *Beowulf*, despite the fact that its overt doctrinal content is minimal: Grendel's mother, she argues, is "a parodic inversion both of the Anglo-Saxon queen and mother, the ideal of which was embodied in the Virgin Mary. . . . In her vengeful mission over the loss of her son, she monstrously inverts an image regarded by the Anglo-Saxons as a religious ideal."[13]

It is easy to overestimate the actual influence that the church exerted on the hearts and minds of the Anglo-Saxon populace at large because our sole con-temporary chronicle of events is the sanguine account of its advance that Bede gives in his *Ecclesiastical History of the English People*, which works towards the conclusion that "many of the Northumbrian race, both noble and simple, have laid aside their weapons and taken the tonsure, preferring that they and their children should take monastic vows rather than train themselves in the art of war."[14] It is difficult to argue against the social dominance of an institution whose most committed members were responsible for the composition and preservation of the only written evidence available to us (although Bede himself gives a different impression of the position of the church in the letter he wrote to Archbishop Egbert not long after the completion of the *History*);[15] in a

---

[12] See, for instance, the divergence of arguments advanced by contributors to *The Dating of Beowulf*, ed. C. Chase (Toronto, 1981). Most literature in OE survives in manuscripts dated to the 10th or later centuries. When a poem took the form in which it is preserved, and the extent to which it preserves archaic elements, is generally impossible to determine with any certainty. I refer comparatively to OE verse, primarily to *Beowulf*, *Maxims* (possibly compiled in the reign of Alfred but containing some proverbs identified as common Germanic), and to three short lyrics, *Wulf and Eadwacer*, *The Wife's Lament* and *The Husband's Message*, which are sometimes dated 8th/9th century. My use of OE verse is assailable because I assume that certain motifs which have OI analogues represent the continuity of a tradition that is of Germanic origin, but I accept that pre-industrial cultures, though conservative, are not static, and I do not intend to imply that OE verse preserves without alteration traditions that were current in the early AS period.

[13] Chance, pp. xiv, xvii, 11, 97.

[14] B. Colgrave and R.A.B. Mynors, ed. and trans., *Bede's Ecclesiastical History of the English People* (Oxford, 1969), p. 561; V.23.

[15] *Councils and Ecclesiastical Documents Relating to Great Britain and Ireland*, ed. A.W. Haddan and W. Stubbs (Oxford, 1871), III, 314–25.

post-colonial age it is perhaps easier to accept that Roman-Christian culture did not succeed in permanently eradicating other cultures from the moment it came into contact with them. All who have an interest in the social position of Anglo-Saxon women will be indebted to Professor Fell for a long time to come. I think, though, that in her understandable disinclination to reproduce in her own study the ecclesio-centric bias of the documentation, she somewhat underestimates the social actualization of the church's heritage of doctrines inimical to women. With the view that the position of women throughout the Anglo-Saxon period was relatively better than it was in the 12th and 13th centuries, I would not disagree as strongly as Klinck did. Klinck concluded from her study of the Anglo-Saxon law codes that "there is a much closer resemblance between the situation obtaining in late Anglo-Saxon England and post-Conquest England than there is between the early and late Anglo-Saxon period. Thus to describe Anglo-Saxon England as a time when women enjoyed an independence which they lost as a result of changes introduced by the Norman Conquest is misleading."[16] One form of decline within the pre-Conquest period was, in fact, indicated by Frank Stenton, when he remarked on the difference between the position of abbesses prior to the 9th century, who ruled over communities comprising both women and men, and abbesses during the later period, when segregated monasticism prevailed: later abbesses, he wrote, "are shadowy figures in comparison with the women who ruled the double monasteries in the seventh and eighth centuries. No woman in the middle ages ever held a position comparable with that of Hild of Whitby."[17] I think, then, that it might be more accurate to speak of a gradual erosion in the position of women, particularly monastic women, from at least as early as the 8th century;[18] doubtless this accelerated in the latter half of the 11th century, although Edward the Confessor's return to England after a long exile in his mother's Norman homeland, and the presence of Norman clerics in England during his reign, suggest that 11th century England experienced some forms of continuity as well as sudden change. As I hope to deal in a later study with the late Anglo-Saxon period, the present collection of essays gives no more than general indications of the ways in which developments in the early Anglo-Saxon period bode ill for women in later centuries and foreshadow the curtailment of the role of the queen.

Southern observed (somewhat troublingly) that "as society became better organized and ecclesiastically more right minded, the necessity for male dominance began to assert itself."[19] The relatively unrepressive attitudes of

---

[16] A.L. Klinck, "Anglo-Saxon Women and the Law," *JMH* 8 (1982), 107–21. Klinck took issue with T.J. Rivers, "Widows' Rights in Anglo-Saxon Law," *American Journal of Legal History* 19 (1975), 208–15, who argued that "the increasing equality of widows with men in England occurred late in the Anglo-Saxon period."

[17] Stenton, 1971, p. 162.

[18] I am thus in agreement with A.L. Meaney, "Women, Witchcraft and Magic in Anglo-Saxon England," in *Superstition and Popular Magic in Anglo-Saxon England*, ed. D.G. Scragg (Manchester, 1989), pp. 9–40, who suggests that condemnation of women engaged in "magical" practices, from *Theodore's Penitential* onwards, served to undermine the relatively more independent and powerful position that they inherited from the pagan past.

[19] R.W. Southern, *Western Society and the Church in the Middle Ages* (Harmondsworth, 1970), p. 310.

Anglo-Saxon churchmen towards the abbesses who ruled the double monasteries – which were proscribed by canon law and no longer founded in the late
Anglo-Saxon period (although a few may have survived from earlier times) –
are one manifestation of the fact that the early church itself was not
spectacularly "right minded"; it had not yet, in other words, become rigorously
"orthodox." But the translation of doctrines inimical to women into pronouncements that claimed the obligatory obedience of the faithful was by no
means a post-Conquest phenomenon, as St Paul witnesses. Before the 10th
century the church in England was more isolated from the development of
continental orthodoxy than it was ever to be again; but Theodore was only one
of a number of influential intermediaries of continental right-mindedness, and
Anglo-Saxon churchmen were not immune from the impulse to regulate that
was historically characteristic of the church's hierarchy. *Theodore's Penitential* is
accepted on good authority as a mid 8th century compilation, embodying a
regulatory tradition that goes back to Theodore (Archbishop of Canterbury
from 669 to 690).[20] I have some reservations about employing it as evidence
because one cannot with any certainty distinguish canons originating in the
time of Theodore from those which originated in the mid 8th century, but the
penitential canons attributed to Theodore are themselves a manifestation of the
social actualization of repressive conceptions of women. Even if attempts to
implement the canons attributed to Theodore were unsuccessful (and there is
internal evidence of women's resistance to ecclesiastical authority) *Theodore's
Penitential* demonstrates the intentions and attitudes towards women that were
harboured by at least some churchmen, which fairly certainly included the most
influential of them. As I have indicated, I also find intimations of enlightened
and encouraging attitudes to women, particularly in the Boniface correspondence, and wish to emphasize the disjunction between the official and private
attitudes of ecclesiastics, but early hagiography, Bede's in particular, also represents a form of social actualization of the view that women constitute a separate
and inferior class. Though I follow the lead of those who have regarded the
customarily powerful and socially influential position of Anglo-Saxon noblewomen as a critically important counterweight to the misogynist strands of
ecclesiastical teachings, it seems unlikely that the two groups of women who
had most contact with the church – monastic women and women at court –
could indefinitely resist the undermining social pressures to which both regulatory and hagiographic literature point. A more significant ameliorating factor
than the benevolent esteem of individual ecclesiastics, I think, was the relatively weak position of the church, which not only rendered churchmen less apt
and less able to regulate women whose families were far more powerful than

---

[20] See esp. P. Meyvaert, "Bede's Text of the *Libellus Responsionum* of Gregory the Great to
Augustine of Canterbury" in *England Before the Conquest: Studies in Primary Sources presented to
Dorothy Whitelock*, ed. P. Clemoes and K. Hughes (Cambridge, 1971), pp. 15–33, who concludes
that *Theodore's Penitential* circulated in England with the text of the *Libellus Responsionum* that
Bede incorporated in his *History*, and that both texts were disseminated from Canterbury. The
compiler of the *Penitential* calls himself "Discipulus Umbrensium," and most ecclesiastical
historians accord some form of credence to this. Haddan and Stubbs, III, 173, for instance,
considered that he was "either a native of Northumbria who had been a disciple of Theodore, or
more probably an Englishman of southern birth who had studied under northern scholars."

male ecclesiastics, but necessitated churchmen's reliance on the support and assistance of royal women, whether abbesses or queens.

It will already be evident, then, that I think that Chance's discussion of literary representations enters a useful qualificatory coda to Professor Fell's study of the social position of Anglo-Saxon women, but regard Chance as having radically overestimated the influence of the church in her assumption that Anglo-Saxons had thoroughly interiorized the iconographical construction of women as types of either Mary or Eve, and in her belief that Anglo-Saxon women were minded to model themselves on Virginal perfection. In part, the following chapters are an attempt to establish the Eve-Mary iconographical construction of women, indeed the very conception of distinctively female stereotypes, as a long – and slow – historical process, which was already under way in the early church and further continued in the vernacular literature of the late Anglo-Saxon period.[21]

For Western Europe in the high and late middle ages, its conceptions of women were timeless and universal truths, inherent in the order of the world since its creation, and for the modern reader of later medieval literature it is an effort to remember that there was once a time when every woman did not automatically assume the lineaments of either Eve or Mary. For the Germanic peoples who had settled England, there was nothing innately given or natural about the Roman-Christian culture that missionaries brought with them in the late 6th and 7th century, or about the Christianized cultures that were introduced from Iona and other regions.[22] The literature of the early Anglo-Saxon period – regulatory, hagiographic and epistolary – offers an opportunity to observe the first, often tentative, steps of indigenous assimilation and promotion of the social and iconographical constructions of women that were to become the established commonplaces of post-11th century Western Europe. But although the conversion of England (still taking place in the late 10th century owing to the disruption attending the 9th century Viking invasion) was a form of cultural imperialism that involved the imposition of alien beliefs and unfamiliar customs, the emissaries of Roman-Christian culture did not operate in a cultural vacuum. Despite the fact that, as the medieval papacy consolidated its position, it wished it to be understood that the dogmas and practices of the church always had been and always would be fixed and unchanging, at all times and in all places, what is historically called Christianity has perhaps never been monolithic and homogeneous, and was far from it in the 7th and 8th centuries.

---

[21] Here too, however, Germanic analogues existed and shaped the development of Eve/Mary iconography. Chance also argues that "Anglo-Saxon poets explain the secular and religious ideal for women by using Germanic and Christian images and concepts" (p. xiv).

[22] As Dietrich, p. 33, notes, "since early Anglo-Saxon society felt the impact of Celtic culture through the Irish church, what is discovered of women in Celtic culture [e.g., what is known of Boudicca] might well have a bearing on the status of women in Anglo-Saxon England," but as early Celtic culture is as elusive as early Germanic culture, the obstacles to determining the influence of Celtic culture on the social position of Anglo-Saxon women seem insuperable. I have attempted, particularly in chs. 2 and 4, to keep in mind the influence of the Irish church in England, and have speculated that it exerted a significant influence on the early Anglo-Saxon cult of Mary; but the difficulties of distinguishing between Irish and Roman (and Gaulish) influences in the early Anglo-Saxon church are well-known, and attempts to distinguish are regarded by some scholars as misguided.

The forms it assumed were, for better and for worse, shaped by the societies from which its converts were drawn. The church in England, tiny and precariously perched on "the remotest islands"[23] was, necessarily, in an interactive mode, and its relationship to indigenous society was not merely accommodating but osmotic.

In a variety of ways, the literature that I am discussing reflects the interaction of a Mediterranean and a Germanic culture. Patristic-derived conceptions of women, I am suggesting, though mapping on to indigenous prejudices and inequalities, established themselves only slowly in Anglo-Saxon England, because they had to contend with the relatively high position that women generally occupied at the most powerful levels of Germanic society. One of the visible consequences of this is the accommodations and compromises to which *Theodore's Penitential* resorts in its attempts to regulate marriage in accordance with the canon law that its compilers accept as orthodox. The emergence of an iconography of Eve, utilizing Germanic anti-types of ideal women, is itself testimony to the power of royal women, being employed as a polemical weapon in the political conflicts of bishops and queens.

But, more broadly, what the assimilation of Roman-Christianity achieved was the alterization of women. Roman-Christianity introduced a number of new conceptions of relationships and identity, and among these was a gender-specific identity for women. The constituting metaphors and subject matter of vernacular literature reflect the social primacy of kinship and comradeship relations, and women as well as men are represented in warrior-heroic modes. Anglo-Saxon culture, then, was more inclined to foreground the likeness of women to men. In the monasteries, the social primacy of kinship and comradeship favoured the acceptance of women religious as sisters in Christ who were members of his body. Just as marriage is conceived in the vernacular literature as a form of *comitatus* relationship, so too monks and clerics regarded monastic women as fellow soldiers in Christ, co-sharers in the struggles and aspirations of a pioneer church whose survival had yet to be assured. The inclusive, corporate, tendencies of early monasticism, operating in conjunction with royal women's customary participation in the rule of kingdoms, as well as a shortage of priests, enabled royal abbesses to share the powers and status of bishops and to exercise some of the offices that were to become the exclusive prerogative of male ecclesiastics. For ecclesiastical culture, on the other hand, marital union, a *signum* of the union of Christ and the church, was the dominant constituting metaphor. Concerned, as a matter of highest priority, to regulate into existence "lawful marriage," the church established marriage as the paramount social bond, contributing in the process to the attrition of kinship bonds, on whose primacy the political influence of noble women rested. Whereas kinship and comradeship as the constituting metaphors of social relations foregrounded women's likeness to men and identity with them, marriage, as mainstream ecclesiastical thinking viewed it, was a fusion of distinctively unalike and unequal beings. Paradigmatic of the mystic union of the body of believers in the headship of Christ, marriage as a *signum* inherently required the construction of

23 HE, III.25.

women as essentially "other" and inferior beings. The distinctively "other" identity the church postulated for women, as is well known, chiefly consisted in the carnal frailty they inherited from Eve. Reiterating from their reading of patristic literature the sexual temptations to which every woman was a provocation, Anglo-Saxon clerics created among their audiences an entirely new erotic consciousness, highly favourable to the replacement of kinship with marital union as the paramount social relation.

The literature of the early Anglo-Saxon period points, but by no means universally, towards the exclusion and marginalization of women, defining the trajectory for the development of a specific female identity. The emblem and the social index of these developments is the double monastery, incorporating both male and female religious and presided over by an abbess. The erotic construction of women first makes its effects felt on the double monastery organization. Canonical prohibitions of the double monastery, requiring the establishment of strictly segregated monasteries, and simultaneously calling for the more rigid enclosure of female religious, explicitly gave expression to the conviction that women were dangerously rampant sexual beings. The implementation of canon law, severing the ranks of male and female "soldiers of Christ," enclosing from the world at large female religious who had once participated in the church's ministry to the laity, graphically epitomizes the construction of a distinctive female identity.

The alterization of women, then, proceeds hand in hand with marriage union's gradual assumption of the dominant position that kinship and comradeship had held, and is an index of the assimilation of Roman-Christian culture. The position of women depended fundamentally on the extent to which the church succeeded in establishing its authority. The first of my chapters deals with Gregory I's letter to Augustine. Documenting the earliest ecclesiastical attempts to regulate women and marriage in Anglo-Saxon society, the letter also concerns the relation of ecclesiastical authority to the individual conscience. This too was a new conception of identity that missionaries introduced, and one which offered, from within Christianity itself, a potential basis for resistance to the implementation of ecclesiastical authority. In relation to the clergy, the status of laymen as well as the status of lay and monastic women declined as the church gained power and influence, claiming the right to order the lives, not merely of those who had chosen to give it their allegiance, but of whole populations. The continental reforms of the mid 8th century to which Boniface was a party represent an increasing bid for ecclesiastical control of both the laity and monastic women; their transmission to England towards the end of Alfred's reign and, more comprehensively, in the late 10th century, is reflected in an increasing misogyny and a decline in the legal status of women. In more than one sense women in Anglo-Saxon society were "involved in mankind," and my reflections on Gregory's letter in chapter I are an attempt to sketch the overall configurations of the impact of the conversion on Anglo-Saxon society and to introduce some of the themes that are taken up in later chapters.

Chapter 2, in viewing *Theodore's Penitential* as a record of cultural negotiation, is particularly concerned with what it reveals of tensions between the church's commitment to the social establishment of marriage as an indissoluble union and the advantages of allowing married women to leave their husbands in order to found monasteries; Bede's account of St Æthelthryth is regarded as a manifestation of these tensions which also points to the disjunction between the official pronouncements of churchmen and their relationships with individual women. Aldhelm's *De Virginitate* demonstrates a further accommodation of official attitudes to actual social conditions – the preponderance of widows and formerly married women as abbesses of double monasteries served to mitigate the church's propensity to regard virginity as the sole source of female sanctity. The discussion of *De Virginitate* in chapter 3 explores Aldhelm's imaging of female religious as soldiers of Christ and brides of the Lamb as a means of defining the broader implications of the adoption of the double monastery organization, and finds, in his warnings to the nuns of Barking on the dangers of self-adornment, an illustration of the way in which the dissemination of misogynist literary traditions ran counter to the corporate tendencies embodied in the double monastery organization. Chapter 4, which examines Boniface's correspondence with monastic women, draws on Bede's *Life of Cuthbert* as well as *Theodore's Penitential* in order to demonstrate the intensification of hierarchical relationships which is a concomitant of the development of sacerdotal elitism. I suggest that the Whitby *Life of Gregory* (which could have been written by a nun) reflects a lingering resistance to this development on the part of the Whitby monastery during the time of Hild's niece and successor, Abbess Ælffled. Chapter 4 is particularly concerned to give substance to the inclusive and egalitarian tendencies of the early church in its examination of the Boniface circle's correspondence, but is obliged to confront a sharp dichotomy between the view of women that Boniface expresses as an episcopal legislator, and the expectations of him expressed by the monastic women to whom he was a friend and teacher in his youth, which are confirmed by his letters to them.

The last five chapters deal with hagiography – for the function of hagiography is not to depict the world as it was but to present an uplifting and edifying version of actuality, and in this sense Bede's *History* is hagiography. In these five chapters, the nature and status of the surviving documentation is particularly under scrutiny. Not much explicit information on the role of women in the early church survives from the early Anglo-Saxon period. Doubtless much that pertained to the history of female religious was destroyed during the Viking invasions and in succeeding centuries. What has been preserved from the missionary period is the literature that recommended itself to later, more orthodox ages; this, as much as accidental destruction or the ravages of invaders, may account for the fact that, both in England and on the continent, very little survives that was written by Anglo-Saxon women, despite the fact that a number of them were famed for their learning. Bede's lengthy chronicle of the English church provides less overt testimony to royal women's political and social involvement than Eddius's brief Life. Set against other sources of information, the hagiographical records appear to have significantly under-represented the contribution made by women to the growth of the church because their authors are, to a greater or less extent, concerned to bring their accounts into line with orthodox conceptions of the role of women, which included the enclosure of female religious and segregated monasteries. Given the actual power and influentiality of royal abbesses and queens, Bede's near silence on the activities of reigning queens and his scanty, unforthcoming coverage of the double monasteries assumes a meaningful aspect, and I conclude that his under-representation of women's social participation reflects an aspiration towards their actual marginalization.

Chapters 5 and 6 deal with power-struggles and power-sharing between bishops and royal women, and focus on Eddius's Life of Wilfrid and Bede's recasting of the relationship of Bishop Cuthbert and Abbess Ælffled in his revision of the Anonymous Lindisfarne Life of Cuthbert. The Life of Wilfrid reflects hostility to the exercise of power by queens not favourably disposed to the church, but a willingness to countenance certain, very limited, forms of participation in the affairs of the church on the part of abbesses and devout queens. Bede's revision of the Anonymous Life of Cuthbert, in keeping with his more highly developed sacerdotal elitism, reflects hostility to the eminence of abbesses, especially their involvement in the mysteries administered by the church. Chapters 7 and 8 examine Bede's History as a record of the contribution to the growth of the church made by abbesses and queens. Chapter 7 recurs to the social implementation of marital theology in drawing out the implications of the fact that, despite Bede's knowledge of at least one papal letter urging an Anglo-Saxon queen to take an active part in the conversion of her husband, reigning queens barely figure in his History. Chapter 8 discusses Bede's account of the double monasteries in the History, with particular reference to his account of Whitby in the time of Abbess Hild. I disagree with Godfrey that the pastoral role of the double monasteries is a self-sufficient explanation for the adoption of the double monastery organization; I accept his suggestion that the double monasteries were conversionary centres, serving the same function as parish churches, but whereas Godfrey considers that the pastoral role of the monasteries necessitated the founding of male communities in proximity to women's houses, I would argue that the pastoral role of monasteries effectively enabled women to exercise an active ministry and to undertake many of the offices that later became the exclusive prerogative of priests.[24] In the light of the significant pastoral role carried out by the double monasteries, Bede's limitations as a chronicler of female monasticism are especially marked.

Rudolph of Fulda's early 9th century Life of Leoba, the Anglo-Saxon nun and kinswoman of Boniface who joined him at the continental mission, helps to demonstrate these limitations. Rudolph's Life yields much more information on monastic women's involvement with lay society in the missionary church. Rudolph's eulogy of Leoba's learning, like Aldhelm's praise of the Barking nuns' scholarship in De Virginitate, also throws into high relief Bede's unforthcomingness concerning monastic women's pursuit of learning. No less than Bede, however, Rudolph is at pains to give the impression that monastic women, even in double monasteries, had no form of contact with monastic men – if this is true, it is difficult to understand why abbesses should have been placed in charge of mixed communities, much less how they contrived to govern them. But Rudolph's portrait of the double monastery where Leoba was educated in England, a century before he wrote his Life, should not be regarded as reliable evidence; the Life everywhere manifests Rudolph's dedication to the implemen-

<hr />

[24] J. Godfrey, "The Double Monastery in Early English History," Ampleforth Journal 79 (1974), 19–32; "The Place of the Double Monastery in the Anglo-Saxon Minster System," in Famulus Christi: Essays in Commemoration of the Thirteenth Centenary of the Birth of the Venerable Bede, ed. G. Bonner (London, 1976), pp. 344–50.

tation of segregated monasticism, which was increasingly insisted upon by continental canons from the mid 8th century onwards. His handling of the relationship of Boniface and Leoba draws on hagiographic convention (I compare it with the relationship of the saint and his sister in Felix's *Life of Guthlac*), but there is good reason to accept as authentic the claim that Boniface expressed the wish to be buried in the same tomb as Leoba. In its treatment of the friendship of Boniface and Leoba, Rudolph's Life is emblematic of the institution of segregated monasticism, a literary enactment of the severance of monastic men and women which is already incipient in Aldhelm's *De Virginitate*.

1

The Conversionary Dynamic:
More Laws for Times Like These

Pope Gregory's Replies to Augustine

In an essay on the conversion written in 1954, Professor Talbot remarked approvingly that "the church in southern England was founded, not by wandering preachers whipping up feverish enthusiasm among a heathen population, but by diplomats, lawyers and architects, who wove Christianity into the framework of the state, and by so doing strengthened it and gave it a chance for development."[1] This cannot be the whole truth, but it appears, unfortunately, to be very close to the truth; the end was held to justify the means, and the outcome was that the character of Christianity was largely determined by the means employed. There are, here and there, signs that the life of the spirit figured rather more in the conversionary appeal of the early church than it did in the reflections of Professor Talbot when he wrote the lines above; and it figured in the Celtic church, which he regarded as so unstable an instrument for making the British Isles safe for Christianity, as much as it did in the Roman church, whose advance in the north of England, if we are to believe Bede, was materially assisted by the aggressive debating skills of Wilfrid at the synod of Whitby.[2] In the late 7th century, when the Anglo-Saxons embarked, in their turn, on a conversionary expedition to the continent, Wihtberht, finding that the Frisians did not want to be converted, made his way back to a hermitage in Ireland, where he gave himself up to the Lord in his accustomed silence.[3] History, however, in any of the senses in which it is either known or knowable to us, is not made by men as little inclined to the play of will as Wihtberht, nor by women either. To accept the official records of the early English church – overwhelmingly concerned with legislative control and administrative ordering – as representative of the considerations that exercised the hearts and minds of its monastic and lay adherents is to be forced to conclude (yet again) that historical Christianity has had exceedingly little to do with faith in Christ. Private correspondence can give a different impression, but it is a surprise to

---

[1] C.H. Talbot, *The Anglo-Saxon Missionaries in Germany* (London, 1954), p. ix.
[2] B. Colgrave and R.A.B. Mynors, ed. and trans., *Bede's Ecclesiastical History of the English People* (Oxford, 1969), III.25. Subsequently referred to as *HE*; translation is from Colgrave and Mynors (cited as C&M), and, occasionally, from L. Sherley-Price, *Bede: A History of the English Church and People*, rev. edn. by R.E. Latham (Harmondsworth, 1984).
[3] *HE*, V.9.

encounter, in the official documentation, occasional testimony to consider-ations that bear a recognizable relation to the Sermon on the Mount, however faint.

The *Libellus Responsionum* in Bede's *History* – the dialogue version of Gregory I's letter of reply to questions from Augustine – is a private communication that has found its way into the public record. Its authenticity has been doubted because Boniface was repeatedly told by Rome that it had no record of such a letter ever having been sent. Boniface was engaged at the time in an argument with the papacy, and Gregory's letter of replies to Augustine's questions was the authority he claimed in support of his position.[4] The obvious conclusion that suggests itself is that Rome could not find the letter because it was not in Rome's interests to search it out. Recent study of the transmission of the *Libellus*, however, shows that it is possible to accept its essential authenticity without calling into question the denials of Rome. Meyvaert concludes that the state-ment explicitly permitting marriages between those related at the third or fourth remove, which was particularly at issue in Boniface's argument with Rome, is an interpolation that occurred when a letter of reply to Augustine was turned into a question and answer dialogue. He suggests that the dialogue form of the *Libellus* originated among the Lombards, a Germanic people to whom prohibited degrees of consanguinity were as obstructively problematic as they were to the Anglo-Saxons. The dialogue form in which Gregory's replies are presented in Bede's *History* – characteristic of Germanic wisdom literature as well as an established convention of Latin literary tradition – thus seems not to have been an original feature, but the adoption of this form heightens the inherently dramatic development of a letter whose authenticity there seems no further cause to doubt.[5]

Augustine's mission made its way to the Kentish court. Missionary policy, both in England and on the continent, was to gain first the protective favour of kings or overlords, and to secure if possible their immediate conversion, so that by their "persuasion and example" their subjects would be brought to follow suit. Wandering preachers who imitated Christ by "whipping up enthusiasm" with-out the protection of secular powers risked meeting the same end as Christ, as Bede demonstrates in his account of the two Hewalds in continental Saxony, who were murdered while awaiting conduct to the regional overlord because the villagers feared that they would be compelled to change their religion.[6] Eddius's Life of Bishop Wilfrid records, with no apparent sense of incongruity, the slaughter that Wilfrid and his companions inflicted in Sussex, when the

[4] *Die Briefe des heiligen Bonifatius und Lullus*, ed. M. Tangl, *MGH ES* I (Berlin, 1955), esp. 33. Translations, unless otherwise stated, are from E. Emerton, *The Letters of Saint Boniface* (New York, 1940).
[5] See esp. Meyvaert, 1971, pp. 15–33, esp. 23–30, 29, n. 4. Meyvaert accepts that Gregory's letter could not be found at Rome because it was not there, but remarks that Tangl, 33, "does not make it clear whether the search was made only in the *Registrum* or in the exemplars of Gregory's other works as well" (p. 15, n. 2). Meyvaert was primarily concerned to refute the argument that the *Libellus* was forged by Bishop Nothhelm: see S. Brechter, *Die Quellen zur Angelsachsenmission Gregors des Grossen* (Münster in Westfalen, 1941), pp. 13–111.
[6] *HE*, V.10.

high priest and his followers tried to capture them as they landed.[7] But the polemical bias of Bede's *Ecclesiastical History of the English People* – dedicated to Ceolwulf of Northumbria – leans to a portrait of the conversion that implicitly establishes Ceolwulf as heir to a tradition of kingship over-ridingly dedicated to the advancement of Christianity amidst almost universal acquiescence.[8] Bede does not conceal the fact that the royal response was sometimes lukewarm or worse, but he offers such edifying examples as Augustine's earliest success, Æthelberht of Kent. It was said of Æthelberht, Bede reports, that he showed greater favour to believers because they were his fellow citizens in the kingdom of heaven, but that he compelled no-one to accept Christianity because he had learnt from his spiritual mentors that the service of Christ was voluntary, and ought not to be constrained.[9]

Pope Gregory's correspondence with the mission gives reason to believe that Æthelberht's instructors and guides to salvation did teach him something of the kind. Gregory himself certainly wished to believe, when he wrote the *Moralia*, that England had not been converted by force of arms but by preaching and miracles.[10] Tempted, initially, by the prospect of early and immediate success, Gregory exhorted Æthelberht to go forth, destroy all pagan idols and spread the faith in the manner of an imperial conqueror like Constantine. But he had thought better of it when he wrote to Mellitus, and had concluded that a gradual evolution of interior conviction was to be sought, instead of the violent eradication of the outward forms of paganism.[11] What Gregory believed ideally should occur, and what actually did occur, are of course two different matters, but they were not perhaps entirely different. According to Bede, both Æthelberht of Kent and Edwin of Northumbria assured the Roman missionaries that customs could not be altered without the consent of their people.[12] In East Anglia the opposition of Redwald's councillors, including his wife, prevented Redwald from abandoning the existing religion in favour of Christian practices; at least three kings who attempted to introduce Christian customs were assassinated.[13] In *Regula Pastoralis*, Gregory emphasized the importance of accommo-

[7] B. Colgrave, ed. and trans., *The Life of Bishop Wilfrid by Eddius Stephanus* (Cambridge, 1927), ch. 13; cf. ch. 41. (Referred to throughout as *Life of Wilfrid*.)

[8] See *HE*, Preface, p. 2. "This prefatory letter is not strictly a dedication but a submission to King Ceolwulf, though a wider readership is already envisaged": J.M. Wallace-Hadrill, *Bede's Ecclesiastical History of the English People: A Historical Commentary* (Oxford, 1988), p. 1.

[9] *HE*, I.26.

[10] See *HE*, II.1. In this, as in his recurrence to the inner disposition of the will in the *Libellus*, Gregory is in a tradition of thought particularly associated with St Augustine; see R.A. Markus, *Saeculum: History and Society in the Theology of St Augustine* (Cambridge, 1970), p. 140.

[11] *HE*, I.32, 30; cf. III.8. R.A. Markus explains how Bede came to preserve these letters in the wrong order: "The Chronology of the Gregorian Mission to England: Bede's Narrative and Gregory's Correspondence," *JEH* 14 (1963), 16–30; "Gregory the Great and a Papal Missionary Strategy," in *The Mission of the Church and the Propagation of the Faith*, ed. G.J. Cuming (Cambridge, 1970), pp. 29–38.

[12] See *HE*, I.25, II.13, II.9. With the doubts expressed by Wallace-Hadrill, 1988, p. 37, cf. the preamble to the 695 Laws of Wihtred of Kent ("with the consent of all, the leading men devised these decrees and added them to the lawful usages of the people of Kent"): ed. F. Liebermann, *Die Gesetze der Angelsachsen* (Halle, 1903), I, 12.

[13] Eorpwold of East Anglia (*HE*, II.15), Sigeberht of Essex (*HE*, III.22), and Peada of Mercia (*HE*, III.24) were all were baptized at the instigation of another, more powerful, king;

dating teaching to the nature of the recipient, and his own change of heart will bear the construction that it had been borne in upon him that secular coercion and destruction of idols was not an efficacious conversionary strategy.[14] In sum, Gregory's proud claim that, in England, the teachings of humble men had prevailed over people whom no show of force could subdue, may not be a mere rhetorical enhancement of the achievements of humble men, but a measure of what Gregory had learnt from his English conversionary experience. The conversion was not an imposition of a monolithic ideology upon a cultural void, but an interactive process, in which Christianity assumed distinctive regional forms.

Practically speaking, the ongoing effect of the two Gregorian missions was minimal; the heritage they left was primarily the ideas that found a sufficient affirmative echo in indigenous culture to lodge themselves in the traditions of the early church.[15] The tradition of interior conviction as a conversionary ideal had been assimilated as a model for action by Bishop Daniel of Winchester. His advice to Boniface on the conversion of the continental Saxons assumes that conversion entails intellectual debate, and he offers Boniface the metaphysical arguments that he considered to be the most persuasive in countering belief in pagan gods.[16] Bede, tailoring his account of the conversion of England to illustrate for the Northumbrian king and people a tradition of necessarily unconstrained adherence to Christianity, helps to ensure that regard for the individual conscience remained current as an ideal for the readers of his Latin work and its English translation.[17]

But the principle of voluntarism could easily be lost sight of. The practice of consolidating supremacy over client kings by requiring their conversion to Christianity was particularly a feature of the policy of Oswiu of Northumbria, a scion of the Celtic church, whose members were chiefly instrumental in spreading Christianity until the resurgence of the Roman church in England that

opposition to Kentish hegemony may also explain the resistance of Redwald's wife and councillors (HE, II.15); see ch. 7, pp. 232–4.

[14] See Regula Pastoralis, III.1–40 (PL 77, 12–130).

[15] Among those who consider that the Gregorian mission was "of decisive importance in the history of English Christianity," is Mayr-Harting, 1972, p. 68. Cf. fn. 21 below.

[16] Tangl, 23. See further C. Plummer, ed., Venerabilis Baedae Opera Historica (Oxford, 1896), II, 57–9.

[17] It was presumably a Canterbury tradition, since Albinus of Canterbury was Bede's chief source, but his commentary on Ezra 7.13 (ed. D. Hurst, CCSL, 119A, 312) shows him to have independently assimilated it, and he appears at times to have reshaped his sources in accordance with it (cf. the conversion of Sussex, Life of Wilfrid, ch. 41; HE, IV.13). For an account of the 5 surviving manuscripts of the OE translation, see T. Miller, ed. and trans., The Old English Version of Bede's Ecclesiastical History of the English People, EETS OS 95, 96 (London, 1890–1), pp. xiii–lix. (Hereafter referred to as OE Bede). For the Latin manuscripts and their circulation in England and on the continent, see C&M, pp. xl–lxxiv. In all OE translations of the History, the status of the Libellus is rendered ambiguous by its appearance at the end of HE, III.1; puzzlingly, since, if it appeared at the end of HE, IV.1, it would imply that it was being associated with the Theodorean canons with which it circulated (see fn. 60). Meyvaert, 1971, pp. 21–31, was unable to determine how long the question and answer form of the Libellus had circulated in England before Bede included it in the History, but establishes that it was in Bede's possession by 721; Meyvaert, "Diversity Within Unity: A Gregorian Theme," Heythrop Journal, 4 (1963), 143, dates the Lombard dissemination to the 7th c. The critical problem, he pointed out, is how the Libellus got to Lombardy.

followed the arrival of Theodore's mission. The utilization of Christianity as a tool of territorial expansion goes largely unremarked by Bede. Ceolwulf was left to draw his own conclusions from the report that, when Peada of Mercia accepted baptism for himself and his people as the price of a marriage alliance with Oswiu, he was assassinated; but once at liberty under their own king, the Mercians willingly gave allegiance to Christ their true king.[18] Bede's own grasp of inner conviction as the essence of authentic conversion, and free choice its necessary pre-condition, did not run deep. For Bede the mystic union of believers in Christ was expressed (particularly in his account of the synod of Whitby) in universal conformity to the same outward observances,[19] and the requirements of meaningful conversion are accordingly met in the prospect of whole populations seeking to follow their leader in exchanging old customs for new.[20]

All in all, Bede's portrait of a conversion accomplished without notable bloodshed or direct coercion is plausible, but the corollary is that what the conversion of England amounted to by the time Bede was writing in 731 was the establishment of monasteries fired by the enthusiasm of a few and the superficial observance of certain selected practices among those sections of the population with whom churchmen had managed to establish contact.[21] When Æthelberht's pagan son succeeded and married his father's wife, his people, no less quick to follow their leader in this, threw aside the constraints of alien marriage customs with evident relief. Needing to explain this, Bede forgets that Æthelberht took the good advice of Augustine, and attributes the reversal to the fact that Eadbald's subjects had originally converted either out of fear of his father or to win his favour.[22] England was converted, not to Christianity, but to the religion of kings. Constituted by clerics as the secular arm of the church, kings more often employed it as a tool of their own policies. The conception of the king as Christ's earthly representative was an absurd paradox, which nonetheless had unacknowledged dimensions of appropriateness; singled out by missionaries to pilot the nation to the baptismal font, it was kings, not missionaries, who paid with their lives for embracing the faith. It was thus fitting that kings should shoulder the burden of guilt for employing the coercion to which ecclesiastics were in principle opposed, as they brought about the universal conformity that ecclesiastics so impatiently desired.[23]

---

[18] HE, III.24.

[19] HE, III.25.

[20] See, e.g., HE, II.14: Paulinus, immediately after the baptism of Edwin, spent 36 days instructing and baptizing people who gathered from the surrounding countryside.

[21] Bede's 734 letter to Archbishop Egbert complains that many remote settlements, although not immune from payment of episcopal dues, have no-one to baptize or teach them: ed. A.W. Haddan and W. Stubbs, Councils and Ecclesiastical Documents Relating to Great Britain and Ireland (Oxford, 1871), III, 317 (hereafter cited as H&S).

[22] HE, II.5.

[23] C. Stancliffe, "Kings Who Opted Out," in Ideal and Reality in Frankish and Anglo-Saxon Society, ed. P. Wormald et al. (Oxford, 1983), pp. 154–76, argues that AS kings who abandoned their kingdoms for monasteries or pilgrimage to Rome reflect Irish influences, running counter to Roman, specifically Gregorian, views on the leading role of kings.

The tensions between Christianity as a state religion and New Testament theology are strikingly represented in Gregory's *Libellus Responsionum*. Gregory was regarded in the early church as, *in absentia*, the apostle to the Anglo-Saxons, but even this fails to convey the full extent of his prestige. Meditating from afar upon their condition, Gregory had accomplished in absence their salvation by sending his beloved son Augustine to dwell among them,[24] and the reverence accorded to him and his writings, given further impetus by the translation of his work in the reign of Alfred, extended its sway into the late Old English period.[25] How fortunate England was in his formative influence is revealed by the papal directives to Boniface during his mission to the continent.

Five of Augustine's nine questions concern the organization of the church, the protection of its property and liturgical differences between Rome and the churches in Gaul. The remaining four do not in any evident way evince Augustine's concern with the difficulties of imparting the message of the gospel to an alien culture. "May two brothers marry two sisters," Augustine enquires, "provided they belong to a family not related to them?" "There is nothing in the sacred writings which seems to forbid it," is the reply. "Within what degree may the faithful marry their kindred?" the questions continue: "And is it lawful to marry a step-mother or sister-in-law?"[26] Step-mothers and sisters-in-law are outruled as marriage partners by conjuring with the Old Testament prohibition against "uncovering the nakedness" of one's father. But the question concerning the precise degree of permitted consanguinity is obviously not met by the sole scriptural passage cited in Gregory's reply, *Leviticus* against "uncovering the nakedness" of one's kindred.[27] Gregory's reply – or, more precisely, the reply contained in the version of the *Libellus Responsionum* that Bede copied into his *History* – measures the distinctly lesser authority of Roman law against the dubious veracity of popular wisdom (that marriages between first cousins do not result in thriving progeny), in order to reach the conclusion that "the faithful should only marry relations three or four times removed."[28]

Obliquely, however, Gregory cautions Augustine that an attempt to impose his rulings on converts, at this early stage, could only be counter-productive. Converts who had already contracted "unlawful marriages" before being baptized were to be warned of their eternal peril but were not be excommunicated; and he advised, in general, that "in these days the Church corrects some things strictly and allows other things out of leniency; others again she deliberately

---

[24] See B. Colgrave, ed. and trans., *The Earliest Life of Gregory the Great by an Anonymous Monk of Whitby* (Lawrence, Ka, 1968), chs. 6, 9–10 (referred to throughout as *Life of Gregory*). See also HE, II.1; cf. I.23. For discussion see P. Meyvaert, *Bede and Gregory the Great* (Jarrow, 1964).

[25] See *King Alfred's West-Saxon Version of Gregory's Pastoral Care*, ed. and trans. H. Sweet, EETS OS 45, 50 (London, 1871); *Bischofs Wærferth von Worcester Übersetzung der Dialoge Gregors des Grossen*, ed. H. Hecht, Bib ags Prosa 5 (Leipzig, 1900).

[26] C&M, p. 83; HE, I.27.

[27] Lev. 18.7, followed by extensive specific prohibitions in 18.8–18, to which, in a general way, Gregory presumably refers Augustine.

[28] C&M, p. 85. This last phrase, in particular, has been considered spurious; its omission does not alter the essential substance of the reply, that marriages of any degree of relationship beyond that of first cousins can be tolerated. Meyvaert, 1971, pp. 23–27, argues that it is an interpolation of Lombard origin.

glosses over and tolerates and by so doing often succeeds in checking the evil of which she disapproves."[29] He made the same point when he instructed the mission to reconsecrate pagan temples instead of destroying them, and advised it to adapt to Christian usage the pagan custom of sacrificing cattle: "It is doubtless impossible to cut out everything at once from their stubborn minds: just as a man who is attempting to climb to the highest place rises by steps and degrees and not by leaps."[30] Gregory's policy of gradualist adaptation to local circumstances looks to the adoption of a more rigorous one as the reward of its success. It was as clear to the British bishops as it is to the contemporary reader of Bede's *History* that Augustine's landing was synonymous with the arrival of an arrogant exercise of power, and they rightly discerned the drift of history that it portended, of which Gregory's council of *pro tem* moderation is prophetic. For, advised by a "holy and prudent" hermit that they would know whether or not to accept Augustine's leadership as a man of God if he had the humility to rise when they approached him, the bishops departed precipitately from the meeting, saying that if he would not rise to greet them at this early stage, he would have even less regard for them once they submitted to his authority.[31]

Augustine's eighth question fairly bristles with enquiry: "Should a pregnant woman be baptized? And when the child has been born how much time should elapse before she can enter the church? And after how many days may the child receive the sacrament of holy baptism so as to forestall its possible death; and after what length of time may her husband have intercourse with her? And is it lawful for a woman to enter the church if she is in her periods or to receive the sacrament of holy communion? And may a man enter a church after relations with his wife before he has washed; or approach the mystery of the holy communion?"[32] The ninth question continues in the same strain. Can it really have been for this that Augustine came so far and so fearfully, bearing messages to the Kentish king that he brought "good news" from Rome?[33]

Gregory, we may say, is captive to the rhetorical terms of Augustine's discourse; indeed, he eventually signals as much, when he chooses to break out of them. His disposition to be a party to Augustine's legislative urge cannot be denied, for it is not entirely confined to the early stages of the letter; but, to a high degree, he is driven to pronounce authoritatively, and on these particular matters, by the pressure of Augustine's questions. But the question is, whose questions are these? Was Augustine also driven from behind to regulate, in his case by his English converts' desire to be regulated? For at the end of the litany of enquiries in question eight, Augustine explains: "All these things the ignorant English people need to know."[34] There are obvious obstacles to gauging what the prior cultural constructs of pre-literate Anglo-Saxons were, but they unquestionably had them. At least some of the matters raised in question eight

---

[29] Trans. Sherley-Price, p. 75; HE, I.27.
[30] C&M, p. 109; HE, I.30.
[31] HE, II.2. Wallace-Hadrill, 1988, p. 54, concludes that Bede regarded British bishops' rejection of Augustine as self-evidently wrong.
[32] C&M, p. 89.
[33] HE, I.23, 25.
[34] "Quae omnia rudi Anglorum genti oportet habere conperta" (C&M p. 88).

seem, by their very nature, unlikely to have forced themselves unaided upon Augustine's attention as being visibly in need of legislation. Augustine's own prior cultural constructs cannot be left out of account. His choice of questions among the many that could, and surely did, occur to his converts reflects the obsessive preoccupations of the early fathers, aided by over-familiarity with *Leviticus*. Such questions perhaps grievously exercised the mind of a monk, with no experience of ministering to lay men and women, who had been sent to convert a pagan people. But carnal profanation of the sacred is not a uniquely Judeo-Christian conception.

The same question can be asked of *Theodore's Penitential* which, according to its preface, is based on the answers that Theodore gave to the Northumbrian presbyter Eoda in answer to *his* questions.[35] The description of Theodore as "a man undoubtedly of extraordinary knowledge for our age" hardly prepares the reader for the *Penitential's* extended treatment of bestiality, masturbation and homosexuality. As the Reverend Plummer rightly remarked in the last century, when he denied Bede's authorship of the penitentials attributed to him: "Evil deeds, the imagination of which may perhaps have dimly floated through our minds in our darkest moments, are here tabulated and reduced to a system. It is hard to see how anyone could busy himself with such literature and not be the worse for it,"[36] although involvement in the act of legislating now appears more harmful to the penitential authors' state of mind than the content of the legislation. A case can be made for denying that *Theodore's Penitential* is admissible evidence for the state of Anglo-Saxon society. Theodore's judgments, for instance, are stated by the preface to be intermixed with penitential material that Theodore declared to be Irish; Pope Vitalian, who despatched Theodore to England was (and rightly, it seems) worried by the thought that he might be harbouring unorthodox Greek notions, and directed Hadrian to accompany him and keep them in check.[37] Theodore's compiler, however, states that "not only many men but also women, enkindled through these decisions with inextinguishable fervour, burning with desire to quench this thirst, made haste in crowds to visit Theodore,"[38] and the compiler, whose aim is to sift out the authentic judgments of Theodore from those which claimed his authority, evidently had among his sources rulings that were framed in response to specific individuals' requests for arbitration.[39]

We may suspect the compiler of exaggerating the number who sought out Theodore, and no doubt it would be unsound to deduce that any single activity mentioned in *Theodore's Penitential* was actually practiced in 7th century England. But *Theodore's Penitential*, as a phenomenon, does not only represent his culturally predetermined belief in the need for legislating, influenced by

[35] Trans. J.T. McNeill and H.M. Gamer, *Medieval Handbooks of Penance* (New York, 1938), pp. 182–215 (cited as McNeill); ed. P. Finsterwalder, *Die Canones Theodori Cantuariensis und ihre Überlieferungsformen* (Weimar, 1929), pp. 287–334, at 287–8 (subsequently referred to as *Theodore's Penitential*).

[36] Plummer, 1896, I, cclvii.

[37] HE, IV.1. Cf. fn. 62.

[38] McNeill, p. 183; *Theodore's Penitential*, Preface, p. 287.

[39] See further ch. 2, fn. 28 and p. 69.

Christianity's early intertwinement with secular power, and his equally predetermined impulse to legislative territorialization of even the most out of the way corners of individual experience. Utilizing conventional categorizations of sin and perhaps preserving the fossilized recollections of unEnglish vices, *Theodore's Penitential* is also a response to existent anxieties on matters laid before Theodore and others like him. Only this will explain the fact that the penitential strays beyond any recognizable concern with public morality and private conscience – as, for instance, in its ruling that if anyone is stung to death by bees, the swarm should be destroyed, but its honey may be eaten.[40]

To existing pagan anxieties, the coming of Christianity added a wide range of new ones. There was much that Anglo-Saxon pagans wanted to know for certain. The Northumbrian councillor's much-quoted comparison of human life to the brief flight of a sparrow through a brightly lit hall, returning to the circumambient darkness whence it came, concludes: "Of what went before this life or of what follows, we know nothing. Therefore, if this new teaching has brought any more certain knowledge, it seems only right that we should follow it."[41] Vernacular literature places high value on the getting of wisdom, and Saturn, turning his mind to death, explains to Solomon in the Old English wisdom dialogue: "There is one matter in this world about which curiosity has disturbed me day and night for fifty years, through the mysterious course of nature, so that my spirit has been sad; it is still the same now, until the eternal Lord should grant me satisfaction from a wiser man."[42] For the new learning brought by Theodore – his Latin and his Greek, the study of literature both sacred and secular, astronomy, computistical calculation and medicine – for this too they made haste in crowds to visit him.[43] But, pervasively, resistance to the changing of old customs is identified by Bede as the major obstacle to the spread of the Roman church among pagan Anglo-Saxons, and bishops of the Celtic church appear in the *History* as foremost of those who were reluctant to abandon the customs that united them in community with the present and the ancestral past. Though Bede is a skilled manipulator of the polemical euphemism, loyalty to customs and traditions is nevertheless a plausible explanation of resistance: "I will not go from here," Byrhtwold declaims on the lost battle field at Maldon, "but I mean to lie at the side of my leader, by the man so dear to me."[44] "Your words and promises are fair indeed," it is given to Æthelberht to reply to the Augustinian mission, "but they are new and uncertain, and I cannot accept them and abandon the age-old beliefs that I have held together with the whole English nation."[45] Writing for a more select, ecclesiastical audience in his *Life of Cuthbert*, Bede allows popular opposition to the new religion to surface, in the villagers' mockery of the Lindisfarne monks caught in a storm: "May God

---

[40] *Theodore's Penitential*, II.xi.6.
[41] Sherley-Price, p. 127; HE II.13. The authenticity of Bede's account is much debated: see D.K. Fry, "The Art of Bede: Edwin's Council," ed. King and Stevens, I, 191–207.
[42] *Solomon and Saturn II* (ASPR VI, 38–48), ll. 247–52; trans. T.A. Shippey, *Poems of Wisdom and Learning in Old English* (Cambridge, 1976), p. 89.
[43] HE, IV.2.
[44] *The Battle of Maldon*, ll. 315–16 (ASPR VI, 7–16). Unless otherwise stated, translations of OE poetry follow S.A.J. Bradley, *Anglo-Saxon Poetry* (London, 1982).
[45] Sherley-Price, pp. 69–70; HE I.25. See also Bishop Colman at Whitby, HE, III.25.

have no mercy on any of them, for they have robbed men of their old ways of worship, and how the new worship is to be conducted, nobody knows."[46]

Presenting itself as the supplanter of tribal rites and practices, Christianity inevitably assumed the aspect of a set of outward observances that needed to be precisely known in order that the community and the individual might continue to secure a favourable relation with the natural and supernatural worlds. Anglo-Saxons were accustomed to being ordered, though perhaps not to total ordering, and a glance at the earliest Kentish law code, almost entirely given over to the regulation of sex and violence in accordance with indigenous customs, makes it clear that the church in England was not the first to instigate regulative ordering of these spheres.[47] In at least some respects the effect of ecclesiastical regulation was to foreground and alter the direction of indigenous preoccupations. On the regulation of marriage priorities coincided, though for entirely different underlying reasons; in terms of its own contractual customs, the earliest Kentish law code is no less concerned than Augustine and Theodore to prevent "unlawful union." Unless we can manage to construe Augustine's "All these things the ignorant English people need to know"[48] as implying that he was astonished to encounter a people entirely untrammelled by the faintest notion of ritual contamination, his question appears to illustrate the manner in which the mental grids of ecclesiastic culture attracted to themselves and assimilated existing indigenous taboos.

The accepted superiority of Mediterranean civilization, nowhere clearly distinguished from the spiritual authority claimed by Rome, also exercised a powerful influence on the willingness of converts to be regulated. Bishop Daniel urged Boniface to point out to disputant pagans that, whereas Christians inhabit the fertile land of the Mediterranean that flows with oil and wine, the pagans and their gods had been banished to the frozen wastelands at the periphery of the world.[49] For King Alfred as for Bede the fruit of learning and material prosperity were, inseparably, the benefits of national observance of Christian custom.[50] It is no accident that the hostility to the new religion that is permitted expression in the *Life of Cuthbert* is attributed to rustic boors. Whether they flocked to an overseas visitor for the new learning, or made haste in crowds to receive his instruction on the new *mores*, the Anglo-Saxon inhabitants of a remote island were being civilized. Augustine's aside in question eight registers the presence of a barbarian race that asked too many questions. Perhaps it implies apologetic distaste for the questions he felt obliged to put before Gregory.[51] Or perhaps, in fact, it reflects scorn for the benighted ignorance of wanting to be dictated to on minute particulars.

[46] *Vita S Cuthberti Auctore Beda*, ed. and trans. B. Colgrave, *Two Lives of Saint Cuthbert: A Life by an Anonymous Monk of Lindisfarne and Bede's Prose Life* (Cambridge, 1940), pp. 142–307, at p. 165. Subsequently referred to as *Bede's Cuthbert*.
[47] See *Ethelbert*: ed. Lieberman, I, 3–8.
[48] See fn. 34; so also the *Capitula* version. For the *Letter* version, see fn. 52.
[49] Tangl, 23.
[50] *Pastoral Care*, Preface, pp. 2–3.
[51] Cf. HE, II.1; cf. also Gregory's image of the confessor as the hand basin at the doorway to the temple in *Regula Pastoralis*, II.5.

Gregory, in answering question eight, draws attention instead to Augustine's own hankering for authoritarian pronouncement in preference to the exercise of his own judgment: "I do not doubt, my brother, that you have been asked questions such as these, and I think I have already given you the answer. But I believe that you merely wish that what you yourself may have thought and felt should be confirmed by my answer."[52] And he calls into question the negatively repressive course on which Augustine is embarked, by turning his enquiry back on him: "Why should a pregnant woman *not* be baptized?" This retort heralds an inspired attempt to subvert the terms of the discourse by redirecting the pursuit of cut and dried administrative answers into a consideration of the doctrinal beliefs that underlie them. Gregory shifts the perspective from the legislation of outward action to the motival origin of action within the individual soul. In doing this, he evokes the transcendence of the law of the Old Testament by the spirit of the New, and the dissolution of the Old Law's certainties based on clearly defined, outward, observances by the New Law's promulgation of the immeasurable and inward sins of the heart.[53]

The overall thrust of Gregory's reply to questions eight and nine is to assert that sin consists, not in action, but in the disposition of the will, a theme brought to summation in his analysis of the original fall as an allegorical paradigm of a process that is essentially interior. The theme is raised early in his reply to question eight, and it is at its most explicit in: "For as in the Old Testament it is the outward deeds that are observed, so in the New Testament careful heed is paid not so much to what is done outwardly as to what is thought inwardly."[54] Gregory thus recasts Augustine's construct of women as contaminating procreative organisms into creatures of God possessed of moral judgment. Defining menstruation as a consequence of the fall like hunger, thirst and weariness, Gregory does not supply the authoritative pronouncement demanded by Augustine's questions (his own or his converts'), but instead makes the judgment of the individual conscience the site of their resolution. He states that women who, after due consideration, do not presume to approach the sacrament when menstruating, are to be commended, but those moved by devotion to receive it are not to be discouraged. With the aid of St Paul's assurance that all things are pure to the pure of heart,[55] he draws his remarks to a conclusion with a decisively rhetorical question: "How can a woman who endures the laws of nature with a pure mind be considered impure?" So too, for instance, in

---

[52] C&M, p. 89. Meyvaert, 1971, p. 28, explains this as a corruption of the *Letter* version, *me* having been introduced in the process of turning it into dialogue form. The *Letter* version reads: "Requisisti si praegnans mulier debeat baptizari . . . vel etiam ad mysterium sanctae communionis accedere: quae omnia apud anglorum gentem fraternitatem tuam arbitror requisitam, cui iam te responsum redidisse non ambigo, sed hoc quod ipse dicere et sentire potuisti credo quia mea apud te volueris responsione firmari." Assuming that Meyvaert is right that Gregory sent his replies to Augustine in the form of a letter which was subsequently cast as a question and answer dialogue, it still seems to hold true that Gregory was replying to questions he understood Augustine to have actually been asked, and that the manner in which these were communicated to him prompted him to make mention of it.

[53] See esp. Matt. 5.27–8.

[54] C&M, p. 95. See fn. 10.

[55] Titus 1.15.

dealing with question nine, on whether a man may receive communion after having an impure dream, and whether, in such circumstances, a priest may celebrate mass, Gregory demonstrates at some length that the answer is to be found through an examination of the conscience and discerning self-judgment.

But what is no less evident than the deflection of Augustine's legislative urge into awareness of the integrity of the individual conscience, is Gregory's tenuous and selective adherence to what he believes is a fundamental Christian tenet. If women, implicitly, have souls no less than men, if women in their relation with the divine can be allowed to exercise their own judgment, and, conceivably, reach the conclusion that they are pure at heart, yet in their relations with their husbands they cannot be trusted to do anything of the kind.[56] Gregory explains that the Old Testament law that a woman may not enter a consecrated place 33 days after the birth of a male child and 66 after the birth of a female is to be understood allegorically, so that, even if a woman were to enter a church to give thanks in the very hour of her delivery, she would do nothing wrong. On the other hand, he states categorically that a man may not approach his wife until her child is weaned. Noting the upsurge (presumably in Rome) of the custom of employing a wet nurse, Gregory attributes it to women's lascivious haste to resume marital relations, and is equally categorical that women must not be allowed to circumvent Old Testament prohibitions in this fashion. Gregory's mental reflexes, in short, have not been uniformly reconstructed in the light of the New Testament, and it is disappointing that, while he is alert to the one-sidedness of Augustine's question concerning whether a man can receive communion after relations with his wife before he has washed, he rectifies the omission by explaining that, as God required men to abstain from women before he spoke to them on Mount Sinai, so much the more should women preserve themselves in purity of body when about to receive the body of God himself.

Augustine's landing in Kent was, among other things, the harbinger of an authoritarian regime. It carried with it also the potential basis for resistance to its own authority, in that it asserted as a basic tenet the primacy of individual conscience. To differing degrees, the exchange between Augustine and Gregory exemplifies the precarious hold that idea had on the minds of those who instigated the conversion. Augustine's questions are evidence of an automatic readiness to shore up an indigenous inclination to embrace the securities of the Old Testament rather than the uncertain freedoms of the New; and it was Anglo-Saxon converts who were largely responsible for furthering missionary teachings. Just as the slow and complex process of the voluntary conversion of the heart was liable to get lost in the desire for mass conversions and the outward semblance of universal adherence, so also the delicate juggling of the judgments of individual conscience against authoritative pronouncement was liable to get short-circuited as the conversion moved along the lines that the British bishops had feared it would. In short, as Christianity became a religion of obligation not choice, the church hierarchy could afford to jettison respect for individuals. The attempt to redirect the conversionary course mapped out by

---

[56] Plummer, 1896, II, 53, considers that Gregory was thinking of nuns; Augustine's questions clearly concern married women.

Augustine's questions is to the greater glory of Gregory, the Great: but a critical view of his replies is not (necessarily) the consequence of a naive Protestantism failing to grasp its own premises – that Christianity is historically constructed, and that the form it assumes at any given place or time represents the fore-grounding of one among the many possibilities offered by its constituent texts (for "no man hath seen God at any time").[57] Gregory shares the view that the individual conscience is fundamental, but he cannot keep it in sight. In the simultaneous attempts to establish the existence of both authority and individ-ual conscience, carried on against a backdrop of requests for minute and precise guidance; in the erratic and tenuous postulation of the primacy of individual judgment; in the reflex undermining of individual judgment on the part of women in particular; in all its aspects, Gregory's *Libellus Responsionum* is an epiphany of the conversion.

Boniface's Questions to Rome

A hundred years and more later, Boniface, whose correspondence with Anglo-Saxon women in England and at the continental mission contributes signifi-cantly to the documentation of the role of women in the early church, headed a new phase of missionary endeavour. The escalating bid for control that followed the Church of Rome's increasing security of survival was accompanied by a corresponding diminution in respect for its adherents. Marriage was by no means the only sphere in which the legislative dynamic operated, but Boniface's interactions with the papacy on the subject of permitted degrees of consan-guinity and relationship offer a numerically quantified measure of the inflation-ary tendencies of Rome's authority. It is a meaningful coincidence that Gregory II also wrote a reply to enquiries from Boniface in which the relation of marriage to kinship figured prominently, for in seeking to establish "lawful marriage" as a matter of the highest priority, the church found itself in conflict with what was to Germanic societies the primary social bond. But whereas Augustine's need to ask reflects the absence of a precise, authoritative definition of the permitted degree of consanguinity, Boniface's suggests an uneasy awareness that the tradi-tions of the church in England that he was accustomed to accept as authorita-tive were in conflict with those of the church in Rome, which claimed a higher authority.[58] No version of Gregory's replies to Augustine *prohibits* marriage within the third degree; even in the versions that omit the statement that modern scholars believe to have been interpolated, the substance of Gregory's reply is that marriage at any degree of relationship beyond that of first cousins can be tolerated. The version that Boniface knew explicitly countenanced marriage within the third degree.[59] He is also likely to have known a version of the penitential canons attributed to Theodore which likewise permitted

---

[57] 1 John 4.12.
[58] Tangl, 26; Boniface's letter of enquiry to Gregory II does not survive.
[59] See Tangl, 33, quoted below.

marriage within the third degree; in England, the *Libellus Responsionum* and the Theodorean canons circulated together.[60]

Theodore's penitential canons, as they survive in *Theodore's Penitential*, have undergone revision, but *Theodore's Penitential* (which is thought to have received its final form in the mid 8th century) points to an earlier ruling on consanguinity that claimed authority from him: "According to the Greeks, it is permitted to marry in the third degree of consanguinity, as it is written in the Law."[61] Characteristically, *Theodore's Penitential* claims authority for rulings that diverge from the canon law of Rome by attributing them to the Greek church, of which Theodore (66 years old when he was sent by Rome to England in 668) had been a member for most of his life;[62] Greek divergences from Rome offered a well-respected precedent for regional variations in ecclesiastical discipline, and therefore justified the *Penitential's* perpetuation of English traditions that did not conform to Roman orthodoxy. Gregory II, approving the fact that Boniface had submitted to him his uncertainties on the degrees of permitted consanguinity, reminded him that the Holy See was the sole fountainhead of all ecclesiastical discipline. In 726, Gregory II's ruling on permitted degrees of relationship was that, "strictly speaking, in so far as the parties know themselves to be related they ought not to be joined together; but since moderation is better than strictness of discipline, especially toward so uncivilized a people, they may contract a marriage after the fourth degree."[63]

Gregory I's accommodating stance lingers on in Gregory II's reply to Boniface, but his answer acknowledges no need to authorize or explain his decision by a citation of scripture, for which Gregory I automatically reaches in the *Libellus Responsionum*. Nor did he trouble to offer the flimsiest text or pretext in support of his reply when Boniface enquired whether a child offered by its parents to a monastery might later leave it in order to marry: "This we strictly forbid, for it is an impious thing to allow children who have been offered to God by their parents to follow their baser instincts for pleasure." *Theodore's Penitential* regards as binding only the monastic vows of an individual who has reached the age of consent; concerning the vowing of infants, it states that it is as well to fulfill such vows, but cattle may be substituted instead.[64] Gregory II was not a man to give rise to a tradition of voluntary conversion accomplished by interior conviction or to endorse the exercise of individual judgment. If the difference between the conversion of England and the continent *is* epitomized by the destruction of the pagan shrine in Northumbria by converts led by their former

---

[60] See Meyvaert, 1971, pp. 24–6. *Theodore's Penitential*, which states that it was compiled by a Northumbrian, is chiefly preserved in continental MSS. Finsterwalder, p. 170, considered that it took its final form among the Boniface circle; Meyvaert and others regard it as a Canterbury text. See fn. 17 for its inclusion in HE.

[61] McNeill, p. 210; *Theodore's Penitential*, II.xii.26. See further below. The Canonical Letters of Basil, highly influential in the Greek church, prohibit only marriage with the sister or brother of a former spouse: see *St Basil: The Letters*, Vol. III, ed. and trans. R.J. Deferrari (London, 1930), 199.23; 217.68, 75, 76, 78.

[62] Wallace-Hadrill, 1988, p. 136, considers it probable that Theodore had lived in Rome a long time as a Greek monk in a Cilician monastery, and was therefore familiar with Latin and Western usages.

[63] Emerton, p. 53; Tangl, 26.

[64] *Theodore's Penitential*, II.xiv.5–6; see also II.xiii.37.

high priest on the one hand, and, on the other, the assault on the sacred groves of the continent carried out by missionaries like Boniface,[65] the difference is at least partly explicable in terms of the degree to which Rome's confidence in its own destiny affected the chain of command.

By 732, Gregory III was instructing Boniface that marriages were not to be contracted within the seventh degree.[66] Gregory II's concessive ruling, like Gregory I's warning to Augustine of the need to tolerate minor infringements in order to eradicate major abuses, merely reflects an assumption of the inferiority of the non-Roman races. Gregory III's letter instructing Boniface to suppress the "filthy and abominable" practice of eating horse flesh, in terms which suggest that the matter was only slightly less urgent than the selling of Christian slaves for pagan sacrifices,[67] is as indifferent to the difficulties Boniface would face in implementing his decrees as it is indisposed to negotiate compromises with pagans. It was under Gregory III that Boniface found himself in trouble for having married a widow to the godfather of her son, who had also adopted the boy. In the laws of Ine of Wessex, wergild compensation for the killing of blood relatives is extended to cover the new, supra-natural, relationships created by the church,[68] quite possibly because these were felt to be comparable with Germanic elective relationships such as blood brotherhood. But there is no suggestion that Rome was regarding the marriage as the equivalent of incest in Germanic terms. It resorted to its imperial Roman heritage, maintaining that under the Christian emperors such a marriage was punishable by death or exile.[69] The distinction between kinship of flesh and blood and the community of spirit was one that the church in England did much to foster. Boniface's puzzlement reveals a much clearer grasp of this distinction – and also his much greater fellow-feeling with those to whom he was joined by membership in the body of Christ: "I cannot possibly understand why, on the one hand, spiritual relationship in the case of matrimonial intercourse can be so great a sin," he wrote to Archbishop Nothhelm of Canterbury, "while, on the other hand, it is well established that by holy baptism we all become sons and daughters of the church, can be shown to be brothers and sisters." Boniface explained to the Archbishop of Canterbury that he wished to understand why the Roman hierarchy objected so greatly to this particular marriage, and therefore asked the Archbishop to inform him if he could find any explanation of Rome's position "either in the decrees of the catholic fathers or in the canons, or in indeed in

---

[65] HE, II.15; III.30. See also *Vita S Bonifatii Archiepiscopi Auctore Willibaldo Presbytero*, trans. Talbot, 1954, pp. 23–62; ed. G.H. Pertz, MGH SS 2 (Hannover, 1829), 331–53, ch. 6. (This Life, completed a decade or so after the death of Boniface, is subsequently referred to as *Life of Boniface*.) The contrast between the conversion of England and missionary activity on the continent, mooted by Wallace-Hadrill, 1988, p. xxii, is less sharp if we recall that Boniface is said to have cut down the sacred oak at the instigation of the Christian faction at Gaesmere.

[66] Tangl, 28. There exists a letter from Gregory I to Bishop Felix of Messana, in which Gregory explains away his permission of marriage within the third degree as a concession to a newly converted race, and states that once they are firmly established in the faith they are to be forbidden to marry up to the seventh generation; H&S, III, 32–3, regard this letter as spurious.

[67] Cf. *Theodore's Penitential*, II.xi.4: "They [Acts 15.29] do not forbid horse [flesh], nevertheless it is not the custom to eat it" (McNeill, p. 208).

[68] *Ine*, 76 (Liebermann, I, 122). For a recent study, see J.H. Lynch, *Godparents and Kinship in Early Medieval Europe* (Princeton, 1986), esp. pp. 242–57.

[69] Tangl, 33.

holy writ."[70] Boniface clearly did not regard the Archbishop of Canterbury as the sole fountainhead of ecclesiastical authority in the British Isles. He made the same request to Bishop Pehthelm in Scotland, and his letter to Pehthelm confirms that his letter to Canterbury diplomatically glosses over the fact that he was far from accepting Rome's view of the case: "As to the nature of this sin, if it is a sin, I was entirely ignorant, nor have I ever seen it mentioned by the fathers, in the ancient canons, nor in the decrees of popes, nor by the apostles in their catalogues of sins. If you have found anywhere a discussion of this subject in ecclesiastical writings kindly inform us, and let us know also your own opinion."[71]

In his letter to Nothhelm of Canterbury, Boniface recalled having read in the replies of Gregory I to Augustine that marriages were permitted within the third degree. He asked Nothhelm if he would obtain for him a copy of Gregory's letter, because he had been told that no such document could be found in the Roman archives. Boniface evidently did not regard this as a sufficient reason to conclude that the letter was spurious. All things considered, he could scarcely ask Nothhelm to support him in a dispute with the pope by affirming that the letter was authentic; he asked Nothhelm, instead, to make every effort to discover whether or not the letter had been proved to have been written by the holy Gregory.

By 742, it was Boniface who was accusing Gregory III of having authorized an irregular marriage, in a letter written to his successor Pope Zacharias. From a canonical point of view, the marriage that Boniface objected to was a case of manifold aggravation; the woman was a former nun who had married her own cousin, whom she had deserted during his lifetime, and she had now married her husband's nephew, to whom she was in any case related by blood, within the third degree. Boniface was still drawing upon the traditions of the English church in his disputes with the papacy. Unexpectedly, however, he asserted that the marriage union in question had been declared "a heinous crime, an incestuous and horrible offence, and a damnable sin" at a synod of London that had been convened by none other than Augustine and the missionary disciples of Gregory. Charging Rome in the same letter with a number of other irregular decisions and oversights, Boniface affirmed, dutifully, that he did not actually believe that such decisions could have emanated from Rome, since he knew that the Holy See had never given a decision contrary to canonical decrees. Speaking of the synod of London convened by Augustine, on the other hand, he stated that Augustine and his fellow bishops had pronounced on the authority of scripture.[72] For Boniface, then, the essence of the matter was that the marriage in question united a man with the widow of his uncle, for which there was a specific scriptural condemnation.[73]

It would be pleasant to think that Boniface was ironically turning the tables on the papacy in the hope of forcing it to admit that it did, on occasions, deviate from its own canons; he was, at the time, attempting to persuade Pope Zacharias to make an exception to canon law on his own behalf, so that he

---

[70] Emerton, p. 63; Tangl, 33. He made a similar request to Abbot Duddo (Tangl, 34).
[71] Emerton, pp. 61–2; Tangl, 32.
[72] Emerton, p. 81; Tangl, 50.
[73] Lev. 18.14.

could appoint his own episcopal successor. If his aim was to force such an acknowledgement, he was singularly unsuccessful; Pope Zacharias agreed that Gregory III could not have authorized the marriage that Boniface described, for the reason that Boniface himself had given.[74] Unfortunately, however, there are inescapable signs that, by 747 at the very latest, Boniface's heart and mind had been overtaken by the role of chief enforcement officer for Roman canonical law into which Rome had cast him.

By 742, Boniface had, presumably, been led to conclude that the Libellus was spurious. His citation of the (otherwise unrecorded) decree of the synod of London reveals that the traditions of the church in England no longer represented for him an authoritative regional alternative that he could draw on to support his individual unease with specific instances of Rome's legislative dynamic; his own country of the mind having been territorialized, he had come to believe instead that current Roman orthodoxy had always prevailed at all times and in all places. But if Boniface had accepted that the Holy See had not and would not ever decree anything contrary to the fathers and the canons (while evidently retaining remnants of the opinion that this was not altogether a good thing), there were still members of the English mission who believed that Gregory's letter of reply to Augustine was authentic, and were spreading that belief through Germany. Zacharias was moved to pronounce on it in 743 – rightly or wrongly, he believed that the dispute had shifted from the third degree to the fourth. Significantly, Zacharias did not rule that Gregory I could not have permitted marriage at the fourth degree because it was against the canons. He said, in effect, that there was nothing in the archives of Rome that proved Gregory I had given such permission, but if he had given it, it no longer applied:

> Nor should we pass over in silence what is spread abroad through the lands of the Germans, which we have been unable to discover in the archives of our church. Nevertheless we learn from men who come from Germany that the holy pope Gregory when, through the grace of God, he enlightened them in the Christian religion, granted them permission to marry within the fourth degree. But within the degrees of blood kinship such marriages are not permissible to Christians. Nevertheless, we are prepared to believe that he allowed this because they were as yet uncivilized and were being invited; although, as we have said above, we have been unable to discover this writing.[75]

Zacharias, then, finally pronounces the official redundancy of concessive tolerance. Papal unwillingness to concede that ecclesiastical customs mutated according to the circumstances of time and place is not surprising; Boniface's inclination to argue on the basis of established regional variation illustrates the challenge that it represented to Rome's commitment to the church as a monolithic entity and itself as the sole authoritative interpreter. But Boniface's

---

[74] Tangl, 51; in the same letter, however, Zacharias permitted Boniface to nominate his successor, emphasizing that it was an act of pure affection, and not to be regarded as setting a precedent.

[75] Acts of the Roman Council, 743 (MGH Conc II.1, 19–21); trans. Meyer, 1971, pp. 15–16.

information concerning Augustine and the synod of London does come as something of a surprise, even when one recognizes that the will to regulate is already fully present in the questions of Augustine that prompted Gregory's replies. The implication of the alleged synod of London is that, within the space of a mere four years, Augustine had discarded the spirit of Gregory's advice by legislating for the imposition of prohibited degrees of relation, and had extended the scope of Gregory's rulings, at least as far as fathers' brothers' wives. If Boniface was correctly informed, Augustine's urge to regulate would seem to have allowed Gregory's policy of accommodation a very short lease of life indeed.[76] Whether or not this synod took place, *Theodore's Penitential* – generally held to have been compiled in England and to have circulated among the Boniface circle on the continent – shows that the period of cultural negotiation continued into the 8th century and beyond. Inevitably, it registers the advance of the more rigorously exacting orthodoxy emanating from Rome in the mid 8th century, but its posture is not a straightforwardly submissive one. The canon on consanguinity quoted above reads in full:

> According to the Greeks it is permitted to marry in the third degree of consanguinity as it is written in the Law; according to the Romans, in the fifth degree; however, in the fourth degree they do not dissolve [a] marriage after it has taken place. Hence they are to be united in the fifth degree; in the fourth, if they are found [already married] they are not to be separated; in the third, they are to be separated.[77]

The superior authority of Rome which this canon formally acknowledges is, as it were, insufficient to altogether supersede the ruling which (suggestively identical with the *Libellus* version of Gregory's replies) claims the authority of the Eastern church; for the compiler has not consigned it to oblivion. His decision to include it makes available an alternative, though lesser, version of orthodoxy to subsequent users of *Theodore's Penitential* (who might conceivably have included abbesses acting as confessors);[78] in effect *Theodore's Penitential* enables the circumvention of some of the more exacting forms of orthodoxy and weakens its claims to supremacy by licensing a pluralism of ecclesiastical discipline that parallels the liturgical pluralism to which Gregory gave his sanction.[79]

That Boniface's propensity to argue with the papacy is a representative reflection of respect for the individual conscience fostered by a Christian tradition in England that claimed its origins in a voluntary conversion achieved by persuasion (and miracles) is a proposition too arguable to argue; it is a possible construction of Boniface's employment of the traditions of his native region that appeal to the customs of a distinctive group did duty for the claims of the

---

[76] Boniface's belief that this synod took place is without substantiation. H&S, III, 33, nevertheless concluded on the strength of his allusion to it that it was "certain" that Gregory's ruling was not acted upon by the English Church even from the beginning (cf. III, 51).

[77] McNeill, p. 210; *Theodore's Penitential*, II.xii.26.

[78] Tangl, 14 (c. 719), is from an abbess who was acting as confessor to both men and women (presumably on her monastic estate); see ch. 4, pp. 134–7.

[79] See Meyvaert, 1963, 141–62.

individual conscience. What is straightforwardly evident in the Boniface correspondence, notwithstanding his capacity for arguing an occasional point, is his own increasing identification with the escalation of regulatory orthodoxy. One manifestation of this is his prohibition of female monastic pilgrimages to Rome, in striking contrast with his earlier role as the teacher and friend of monastic women.[80] On them the proliferation of increasingly more restrictive legislation would bear most heavily.

Further to Pope Gregory's Replies

While there are ways in which it is true that individualism in Western Europe is the discovery of the 12th century or the creation of the 13th, the matrix for it was offered, on the eve of the conversion of England, in Gregory's affirmation that individual self-judgment is of the essence of the New Testament. In this, as in much else, the 12th and 13th centuries represent the coming to fruit of seeds long planted in the ground. The rise of individualism is no longer apt to have about it the aura of a rosy dawn as it once did for historians able to celebrate the progress of Western Europe. For Foucault, "history is the play of rituals of power, humanity advancing from one domination to another,"[81] and confession, as obligatorily instituted in the early 13th century, is a fundamental strategy of domination in the construction of Western Man. From this it follows that our very individualism is so tainted in its origins and development that the only possibility for averting total ordering is to get rid of it: "Maybe the target nowadays is not to discover what we are but to refuse what we are. . . . not to try to liberate the individual from the state, and from the state's institutions, but to liberate us both from the state and from the type of individualization that is linked to the state. We have to promote new forms of subjectivity through the refusal of this kind of individuality which has been imposed on us for several centuries."[82] He offers himself, I take it, as an example of the toll that history has taken on the freedom to imagine when he proposes, as an alternative to what history has made us, a different form of individualism. With the devaluing of Western individualism, not infrequently coupled with nostalgia for the communality of more traditional, non-Western cultures, the rise of individualism is in a fair way to becoming again the equivalent of the Original Fall. In Anglo-Saxon lyric the impact of individualism registers in the lament of solitary exiles severed from kindred and *comitatus*, whose conscious misery at having been cut adrift from the joys of communality, irrevocably lost, is the emblem of Edenic

---

[80] See ch. 4, pp. 130–3, 137–50.
[81] M. Foucault, *The History of Sexuality I: An Introduction*, trans. R. Hurley (New York, 1978), p. 36.
[82] "Afterword," in *Michel Foucault: Beyond Structuralism and Hermeneutics*, H.L. Dreyfus and P. Rabinow (Chicago, 1983), p. 216.

severance from God, from which they seek escape by restoration to community in the company of the saints.[83] After such knowledge, what forgiveness?

Gregory's *Libellus Responsionum* enables the claim to be made that individual self-knowledge, as he posited it, runs counter to the dynamic of authoritarian ordering, and that, in his construction, it carries with it a potential for the defence of individual self-determination in as much as the individual con-science, by virtue of its privileged knowledge of an inner life hidden from the sight of others, is the ultimate judge of actions. How it could operate is illustrated by Goscelin's account of what Edith of Wilton said to the Bishop of Winchester when he criticized the fine clothing she wore and pointed out that Christ takes no delight in outward appearances, because it is the heart alone that he asks: "Quite so, my lord, and I have given mine." Goscelin claimed that his late 11th century Life of Edith, written some hundred years after her death, was based on earlier lives and the oral traditions of the nuns of Wilton.[84] Hagiographers being, arguably, the least reliable of chroniclers, this is not quite as good as having it from Edith herself. The letter of Abbess Eangyth to Boniface does represent first-hand testimony to individual self-defence, in her rejection of those who cite canon law in opposition to her desire to make a pilgrimage to Rome as "those who glory in appearances and not in heart."[85]

The modes of Germanic society with which early Christianity found a point of contact were those of warrior heroism; the metaphoric campaign of soldiers of Christ against Satan, waged in the spirit by the desert fathers, had already been sharpened to prominence and literalized by the persecution of Christians, in the objective and subjective genitive. Heroic age Christianity was less concerned with the submission of the will to God than the cultivation of the will to resist foes internal and external. Alcuin, urging Archbishop Eanbald of York to imi-tate the passion of Christ in his resistance to the Northumbrian king, was not urging him to embrace martyrdom but exhorting him to have the same courage in fighting the good fight as Christ displayed when he took up his cross to do battle with the powers of darkness.[86] Warrior-heroic modes could be, more or less, indiscriminately applied to both men and women: "For all soldiers of Christ of either sex have despised temporal troubles and tempests and have held the frailties of this world as naught," as Boniface explained to Abbess Bugga.[87] Alcuin wrote in similar terms to Abbess Æthelburg: "I have heard of the troubles that you and almost all of the servants of God are suffering, now that your rulers are not kings but tyrants. . . . If the old enemy does not find a place to tempt you within, he looks for one outside, to weaken your spiritual courage, and you must resist him bravely."[88] Notable builders of churches for the greater glory of God and the provision of defensive fortification, early monastic women

---

83 That is, a Germanic lyric theme of the grief of the last survivor fuses with a patristic *topos*; see esp. *The Wanderer* (ASPR III, 134–7).

84 *Life of Edith*, ch. 12: ed. A. Wilmart, "La Légende de Sainte Édithe en prose et vers par le moine Goscelin," AB 56 (1938), 5–101, 265–307.

85 Tangl, 14; see further pp. 146–8.

86 *Epistolae Karolini Aevi II*, ed. E. Duemmler, MGH Epist 4 (Berlin, 1895), 232. Selected letters are translated by S. Allott, *Alcuin of York* (York 1974).

87 Emerton, p. 171; Tangl, 94.

88 Allott, p. 57; Duemmler, 300.

were being encouraged to labour in building in the soul a fortress of free will, where, strong in the knowledge of self which is the knowledge of God, they could, like Edith of Wilton, take up their existential *estancia*.[89]

In its indiscriminately heroic representation of men and women, which submerges – or ignores – differences of gender, Anglo-Saxon literature is in striking contrast with later, romance modes of representation. Writing shortly after the conquest, Goscelin is poised between two worlds. The story of Edith of Wilton was retold in the 12th century by the Anglo-Norman chronicler William of Malmesbury,[90] but the effect is crucially different, for the bishop is not halted in his tracks by her certain knowledge of the state in which she stands. William's Edith is a witty young lady who parries the reproof with an *argumentum ad hominem*, observing that a mind might be as pure beneath her vestments as the one he bears beneath his tattered furs. The bishop, blushing, is silenced by her lively repartee and, possibly even, subliminally overcome by female charm. Edith wins her point, but William does not easily forget that an abbess is a woman.

With the view that the position of women was, relatively speaking, more favourable throughout the Anglo-Saxon period than in later centuries, I am in agreement. That they owed this relatively favourable position chiefly to Germanic custom seems certain, although – incidental no doubt to the occupation of centre-stage by rituals of power – every change has brought with it apparent benefits that assist its acceptance, and at least some of the early English abbesses who were famed for their learning are likely to have been under the impression that they were beneficiaries of the advance of Roman civilization under the auspices of the Church of Rome. Be that as it may, the ecclesiastical bases for eventually undermining the position of women were already being laid in the conversion period, and the coming to power of a Norman church hierarchy – already influential in any case during the reign of Edward the Confessor – may have accelerated the effects of the Benedictine Reform movement in England, but does not represent an essential change in direction.[91]

The bases for undermining the authority of individual women as judges of their own interior disposition are present in Gregory's replies, in the assumption that women are relatively more corrupt and cannot be permitted to exercise their own judgment in matters pertaining to their own sexuality. They are present too in Augustine's questions, which elevate sexuality, particularly female sexuality, to unique prominence as an offence against all that is sacred. *Theodore's Penitential* is in many respects a more striking example of enlightened attitudes than the *Libellus Responsionum*. But how little cognizance it took of Gregory's provision for women using their own judgment in relation to the divine is evident in its handling of the topics that Augustine had raised. On the question of women taking communion while menstruating Gregory stated: "Let women make up their own minds and if they do not venture to approach the sacrament . . . they are to be praised for their right thinking: but when as the

---

[89] See further ch. 3, pp. 106, 109.
[90] *De Gestis Regum Anglorum*, ed. W. Stubbs, RS 90 (London, 1887), I, 269. William's term for Edith is *puella*.
[91] See Introduction, p. 7.

result of the habits of a religious life they are carried away by the love of the same mystery, they are not to be prevented." *Theodore's Penitential* decrees: "Women shall not in the time of impurity enter into a church, or communicate – neither nuns nor laywomen; if they presume [to do this] they shall fast for three weeks."[92] Gregory stated that the Old Testament law on purification after childbirth is to be understood allegorically, for if a woman were to enter a church at the very hour of her delivery in order to give thanks, she would not be guilty of any sin. *Theodore's Penitential* continues, in its own, very different, strain: "In the same way shall they do penance who enter a church before purification after childbirth, that is, forty days."[93] Gregory's respect for the individual judgment of men in the matter of purification following marital relations survived no better. Gregory explained that "although different nations think differently in this matter and appear to observe different rules, yet it has always been the custom of the Romans from ancient times, after intercourse with one's wife, to seek purification by washing and reverently to abstain from entering a church for a brief period."[94] This alone was perhaps sufficient reason for *Theodore's Penitential* to decree flatly: "A husband who sleeps with his wife shall wash himself before he goes into a church."[95] It is worth recalling that Gregory's *Libellus Responsionum* is, in origin, a private communication on pastoral ministry, whereas penitential canons, like contemporary legislation, are not generally designed to convey the subtle complexity of their actual implementation. But *Theodore's Penitential*, as I have indicated, does have a negotiable mode, and, given that these particular rulings must have been directly derived from the *Libellus*, which circulated with the penitential canons, it is all the more remarkable that they are couched in such crudely authoritarian terms. They spring, presumably, from a *milieu* in which the whole of the *Libellus* – including its remarks on women – was held to represent a policy of indulgence that had been superseded.[96]

The bases for an ultimate deterioration in the position of women are present in a more general way in the *Libellus Responsionum*'s pervasive reflection of the importance that the marriage bond assumed in ecclesiastical thinking. In its social establishment of the marriage bond, the church effectively brought into being the postlapsarian condition as it had been extrapolated from Genesis. It is therefore altogether fitting that in the beginning, at the very genesis of the church in England, Gregory explained the nature of sin to Augustine as a psychomachic repetition of the original fall. Specifically, the original fall is understood, in his explanation, to have consisted in succumbing to the sexual temptation of a woman; within the individual, sin consists, metaphorically, of the procreative copulation of the spirit and flesh, of whose marital union the individual is constituted: "The Evil Serpent suggested the first sin, and Eve, as flesh, took physical pleasure in it, while Adam, as spirit, consented. . . . For when the Evil Spirit suggests a sin, no sin is committed unless the flesh takes

---

92 McNeill, p. 197; *Theodore's Penitential*, I.xiv.17.
93 McNeill, p. 197; *Theodore's Penitential*, I.xiv.18.
94 C&M, pp. 93–5.
95 McNeill, p. 211; *Theodore's Penitential*, II.xii.30.
96 See Meyvaert, 1971, 25–6. *Theodore's Penitential*, Preface, p. 288, makes it clear that Bk. II, in which these rulings appear, belongs to a later stratum of compilation.

pleasure in it; but when the flesh begins to take pleasure, then sin is born; and if deliberate consent is given, sin is complete."[97]

The missionary church's idea of marriage was a mysterious union in which two distinct corporeal entities inextricably merged and lost their distinctness of being to become a single entity, and as the process was irreversible, it followed that it ought not to be repeatable by either party outside the marriage. How literally this idea could be rooted in the mind is evident from the fact that what makes a man's marriage to his step-mother or his sister-in-law an abomination in Gregory's reasoning is not consanguinity, for there is none; the reason it is prohibited is that, because husband and wife are one flesh, a man's marital union with his father's wife is indistinguishable from homosexual incest with his father. Gregory's letter illustrates both the centrality of marriage union as a constituting metaphor for religious experience and theological discourse; and, even more importantly, the pervasive tendency to blur metaphoric with objective levels of reality. Marital union is not only employed by Gregory to express the relation of spirit and flesh. He also uses it to define the nature of episcopal consecration, as well as the condition of women – though not men – receiving communion: "How much the more should women preserve themselves in purity of body when about to receive the body of Almighty God himself, lest they be overwhelmed by the very greatness of this inestimable mystery?"[98] By an undoubtedly meaningful paradox, Paul employed as a constituting metaphor for the relation of Christ and his church the relation which the church generally regarded as the most corrupt. Noticeably conscious of the gulf that separated the mystic marriage from the human institution that figured it, Paul nevertheless opted finally for the social actualization of his metaphoric paradigm: "For this cause shall a man leave his father and mother, and shall be joined unto his wife, and they two shall be one flesh. This is a great mystery: but I speak concerning Christ and the church. Nevertheless let every one of you in particular so love his wife even as himself; and the wife see that she reverences her husband."[99]

Whenever the early church turned its attention from the engrossing business of ordering its own affairs to ordering society, the establishment of "lawful marriage" was a paramount concern. To all appearances it regulated to confine sexual activity to "lawful marriage" merely for the sake of regulating what it would rather have stamped out altogether, but what was at stake, in as much as the process was ultimately purposive, was the figurative dimensions of its particular conception of marital union.[100] Actual social relations in Anglo-Saxon

---

[97] Sherley-Price, p. 83. There is, of course, nothing original about Gregory's allegorization of the fall, and his conception of the nature of the original fall was the one which dominated; but there were other conceptions of the nature of the fall available, and the view that the original fall consisted in concupiscence is by no means one to which Gen. 3 inexorably points. For extended discussion of patristic and late antique views on sexuality, see K.E. Borresen, *Subordination and Equivalence: The Nature and Role of Women in Augustine and Thomas Aquinas*, trans. C.H. Talbot (Washington, 1981); P. Brown, *The Making of Late Antiquity* (Chicago, 1978); E.R. Dodds, *Pagan and Christian in an Age of Anxiety* (New York, 1970), ch. 1; R.R. Reuther, *Religion and Sexism* (New York, 1974).

[98] Sherley-Price, p. 81.

[99] Eph. 5.31–3. For a study of Paul's views on women and marriage, see G. Delling, *Paulus' Stellung zu Frau und Ehe* (Stuttgart, 1931).

[100] The early church accepted secular contracts of marriage as binding, but marriage could be

England were different from the ones with which missionaries were familiar, and
certainly different from the ones they were accustomed to employ as metaphors.
It may be safely concluded that the Anglo-Saxons with whom the church came
into contact also differed in not sharing its conception of marriage as an indissoluble and exclusive union by which two people became mystically one.[101] The
task for the church was to find proximate channels for imaging humanity's
incorporation into the body of Christ while at the same time working towards
the construction of a social reality that conformed, at least visibly, to the
conception of exclusive and indissoluble union. What it found to hand was not
paradigms for the individual relation of the soul to God, but the relation of the
warrior chief and his *comitatus*; a more apt vehicle for union of the body of
believers in the headship of Christ, despite its disjunctions, than the marital
relation that Paul employed.[102]

For Anglo-Saxon society the primary bond was kinship, and marriage a
contractual relation between families; and, indeed, amongst members of the
same family – the fact that the permitted degrees of consanguinity in marriage
formed a vital question for both Augustine and Boniface is an index of the
collision between what was for ecclesiastical culture the primary relational
bond, and its chief indigenous rival in Germanic societies. Against the kin-
group as the entity responsible in law, the penitentials asserted the moral
responsibility of the individual.[103] The detachment of the individual from identity with the kin-group was also an essential pre-requisite for the emergence to
prominence of marriage as the exclusive union of two separate beings: "for this
cause shall a man leave his father and mother, and shall be joined unto his
wife." The forsaking of kindred was also the condition prescribed for entry to
the monastic life; "leave father and mother and follow me."

Familial relations are a no less vital constituting metaphor in the New Testament than marital union, and the social dominance of kinship offered an
opportunity for making kinship rather than marriage a *signum* of mystic union –
for we are, as Paul affirmed, "members of his body, of his flesh, and of his bones."
Boniface, in urging the English church to pray for the conversion of the Saxons,
because, as the Saxons themselves were wont to say, "We are of one blood and
one bone," seems to understand the physical oneness of the human race as the
means through which mystical membership in the body of Christ is

---

regarded as a *signum* of the relation of Christ and the Church without being a sacrament: see
J.M. Wallace-Hadrill, *The Frankish Church* (Oxford, 1983), pp. 403–11.

[101] The matrimonial arrangements and conceptions of the various early Germanic peoples
remain controversial because of the insufficiency of documentation, but there appears to be
general agreement on the existence of separation and polygyny.

[102] This is not to overlook the probability that the lord-*comitatus* relationship depicted in
vernacular literature represents not purely secular ideals, but ideals which have been re-shaped
by their employment as ecclesiastical metaphors: see R. Woolf, "The Ideal of Warriors Dying
with Their Lord in the *Germania* and in *The Battle of Maldon*," ASE 5 (1976), 63–81.

[103] See esp. T.P. Oakley, *English Penitential Discipline and Anglo-Saxon Law in Their Joint Influence*
(New York, 1923). Even in the late AS period, the distinction is by no means clear-cut. Secular
law codes sometimes operate with a conception of individual responsibility, whereas Wulfstan's
penitential handbook allows vicarious penance: ed. R. Fowler, "A Late OE Handbook for the
Use of a Confessor," *Anglia* 83 (1965), 1–34.

apprehended.[104] But against all "mere" earthly attachment – above all, against the kinship of flesh and blood – the early church postulated membership in a spiritual community, entirely distinct from earthly kinship and free from the taint of corporeality. Into this immaculate new family the nuns of Barking had been born again by ecclesiastical teaching, and had become "adoptive daughters of regenerate grace brought forth from the fecund womb of ecclesiastical conception through the seed of the spiritual word."[105] The English penitentials are less active than the Irish in driving in the wedge between natural kinship and devout community:

> Anyone therefore whom the devil has mocked by means of grief and sorrows, such as the loss of friends or relatives or of anything else, so that he allows him to do nothing good, but (only) to despair, let him first keep a three days' fast without food or drink; if he relapses into the same state afterwards, it is forty nights on bread and water. If he should be in grief and sadness so that he cannot be roused, the monk does penance in another place on bread and water, and returns no more into the community of the brethren, until he be joyful in body and soul.[106]

English hagiography is most explicitly concerned to affirm the primacy of spiritual relations over those of the flesh where the church's retention of family-owned lands is threatened – as it was by the practice of abbots appointing their kinsmen as their successors. Benedict Biscop, in *History of the Abbots*, advising his monks on the appointment of his successor, is particularly insistent on the distinction between carnal and spiritual community, despite the fact that both of the co-abbots Benedict had appointed during his life were related to him:

> For just as those who beget children by carnal generation must be governed by earthly and carnal considerations in their choice of an heir for an earthly and carnal inheritance, so must they who, in a spiritual sense, bring forth children of God by the seed of his spiritual word, be guided by spiritual criteria. Let them reckon the eldest son among their spiritual children him who is endowed with more abundant spiritual grace, just as parents according to the flesh recognize that their firstborn has pride of place among their offspring and must be preferred to the rest when they share out their inheritance.[107]

But, pervasively, the attempt to differentiate kinship in Christ from kinship of flesh and blood has the effect of testifying to the strength of those attachments. "I confess," wrote Alcuin to Abbot Æthelheard, "that I have wearied myself to

---

[104] Tangl, 46; cf. Eph. 5.30.
[105] *De Virginitate*, ch. 2. Trans. M. Lapidge and M. Herren, *Aldhelm: The Prose Works* (Cambridge, 1979), pp. 59–132 (cited as L&H), at pp. 59–60: ed. R. Ehwald, MGH AA 15 (Berlin, 1919), 226–323.
[106] *Old Irish Penitential*, VI.2–3; trans. D.A. Binchy, in L. Bieler, ed. and trans., *The Irish Penitentials* (Dublin, 1963), pp. 258–77, p. 274.
[107] *Historia Abbatum Auctore Baeda*, trans. J.F. Webb and D.H. Farmer, *The Age of Bede*, rev. edn. (Harmondsworth, 1983), pp. 185–210, at p. 197; ed. Plummer, 1896, I, 364–87, ch. 11. (Subsequently referred to as *History of the Abbots*). Benedict Biscop's speech echoes *Rule of Benedict*, chs. 2, 58: ed. A. de Vogüé, *La Règle de Saint Benoît* (Paris, 1972).

exhaustion in grieving after you and been saddened to tears by your absence. I have not been so exhausted during my life abroad by affection for a brother or sister after the flesh as I have by an overwhelming longing for you, my spiritual brother." In his incarnational theology Alcuin was unusual, finding no tension between human and divine love: "I have written to you, my brother, that you may know how I love you, if you can; for I confess I cannot express it, and maybe you cannot say how you love me, but God knows, for he poured this love in our hearts."[108] Ecgburg, familiar with the oppositional view of earthly kinship and heavenly community, was less certainly able to integrate the *caritas* inspired by Boniface as an apostle of light with the affection she felt for him on account of his friendship with her dead brother; and although she struggled to find comfort in the belief that her sister, in making the pilgrimage to Rome had secured herself a place in heaven by placing her love for Christ above all earthly ties, her grief for the loss of her sister still remained.[109] Felix's *Life of Guthlac* sharpens the tensions to a paradox – the hermit saint reveals at his death that he has avoided the presence of his sister during his life in order that he may spend eternity in her company.[110]

The conception of a community of spirit distinct from and superior to kinship of flesh and blood in itself undercut the primacy of kinship bonds. The conception of members of a family as individuals whose moral responsibilities transcended family loyalties further weakened the hold of kinship bonds. It would probably be wrong to attribute to members of the church hierarchy a deliberate programmatic intention of undermining ties of kinship among the laity, but in identifiable and pragmatic ways family solidarity presented the chief obstacle to the ecclesiastical regulation of society, including the establishment of "lawful marriage." Unless they could persuade secular powers to back their rulings, bishops were reliant on their power to excommunicate; in the last resort social ostracism, isolation from family support, was a more effective weapon than exclusion from the church – as Bishop Cedd illustrates, in his attempt to dissolve the uncanonical marriage of one of Sigeberht's kinsmen by coupling his ban of excommunication to the decree that no-one should enter his house or eat at his table.[111] An early Irish penitential decrees: "If anyone gives his daughter in honourable marriage, and she loves another, and he connives with her and receives a bride-price, both shall be excluded from the church."[112] Women had most to lose from the attrition of kinship bonds – their political influence derived from their family connexions and, having less access to force of arms, they were more reliant than men on the protection and support of their families. Individuals could be more easily constituted under the authority of churchmen, and female individuals under the authority of husbands.

By the 12th century, marriage and hetero-eroticism had emerged as the dominant constituting metaphors of religious experience. Soldiers of Christ had,

[108] Allott, p. 16; Duemmler, 9.
[109] Tangl, 13.
[110] *Felix's Life of Saint Guthlac*, ed. and trans. B. Colgrave (Cambridge, 1956), ch. 50. Subsequently referred to as *Life of Guthlac*.
[111] *HE*, III.22.
[112] "First Synod of St Patrick," 22; ed. and trans. Bieler, pp. 54–9, at p. 57.

practically to a woman, become brides of the Lamb. So too the loving couple had displaced kinship and comradeship as the focus of vernacular literary attention; eroticism replaced familial feeling as the profane rival of *caritas*. The emergence of heterosexual union as the paramount relational bond was, no doubt, as C.S. Lewis assured us, one of the few real changes in human sentiment.[113] But there is nothing sudden or inexplicable about it. It is the triumphant culmination of a conversionary process begun centuries earlier, and the time it took confirms not merely the view that nothing is natural or innate, but that on the way to dominance marriage had travelled a hard and difficult route through fairly inhospitable terrain.

It was an essential aspect of the social actualization of the ecclesiastical conception of marital union that gender distinction should be foregrounded. The usefulness of the idea of mystic marital union as metaphor is that it provides for the unitary fusion of otherwise irreconcilable antinomies, whether the conjunction involved is the union of God and Man or the simultaneous co-existence of Justice and Mercy within the nature of God.[114] Thus Alcuin, whose letters are pervaded by his familiarity with exegesis of *Canticles*, points the way forward in his letter to the heir-apparent of Offa of Mercia. With an eye to Ecgfrith's education as a Christ-king, Alcuin urged him to learn authority from his father and compassion from his mother, "from him how to rule the people in justice, from her how to feel pity for those who suffer, from both the devotion of the Christian religion."[115] The indiscriminate representation of women in warrior-heroic modes submerged gender distinctness, and the indigenous constitution of relations between men and women on the paradigm of kinship and warrior *comitatus* relationship helped to foreground indissolubility and likeness rather than the hierarchical fusion of distinct beings in the conception of marriage union. Early Christianity, coalescing with male warrior culture, discovered not only points of contact with it, but also its inherently unconvertable nature. Ultimately, women would gain a distinct identity largely arising from the role of non-combatants that they shared with clerics. Lending themselves far more readily to a relationship with Christ that was metaphorically conceived as a marital union, women were also better placed than warriors to love their enemies, bless those that cursed them, and pray for those who persecuted them, although, to the inheritance of the beatitudes, male religious orders were generally believed to have a prior claim.

But, inevitably, the emphasis in the construction of female alterity settled eventually upon the corrupt and uncontrolled sexuality, which, as it had caused the original fall, remained a paramount and barely resistible provocation to sin. Anglo-Saxons were not significantly overwhelmed by the concupiscence of our first parents as an explanation of the original wrong that had accumulated to produce the unquestionably lamentable state of the world in which human beings found themselves. In a society in which the blood-feud was endemic, the law codes were as concerned to regulate violence as ecclesiastical canons were

---

113 *The Allegory of Love* (New York, 1958), p. 11.
114 Cf. Ps. 84.11.
115 Allott, p. 48; Duemmler, 61. Gregory, in *Regula Pastoralis*, II.6, exhorted episcopal rulers to combine the loving-kindness of a mother with the correction of a father.

to regulate sex; it was a more persuasive explanation that the world's troubles originated with a man's striking of the first murderous blow:

> Feuding has existed among mankind ever since earth swallowed the blood of Abel. That was no one day strife: from it the drops splashed abroad, great wickedness among men and malice-mingled strife among nations. His brother killed his own; but Cain kept no prerogative over murder. After that it became widely manifest that chronic strife was causing harm among men so that far abroad through the earth its inhabitants suffered a contest of arms, and devised and tempered the destructive sword.[116]

As a more or less necessary corollary of the establishment of the man-woman union as paramount – if only because some rather powerful form of attraction was needed to compete with kinship affinities – the preoccupations of the early fathers were visited upon the minds of everyone, and the days of the double monastery, where soldiers of Christ of both sexes fought side by side, were numbered.

The operation of individual judgment, as understood by Gregory, and even more so the defence of the individual judgment against authoritarian prescription, is critically dependent on knowledge of the constituting texts of ecclesiastical culture. Gregory's provision for individual judgment on the part of lay men and women could be regarded as an aspect of his own pastoral inexperience.[117] A woman who was to determine that she did nothing wrong in entering a church immediately after childbirth, needed to know not only the scriptural injunctions against it but, more importantly, the tradition of allegorical interpretation of the Old Testament that nullified the literal meaning of those injunctions. For an informed judgment on the rectitude of their interior disposition, and their ensuing actions, early Anglo-Saxon women, particularly monastic women, were in a strong position.[118] The posture of the conversionary ministry was an educational one, and knowledge of the written word synonymous with knowledge of God. Converts, especially converts to the monastic life, appeared in their thousands only when chroniclers like Bede estimated the numbers that the first wave of missionaries baptized in a day. After Theodore arrived and educated more teachers in the school he set up, "all who wished for instruction in sacred studies had teachers ready at hand."[119] Female religious, in theory debarred from active ministry (though not in practice) made a significant contribution to the conversion by educating missionary teachers, both at home and abroad.[120] Their services were less required for furthering the conversion of England after the advent of Theodore, but – still encouraged to pursue knowledge of God in knowledge of the written word – they could and did keep

---

[116] *Maxims I* (ASPR III, 156–63), ll. 192–200; trans. Bradley, p. 350.

[117] In *Regula Pastoralis*, where Gregory defines numerous classes and categories of people, all requiring different handling by the episcopal ruler, difference of gender heads the list; men should be spurred to great achievements by heavy obligations, but gentle treatment should be employed to bring about amends in women (III.1).

[118] For a survey of monastic women's education, see Fell, 1986, pp. 109–28.

[119] C&M, p. 335; HE, IV.2.

[120] See HE, IV.23; see further ch. 8, pp. 257, 261–70.

pace with their male counterparts. The nuns at Barking were studying the mystic commentaries of the fathers, as well as the scriptures;[121] Leoba, at the continental mission, also studied canon law, which, as Boniface had cause to know, was more seminal to an understanding of the true nature of Christianity than knowledge of Holy Writ.[122] Monastic women were among those who "flocked" to the teaching of Boniface,[123] and it is even possible that the "all" who gained, at their desire, instruction in the new learning brought by Theodore, meant what it ought to mean. But this state of affairs depended on the freedom of contact and freedom of movement that was more generally available to women religious in the age of double monasteries; with the re-establishment of monasticism after the Viking invasions came reformed continental pressures towards enclosure and segregation, whereby monastic women gradually lost contact – direct contact at very least – with succeeding forms of new learning.[124]

Changed too, by the later 10th century, was the role of learning in the knowledge of God. The English preface to the *Rule of Benedict*, apparently addressed to learned persons imported from the continent, asserted: "It certainly cannot matter by what language a man is acquired and drawn to the true faith, as long only as he comes to God. Therefore let the unlearned natives have the knowledge of this holy rule by the exposition of their own language, that they may the more zealously serve God and have no excuse that they were driven by ignorance to err."[125] Certainly it does not matter in what language anyone comes to know God, but the knowledge of God made available in the vernacular, to female religious and laity alike, with the exception of some of the work of Ælfric, was overwhelming limited to moral hortation essentially designed to ensure that no-one had any excuse for not doing what was demanded of them. This is not to suggest that the learned tradition of female monasticism ceased to exist altogether in the late Old English period; not coincidentally, one of the convents where it survived was Wilton, the *alma mater* of Edith, whose deflection of her bishop's reproof is reported by Goscelin.[126]

---

121 *De Virginitate*, ch. 4.
122 *Vita Leobae Abbatissae Biscofesheimensis Auctore Rudolfo Fuldensi*, trans. C.H. Talbot, 1954, pp. 205–26; ed. G. Waitz, MGH SS 15.1 (Hannover, 1887), 118–31, ch. 11 (subsequently referred to as *Life of Leoba*).
123 *Life of Boniface*, ch. 2. Tangl, 13, is a letter from a woman who had been taught by Boniface.
124 Asser's *Life of Alfred*, chs. 92, 98, says that Alfred founded segregated monasteries. Trans. M. Lapidge and S. Keynes, *Alfred the Great* (Harmondsworth, 1983), pp. 67–110; ed. W. Stevenson, *Asser's Life of King Alfred*, 2nd edn. (Oxford, 1959). W. Levison, *England and the Continent in the Eighth Century* (London, 1946), p. 257, n. 3, notes that double monasteries may have survived in the late 10th c. diocese of Oswald. The 12th c. foundations of the Gilbertine order were different in kind: see ch. 9, fns. 11, 150.
125 Ed. and trans. D. Whitelock, *An Account of King Edgar's Establishment of the Monasteries*, in *Councils & Synods*, ed. D. Whitelock et al. (Oxford, 1981), I.1, 142–55 (subsequently cited as Whitelock), at 152.
126 Edith, wife of Edward the Confessor, was educated at Wilton: see *The Life of King Edward who Rests at Westminster*, ed. and trans. F. Barlow (London, 1962), p. 46 (subsequently referred to as *Life of King Edward*). Wilton's high standard of learning is shown by the *Liber Confortatorius* that Goscelin wrote for Eve after she left Wilton to become an anchorite: ed. C.H. Talbot, *Studia Anselmiana* 37 (1955), 1–117. That the new learning in the late AS period was often made available in the vernacular may suggest that standards of learning had, universally, declined by then; but whereas the Latin learned tradition evidently survived at some male

The Benedictine Reform in the late Anglo-Saxon period was the final stage of the conversion. Irrespective of the setbacks caused by Danish invasion and Danish settlement, the scale and degree of regulatory control at which the reformers aimed, and the degree of regulation, was one that the church in England had never before achieved. Eleventh century Anglo-Saxons were no less willing to be imposed upon by superior overseas ways than their forebears had been. It was already long since Archbishop Fulk of Reims had written to King Alfred to point out, with undisguised contempt, that, as for the traditions that the English race had derived from Gregory, the time had come to put away such childish things and face up to the more comprehensive demands of a new, definitively post-apostolic, era of Christianity:

> Certainly St Augustine, the first bishop of your people, sent to you by the blessed Gregory, your Apostle, neither could demonstrate in a short time the decrees of the apostolic ordinances, nor wished suddenly to burden a rude and barbarous race with new and unknown laws; for he knew how to have regard to their weakness, and to say with the Apostle, as it were to little ones in Christ: 'I gave you milk to drink, not meat'. . . . But as time passed and the Christian religion grew, Holy Church would not and had no right to be content with these things, but only with the model received from those Apostles, their masters and founders, who after the propagation and diffusion of the evangelical teaching by the celestial master himself, accounted it not superfluous and useless, but necessary and beneficial, to establish the faithful more perfectly with the frequent admonitions of their letters and to strengthen them more firmly in the true faith, and to deliver to them more abundantly a way of living and a pattern of religion.[127]

Even with the best will in the world, and with no deliberate intention to avoid educating the laity to a point at which it could argue with the ecclesiastical hierarchy on equal terms, it was practically impossible to ensure interior conviction or educate for individual judgment. It was out of the question to even attempt it at anything like the speed with which reformers wished to see the conduct of the nation at large brought into line with the exacting standards of continental orthodoxy. Though Alfred cannot be regarded as having been moved by the best will in the world, yet he was surely a man of good will, and even Alfred thought it practically possible to aim only at vernacular literacy for young men from families able to spare them from other labours, and instruction in Latin for potential members of religious orders – or perhaps he did mean "young persons."[128] By the time the universities were founded, female religious

---

houses, Wilton is the only convent in the late AS period known to me that ranks as a centre of learning with the early double monasteries (see ch. 8, fn. 41).

[127] Trans. D. Whitelock, *English Historical Documents*, 2nd edn. (London, 1979), I, 884 (subsequently cited as *EHD*); *Cartularium Saxonicum*, ed. W. de G. Birch (London, 1887), II, 555 (for 556).

[128] See *Pastoral Care*, Preface, p. 6 ("eal sio gioguth the nu is on Angel kynne friora monna"). Fell, 1986, pp. 17–19, 100, cautions against imposing gender specificity in the reading of OE, particularly in this instance, and points out that education among Alfred's own children was not confined to his sons (*Life of Alfred*, ch. 75).

had definitively lost the opportunity to participate in any way in the elite status which male clerics were consolidating for themselves; in relation to clerics, their position declined with the laity's. For women religious, as for the laity, the content of the devotional life would come to be filled less with knowledge of the word which is knowledge of God and more with the mystic contemplation of the individual soul's union with the bridegroom Christ. The individual's privileged knowledge of the interior life continued to serve devout women, from Christina of Markyate to Margery Kempe, as a means of defending an irregular manner of life.[129] But the proliferation of authenticating visions is a sign that individual judgments needed rather substantial buttressing against authority. If the letter of Edwin of New Minster does preserve an episode that dates from the 980s, the signs were by then already at hand. Refused his abbot's permission to visit St Cuthbert's shrine at Durham, Edwin "went on his own say-so, and took himself north" after the saint appeared to him in a vision.[130] In the final analysis, if monastic women appear to have been held in relatively high regard in the early church, it is because there was generally more regard for individuals when the Church Militant filled its ranks less with conscripts than with volunteers.

---

[129] Life of Christina of Markyate, ed. and trans., C.H. Talbot (Oxford, 1959); The Book of Margery Kempe, trans. B.A. Windeatt (Harmondsworth, 1985). The limitations of Christina's success are observed by A.K. Warren, "The Nun as Anchoress: England 1100–1500," in Medieval Religious Women, ed. J.A. Nichols and L.T. Shank (Kalamazoo, 1984), I, 200.

[130] F.E. Harmer, ed. and trans., Anglo-Saxon Writs (Manchester, 1952), 113. Harmer, pp. 387–95, concludes that, although the writ itself is a 12th c. fabrication, a tradition of an unauthorized visit to Durham may have existed by the early 11th c.

2

"Some Special Irregularities of Marriage": *Theodore's Penitential* and the Case of St Æthelthryth

Introduction: Marriage Union

The high priority that the missionary church attached to the establishment of "lawful marriage" that is evident in the *Libellus Responsionum* was also manifested at the 673 Council of Hertford. Theodore, who presided over the council, called on the assembled bishops to enact ten canons that he had selected from a book of canon law; these ten, he said, were of the utmost importance. For Theodore, as for Augustine, the really vital business of the church was its own internal organization. All but one of his canons concern administration and discipline within the church. Last of all, however, the council decreed: "That nothing be allowed but lawful wedlock. Let none be guilty of incest, and let none leave his own wife except for fornication, as the gospel teaches. If anyone puts away his own wife who is joined to him by lawful matrimony, he may not take another if he wishes to be a true Christian; he must either remain as he is, or else be reconciled to his own wife."[1]

Simple and all but absolute, Theodore's ruling on marriage at the Council of Hertford draws for its authority on one of the few statements that Christ made on the subject.[2] Setting aside men's freedom to divorce their wives under Mosaic law as a concession that had been made to their hardness of heart, Christ condemned divorce and remarriage for any reason other than the adultery of a wife. Theodore's canon likewise countenances divorce and remarriage solely on the grounds of a wife's adultery. But, in condemning remarriage and approving reconciliation as an alternative to divorce, the canon echoes 1 Cor. 7.10–11. The difference is that Paul – addressing himself to both men and women – claimed divine authority for prohibiting divorce and remarriage for any reason at all: "And unto the married I command, yet not I, but the Lord, Let not the wife depart from her husband: But and if she depart, let her remain

---

[1] HE, IV.5: "Decimum capitulum pro conjugiis: Ut nulli liceat nisi legitimum habere coniugium; nullus incestum faciat, nullus coniugem propriam nisi, ut sanctum euangelium docet, fornicationis causa relinquat. Quod si quisquam propriam expulerit coniugem legitimo sibi matrimonio coniunctam, si Christianus esse recte voluerit, nulli alteri copuletur; sed ita permaneat, aut propriae reconcilietur coniugi" (C&M, p. 352). Basil's Canonical Letters (see fn. 19) are among the sources suggested.

[2] See Matt. 5.31–2, 19.5–9; Mark 10.11–12; Luke 16.18.

unmarried, or be reconciled to her husband: and let not the husband put away his wife." Paul may be regarded here as having effectively interpreted the letter of Christ's words in the spirit of New Testament charity. In Theodore's canon, then, permission for a man to remarry in the case of a wife's adultery is contextualized as a concession to human imperfection, and the canon is in line with 1 Cor. 7.10–11 in its intention to affirm that marriage is a union which is unique and indissoluble, even in the face of the most extreme breach imaginable, the adultery of a wife: "Wherefore they twain are no more twain, but one flesh. What therefore God hath joined together, let not man put asunder."[3]

When Paul dilated on organic union in Eph. 5.22–33, he moved from the simple union of flesh to an innately hierarchical conception of the union of head and body. On the one hand, Paul was conscious of the absolute alterity of divine and human spheres: that husband and wife were one flesh was "a great mystery," but only in the sense that their union figured the union of Christ and the church. He nevertheless asserted it as imperative that the earthly institution should make manifest the mystic union that it figured, by the subordination of the wife to her husband's headship; more precisely, to her husband's *loving* headship. In effect, the inequality of the social institution as Paul knew it, by its employment as a metaphor for Christ and his church, was given a powerful metaphysical endorsement, and patriarchy, generally without the benevolence that was an intrinsic part of Paul's definition of union, became a monolithic paradigm for this world and the next: "Nevertheless let every one of you in particular so love his wife even as himself; and the wife see that she reverence her husband."

Without the introduction of the head-body hierarchy, however, the conception of marriage as an exclusive and indissoluble union of two fleshes offers a potential basis for regarding the relationship as a union of equals. In their commitment to affirming the indissolubility of marriage, ecclesiastics sometimes promoted the image of marriage as a union of identical and equal entities, particularly in societies where the indigenous status of women was relatively high.[4] The authorizing texts and canons available to them were varied; Paul, for instance, in exhorting both men and women not to abandon their spouses, is recognizing the logic of a marital fusion of identities – that what holds true for one partner must hold true for the other. So, too, in asserting that "the wife hath not power of her own body, but the husband: and likewise also the husband hath not power over his own body, but the wife," Paul realizes that the condition of unified entities cannot be distinguished. In 9th century Wessex, the priest Asser deplored the court's refusal to permit the king's wife to share the throne or hold the title of queen, alleging that their refusal was contrary to the custom of all Germanic peoples.[5] Although penitentials give every appearance

---

[3] Matt. 19.6, cf. Eph. 5.31.
[4] I do not intend to imply that the absence of a homogeneous construct of women in marriage was peculiar to AS England. Wallace-Hadrill, 1983, p. 409, points out that Jonas of Orleans (*PL* 106, 170–92) was "particularly insistent on equality within marriage, for which he could find much support in the conciliar legislation from the mid eighth century onwards." In the 12th c., Hugh of St Victor found confirmation for regarding marriage as a union of equals in the fact that Eve was created from the side of Adam, rather than his head or feet (*De Sacramentis Christianae Fidei, PL* 176, 284).
[5] *Life of Alfred*, chs. 13–14.

of seeking to minimize the incidence of sexual activity as an end in itself, Paul's conception of marriage as a *signum* of the union of Christ and the church exerted a powerful pressure towards regulating the earthly institution of marriage in order to make it conform in outward appearance to the transcendental reality it signified. Asser was conceivably aware of moves towards a sacramental definition of marriage through Wessex links with Frankish clergy.[6] The unexpected direction of his concern with the status of the queen is explicable if his intention was to promote marriage as an emblem of the union of Christ and his church, whereas the royal marriage in Wessex, far from offering an exemplary model, displayed none of the customary indigenous forms that affirmed the unity of the royal pair.

The conceptions of marriage as a social institution that missionaries sent from Rome had derived from their own cultural experience were different from those of the Anglo-Saxon societies with which they came into contact, and the figurative terms in which the church envisaged marital union were alien. Asser's remarks suggest that, in the early Anglo-Saxon period, the idea of marriage union that the church promoted made use of available indigenous conceptions, and in consequence emphasized the identity of being and indivisibility of two people who were joined as one, rather than the hierarchy of being that inheres in organic union conceived as a fusion of head and body. What early hagiography and vernacular literature chiefly know of the indissolubility of human relations is the bonds of kinship and comradeship. In *Maxims I*, the pragmatic need for physical inseparability shades into a more metaphysical conception of an enduring relational bond: "The man who has to live by himself is miserable. . . . It would be better for him to have a brother, for them both to be the sons of one man, one nobleman, if they were to have to attack a boar or overpower a bear; that is an animal with cruel paws. The warriors should always carry their equipment with them and all sleep in a body. Let no-one separate them by slanders before death parts them."[7] No-one who has read *The Battle of Maldon* can forget the vows that they spoke on the battle-field when their leader lay slain, for at that point "they all desired one of two things, to give up their lives or avenge the man they had loved."[8] But no less important is the vow that Offa had made earlier to his lord: "that they should both ride home safe to the fortress or perish in war." Warrior vows of loyalty are vows of physical inseparability in death *and* in life, pledges to share the same fate. In the event, Offa and his lord do both perish in war, and Offa's vow finds fulfilment in his physical proximity to Byrhtnoth in death – Offa, the poet relates, lay close beside his lord in a manner befitting a thane.[9] For Aldhelm, urging the abbots of Bishop Wilfrid to accompanying him into exile, the warrior *comitatus* was, ideally, indissolubly involved in its leader's fate, for better or for worse: "If worldly men, exiles from divine teaching, were to desert a devoted master, whom they had embraced in prosperity but once the opulence of good times began to diminish and the adversity of bad fortune began its onslaught, they preferred the secure

---

6 See ch. 7, esp. fns. 45, 49, 61.
7 *Maxims I*, ll. 172–80; trans. Shippey, p. 73.
8 *The Battle of Maldon*, ll. 207–8.
9 See *The Battle of Maldon*, ll. 288–9.

peace of their dear country to the burdens of a banished master, are they not deemed worthy of the scorn and mockery of all?"[10]

That the constitution of marriage (or "male-female union") on the paradigms of warrior relations was an indigenous Germanic impulse is evident in the Old Icelandic literature of later centuries, and perceptible in the Old English love-lyrics of the 9th (or possibly 8th) century.[11] Although these three lyrics have been widely interpreted as allegories deriving from exegesis of *Canticles*, the erotic union of flesh – on which traditional exegesis of *Canticles* hinges – is central to the conception of union in only one of them. The union of flesh *is* the essence of the union whose severance *Wulf and Eadwacer* laments, in terms that revert ironically to the injunction that no man may put asunder that which God has joined.[12] *The Husband's Message* and *The Wife's Lament*, however, depict union by variations of the theme of sharing a common fate in accordance with fidelity to vows; the absence of vows in *Wulf and Eadwacer* is perhaps a concomitant of the extra-marital nature of its severed union. But in *Wulf and Eadwacer*, as in *The Wife's Lament*, union is imaged as man and woman sharing a common condition, which transcends physical separation: "Wulf is on one island and I am on another." The woman who voices *The Wife's Lament* recalls the mutual vows that she and her lover/husband often made, that "nothing but death should come between us." Estranged from him and separated by distance, she rises in her final curse to demand the indissoluble continuance of their vows of union; as she sits on land, a solitary exile lamenting by a cave in a wilderness, so may he sit by sea, "under a stony pile, rime-encrusted by the storm, drenched in water in a drear dwelling."[13] In *The Husband's Message*, the courtly message requesting the woman to take ship and join the man who awaits her, under-pinned by reminders of the vows that they once spoke, has as its definition of sharing a common fate the sharing of treasure and overlordship that he has won in another land – as once they held a city, inhabited one country, he is in hopes that God will grant that they two together may thereafter distribute treasure to the warrior retinue.[14]

Marriage union in the comradeship mode, then, involves joint possession and lordship, but is not necessarily equal. The underlying relational model of *The Wife's Lament* is that of lord and retainer, more precisely, the relation of the lord and his particular intimate, as represented by the mutual vows of Offa and Byrhtnoth in *The Battle of Maldon*; to the woman in *The Wife's Lament*, the man

[10] *Epist* 12; trans. L&H, pp. 169–70: ed. Ehwald, 500–2.

[11] See F. Roeder, *Die Familie bei den Angelsachsen, I: Mann und Frau, Studien zur Englischen Philologie* 4 (Halle, 1899), pp. 84ff.

[12] *Wulf and Eadwacer* (ASPR III, 179–80): "thæt mon eathe tosliteth thætte næfre gesomnad wæs,/ uncer giedd geador" (ll. 18–19). For discussion of these lines as a verbal echo of OE translations of Matt. 19.6, see J.B. Spamer, "The Marriage Concept in *Wulf and Eadwacer*," *Neophilologus* 62 (1978), 143–4. This short lyric has been debated at length; that its speaker is a woman and male-female relationship its subject is widely accepted. Interpretation of the poem as a mother's lament for her son, although less wildly idiosyncratic than some which have been proposed, founders on ll. 18–19.

[13] Trans. Bradley, p. 385; see *The Wife's Lament* (ASPR III, 210–11), esp. ll. 21–5, 42–50. Here, too, the identity of the *dramatis personae* has been disputed; few would now argue that, notwithstanding the feminine forms, the speaker is a man.

[14] See *The Husband's Message* (ASPR III, 225–7), esp. ll. 14–19, 32–9. See fn. 16.

is a *frea* ("lord") as well as a *freond*. There being no contemporary documentation of pre-Christian Anglo-Saxon society, it is impossible to determine how far the conception of union in these lyrics is the product of ecclesiastical influence – their imaging of a union that persists despite physical absence, which is a prominent theme of the correspondence of the Boniface circle, seems particularly likely to represent the influence of a Christian conception of spiritualized, humanly transcendent relationships.[15] The modelling of man-woman relationships on the lord-retainer relation fairly certainly does point to the existence of an indigenous hierarchy in marriage rather than a shift from an egalitarian comradeship model prompted by ecclesiastical thinking.[16] But like Asser' fulminations on the Wessex court's refusal to grant formal equality of status to the queen, what these lyrics suggest is that the organic union of ecclesiastical culture, fusing with warrior culture's loyal adherence through thick and thin, produced an ideal of marriage union as a one-ness and likeness of identity, a sharing of the same fate that persisted beyond physical separation, in life and in death.

As is well known, the conception of marriage as the subordination of an inferior female Body to a male Head ultimately prevailed; converts, drawn from societies in which the position of women was generally inferior, found ample sanction for the importation and enhancement of their prior views of women in the New Testament as well as the Old, and the more influential among them contributed their own writings as further authorization. But assimilation of the construct of marriage as an organic but innately unequal union advanced only by degrees; pre-Conquest England affords no such bizarrely selective interpretations of the indissoluble oneness of flesh as Glanvill's 12th century laws, which allow a woman to bring a charge in only two cases: in the case of rape, because it is an injury to her person, and in the case of murder of her husband, "because husband and wife are one flesh."[17] Gregory's replies to Augustine in the *Libellus Responsionum* illustrate the culturally interactive nature of the conversion. *Theodore's Penitential*, I want to suggest, illustrates the way in which the indigenous position of women – and the temperamental predilections of individual ecclesiastics – helped to foreground the non-hierarchical potentialities of scriptural texts, acting, for a time, as a check on the full implementation of an unequal and discriminatory conception of marital union. What *Theodore's Penitential* demonstrates, in other words, is that Theodore and the later compilers and revisers who contributed to the *Penitential* were having to compromise their own dogmas and to accommodate to the exigencies of a society whose conceptions of marriage were different from those of canon law, and in which the position of women was relatively high. Orthodoxy itself was not monolithic,

---

15 See ch. 4, pp. 113, 130–2, 137–43.
16 My shift from "male-female union" to "marriage" may seem to ignore the fact that some readers of *The Husband's Lament* regard the couple as betrothed rather than married. As the Church regarded betrothals as binding (*Theodore's Penitential*, II.xii.34) and was far from insisting on nuptial benedictions in the 9th c. (Wallace-Hadrill, 1983, 406–11), it is unlikely that the distinction signified in the AS period.
17 *The Treatise on the Laws and Customs of the Realm of England Commonly Called Glanvill*, ed. and trans. G.D.G. Hall (London, 1965), XI.1; XIV.1, 3, 6.

and the various, sometimes conflicting, rulings on marriage and women that make up *Theodore's Penitential* spring ultimately from divergent conceptions of Christianity. In some cases the legislators are conscious of deviating from the orthodoxy of Rome, and authorize their rulings by adducing the principle of regional variation; for, by claiming the authority of "the Greeks," the canonists not only give the impression (probably specious in most cases) that their rulings originated with Theodore of Tarsus, but evoke a precedent for Anglo-Saxon regional variation from Roman orthodoxy.

Background to *Theodore's Penitential*

Theodore's Penitential,[18] then, does not represent a simple dogmatic promulgation of a monolithic orthodoxy. The fact that its legislators are effectively choosing among a variety of possibilities and interacting with local circumstances becomes more clearly evident if we compare the penitential canons of different regions. New Testament texts pertaining to marriage, as I have indicated, are in any case highly divergent, and canonical attitudes to divorce, remarriage and adultery differed considerably. One strand of interpretation with which Theodore was familiar is represented by the Canonical Letters of Basil – he was highly influential in the Eastern Church, and is cited as an authority by *Theodore's Penitential*.[19] Basil is unusual in registering his awareness of the fact that penitential practice was determined more by social attitudes than by revealed truth; more precisely, existing social custom determined the choice of authorizing scriptural texts, and, by its adoption as the custom of the church, it gained further sanction. Basil explains that, logically, Christ's condemnation of divorce except in the case of adultery applies to both men and women; but custom – for which scriptural authority can also be found – regards more seriously the adultery of a woman.[20] How seriously Basil's society regarded female adultery is evident from his explanation that the church has never required full public penance on the part of a woman who has confessed to adultery, lest this should result in her death; whether at the hands of her husband or of secular authorities is unstated.[21] Basil thus accepts that wives who commit adultery are divorced by their husbands, but rules that wives must continue to bear with husbands who commit adultery. Further, he decrees that a woman is on no account to leave her husband, even if he is a pagan, and he cites, as his authority, 1 Cor. 7.14, "the unbelieving husband is sanctified by the

---

[18] *Die Canones Theodori Cantuariensis und ihre Überlieferungsformen*, ed. P.W. Finsterwalder (Weimar, 1929), pp. 285–334. Translation throughout is from J.T. McNeill and H.M. Gamer, *Medieval Handbooks of Penance* (New York, 1965), pp. 182–215 (cited as McNeill).

[19] See *St Basil: The Letters*, ed. and trans. R.J. Deferrari (London, 1930), III, 5–47, 103–35, 241–267 (subsequently referred to as *Basil*). These canonical letters (188, 199, 217), dated 374–5, formed the nucleus of ecclesiastical discipline in the Greek church in the 6th c.

[20] *Basil*, 188.9, 199.21.

[21] *Basil*, 199.34.

wife," despite the fact that Paul also counseled against men divorcing pagan wives, on the same grounds.[22]

Theodore's Penitential makes it clear that the exclusively masculine reference of the law on marriage enacted by his bishops at Hertford is not intended to convey universal applicability; it assumes a patriarchal society in which the initiation of divorce by a woman is an eventuality beyond expression.[23] On the other hand, viewed against Basil's Canonical Letters, the injunction to reconcil-iation with an adulterous wife that Theodore urged upon husbands at the Council of Hertford is striking. Effectively, Theodore required, on the part of a man, an exercise of charitable forgiveness within earthly marriage comparable with Christ's forgiveness of the sinful bride of the mystic union – for him, as for Paul, the union of husband and wife was not only a figure of Christ's headship over the church, but also of his love for it. In this, Theodore's canon is entirely different from the canons attributed to St Patrick. These *oppose* reconciliation between a husband and a wife who has committed adultery. Ironically, their opposition to reconciliation is based on the premise that husband and wife are one flesh – they cite as their authority a Pauline statement on fornication: "He who is joined to a harlot is made one body." Hostility to adulterous women goes hand in hand here with a willingness to enable men who divorce them to contract a second marriage: by conjuring with a quotation from the Old Testa-ment, " 'An adulteress shall be stoned,' that is, she shall die for this fault," the canons attributed to St Patrick are able to conclude that there is nothing to prevent a man from remarrying if his wife has committed adultery, because it is as if the wife is dead.[24]

Different again is the *Penitential of Finnian*, which may have been among the Irish penitentials in use in the north of England, and may even have been the Irish penitential on which the compiler of *Theodore's Penitential* drew. The *Penitential of Finnian* sticks to the letter of 1 Cor. 7.10–11, in prohibiting remarriage to anyone, man or woman, who has renounced an adulterous part-ner. Here, respect for the absolute principle of the uniqueness of marriage union has triumphed over the canonist's generally discriminatory attitude to women, as it so clearly has not in the canons attributed to St Patrick. But it is abun-dantly evident that formal parity in canon law was no guarantee that men and women would be treated equally unless the legislator's understanding of *caritas* outweighed his bias against women. The *Penitential of Finnian's* idea of Christ-like forgiveness in marital reconciliation is that, if a woman commits adultery and is truly repentant, it is fitting that her husband should take her back; but, as well as losing her dowry, she is to go into service to her former husband as long

---

[22] *Basil*, 188.9.

[23] See below, fn. 53.

[24] "Second Synod of St Patrick" 26, quoting 1 Cor. 6.16 and Lev. 20.10 (ed. and trans. Bieler, pp. 184–97). The Irish canons employed in the compilation of *Theodore's Penitential* (see fn. 28) are generally thought to have been *Penitential of Cummean*, either in the form known to us or in a slightly different text; ed. and trans. Bieler, pp. 108–36. *Penitential of Finnian*, the earliest penitential (pre 591), is also regarded as a possible source (ed. and trans. Bieler, pp. 74–96). *Cummean*, II.29, adjudges one year's penance for a woman who returns to be reconciled with her husband after deserting him, and the same penalty for a man if he has remarried; this impression of formal impartiality suggests that the canon assigning penance only for a man who commits adultery (also one year) is intended to apply equally to women (*Cummean*, II.23); see fn. 53.

as he lives, and is to make amends in place of a male or female slave in all piety and subjection. On the other hand, if a wife is dismissed by her husband in favour of another woman, she must wait for him in patient chastity in the hope that God will bring him to a change of heart.[25]

The Irish penitentials, like Theodore's, are products of an era in which no single body of scriptural exegesis had established itself as universally authoritative; 9th century condemnations of most of the penitentials that were in circulation on the continent mark the advance to monolithic dominance of an ever-increasingly more demanding orthodoxy.[26] Such penitentials, then, represent regional versions of Christianity. But the differences between the penitential that derives from Theodore, whose Greek background rendered him somewhat suspect to the Roman hierarchy that sent him to England, and the *Penitential of Finnian*, which reflects the ascetic hostility to women that had developed in the Celtic church, are not simply attributable to different regional traditions of Christianity. Something must be allowed, particularly in the relatively fluid conditions of the conversion period, for individual differences in apprehending the nature of Christianity, even among members of the same local tradition – and it is, finally, the values of individual compilers that the early penitentials enshrine and promulgate.

More significantly, further distinctively local versions of Christianity were shaped by the indigenous cultural values of the societies with which missionaries came into contact. At the Council of Hertford, Theodore nailed his colours to the mast with a formula whose underlying opposition to multiple marriage is as evident as its assumptions about the legal and social position of women. *Theodore's Penitential* reveals Theodore and/or his revisers (for their work cannot be confidently distinguished from Theodore's thoughts and second thoughts, even where clear differences in underlying principles are involved) battling it out at the cultural interface, and severely under pressure in confrontation with a social actuality far more complex than anything that the simple dogmatic pronouncement of the Council of Hertford was framed to meet.[27]

---

[25] *Finnian*, 42–5.

[26] Erroneous penitentials causing the destruction of the souls of the unlearned by the imposition of light penalties for grave sins were condemned by the Councils of Chalon (813) and Paris (829). The authority of Theodore, however, continued to command respect; Regino of Pruem, who (in 906) was among the first to recommend the use of penitentials in the period following these councils, specified the use of penitentials compiled either by Theodore or by Bede. Despite condemnation, continued copying of the older penitentials throughout the 9th c. shows that they remained in use. The general lines of development are outlined by P.J. Payer, *Sex and the Penitentials: The Development of a Sexual Code* (Toronto, 1984), pp. 55–71. In the late OE period, copies of the vernacular *Confessional of Pseudo-Ecgbert*, deriving from *Theodore's Penitential* and *Cummean*, survived side by side with penitentials influenced by continental reforms (see fns. 36, 43). For the transmission of OE penitentials, see A.J. Frantzen, "The Tradition of Penitentials in Anglo-Saxon England," *ASE* 11 (1982), 23–56.

[27] The manuscript tradition of early penitentials is notoriously complex. A number of penitentials were associated with Theodore's name; the work to which I refer (see fn. 18) is generally accepted as his. *Theodore's Penitential* had probably attained the form in which it survives c. 741. Penitential material, mediated through both Roman and Irish missionaries, and re-formed in the crucible of Anglo-Saxon society, was transmitted to the continent, particularly by the Boniface mission, where it doubtless underwent further transmutations in its interaction with

The Prologue to *Theodore's Penitential* confirms the view that it documents an ongoing legislative interaction with concrete social actualities.[28] Although the *Penitential* contains much that is not unique to it, then, its pronouncements on marriage do not represent the fossilized preservation of a tradition of penitential canons whose existence was purely literary.[29] There were, however, obstacles to their implementation. *Theodore's Penitential* moves freely from the regulation of individual conscience to social legislation, but the authoritative tone of ecclesiastical administrators should not mislead us into thinking that the unaided power of the word was sufficient to create a world that conformed to their wishes. The *Penitential's* itemization of penances for him who is married three or more times, for him who puts away his wife and remarries, and for her who deserts her husband and returns to him undishonoured, are evidence that an ecclesiastical council's decrees are no more reliable as a guide to social actuality than the idealizations of epic literature. For the imposition of ecclesiastical law on the recalcitrant, bishops were reliant on secular power. Despite Augustine's concern with the establishment of "lawful marriage," there is no trace of his influence in the law codes of his royal convert, Æthelberht of Kent, nor is ecclesiastical influence discernible in the code of Hlothere and Eadric, who ruled in Kent when Theodore was Archbishop of Canterbury. The 695 law code of Wihtred of Kent – a hundred years after the landing of Augustine – is the earliest surviving secular code on which the ecclesiastical regulation of marriage has succeeded in making an impact. Under the influence of Theodore's successor, Wihtred and his councillors decreed that without "lawful marriage" there could be no communion, and no *communitas* either: "Men living in illicit cohabitation are to turn to a right life with repentance of sins, or to be excluded from the fellowship of the church. Foreigners, if they will not regularize their marriages, are to depart from the land with their goods and their sins."[30]

converts, except where force of arms circumvented the conversionary process. Finsterwalder, pointing to the multiplication of copies of *Theodore's Penitential* on the continent, considered that it took its final form in the Boniface circle (pp. 168–74), but the prologue's account of the work's composition is generally accepted as authentic. Theodore's direct responsibility for judgements in *Theodore's Penitential*, even for those which specifically claim his authority or Basil's, is open to doubt because the standing of penitential canons depended entirely on the authority they claimed. As Theodore's direct responsibility made no difference to the standing of the canons that claimed authority from him, the question of levels of revision, though it affects their date of currency, is much less significant than the possibility that *Theodore's Penitential* could contain canons that reflect distinctively continental *mores*, and my interpretation of Æthelthryth's Life in the light of *Theodore's Penitential* is necessarily tentative.

[28] The Northumbrian disciple states, in the Preface, that his work is based on Theodore's replies to the questions of Eoda, supplemented by Irish canons, and that Book II incorporates Theodore's pronouncements on specific cases brought to him; these judgments had evidently been reshaped to suit the inclinations of ecclesiastical administrators, since they had given rise to what the Northumbrian disciple regards as a body of confused and contradictory material, upon which he, in turn, has imposed his own preferences by selecting as he sees fit.

[29] The view that penitentials existed in a direct relationship to social behaviour is now the more common one: see, e.g., R. Kottje, "Ehe und Eheverständnis in den vorgratianischen Bussbüchern," in *Love and Marriage in the Twelfth Century*, ed. W. van Hoeck and A. Welkenhuysen (Louvain, 1981), pp. 8–40.

[30] For these three codes, see Liebermann, I, 3–14; trans. Whitelock, *EHD*, I, 391–8.

Employing the gradualist policy that Gregory recommended to Augustine, Wihtred and his council introduced monetary fines only for illicit unions that were entered into subsequent to their law code taking effect; and it is by no means certain that they intended that all illicit unions contracted in the future were to be summarily terminated, or whether they meant that the nobly-born, having paid a fine twice that imposed on the *ceorl* class, were to be permitted to continue in illicit union. Given that the establishment of lawful marriage was still in its infancy, Wihtred and his council can scarcely have undertaken to bring their power to bear against all of the many and varied forms of marriage and remarriage that *Theodore's Penitential* declares unlawful; Wihtred's law code presumably refers only to the marriages within prohibited degrees of consanguinity that were proscribed by the Council of Hertford. For the most part, the canons of *Theodore's Penitential*, on marriage as on all other matters, can only have been binding on those who voluntarily sought out a confessor.[31]

Theodore's Penitential

Despite the fact that Council of Hertford condemned all multiple marriages, Book II of *Theodore's Penitential* promulgates a number of concessions permitting remarriage. One set of canons permits a man to remarry in the event of desertion by his wife, forcible captivity from which she cannot be redeemed, and abduction by an enemy from which she cannot be recovered.[32] A woman may remarry if her husband is enslaved for theft, fornication or any crime; but only if the enslaved man was her first husband.[33] The appearance of a greater number and variety of specific concessions that refer exclusively to men is, in part, a reflection of the greater liability of women to be constrained against their will from their husbands; but the relatively greater attempts to limit the number of marriages that women could lawfully contract doubtless reflects the conviction that women at least could and should be be regulated according to ecclesiastical principles. Another group of canons in Book II, however, which cover captivity in time of war, allow both men and women to remarry on equal terms. The same group of canons also requires both men and women to abandon the subsequent marriage if it should happen that the original partner returns from captivity.[34] The *Penitential* also deals with the case of a man whose wife has been abducted by one of his enemies and is returned to him after he has remarried. In this case, the *Penitential* rules that the man is to hold to his subsequent marriage; but his erstwhile wife is permitted to remarry. Here, however, the qualification resurfaces; she may remarry only if the dissolved marriage was her first.[35]

---

[31] For *Dialogue of Egbert's* claim that annual confession was customary from the time of Theodore, see ch. 4, fn. 27.
[32] *Theodore's Penitential*, II.xii.20–1, 24.
[33] *Theodore's Penitential*, II.xii.9.
[34] *Theodore's Penitential*, II.xii.22–3.
[35] *Theodore's Penitential*, II.xii.25.

In this section, then, the *Penitential* is very evidently grappling with the raw material of life, and its grasp of the existential complexities arising from abduction and captivity is in marked contrast to Book I's bald statement of penance for a woman who deserts her husband and returns undishonoured.[36] The *Penitential*'s provisions for the remarriage of both men and women in circumstances beyond their control demonstrate the existence of at least one influential confessor (whether or not Theodore himself) whose capacity for humane response triumphed over dogmatic dedication to absolute principles when faced with concrete situations. In the society for which *Theodore's Penitential* was framed, the right of remarriage was a more pressing issue than the right of divorce, particularly as the hazards of existence rendered women of marriageable age disproportionately few in number;[37] the relatively greater unwillingness to sanction multiple marriages contracted by women marks the ideological limits of the *Penitential*'s accommodation to demographic exigencies. Demographic imbalance, however, does not obviate reasons for wanting a divorce. Book II permits a woman to remarry if she can prove that her husband is impotent; but it contains no provision for divorce from a barren wife.[38] Despite the more liberal provision for men to remarry in circumstances beyond their control, the *Penitential*'s ruling that a man may divorce a pagan wife who refuses to be converted[39] is the sole point at which it diverges from the Council of Hertford's decree that a man may divorce his wife only on the grounds of adultery.

The coming of Christianity, monastic in its emphasis, added to the life-choices of Anglo-Saxon women, and the *Penitential*'s regulation of marriage is, inevitably, borne in upon by issues affecting entry to the monasteries; I want now to pursue its regulation of women and marriage through a brief survey of the legislation on widows, unmarried women and wives that relates to monasticism. *Theodore's Penitential* is generally much less disposed to coerce and regulate adherents than post-12th century churchmen were, but the early church was, understandably, inclined to facilitate an increase in the number of women entering the monastic life. The overall conclusion to which the *Penitential* points is that widows and married women were much more attracted to the monastic life than virgin daughters; the shortage of women of marriageable age doubtless played a significant part in this. The foundation of monasteries by royal women had obvious advantages for the early church. Royal women who wanted to leave their husbands in order to found monasteries thus presented a

---

[36] *Theodore's Penitential*, I.xiv.13; so also *Cummean*, II.29. In its social adaptations, *Theodore's Penitential* is in contrast with *Basil*, which rules that a man deserted by his wife can be pardoned if he remarries, but a wife left by her husband is an adulteress if she cohabits with another man before he is known to be dead, although soldiers' wives have some excuse for presumption of death (see 199.31, 35, 36, 46, 48). Some of the provisions for remarriage in *Theodore's Penitential* are repeated in the late OE *Confessional of Pseudo-Ecgbert*, ed. R. Spindler (Leipzig, 1934), pp. 181–3. *Penitential of Pseudo-Egbert*, ed. J. Raith (Hamburg, 1933), which embodies continental reforms, is more restrictively orthodox on this, as on all other matters (see Raith, p. 25).
[37] See D. Herlihy, "Life Expectancies for Women," in *The Role of Women in the Middle Ages*, ed. R.T. Morewedge (London, 1975), p. 8. See also Introduction, fn. 4.
[38] *Theodore's Penitential*, II.xii.33; divorce from a barren wife is specifically prohibited by *Cummean*, II.28, and *Finnian*, 41.
[39] *Theodore's Penitential*, II.xii.18–19.

particularly challenging problem to ecclesiastical legislators struggling to adhere to the dogma that marriage was an exclusive and indissoluble union.

Aldhelm's *De Virginitate* confirms the impression that formerly married women, both separated and widowed, were significantly well-represented in the monasteries.[40] The *Penitential*'s provisions for remarriage by women suggest that its compilers were not deliberately intent on pressuring women to enter monasteries if misfortune had separated them from their husbands (although its tendency to limit to two the number of marriages that a woman may lawfully contract seems likely to have accounted for some of the formerly married women who entered monasteries). Whereas Paul, attaching unique sanctity to virginity, and convinced that a woman who had already been married was even more prone to lapse from a vow of chastity than one who had not,[41] was reluctant to accept widows into the religious life, *Theodore's Penitential* resorts to the principle of regional variation from Roman orthodoxy to sanction the place of widows in the monastic life: "The Greeks bless a widow and a virgin together and choose either as an abbess. The Romans, however, do not veil a widow with a virgin."[42] This suggests an encouraging attitude to widows taking the veil, but the *Penitential* gives no reason to suppose that the relative numerousness of widows in the early Anglo-Saxon monasteries reflects coercive ecclesiastical legislation.

In contrast to the *Penitential*, which regularly permits women to contract two successive marriages, later ecclesiastical legislation asserted a single marriage as normative – already in the late Old English period, there are signs of a climate of opinion relatively more unfavourable to women contracting a second marriage.[43] On widows, the *Penitential* rules only that they may remarry after a year; widowers are permitted to remarry after a month,[44] but – unlike the ecclesiastical and secular legislation of the late Anglo-Saxon period, which reveals a marked determination to compel women to wait a year before remarrying – *Theodore's Penitential* contains no penalties or sanctions against widows who remarry within a year. Legislation of the late Anglo-Saxon period, however, is

---

[40] *De Virginitate*, esp. chs. 18–29, 58. See further ch. 3, pp. 80–2, 84, 107–8.

[41] See 1 Tim. 5.11–12.

[42] McNeill, p. 201; *Theodore's Penitential*, II.iii.7. Cf. *Basil*, 199.18, which clearly prefers virgins and agrees with Paul on the undesirability of readmitting young widows.

[43] OE *Confessional* echoes *Theodore's Penitential* in permitting a husband to divorce a wife for adultery, and permits both parties to remarry; but in ruling that a woman may not divorce her husband even for adultery, it omits the concession that enables her to do so to enter a monastery (Spindler, pp. 181, 185). It also follows *Theodore's Penitential*, II.xii.8, in allowing separation, by mutual consent, to enable one partner to enter a monastery, and in ruling that, if it was a first marriage, the remaining partner may remarry while the monastic partner is still alive; but unease is manifested in its assertion that this arrangement is *not* acceptable among the Greeks (Spindler, pp. 180–1). OE *Penitential*, carefully specifying applicability to both men and women, prohibits anyone to remarry whose spouse remains alive, and permits only one subsequent marriage after the death of a spouse (Raith, p. 27). In contrast with the numerous and varied provisions for separation and remarriage that OE *Confessional* repeats from Theodore (see fn. 36), OE *Penitential* allows couples to separate, by common consent, only for reasons of ill-health or to enter a monastery, and on condition that they obtain episcopal permission (Raith, p. 65). The ruling in OE *Penitential* is the one that 11th c. reformers such as Wulfstan struggled to uphold.

[44] *Theodore's Penitential*, II.xii.10.

simultaneously concerned to prevent secular coercion of widows, and asserts that they should not be forced to remarry or to enter a monastery against their wishes.[45] Theodore's Penitential makes no attempt to assist widows by preventing their forcible remarriage – its silence perhaps confirms the view that in so far as widows who embraced monasticism were responding to external pressures, the pressures inhered in the difficulties that widows without the backing of their own family experienced in retaining possession of property against the king and their husbands' kindred.[46]

Not surprisingly, Theodore's Penitential evinces interest in facilitating the monastic aspirations of the unmarried, since the growth of the church was, conventionally, apt to be measured by its virginal monastics.[47] The Penitential formulates the principle of individual autonomy; beyond the age of majority (variously defined by different manuscripts of the Penitential), daughters (and sons) are held to be no longer in the power of their parents, but have power of their own bodies, and may not be given in marriage against their will. This principle is not invoked solely to limit the power of parents to obstruct the monastic aspirations of their daughters and sons; the Penitential rules that a daughter who refuses to marry a man to whom she is betrothed may either enter a monastery or be betrothed to another man.[48] The 1023 law code of Cnut decrees that no woman, widow or maid, is to be forced to marry a man she dislikes. This legislation appears rather more likely to reflect a penitential tradition affirming that an unmarried woman has power over her own body than to represent the first stirrings of chivalric attitudes to women.[49] In formulating the principle of an unmarried daughter's power over her own body, Theodore's Penitential runs directly counter to the canons attributed to St Patrick, which extend patriarchal headship from marital union to familial relations. They state that, because the head of the woman is the man, what the father wishes, the daughter shall do; the will of the daughter is to be enquired after (presumably in choosing her a husband), but only because "God left man in the hand of his own council."[50] Theodore's Penitential, in casually accepting a betrothed woman's refusal to marry the man of her parents' choice as the basis from which it legislates, has every appearance of taking for granted an established social custom, and its employment of the principle of individual autonomy as the means of swelling the ranks of virgins in the monasteries is thus explicable as the response of a well-disposed legislator to a social climate not outstandingly characterized by the coercion of its young. Like its negotiable stance on the vowing of infants to monasteries, the Penitential's legislation on

---

[45] See II Cnut, 73–4 (Liebermann, I, 308–71); see fn. 67.

[46] See fns. 67 and 95; see also pp. 80, 138–40, 255–6. Boniface's claim that, even among the pagan Wendts, the marriage bond was so highly regarded that widows who committed suttee were esteemed (Tangl, 73), suggests the possibility of a point of contact between indigenous loyalties and Christian exclusiveness which might help to explain the attraction of monasticism for widows.

[47] See fn. 42.

[48] Theodore's Penitential, II.xii.34–7.

[49] II Cnut, 74. Opposition to enforced marriages for the sake of the bride price, rather than specific concern with wards of the king, seems indicated here; cf. the seeming euphemism, "remuneration for rearing the bride," in Be wifmannes beweddunge (Liebermann, I, 442–4).

[50] "Second Synod of St Patrick," 27; Ecclus. 15.14.

unmarried women's entry to the religious life is consistent with the tradition of baptismal voluntarism reflected in the documentation of the Gregorian missions.[51]

The formerly married women who entered monasteries included women whose separation from their husbands was an act of deliberate choice. Whereas the *Penitential* reveals no attempt to assist or constrain widows to enter monasteries, and makes no very strenuous efforts to secure the postulancy of unmarried women, Book II shows a marked inclination to accommodate married people wishing to enter monasteries, and evident signs of problematic strains. Notable also is its relatively generous treatment of female adultery.

Book II permits a man to remarry if he divorces his wife for adultery, although the Council of Hertford's opposition to this course of action lingers on in the proviso that he may remarry only if the wife who is renounced was his first wife.[52] Book I manifests a severe and discriminatory attitude to female adultery. The penance for a man who commits adultery is three years, but for a woman, it is seven – this judgment is accompanied by one of the rare citations of authority, which, elsewhere in the *Penitential*, are an index of contentious rulings.[53] But despite Book I's ruling, and despite the fact that Christ condemned marriage to a woman whose husband had divorced her for adultery, Book II permits women divorced on grounds of adultery to remarry after five years, provided that they

---

[51] For *Theodore's Penitential*, II.xiv.5–6, see ch. 1, p. 28. Basil advised that monastic vows were less likely to be broken if the church refused to receive children vowed by their parents and accepted only women over 17 with a vocation (199.18). It is true, however, that the only information Bede gives concerning the circumstances in which an unmarried woman became a nun is the report that King Oswiu vowed his infant daughter, Ælffled, to a monastery in the hope of gaining divine aid against Mercia (*HE*, III.24). Whether ecclesiastical compulsion was brought to bear appears to have depended on social status – with Wilfrid's employment of a secular official to forcibly recover a child vowed by his British mother, cf. the report that noblemen gave their sons to Wilfrid to instruct, leaving him to decide whether they were better suited to the service of God or of the king (*Life of Wilfrid*, chs. 18, 21).

[52] *Theodore's Penitential*, II.xii.5.

[53] *Theodore's Penitential*, I.xiv.14: "and this matter is stated in the same way in the canon." (The 3 years penance in I.xiv.15 appears to apply to an unmarried woman who commits adultery with a married man). Penance for adultery by married men is given as 3 years, with variations according to circumstance, in I.xiv.9–12 (cf. I.ii.1). The canons referred to in I.xiv.14 could mean the Irish canons or Basil's: the attitudes of both are clearly discriminatory, but they offer little positive evidence of discriminatory penalties (see fn. 24). The issue is complicated by the fact that masculine reference could, sometimes, imply universal application; as in the case of Basil, 217.58, whose relatively heavy 7/15 year penalty Theodore may be echoing (see Deferrari, pp. 248–51). Payer, p. 15, says that "before the 9th century penitential canons were usually addressed to one person, most frequently to the male in a heterosexual union. In the absence of general rules of interpretation I have assumed that such canons applied solely to the person to whom they were addressed." Payer, p. 131, however, observing the contrast between the 7 year penance for women in *Theodore's Penitential*, I.xiv.14, and the 3 years for men in I.xiv.9, says: "Is this . . . discrimination, or is it more likely an example of the collector's penchant for completeness?" Payer's consistent foregrounding of the methodological rigour required in order to interpret the evidence of the penitentials makes all the more startling his failure to recognize that they also present a problem of interpretation in the area of gender specificity, a problem which, inasmuch as it has critical bearing for the development of the construct of individualism for Western Woman, is of not inconsiderable significance.

undertake to do penance.[54] Book II also rules that, if a woman is an adulteress and her husband does not wish to live with her, she is to have a fourth part of her inheritance if she enters a monastery; otherwise she receives nothing.[55] The inducement for a repentant adulterous wife to enter a monastery is evident (although significantly moderated by the provision for her remarriage). Nevertheless, the canonist's disposition to accept a woman divorced for adultery into the religious life is as consistent with the counsel of reconciliation that the Council of Hertford laid upon husbands as it is in contrast with the canons attributed to St Patrick and the *Penitential of Finnian*.

Theodore's Penitential states that a husband has the right to choose whether he is reconciled to an adulterous wife and that "her punishment does not concern the clergy".[56] This canon clearly reflects the doctrine that a married woman is in the power of her husband. So also, Book II rules that, if a woman remarries after having vowed not to take another husband, and she then wishes to fulfill her vow of celibacy, it is for her husband to decide whether or not she may do so.[57] The same doctrine undoubtedly underlies the *Penitential*'s reluctance to countenance divorce initiated by a woman. Book II asserts that "a woman may not put away her husband, even if he is a fornicator, unless, perchance, for the purposes of entering a monastery. Basil so decided."[58] This ruling is apt to create the impression that Theodore, wanting to give a form of legality to married women abandoning their husbands to enter a monastery, dredged up a liberalization of canon law from the depths of his Greek experience. Only Theodore is likely to have invoked the authority of Basil – the *Penitential*'s usual formula for rulings that diverge from Roman orthodoxy is "according to the Greeks." But Basil is not known to have decreed in favour of married women seeking separation for the purposes of entering a monastery, and the evidence of his Canonical Letters is overwhelmingly against any disposition to do so.[59] Basil's authority can only vouch for the patently inequitable ruling that denies women the permission to divorce on grounds of adultery that is given to men – an inequity

[54] *Theodore's Penitential*, II.xii.5: "Si cuius uxor fornicata fuerit, licet dimittere eam et aliam accipere; hoc est, si vir dimiserit uxorem suam propter fornicationem, si prima fuerit, licitum est ut aliam accipiat uxorem; illa vero, si voluerit penitere peccata sua, post V. annos alium virum accipiat" (Finsterwalder, p. 326). *Fornicatio* is employed loosely by the penitentials for all manner of sexual irregularities (Payer, pp. 142–3); but the terminology of this canon is the same as that used by the Council of Hertford (see fn. 1), and by the canon which immediately follows it (II.xii.6, see fn. 58).

[55] *Theodore's Penitential*, II.xii.11.

[56] McNeill, p. 209; *Theodore's Penitential*, II.xii.12. This, presumably, does not nullify *Theodore's Penitential*, I.xiv.4, which provides penance for a man engaging in marital relations with a wife to whom he has been reconciled who is still carrying out penance for adultery.

[57] *Theodore's Penitential*, II.xii.14, cf. I.xiv.7; see also I.xiv.5–6.

[58] McNeill, pp. 208–9. *Theodore's Penitential*, II.xii.6; "Mulieri non licit virum dimittere licit sit fornicator, nisi forte pro monasterio. Basilius hoc iudicavit" (Finsterwalder, p. 327). See fn. 54.

[59] Cf. the appeal to "the canons" for the unequal penance for female adultery in *Theodore's Penitential*, I.xiv.14 (see fn. 53). Basil's recognition that custom, not scripture, decrees inequality in matters of divorce, could be construed as authorizing exceptions to the rule that women may not divorce their husbands for adultery, but his lack of enthusiasm for monastic widows (see fn. 42) tends to confirm that his name has been taken in vain here. Lapidge and Herren, pp. 51–8, who take this canon to signify that Theodore produced a Greek precedent in order to create a loophole in Roman orthodoxy, also appear to have been unable to find a source for it in the Canonical Letters.

which, as Basil had pointed out, was contrary to the logic of the scriptures. What the canon conveys is that Theodore was bent on upholding the principle that a woman may not divorce her husband but, under extreme pressure from female converts – and royal women were surely the only ones in a position to force this concession – Theodore made a special exception for cases where the woman wanted to enter a monastery.[60]

No less obviously contentious are the two canons that immediately follow this, which also represent a concession facilitating entry to monasteries in response to pressure from married converts. These canons declare that a marriage may only be broken by the consent of both partners, and state that, "according to the Greeks," and even though "this is not canonical," either party to a marriage may give the other permission to enter a monastery, and then remarry; but this concession applies only to first marriages.[61] Continental orthodoxy made no exceptions for first marriages; remarriage was lawful only after the death of the husband or wife who had abandoned a marriage to enter a monastery. *Theodore's Penitential*, then, is patently invoking the principle of regional variation – Greek custom – to justify Anglo-Saxon deviation from continental orthodoxy. The *Penitential*'s provision for separation by mutual consent effectively supersedes the canon that prohibits women from initiating a divorce, limiting its application to cases in which the husband opposes his wife's departure – that may well have been the contingency that it was originally framed to meet. The provisions for remarriage when a marriage has been dissolved by mutual consent, though advertised as highly tenuous, remove, at least in the case of a first marriage, the most pressing grounds for opposing a spouse's departure to a monastery.[62] A subsequent canon in Book II further liberalizes the provisions for dissolution of marriages by mutual consent, stating that a married couple may agree to separate if one wants to enter the monastery and the other does not, or if one is broken in health and the other is not.[63] Though Bede's account of Dryhthelm's entry to a monastery suggests that, in practice, mutual consent was something men took for granted, his account of Sebbi's wife, who refused her consent until old age was upon them both, may be a no less telling social indicator.[64]

The canons in Book II which place a married woman in the power of her husband and which carry with them, as a consequence, a relatively much greater restriction on married women's self-determination and freedom of movement, are consistent with Book I's patriarchal attitudes, which are also reflected in the higher penance for female adultery. This aspect of the *Penitential* comes as no surprise if we regard the most viciously repressive of the early fathers as

---

[60] For judgments claiming authority from Theodore and Basil, see fn. 27.

[61] *Theodore's Penitential*, II.xii.7–8.

[62] This concession seems likely to have been made in response to a powerful man in need of an heir, such as Æthelthryth's husband, Ecgfrith of Northumbria. That Greek precedent was invoked to appease orthodox clerics, such as Bishop Wilfrid, is unlikely; Wilfrid opposed pluralism at Whitby (*HE*, III.25), and his hostility to Ecgfrith's second wife is explicable without the hypothesis that he had canonical objections to the marriage (see ch. 5, pp. 166–8, 176–7).

[63] *Theodore's Penitential*, II.xii.13.

[64] See *HE*, IV.11, V.12. For discussion of the phenomenon, see M. Lapidge, "A Seventh-Century Insular Latin Debate Poem on Divorce," *Cambridge Medieval Celtic Studies* 10 (1985), 1–23.

having established a line of thought to be undeviatingly followed in the treatment of women; the elements of Book II which display a greater generosity of
spirit reveal that this is not the case. The insistence that marital separation
requires the consent of both partners could be regarded as having been authorized by the scrupulous book-keeping that occasionally characterizes Paul's
remarks on marital relations – as for instance, when he asserts that the wife is in
the power of her husband, and that the husband is also in the power of his wife.
In principle, and in its potential ramifications, the insistence that the dissolution of a marriage requires the consent of both partners is entirely different from
the patriarchal conception of marriage which places the wife in the power of her
husband. The early law codes, to which I now turn, help to illuminate the social
accommodations made by the Penitential and the social dislocations that the
ecclesiastical establishment of "lawful marriage" entailed.

Had Anglo-Saxon society resembled the one to which Christ's words were
addressed, as Theodore appears to have assumed it did when he convened the
Council of Hertford – if, in other words, women were apt to find themselves
abandoned without financial support and protection by men who were in the
habit of casting one wife aside in favour of another – the conversion of England
could be said to have carried with it a potential for improving the position of
women. But married women appear to have retained their identity as members
of their own family group and, although women who had no powerful family of
their own to back them were undoubtedly vulnerable, family support constituted its own sanctions against a woman being cast aside against her will, if
only because it represented an affront to family honour. It may not have been
the whole truth, or even the truth at all, that Penda of Mercia waged war on
Cenwealh of Wessex because the wife he had repudiated was Penda's sister, but
Bede evidently considered that a plausible motive for a war between two pagan
kings. Alcuin, predicting that the Northumbrian king's public rejection of his
wife would lead to the loss of his throne, need not have been relying on a bolt
from heaven.[65] Accordingly, the benefits of ecclesiastical regulation of marriage
were most probably felt, if at all, by women who belonged to the least powerful
social classes.[66]

On the other hand, one definable area in which ecclesiastical influence
significantly reduced the freedom, and the status, of married women was in
prohibiting them from divorcing their husbands, except, under sufferance, to
enter a monastery. The indications are that Anglo-Saxon marriage was a contract entered into and terminated by mutual agreement – the Penitential's insistence that a marriage can only be dissolved by mutual consent, if not directly
prompted by indigenous, contractual conceptions of marriage, is likely to have
been at least as recognizable to early Anglo-Saxons as a point of cultural contact
as ecclesiastical attempts to place women in the power of their husbands. The
earliest surviving laws, those of Æthelberht of Kent, though they date from the
time of Augustine, reflect indigenous custom in ruling on settlement in the
event of marital separation. They deal only with separation initiated by a

---

[65] See HE, III.7; Duemmler, 122.
[66] The issue is particularly complicated by the practice of polygyny by men of the highest rank:
see M. Clunies Ross, "Concubinage in Anglo-Saxon England," P&P 108 (1985), 3–34. S.F.

woman, and state that a woman who leaves her husband is entitled to half of the joint property, unless the husband wishes to keep the children, in which case her entitlement is one third.[67] *Theodore's Penitential* confirms the initiation of divorce by women, in ruling that a man may remarry "if his wife leaves despising him and is unwilling to return and be reconciled."[68] Theodore's reluctant concession on divorce initiated by women strongly suggests, then, that the pressures brought to bear on him were not simply fueled by women's desire to enter monasteries, but arose from the fact that he was virtually depriving them of their customary freedom to leave their husbands. Though it has been assumed that the name of Basil was invoked to authorize a ruling to which other bishops – notably Bishop Wilfrid – might object,[69] the objections are more likely to have been raised by women.

Æthelberht's law code also states that if a freeman lies with the wife of another freeman he is to compensate him and procure for him another wife.[70] This is in keeping with the law code's general treatment of sexual transgressions as an offence by a man against the woman's protector (whether husband, kindred or overlord).[71] Such provisions, like the existence of the bride price, are not necessarily the expression of a prevailing view of women as goods and chattels, any more than the wergild provision of monetary compensation for killing and injuring both men and women is evidence of a perception of human beings as commodities.[72] What they do suggest is that women were not recognized as individual entities in law and were, presumably, thought of as in some way incorporated in the identity of their kindred or husband.[73] The ecclesiastical

---

Wemple, *Women in Frankish Society* (Philadelphia, 1981), pp. 97–126, concludes that monogamy increased women's security but diminished their role in the public sphere.

[67] *Ethelbert*, 79–80: "If she wishes to go away with the children, she is to have half the goods. If the husband wishes to keep [the children], [she is to have the same share] as a child." Though marital separation is unlikely to have ceased to occur after Æthelberht's reign, his code is unique in its provisions for divorce settlement, and later codes echo only the provisions for widows which are found in *Ethelbert*, 78, 81; cf. *Hlothere and Eadric*, 6; *Ine*, 38; *II Cnut*, 70. These laws reflect conflict between widows and their husband's kindred, not merely over custody of the male heir, but over conjugal property as well, and *II Cnut*, 73, is evidently making use of the resentment that a dead man's family were likely to feel when his wife inherited (especially if she remarried) when it decrees that, if a widow contravenes ecclesiastical law by remarrying within a year of her husband's death, the property she inherited from him is to be forfeited to his kinsmen. *II Cnut's* concern to protect widows is at least in part attributable to the fact that the scriptures give them particular status as deserving recipients of charity. The absence of any legal provision for wives deserted by their husbands can be variously interpreted.

[68] McNeill, p. 210; *Theodore's Penitential*, II.xii.20 (cf. I.xiv.13, from *Cummean*, II.29). *Theodore's Penitential*, II.xii.35, reveals that women also refused to live with men to whom they were betrothed.

[69] See fns. 59, 62.

[70] *Ethelbert*, 31; cf. 85 ("If anyone lies with the woman of a servant while her husband is alive, he is to pay a two-fold compensation").

[71] See *Ethelbert*, 10–12, 14–16, 75–6, 82–5.

[72] Cf. R. Hill, p. 69 (the support she draws from *Theodore's Penitential*, II.xii.35, is illusory). As Fell, 1986, p. 16, observes, the connotations of (*ge*) *bycgan* were not necessarily those of MnE "buy." See also fn. 49 above, and Introduction, fn. 4.

[73] *Ethelbert*, 73, however, offers one of the instances of a penalty specifying direct female responsibility, which, like the immediately adjacent legislation (*Ethelbert*, 32–74), may refer to injury inflicted by violence; cf. C. Fell, "A *friwif locbore* Revisited," *ASE* 13 (1984), 157–65.

conception of individual moral responsibility for actions, of which the penitentials are the instrument, constituted a pressure towards the eventual emergence
of the individual, instead of the kin-group, as the entity responsible in law;[74] the
late Old English law codes, as I have indicated, also echo the *Penitential*'s
formulation of the principle that daughters over the age of majority have power
over their own body. But in the case of married women, development of a
distinct legal identity is hampered by ecclesiastics' simultaneous promotion of
the power of the husband. The tensions can be seen in the Laws of Ine, which
effectively rule that a woman is not automatically guilty of her husband's crimes,
because his headship deprives her of full autonomy: "If a husband steals any
cattle and brings it into his house, and it is seized therein, he is guilty for his
part, but without his wife, because she must obey her lord: and if she dare swear
an oath that she did not taste the stolen meat, she is to receive her third
portion."[75] That married women are barely regarded as individual entities by the
law codes is not inconsistent with the existence of a traditional, Germanic form
of patriarchy that meshed with the ecclesiastical doctrine of the power of the
husband, just as the Kentish law code's assumption that all women are under
male protection can (though perhaps too readily) be taken to mean that they
were universally under male control; but the absence of an independent legal
identity is not a comprehensive guide to the actual and social position of
women.

The Kentish legislation that requires a man who lies with another man's wife
to compensate her husband and procure him another wife could signify automatic rejection of a wife who committed adultery; or worse. Boniface wrote
that, in Saxony, an adulterous woman was compelled to take her own life and
that her seducer was hung over her funeral pyre; and sometimes, he claimed, an
adulterous woman was set upon and left for dead by the women of her community. This has been taken as evidence of the savagely high value that Germanic society in general placed on female chastity, although Boniface offered it
as polemical proof of respect for the marriage bond even among pagans.[76]
Theodore's Penitential evinces an ecclesiastical attitude to female adultery with
the potential for ameliorating barbarity. But customs among the various Germanic tribes who settled England are unlikely to have been homogeneous. One
form of popular response is shown in the vernacular poem *Maxims I*, in the
portrait of the wife of the Frisian sailor, where the promiscuity of a wife is
presented as breaking faith with vows and productive of an ill reputation;
serious enough in the secular value-system, but not life-threatening.[77] *Theodore's*
Penitential, which claims to be the work of a Northumbrian, does not imply a

---

[74] Ecclesiastical conceptions of individual moral responsibility presumably underlie the appearance, in Alfred's laws (885x889), of legislation on sexual offences in which women are agents
(*Alfred*, 18). For instances of canons specifying application to both men and women in late OE
penitentials, see OE *Penitential of Pseudo-Egbert* (fn. 43 above), and "Late OE Handbook" (fn.
78); cf. fn. 53.

[75] *Ine*, 57, which needs to be read against *Ine*, 7.1: "If he steals with the knowledge of all his
household they are all to go into slavery" (Liebermann, I, 90–123). Cf. *II Cnut*, 76.

[76] Letter to Æthelbald of Mercia (c. 746), Tangl, 73. Boniface did not necessarily understand
the significance of the customs he observed.

[77] *Maxims I*, ll. 93–104.

background of customarily savage attitudes to female adultery.[78] On the contrary, there would seem to be little point in the provisions covering reconciliation with a wife who had committed adultery, permission for her remarriage, and entitlement to a quarter of the joint goods if she chooses to enter a monastery, if a woman who had committed adultery was an abomination in the eyes of all right-thinking pagans. The ruling that a wife divorced for adultery is to have a share of the joint property if she enters a monastery is clearly based on the same custom of apportioning property in the event of separation as Æthelberht's law code; it looks difficult to enforce, unless a woman's entitlement to property, whatever the grounds of separation, was firmly established. The difficulties of enforcement disappear, however, if we accept that the *Penitential*, in stipulating that adulterous women who do not enter a monastery are to have nothing, was attempting to secure exclusively for women who entered monasteries an entitlement to property that applied universally when a marriage was terminated.[79] While the Kentish law code's decree that a freeman who lies with another freeman's wife must compensate him and obtain him another wife can be construed as dire in its implications for the position of women in pre-conversion England,[80] it seems more likely, in view of the *Penitential*'s handling of adultery, to represent a provision for divorce and remarriage.[81] This legislation, then, like the Kentish law code's ruling on the property entitlement of women who leave their husbands, reflects an indigenous contractual construct of marriage that was capable of coalescing with the mutual consent strand of received Christianity to ameliorate the weight of patriarchal tradition that it simultaneously imported.

The Case of St Æthelthryth

The *Penitential*'s wrestling with the competing claims of marital orthodoxy and the monastic aspirations of married women gives particular interest to Adomnan's *Life of Columba* and Bede's *History*, which offer two, highly contrasted,

---

[78] AS attitudes undoubtedly varied according to time and place (as Asser's report of the uniquely low status of the Wessex queen in Alfred's time demonstrates, see fn. 5), and possibly amongst individuals. *Alfred*, 42.7 (Liebermann, I, 26–89), like *Ethelred*, 31, leaves us to our own imagination by its silence concerning the fate of the women involved, when it rules that a man can fight without incurring a blood-feud if he finds his (legal) wife, daughter, sister, or father's wife under a blanket or behind closed doors with a man; "Late OE Handbook" (Fowler, p. 21) and *OE Penitential* (Raith, p. 17), which assign 3 years penance to a man who kills his wife in a jealous rage, if she is innocent, are highly disturbing, but it would be rash to employ this to fill all of the silences. Much more disturbing is *II Cnut*, 53, which decrees that an adulterous woman's property is to be forfeited to her husband and she is to lose her nose and ears, whereas male adulterers are merely to be fined and do penance; Scandinavian or Flemish influence might account for this – Wulfstan, who drafted *II Cnut*, is also thought to have compiled "Late OE Handbook," which merely gives the penance for adultery as 7 years "whether it be a woman or a man" (Fowler, p. 22).
[79] Dryhthelm, who assigns his wife a third of the property when he enters the monastery (*HE*, V.12), reveals Bede's approval of the arrangement in these particular circumstances.
[80] See fn. 78.
[81] Fell, 1986, p. 64, takes the same view.

accounts of the response of a spiritual advisor to a married woman refusing to consummate her marriage. Adomnan's Life of Columba relates that a layman complained to the saint that his wife refused to consummate the marriage; Columba exhorted her to remember that husband and wife were bidden by the gospel to become one flesh. The wife replied that she was willing to do anything rather than be joined with a husband who was so repulsively ugly. She was, she said, fully prepared to continue to carry out her wifely duty of managing the household, but, if Columba wished, she would even cross the seas and enter a monastery. This Columba forbade, on the grounds that she was bound by the will of her husband as long as he was alive, and none could separate what God had lawfully joined. He did, however, fast and pray with the couple, in consequence of which the woman's feelings towards her husband changed, overnight, to love.[82]

That the monastery assumes the aspect of the sole possible escape from an undesirable marriage, in this patently tendentious anecdote, calls for cautious handling as evidence of the general position of married women or their motives for entering monasteries; there is no other form of separation that a woman characterized as willing to be guided by Columba could plausibly suggest. For one of the striking aspects of the anecdote is that it is not fear that prevents the woman from leaving her husband – she is prepared to undertake the most penitential form of entry to the religious life, by going into exile in a foreign land. As presented by Columba's hagiographer, the wife is inhibited from leaving by a felt need for ecclesiastical sanction, which is consistent with the characterization of her as conscientiously concerned to execute a wife's managerial duties. Noticeably, Columba, in this account, is not a purely authoritarian spiritual mentor; he reflects the hagiographic ideal of the confessor as a Christ-like mediator of divine caritas.[83] His role is to effect mystically (by prayers and fasting) a marital union figuring the union of Christ and his church which is both hierarchic and affectional – he embodies, as it were, the ecclesiastical capacity to join together husband and wife in Christ.

Polemical commitment to marriage as a union whose indissolubility endures eternally is manifested elsewhere in the Life of Columba, in the account of one of the saint's eschatological visions: he sees the soul of a woman battling on the side of the angels to secure the posthumous salvation of her husband, whose soul was being attacked by demons. Submerged discouragement of the dissolution of pagan-Christian marriages is also evident in this vision, since it offers an emblematic illustration of the husband saved by the believing wife.[84] In the anecdote of the lay woman and her husband there are no apparent hesitations or tensions in affirming, as a principle overriding the ascetic ideal of chastity as the highest state, that marriage is an indissoluble union, which, as a union of the flesh, permits of no physical severance; even when, it would seem, the marriage has

---

[82] Adomnan's Life of Columba, ed. and trans. A.O. Anderson and M.O. Anderson, rev. edn. (Oxford, 1991), II.41. Adomnan (d. 704) was Abbot of Iona, which had a shaping influence on the church in Northumbria in the latter half of the 7th c.

[83] See further ch. 4. Readers of Foucault, 1978, will not need me to explain the nature and extent to which I differ in my view of confession, whose pre-13th c. existence does not fall within Foucault's scope.

[84] Life of Columba, III.10.

never been consummated. In the ideal world of hagiography, spiritual mentors are not exercised by the advantages of accommodating prospective entrants to the monastic life (though the advantages were undoubtedly more evident when the monastic postulants were royal). Set against the pressures surfacing in *Theodore's Penitential*, the narrative has the appearance of deliberately denying that a wife's separation from her husband is ever acceptable for any reason, because it contravenes what is here regarded as the inalienable rights of a husband as the head of the wife.

Of more particular interest in the light of *Theodore's Penitential* is Bede's account of St Æthelthryth.[85] Among the early abbesses that Bede mentions in his *History*, Æthelthryth alone commands his enthusiasm. He is indeed at considerable pains to promote her cult, incorporating a verse panegyric of his own composition. Bede's partiality for Æthelthryth is to a high degree explained by the fact that, in having chastely spurned the marital embrace for the heavenly bridegroom, she fits the model of female sanctity defined by the overwhelming majority of Roman saints Lives as the preservation of virginity against heavy odds; a mould into which widows, from whose ranks the abbesses of the early English church were chiefly drawn, could not plausibly be cast. Nor, on the whole, could formerly married monastic women. Given the importance that Bede consistently attaches to the influential example of kings, such as the fashion for pilgrimage created by Ine,[86] Æthelthryth, as a reigning queen who embarked on the monastic life, represented a polemical opportunity too good to miss. The view was clearly shared by Bishop Wilfrid, who, if he was not the originator of the cult of Æthelthryth, was a source for her hagiography, and presumably responsible for the particular form given to the circumstances in which she entered a monastery.[87]

Despite the profusion of comparisons to Roman virgin martyrs with which Bede lauds Æthelthryth in his verse panegyric, her preservation of her virginity is for him a prodigious feat before which faith needs the aid of understanding: "And there is no reason to doubt that such a thing could happen in our day, since reliable histories record it as having happened on several occasions in the past through the grace of the Lord"[88] – although we are given to understand that it is the scepticism of others that led Bede to make enquiries of Bishop Wilfrid. Bede reports that Æthelthryth was first married to a Welsh prince, who, however, died shortly after the marriage. That she preserved the glory of perpetual virginity through her twelve years of marriage to Ecgfrith of Northumbria was personally vouched for by Bishop Wilfrid; for the king, knowing Wilfrid's influence with the queen, promised him much wealth and estates if he would persuade Æthelthryth to consummate the marriage; and the incorruptibility of her body in death, for which Wilfrid could also personally vouch, is proof of it. Long did Æthelthryth beg the king to allow her to retire from worldly affairs

---

[85] See fn. 27.
[86] *HE*, V.7.
[87] Bede's Life of Æthelthryth may also reflect Ely's familiarity with continental hagiography; see ch. 8, fn. 30.
[88] Trans. Sherley-Price, p. 238; *HE*, IV.19.

and serve Christ, and, having gained his reluctant consent, she entered a monastery that was ruled by his aunt, where she received the veil from Wilfrid, and a year later returned to her East Anglian homeland and became the abbess of a monastery she founded at Ely.[89]

To doubt this story is perhaps to be as vulgar minded as Bede. The excuse must be that Ecgfrith, though contracting a subsequent marriage with Jurmenburg, died without heirs; and as the question of Ecgfrith's successor can have been no less vitally important at the Northumbrian court than it was to his sister Abbess Ælffled, who implored Bishop Cuthbert to prophesy on this matter,[90] Ecgfrith's reluctance to part with Æthelthryth is likely to have been seriously overstated. In view of the importance attached to royal heirs, the *Penitential*'s wisdom in permitting remarriage to those who consent to the departure of a spouse for the monastery, albeit against the canonist's better judgment, is apparent: the limitation of this concession to first marriages would, of course, have prevented Æthelthryth from receiving ecclesiastical sanction for a further marriage, had she been so disposed[91] – though she was considerably older than Ecgfrith. Puzzling, too, is the prospect of a woman intent on maintaining perpetual virginity who contracted not one, but two, marriages. Readers of Bede who have assumed that his account of Æthelthryth obliquely reveals how little say royal women had in the contracting of marriages have been willing to accept the veracity of Æthelthryth's Life. Æthelthryth's second marriage, which took place during the reign of her uncle, might have been compelled by a pressing need for an alliance with Northumbria; some five years earlier, Ecgfrith's father, Oswiu of Northumbria, had inflicted a crushing defeat on East Anglia and its allies.[92] But no such explanation for her first marriage offers itself. What does emerge from Bede's *History* is that not all of the daughters of Anna of East Anglia were obliged to marry; Anna's fame for holiness appears, indeed, to rest chiefly on the numerousness of his monastic daughters. Among the many East Anglian royal women who entered Frankish monasteries was Æthelthryth's sister, the virginal Æthelburg, similarly discovered to be uncorrupted at death.[93]

It is evident that, under the terms laid down by *Theodore's Penitential*, a queen wanting ecclesiastical sanction for leaving her husband and returning to her homeland could choose only between entry to a monastery or the plea of ill-health. Equally, a queen's adoption of one of these two courses of action was the only way that her husband could hope to remarry and beget legitimate heirs, if it chanced that ecclesiastical sanction was a consideration that weighed with him. Although we may suspect Bede of having exaggerated the extent of early Anglo-Saxon enthusiasm for monasticism, there is no necessity to outrule its

[89] HE, IV.19. *Life of Wilfrid*, ch. 39, claims Ecgfrith's aunt as a supporter of Wilfrid.
[90] *Vita Sancti Cuthberti Auctore Anonymo*, III.6; ed. and trans. B. Colgrave, *Two Lives of Saint Cuthbert: A Life by an Anonymous Monk of Lindisfarne and Bede's Prose Life of Cuthbert* (Cambridge, 1940), pp. 60–139. (This Life, written by a Lindisfarne monk *c*. 700, is subsequently referred to as *Anon Cuthbert*.)
[91] See fn. 62.
[92] Æthelthryth's father, Anna, was killed by Penda of Mercia in 654 (HE, III.18); her uncle was defeated by Oswiu in the following year (HE, III.24). See fn. 96.
[93] HE, III.7, 8. See fn. 87.

existence altogether. Alternatives to the official version of Æthelthryth's twelve-year marriage nevertheless suggest themselves. Book II of the *Penitential*, for instance, conceivably casts some light on the situation in its ruling on widows' vows, particularly its ruling on women who remarry after having vowed not to take another husband, and then, moved by penitence, wish to fulfill their vow of celibacy. In such cases, Book II decrees, it is in the power of a woman's husband to determine whether or not she may fulfill her vow; Book I, in the same doctrinal vein, states that a woman may not take a vow of chastity without the consent of her husband.[94] Nevertheless, the *Penitential* records that Theodore did give judgment on a specific case. To a woman who, after eleven years of marriage, confessed to having made such a vow, he gave permission to cohabit with the man.[95] Æthelthryth founded her monastery at Ely in the same year as the Council of Hertford, by which year Theodore is known to have been in the north.[96] That her marriage with Ecgfrith is said to have ended after 12 years may be a mere coincidence, and an imperfect one at that.

Theodore's case differs slightly, but significantly, from the state of affairs that Bede relates, in involving the desire to renounce a sexual union contracted in breach of a vow of celibacy. It is of interest not only because it suggests one kind of situation that could have provided the factual underpinning of the hagiography of Æthelthryth, but also because the attributed stances of Bishop Wilfrid and Æthelthryth are markedly at odds with ecclesiastical promotion of the doctrine that a wife is in the power of her husband, enshrined in the *Penitential* as a general principle, and brought to bear by Theodore in his ruling on a specific case involving a woman's vow of celibacy. Though Bede does not explicitly claim that Wilfrid positively encouraged Æthelthryth, Wilfrid would at very least seem from Bede's account to have credited himself with a noble unworldliness in failing to bring an acknowledged influence to bear on her when Ecgfrith offered him lands and wealth. Wilfrid is widely assumed to have lost Ecgfrith's favour and been banished from court for supporting the queen against his wishes. The actual extent of Wilfrid's instrumental influence on Æthelthryth may be doubted; to have encouraged her to leave for a monastery if the king wished her to stay would certainly have been disinterested, since

---

[94] *Theodore's Penitential*, I.xiv.7.

[95] See McNeill, p. 209; *Theodore's Penitential*, II.xii.14–15. "Mulier quae vovit, ut post mortem viri eius non accipiat alium, et mortuo illo praevaricatrix accipiat alium, iterumque nupta, cum ea penitentia mota implere vult vota sua, in potestate viri eius est, utrum impleat an non. Ergo uni licentiam dedit Theodorus, quae confessa est votum, post XI. annos nubere cum illo viro" (Finsterwalder, p. 328). This appears to mean that Theodore invoked his power to nullify vows made by seculars without episcopal consent (cf. I.xiv.5–7), and sanctioned an already existing sexual relationship. OE *Confessional*, in echoing this (Spindler, p. 186), understands it to mean a vow made during the lifetime of the first husband; such vows could affect a widow's inheritance of property. Ealdorman Alfred (871x888) willed the bulk of his property to his wife, provided she remained unmarried in accordance with their verbal agreement (Harmer, 10). See also fns. 46, 67.

[96] See ASC, 673: reference, unless otherwise stated, is to the Parker manuscript, ed. J.M. Bately, *The Anglo-Saxon Chronicle: MS A* (Cambridge, 1986). This entry, and Bede's report that Æthelthryth spent a year's novitiate at Coldingham, are the sole basis for the 660 dating of her marriage. Theodore began his tour of England in 669 (*HE*, IV.2); that he spent a considerable time in Northumbria, is probable, and he visited it more than once.

Wilfrid's position at court depended on his friendship with Æthelthryth. That, at any rate, is the conclusion that begs to be drawn from the account of Wilfrid's devoted hagiographer, Eddius.

Eddius, in his account, claims for Wilfrid a charismatic ambience that extended far beyond the influence over Æthelthryth that Bede mentions. So large does he loom in Eddius's Life that Æthelthryth's reputation for saintly purity – rather ambiguously couched – is merely incidental. Somewhat in the manner of Columba in Adomnan's Life, Wilfrid mystically held together husband and wife, for as long as they were both obedient to his bidding, and his good influence radiated outward to the kingdom at large, bringing peace and prosperity to all: were it not for that fact that Eddius attributes to Wilfrid the king's victories in battle, it would be evident that the presence of Wilfrid was identical with the peace that signifies Christ's continuing presence in the world. But when the king and the bishop fell out, the royal marital union fell apart, and the king and kingdom went to the bad:

> Now in those days, the pious King Ecgfrith, and his most blessed Queen Æthelthryth (whose body still remaining uncorrupted after death, shows that it was unstained before, while alive) were both obedient to Bishop Wilfrid in all things, and there ensued, by the aid of God, peace and joy among the people, fruitful years and victory over their foes. . . . So when King Ecgfrith lived in peace with our bishop, the kingdom, as many bear witness, was increased on every hand by his glorious victories; but when the agreement between them was destroyed, and his queen had separated from him and dedicated herself to God, the king's triumph came to an end during his own lifetime.[97]

The likelihood that it was the queen, rather than the bishop, who held the role of influential linchpin in this triangular relationship seems confirmed by the fact that Wilfrid's subsequent downfall and exile was accomplished at the instigation of Æthelthryth's successor, Ecgfrith's second wife, Queen Jurmenburg[98] – objections by Wilfrid to the unorthodoxy of Ecgfrith's second marriage scarcely need to be hypothesized to explain his later conflict with Jurmenburg.[99] Wilfrid, not to put too fine a point on it, had a vested interest in the continuance of a royal marriage where he had the favour of the queen; when Æthelthryth departed from the court, so did Wilfrid, and Eddius's enigmatic report will bear the construction that Æthelthryth as well as Wilfrid was not on particularly amiable terms with Ecgfrith by the time she left. Æthelthryth's refusal to consummate her marriage – whether sustained for twelve years or featuring only in its termination – may not have been the direct, all-sufficient explanation of the end of the accord between Ecgfrith, his queen, and her bishop, that the combined hagiographical accounts of Bede and Eddius lead us to believe it

---

[97] Colgrave, p. 41; Life of Wilfrid, ch. 19. Æthelthryth's gift to Wilfrid of lands at Hexham may have coincided with her entry to Coldingham, but cannot be exactly dated: see M. Roper, "Wilfrid's Landholdings in Northumbria," in St Wilfrid at Hexham, ed. D.P. Kirby (Newcastle-upon-Tyne, 1974), pp. 72–3, 169–71.
[98] Life of Wilfrid, ch. 24.
[99] See pp. 166–8, 176–7.

was.[100] But however much it is open to doubt that Wilfrid's influence was responsible for piloting Æthelthryth through an unconsummated marriage to the safety of a monastery and enduring fame for virginal sanctity, his role in Bede's Life of Æthelthryth – where he effectively bestows ecclesiastical sanction on Æthelthryth's refusal to consummate her marriage in accordance with the wishes of her husband – illustrates the extent to which the penitential canons of one bishop-confessor are no guide to the attitude that another bishop-confessor might adopt towards particular individuals, and especially royal individuals. Anomalous as Wilfrid's stance is in Bede's account, however, his presence at least ensures that Æthelthryth, in opposing her husband's desire to consummate the marriage, is seen to be acting under ecclesiastical headship. Ecgfrith's eventual consent, reluctant or otherwise, is both canonically correct and usefully mitigates her opposition to him.

The beatification of Æthelthryth makes it possible for Bede to rejoice in a native female saint who, though permitted to depart by a regretful husband, whose overtures amounted to nothing more than attempting to bribe a bishop to act as a go-between, is yet worthy to be compared with martyrs who braved unflinchingly the torments of wild beasts and tyrannical persecutors. That Bede was unable to find among his sources something more straightforwardly analogous to the Roman Lives of female saints, not a single daughter refusing to be coerced into the bestial embrace of a persistent suitor by obdurate parents, nor gallantly withstanding the frenzied onslaughts of a pagan husband with whom she has been forced into marriage, entirely against her will, suggests that the conversion of England was not marked by domestic conflict between parents and the monastic aspirations of their daughters, and this silence makes it likely that the post-Conquest Lives of early Anglo-Saxon women saints have needed a certain amount of artistic licence to bring them into conformity with the notion of Virginity Preserved as the essential definition of female sanctity, of whose establishment Bede is the harbinger.[101] Compared though Æthelthryth is to Cecilia facing martyrdom, she does not resemble her in having converted her

---

[100] Eddius's remarkably enigmatic report in ch. 19 would have been impenetrable had not Bede written his Life of Æthelthryth; this, too, suggests that the matter may have been less clear-cut than it seems in HE, IV.19.

[101] Parental opposition and/or unwelcome suitors figure in the post-Conquest Lives of many of the early AS women who were revered as saints, such as Werburg of Chester and Withburg of Dereham. Where information was wanting, hagiographers were particularly likely to resort to the model of the Roman virgin martyrs: see, e.g., F.M. Stenton, "Frideswide and her Times," in Preparatory to Anglo-Saxon England, ed. D.M. Stenton (Oxford, 1970), pp. 224–33. For the post-Conquest tradition concerning the trials of St Osyth (7th c.), said to have parted with her husband to become the founder of Chich, see D. Bethell, "The Lives of St Osyth of Essex and St Osyth of Aylesbury," AB 88 (1970), 85–7. Goscelin's Life of Mildrith, chs. 10–15, relates that she was sent to study at Chelles, where the abbess attempted to force her to marry a relative of hers: ed. D.W. Rollason, The Mildrith Legend: A Study in Early Medieval Hagiography in England (Leicester, 1982), pp. 108–43. The motif reappears in his Life of the 10th c. nun, Wulfhild, except that, in her case, the abbess is her aunt: ed. M. Esposito, "La Vie de Sainte Vulfhilde par Goscelin de Cantorbéry," AB 32 (1913), 10–26, ch. 2. Roman virgins and martyrs far outnumber AS female saints – none of whom conforms to classic type – in the 9th c. Mercian Old English Martyrology: ed. G. Kotzor, Das altenglische Martyrologium (Munich, 1981). See further ch. 8, pp. 246–50.

husband to the religious life by the preservation of her vow of chastity, for the conversion as presented by Bede was the achievement of bishops and kings; but she is nevertheless the closest analogue in the annals of the early English church to the continental queens whose means of converting their husbands Theodore would have found it a hard struggle to countenance.

As a married woman who separated from her husband to enter a monastery, Æthelthryth is the representative emblem of the formerly married women who accounted for a significant number of female religious in the conversion period, a phenomenon made possible only by customary freedom of separation and the tenuousness of the ecclesiastical conception of marriage as an indissolubly binding union in which women were in the power of their husbands. The phenomenon is represented in its most orthodox possible form in Æthelthryth's official biography – an unconsummated marriage and a wife who, though opposing her husband in this respect, yet dutifully sues for permission to depart; in which also no mention is made of Ecgfrith's subsequent remarriage. During Bede's lifetime, Queen Cuthburg parted from her husband Aldfrith of Northumbria, and returned to Wessex to found a monastery at Wimbourne,[102] but whereas Ecgfrith's second marriage also failed to produce an heir, Aldfrith of Northumbria was succeeded by his – and presumably Cuthburg's – son. Bede's failure to mention Cuthburg is consistent with his lack of enthusiasm for formerly married monastic women in all but the most exceptional and impeccably childless form; in celebrating the perpetual virginity of a married woman who left her husband to found a monastery, Bede gives a mythic, idealizing form of expression to the preponderance of widows and formerly married women among the founders of female monasticism.[103] Domne Eafe, another of the early monastic founders who parted from her husband, returned to her homeland, according to one version of the Mildrith Legend, saying that she set a higher value on the Kentish mausoleums of Augustine and his companions than the Mercian palaces, and that she preferred the company of Theodore and Hadrian to that of the uncouth Mercians. But most of the various hagiographical versions of this separation reflect a more conservative orthodoxy on marriage, and represent Domne Eafe and her husband as having parted in order that they might both enter a monastery.[104] This goes further than canon law required; even the most conservative orthodoxy did not oblige both partners to a dissolved marriage to enter a monastery. But married couples separating so that they may both enter a monastery embodies to the fullest the conception of marriage as a union whose essential indissolubility persists despite physical severance: Bede's account of Sebbi, who assumes that the wife who finally gives her consent to his entering the monastery will herself take on the service of God, represents one means – whether actual or polemical – of reconciling the existence of formerly married monastics with the theology of marriage.

[102] See ASC, 718.
[103] For formerly married abbesses, see ch. 5, fn. 110. It is not evident from HE, IV.23, that Hild's sister, Hereswith, was among the women who left their husbands for a monastery (cf. HE, III.24); for Bede's general unforthcomingness on the marital status of women religious, see ch. 8, fn. 32.
[104] Versions of the Mildrith Legend are collated and summarized by Rollason, 1982, pp. 73–87.

The life of Æthelthryth represents in concrete form the tensions evident in *Theodore's Penitential* between a conversionary church's desire to accommodate the monastic aspirations of royal women and its determination to uphold the construct of marriage as a unique and indissoluble union in a society not hospitable to its reception. As a hagiographic celebration of a married woman rejecting both the power of a husband and the marriage bond itself, the exemplary thrust of the life of Æthelthryth is in direct opposition to ecclesiastical ambitions regarding the institution of marriage. Somewhat irregular in relation to the orthodoxy of the time in which it was formulated, the life of Æthelthryth became increasingly awkward as an *exemplum*.

Alcuin felt a certain amount of pride in the saint that his homeland had produced, and sent a copy of Bede's panegyric verses on Æthelthryth from the court of Charlemagne to his friend Bishop Arno with warm commendations.[105] But his unease with a hagiographical ideal of a married woman at odds with her husband is revealed by the fact that Alcuin's *Song of York* has sunk without trace Ecgfrith's unconsenting resistance to his wife's refusal to consummate their marriage. In the *Song of York*, Æthelthryth assumes the aspect of a woman converter – a type of woman conspicuously lacking in the work of Bede – who, Cecilia-like, transforms carnal marriage into spiritual union: "How pure was her faith, how wondrous his patience! He was won over by her prayers, and she by love of God! Afire, both of them, with inward flames of the holy Faith, in chastity they remained together as husband and wife."[106] The authority of Bede ensured for Æthelthryth an enduringly eminent place; she is the only native female saint who is included in the extensive collection of Lives of Roman virgin martyrs that Ælfric translated into the vernacular in the late 10th century, and national pride lives on: "The English race is not deprived of the Lord's saints when there lie buried in England such saints as this holy king [Edmund] and the blessed Cuthbert, and Saint Æthelthryth at Ely, and her sister also."[107] But the age of a pioneering church willing to compromise its ideology of marriage to enable royal women to enter the monastic life had passed. Even the *Confessional of Pseudo-Ecgbert*, distinctly backward-looking in many respects, reproduces from *Theodore's Penitential* the ruling that women may not divorce their husbands, even for adultery, but omits the concessive exception for those entering a monastery.[108] Ælfric retains the evidence of Ecgfrith's discontent, but

---

[105] Duemmler, 259. Here, as in *Song of York* (see fn. 106), Alcuin's pride in Bede's hymn surpasses his pride in Æthelthryth.

[106] P. Godman, ed. and trans., *Alcuin: The Bishops, Kings, and Saints of York* (Oxford, 1982), p. 64, ll. 760–63. Æthelthryth's marriage to the Welsh prince is amongst the inconveniences that Alcuin's higher standards of orthodoxy have found it necessary to shed; see Godman, pp. 62–6.

[107] *Ælfric's Lives of Saints*, ed. and trans. W.W. Skeat, EETS OS 94, 114 (London, 1890–1900), II, 332. Ælfric refers, not to Æthelthryth's widowed sister, Seaxburg, with whom Bede associates her (HE, IV.19), but to the uncorrupted virgin saint, Withburg of Dereham, closely linked with Æthelthryth's cult following her translation to Ely in the late 10th c. Bede was responsible for the literary fame of Æthelthryth; her 10th c. cult at Ely is the creation of the Ely monks who possessed her relics, but a written Life is generally held to be essential for the creation of a cult. For the socio-political implications of the cult of Æthelthryth and her sisters, see S.J. Ridyard, *The Royal Saints of Anglo-Saxon England* (Cambridge, 1988), pp. 50–73, 176–210.

[108] See fn. 43.

adds an account of a married man, beside whom Æthelthryth's achievement pales somewhat, for he, having fathered children, remained chaste for 30 years, after which he entered a monastery. The Life of Æthelthryth has become in Ælfric's work a moral *exemplum* of the chastity in marriage for which all married couples should strive.[109] It is a somewhat paradoxical utilization of Æthelthryth's Life but, in shifting the emphasis from marital obligations denied to endurance within the married state, it asserts the indissoluble character of the bond whose establishment, high on the agenda of the conversionary church, was being more rigorously pursued in Ælfric's time by reforming churchmen who felt less need for accommodation.

[109] See *Ælfric's Lives of Saints*, ed. and trans. W.W. Skeat, EETS OS 76, 82 (London, 1881–5), I, 432–4, 440. Chaste marriage is foreshadowed by Alcuin, who makes no mention of Æthelthryth's entry to a monastery.

3

Aldhelm's *De Virginitate*:
Soldiers of Christ and Brides of the Lamb

Introduction: Aldhelm's Dedication and the Barking Community

Aldhelm's prose *De Virginitate* was written in the late 7th or, more probably, early 8th century in response to letters from the nuns and Abbess Hildelith at the double monastery at Barking.[1] The double monastery – housing both nuns and monks and presided over by an abbess – was widely, perhaps universally, preferred to single-sex establishments for women in the early Anglo-Saxon period.[2] Aldhelm's preamble records his pleasure in receiving the nuns' recent letters to his humble self: "The mellifluous studies of Holy Scripture were manifest in the extremely subtle sequence of your discourse," he assures them, and he has much admired their "extremely rich verbal eloquence and the innocent expression of sophistication."[3] The elaborately prolix courtesy that habitually afflicts Aldhelm's style of address is here of a piece with his avowed purpose of lauding the state that his audience has embraced, and the flattering humility of his posture is attributed to their reputation for sanctity and learning. Although the egalitarian strain of Christianity dictated that aristocratic nuns

---

[1] Trans. M. Lapidge and M. Herren, *Aldhelm: The Prose Works* (Cambridge, 1979), 59–132; ed. R. Ehwald, MGH AA 15 (Berlin, 1919), 226–323. Subsequent references are to Aldhelm's *De Virginitate* in the translation of Lapidge and Herren (cited as L&H) unless otherwise stated. For dating, see fns. 15, 41.

[2] For studies, see M. Bateson, "Origin and Early History of Double Monasteries," *TRHS* NS 13 (1899), 137–98, esp. 168–83; S. Hilpisch, *Die Doppelklöster: Entstehung und Organisation* (Munster, 1928); S.E. Rigold, "The 'Double Minsters' of Kent and their Analogies," *Journal of the British Archaeological Association* 3rd ser. 31 (1961), 27–37; J. Godfrey, "The Place of the Double Monastery in the Anglo-Saxon Minster System," *Famulus Christi: Essays in Commemoration of the Thirteenth Centenary of the Birth of the Venerable Bede*, ed. G. Bonner (London, 1976), pp. 344–50. I have not seen D.B. Schneider, "Anglo-Saxon Women in the Religious Life: A Study of the Status and Position of Women in an Early Medieval Society" (unpubl. PhD diss., Cambridge University, 1985). Whereas there is no evidence of any early AS foundation exclusively for women, at least a dozen monasteries ruled by abbesses are known to have been "double" (Barking, Whitby, Ely, Thanet, Sheppey, Lyminge, Leominster, Wimbourne, Much Wenlock, Coldingham, Repton, Bardney); some (e.g., the double monastery from which Tangl, 14, originated) have not been identified. (For the uncertain status of Bath, see P. Sims-Williams, *Religion and Literature in Western England, 600–800* [Cambridge, 1990], pp. 120–1, who also identifies Bradley as a double monastery, pp. 237–42). Bateson, 164, states that in England, but not on the continent, they were invariably ruled by an abbess: *Theodore's Penitential*, II.vi.8 ("It is not permissible for men to have monastic women nor women, men") suggests otherwise.

[3] L&H, p. 59; chs. 1, 2.

were formulaically honoured by Bede and others for being no less noble in virtue than in birth, the family connexions of the nuns of Barking, with one of whom Aldhelm claims kinship, were perhaps not wholly irrelevant either. The alteration in the attitude of later medieval clerics, however, whose addresses to female religious are generally characterized by didactic condescension and authoritative regulation of the manner of life, is less indicative of a change in the social classes from which female religious were drawn than it is of the relative rise in the status of ecclesiastical men.

Obedience to the behest of a patron as a means of recommending one's literary productions was a topos familiar to Aldhelm from his much paraded classical studies, and became formulaic in hagiography as a means of protesting the author's humility in spite of the self-assertion innate in the act of setting pen to parchment; but Aldhelm's reiterated claim to be responding to requests for a work on virginity is, so far as we can tell, authentic. The service of ladies that has *fine amour* lovers from the 12th century on making lyrics to their mistresses' eyebrows, and clerical poets like Chrétien obediently delivering their compositions at the instructions of aristocratic women patrons, is provocatively reminiscent of earlier literary labours of clerics for women religious, of which the passionate-platonic poems of Fortunatus for Abbess Radegund are the most striking. In the later chivalric world women as audiences of literature, like women as audiences of tournaments, are a spur to the performance of deeds of renown. In the more assertively constituted modes of the heroic world, where the assumption of stasis as a normative condition renders action a portentous affair requiring prodigious effort, it is the office of women to spur on their menfolk to achievement by constant urging: Alcuin, on the completion of the commentary on the Gospel of St John that he dedicated to to the royal nuns, Gisla and Rodtruda, betrays his entirely unconscious innocence of erotic dimensions to the enterprise: he had, explains, wanted to write it thirty years ago, but his pen did not stir, because there was no one to raise it.[4] Aldhelm evidently desires to render De Virginitate yet more fulsomely, in verse, but professes himself reluctant to "sweat in vain under the burden of subsequent composition," unless the nuns of Barking "deign to stimulate [him] with just as many repeated letters written as [they] were good enough to resolutely elicit the preceding text of this little book with."[5] That the Carmen De Virginitate survives, and in a large number of copies is, presumably, evidence that provocation was forthcoming.[6]

Such literary compliments to women are, no doubt, sincere tokens of admiring regard, even if they are less substantial assurances of friendship than Alcuin sent to Bishop Beornred with the two Lives of their kinsman Willibrord that he composed: "If I were not impelled by a love which never refuses, I would not dare to touch such a task. . . . Both were dictated in stolen hours at night, as I have been too busy during the day."[7] Aldhelm is neither the first nor last of the

---

[4] Duemmler, 214. Sims-Williams, 1990, p. 197, discerns a connexion between AS clerics as instructors of women and Jerome's writing at the request of women in Rome.

[5] L&H, p. 131; ch. 60.

[6] For manuscripts of the metrical De Virginitate, see Ehwald, 349; M. Lapidge and J.L. Rosier, trans., Aldhelm: The Poetic Works (Cambridge, 1985), p. 256, n. 11. See fn. 44.

[7] Allott, p. 154; Duemmler, 120.

furnishers of literature for female religious to apologize at length for tardiness in the fulfilment of their requests, and Aelred's sister can scarcely have felt such a pressing need for the rule of life that Aelred produced for her shortly before her death in her fifties as she did when she took the veil in her youth.[8] Protestations of having laboured amidst manifold claims upon the attention – in Aldhelm's case the practical business of pastoral care and the burdens of office – natural no doubt in an author, inasmuch as they enhance the value of his work as well as his sacrificial regard for his audience, are common and not gender-specific. Aldhelm, asking as a reward of his labours the intercessory prayers of his audience, reflects, as Boniface was to do in more deeply felt ways, Gregory's conception of the monastic orders as his supportive anchor in the troubled sea of life.[9] Pray for me, Aldhelm asks, "so that I, who seem to vacillate shakily and uncertainly in the condition of my own merits and the weakness of my faith, may deserve to be sustained blessedly and fixedly, borne up on the stable column of your patronage."[10] The implication that the nuns at Barking, engaged in study and prayer, are the ones who are to be envied from the point of view of an ecclesiastic weighed down by secular concerns, demands to be turned on its head, since women were barred from secular orders. Early monasteries, including the female communities of double monasteries, do in fact appear to have engaged in pastoral work, but female religious, particularly if expected to observe strict enclosure, were officially confined to a contemplative role.[11] But as it was a conventional conviction that the contemplative life surpassed the active, and as "the troublesome business of worldly affairs" was likely to have been no less real for Aldhelm than we can readily believe that it was for Boniface, apologizing more than once for his slowness in providing scriptural passages as a form of guidance to meditation,[12] the point of view was one that individuals might have held neither insincerely nor with deliberately repressive intention.

As a consequence of steady pressures towards the segregation and enclosure of female religious which rendered abbesses dependent on their bishop for transactions with the world at large, abbesses' authority over their establishments passed ultimately to bishops, a development accompanied by a decline in the prestige of abbesses and their communities.[13] In the lifetime of Aldhelm, however, episcopal oversight of monasteries was a contentious issue, irrespective of their constitution.[14] The distinction he draws between "those living cloistered

---

8 *De Institutione Inclusarum*: ed. C.H. Talbot, CCCM 1 (Turnhout, 1971), 637–82.
9 *Moralia*: PL 75, 511 (cf. *HE*, II.1); Tangl, 30, 66.
10 L&H, p. 131; ch. 60.
11 For the double monasteries' pastoral role, see fn. 101. The office of deaconess, said to have existed in the Eastern church (J.G. Davies, "Deacons, Deaconesses and Minor Orders in the Patristic Period," *JEH* 14 [1963], 1–11), was outlawed by 5th and 6th c. bishops in the West, and it is unclear whether the title, continuing in use, signifies ordination or merely marriage to an ordained man (see Wemple, 1981, 136–48).
12 L&H, p. 130; ch. 59: Tangl, 27, 94.
13 See J.T. Schulenburg, "Strict Active Enclosure and its Effects on the Female Monastic Experience (ca 500–1100)," in *Medieval Religious Women*, ed. J.A. Nichols and L.T. Shank (Kalamazoo, 1984), I, 51–86.
14 See H&S, III, 314–25, esp. 322; cf. the synod of Hertford, *HE*, IV.5.

under the discipline of the monastery," and "ecclesiastics whose clerical sphere of duty is under the control of a bishop," suggests that he may already have been elevated to a bishopric when he wrote De Virginitate, and was conscious that the scope of ecclesiastical jurisdiction was a matter in which it behoved him to tread carefully:[15] in his episcopal capacity, he guaranteed free elections to all congregations in his see, specifically including Wimbourne, "over which Cuthburg, the king's sister, presides."[16] Barking, however, did not fall within Aldhelm's see. The request of the Barking nuns was presumably prompted by his personal ties with the monastery through his kinswoman. Presumably, too, his reputation for learning had already been established by his studies under Hadrian at the Canterbury school established by Theodore.[17]

Aldhelm's works, especially De Virginitate and his textbook on metrics, were much studied throughout the Anglo-Saxon period, and the pervasive influence of his cumbersomely aureate style is reflected in the letters of women in correspondence with Boniface. Posthumously, then, Aldhelm became the conventual teacher par excellence.[18] The means by which women's religious houses originally became centres of learning, however, is by no means clear – but it is clear that the establishment of monastic schools must have required a good deal more fraternization between monastic men and women than the prevailingly orthodox sources intimate. In the North, Hild, the founder abbess of Hartlepool and Whitby, whose monastic schools contributed significantly to the growth of the church by educating priests and bishops, is most likely to have been taught by Bishop Aidan, from whom she received the veil.[19] Later tradition claims that Hildelith was educated in France, and came to Barking to establish the continental system of monastic discipline at the invitation of Eorcenwold, the Bishop of London, whose sister was the first abbess of the monastery. Bede informs us that, before the establishment of female monasticism in the south of England, women of the East Anglian and Kentish royal houses were obliged to travel to Frankish monasteries;[20] the early Life of Bertila of Chelles says that English rulers appealed to her for teachers and founders of monasteries, and she sent them both women and men, as well many books.[21]

The tradition that Hildelith was educated in a Frankish monastery offers, then, an explanation for the existence of a monastic school at Barking that is both plausible and untroubling to the orthodox sensibilities of a later age; it may, equally, represent the fictionalization of a hagiographer with access to the

[15] L&H, p. 127; ch. 58. Aldhelm was Bishop of Sherbourne, c. 705–9. Lapidge and Herren conclude that De Virginitate is "impossible" to date (pp. 14–15, 10), but believe that it pre-dates his episcopacy (p. 183, n. 25); see fn. 41.

[16] Charter 5; ed. Ehwald, 515.

[17] See Epist 2, 6, 9 (trans. L&H, pp. 152–70).

[18] See L&H, pp. 1–4.

[19] HE, IV.23.

[20] HE, III.8.

[21] Vita Bertilae Abbatissae Calensis, ed. W. Levison, MGH SRM 6 (Hannover, 1913), 95–109, ch. 6. Bertila was abbess of Chelles c. 658–705. P. Sims-Williams, "Continental Influence at Bath Monastery in the Seventh Century," ASE 4 (1975), 1–10, finds evidence for a monastery with a continental abbess founded by a Hwicce sub-king in 675. Another (Liobsynde) was party to an exchange of land with Milburg of Much Wenlock, c. 680; see R. Whitelock, "The Pre-Viking Age Church in East Anglia," ASE 1 (1972), 12.

same circumstantial information as we have.[22] Aldhelm's epistolary communication with the nuns of Barking evidently sprang from direct contact with them, since he greets a number of them by name; he also knows the curriculum that was taught by Hildelith. Boniface, too, was in direct contact with Barking, for the account of the vision of a monk at Much Wenlock that he obtained at the request of Abbess Eadburg was given to him by Hildelith.[23] Boniface was undoubtedly a teacher of monastic women – the earliest Life of Boniface explains that many were attracted to his teaching by his far-spread fame, and that the nuns, though not always able to attend his lectures, "stimulated by his vast wisdom and his spirit of divine love, applied themselves with diligence to the study of the sacred texts, scanning page after page as they meditated on sacred and hidden mysteries."[24]

Aldhelm's treatise is itself evidence of the high standard of learning at Barking, and in recommending his audience to read the *Collationes Patrum* of Cassian and Gregory's *Moralia in Job*[25] he testifies indirectly to the resources of Barking's library. But *De Virginitate* is also an index of the relatively free interaction between male and female religious in the early church. The language in which Bede describes the revival of learning under Theodore is, unexpectedly, inclusive,[26] and the report that nuns in the early eighth century travelled to hear Boniface teach at Nursling suggests that direct contact between Barking and the nearby Canterbury school was not altogether inconceivable, however strongly the Penitential that bears Theodore's name enforces the conclusion that he was also instrumental in introducing a more rigorous conception of orthodoxy. But the difference between the curriculum taught by Theodore and Aldhelm's enumeration of the subjects studied at Barking under Hildelith might be of telling significance. Whereas Bede states that Theodore taught astronomy and computistical studies as well as sacred and secular literature, Aldhelm mentions only study of the scriptures, exegetical commentaries, and grammar, together with "old stories of the historians and the entries of the chroniclers"[27] – to the last of these studies, the Barking chronicle-history that Bede used as a source for his *History* possibly owed its inspiration.[28] But if the Barking curriculum, as Aldhelm describes it, suggests limitations on its direct contact with the new learning brought by Theodore, it had in Aldhelm a useful intermediary link; his deferential attentiveness and tributes to Barking's own accomplishments demonstrate, however, that interaction between the male and female *literati* of the early church was not as one-sided as the existence of a didactic work written by a male ecclesiastic for female religious inherently suggests.

[22] See C. Horstmann, ed., *Nova Legenda Anglie* (Oxford, 1901), II, 34–5.
[23] Tangl, 10 (716). This claim is not contradicted by the letter's presentation of the account as the testimony of one who heard it first-hand from the Wenlock monk; Boniface is recording *verbatim* the testimony of the original witness.
[24] Trans. Talbot, 1954, p. 31; *Life of Boniface*, ch. 2.
[25] Ch. 14.
[26] *HE*, IV.2.
[27] L&H, pp. 62; ch. 4.
[28] *HE*, IV.11, draws on the Barking *Libellus* for the account of King Sebbi; D.P. Kirby, "Bede's Native Sources for the *Historia Ecclesiastica*," *BJRL* 48 (1965–6), 360, traces the account of Eorcenwold (*HE*, IV.6) to the same source.

In the prose *De Virginitate*, Aldhelm addresses himself particularly to the relative merits of virginity and marriage, an issue complicated by the number of formerly married women who had embraced the monastic life.

In the opinion of Basil, the growth of the church was measured by its crop of virgins. But for such time as the harvest remained small, he was inclined to regard back-sliding with indulgence, counselling, however, that many difficulties could be avoided by accepting as postulants only women over seventeen with a firm vocation.[29] *Theodore's Penitential* adopts the same kind of liberal-pragmatic position. It rules that men and women who have taken monastic vows and then abandoned them ought not to be promoted to a high rank in the church; but it takes it for granted that they can re-enter a monastery if they wish to do so.[30]

Whereas the indications are that unmarried Anglo-Saxon women were not attracted to monasticism in significant numbers,[31] widows, and particularly royal widows, were. For the apparent predominance of widows in the early Anglo-Saxon monasteries, materialist explanations are not far to seek. It is evident from the law codes that a widow's inheritance of her husband's property was apt to be resented by her husband's family; the church offered an alternative form of protection if her own family were dead or otherwise unable to aid her in maintaining possession of property against her husband's relatives.[32] Secular powers, particularly the king, represented no less of a threat to landed women unable to draw on influential family ties.[33] Further, in the late Anglo-Saxon period, if not earlier, a woman's vow to remain unmarried after the death of her husband was in some cases a condition of her inheritance of property;[34] although Boniface's account of *suttee* amongst the Wendts suggests the possibility that widows' vows could on occasions have been generated by warrior ideals of loyalty operating in the sphere of marital relations.[35] A rich harvest of widows was not, for conventional labourers in the vineyard, cause for much rejoicing, and Basil was not alone in eschewing young widows in the religious life on the recommendation of St Paul.[36] Nevertheless, *Theodore's Penitential* makes one of its accommodations to local circumstances by adducing the principle of regional variations: the Greeks, it states, regard widows and virgins as equally fit to be abbesses, although the Romans do not regard them in the same light.[37]

The category of formerly married women, however, did not only include

---

[29] *Basil*, 199.18.

[30] *Theodore's Penitential*, I.ix.2–3; cf. II.iii.7.

[31] See ch. 2, p. 71.

[32] See ch. 2, fn. 67.

[33] See esp. Tangl, 14, discussed in ch. 4. The apocryphal story of Trajan's assistance to a widow unable to obtain wergild for her son in *Life of Gregory*, ch. 29, had significant implications for monastic women.

[34] See ch. 2, fn. 95, for Ealdorman Alfred's will.

[35] Tangl, 73. Cf. *Brennu-Njáls Saga*, ch. 129, Bergthora's refusal to leave her husband when the house is set on fire, because they had vowed to share the same fate: ed. E.O. Sveinsson, *Íslenzk Fornrit* 12 (Reykjavik, 1954).

[36] 1 Tim. 5.9–15 (i.e., under the age of 60).

[37] *Theodore's Penitential*, II.iii.7.

widows. The presence in the monasteries of women who had divorced their husbands, a problematic issue for *Theodore's Penitential*, and raised to the level of art in Bede's hagiographic enthusiasm for the twice-married and ever-virginal Æthelthryth,[38] created a further, unconventional dimension to the long-standing debate on marriage versus virginity. Aldhelm's approach is two-pronged, concerned not only with the relative merits of the virgin state and married life, but also with the relative merits of virginal and formerly married nuns, both widows and divorcees. His treatise is of particular interest in demonstrating the manner in which the numerical weight of formerly married monastic women served to mitigate the high valuation of female bodily intactness. Whereas Bede, for instance, endorses and promotes the valorization of physiological virginity in his account of Æthelthryth, Aldhelm keeps in currency the moral and psychological conception of purity – a conception which, though formulated by Augustine, scarcely achieved the status of a mainstream view in considerations of female sanctity throughout the middle ages.[39] Equally of interest is Aldhelm's concomitant affirmation of the freedom of the will.

In pursuing his subject, Aldhelm may have been responding to questions raised in the letters he received. Hildelith herself was probably a formerly married woman, since she is among the abbesses whom Bede does not hail as *virgo*;[40] and Cuthburg, one of the women Aldhelm greets by name, has been identified with the sister of the Wessex kings Ingeld and Ine, who parted from her husband Aldfrith of Northumbria and founded the monastery at Wimbourne (it being the expectation – at least on the part of modern commentators – that founding abbesses were all sufficiently orthodox to spend a year's novitiate in another establishment).[41] The identification is attractive, since a Barking education for Cuthburg of Wimbourne would establish the seminal origins of the monastic school at her monastery, which produced Leoba, depicted by her later hagiographer as the very model of the learned nun.[42] But whether or not the Cuthburg greeted by Aldhelm was the former wife of Aldfrith, the preponderance of aristocratic women among both categories of formerly married female religious adds point to the fact that Aldhelm steers a diplomatic path in his treatment of a matter which in any case required, as

---

[38] *HE*, IV.19–20.
[39] For the traditional aspects of Aldhelm's conception of virginity, see M. Byrne, *The Tradition of the Nun in Medieval England* (Washington, 1932), pp. 25–43; Lapidge and Herren, pp. 51–8, draw attention to its novelty. C.W. Atkinson " 'Precious Balsam in a Fragile Glass': The Ideology of Virginity in the Later Middle Ages," *Journal of Family History* 8 (1983), 131–43, argues that there was an increasing tendency to regard virginity as a moral and psychological attribute from the 13th c. onwards; she attributes the desuetude of Augustinian conceptions to the influence of popular, superstitious beliefs.
[40] C.E. Fell, "Hild, Abbess of Streonæshalch," in *Hagiography and Medieval Literature: A Symposium*, ed. H. Bekker-Nielsen et al. (Odense, 1981), p. 79, remarks that Bede "rarely misses the opportunity to use the title 'virgin.' "
[41] See *ASC*, 718. Proof of this identification would date *De Virginitate* to 697x705 (see fn. 15), there being no suggestion that the 8 year old who succeeded Aldfrith was illegitimate (*Life of Wilfrid*, ch. 60), despite the later hagiographic tradition that Cuthburg's marriage was unconsummated.
[42] That Leoba was taught by an Abbess Eadburg (Tangl, 29) need not mean that she was later educated at Thanet; see ch. 9, fn. 24.

1 Cor. 7 had demonstrated, the full exercise of Paul's characteristic genius for circling around a question until he could by common consent be deemed to have it trapped.

Soldiers of Christ

Aldhelm conjures with the figurative dimensions of "brides of Christ," a metaphor whose emergence as the dominant vehicle of devotional experience from the 12th century onwards accompanies the establishment of the marriage union in place of kinship and comradeship bonds as the primary societal relationship. But for Aldhelm, the nuns of Barking are pre-eminently soldiers of Christ. Some teachers (Alcuin in particular) present themselves in the role of nourisher and nurturer, for the fruits of learning are the spiritual obverse of the fruits of the fall.[43] The nuns at Barking under the tutelage of their abbess were capable of gathering their own food. Likened to a swarm of bees, they are veritably stuffing themselves to the full on the sweets of learning, although Aldhelm adopts briefly the role of provider when, dangling before them the prospect of a metrical De Virginitate, he explains that prose differs from metre "as sweet new wine is different from heady mead."[44] Overall, though, Aldhelm as teacher falls into the mode of battle leader putting heart into the troops by laudatory commendation and spurring them on by his guidance to yet greater achievement. But his courtliness does not desert him as he exhorts virgins of Christ and raw recruits to fight with muscular energy against the horrendous monster of pride and the seven wild beasts of the virulent vices, whose spiritual weapons batter repeatedly the shield wall of the young soldiers of Christ: "Let us not sloppily offer the backs of our shoulder-blades to these enemies after the fashion of timid soldiers effeminately fearing the horror of war and the battle call of the trumpeter," he urges, "but boldly offer our foreheads armed with the banner of the Cross."[45]

This is stirring stuff, but it is not only against the deadly sins that the nuns of Barking are locked in combat, for as Aldhelm explains with a gospel quotation, the kingdom of Heaven is seized by violence and the violent bear it away. Aldhelm pictures the nuns engaged in intellectual pursuits, with their remarkable mental dispositions roaming and traversing the scriptures, the secular historians and the grammarians, as an army of plundering bees, raiding the

---

[43] See esp. Duemmler, 121.
[44] L&H, p. 131; ch. 60. The metrical De Virginitate was written for a wider audience (fn. 6). Virtually all that is germane to the present discussion – dedicatory and related material, Aldhelm's consideration of adornment and the nature of virginity – is omitted from the metrical version, although the tripartite division figuring those who have scorned matrimony (ch. 19) is retained. This confirms that the didactic concerns of the prose De Virginitate were specifically framed for Barking, but the conventions of the opus geminatum are also operative: see G. Wieland, "Geminus Stilus: Studies in Anglo-Latin Hagiography," in Insular Latin Studies, ed. M.W. Herren (Toronto, 1981), pp. 113–33; P. Godman, "The Anglo-Latin Opus Geminatum: From Aldhelm to Alcuin," MÆ 50 (1981), 215–29.
[45] L&H, p. 68; ch. 11.

flowers of the meadow and returning with their loot to build and furnish their waxen castles. Exercising the subtle industry of their minds and lively intelligence through their assiduous perseverance in reading, they are also, to an imagination run riot on classical literature, like wrestlers in the gymnasium sweating and striving under the eye of an instructor, all seeking the crown of victory by their exertions; archers unerringly demonstrating their keenness of aim; panting runners seeking to overcome all others in a quest for the palm of victory, and so on.[46] Aldhelm calls polite attention to the allegorical and inner dimension of these figures, although, in the early church, and particularly the Celtic church, the physically strenuous ascetic practices of soldiers of Christ seem to have assumed an importance parallel to the heroic martial exertions of followers of the lords of this world: ascetic practices, such as those Bede recounts of Dryhthelm, were, in the context of a warrior society, undoubtedly impressive as a means of lay conversion.[47]

This competitive exhibition of prowess for the crown of victory under the watchful eye of Christ, whose earthly representative is the abbess herself, surfaces again when Aldhelm deals with the issue of virgin nuns versus the formerly married. Whether or not the nun's letters conveyed to Aldhelm that Barking was wracked with status struggles, after he had read them "with a certain natural curiosity about hidden things – as, it is said, is innate in me,"[48] it is through the metaphors of combat and hierarchy that he pursues his enquiry. Aldhelm effectively upholds both sides of the putative debate, on the basis of a distinction of carnal and spiritual chastity. Whereas virginity is singled out among the other ranks of virtues to wield the sceptre of the highest sovereignty by Our Lord's preference for it, yet, in respect of marriage, comparisons, albeit much prolonged by Aldhelm, are not to the point. And though those who from their first infancy have preserved the unbreached barriers of their modesty might seem to have a head start in the race for the victor's crown of heaven, yet nevertheless they are liable to succumb to pride, for she, like a fierce queen, is known to usurp for herself the authority of tyrannical power; so that it thus transpires that the inferior station of life, that of the formerly married, advancing on all fronts little by little, takes the place of the superior grade as it languishes tepidly, and, urged on by the goad of the most bitter remorse, obtains its wish and overtakes the once superior victor. Though, in the person of Mary and Anna, the grades of virgins and widows were honoured in the very beginning at the divine nativity, yet, on the other hand, to those who combine in themselves carnal and spiritual virginity, all the sublime loftiness of the wedded takes second place; though, further, bodily purity itself can by no means serve to re-open the door of Paradise. But further also, St Paul says that the virgin thinks only of the things of the Lord and the married woman of the things of the world; so that it would seem that the kingdom of heaven is now in a certain sense seized by violence beforehand by the male and female followers of intact virginity, and we would seem to have reached a resounding conclusion in favour of virginity of either one sort or the other when Aldhelm trumpets: "Let us also run together with harmonizing desires for action, thereafter expecting the prize

---

[46] Chs. 2–3.
[47] *HE*, V.12; see L. Gougaud, *Christianity in Celtic Lands*, trans. M. Joynt (London, 1932), p. 95.
[48] L&H, p. 59; ch. 2.

for patience from the true athlete watching the course of this struggle, the prize which without doubt that person shall then deserve to receive when the time of his contest is completed, who is now seen in no way to flag in maintaining his virginity."[49] But Aldhelm then produces a tripartite division from "a certain volume," into virginity, chastity and conjugality – hierarchically ranked, but all known to bear arms for one commander in chief.[50] In this schema, chastity is that which "having been assigned to marital contracts, has scorned the commerce of matrimony for the sake of the heavenly kingdom" – the explanation of "chastity," then, neatly takes into account the presence of divorced women as well as widows, who normally occupy second place in such schemas. This schema, since Aldhelm is "lacking in the firm support of the scriptures," he quickly abandons for an extended eulogy of virginity in the shape of a martyrology in which figure saints belonging to all the categories and conditions that he has mentioned, only to return to a conclusion which foregrounds a definition of virginity which is essentially spiritual and not carnal: as, for instance, in his quotation from Augustine: "The sanctity of the body is not lost provided that the sanctity of the soul remains, even if the body is overcome, just as the sanctity of the body is lost if the purity of the soul is violated, even if the body is intact."[51]

Aldhelm's discourse is not designed to bring paradoxes to articulate clarity, and he has every reason for not coming down clearly on one side or the other. He cultivates multivalent significances, respectfully leaving their discovery and resolution to the intelligence of his hearers, and hoping, fairly certainly, that his exhibition of literary prowess will occasion both delight and admiration. While he sporadically acknowledges monastic life as corporate, united in its spiritual purposes as an army in the face of a common enemy, the over-riding impression is not spiritual *comitatus* and fellowship with Christ in the bonds of the Holy Spirit, but individualistic aspiration and competitive vying shaped by the warrior ethic and the importance attached to gaining renown: the fact of service to a common overlord does not seem to have obviated this in the secular ethos either. One dimension of ecclesiastical use of heroic figurative language is to signify the conversion of warrior ethics to the peace of God – Bede, for instance remarks that Oswiu founded monasteries in order that earthly warfare might be turned into heavenly warfare.[52] This particular form of conversion was far more readily accomplished at a verbal level than in actuality, and in practice, as Aldhelm's work reveals, the employment of heroic rhetoric does not effect the conversion of the warrior ethic but tends rather to make the monasteries a locus for its sublimated perpetuation.

Aldhelm's image of the nuns as a swarm of bees in their intellectual pursuits is later redeployed to figure voluntary obedience to the call of a leader (signifying

[49] L&H, p. 75; ch. 18.

[50] Ch. 19; a similar three-fold division is briefly enunciated in *Passio S Victoriae*, but the elaboration and application are Aldhelm's (L&H, p. 194, n. 10).

[51] L&H, p. 129; ch. 58 (*De Civitate Dei*, I.18); like Aldhelm, Augustine was moved to a re-assessment by the actualities of pastoral experience (the plight of women who had been raped during the sack of Rome).

[52] HE, III.24; see fn. 109.

both Christ and the abbess). By this Aldhelm recalls the secular-heroic ideal of the willingness of warriors to embrace even exile from their homeland if their leader bids them follow.[53] It was evidently easy enough to regard bees as Valkyrie-like women flying though the air armed with poisonous spears and humming a battle chant: the Old English charm for persuading them to settle respectfully addresses them as "victory women."[54] But when Aldhelm drew upon this same image for rhetorical ballast in his letter to the abbots of Wilfrid when their bishop was exiled by the king, he fairly certainly did not think of warfare as a customary occupation of women. Aldhelm urges the abbots to follow the example of the bees who, when their leader departs, throng forth in swarms "excepting only the female servants of their former homes who are left behind for the propagation of future offspring."[55] Aldhelm may just possibly be essaying here a class distinction between the heroic assertion of the free born and the timorous passivity of the servile classes which cuts across gender distinction: but given that Aldhelm is attempting to goad into action an exclusively male audience, this is a somewhat slender hope. The female and the servile are established alike as the antithesis of warrior courage.

Tacitus, describing the Germanic peoples on the continent in the first century, implies a conception of marriage as a relation modelled on the same lines as male comradeship. The bride, he says, brought weapons to her husband, signifying that she was coming to share his lot: "A woman must not imagine herself free to neglect the manly virtues or immune from the hazards of war. That is why she is reminded, in the very ceremonies which bless her marriage at the outset, that she is coming to share a man's toils and dangers, that she is to be his partner in all his sufferings and adventures, whether in peace or war."[56] Despite this assertion of partnership in peace and war, Tacitus makes no mention of women warriors among the Germanic tribes. The customary role of women in war, as he describes it, was to incite their menfolk by their proximity to the fighting – warriors were stirred to greater efforts when they could hear the lamentations of women and children, he reports. And further: "It stands on record that armies wavering on the point of collapse have been restored by the women. They have pleaded heroically with their men, thrusting their bosoms before them and forcing them to realize the imminent prospect of their enslavement – a fate which they fear more desperately for their women than for themselves."[57] Tacitus, describing continental Germanic tribes in the pre-migration period, from second-hand accounts, is not universally regarded as a reliable testimony to Anglo-Saxon mores in the conversion period. But the veracity of his pointers towards the conception of Germanic marriage on the paradigm of kinship and male comradeship (which are more or less synonymous) is born out both in the surviving Anglo-Saxon literature and the much

53 Chs. 4, 6.
54 "For a Swarm of Bees" (ASPR VI, 125), l. 9. For the relation of *sigewif* to the Teutonic concept of Valkyrie and *idisi*, see H. Damico, "The Valkyrie Reflex in Old English Literature," *Allegorica* 5 (1980), 149–67. For its survival in OE, see also H. Stuart, "The Anglo-Saxon Elf," *Studia Neophilologica* 48 (1976), 313–20.
55 L&H, p. 169; *Epist* 12.
56 Trans. H. Mattingly, *Tacitus on Britain and Germany* (Harmondsworth, 1962), p. 116; ed. R.P. Robinson, *The Germania of Tacitus* (Middletown, Conn., 1935), ch. 18, see also ch. 46.
57 Mattingly, p. 107; *Germania*, ch. 8, see also ch. 7.

more prolific Old Icelandic sources. More commonly, perhaps, the wife's sharing of the lot of her husband was modelled on the loyalty of the retainer to his lord, whose endurance Aldhelm held up as an example to the abbots of Wilfrid: "If worldly men, exiles from divine teaching, were to desert a devoted master, whom they embraced in prosperity, but once the opulence of good times began to diminish and the adversity of bad fortune began its onslaught, they preferred the secure peace of their dear country to the burdens of a banished master, are they not deemed worthy of the scorn of scathing laughter and the noise of mockery from all?"[58]

The Anonymous Lindisfarne *Life of Cuthbert* mentions Queen Jurmenburg accompanying Ecgfrith on his campaign against the Picts as far as Carlisle, where she awaited the outcome of the battle.[59] Bede notes that Queen Cynewise of Mercia held the son of Oswiu hostage at the capital while her husband Penda was away fighting Oswiu in Northumbria.[60] Hæsten's invading Danish army in the reign of Alfred was evidently accompanied by women and children, but the *Anglo-Saxon Chronicle* says that they remained in the fortress while the army was on campaign.[61] What these instances represent is division of spheres within a form of comradely solidarity, a sharing of the same fate by participation in the same enterprise. So too, in *Maxims I*, whose ideal of the noble lord and lady is closely reflected in the depiction of Wealhtheow in *Beowulf*, there is an implicit division between the warrior *comitatus* of the Lord, whose sphere is the battle-field, and the social, peacetime *comitatus* that the Lady weaves by the distribution of the cup in the hall. The Lady, in other words, exercises a parallel leadership in support of her husband's lordship, which interlocks in the hall with his; for *Maxims I*, the noble lord and lady are "rulers together," a role dramatized by Wealhtheow's assumption of her seat beside her husband when she has finished circulating the cup.[62]

The warrior woman, in the sense of an active combatant is, then, difficult to discern in Anglo-Saxon records, though her existence in cognate warrior cultures of the British Isles – Celtic and Viking – in forms that are not simply mythological and literary, makes it reasonable to presume her existence.[63] In part, the Anglo-Saxon warrior woman is rendered difficult to discern by the paucity of documentation, particularly in the conversion period. With the existence of the woman military leader and commander of troops we are on firmer ground. King Alfred's daughter, Æthelfled, the Lady of the Mercians,

---

[58] L&H, pp. 169–70; *Epist* 12. Cf. the woman in *The Wife's Lament*, whose relation to her *frea* and *freond* from whom she is parted is that of a retainer; loyal to the vow they have both sworn, that nothing but death will separate them (ll. 21–5), she wanders far to find him when he journeys forth.

[59] *Anon Cuthbert*, IV.8.

[60] *HE*, III.24.

[61] *ASC*, 893.

[62] *Maxims I*, ll. 81–92 ("boldagendum bæm ætsomne"). Cf. *Beowulf*, ed. and trans. M.J. Swanton (Manchester, 1978), ll. 640–1, 1232. For throne-sharing, see pp. 152–5, 208–20.

[63] For a 9th c. woman buried with a spear at Gerdrup, see Fell, 1986, p. 130; for one buried at Asnes with armory and a horse, see U. Dronke, ed. and trans., *The Poetic Edda* (Oxford, 1969), p. 58. Dronke also documents shieldmaids and Valkyrie in Viking legend, and the "Red-haired maid," who commanded a fleet in the 10th c. Norse raids on Munster. See also H. Damico, *Beowulf's Wealhtheow and the Valkyrie Tradition* (Madison, Wis., 1984), pp. 194–6. For Celtic warrior women, see fn. 73.

commanded Mercia's campaign against the Danes in the early 10th century. But the *Mercian Register* chiefly records that she built fortifications, and does not explicitly state that she led an army into battle, and a similar uncertainty hovers over the *Anglo-Saxon Chronicle* entry for 722, which states that Æthelburg destroyed the forts that her husband Ine had built at Taunton.[64] The Lady of Mercia appears to have assumed command of campaigns even before the death of her husband.[65] We are not bound to deduce that this was because her husband was incapacitated towards the end of his life, even though it is true, generally, that male absence or incapacity tends to be a pre-condition for the woman defensive commander; and in the post-Conquest period, for which the records are fuller, we find, not active campaigners (with the notable exception of the Empress Mathilda), but women who assume military command because their castles have been besieged during the absence of their husbands.[66] In Old Icelandic, too, the woman avenger of her kindred, like Grendel's mother in *Beowulf*, is a traditional figure, but one whose appearance depends on the extremity of her status as last survivor, bereft of all male kindred who would otherwise prosecute the blood-feud on her behalf.[67] So also, the woman referred to in the 996 charter of Æthelred, who is reported as having killed the king's thane and 15 others, was a widow attempting to hold possession of some disputed land which her husband had claimed.[68] The woman military commander acting as the saviour of her people was an accepted, even an admired figure, just as the woman avenger is sympathetically regarded in Old Icelandic. The eulogistic portrayal of the Old Testament Judith as a leader of national resistance in the 10th century Old English vernacular epic has the appearance of being prompted by contemporary actuality;[69] Aldhelm, depicting her in an *exemplum* as a widow vowed to chastity, and feeling a need to excuse her emergence from seclusion, explains that "she did it grieving for her kinsfolk with the affection of compassion and not through any disaffection from chastity."[70] The terse report of the Lady of Mercia's campaign conveys the reverse of disapproval; whatever the precise form her leadership took when

[64] See Mercian Register (MR), 910–18, ed. S. Taylor, *The Anglo-Saxon Chronicle: MS B* (Cambridge, 1983), 49–50. The entry for 917 reads: "Her Æthelflæd Myrcna hlæfdige Gode fultmigendum foran to Hlafmæssan begeat tha burh mid eallum tham the thærto hyrde, the ys haten Deoraby; 7 thær wæron eac ofslegene hire thegna feower the hire besorge wæron binn tham gatum." The entry for 916 states: "7 thæs ymb .iii. niht sende Æthelflæd fyrd on Wealas 7 abræc Brecenanmere 7 thær genam thæs cinges wif feower 7 thritiga sume." Such formulations, if used of a king, would probably seem straightforward. Æthelfled's defensive campaigns are not clearly distinguishable from reclamation of former Mercian territories; see fn. 71.
[65] MR, 910–11, records the death of the Lord of Mercia in the year following an entry concerning Æthelfled's building of a borough at *Bremesbyrig*.
[66] The earliest English record is in *The Peterborough Chronicle*, 1075: ed. C. Clark, 2nd edn. (Oxford, 1970). See fn. 76.
[67] For Grendel's mother as avenger, see *Beowulf*, ll. 1258–78; for the earliest of the OI female avengers, see Guthrun in the Eddic lay, *Atlakvitha*, ed. and trans. Dronke, pp. 1–12 (dated 9th or 10th c.), who avenges the death of her brothers at the hand of her husband.
[68] A.J. Robertson ed., *Anglo-Saxon Charters*, 2nd edn. (Cambridge, 1956), 63; the child/son accompanying her was, presumably, too young to be regarded as a party to her resistance.
[69] *Judith*, ASPR IV, pp. 99–109. Ælfric, during the 990–1010 crisis under Æthelred, saw Judith as an example of national resistance to pagan invasion; *The Old English Version of the Heptateuch*, ed. S.J. Crawford, EETS 160 (London, 1922), p. 48. Cf. his homiletic account, fn. 92.
[70] L&H, p. 127; ch. 57.

"with the help of God she obtained the borough called Derby, with all that belonged to it, and there also four thanes who were dear to her were killed within the gates," her command of Mercian forces appears to have seemed so self-evidently right to the chronicler as to require no explication, and he affirms that she was the lawful ruler of Mercia.[71] The recording of her deeds in the matter-of-fact style normally characteristic of the *Anglo-Saxon Chronicle* points to a climate of opinion far more favourable than that implied by the Anglo-Norman chroniclers, who depicted Æthelfled as no less prodigious, and more amusing, than Dr Johnson's preaching dog.[72]

But there is little doubt that women warriors are made additionally difficult to discern in the surviving records by the censoring effect of ecclesiastical disapproval of their active engagement in violence. There is no legislation in England comparable to the late 7th century Irish *Law of Adomnan*, though there are hints of similar influences at work. The law code enacts penalties for the slaying of women, as well as clerics, children and the witless – those, in other words, regarded as unable to defend themselves. Even more striking however, is the fact that the code also enacts penalties for the employment of women in armies: "If women be employed in an assault or in a host or fight, seven *cumals* for every hand as far as seven, and beyond that it is to be accounted as the crime of one man."[73] The preamble locates the law code within a context of regard for women derived from a cult of Mary, not in the aspect of heavenly mistress, which is the focus of later medieval devotion, but in her aspect as mother, and the source of all life. Adomnan was visited by an angel, who said to him:

'Go forth into Ireland, and make a law in it that women be not in any manner killed by men, by stabbing or any other form of death, either by poison, or in water, or in fire, or by any beast, or in a pit, or with dogs, but that they shall die in their lawful bed. Thou shalt establish a law in Ireland and Britain for the sake of the mother of each one, because a mother has borne each one, and for the sake of Mary mother of Jesus Christ through whom all are. Mary besought her son on behalf of Adamnan about this Law. For whoever slays a woman shall be condemned to a twofold punishment . . . . for the sin is great when any slays the mother and sister of Christ's mother, and the mother of Christ, and her who carries the spindle and clothes everyone.'[74]

---

[71] Her establishment of a powerful and autonomous Mercia was in conflict with the territorial ambitions of her brother, Edward of Wessex, who invaded Mercia at her death and led away in captivity her daughter Ælfwynn, whom *MR*, 919, appears to regard as heir to Æthelfled's rule. F.T. Wainwright, "Æthelflæd, Lady of the Mercians," in *The Anglo-Saxons: Studies in Some Aspects of Their History and Culture*, ed. P. Clemoes (London, 1959), pp. 53–69, plausibly explains the non-reporting of her campaigns in ASC (A) as a consequence of these broader political conflicts.

[72] See Bandel, 113–18.

[73] *Law of Adomnan*, trans. McNeill, pp. 135–9; ed. K. Meyer *Cáin Adamnáin: An Old-Irish Treatise on the Law of Adamnan* (Oxford, 1905), 52. Meyer, p. viii, thought that both code and preamble were 9th c., but later scholarship concludes that the terms of the Law were set forth at a synod at Tara (697) under the influence of Adomnan, Abbot of Iona (679–704). Northumbrian contact with the church in Ireland, both directly and via Iona, continued throughout the 8th c.

[74] McNeill, pp. 135–6.

The preamble is a later, perhaps 9th century, addition to the law code, but the conclusion still holds that, in order for the church to embrace women (and particularly widows) as the subjects of its particular protection and compassion, it was first necessary to ensure that they laid down their arms and assumed the non-combatant status to which the religious orders themselves were bidden. In short, the historic and actual precondition of ecclesiastical chivalry to women was their complete defencelessness.

Adomnan's concern with the plight of the defenceless is confirmed by an episode he includes in his *Life of Columba*, when the saint, a young deacon at the time, was walking with his aged master. The account offers an a epiphany of the way in which physical powerlessness created a form of identity between women and ecclesiastics – though it reveals much more than that:

> It happened one day that a certain cruel man, a pitiless oppressor of the innocent, was pursuing a young girl, who fled upon the level surface of the plain. When by chance she saw the aforesaid young deacon's master, the aged Gemman, reading on the plain, she ran straight to him for protection with all the speed she could. Alarmed by this sudden happening he called to him Columba, who was reading at a little distance, so that together they might to the extent of their power defend the girl from her pursuer. But as soon as the man came near, showing them no reverence he killed the girl with a spear, under their robes. And he left her lying dead upon their feet, and turning away began to depart.
>
> Then the old man in great distress of mind turned to Columba, and said: "For how long, holy boy, Columba, will God, the just judge, suffer this crime, and our dishonour, to go unavenged?" Thereupon the saint pronounced this sentence upon the miscreant: "In the same hour in which the soul of the girl whom he has slain ascends to heaven, let the soul of the slayer descend to hell." And more quickly than speech, with that word, like Ananias before Peter, so also before the eyes of the holy youth that killer of innocents fell dead on the spot. The fame of this sudden and dreadful vengeance was immediately spread abroad throughout many provinces in Ireland, to the wonderful renown of the holy deacon.[75]

Adomnan's narration illustrates very clearly the extent to which ecclesiastics relied, whether for the protection of women or themselves – and, in general, for the imposition of their values on society – on the awe they could inspire by their reputation for the possession of non-material powers. This helps to explain, though does not entirely obviate, the fact that for Adomnan the outrage perpetrated consisted not merely in the fact that the murderer was "a pitiless oppressor of the innocent," but that he failed to respect the ecclesiastics who attempted to extend their protection.

Dimly, it is possible to discern throughout the Anglo-Saxon period the process by which the ecclesiastical construct of women as helpless non-combatants emerged to triumph in the *Encomium* which Queen Emma commissioned in honour of herself, probably for an ecclesiastical audience, in 1042; for when

---

[75] Anderson, p. 131; *Life of Columba*, II.25.

Emma resisted King Harold's repossession of the royal regalia and treasure, she had the Wessex household troops with her, but the episode has no conceivable place in the Encomium's portrait of Emma, looking forward as it does to the heroines of later romance in its depiction of her as a wronged innocent aided by Providence alone.[76] The first stirrings of ecclesiastical chivalry to women are evident in the work of Bede. To his revision of the Anonymous Life of Cuthbert, he adds a depiction of the episcopal saint's concern to ensure the flight of Queen Jurmenburg to safety when he divined clairvoyantly that her husband Ecgfrith had been killed and the battle lost.[77] In the History, Bishop Paulinus appears as the protector of the widowed Æthelburg, in an episode somewhat reminiscent of the ending of the Finnsburg lay, where the Danes triumphantly carry their princess back to her people after the defeat of her husband and his followers.[78] Bede relates that Bishop Paulinus, who had accompanied Æthelburg of Kent to guard her against the corruptions of paganism when she married Edwin of Northumbria, escorted her and her children back to her homeland when Edwin and his Northumbrian army fell in battle. He was defeated by Penda and Cædwalla, who acted in a manner that Bede wishes to have understood as specifically characteristic of pagan conquerers, by sparing neither women nor children, but putting them all to death with ruthless savagery.[79]

No less material to the safe escape of Æthelburg and her party, one feels, was the presence of Bass, a retainer of King Edwin, renowned for his bravery, who also accompanied them back to Kent. The presence of Bass as co-protector on this chivalrous undertaking marks a point of cultural coalition. Clerical chivalry to women fuses with a tradition of Germanic sympathy for women as the particular sufferers in war, which is evinced in Beowulf's backdrop of mourning women,[80] and remarked as early as Tacitus, in his account of the continental tribes, stirred into battle by the prospect of enslavement "which they fear more desperately for their women than for themselves." Just as Tacitus asserts that Germanic warriors were stirred to military valour when they could hear close by the lamentations of women and the wailing of children,[81] so the aged Swedish king in Beowulf, having rescued his queen from the invading Geats, retreats behind the ramparts when he realizes that he cannot "defend hoard, women and children from the war-voyagers" in open battle.[82] The ecclesiastical view of warrior women as morally perverse has its echo in indigenous culture too. The Beowulf poet was familiar with the existence of warrior women, even though it

[76] See Encomium Emmae Reginae, ed. and trans. A. Campbell, RHS Camden 3rd ser. 72 (London, 1949), esp. III.1–7 (subsequently referred to as Encomium). With the Encomium's depiction of the accession of Emma's son, Harthacanute, as a triumph for Emma's nebulous good influence, cf. ASC 1035 (C), which suggests that she offered armed resistance to Harald while she was acting as regent for her son. But the aged queen in the early 11th c. Chronicle of Thietmar of Merseburg, who holds London against the Danes after the death of Æthelred, grieving for her husband and defender, is not Emma-Ælfgifu (cf. EHD, I, 347), but Æthelred's first wife, Ælfgifu of Northumbria: ed. R. Holtzmann, MGH SRG NS 9 (Berlin, 1955), VII.40.
[77] Bede's Cuthbert, ch. 27.
[78] Beowulf, ll. 1151–9.
[79] See HE, II.20.
[80] Renoir, 1975, pp. 224–51, offers a comparative study of female grief in Germanic literature.
[81] Germania, chs. 7, 8.
[82] Beowulf, ll. 2953–7.

is not certain whether he regarded them as more or less terrifying than warrior men:[83] but the salient point about Grendel's mother is that she is a troll-wife, a species of monster. *Beowulf*, particularly if it took its final form in the 10th or 11th, rather than the 7th or 8th century, is more likely to represent the fusion of Germanic and Christian culture than to preserve archaic attitudes in their original purity.[84] But the warrior woman can never have been other than a rarity, always liable to be construed as uncanny. Guthrun in the Eddic lays, linked with the Norns and Valkyrie, is also the woman who "wept not as other women do," and achieves violent revenge for her brothers, in the manner of a man, at the cost of not being a woman: there will, the narrator remarks, "never be another warrior in chain-mail like her."[85]

Though Aldhelm inserts a brief reminder that the martial and athletic exertions he conjures up to depict the pursuit of learning are allegorical figures for the inner and spiritual life, he gives no sign that he sees anything paradoxical or incongruous about constituting female religious as soldiers of Christ. The obvious inference to be drawn from his letter to the abbots of Wilfrid is that nuns as soldiers of Christ are honorary men, exceptional prodigies who have triumphed over their female nature. But, in the context of his address to the nuns of Barking, Aldhelm betrays no sign of seeing the matter thus. His path was no doubt eased by his familiarity with the *Psychomachia* tradition, in which the female personification of the vices and virtues in conflict within the soul rises, apparently unreflectingly, from the grammatical gender of *anima*.[86] Early rules for women, such as the rule that Caesarius wrote for his sister, similarly make casual use of Paul's *miles Christi* metaphor; the *Rule of Benedict*, used alike by communities of men and women, has nothing specifically to say to, or about, women religious as a separate class. This, we may say, reflects the assumption of the experience of male religious as normative, a casually oblivious disregard of a marginal group. But the implications can perhaps be pursued further than this.

The female protagonists who are presented in the heroic mode in *Elene*, *Juliana* and *Judith*, are quasi-allegorical *milites Christi*, though in differing ways.

---

[83] *Beowulf*, ll. 1279–87. "Her violence, the violence of a woman in battle was the lesser – by just as much as the strength of females is compared with a male when the . . . sword forged by the hammer, the broad sword blade shears through the . . . boar image above the helmet" (Bradley, p. 445). Taken literally, as F. Klaeber ed., *Beowulf*, 3rd edn. (Boston, 1950), p. 181, points out, this "seems at variance with the facts, for the second fight is far more difficult for Beowulf than the first."

[84] For Grendel's mother as "an inversion of the Anglo-Saxon ideal of woman" (Chance, pp. 95–108), and the dating of *Beowulf*, see p. 6.

[85] *Atlakvitha*, st. 29–44. Guthrun's tearlessness connects her with the Norns; for her unnatural tearlessness, see also *Guthrúnarkvitha I*, ed. H. Kuhn, *Edda*, 4th rev. edn. (Heidelberg, 1962), I, 202–6. Proverbially, the Norns do not weep for the griefs of the human race whose fate they weave (*Atlakvitha*, st. 16); so Guthrun, preparing dry-eyed to set fire to the Huns and their hall, recalls the "doom of the Gods" of Nordic mythology.

[86] Prudentius' *Psychomachia* was much studied in the period, but Aldhelm's direct knowledge eludes proof (Lapidge and Rosier, p. 100). J.P. Hermann, *Allegories of War: Language and Violence in Old English Poetry* (Ann Arbor, 1989), examines the psychomachia theme in OE, arguing that "representation of spiritual life as a violent conflict is complicitous with social violence," pp. 1–2, but the fact that the protagonists of three of the five poems that he studies are women does not have significance for him.

Cynewulf's Juliana is a virgin martyr characteristic of the persecution period, and her defiance of her earthly and demonic assailants depends more fundamentally on the heroic exercise of the will than the exertion of brute force, to which her antagonists are obliged to resort for their purely mundane, and short-lived, triumph.[87] Cynewulf's Elene, on the other hand, is herself an active persecutor, an imperial conqueror forged in the mould of her son Constantine, subjugating the enemies of the cross. Her success in wresting the True Cross from the Jews is, in a manner of speaking, a triumph for her implacable will, but nevertheless entails her willingness to resort to force of arms, and she employs her accompanying warrior band to imprison Judas in a pit.[88] Elene is a type of the Church Militant, who was conceived in an era when the enemies of Christianity took forms that were not only supernatural and psychomachic, for Cynewulf was writing during a period of Viking invasions. She serves as a paradigmatic *exemplum* for Christians, and particularly perhaps for Christian queens; when Gregory the Great wrote to urge the king and queen of Kent to take a leading part in the conversion, he offered Elene as a role model to Queen Bertha, just as he urged her husband to become another Constantine,[89] and the *Mercian Register* notes that the Lady of Mercia began her fortifications on the eve of the Invention of the Cross.[90]

Elene is evidence of the absence of a cultural construction of mercifully gentle femininity; for the figurative significance of the heroic presentation of female saints does not negate its literal implications. Cynewulf and the late Old English homily "De Inventione Sanctae Crucis" ultimately derive their army-leader portrait of Elene from the same Latin source, but he, like the homilist, enhances her militancy.[91] As other 11th and 12th century vernacular homilies of the Invention show, the legend does not inherently require Elene to be cast in a heroic mode; like Ælfric's homiletic account of Judith,[92] the non-heroic presentation of Elene marks the development of a distinctive gender construction of women which is clearly delineated in the *Encomium* of Emma.[93] Significantly, the presentation of women in the same, militantly assertive modes as men also characterizes the depiction of women who have no allegorical dimension. Hildegyth, in her speech to Waldere, declaims in a manner indistinguish-

---

[87] *Juliana*, ASPR III, 113–33. C. Schneider, "Cynewulf's Devaluation of Heroic Tradition in *Juliana*," ASE 7 (1978), 107–18, argues that the depiction of Juliana represents a new, specifically Christian, form of heroism, because it denigrates physical force and recommends passive strength. Awareness of the inherent paradox of martial-heroic Christianity is not confined to female hagiography, and is central to *The Dream of The Rood* (ASPR II, 61–5). Cf. A.H. Olsen, "Cynewulf's Autonomous Women: A Reconsideration of Elene and Juliana," ed. Damico and Olsen, pp. 222–32.

[88] See *Elene* (ASPR II, 66–102), ll. 574–709.

[89] H&S, III, 17–18.

[90] MR, 912.

[91] See *The Old English Finding of the True Cross*, ed. and trans. M. Bodden (Cambridge, 1987), esp. p. 55.

[92] Ælfric's Homily on Judith, written for an anchoress and essentially concerned with chastity, exploits none of the heroic potential of the material: ed. B. Assmann, *Angelsächsische Homilien und Heiligenleben*, Bib ags Prosa 3 (Kassel, 1889), pp. 102–16.

[93] See *Legends of the Holy Rood*, ed. R. Morris, EETS OS 46 (London, 1871); *History of the Holy Rood Tree*, ed. A.S. Napier, EETS OS 103 (London, 1894).

able from the warriors on the battlefield at Maldon.[94] Wealhtheow, addressing Hrothgar on the future disposition of the kingdom, does not employ persuasion, but speaks in the hortatory accents unvaryingly characteristic of the world she inhabits: "And when you must go forth to face the decree of Providence, leave the people and the realm to your kinsmen!" Soliciting the support of Beowulf for her sons, she does not appeal to sympathy for the weak, but asserts her position of strength as the distributor of treasure and mead: "Distinguish yourself by strength and be kindly disposed to these boys by giving them good counsels! I shall keep your reward for this in mind. . . . The men of this court, having drunk to it, will do as I bid."[95] The depiction of Wealhtheow as throne-sharer with the king, exercising a lordship of the hall that parallels his, reflects the constitution of married women as comrades, sharers with their husband in a joint pursuit. The indiscriminately heroic portraiture of women, though underlain by a gender-based distinction that removes them from the sphere of active combat, is at the same time a convention which foregrounds male-female identity, submerging differences.

Aldhelm cannot be said to regard male monasticism as normative. There are central ways in which he embodies his consciousness of Barking as a double monastery, most evidently in the martyrological section's inclusion of both male and female saints. His treatise is in fact a rather exceptional case of a work written for a mixed audience which addresses itself primarily to women. His casting of the nuns of Barking as soldiers of Christ can also be regarded as reflecting a conception of female religious as partners in a joint enterprise. Seemingly owing their origins in the north of England to Irish models, and regarded by *Theodore's Penitential* as a custom unorthodox but too well-established in England for it to be worth attempting to suppress them, double monasteries nevertheless continued to be founded by those who had strong ties with the Roman Church: Æthelthryth, for instance, though closely associated with Bishop Wilfrid, founded a double monastery at Ely when she returned from the north to her East Anglian homeland.[96] Pragmatic reasons have been offered

---

[94] *Waldere*, ASPR VI, 4–6.

[95] Trans. Bradley, p. 444; see *Beowulf*, ll. 1178–80, 1216–31. Cf. A.L. Klinck, "Female Characterization in Old English Poetry and the Growth of Psychological Realism," *Neophilologus* 63 (1979), 597–610, who views the heroic depiction of women in OE poetry as mechanically conventional, arguing that the passive female protagonists of *Genesis B* and *Christ I* prompt the poets to a new individualization and originality.

[96] See *HE*, IV.19–20. Some argue for Gaulish models in southern England (esp. Rigold, 27–37), particularly as Æthelthryth's kinswomen entered Gaulish double monasteries (*HE*, III.8); Gaulish influence through association with Wilfrid is also suggested: see P. Wormald, "Bede and Benedict Biscop," ed. Bonner, p. 144. P. Hunter Blair, "Whitby as a Centre of Learning in the Seventh Century," in *Learning and Literature in Anglo-Saxon England: Studies Presented to Peter Clemoes*, ed. M. Lapidge and H. Gneuss (Cambridge, 1985), pp. 7–9, 30–2, argues for Gaulish influence on Hild, even though she did not succeed in reaching Chelles (*HE*, IV.23). Bateson, 150–6, assumes that double monasteries in England derived from Aidan's influence on Hild's foundations, and attributes the double monasteries at Faremoutiers, Chelles and Andelys to Irish inspiration, but concludes: "St Columban's followers introduced no new and peculiarly Irish system of monastic organization when they founded such houses. They arose, it would seem, in many countries and at many times as the natural sequel to an outburst of religious enthusiasm" (149–50). The last known double monastery founded before the Viking raids was at Winchcombe, 798 (see Levison, 1946, pp. 249–59).

for the existence of the double monasteries; sometimes, one suspects, in the belief that to have explained that the double monastery organization was a matter of practical necessity is to have satisfactorily explained it away. A 1919 report to the Archbishop of Canterbury on the ministry of women stated: "It is difficult to regard these religious houses . . . as anything but nunneries in connection with which there were communities of brethren to do such work and perform such services as the nuns could not do or perform themselves."[97] Bede, too, preferred to regard the double monasteries as strictly segregated communities which happened to have been built in close proximity, but his account of Coldingham is not the only reason for believing that this was not the case.[98] The need for a priest to conduct services and minister to the nuns scarcely seems to necessitate the presence of a community of men.[99] Protection against attack, assistance with heavy labour – these are roles that would have been better performed by monastic servants who did not labour under the inhibition of knowing that it was unworthy of a man of God to wield any weapon more life-threatening than a heavy stick.[100] Communities of female monastics have, after all, for most of their history, managed with the assistance of a chaplain and the employment of lay workers. A more plausible explanation is that the monasteries were in effect pastoral centres and, because women were prohibited from preaching, adjacent male communities were founded nearby. In this case, however, the presence of female communities appears superfluous – if the object of religious communities was to minister to the laity and the laity could only be properly ministered to by men, there was nothing to be gained by endowing female houses; one would expect to find nuns left to live in obscure seclusion.[101] Whatever pragmatic reasons there may have been for the origins and continued existence of the double monasteries, the fact that it was ever a conceivable form of monastic organization testifies to a certain pioneering willingness to be inclusive on the part of the early church (which in the case of the Irish church

[97] A.T. Thompson, "Double Monasteries and the Male Element in Nunneries," in *The Ministry of Women: A Report by a Committee Appointed by His Grace the Lord Archbishop of Canterbury* (London, 1919), p. 418.

[98] On the education of priests at Hild's monastery (*HE*, IV.23), and other forms of male-female association, see ch. 8.

[99] Bateson, 138–9, argues that women's houses were founded in proximity to existing male communities from the very beginnings of Christian monasticism in order to give them access to a priest for their services; this does not account for the persistence of the model. Evidence for the nature of the male communities at double monasteries is slight. M. Deanesly, "English and Gallic Minsters," *TRHS*, 4th ser. 23 (1941), 25–69, argues that the male communities were not regular monks but secular clerks; Hilpisch, pp. 48–50, takes a more qualified view. Presumably, both male and female communities were highly diverse; but whether or not the men were regular monks made no difference to reformers' attitudes.

[100] *HE*, III.18. Given the social status of the women who founded double monasteries, it is not surprising that they "made use of the indispensable services of men in a rough age" (Godfrey, p. 346); Bede reports that Seaxburg sent some monks to find a coffin for Æthelthryth (*HE*, IV.19), but Whitby had a distinct community of monastic servants (*HE*, IV.24). Protection of female religious and a chivalrous desire to relieve them of the rigours of life were among the stated motives of the men who established strictly-segregated male-female houses in the 12th c. at Fontevrault and in England; see ch. 9, fn. 150.

[101] Godfrey, pp. 344–50, regards double monasteries as centres for implementing AS kings' commitment to the conversion of their people; curiously, he assumes that it was acceptable for women to baptize and teach, but not to preach (see ch. 8, fn. 10).

was certainly short-lived).[102] It was a willingness aided and encouraged in Anglo-Saxon society by the traditionally high level of participation by women, which is implicit, for instance, in Bede's complaint concerning the "family monasteries" – that men had set up monasteries for themselves and made their wives abbesses of others,[103] and implicit also in Eddius's Life of Wilfrid where royal couples are described as having acted jointly in outlawing the bishop.[104] Women's establishment of double monasteries whose purpose was to aid the conversion and minister to the laity in itself affirms their expectation of involvement in the active life of the church.

Gregory's Libellus Responsionum makes an effort to remind Augustine that, with respect to the missionary salvation of souls, women should not be overlooked, and Aldhelm's occasional references to "believers of both sexes," for which there are parallels even in Bede, is an index of the same deliberate inclusiveness of the conversion period. Despite the polemically sanguine picture painted by Bede's History, the monastic orders in England were a tiny minority in the midst of a population on which Christianity had yet to make a deep impression. Female religious were, in a very real sense, comrades in a joint struggle – albeit there was an underlying division of spheres whereby the official exclusion of women from the active ministry and their confinement to contemplative pursuits placed them in somewhat the same position as Queen Jurmenburg awaiting the outcome of the battle at Carlisle. The egalitarian and inclusive impulses of early Christianity still find expression in a letter of Alcuin's written in the 790s accompanying the translation of a devotional book for a layman, to whom Alcuin expresses his assurances that the kingdom of heaven is open to all equally, irrespective of social status or gender, to members of the laity no less than to those in religious orders – a fundamental truism, but not one that is urged with much personal warmth in the later middle ages.[105]

That the portrayal of women in warrior-heroic modes in both ecclesiastical as well as secular literature represents a pervasive appropriation of women to male cultural forms and values, which precludes the emergence of a specifically female culture, goes without saying. But the foregrounding of likeness is accompanied by an approximation – a rough approximation certainly – to a condition of equality, and particularly by comparison with the post-Conquest period, whether we measure that in terms of the tenor of address that an early cleric like Aldhelm employs in writing for female religious, or married women's property rights. Submerging gender distinctness in the union of soldiers of Christ, the double monastery was a potential locus for the development of a common identity, and its passing marks a stage in the constitution of female

---

[102] The second order of Irish saints (543–99) reputedly shunned the society of women and shut them out of their monasteries; this may not mean that they rejected double monasteries, and one apparently survived at Kildare in the 8th c. (Bateson, 165–7). Celtic ascetics occasionally cohabited as a trial of virtue, and it is suggested that double monasteries perpetuate such arrangements: see R. Reynolds, "Virgines subintroductae in Celtic Christianity," HTR 61 (1968), 547–66, and L. Gougaud, "Mulier Consortia: Etude sur le Syneisaktisme chez les ascetes Celtiques," Ériu 9 (1921), 147–56.
[103] Letter to Archbishop Egbert (H&S, III, 321): Bede's essentially patriarchal conception of this is open to doubt (see fn. 176).
[104] Life of Wilfrid, chs. 24, 40.
[105] Duemmler, 305.

alterity – Jonas reports that at Brie no distinction of the sexes was recognized, and that the abbess treated monks and nuns as equal;[106] the Life of Gertrude of Nivelles claims that the nuns at her 7th century double monastery were tonsured in the manner of monks.[107]

The constitution and progressive foregrounding of gender-distinction, already evident to varying degrees in the earliest Anglo-Saxon records, proceeds, most discernibly where ecclesiastical culture dominates, tied to an evaluative hierarchy. Specifically female characteristics are constituted upon non-warrior traits and values – they are grounded upon the status of non-combatants that women shared with ecclesiastics. The later medieval ideal woman, merciful and gentle, emotionally susceptible and compassionate towards suffering, represents a shift, but is not a world away from heroic age woman as chief mourner of fallen kinsmen by virtue of her position as the particular sufferer in war.[108] The medieval lady of romance, most frequently found retired to the seclusion of her chamber or the enclosure of her tower, an automatic provocation in her helplessness to chivalric deeds of arms, is a descendant of the religious orders withdrawn behind their walls to contemplation, dependent for their protection on the secular arm – Bede's *real* complaint about the establishment of monasteries as havens to avoid taxes and military service to the king emerges with his expression of fears regarding the shortage of defenders in the event of an invasion.[109] Enlistment in the ranks of the "soldiers of Christ" did not remove the stigma of being a professed non-combatant in a warrior society: enforced tonsuring was not merely a means of deposing unpopular kings but a form of insulting disparagement, for which Alfred's law code provides heavy penalties.[110] Sebbi, who was prevented from entering a monastery by his wife's refusal to agree to a separation, was widely rumoured to have a temperament more suited to a bishop than a king, and there is a moving consistency in the report that he wanted no-one at his death-bed besides a bishop and two servants, lest by some word or gesture he should betray his suffering.[111] In being – as a general rule – non-combatants, women and ecclesiastics had the basis for a promising alliance against warrior society; the establishment of double monasteries may be said to represent a form of alliance. But ultimately, by a possibly inevitable

[106] See Jonas's Life of Fara, *Vitae Columbani Abbatis Disciplorumque Eius*, ed. B. Krusch, MGH SRG *in usum schol* (Hannover, 1905), 257–79, II.19. (Subsequently referred to as as *Jonas's Life of Columban*.)

[107] *Vita S Geretrudis*, ed. B. Krusch, MGH SRM 2 (Hannover, 1888), 453–74, ch. 3. The 11th c. Life is not universally regarded as reliable; Bateson, 158, n. 1, cites earlier legislation on the tonsuring of nuns.

[108] With Hildeburg as chief mourner for her son and brother and the Geatish woman's dirge at Beowulf's pyre (*Beowulf*, ll. 1071–80, 1114–18, 3150–5), cf. Chaucer's Prioress as the mourner for dead and bleeding mice in the *General Prologue*, ed. L.D. Benson, *The Riverside Chaucer* (Oxford, 1988), p. 25.

[109] Letter to Egbert (H&S, III, 320); cf. *HE*, V.23, where Bede declines to speculate on the consequences of Northumbrian enthusiasm for monasticism. Bede's account of the East Anglian army's defeat by pagans when the monk-king Sigeberht, forced out of retirement to lead it, refused to wield anything but a heavy stick (*HE* III.18), illustrates the dilemma.

[110] *Alfred*, 35.3–6. Ceolwulf of Northumbria's tonsuring by his Mercian captors in 731 (northern annals of *Historia Regum*) is a straightforward example of disparagement.

[111] *HE*, IV.11.

paradox, clerics would come to regard the emotionality and timorousness of women as one further manifestation of their "natural" inferiority.

From the twelfth century on, cultivation of emotional response and pity for suffering focused on the image of Christ crucified (already discernible in the pre-Conquest period), became central to the devotional life, as mercy and pity became the hallmarks of true aristocratic *gentilesse*. The cultivation of compassion for the sufferings of Christ on behalf a suffering world, itself a product of male monastic culture, is by no means offered exclusively to women, either religious or lay, as a form of devotional life; but it may be said that both Aelred and the author of the *Ancrene Wisse*, in presenting Christ the suffering lover as an icon for meditation, register their sense, apparent in other ways, of the specific and distinct nature of female religious.[112] That the world has always needed all the compassion that it can get, I do not doubt. That clerical chivalry to women took positive and protective forms of which there was need, this too I do not doubt, nor even its good intentions, notwithstanding the humanly imperfect motives that inform Adomnan's account of Columba as a young deacon. But it is also the case that the heroic forms which Christianity assumed in its early coalition with warrior society have the appearance of offering more support to the strength and independence of women religious, and women generally, than the postures that accompanied emotional piety. As Aldhelm exhorts his soldiers of Christ to strenuous resolve in fighting the good fight and resisting attacks on their fortress of faith, Boniface wrote to Bugga, assailed in her quest for retired contemplation by the demands of seculars, to urge her to the exercise of a heroic will made stronger to resist despite the physical deterioration of age.[113] Female saints like Juliana oppose not only demons but governors, and the heroic will to unyielding resistance, once developed, need not confine itself to disposing of the horrendous monster of pride. Alcuin, writing to an Abbess Æthelburg in England, conflates, in a manner typical of his age, demonic forces and their human agents when he urges her to regard the king's attacks on monastic possessions as an attempt by Satan to undermine by external events the fortitude of those who have successfully resisted his machinations within the soul.[114] Boniface's letter to Æthelbald of Mercia, condemning the financial and sexual rapacity of his dealings with the monasteries,[115] is one of many evocations of the extent to which monastic communities needed to cultivate the heroic will to resist; encouragement was, not unnaturally, forthcoming from the ecclesiastical hierarchy where secular powers were involved. Constituting ecclesiastical authorities on the wrong side of the divide that separates good from evil required a certain amount of theological expertise which it was not beyond the wit of heroic wills to accomplish.[116]

---

[112] See esp. *De Institutione Inclusarum*, ch. 27; *Ancrene Riwle*, Pt. 7, ed. E.J. Dobson, *The English Text of the Ancrene Riwle*, EETS OS 267 (London, 1972), esp. pp. 284–8.
[113] Tangl, 94.
[114] Duemmler, 300.
[115] Tangl, 73.
[116] See ch. 4, pp. 146–8.

Brides of The Lamb

As Soldiers of Christ the nuns of Barking are lauded and urged on to greater efforts in fighting the good fight, in which Pride, according to the conventional schema of vices, looms largest as an enemy. But in their aspect as Brides of the Lord, they are warned against the wearing of fine clothing and self-glamorization. Isaiah 61.10 likens the soul clothed in the garments of salvation to a bridegroom decked in ornaments and a bride adorned with jewels. The conception of the religious life as a renunciation of care lavished on decking the body in outer garments for the sake of cultivating inner and spiritual adornments for the soul is not, intrinsically, suited *only* to female religious. Alcuin taxed the monks at Lindisfarne for having abandoned their calling in the same metaphoric terms: "Let your garments be suitable to your order. . . . It is better to adorn with good habits the soul which will live for ever, than to deck with choice garments the body which will soon decay in the dust." Here, and in Alcuin's reproaches to King Æthelred of Northumbria, attention lavished on outer garments does not emblematize carnality but *cupiditas*, a self-regarding pride and worldliness that obviates compassion for others: "Consider the dress, the way of wearing the hair, the luxurious habits of princes and people. . . . What also of the immoderate use of clothing beyond the needs of human nature, beyond the custom of our predecessors? The prince's superfluity is the poverty of the people. Some labour under an enormity of clothing, others perish with cold; some are inundated with delicacies and feasting like Dives clothed in purple, and Lazarus dies of hunger at the gate. Where is brotherly love? Where is the pity which we are admonished to have for the wretched?"[117]

As Brides of the Lord, however, female religious are peculiarly apt to be bidden to deck themselves in spiritual garments, and to be accused of perversion of their calling by the wearing of outward finery. Paul had already characterized self-adornment as a specifically female vice, in 1 Tim. 2, for instance, where egregious self-presentation on the part of women transgresses against the condition of modest and submissive invisibility he regards as proper for them. Aldhelm, in electing to warn particularly against the wearing of fine clothing and personal adornment, and liberally quoting from patristic commentaries on the garments of salvation, whose bias is the same as Paul's, promulgates the view that women are especially prone to succumb to the temptations of the flesh and to act as agents of sexual temptation.[118] Ironically, Judith figures in a moral exemplum in Aldhelm's work, not as a soldier of Christ who slew evil incarnate in beheading Holofernes, but as a *femme fatale* who lured him to his death by the innate beauty of her face and her bodily adornment.[119]

This theme, whose full treatment is reserved for the conclusion, also surfaces

---

[117] Trans. Whitelock, EHD I, 843, 846; Duemmler, 20, 16.

[118] Patristic treatises on virginity (e.g., Cyprian's De Habitu Virginum, PL 4, 335–64, on which Aldhelm draws) typically harangue women on the subject of adornment, but the purely laudatory form of the metrical De Virginitate confirms Aldhelm's familiarity with alternative modes, possibly Fortunatus's De Virginitate, which Wallace-Hadrill, 1988, pp. xxviii–xxix, believes to have influenced Bede's hymn to Æthelthryth (HE, IV.20).

[119] Ch. 57.

early on in Aldhelm's handling of the question of virginity versus marriage. Aldhelm joins the ranks of the unimaginative to whom Paul's statement – that the unmarried woman and the virgin think only of the things of the Lord but she that is married thinks of the things of this world – can mean only one thing.[120] He embarks on a contrast between the chaste adornment of the self in virtues and the kindling of marital wantonness with necklaces, bracelets and rings, the curling of tresses and the painting of the face. Nor can he conceive of any reason why fine clothing should be worn *except* for the purpose of entice-ment.[121] In the secular value system of *Maxims I*, fine adornments are an obliga-tory sign of aristocratic status, for both men and women.[122] Jewelry, as much a part of the conventional poetic repertoire for depicting women as arms and armour are for the depicting of warriors, can assume the aspect of a parallel accoutrement that conveys power and status. Elene, characterized as a battle leader in Cynewulf's 9th century epic is, in her dazzling jewels, an intimidating presence that quells the will to resist; Jurmenburg, wearing about her neck the reliquary seized from Wilfrid after she instigated his banishment, bears the talismanic sign of her triumphant appropriation of his powers.[123] The status-bearing function of outer adornment surfaces noticeably in the late Anglo-Saxon period when the laicization of monastic ideals requires accommodations that render crucially useful the distinction between outer and visible clothing and the inner purity of the heart's intentions. Edward the Confessor, according to the earliest Life, was careless of his own appearance but welcomed the fine embroidered garments provided by his queen as a means of commanding the honour necessarily due to his elevated office.[124] If Goscelin's account of Edith of Wilton's retort to episcopal criticism of her fine clothing characterizes a habit-ual proclivity on the part of Anglo-Saxon royal abbesses,[125] it is a plausible construction that what it represented was a straightforward transference of their social standing and its visible signs from the kingdom at large to the rule of their monastic foundations. Although Aldhelm's *exempla* are biblical – the whore of the Apocalypse pouring out intoxicating drink, for instance – he is thought to have his eye on the contemporary scene when he descends to specifics in the wearing of jewelry, the manner of curling the hair and the painting of the face, and so on.[126] It is evident, however, that Aldhelm has no particular reason for believing that his condemnation of self-adornment is targeted to an existent condition at Barking. Like Alcuin – who never misses the opportunity to offer what he regards as suitable moral hortatory reminders in his letters to members of religious orders and the laity in places as far distant as his English homeland, some of whom he may never have met, and whose manner of life, in all cases, cannot have been known to him – Aldhelm is influenced by the conception of preaching, particularly deriving from Gregory's emphasis on the principle of appropriateness to audience, which associates liability to particular abuses with

---

[120] 1 Cor. 7.34.
[121] Ch. 58.
[122] See *Maxims I*, ll. 125–6.
[123] *Life of Wilfrid*, ch. 34; *Elene*, ll. 259–75, 320–31.
[124] *Life of King Edward*, p. 41.
[125] *Life of Edith*, ch. 12.
[126] Chs. 17, 58. See R.I. Page, *Life in Anglo-Saxon England* (London, 1970), pp. 166–9.

particular categories and classes of people.[127] To the full ramifications of Aldhelm's ultimate retreat from didacticism I will return, but his withdrawal from the subject is based precisely on the essential difference between categories and individuals, a distinction which he is pedantically pleased with himself for recognizing: "The common generality of the many ought not rightly to be censured where the particular characteristics of individuals cannot be blamed; for indeed genus and species, that is to say the general and the particular, differ a good deal from each other."[128] Aldhelm, in short, is well aware that he is not attacking an abuse that he knows to be current among his audience; he is merely exercising his clerical-Christian duty of proselytizing in and out of season; if the cap happens to fit, it is possible that the inhabitants of Barking will consent to try it on.

That Aldhelm elects to warn the nuns of Barking against self-adornment in ways that identify women as agents of sexual temptation may seem unsurprising in view of the weight of patristic tradition to which he is heir, and from which he quotes prolifically. But there are signs that early Anglo-Saxon society was not especially fertile ground for the development of a stereotype of woman as seductive temptress. Even the belief that the world's evils originate from our first parents' having fallen prey to concupiscence had not taken universal hold. *Maxims I* has assimilated to its store of traditional wisdom, not the fall in Eden, but Cain's murder of Abel; to a warrior society pervaded by the blood feud, a man's striking of the first murderous blow, compounded in its malignity by the betrayal of kinship loyalties, was a more persuasive explanation of the world's ills than the relationship between a man and a woman in a garden. The same myth of origins is adduced in *Beowulf*.[129]

Woman as temptress employing sexual seductiveness, her physical attractions and adornment, was not an automatic stereotype even for an ecclesiastical writer evidently familiar with the patristic material for creating it. Eddius begins his account of Wilfrid's downfall and exile from Northumbria by explaining that Satan, "taking his usual weapons, sought first the weaker vessel, the woman," that is, Ecgfrith's queen, Jurmenburg. But Jurmenburg's stratagem does not consist of bringing to bear the charms of her person. It takes the form of inflaming the king to self-aggrandizement, of rousing him to an envious desire to possess the immensity of Wilfrid's riches. The weapons she fights with are words – "shooting poison arrows of speech from her quiver into the heart of the king . . . she eloquently described to him the all the temporal glories of St Wilfrid, his riches, the number of his monasteries, the greatness of his buildings, his countless army of followers arrayed in royal vestments and arms. With such shafts as these the king's heart was wounded."[130] There is a case to be made that sexual provocation in the Anglo-Saxon world-view expressed itself as a challenge to combat rather than as an alluring enticement. The prostitutes of Ireland (literal or allegorical), against whom Aldhelm warns a former pupil in one of his letters, adorned like chariots with metal bosses in their burnished leg

---

[127] *Regula Pastoralis*, III.1–40.
[128] L&H, p. 128; ch. 58.
[129] *Maxims I*, ll. 192–200; *Beowulf*, ll. 86–114.
[130] Colgrave, p. 49; *Life of Wilfrid*, ch. 24.

bands and bracelets, are dressed to kill in a manner befitting a warrior ethos.[131] The women in those Old English Riddles that rely on *double entendre* – the woman vigorously manipulating the object that is "really" an onion, the woman who energetically thumps the tumescent "dough," for instance – are described as "arrogant" or "proud minded."[132] But the sexual dimensions of combat do not seem to be operative in the description of Jurmenburg, nor do her weapons have anything to do with the erotic wounds of *Canticles*; what she inflicts are the wounds of the sin of avarice.

Eddius's early 8th century conception of woman as tempter is similar in kind to the presentation of the fall in the 9th century vernacular poem, *Genesis B*. Eve's error in *Genesis B* is an intellectual error. She acted "out of loyal intent," but was deceived by the serpent into believing that he was an emissary of God; and the fall of Adam consists in being won by verbal exhortation to the view that eating the apple is a means to gain the favour of his divine overlord.[133] In the role of aristocratic woman as hostess at the feast and cup-bearer, ecclesiastics found an indigenous *locus* for the development of a female tempter associated with the weakness of the flesh.[134] But, like Hildegyth before the battle in *Waldere*, like Wealhtheow in the hall in *Beowulf* – indeed, like the nuns of Barking, invited by Aldhelm to deign to stimulate him to write a metrical version of *De Virginitate* with just as many letters as they have brought to bear in eliciting the prose version – the first woman's role in *Genesis B* is to urge representative man by eloquence to perform a deed that will enhance his own prestige. The conception of woman as tempter, in other words, adverts to her role as *agent provocateur* in the pursuit of renown, which Tacitus claimed to be the role of Germanic women on the battlefield.[135]

The female allurement syndrome that Aldhelm brings into play in *De Virginitate* also figures in the one scandal reported of the double monasteries; Bede, writing some thirty years later, includes it in his *History*. The abuses that flourished at Coldingham, as related by Bede, were obviously not so open and flagrant that they had been spread by rumour. They were unknown even to the abbess, Æbbe, sister of King Oswiu, whose reputation is thereby spared for posterity, particularly as it was not until after her death that the Coldingham monastery was destroyed by fire – this being, in Bede's view, an unquestionable manifestation of divine justice. It was not even known to Adomnan, who was staying at the monastery, what was really taking place within the walls, until it was revealed to him in a vision.

Precisely what Bede is not claiming is that the inhabitants of the double monastery at Coldingham were united in carnality – not explicitly, anyway. We can make what we like of the fact that the Adomnan's angelic visitor who had had a good look around the interior of Coldingham reported that men and

---

131 *Epist* 3.

132 Exeter Riddles, 25, 45.

133 See *Genesis B* (ASPR I, 9–28), esp. ll. 704–722. Opinions differ as to whether or not the poet regards Eve as *culpably* deceived; see pp. 190–1.

134 See pp. 156–60, 205–7.

135 For a comparative study, see M. Murphy, "Vows, Boasts and Taunts, and the Role of Women in Some Medieval Literature," *English Studies* 66 (1985), 105–12.

women alike were either sunk in sleep, heedless of their vigils, or awake only to sin, but what follows is that even the cells had been converted into places for eating, drinking, gossip or other amusements:[136] the inhabitants of Coldingham, in short, were engaged in feasting, which Alcuin routinely warns monks against, since it is the vice of worldly, warrior society that he associates with monks as a class,[137] and which still exercises the compilers of the *Regularis Concordia* in the 10th century, for whom segregated monasteries were the established norm.[138] The nuns of Coldingham, however, according to Bede, spent their time weaving fine clothes; more precisely, they reverted to the carnal dimension of their metaphorical state, for they adorned themselves like brides, thereby imperilling their vocations, or – worse having come to worse at this point – struck up friendships with outsiders.[139] The reputation of the monks at Coldingham is, beyond a certain point, preserved along with that of the abbess.

Bede, silent in his *History* concerning the far greater monastic scandal that he urged Bishop Egbert to rectify (the setting up of monasteries by members of the laity for the purposes of tax evasion, where they continued their lives in marital union with brief interruptions for liturgical devotions),[140] is suspiciously forthcoming about the reason why it is desirable to publicize this one. The story illustrates God's certain judgment on all who heedlessly continue in their wickedness, despite his merciful dispatchment of a warning prophet. The source that Bede names – an exceptional manoeuvre, considering that it is not a saint's reputation for performing miracles that is at issue here – is the conveniently dead priest, Eadgisl, who had been living at Coldingham at the time, and who sought refuge after the destruction of Coldingham at Bede's own, single sex, monastery. The real moral of the story is that, in the opinion of Bede, women were much too dangerous to share a monastery with. Post-Conquest ecclesiastical traditions claimed Cuthbert as a misogynist; at Durham, where women were forbidden to approach his shrine, Simeon explained that it was because of the scandalous behaviour at Coldingham that Cuthbert himself had refused to allow women to enter the church at his Lindisfarne monastery.[141] This is a libel on Cuthbert, who is reported by the Anonymous Lindisfarne Life to have been on friendly terms with several women religious, though Bede, in his rewriting of the early Life, is at pains to reduce these friendships to purely official interactions.[142] But Simeon's polemical invention contains a tellingly approximate insight. The long term effect of repeating such scandals was undoubtedly to assist in the creation of a climate of opinion that favoured segregated monasticism – and the stricter enclosure of female religious.[143]

---

[136] *HE*, IV.25.

[137] See, e.g., Duemmler, 16, 20 (quoted above); Aldhelm, *Epist* 11.

[138] *Regularis Concordia*, ed. and trans. T. Symons (London, 1953), pp. 7, 8.

[139] This complex play on the Ave/Eva aspects of garment weaving recalls Prov. 31.10–31.

[140] H&S, III, 321.

[141] *Symeonis Monachi Opera Omnia*, ed. T. Arnold, RS 75 (London, 1882) I, 59. B. Ward, *Miracles and the Medieval Mind* (Oxford, 1982), pp. 61–2, 233–4, explains the Durham tradition as part of a campaign to restore monastic rule.

[142] See pp. 128–9, 189–90, 199–207.

[143] For the prohibition on the founding of double monasteries by the 787 Second Council of Nice, see Bateson, 163; existing foundations were permitted to continue under rigorously

Aldhelm's warnings against the dangers of self-adornment are obviously not, like Bede's story, a thinly disguised polemic against the double monasteries, but his promulgation of the view that nuns as a class are liable to be guilty of decking themselves out fine, with all that that entails, erects a countervailing force to the willingness to accept them as comrades-in-arms in the service of God which is implicit in his *miles Christi* metaphor. By giving currency to the view that women embody the temptations of the flesh, he effectively adds weight to orthodox pressures for the establishment of monastic segregation. As the double monasteries were not in accordance with the practices of the Roman church (or Greek, for that matter), for precisely the reasons that Aldhelm is putting into circulation, they were doomed, sooner or later, from the moment that Theodore decreed: "It is not permissible for men to have monastic women, nor women, men; nevertheless we shall not overthrow that which is the custom in this region."[144] The implementation of the Benedictine Reform depended heavily on first-hand and pervasive contact with more rigidly orthodox continental clerics, made confident of their own authoritative rightness by their membership of a church that had succeeded in establishing itself. The suppression of provincial variations in the conversion period was a slower process, more dependent upon indigenous internalization of Roman attitudes.

To postulate the entire innocence of the double monasteries – to suggest that *Theodore's Penitential*, in prescribing penalties for the sexual irregularities of both monks and nuns,[145] is not responding to an actual situation, but merely reflects an orthodox mental set – is to postulate the double monastery as a site for the successful recovery of the innocence of our first parents. Aldhelm, I shall later suggest, gestures in this direction: his weaving together of the portraits of male and female saints into a heavenly crown of virginity, behind which lies the union in virginity which Christ accomplished on the cross when he commended his mother to his disciple John, is an image of the transcendental reality of the Barking double monastery. The monastic life was conventionally conceived as an attempt to recover paradise, but to suggest that the double monastery might have succeeded in this recovery is merely to run the risk of being accused of having fallen into a particularly naive form of nostalgic romanticism; and this is not quite what I am suggesting. Nevertheless Eddius's failure to reach automatically, in his account of woman as tempter, for the modes of sexual seduction – and the near absence of sexuality as a subject in the literature of the Anglo-Saxon period – is consistent with the Germanic conception of marriage as an analogue of kinship and comradeship, and not as the union of the flesh which is of such over-riding concern in Gregory's *Libellus Responsionum*. Again, this is not, precisely, to raise the spectre of chaste Germanic

---

segregated conditions. The revival of monasticism under Alfred appears to have followed continental orthodoxy; see ch. 9, fns. 11, 12.

[144] McNeill, p. 204; *Theodore's Penitential*, II.vi.8 (see fn. 2). Godfrey, p. 346, notes the likelihood that Theodore knew of Justinian's prohibition of double monasteries in the *Novellae* (565): ed. R. Schoell and G. Kroll (*Corpus Juris Civilis III: Novellae*, Berlin, 1963; repr. 1988), p. 133. It also rules that men must not be buried in nunneries and, where the services of men are required for the burial of nuns, only the female gatekeeper and the abbess may be present; commemoratory feasts for the dead are to be celebrated by the sexes in separation.

[145] *Theodore's Penitential*, I.viii.6.

womanhood, a phenomenon which is so evidently, in both Tacitus's account of the continental Germans, and Boniface's allusion to the Wendts, a product of the particular polemical axe they are grinding.[146] If the early Anglo-Saxon laws are either largely silent on the sexual misconduct of women, or conversely appear to hold them guilty of sexual crimes committed against them, it is because what is at stake in secular conceptions is not individual guilt but loss of female honour, which is inextricably bound up in family honour.[147] The point is rather that, just as the vernacular and ecclesiastical conventions of depicting women in the same warrior-heroic modes as men emphasize common ground, submerging the fact that women were distinct by the rareness with which they were active in combat, so too the literary conventions of portraiture are inimical to the foregrounding of specifically female sexuality. It is a somewhat misleading way of putting the matter to assert that "sex is not a biological referent but a historic construct."[148] But woman as sexual tempter, and its underlying concomitant of highly focused consciousness of female sexuality, is a cultural construct, and the monastic culture of the conversion period is the site for its development. Unlike the woman warrior as moral perversity, this construct has no clearly discernible counterpart in indigenous culture beyond simple biology and the fact that women's non-marital sexual relations evidently constituted loss of individual and family honour, whereas there is scarcely a suggestion that men could incur dishonour in the same way. As an alterizing construct, further sharpened in the late Anglo-Saxon period by the Benedictine reformers, the ramified consequences of woman as sexual tempter go far beyond the implementation of orthodoxy in the segregation of the monasteries. The appearance of 12th century costume which emphasizes and reveals a distinctively female form, in contrast to the heavily draped, if adorned, Romanesque fashion in female clothing, emblematizes, and is indeed a pre-requisite of, the triumphant emergence of hetero-eroticism and marriage as the dominant social relationship. Tacitus, however, offers an even sharper point of contrast in his description of the costuming of the continental Germans. "The dress of the women differs from that of the men in two respects only. The women often wear undergarments of linen, embroidered with purple, and, as the upper part does not extend to sleeves, forearms and upper arms are bare."[149]

The conception of monastic women as other, and especially as a morally dangerous force needing to be contained and marginalized, inevitably precipitates an increasing loss of dignity and respect, over and above the concomitant loss of contact with the centres of male monastic scholarship. Aldhelm, remarkably, despite having fallen victim to a patristic tradition of prior equation of the clothing syndrome with women, gathers himself together for an oration against the vanity of both sexes. His catalogue wanders off from a consideration of specifically male attire into specifically female primping and adorning (though the precise point at which it wanders off must be determined by individual opinions of the degree of self-glamorization in which Anglo-Saxon male

---

[146] Germania, ch. 19; Tangl, 73.
[147] See ch. 2, pp. 63–5.
[148] Foucault, 1978, p. 42.
[149] Trans. Mattingly, p. 115; Germania, ch. 17.

religious were likely to engage).[150] The bulk of his condemnation, though quoting Gregory's "Consider what a fault it would be for men to want what the shepherd of the church took care to avert even women from," is addressed to women. Aldhelm's recollection of the shameless impudence of vanity of both sexes, however, demonstrates the way in which the double monastery, to some degree, serves as a limitation on the alterizing identification of women religious with particular frailties, and functions as a pressure towards the perception of frailty as a shared human condition. Segregated and enclosed, women religious cease to be comrades fighting soldier to soldier and become absent fiends.

The most striking aspect of Aldhelm's inclusion of moral reproof in his work of laudation, however, is the apologetic and even deferential air with which it is offered. There are signs, even before Aldhelm begins to retreat from his didactic posture, that automatic deference to his strictures is not something he feels he can expect. Despite the fact that Aldhelm has quoted at length from patristic writers and cited no less an authority than Gregory, the revered apostle to the English, it is evident when he offers the example of Judith that the word of a male ecclesiastic, bishop or not, is insufficient unless it has the authority of the scriptures behind it: "So you see, it is not by my assertion but by the statement of scripture that the adornment of women is called the depredation of men."[151] As Aldhelm launches into his peroration, he remarks, defensively, that it were best not to prolong the subject lest he should meet with the derision and insults of the undisciplined, who prefer their faults negligently glossed over than mildly reproved. He offers, in excuse, an old chestnut, that the wounds of a friend are better than the kisses of an enemy. He is also in hopes that he will gain the indulgence of mercy from everyone, since he has named no-one in particular. Asserting the distinction between genus and species and conceding that the generality cannot rightly be censured if individuals are without blame, he is finally reduced to acknowledging that his warnings have no foundation in facts known to him. And, having effectively retracted his censures, he comes close to admitting that they are almost beside the point, before he changes the subject entirely: "But as I was about to speak of the glory of intact virginity, I began to harangue unnecessarily about the covering of garments – almost superfluously, since I have decided to discourse only on the renown of chastity, insofar as the freely given grace of God assists, abandoning for a little while the preoccupation with other things."[152]

At the deepest level of analysis, Aldhelm's condemnation of attention given

---

[150] "This sort of glamorization for either sex consists in fine linen shirts, in scarlet or blue tunics, in necklines and sleeves embroidered with silk; their shoes are trimmed with red-dyed leather; the hair of their forelocks and the curls at their temples are crimped with a curling iron; dark-grey veils for the head give way to bright and coloured head-dresses, which are sewn with interlacings of ribbons and hang down as far as the ankles. Fingernails are sharpened after the manner of falcons or hawks" (L&H, p. 127; ch. 58). Boniface deplored youths clad in purple garments in the monasteries and detected the mark of Antichrist in the wearing of wide stripes and scarlet borders (Tangl, 78).

[151] L&H, p. 127; ch. 57; the authority of scripture was itself arguable, since the phrase on which Aldhelm bases his claim is not found in the Vulgate, but in a *Vetus Latina* version (L&H, p. 197, n. 32).

[152] L&H, pp. 128–9; ch. 58.

to bodily covering *is* irrelevant. For although he has moralized that the wearing of external finery nullifies the interior beauties of the soul, Aldhelm deconstructs his own concern with outer, literal and bodily garments by putting the emphasis back upon intentionality as the crucial determinant of good and evil, and defines the inward and invisible life of the spirit as a separate reality, transcending physical, exterior, and purely carnal matters such as the literal condition of the body. Aldhelm asserts finally that true virginal virtue exists within the province of the fortress of the mind, and is, as he has already made plain, entirely distinct from mere bodily intactness. The spirit, resolutely disposed to good by an act of free will, remains triumphantly inviolate in despite of physical and exterior circumstances: "For every privilege of pure virginity is preserved only in the fortress of the free mind rather than being contained in the restricted fortress of the flesh; and it is beneficially safe-guarded by the inflexible judge of the free will, rather than being diminished out of existence by the enforced servitude of the body."[153] And he quotes further both Augustine and Prosper of Aquitaine to the effect that "the sanctity of the body is not lost provided that the sanctity of the soul remains, even if the body is overcome."[154] This goes further than simply tipping the scales back again in favour of the formerly married, in its recognition that the spirit, not the flesh, is paramount in the religious life, and the disposition of the will, not actions themselves, are the proper focus of moral evaluation. Aldhelm, like Gregory in his letter of reply to Augustine, ultimately reaches past the enforced regulation of outward conduct to affirm that sin consists in the disposition of the will, which has as its correlative that all things are pure to the pure of heart.[155] Edith's reply to the Bishop of Wilton, like Eangyth's dismissal of those who cite canonical prohibitions in opposition to her pilgrimage as "glorying in appearances but not in heart," is rooted in a theological tradition of highly respected origins that had considerable currency throughout the period.[156]

Aldhelm, then, retreats finally from authoritative didacticism and definitive categorizing pronouncements, and foregrounds the interior life of the individual and the exercise of freedom of the will. His apologetic and respectfully deferential air is certainly not class free. But more important than this is the status the nuns of Barking have by virtue of his respect for their learning. Learning as the essence of the religious life, especially the conception of the study of the scriptures as the means to know God, is an attitude that is characteristic of a church engaged in the work of conversion. Characteristic of a conversionary ethos also is a strong fundamentalist strain, the acceptance of only that which has scriptural authority: when Bishop Lul of Mainz excommunicated Abbess Switha for defying his authority by permitting members of her community to return to their families, he was doubtful that she was any more disposed to accept his authority than she had been hitherto, and called on the support of a gospel text that she seemed to him to have forgotten: "Who spurns you, spurns me."[157] So long as these conversionary attitudes predominated, women religious

---

[153] L&H, p. 129; ch. 58.
[154] *De Civitate Dei*, I.18; Prosper, *Epigrams*, 51, 76 (so Ehwald, 319).
[155] *HE*, I. 27.
[156] Tangl, 14; see pp. 34, 146-8.
[157] Tangl, 128; Luke 10.16.

were in a strong position to take issue with ecclesiastic attempts to regulate the manner in which they pursued the life of the spirit, and abbesses were in a position to participate on equal terms with bishops at ecclesiastical councils. The Life of Leoba, who joined Boniface at the continental mission, mentions her attendance at episcopal councils, and adds to her studies the whole of canon law, which, as Boniface had cause to know, was already regarded by Rome as a more authoritative definition of Christianity than the scriptures.[158] As isolation of women religious from the centres of monastic scholarship through the steady growth of pressures towards enclosure made the cultivation of piety appear more appropriate to their condition, they were increasingly less in a position to assert their right to the individual freedom of the spirit that Gregory understood as fundamental to Christianity. Male monastic orders were rather better placed for resisting complete colonization of the will and retaining areas of licence for themselves. To the Augustinian canon who wrote the *Ancrene Wisse* for three aristocratic women about the year 1300, their request for a rule of life was, in itself, evidence of their failure to understand that the true religious life consists in the inward observances. The *Ancrene Wisse* affirms the primacy of the interior disposition, and the unbinding nature of all man-made rules for those who, loving God, may do what they will. For all that, the author is not behind-hand in providing a rule of life which dictates to a very high degree, in specific particulars, what the female anchorite may and may not do within the limits of her strict enclosure.[159]

But of much greater and underlying importance as a condition of the conversionary period determining Aldhelm's attitude to the nuns of Barking is the fact that at the time he wrote, the church in England, and hence its ecclesiastical hierarchy, had no automatic and inalienable hold on the lives, inner or outer, of its members. Its authority was far from absolute and unquestioned, and in so far as baptism and entry to a monastic order was not an act of free choice, the compulsions were secular ones. Aldhelm, even as a bishop, was a member of a ruling elite only in so far as he was connected by birth to the reigning house of Wessex.[160] It is one view of the medieval monastic orders that the involvement of their members in secular affairs, and flagrant disregard of canonical injunctions or the rule of the order, represents decadence, whereas automatic deference and obedience bears witness to the quality of religious life and manifests the voluntariness of religious vocations. There seems to me a case to be made that the opposite holds true.

The plain meaning of St Paul's elevation of virginity above marriage in 1 Cor. 7 is that Paul knows he is without the authority of either the teachings of Christ or post-apostolic revelation for the absolute rightness of his statements, and that he speaks of himself out of his own personal preferences and experience, albeit strongly inclined to the view that the deity shares his conviction that the world would be a better place if everyone were like Paul: "Now concerning virgins I have no commandment of the Lord: yet I give my judgment as one that hath obtained mercy of the Lord to be faithful." The same holds true of his

---

[158] *Life of Leoba*, ch. 11.
[159] See *Ancrene Riwle*, Prologue and Pt. 8.
[160] For Aldhelm's elevation, see fn. 15; for his royal connexions, see Lapidge and Rosier, p. 6.

preference for chaste widowhood above remarriage: "She is happier if she so abide, after my judgment: and I think also that I have the Spirit of God." Aldhelm accepts Paul's hierarchical ranking – but only provisionally, on his way to a conclusion that transcends them; and he understands the general implications of Paul's remarks better than later ages, for whom the unsupported opinion of Paul was a commandment in itself.[161] What Aldhelm understands Paul to mean by the statement that he has "no commandment to give concerning virgins" is: "that gift has greater merit which is given with the free will by spontaneous choice, than what is ordered to be fulfilled by the rigid command of a forcible precept." So too, in interpreting "He that can take, let him take it," Aldhelm explains that the evangelist urges not by the rigid stimulus of precept but the gentle counsel of suggestions, so that "individuals dedicated by the free will of their own choice and endowed with consciousness of their election may be able to test the capacity of their strength and, exploring the quality of their own virtue, may strive to endure the long drawn-out exertion of patience."[162] Such conscious respect for choice, such preference for persuasion and not compulsion, such an awareness of the spiritual life as an inwardly prompted dynamic, which seems, even, to suggest that those who have once entered upon the monastic life of chastity may, as a matter of pure human frailty, be prone to return to the secular life – this is a far cry from the post-Conquest considerations of women religious which assume that the dedication of the self to the religious life constitutes the acceptance of a compulsory obligation from which there is no permitted escape and that the life itself must be regulated in every minute particular.

It is not only a post-Conquest assumption. Wulfstan's legislation on widows in the *Institute of Polity* was not, one hopes contrary to appearances, directed to *all* widows in the belief that the laws which placed them and their property under the protection of the church, provided that they adhered to the canonical prohibition against marrying within a year, gave the church the right to direct their manner of life entirely.[163] Wulfstan's legislation, presumably, was directed only to all widows who had vowed before a bishop that they would not re-marry. The assumption of dictatorial control over even this, informally constituted group, marks the gaining of considerable territory in an inexorable advance: "It is right that all widows follow earnestly the example of Anna who was serving God in the temple night and day. And they should fast and pray and with sorrowing mind call to Christ and give alms frequently and please God with all their might in words and deeds and gain their eternal reward."[164]

---

[161] Chaucer's *Wife of Bath's Prologue* is a well-known exception (ed. Benson, p. 106).
[162] L&H, p. 74; ch. 18 (Matt. 19.12).
[163] See esp. V *Ethelred*, 21–21.1, which places widows under the protection of "God and the king," on condition that they "conduct themselves rightly," and II *Cnut*, 70–2; cf. ch. 2, fn. 67.
[164] *Die "Institutes of Polity, Civil and Ecclesiastical"*, ed. and trans. K. Jost (Bern, 1959), pp. 136–7; cf. 1 Tim. 5.5–6.

Postscript: The Communion of Saints

Having in mind the constitution of the Barking double monastery, Aldhelm includes in the martyrology of *De Virginitate* both male and female saints, who are drawn from the various classes that he dilates upon; virgins, the formerly married and the widowed. The female saints, inevitably, are for the most part virgins assailed by the horrendous persecutions of suitors and governors, though some variety is provided by exemplars such as Constantina, the teacher and converter, and the learned Eustochium.[165] By the martyrology's inclusion of a gallery of male saints, the nuns of Barking become the heirs and followers of a tradition of sainthood more fully and humanly varied. Aldhelm's martyrology of male and female saints signifies the communion of saints; it represents the union of all varieties of virginity into a mystic One, compounded of male and female but beyond specificity of gender: "there is neither male nor female: for ye are all one in Christ."[166]

One of the figurative dimensions of Aldhelm's inserted martyrology is the construction of a tower. The male saints, placed first, are the foundations, supporting the edifice of chaste behaviour with anything but a crumbling foundation of integrity. On top of this are placed "the second sex" – the term is chronological rather than evaluative, for they, being "equally distinguished," form the upper story, whither Aldhelm's verbal foot-steps tend.[167] The tower of virginity is the summation of images Aldhelm uses elsewhere: the waxen castle in which the nuns, pursuing their studies like bees, store the fruits of contemplation, for instance; the fortress of the free mind; the stable column of patronage constituted by the nuns' store of merits, on which Aldhelm hopes to be raised up by their prayers of intercession. The tower is thus the mystical Church. It is the tower of faith and temple of the Holy Spirit, the kingdom of heaven within: "With the help of your bridegroom Christ, carry through in your beautiful old age to the glory of God the building of the gospel tower begun in your early youth, so that at the coming of Christ you may be found worthy to meet him among the wise virgins," as Boniface wrote to Bugga when he urged her to persevere notwithstanding the assaults of secular powers.[168] Aldhelm's tower is the tower of David, a symbol of Mary, the foremost of the female saints, who is "a garden of faith, a fountain shut up," and thus a type of paradise.[169]

The configurations of Aldhelm's martyrology are circular as well as vertical. The male saints do not only form a supportive foundation of the tower but also constitute an enclosing circle, because they follow as well as precede his Lives of female saints. For Aldhelm is constructing in his martyrology the heavenly crown of victory for which he bids his audience to strive. He is "weaving a crown of virginity, embroidering a braid that cannot be unplaited."[170] The virgin crown then, is an emblem of mystical marriage, wherein there is neither

---

[165] Chs. 20–54.
[166] Gal. 3.28.
[167] L&H, p. 106; ch. 39.
[168] Emerton, p. 172; Tangl, 94.
[169] L&H, p. 106; ch. 40 (Cant. 4.4, 12).
[170] L&H, p. 106; ch. 39.

male nor female but a perfect union in chastity. The crown is thus the pictorial symbol of Christ's conjoinment of Mary and John to one another and himself. Thus Aldhelm expresses, by means of an *enigma*, Christ's commendation of Mary to the disciple John as they stood at the foot of the cross:

> Christ, having suffered on the cross
> And the hiding places of death,
> Himself a virgin commended a virgin
> To a virgin for safe-keeping.[171]

Of this episode at the cross, John 19.26–7 relates: "When Jesus therefore saw his mother, and the disciple standing by whom he loved, he saith unto his mother, Woman, behold thy son! Then saith he to the disciple, Behold thy mother! And from that hour that disciple took her unto his own home." Pragmatic reasons have been adduced to explain the adoption of the double monastery as a form of organization. It will also bear an emblematic construction as the communion of the saints, wherein a presiding Marian abbess and her sorority were entrusted to the care of the monastic brothers of John. The imagery of Aldhelm's *enigma* is nuptial, but the dimensions of relation are manifold; for Mary is also "the mother and sister of the Son," and Christ was "mindful of reverence to his mother," and therefore "dutifully enjoined the disciple who was awaiting the outcome of things among the dangers [presented by] the perfidious soldiers to look after his mother." Many of the early abbesses were widowed mothers, and an emblematic construction of the abbess as a mother, protected by the surrogate sons of Christ, was capable of fusing with the protective chivalry to women based on reverence for Mary as mother (and sister) which is promoted by the Law of Adomnan: widows, of course, were conventionally regarded as having a particular claim on ecclesiastical protection – those, at least, who were "widows indeed."[172] In the light of the ultimately Celtic origin of the double monastery, the Celtic church's allegiance to Christ's favourite disciple John, rather than to Peter, is of particular interest, for his role at the foot of the cross, as surrogate-protector of Christ's mother, lends a form of affirmation to the view that John was the true apostolic successor of Christ.[173]

Aldhelm's weaving together of the portraits of male and female saints, behind which lies the union in virginity accomplished by Christ on the cross, offers an image of the transcendental reality of the Barking double monastery. Barking, in fact, was a twin monastery as well as a double monastery, linked by a gesture of fraternal unity with Chertsey, for according to Bede it was founded by Eorcenwold for his sister Æthelburg; he built one monastery for himself and one for her, before he became Bishop of London.[174] Within the walls, like a garden "enclosed about," the double monastery, containing male and female religious united in chaste union, is implicitly a site for the recovery of paradisial innocence. Aldhelm's nuptial construction of the double monastery is a good

---

[171] L&H, p. 64; ch. 7.
[172] 1 Tim. 5.3–16. See fn. 33.
[173] For the emblematic status of abbesses, see pp. 164–5, 172–5, 183–4, 188–9, 206, 263, 281–2, 290–7.
[174] See fn. 176. Cf. the adjacent Lindsey monasteries of Æthelhild and her brother Ealdwine (HE, III.11); there are various patristic analogues.

deal more hazardous than the familial metaphors to which the organization also lent itself, since ecclesiastical councils held the fall to be irreversible.

Some such considerations conceivably underlay the actions of Hildelith of Barking reported in Bede's *History*. Hildelith had the bones of Christ's servants who were buried at Barking, both male and female, exhumed and transferred to a single tomb within the church, which was dedicated, as it happens, to the blessed Mother of God.[175] Both Bede and Hildelith may have been unaware of any canonical opposition to the posthumous proximity of members of religious orders of the opposite sex. Bede's proffered explanation – the restricted space on which the monastery was built – suggests to me that Bede, whose orthodox aversion to desegregated monasticism is evident in the account of the judgment that befell Coldingham, felt that a justifying gloss was needed for this action.[176] Hildelith's action has a deliberately polemical appearance, particularly in view of the fact that Bede also reports that the establishment of separate graveyards for men and women took place under Hildelith's predecessor in accordance with the will of heaven. When the plague struck the monks' quarters at Barking, Abbess Æthelburg circumspectly enquired of the nuns where they wished to be buried, but elicited no very definite answer. However, while Æthelburg and the nuns were visiting the graves of the monks one night, a light from heaven appeared, and directed them to a place some way off, to the south side of the convent, westward of the oratory.[177] Burial of monks and nuns in the same cemetery was customary at double monasteries;[178] conceivably, the establishment of separate graveyards at Barking in the time of Æthelburg reflected the influence of Theodore, since Justinian's prohibition of double monasteries, which is thought to underlie Theodore's pronouncement on them, also prohibited burial of monks and nuns in the same graveyard, as well as their attendance at the same funeral.[179]

Hildelith's symbolic affirmation of the innocent communion of the saints, in death at the very least, appears to have been validated. Bede culls from his Barking source the information that a heavenly light was often seen at the single tomb in which Hildelith joined together the male and female monastics of Barking, and a wonderfully fragrant scent was often evident – this last commonly appears as a sign attending the physical incorruption of the body

---

[175] HE, IV.10. The nuns' or main church of double monasteries was commonly dedicated to Mary, the monks' to one of the apostles (Bateson, 136–164, esp. 143). The typological connexion is assisted by the fact that abbesses built and dedicated churches to Mary: e.g., Barking (HE IV.10); Lyminge (Birch, 97); Thanet (Birch, 96); Sheppey (Birch, 91); and Bugga's church in Wessex (Aldhelm, *Carm Eccles* 3, trans. Lapidge and Rosier, pp. 48–50; ed. Ehwald, pp. 14–18).

[176] Barking was not, as such, short of land. Eorcenwold's grant of privileges and confirmation of lands to Barking (695) lists substantial grants from OEthelred of Essex, Cædwalla of Wessex, Wulfhere and Æthelred, kings of Mercia, and a woman called Cwengyth, as well as some land that had been granted to Eorcenwold (Birch, 87). Charters of Cædwalla and OEthelred are extant (Birch, 81, 82); although Bede says that Eorcenwold founded Barking for Æthelburg, both charters specify that the land is granted to Æthelburg; see further ch. 8, p. 260.

[177] HE, IV.7.

[178] Bateson, 140.

[179] See fn. 144. Bede records the presence of monks and nuns at Eorcengota's burial (HE, III.8), and at Æthelthryth's translation (HE, IV.19), but in the latter episode they are carefully segregated (on either side of the coffin). For the difficulties created by Boniface's instructions that Leoba was to share his tomb, see ch. 9.

that makes manifest a saint's lifelong chastity. The tomb erected by Hildelith was also the site of other miraculous events; for an account of these heavenly signs, Bede refers his readers to the Barking *Libellus* from which his account is drawn. The fact that Bede chooses not to relate any of the miracles that occurred at Hildelith's desegregated tomb, but goes on to record a miracle of healing that took place in the nuns' burial ground is, perhaps, pure coincidence rather than a demonstration of monachistic preference.

4

Confessors and Spiritual Mentors: Hagiographic Ideals and the Boniface Circle

Introduction

The present chapter, focusing on conceptions of spiritual guidance and support – including the exercise of the confessional by female religious – looks at some of the forces that secured monastic women's inclusion in and ultimate exclusion from "community in Christ." Some members of the early church took seriously the idea of the church as a body of believers who, irrespective of sex, class or age, were knit together by the spirit of love, and made one in Christ. The sense of belonging to a community joined together by *caritas* is pervasively expressed in the correspondence of the Boniface circle. Though divided by distance, members of the religious orders in England and those at the continental mission felt themselves to be united in Christ. They were part of the same conversionary endeavour, and their mutual prayers provided, in absence, the existential solidarity and comfort in a hostile world that secular society derived from the physical presence of kindred. So Wihtberht, newly arrived at the continental mission, wrote back to the monks he had left behind in Glastonbury, offering them consolation for absent friends, by way of consoling himself:

> You know, brothers, that no earthly distance of land divides us whom the love of Christ unites. . . . Be assured that our labour is not in vain in the Lord, and that you will share the rewards. For God almighty through his mercy and your merits completes the good effects of our work, although living here is very perilous and full of hardships in almost every way, in hunger and thirst, in cold and the attacks of pagans. Therefore I ask earnestly, pray for us, 'that speech may be given us in the opening of our mouths,' and permanence and success to our work.[1]

Wihtberht, in affirming the mystic one-ness of all who are joined together by the love of Christ, did not have in mind only his brother monks; to them he sent greetings, but he also asked that news of his safe arrival be conveyed to the

---

[1] Trans. Whitelock, *EHD*, I, 826; *Die Briefe des heiligen Bonifatius und Lullus*, ed. M. Tangl, MGH ES I (Berlin, 1955), 101. Selected letters are translated by E. Emerton, *The Letters of Saint Boniface* (New York, 1940), and E. Kylie, *The English Correspondence of Saint Boniface* (New York, 1913); other translations are occasionally cited in this chapter.

double monastery at Wimbourne and its the abbess, whom he thought of as "my Mother, Tette."

The social primacy of kinship bonds gave emotional potency to the familial metaphors employed to express community in Christ. Aldhelm hailed the nuns at Barking as members of a new, elective, family, whose unity, wrought by the spirit, surpassed the unity created by kinship of flesh and blood. As voluntary exiles for Christ who had forsaken earthly kindred, the nuns of Barking were, in ideal terms, re-begotten by the Word, and had become daughters of Christ.[2] But although, in the ideal conception of the religious life, kinship of flesh and blood and membership in the family of Christ were regarded as antithetical, in prac-tice members of religious orders were not infrequently related by blood, and exile for Christ – whether in the form of entry to a monastery, pilgrimage to Rome, or joining the continental mission – appears to be have been motivated as much by the need for family solidarity as by the desire to renounce earthly ties. Leoba, who, as a young nun, wrote to ask Boniface to remember his kinship relation to her, because she had neither father nor brothers, later went over to Germany to join him at the mission.[3] Lul, like Willibald, made the pilgrimage to Rome in the bosom of his family, traveling in the company of his male kinsmen; finding himself alone in the world when the plague claimed all of his relations, Lul too attached himself to the mission.[4] Community among the religious orders was an inextricable fusion of *caritas* and the affection of blood relatives; those who were without surviving family found a substitute for their loss in the monastic *familia*. Ties of kinship, then, actual or surrogate, provided an underpinning to community in Christ, adding emotional warmth to the metaphysical family solidarity that united the sons and daughters of Christ.

The inclusive, familial, conception of Christian community is characteristic of the church in its pioneering phase – the solidarity of male and female religious connected with the missionary church struggling for survival on the continent in the early 8th century replicates conditions in England before the arrival of Theodore, when the position of the church was particularly insecure. The acceptance of monastic women as participants in a shared endeavour and members of the family of Christ made it possible for women, particularly abbesses, to carry out some of the offices of bishops and priests. Participation in secular power on the part of royal women, from whose ranks early abbesses were chiefly drawn, also played a significant part in enabling them to share in sacerdotal powers. The essential pre-condition of acceptance of monastic women as fellow members of the church, and of their exercise of sacerdotal offices, however, was the absence of a conception of women as unholy beings who embodied sexual temptation and profaned the sacred mysteries of the church. The emphatically familial conception of the religious orders served, for a time, to mitigate the development of female alterization.

The portrayal of the saint as spiritual guide in Bede's *Life of Cuthbert* and Felix's *Life of Guthlac* also testifies to the currency of an ideal of community in Christ – the saint in these two Lives is a Christ figure who effects the cure of souls by compassionate identification with the suffering that is the common lot

---

2 *De Virginitate*, ch. 2.
3 Tangl, 29.
4 Tangl, 98.

of humanity. Bede's *Life of Cuthbert*, however, is a contribution to the growth of episcopal authority and increasing sacerdotalism in England. For Bede, male ecclesiastics are an elite caste, and their exclusive possession of supernatural powers elevates them to a position of superiority far above both the laity and female religious. Boniface's correspondence with women demonstrates his acceptance of monastic women as fellow members of the community wrought by Christ; his appeals for their intercessory prayers reveal that, for him, the ministry of all believers encompassed women as well as men. But in the letter he wrote to the Archbishop of Canterbury towards the end of his life, urging him to prevent women religious from undertaking the pilgrimage to Rome because their sexual license had become a public scandal,[5] the inclusive, egalitarian conception of community in Christ has given way under the combined pressures of an elitist conception of ecclesiastical office and a hostile and derogatory attitude to women. Boniface's letter to Canterbury, then, signals the end of the pioneering era on the continent and points the direction of future developments within the church.

The Confessor as Friend: Hagiographic Ideals

"I know," the Wanderer soliloquizes, "that it is a noble custom in a warrior that he keep fast his thoughts, guard the treasure-chamber of the heart, no matter what he thinks."[6] King Sebbi, afraid that the sufferings of a painful death might wring from him an involuntary word or gesture, wanted no-one present at his death-bed except a bishop and two attendants.[7] For the sufferings of mind and body, heroic honour demanded concealment. Public ignominy was the lot of those whose failings were public knowledge. *Solomon and Saturn* evokes the grief of the mother whose son has gone to the bad – time and again she weeps for his loss of honour, and the son, rejected by his lord, is a social outcast who keeps to his own house, sunk in gloom.[8] Penitential doctrine, on the other hand, teaches that the only cure for the soul is to make known the wounds of the heart with visible weeping. "Let there be not left within the den of my heart any jot of my abject guilts," runs the penitent's prayer in *Judgment Day II*: "Let that which was concealed be known to the light of day, and all be discovered in plain words."[9]

The introduction of Christianity to warrior society effected a collision between shame culture and guilt culture that outlasted the Middle Ages. It produced some curious hybrids. Alcuin, writing to reproach a former pupil for what he could only describe as his addiction to deplorable boyhood habits that he should never have acquired in the first place, was torn between lament for lost reputation and moral castigation of vice: "What is this I hear about you, my son, not from one person whispering in a corner but from crowds of people

---

[5] Tangl, 78.
[6] *The Wanderer*, ll. 11–14.
[7] *HE*, IV.11.
[8] See *Solomon and Saturn II*, ll. 374–84.
[9] See *Judgment Day II* (ASPR VI, 58–67), ll. 26–48.

laughing at the story."[10] As is well known, Western Europe preferred the Celtic system of private penance to the public penance favoured by Rome, and when annual confession became obligatory for the laity in 1211, private penance prevailed. The entrenched conception of a secret self, engendered by concern for public reputation, is not of course a self-sufficient explanation of the historical prevalence of private penance, but was nevertheless an influential factor in the social assimilation of confessional practice.

The constraints of silence imposed on warrior society by the dictates of honour exacted a heavy toll: "Sorrow will eat out the heart unless you can tell someone all that is in your mind," states the traditional wisdom of the Old Icelandic *Havamal*.[11] To entrust another with the secrets of the heart is thus the epitome of friendship: "It is a sign of the greatest intimacy when a man determines to reveal all that is in his mind to someone."[12] The confessor made his way into Anglo-Saxon society as a wise and trusted friend. Privy to the secrets of the heart, he could console and advise. In the literature of the Anglo-Saxon period, authority figures of all kinds – secular as well as ecclesiastical, parents and elder kinsmen as well as overlords – are constructed in the same mould as the spiritual guide. They are friendly mentors, who extend to those who are under their protective leadership a version of the confessor's "council and consolation." The essential similarity in the conception of secular and ecclesiastical authority no doubt reflects the church's impulse to reconstitute secular authority in its own terms, beginning with the conversion of royal power to ecclesiastical protection by casting the king as a vicar of Christ. But the conception of the "friendly lord" as an existential guide and sympathetic confidant possibly predates the arrival of Christianity.[13]

The dramatic persona of *The Wanderer*, for instance, is a lordless exile. Sorrowing at heart for his native land, and his kinsmen, he is existentially adrift as he trecks the frozen wasteland in search of another lord. He laments the loss of his beloved lord's guiding words. His search for another lord is a search for a

---

10 Allott, p. 134; Duemmler, 294.

11 *Hávamál*, st. 121; ed. and trans. D.E.M. Clarke (Cambridge, 1923), p. 75. Clarke concludes that "the bulk of [*Hávamál*] must be assigned to the heathen period" (p. 12).

12 *Hávamál*, st. 124.

13 An Irish saying attributed to St Brigid, and to St Comgall, held that "anyone without a soul friend [*anmchara*] is like a body without a head" (see W. Stokes, *The Martyrology of OEngus the Culdee*, HBS 29 [London, 1905], pp. 65, 183). McNeill, p. 25, concludes that the Brahman codes show the presence of directors of conscience, and that resemblance between the Brahman *acharya* ("spiritual guide") and the Irish soul friend or confessor "is so close as to point with reasonable certainty to a racial [Indo-European] institution of great antiquity." Such a conception of existential/spiritual guidance need not, however, have included confession of sin, as R. Pettazzoni, "Confession of Sins in the Classics," HTR 30 (1937), 1–14, pointed out. Edwin's encounter with the mysterious stranger who assured him he understood the cause of his grief, and, promising him that he would escape the threats against his life and recover his kingdom if he pledged to obey his advice in future, laid his hand on Edwin's head as the sign by which Edwin would recognize him when they met again (*HE*, II.12), confirms the indigenous existence of an authoritative spiritual guide who claimed a form of lordship (obedience to his advice) whose niche was filled by ecclesiastics (literally, in Edwin's case, since it was by claiming to be the re-manifestation of his mysterious visitant that Paulinus secured Edwin's conversion), but does not assist with the question of whether or not this figure was identified with the secular overlord before the conversion of England.

friend in whom he can confide the secret sorrows locked fast within his heart, who will cheer and comfort him.[14] But amidst the crumbling insecurity of all earthly things, consolation is to be found only in the father of heaven. Inasmuch as *The Wanderer* re-orientates the exile's quest for the guidance and consolation of an earthly lord towards the lordship of God, it illustrates the process by which conceptions of secular authority were reconstituted along ecclesiastical lines. As a friendly confidant who provides existential direction and comfort, the office of the secular lord parallels that of the confessor; perhaps by this the speaker foreshadows his perception of a divine consolation that transcends the failure of secular comfort. But the effectiveness of the poem's strategy depends upon recognizable resemblances – upon the existence of an essentially secular conception of the lord as a confidential intimate whose protective guidance and consolation could be transcendentally reconceived.

The wife of the king exercised a form of protective leadership parallel to that of an overlord. King and queen in *Maxims I* are "rulers together," and the queen's role – defined in entirely secular terms – includes the typical offices of a leader: her role is to cheer and advise, and she must know how to keep secrets.[15] Eanfled, too, in the *Life of Wilfrid*, is defined as a leader-figure. When Bishop Wilfrid, in his youth, sought to enlist in her service he asked if he might serve God "under her council and protection." Eanfled was evidently a joint ruler with an independent retinue – Wilfrid gathered an armed retinue when he went to seek service with her. But Eanfled set Wilfrid on the path of his ecclesiastical career by sending him instead to act as a servant to a former royal retainer who had become a monk at Lindisfarne. Wilfrid's hagiographer presumably intends Wilfrid's request to serve under Eanfled's council and protection to have quasi-ecclesiastical connotations, since he is attempting, despite Wilfrid's accompanying armed band, to maintain the pious fiction that, from the very outset, Wilfrid had intended to serve God. But the distinction between royal and monastic overlordship was generally somewhat blurred, owing to the notorious propensity of rulers to regard the monasteries they endowed as their own property, and the leadership of Eanfled, who persuaded her husband Oswiu to endow a monastery in compensation for the murder of her uncle,[16] may have

---

[14] See *The Wanderer*, esp. ll. 25–9, 37–8 (I follow those who interpret *mine wisse*, l. 27, sometimes emended to *min mine wisse*, as "would know my thought"). King Hrothgar's warning to Beowulf (*Beowulf*, ll. 1700–84) may reflect the influence of ecclesiastical conceptions of royal failings, but offers, formally, an example of the secular lord's guiding advice. The old father's advice to his son on the importance of choosing a wise advisor, *Precepts* (ASPR III, 140–3), ll. 23–6, also appears to refer to a secular lord.

[15] See *Maxims I*, ll. 84–92: "ond wif getheon,/ leof mid hyre leodum, leohtmod wesan,/ rune healdan ... ond him ræd witan/ boldagendum bæm ætsomne." Shippey, p. 69, translates: "and his wife [should] be a success, liked by her people; she must be cheerful, keep secrets ... and know what advice to give him as joint master and mistress of the house together" (cf. Wealhtheow's advice on noble conduct, which extends beyond the king, *Beowulf*, ll. 1162–231; see further pp. 153–5.) In view of OE *leodrune* and *burgrune*, "women skilled in the arcane knowledge, or mysteries, of a community," *rune healdan* could be construed as "cultivate wisdom," but, in this definition of the queen's social responsibilities, "keep secrets" seems nearer the mark.

[16] See *HE*, III.24.

readily lent itself to a quasi-ecclesiastical, or even Marian, construction because she had a controlling interest in monastic foundations.[17]

Eddius's *Life of Wilfrid*, in its depiction of Eanfled, is unique in its indication that the leadership of queens, as well as kings, was being reconstituted by the church. Only in the late Anglo-Saxon period was the queen's customary participation in the overlordship of her husband formally co-opted for ecclesiastical purposes. The reformist bishop, Æthelwold, in his *c.* 970 prologue to *Regularis Concordia*, bestowed upon the queen the role of protector of convents, paralleling the king's role as protector of the monasteries. When King Edgar, like a Good Shepherd had rescued the monasteries from the jaws of wolves, the prologue explains, "he saw to it wisely that his Queen, Ælfthryth, should be the protectress and fearless guardian of the nuns."[18] The queen's role as co-protector of the monasteries is embodied in the depiction of Queen Edith in the 11th century *Life of King Edward*. The identification of the queen with Mary, Queen of Heaven, embryonically present in the *Life of Wilfrid*'s account of Eanfled, has been fully implemented in the *Life of King Edward*. As Edward, the Christ-king, attends to the building of Westminster monastery, his Marian consort mirrors his loving care for the church by labouring over the renovation of the Wilton convent.[19] The queen's partnership with the king in the guardianship of the church also extends to advice on its internal affairs – the author laments that both Edith and the king had warned in vain of the need to eradicate abuses within the church.[20] But Edith is also a leader in the secular realm, who gives council and comfort to the court. Figuratively, she assumes the aspect of a battle leader, warding off troubles with her resourceful advice and putting heart into the troops. When Edith's brothers quarrel, the twin pillars of the kingdom totter. Edward goes into a fatal decline and, as Edith is likewise overwhelmed by the troubles of the kingdom, her much-praised powers of advice fail her; the court, bereft of leadership, weeps helplessly with her. Whereas when misfortunes had attacked the court in the past, the author explains: "she had always stood as a defence, and had both repelled all the hostile forces with her powerful counsels and cheered the king and his retinue."[21] Just as the ecclesiastical constitution of the king as a Christ-figure whose offices parallel those of a bishop confessor builds upon an existing conception of the "friendly lord," so too the late Anglo-Saxon conception of the queen as a Marian consort of the king and co-protector of the church builds upon a secular conception of the queen as a joint ruler exercising a leadership role parallel to her husband's by giving advice and consolation.

Bishops, above all, charged with ultimate responsibility for both lay and monastic society, assumed the aspect of friendly, but hierarchically superior, mentors. For hagiographers, they are the natural companions of kings (and occasionally queens), who find in bishops the wise and sympathetic guidance which, ideally,

---

[17] *Life of Wilfrid*, ch. 2; for further discussion of this episode, see pp. 168–9, 226; for royal couples' overlordship of the monasteries, see pp. 212–14.
[18] Symons, *Regularis Concordia*, p. 2.
[19] *Life of King Edward*, pp. 44–8.
[20] *Life of King Edward*, p. 77.
[21] Barlow, *Life of King Edward*, p. 54.

they themselves extended to their own subjects. Abbesses are befriended on the same terms. Bede assures us that Ælffled at Whitby found Bishop Trumwine a great help in the running of her monastery, as well as comfort in her own life,[22] and that Bishop Aidan and other devout men visited Hild, as an expression of their affection and in order to give instruction.[23] Bede's depiction of abbesses under episcopal leadership reflects his polemical dedication to affirming the supreme authority of bishops; for royal women, accustomed to participate in the rule of the kingdom, continued as abbesses to hold a position of headship in the ecclesiastical sphere comparable with that of a bishop, and their adoption of sacerdotal roles – such as the administration of confession – represents, as I later want to suggest, one of the ways in which, as rulers of double monasteries, abbesses shared the authority and powers of bishops in much the same way as queens exercised joint overlordship in the kingdom at large.

The hagiographic depiction of bishop-confessors as spiritual leaders who combine sympathetic comfort with corrective guidance suggests their role as the earthly representatives of God, in whose judgment mercy and justice are mystically united, although mercy prevails over all. Ultimately, the ideal of the bishop-confessor derives from Gregory's *Regula Pastoralis*. In the *Regula Pastoralis*, Gregory dilated upon the dualism of the sacerdotal role in terms of the bishop-priest's position as the intermediary between God and humanity. On the one hand, Gregory's ideal pastor is united with God in contemplation; on the other, he is involved in humanity, and through his empathetic identification with the sufferings of his flock, he unites them to God. As Christ's earthly representative, then, the pastor reiterates in his ministry the salvation that was accomplished by the incarnation. Though he is set apart from his fellow humans, and drawn upwards by the transcendent relation with the divine that he cultivates in meditation, his task is not to dissociate himself from the human condition but to share it.[24] The confessor, Gregory explains, is like the basin placed before the temple so that all who enter it may wash their hands and feet, and he need not fear if he himself is tempted by the sins confessed to him, because the more he is afflicted by the temptations of others, the more readily will God grant him deliverance from his own.[25] But while Gregory's ideal pastor shares equally in the human condition, it is inherent in his role as divine intermediary that he does not share it as an equal, and the unique spiritual authority claimed for the ecclesiastical shepherd inevitably makes him the hierarchical superior of his flock. Gregory, however, was much exercised by the corrupting effects of power, and it is in keeping with his fundamental conception of the sacerdotal role that he attempts to maintain a balance between God-like supremacy in authority and Christ's sacrificial humility in embracing human nature: the pastor, he asserts, should not dwell upon his elevated rank and authority, but should bear in mind how much like others he is because of

---

[22] HE, IV.26.
[23] HE, IV.23.
[24] *Regula Pastoralis*, esp. II.1–11.
[25] *Regula Pastoralis*, II.5. It is generally agreed that Gregory refers here to the sacrament of penance and to confession. For the problematic character of penance in his time, see E. Göller, *Papsttum und Bussgewalt in spätrömischer und frühmittelalterlicher Zeit* (Freiburg, 1933), pp. 125–97, esp. pp. 192–7.

the human nature that he shares with them; he should find joy not in ruling others, but in helping them, for the Old Testament archetypes of bishops were not kings of men, but shepherds of flocks.[26]

The arrival of Theodore gave impetus to penitential practice among the laity. According to the *Dialogue of Egbert*, annual confession had already been established as a custom among the laity in the 8th century since the time of Theodore.[27] The *Dialogue of Egbert* fairly certainly exaggerates the influence of Theodore, with the intention of validating the Benedictine reformers' attempts to institutionalize confession in the late Anglo-Saxon period by a retrospective idealization of the past. Bede's letter to Archbishop Egbert, though urging him to implement a programme of basic religious instruction for the laity, makes no reference to the institution of confession.[28] But, in his rewriting of the Anonymous Lindisfarne *Life of Cuthbert*, Bede made a number of additions whose overall effect is to present Cuthbert as engaged, at every stage of his life, in evangelizing and ministering to the laity – an aspect of Cuthbert that barely figures in the Anonymous Life.[29] Bede's additions include a passage, suggested to him by the Evagrian *Life of Antony*, in which he describes the saint as the advisor and consoler of the crowds of visitors he attracted, who were irresistibly moved to confide in him.[30] The description is echoed in Felix's *Life of Guthlac*. These two Lives, then, especially Bede's rewriting of the Lindisfarne Life, suggest at very least a polemical interest in encouraging the development of lay confession, if not an actual growth in penitential practice.[31] Bede's rewriting of the Lindisfarne Life – ostensibly undertaken to incorporate testimony to the life and miracles of Cuthbert that was not available to the Anonymous author[32] – effectively brings the earlier Life's portrait of the saint into conformity with his own conception of sanctity, which was to prove historically dominant. The sanctity of Bede's Cuthbert does not consist in his compassionate identification with humanity, but in his transcendence of the human condition; his possession of miraculous powers is the crowning proof of his godlike and inhuman virtue.

---

[26] *Regula Pastoralis*, II.6.

[27] *Dialogue of Egbert*, 16: ed. H&S, III, 403–13. Watkins, II, 636, 654, who accepts the 8th c. derivation of this work, observes that its assignment of annual confession to the period before Christmas, instead of Easter, resembles Eastern usage and may therefore represent the influence of Theodore.

[28] H&S, III, 314–25.

[29] For an account of these, see A. Thacker, "Bede's Ideal of Reform," in *Ideal and Reality in Frankish and Anglo-Saxon Society*, ed. P. Wormald et al. (Oxford, 1983), pp. 130–53, esp. pp. 138–43; C. Stancliffe, "Cuthbert and the Polarity between Pastor and Solitary," in *St Cuthbert, His Cult and His Community to AD 1200*, ed. G. Bonner et al. (Woodbridge, 1989), pp. 21–44.

[30] *Bede's Cuthbert*, ch. 22 (echoed in ch. 26); *Life of Guthlac*, ch. 45. B. Colgrave, ed. and trans., *Two Lives of Saint Cuthbert: A Life by an Anonymous Monk of Lindisfarne and Bede's Prose Life* (Cambridge, 1940), pp. 142–307; *Felix's Life of Guthlac* (Cambridge, 1956).

[31] The passage is retained in Bede's abridgement of Cuthbert's Life in HE, IV.27. Tradition credits Bede himself with authorship of a penitential work; see B. Albers, "Wann sind die Beda-Egbert'schen Bussbücher verfasst worden, und wer ist ihr Verfasser?" *Archiv für Katholisches Kirchenrecht* 81 (1901), 393–420. But Bede's responsibility for any of the penitentials attributed to him now seems unlikely; see A.J. Frantzen, "The Penitentials Attributed to Bede," *Speculum* 58 (1983), 573–97.

[32] See *Bede's Cuthbert*, Prologue, pp. 142–4.

At the same time, Bede emphasizes Cuthbert's hierarchical superiority and official role.

Bede's portrait of Cuthbert is a didactic *speculum* for bishops, offered in the first instance as a role model for the imitation of Cuthbert's successor to the Lindisfarne see, Bishop Eadfrith, to whom Bede's Life is dedicated. Cuthbert, in Bede's Life, exemplifies the dignity and elevated responsibilities of the episcopal office that Bede was later to urge upon Egbert of York in the hortatory letter he wrote to him. Bede's Cuthbert, then, represents his ideal of a bishop, and, in recasting the homely ascetic of the Anonymous Life, he promotes a conception of episcopal authority that would radically alter the nature of relationship within the community of Christ. Bede's version of the episode in the Anonymous Life in which an eagle descends from the sky with a fish when Cuthbert is exercised by the problems of finding lunch is symptomatic of his instinctively hierarchical world-view. In the Anonymous Life, Cuthbert regards the eagle as a fellow creature; the eagle is "our fisherman," and Cuthbert sees to it that the eagle gets a share of the fish because he is hungry too.[33] But for Bede, Cuthbert's relation to the natural world is one of mastery. Nature obeys Cuthbert because he obeys God;[34] the eagle is thus a ministering servant, and therefore female, and is given some of the fish as a reward for her dutiful service to the episcopal saint.[35]

The authoritarian legalism of *Theodore's Penitential* evokes, all too vividly, the purely regulatory and corrective office of the confessor. Bede and Felix depict their confessor saints as the consolers of all sorrows through their Christ-like consolation of human suffering. They are Comforters, manifestations of the Holy Spirit, whose presence in the world, in accordance with the promise of Christ, fills the void left by his absence. Bede – evidently conscious of resistance to the practice of confessional self-exposure – presents Cuthbert as so radiant with angelic love that no-one would conceal from him the secrets of the heart, because it seemed impossible that anything could remain hidden from his sight.[36] Those who were drawn to Cuthbert by the report of his miracles confided in him all manner of troubles, and received consolation. They revealed to him:

> either the sins they had committed or the temptations of devils to which they were exposed, or else revealed the common troubles of mankind by which they were afflicted, hoping they would get consolation from such sanctity. Nor did their hope deceive them. For none went away from him without enjoying his consolation and none returned accompanied by that sorrow of mind which he had brought hither.[37]

In Felix's version of this description in the *Life of Guthlac*, confession of sin and release from its burden is even more thoroughly submerged in the holy man's

---

[33] *Anon Cuthbert*, II.5 (dated 698x705).

[34] *Bede's Cuthbert*, ch. 21.

[35] *Bede's Cuthbert*, ch. 12.

[36] *Bede's Cuthbert*, ch. 9; the Latin source of OE *Judgment Day II* (quoted above) is traditionally attributed to Bede (*De Die Judicii*, ed. J. Fraipont, CCSL 122 [Turnhout, 1965], 439–44).

[37] Colgrave, p. 229; *Bede's Cuthbert*, ch. 22.

consolation of the sorrows to which the human race is heir, and is merely one aspect of his comprehensive cure of souls:

> Those who were afflicted by sickness of the body, by the obsession of evil spirits, by the acknowledgement of sins committed, or by reason of any of the other wrongs by which the human race is surrounded, believed that according to their several necessities they would get consolation from a man of such sanctity; nor were they deceived by vain hope. For no sick man went away from him without relief, no afflicted person without healing, no sad ones without joy, no weary ones without encouragement, no mourners without comfort, no anxious ones without counsel.[38]

Felix and Bede, then, where they echo the Life of Antony, depict their saints as healers of human grief, whose thaumaturgic powers are derived from their outstanding holiness. Confession of sin and release from its burdens, like the wise and sympathetic advice of a spiritual mentor, is only one aspect of their consolatory role. Their role is not corrective or regulatory, and they do not exercise a formal, sacerdotal ministry, for they do not ascribe penance or pronounce absolution; instead, they effect deliverance from all manner of suffering by the wisdom and healing powers that are the attributes of holiness. This non-official and non-sacramental conception of the saint-confessor, sought out by the laity as spiritual confidant and advisor because of his reputation for sanctity, parallels the lay popularity of famous ascetics as confessors in the early Irish church, who were not necessarily priests.[39] In adopting the Life of Antony's account of how crowds flocked to St Antony and were miraculously transformed by his beatific presence, Bede and Felix are presumably giving artistic form to actual lay practices in Northumbria and East Anglia in the late 7th and early 8th century.[40]

Bede's emphatic sacerdotalism, however, is revealed by a subsequent addition to the Anonymous Life of Cuthbert, in which he presents Cuthbert's confessorial role as a specifically priestly office, associated with his sacramental ministry, and linked with the administration of penance. Bede adds a description of Cuthbert as priest-celebrant. Cuthbert, he says, always wept in imitation of Christ when he celebrated the sacrifice of the innocent victim, and drew his congregation to join with him by his heart-felt sighing. As liturgical celebrant, Cuthbert is an intermediary between God and humanity; his tears of compassion unite suffering humanity to Christ on the cross, who shared humanity's suffering in order to redeem it. So too in the description of Cuthbert exercising the confessional, which is linked to this account of him as priest-celebrant, Cuthbert is an Agnus Dei, who takes away the sins and sufferings of the world. But in this clearly sacramental and official definition of Cuthbert's confessorial role, his ministrations are shown to be regulatory and corrective: when penitents confessed their sins to Cuthbert, Bede says, "he shed tears of pity for their weakness, and

---

[38] Colgrave, p. 139; Life of Guthlac, ch. 45.
[39] See McNeill, p. 28, who also points out that "confession in the Eastern church had often been made to monks whose asceticism recommended them to penitents," and that the Penitential of Columban enjoins confession to a priest.
[40] Cf. Evagrian Life of Antony, ch. 28 (PL 73, 150–2).

though himself righteous, by his own example would show the sinner what to do."[41] Though Bede's depiction of Cuthbert as priest-confessor clearly draws on the *Regula Pastoralis* ideal of the pastor as an intermediary between humanity and the divine, Bede (characteristically) emphasizes Cuthbert's human transcendence when he depicts him as an official confessor – Cuthbert's compassion for suffering is the pity of a superior nature for weaknesses that he himself does not share.

Guthlac, on the other hand, as a former monk turned hermit, approximates quite closely to the Irish holy man. He is ordained only towards the end of his life, after much coaxing from Bishop Headda.[42] In the light of Bede's sacerdotalist handling of Cuthbert, Bishop Headda's insistence on ordaining Guthlac may well represent a movement, in the early 8th century, to put a stop to the informal pastoral ministries of the men – and women – whose influence on the laity derived solely from their personal sanctity, and to make their practitioners, where it was possible, part of the official church hierarchy. Felix does regard Guthlac's ordination as endowing him with additional grace, but his view of the priesthood is primarily meritocratic; for him, Guthlac's ordination is an a honour bestowed in recognition of his sanctity, and a confirmatory tribute to the divine origin of his supernatural powers. It is, however, not without significance that Guthlac's ordination precedes his consolatory ministrations to the exiled King Æthelbald. In the *Life of Wilfrid* – where the relative powers of ecclesiastical and secular authorities are noticeably at issue in Wilfrid's conflicts with kings – Wilfrid, in his youth, becomes the "soul friend" of the Deiran sub-king, Alhfrith, and is immediately ordained as a priest.[43] Wilfrid's elevation to an ecclesiastical office serves here to bestow on him the status appropriate to an intimate companion and spiritual advisor of a king. Felix, whose *Life of Guthlac* is dedicated to an East-Anglian king,[44] also appears to reflect the attempt to claim a form of parity between secular and spiritual powers through official rank in an ecclesiastical hierarchy.

Whereas Bede's portrait of Cuthbert as priest-confessor depicts his cure of souls as a superior nature's compassion for human weakness, Felix's Life, by contrast, explains Guthlac's spiritual healing in terms of his empathetic participation in suffering by his identification in *caritas* with those who suffer. None went unconsoled from Guthlac, Felix explains, because as he abounded in true charity, he shared the suffering of everyone. Felix's generalized delineation of Guthlac as ideal confessor is concretely elaborated in his account of Guthlac as the comforter of the exiled king Æthelbald. As a solitary hermit, living in voluntary exile for Christ amidst uninhabited fenlands, Guthlac is, even more evidently than the itinerant ascetic Cuthbert, the natural refuge and the friend of all who are outcast from earthly joy, and particularly the exiled king, Æthelbald of Mercia. Significantly polemical, in terms of the attempts to constitute kings under the guiding mentorship of ecclesiastics, is the fact that Guthlac's relationship with the king demonstrates the superiority of spiritual over earthly leadership. The confessor-saint is able to give Æthelbald advice and consola-

---

[41] Colgrave, p. 213; *Bede's Cuthbert*, ch. 16.
[42] *Life of Guthlac*, ch. 47.
[43] *Life of Wilfrid*, chs. 7, 9.
[44] *Life of Guthlac*, Prologue, p. 60; Ælfwold of East Anglia's regnal dates are *c*. 713–49.

tion when the king, having reached the limits of his own purely human resources, is no longer able to offer leadership to his followers and is himself existentially directionless: Æthelbald comes to Guthlac "amid doubts and dangers, when his own endurance and that of his followers was failing and when his strength was utterly exhausted . . . in order that, when human counsel had failed, he might seek divine counsel." Guthlac interrupts Æthelbald's account of his troubles: "I am not ignorant of your miseries since the beginning of your life." He reveals that, in sympathy with Æthelbald's sorrows, he has prayed to God and received certain knowledge that Æthelbald's kingdom will be returned to him in the fullness of time, and counsels him to trust in providence to make good his own insufficiencies: "And so be strong, for the Lord is your helper, be patient, lest you turn to a purpose you cannot perform."[45]

Guthlac's knowledge of the sorrows of the human heart is more evidently a manifestation of god-like omniscience than Cuthbert's irresistible power to move the laity to confide their private sorrows to him because his angelic countenance inspired the belief that nothing could be invisible to him. (Though neither Guthlac or Bede's Cuthbert are quite so god-like as the renegade Gaulish priest Aldebert, who appears to have been carried away by the divinity bestowed on him by his ecclesiastical office – or perhaps he was just satirically averse to it. For Aldebert consecrated churches in his own name, distributed clippings of his hair and nails as relics, and when approached to hear confessions, he replied: "I know all your sins; your secret deeds are open to my gaze. There is no need to confess, since your past sins are forgiven. Go home in peace: you are absolved.")[46] Guthlac's knowledge of the human heart is an aspect of his knowledge of all that is unseen and invisible – as he can discern the past sufferings of Æthelbald's whole life, he is able to comfort and advise him because he has prophetic insight into the future. This visionary gift is understood by Felix as a gift that is added to those who have the gift of compassionate empathy with suffering humanity. But Felix's *Life of Guthlac* and Bede's *Life of Cuthbert* mark an advance towards the conception of miracle-working as the defining hallmark of sanctity – in both Lives, ministering to the laity is itself an exercise of supernatural faculties.[47] In Bede's *Life of Cuthbert*, miracle-working as ultimate proof of sanctity and sacerdotalism go hand in hand, defining the episcopal saint as a superior being set apart from his fellow men by his possession of divinely-given powers.

In a letter to Augustine, Gregory expressed his fear of the corrupting effect of

---

[45] Colgrave, pp. 149–51; *Life of Guthlac*, ch. 49, see also ch. 52. In accordance with Guthlac's prophecy, Æthelbald recovered the Mercian throne, and erected the shrine to which Guthlac's remains were translated; Boniface's 747 letter of reproof to Æthelbald (Tangl, 73) reveals that, in later life at least, the king was much less amenable to ecclesiastical guidance than the Life paints him. Guthlac's role in this episode has striking parallels with the spirit-guide who appears to the exiled Northumbrian king in HE II.12; see fn. 13.

[46] Talbot, 1954, p. 110; Tangl, 59.

[47] I am not in fundamental disagreement with B. Ward, "Miracles and History: A Reconsideration of the Miracle Stories used by Bede," ed. Bonner, pp. 70–6. She argues that Bede "was not primarily interested in the external marvelousness of miracles. . . . It was what was signified that mattered" (pp. 71–2). My emphasis differs because I am concerned with the didactic significance Bede gives to the miraculous in his Life of Cuthbert.

miracles on those who performed them. Gregory could not but rejoice that Augustine had secured the conversion of many by means of a miracle. But those who perform miracles, he pointed out, were liable to glory in their own powers and presumptuously exalt themselves, forgetting that they were the mere instruments of the power of God. Gregory therefore urged Augustine to examine his conscience carefully, lest the very thing which had brought him honour in the eyes of the world should cause him to fall into the sin of pride. He was particularly concerned that Augustine should not regard the performance of miracles as a sign of election. In keeping with *Regula Pastoralis'* emphasis on the pastor's identification with his fellow humans, Gregory discouraged Augustine from rejoicing in the possession of superhuman powers which set him apart from others, for true disciples rejoice only in the eternal joy which is shared in common by all who inherit eternal life. Not all of the elect work miracles, he assured him; the only infallible sign that distinguishes those chosen by God is their union in *caritas*, for which the supporting text is: "In this shall it be known that you are my disciples, if you love one another."[48]

The Whitby *Life of Gregory*,[49] taken together with the account of its founder, Abbess Hild, in Bede's *History*,[50] indicate that Whitby espoused a view of episcopal sanctity and authority very different from the one that Bede was promoting. For this view the writings of Gregory afforded support, and the Life's celebration of Gregory as (by proxy) the apostle of the English[51] does not demonstrate that Whitby had wholeheartedly transferred allegiance to Rome following Wilfrid's purported rout of the Celtic faction at the Whitby synod in 664;[52] the writings of the Pope to whom the Roman church in England traced its origins are used to give indisputable authority to the Life's opposition to conceptions of episcopal sanctity that were being promoted by ardent Romanists like Bede. Hild evidently played an active and leading part in the early Northumbrian church, particularly before the resurgence of the church under Theodore. Bede, unsurprisingly in the light of his views on sacerdotal power and episcopal authority, tells us next to nothing of the contribution to the growth of the church and the participatory role of abbesses like Hild. But he allows us to glimpse the importance of Whitby as a conversionary centre during the abbacy of Hild when he intimates that many priests and five bishops were educated at her double monastery; his commitment to the superior dignity of bishops and priests, however, prevents him from identifying Hild as their teacher. His reference to Hild's role as advisor to the laity indicates that engagement in pastoral ministry had yet to become the exclusive prerogative of churchmen. The

---

[48] *HE* I.31 (John 13.35). As C.W. Jones, *Saints' Lives and Chronicles in Early England* (Ithaca, NY, 1947), p. 89, points out, Bede's abridgement of this letter (H&S, III, 16) downplays Gregory's insistence that miracles are extrinsic to Christianity and valueless in relation to works; it also suppresses his assertion that *caritas* alone defines the elect.

[49] B. Colgrave, ed. and trans, *The Earliest Life of Gregory the Great by an Anonymous Monk of Whitby* (Lawrence, Ka, 1968), esp. chs. 3–8.

[50] *HE*, IV.23–4.

[51] *Life of Gregory*, ch. 6.

[52] *HE*, III.25. For Hild's support of the Celtic party at Whitby and later opposition to Wilfrid's reinstatement (*Life of Wilfrid*, ch. 54), see further pp. 180–4. Whitby had dedicated an altar to Gregory, and the cult of Abbess Ælffled's grandfather, Edwin of Northumbria, is linked with him (*Life of Gregory*, chs. 18–19).

Whitby *Life of Gregory*, dating from the abbacy of Hild's niece, Ælffled, and possibly written by a Whitby nun, suggests, by its concern with the role of miracles in conversion, that Whitby under Ælffled continued to be actively involved in the conversion of the laity and engaged in some forms of pastoral ministry.[53] The Whitby *Life of Gregory*, however, in addressing the role of miracles, is more broadly concerned with the nature of sanctity.

The Whitby *Life of Gregory*, though striving to avoid uncharitable contention, gives every appearance of adopting a position in relation to a current polemical debate on the nature of sanctity. Let none wonder, the author remarks, that Gregory is acclaimed for his sanctity, despite the fact that he performed few miracles, and even though "many are accustomed to judge the lives of saints by their miracles and to measure their merits and holiness by the signs they perform."[54] The Whitby Life follows Gregory in asserting that sanctity is not necessarily attended by miracle working and supernatural signs, and that saints who do not perform miracles are equal to those who do. It also broadens the definition of the miraculous to include the saint's transformation of his own human nature in imitation of Christ, and the transformation that the saint brings about in others through his teaching and the example of his life. Here too, the authority of Gregory is adduced as support; the author explains that Gregory considered that miracles consisting of the invisible and interior operation of grace were of greater value – because they are more truly spiritual in nature – than the miracles which consist of objective manifestations of supernatural power and are apprehended through the senses.[55] The Whitby sources Bede drew on for the account in his *History* evidently reflected the same view of miracles. Apart from a vision of Hild's soul ascending at her death, witnessed by two nuns, the only miraculous element in Bede's account of Whitby is the story of the poet Cædmon, and the miracle in this story consists entirely of the invisible and interior operation of grace, since Cædmon is inspired to the composition of devotional poetry in a dream, and subsequently converts from a secular to a monastic way of life.[56] It is also consistent with the Whitby Life's preference for conversion by teaching and example that Bede, in his *Life of Cuthbert*, intimates that Whitby accepted with equanimity the disappearance of a girdle that Cuthbert had given to the Abbess Ælffled, by whose aid she performed two miracles of healing, because Whitby did not want the girdle to attract to the monastery people who merely sought a cure for physical ills.[57]

The Whitby *Life of Gregory*, then, claims Gregory as the exemplar of a type of sainthood that is miraculous only in imitating the love and humility by which God became one with humanity, and in its power to move others to the same form of imitation: "That power which can only produce amazement by what is heard and seen is of a baser kind than that which avails itself of the meek and lowly Christ and the love which Christ himself ever has. Therefore we place

---

[53] See further ch. 8, pp. 180–5, 268, 270.

[54] Colgrave, p. 77; *Life of Gregory*, ch. 3.

[55] See *Life of Gregory*, chs. 4–6.

[56] See further pp. 248–9, 263–7.

[57] See *Bede's Cuthbert*, ch. 23. According to Bede, Whitby feared that undeserving pilgrims who sought miraculous cures would question Cuthbert's sanctity.

first as a sign of the sanctity of [Gregory] that he followed the example of him who is the beginning of all things."[58] The Whitby author's incarnational conception of sanctity is accompanied by a consciousness of the paradox inherent in the existence of an ecclesiastical hierarchy. The paradox finds a resolution in a meritocracy of humility; the author claims Jerome's authority for the axiom that they are worthiest of ecclesiastical office who feel themselves the most unworthy.[59] Gregory is thus regarded by the Whitby author as having demonstrated the essence of his sanctity in his attempt to resist his elevation to the apostolic throne, wherein he imitated Christ's rejection of an earthly throne: "For it was Christ himself who, when his apostles asked him who was the greatest in the kingdom of heaven, answered that it was the meek."[60]

The sanctity of Hild, as Bede's History derived it from his sources, echoes the Whitby hagiographer's conception of sanctity. Hild's sanctity does not consist in miracle-working but in the inspiring example of her holiness of life and her teaching, in which she promoted peace and love above all. Whitby, Bede intimates, eschewed social distinctions and cultivated an egalitarian and collectivist ethos – there was neither wealth nor poverty, for, following the example of the apostolic church, members of the community owned all things in common.[61] Whitby's understanding of Christianity appears antithetical to Bede's conception of the church as an official, hierarchical institution, and the long term effect of the emergence of a priestly caste was to reduce the participation in the life of the church of double monasteries such as Whitby, and to give superior status to the priests and bishops that abbesses like Hild had once educated.[62] The Whitby Life of Gregory's affirmation of the primacy of personal sanctity, especially humility, then, has the appearance of a polemical statement of the Whitby monastery's resistance to the developing conception of the power and authority inhering in sacerdotal office which Bede is at pains to promote.[63]

Bede's revision of the Anonymous Lindisfarne Life of Cuthbert for the edification of Bishop Eadfrith reveals the way in which the ideals of episcopal sanctity in these two Lives – the one hierarchical and transcendent in orientation, the

---

[58] Colgrave, p. 85; Life of Gregory, ch. 7.

[59] Colgrave, 1965, p. 144, was unable to confirm the attribution to Jerome.

[60] Colgrave, p. 85; Life of Gregory, ch. 7, see also ch. 8.

[61] HE, IV.23.

[62] Thacker, 1983, pp. 130–1, argues that Bede wished to see "an intellectual and moral elite of teachers distinct from the ordained sacerdos." Inasmuch as Bede wanted all heads of households, lay and religious, to instruct those under their rule in Christian teachings, he did not regard evangelization as the exclusive province of the sacerdos (characteristically, participation extends only to those in authority); but, as Thacker indicates, Bede never lost sight of the distinction between this "intellectual and moral elite of teachers" and the ordained sacerdos. See further, ch. 8, fn. 136.

[63] On grounds of dating, Life of Gregory (704x14) cannot be responding to Bede's Cuthbert (721), only to the views of episcopal sanctity it enshrines. Thacker, in an unpublished D.Phil. thesis (see D.W. Rollason, Saints and Relics in Anglo-Saxon England [Oxford, 1989], p. 65), argues that the Whitby author had written sources from Rome, possibly intended as the basis for a Life which was never written or is now lost. Divergent views on miracles were held by the early fathers – strict followers of Cassian denied altogether that a holy man could be recognized by miracles; see O. Chadwick, John Cassian: A Study in Primitive Monasticism, 2nd edn. (Cambridge, 1968), pp. 51, 100.

other inclining towards egalitarian corporateness – take effect in entirely dissimilar conceptions of ministering to the laity. In the account of the healing of Hildmer's wife, the author of the Anonymous Life extrapolates the motives of Hildmer with intuitive sympathy. The author of the Anonymous Life understands the humanly invisible, not by an alleged supernatural faculty, but by identifying in love with his fellow human beings, and as he was a member of Cuthbert's *familia*, his view of the event is likely to have derived directly from Cuthbert. The Anonymous author understands that Hildmer conceals the nature of his wife's illness because fits of the kind that she was suffering were attributed to demonic possession, and Hildmer therefore felt that her illness reflected dishonour upon them both: "He was ashamed to declare that a woman so religious was oppressed by a devil." The author also understands that Hildmer weeps when Cuthbert insists on accompanying him to his home for two reasons; he weeps because he has failed to protect his wife from the shame of being seen by Cuthbert in a physically degraded condition, and because he expects that she will die and is therefore grieving for his own loss and his children's loss of a mother. No less striking than this unjudgmental comprehension of entirely "secular" motives, is the author's sympathetic acceptance of demonic possession as a widely shared phenomenon: Hildmer did not know, he explains simply, "that such a trial is wont to fall frequently upon Christians."[64]

In his letter to Archbishop Egbert, Bede urged him to restrain himself with pontifical dignity from idle conversations, and to meditate on devotional works, so that his speech might be elevated above common diction – for it is unseemly, he assured the archbishop, for the sacred vessels of the altar to be profaned by common-place usage.[65] Human sympathy was apparently no less inimical to the dignity that Bede considered appropriate to ecclesiastical rank. Even Hildmer, as a devout layman, has turned unfeelingly pious in Bede's Life. He is solely concerned with his wife's devout standing in the eyes of the saint, and weeps only because he fears that Cuthbert will think that her devotion to the service of God has been an empty pretence. With the role of judgmental superior, Bede's Cuthbert is entirely at ease: "Do not weep as if I were about to find your wife in such a condition as I would not wish," he instructs graciously, and the consolation that Bede's Cuthbert offers – more in the nature of impersonal pedagogic instruction – is not calculated to identify him as a fellow Christian with the sufferings experienced by Hildmer's wife: "It is not only the wicked who are subject to such torments, but sometimes in this world, by the inscrutable judgments of God, the innocent are taken captive by the devil, not only in body but in mind."[66]

Bede is no less concerned to free his saint from the taint of human affection in his version of Cuthbert's relations with female religious: though Bede's assimilation of patristic concepts of women as morally dangerous is also evident here.[67] Bede dispels any suggestion that Cuthbert mingled on familiar and friendly terms with monastic women. His visits are presented as an aspect of his official pastoral ministry. Whereas the Lindisfarne Life explains that Cuthbert

---

[64] Colgrave, p. 93; *Anon Cuthbert*, II.8.
[65] H&S, III, 314–15; Bede also urged the Archbishop to read *Regula Pastoralis*.
[66] Colgrave, pp. 205–7; *Bede's Cuthbert*, ch. 15.
[67] See further pp. 101–2, 199–207.

frequently visited the nun Censwith because she had brought him up from childhood and was like a mother to him, Bede adduces her devotion to good works to justify Cuthbert's attentions, and locates his visits within the sphere of official duty by explaining that he chanced one day to be in Censwith's village in the course of his missionary perambulations.[68] The Lindisfarne Life merely mentions that Cuthbert was staying at the monastery of the Abbess Æbbe because she had invited him. In Bede's version, the abbess, rendered worthy of special favour by the piety for which she is everywhere honoured and her relationship to King Oswiu, has prevailed on Cuthbert to visit for the purpose of preaching to her and her community; though the reluctance with which he answers the call of duty is implicit in the explanation that he could not refuse a request that was made to him in all charity of heart.[69] Like Bishop Aidan who, according to Bede, guided the efforts of Hild, and Bishop Trumwine who helped Ælffled to run the Whitby monastery, Bede's episcopal saint is the friendly, but hierarchically superior, mentor of monastic women.

The difference between the conceptions of episcopal sainthood represented by Bede's rewriting of the Life of Cuthbert on the one hand, and the early Lindisfarne and Whitby Lives on the other, are neatly emblematized by the story Bede tells in his History of Theodore's influence on Bishop Chad: "Because it was the custom of the reverend Bishop Chad to carry out his evangelistic work on foot rather than on horseback, Theodore ordered him to ride whenever he was faced with too long a journey; but Chad showed much hesitation, for he was deeply devoted to this religious exercise, so the archbishop lifted him on to the horse with his own hands since he knew him to be a man of great sanctity and he determined to compel him to ride a horse when necessity arose."[70] For Theodore, it seems, imitation of Christ was an inadequate qualification for a bishop, and the inward and invisible grace that was evident to him needed to be made manifest to the laity by outward and visible signs; in hoisting Bishop Chad into the saddle to assume the reins of office, Theodore elevated him above the level of ordinary humanity, with whom in all humility Chad had been accustomed to identify himself, and identified him instead with the secular aristocracy. Chad was a disciple of Bishop Aidan, who had been better able to resist the same temptation when it was offered by King Oswine, for Aidan gave away Oswine's gift of a horse and royal trappings to a poor man who asked him for alms.[71] The ideals of sanctity of the Lindisfarne and Whitby Lives can thus be located within the Celtic traditions of Christianity that their authors inherited, since Aidan was responsible for the founding of both monasteries; and, despite the Whitby author's employment of Gregory as an exemplar of episcopal sanctity, I have suggested, the Life represents the employment of a Roman authority to oppose positions that were promoted by those who identified themselves with Rome.

Roman adherents were, perhaps, inherently more likely to insist on the elite status and authority of bishops – Theodore's concern to manifest the dignity of

---

68 Cf. Bede's Cuthbert, ch. 14; Anon Cuthbert, II.7.
69 Cf. Bede's Cuthbert, ch. 10; Anon Cuthbert, II.3.
70 C&M, p. 337; HE, IV.3.
71 HE, III.14.

episcopal office in secular forms is anticipated by Wilfrid, whose predilection for surrounding himself with mounted retinues is of a piece with his attempts to claim authority over kings by virtue of the power to bind and unbind that he possessed through the Petrine succession.[72] But, as Gregory's ideal of the pastor shows, the difference between the Celtic and Roman traditions was not absolute. The egalitarian model of sanctity was evidently current in the predominately Roman traditions of Wearmouth. It is represented in Bede's *History of the Abbots* by the portrait of Eosterwine, who is said to have identified so completely with his brother monks that he took a positive delight in sharing their work, and often stopped as he went about the monastery to help them with their ploughing, hammering and winnowing.[73] The fact that Bede's appreciation of Eosterwine is mediated through the Benedictine Rule's ideal of monastic community as a return to the fraternal poverty that characterized the apostolic church, when all things were held in common,[74] is a sufficient reminder of the continued availability of the egalitarian model of sanctity within the Roman church. Bede's rewriting of the Anonymous Life, then, is not so much representative of a difference in spirit between Roman and Celtic traditions as a chronological shift which is heralded by the arrival of Theodore, whose insistence on investing episcopal office with the trappings of secular authority offered a powerful encouragement to an egregiously inhuman and hierarchically authoritarian construction of episcopal sanctity. The same chronological shift is observable in the correspondence of Boniface, who, elevated to a bishopric on the continent, adopts, in the last decade or so of his life, public postures which are inimical to his earlier and private conception of women as fellow members of the community of Christ.

Monastic Women as Spiritual Mentors

The humane, egalitarian strain of Christianity predominates in the correspondence of Boniface and his associates, whose origins were predominately West Saxon. Boniface, according to Rudolph of Fulda, wanted to be buried beside his kinswoman Leoba who had shared his labours in the mission to the continent, so that, as they had served Christ with equal zeal, they might together await the resurrection.[75] Boniface's regard for Leoba as a comrade-in-arms in the service of Christ is confirmed by his correspondence. Boniface addresses monastic women as companions in the same spiritual endeavour, who labour under the same, embattled, conditions of human existence. The corollary of this solidarity is a pervasive affirmation of unity in the bonds of the Holy Spirit that transcends physical separation. Divided by distance, Boniface and his circle are nevertheless united by a love that partakes of the nature of Christ's love, and in which

---

[72] See *Life of Wilfrid*, esp. chs. 2, 21, 24, 37–9.
[73] *History of the Abbots*, ch. 8.
[74] Acts 2.44, 4.32; *Rule of Benedict*, chs. 33, 2, 58.
[75] *Life of Leoba*, ch. 17.

Christ is present. The vehicle of this union is the confraternity of prayer.[76] Daniel of Winchester's letter to Boniface, like Wihtberht's letter to the monks at Glastonbury, gives explicit expression to the underlying assumptions of the correspondence between English monasteries and the continental mission: "Although we are separated by the vast extent of land and sea and the wide diversity of climate, the same scourge of sorrows afflicts us. The work of Satan is the same there as here. Wherefore I earnestly pray that we may fortify each other by mutual exchange of prayers, ever mindful of 'Where two or three are gathered together [there am I in the midst of you].' "[77]

Consoler and advisor to the monastic women to whom he was a "brother in the spirit rather than in the flesh," Boniface also confides in them his sense of his own insufficiencies, and asks them to support him in his missionary labours by interceding for him in their prayers: "Intercede for us," he urges, "for because of our sins, the way of our wandering is beset by tempests of many kinds."[78] He writes in gratitude, too, for the support monastic women had given by sending gifts and by copying books that he needed. To Abbess Eadburg he confided that on every hand there was "struggle and grief, fighting without and fear within," and he thanked her for having brought light and consolation to an exile in Germany by the books that she had sent him. "Pray for me," he asked, "because, for my sins, I am tossed by the tempests of a perilous sea."[79] To his old friend Abbess Bugga – and no friend was dearer to Boniface than an old friend[80] – he sent consolation and advice on hearing that secular interference in the affairs of her monastery had robbed her of the contemplative peace she had hoped to find in an anchorage. His consolation and advice are not the hortations of a pedagogic superior but spring from his identificatory sympathy with a friend experiencing troubles not dissimilar from his own: "So now, my revered sister, in sympathy with your misfortunes and mindful of your kindness to me and of our ancient friendship, I am sending you a brotherly letter of comfort and exhortation."[81] In giving comfort, he affirms his sense of mutual dependence in the midst of shared difficulty, asking her to pray for him, in return for his prayers, so that his soul may escape the dangers that surround it.

The missionary nun to whom Boniface addressed the most urgent of his appeals is not named. Boniface was probably writing to Leoba, since this appeal echoes a letter dating from the same period that Boniface addressed to Leoba and two of her companions, in which he expressed his fear that his missionary efforts would come to nothing.[82] In the appeal to the unnamed nun, as in his letter to Leoba and her companions, Boniface affirms a mutuality of dependence on supportive encouragement. Like Bishop Daniel, he assumes the experience of suffering as the unifying condition of humanity; as those who labour for

---

[76] I refer to confraternities in the non-technical sense, as well as to the formally instituted Confraternities discussed by Levison, 1946, pp. 101–3.
[77] Emerton, p. 121; Tangl, 64 (Matt. 18.20).
[78] Emerton, pp. 121–2; Tangl, 65.
[79] Emerton, p. 61; Tangl, 30; see also 35.
[80] See esp. Tangl, 34.
[81] Emerton, p. 171; Tangl, 94. "Bugga" is a cognomen for -burg, but the woman addressed as Bugga in this letter need not be identical with the Abbess Eadburg to whom Tangl, 30, 35, 65, are addressed.
[82] Tangl, 67.

Christ in the same endeavour have a single identity through their union in Christ, Boniface assumes that the unnamed nun shares the despair of success that he feels, and he extends to her the consolation that he asks for himself:

> We beg that we may be consoled and rescued through your prayers. . . . We trust in the Lord that through your loving prayers we may deserve to find pardon for our sins and rest from storms, since the apostle James, who is true to his word, has said: "Confess your faults one to another, that ye may be healed. The fervent prayer of the righteous man availeth much". . . . I beg you not to refuse because I have made this same request before; I should ask again and again, since I would have your prayers never cease. Daily tribulations make me seek divine comfort from my brothers and sisters. I fear, moreover, that the temptations of Satan are the same there as here. In the words of the apostle: "Be ye steadfast, immovable, always abounding in the work of the Lord, inasmuch as ye know that your labour is not in vain in the Lord."[83]

It is true that, in his disputes with the papacy, Boniface wrote to his fellow ecclesiastics for advice. It is also true that there are no surviving letters from monastic women offering him supportive encouragement of the kind that he gives in this letter. But in his letters to monastic women Boniface charac-teristically does not present himself as an official spiritual mentor. He is instead, as he affirms by his quotation of James 5.16 in this letter to the missionary nun, a participant in the ministry of all believers, who confess to one another their shared human weakness, and derive forgiveness and support from one another's prayers. Where the church struggled for survival, at the continental mission and in England, mutual interdependence prompted a vision of the church, not as an officially constituted hierarchical entity, but as a mystical unity wrought through the love and suffering of Christ for humanity, which equalized the value of all of its members and endowed them with the power to exercise an efficacious ministry by their identificatory empathy.

Bede may never have encountered in the flesh his idea of Christ incarnate; some who knew Boniface believed that they had. Abbess Eangyth was one of them. Eangyth wrote to Boniface in the early years of the mission on behalf of herself and her widowed daughter to ask his advice on a pilgrimage to Rome that she wished to take. Her letter (c. 719) pre-dates Boniface's elevation to a bishopric. Some of Boniface's friendships with women religious in England stem from his earlier role as a monastic teacher; the report that Boniface taught both monks and nuns before he left England for the continent serves to confirm both the inclusiveness of Boniface's own conception of Christian community and the freedom of monastic women to participate in the acquisition of learning.[84] Ecgburg, seeking consolation from Boniface, bases her request, in part, on their former relation as pupil and teacher.[85] Eangyth, however, addresses Boniface as a personal friend. Like King Æthelbald in the *Life of Guthlac*, Eangyth is a leader

---

83 Kylie, pp. 147–8; Tangl, 66.
84 See *Life of Boniface*, ch. 2.
85 Tangl, 13.

seeking leadership. Borne down by a multitude of miseries – the difficulties besetting her in the rule of her monastery – she seeks comfort and counsel when her own powers of direction have failed:

> Every man uncertain of his purpose and distrustful of his own counsel, seeks a faithful friend whose advice he follows since he distrusts his own; and such faith has he in him that he lays before him the secrets of his heart. As has been said, what is sweeter than having someone with whom one can converse as oneself?[86] Therefore on account of the pressing miseries we have not insisted on to the full, we needs must find a true friend, one whom we can trust more than ourselves; who will treat our grief, our miseries and our poverty as his own, who will sympathize with us, comfort us, support us by his words and raise us up by wise counsel. Long have we sought him. And we believe that in you we have found the friend whom we longed for, whom we wished for, whom we desired.[87]

Though Eangyth looks to Boniface for superior guidance, the basis of her request is a personal relationship based on mutuality. Her choice of Boniface as a confidant recalls the *Havamal*'s maxim, that it is a sign of the greatest intimacy to reveal all that is in one's heart; with just such a conception of the trusted friend as confidant, I have suggested, the role of the official ecclesiastical confessor coalesced. So much did Boniface identify with Eangyth's conflict with ecclesiastical authority, that he echoed Eangyth's words in a letter to Bishop Daniel asking for advice on his conflicts with Rome. Like Eangyth, Boniface in his letter to Daniel presents the desire to unburden the troubles of the heart to an intimate friend as a popular, non-ecclesiastical, conception: "It is a well-known custom among men, when anything sad or burdensome happens to them, to seek for comfort and advice from those in whose friendship and wisdom they have especial confidence. And so I, trusting in your well-proven fatherly wisdom and friendship, am laying before you the troubles of my weary mind and am asking for your advice and comfort."[88] Eangyth's request for advice, although it involves a question of canon law, is not addressed to Boniface as a member of the official church hierarchy, but is located within the ministry of believers. The conception of the trusted friend as the chosen recipient of confidences blends in her letter with the ideal of the Christ-like confessor and consoler of sorrows that shapes Felix's hagiographical portrait of Guthlac and fails to find expression in Bede's depiction of Cuthbert's pastoral ministry; Eangyth's expectation of Boniface as a friend is that he will identify through the spirit of *caritas* with her troubles. As *caritas* is to love others as oneself, the identity of being that it brings about, in the belief of Eangyth, creates a perfect understanding of another.

---

[86] So also Boniface to Archbishop Cuthbert: "It is written in the book of Solomon, 'Blessed be he that finds a true friend with whom he can speak as with himself.'" (Tangl, 78). According to Tangl, the source of this is Ecclus. 25.12.

[87] Trans. Eckenstein, pp. 128–31, at p. 130; Tangl, 14.

[88] Emerton, p. 114; Tangl, 63.

Eangyth's expectations of Boniface as spiritual advisor and confidant have an additional dimension of interest, since Eangyth herself appears to have exercised a confessional ministry. She describes this in formal, sacerdotal terms. Among the many burdens of her monastic rule that she enumerates is: "care for the souls of those of either sex and of every age which have been entrusted to us. For this care involves ministering to many minds and various dispositions, and afterwards giving account before the supreme tribunal of Christ both for obvious sins in deeds and words, and for secret thoughts which men ignore and God alone witnesses." Eangyth is echoing the Benedictine Rule's account of the duties of an abbot. The *Rule of Benedict*, in exhorting the abbot to be a pastor in the manner of Christ, emphasizes the burdens of office rather than the exercise of authority and warns abbots at some length of the weighty responsibility they bear in being answerable at the Last Judgment for the souls entrusted to their care.[89] Eangyth, then, models her monastic leadership directly on the role accorded to an abbot, whose cure of souls derived naturally from the fact that he was an ordained priest. But the Benedictine Rule speaks only of the abbot's responsibility for the words and deeds of his monastic community; Eangyth adds a specifically confessorial dimension to her office in assuming responsibility for "the secret thoughts that men ignore and God alone witnesses." A further significant difference is that Eangyth's ministry extends to both sexes – the nuns and monks of her double monastery, and perhaps also the men and women on the monastic estates. Her letter thus points to the actuality of the rule of an abbess of a double monastery. Although Bede's *History* is concerned to give the impression that male and female houses at double monasteries were self-contained, non-communicating establishments,[90] Eangyth's ministry clearly encompasses both, and she can scarcely have carried out her pastoral responsibilities for the whole of her community under the kind of rigidly segregated conditions that Rudolph of Fulda claims to have existed under Abbess Tette at Wimbourne where, according to Rudolph, women were strictly prohibited from entering the men's quarters, and the only men permitted to enter the women's quarters were priests, who were required to withdraw immediately they had said mass.[91] Eangyth's exercise of the confessional also suggests that the need for resident priests to minister to communities of nuns does not account for the adoption of the double monastery organization – rather, abbesses of double monasteries would appear to have taken over some of the offices of priests.[92]

On the continent, in the first half of the 6th century, Abbess Fara at Brie is said to have heard the confessions of the men and women at her double monastery; she is also said to have had the power to excommunicate.[93] The formal administration of confession by women was sufficiently common for it to be declared uncanonical by *Theodore's Penitential*, and it may be that the compiler of the *Penitential* finds it worthy of note that women as well as men came to Theodore to enquire into his judgments because he is referring, not to members

89 *Rule of Benedict*, ch. 2; see also chs. 27, 64.
90 See ch. 8, pp. 245–6.
91 *Life of Leoba*, chs. 2–3; see further ch. 9, pp. 271–5.
92 See further pp. 96, 163–5, 170–2, 179–85, 203–7, 244, 280, 290.
93 *Jonas's Life of Columban*, II.19; see also Bateson, 51, 155.

of the laity, but to people who acted as directors of conscience and wished to learn the rulings of Theodore. *Theodore's Penitential* includes a section entitled "The Rite of Women, or their Ministry in the Church." Most versions of the Penitential contain under this rubric a ruling on the exercise of the confessional which states: "According to the canons it is the function of the bishops and priests to prescribe penance." A few manuscripts have, in place of this canon: "No woman may adjudge penance for anyone, since in the canons no one may [do this] except the priests alone."[94] The minority reading is fairly certainly of a later date, since it represents a more developed sacerdotalism, explicitly prohibiting women from exercising authority which is deemed to reside exclusively in men who are ordained. The reading preserved in the majority of manuscripts, on the other hand, appears to belong to the period of compromise, when uncanonical practices – like the double monastery organization itself – were tacitly permitted to continue because they were well-established regional customs and bishops were either unwilling or unable to suppress them;[95] for the statement that "according to the canons it is the function of bishops and priests to assign penance," falls short of positively debarring women from exercising the confessional.

In his account of Abbess Hild in the *History*, Bede relates: "So great was her prudence that not only ordinary people, but also kings and princes, sometimes sought out and received her advice when in difficulties."[96] Subsequently, he reports that Hild was called "Mother" by all who knew her. Bede's remarks are apt to suggest that Hild fulfilled the role of a local wise-woman, offering motherly advice on practical problems. In view of the adoption of a confessorial office by abbesses of double monasteries, however, it is likely that Hild's advice was not confined to purely secular matters, and that Bede has attempted to gloss over her role as spiritual advisor to the laity because it conflicted with his sacerdotalist convictions. But whereas Eangyth's letter suggests a formal conception of a director of conscience, derived from the spiritual authority that the *Rule of Benedict* invests in abbots, Bede's terse allusion to Hild's role as advisor to members of the laity who were in difficulties suggests the kind of informally constituted ministry that underlies the hagiographical idealization of Cuthbert and Guthlac as consolers of the sins and sufferings to which the human race is heir, who inspired the laity to seek them out and confide in them because of their reputation for holiness. Hild's role as advisor to the laity presumably reflects the Celtic traditions in which Whitby was founded: in the early Irish church, women ascetics, as well as men, occasionally acted as confessors and spiritual guides. Nor were their ministrations confined to the laity. The earliest Life of the 6th century saint, St Brendan, relates that he made his confession to a woman ascetic and teacher called St Ita,[97] and St Columban – the founder of

---

[94] *Theodore's Penitential,* II.vii.2; see McNeill, p. 205.

[95] See *Theodore's Penitential,* II.vi.8.

[96] C&M, p. 409; HE, IV.23.

[97] *Vita Prima Sancti Brendani,* ed. C. Plummer, *Vitae Sanctorum Hiberniae* (Oxford, 1910), I, 98–151, ch. 71. The Lives may have taken shape in the 12th c., but "contain earlier, sometimes primitive, materials" (Plummer, I, lxxxix). In the later middle ages, women anchorites acted as advisors to the laity, recluses having (paradoxically) become more socially accessible than monastics; see A.K. Warren, *Anchorites and their Patrons in Medieval England* (Berkeley, 1985), pp. 108–11, 163, 178, 203–6, 281.

Abbess Fara's monastery – is said, in his youth, to have sought out the spiritual advice of a woman who was famed for her holiness of life.[98] Bede's foregrounding of the "kings and princes" who sought Hild's advice recalls the link between kings and socially marginal advisors drawn in Felix's *Life of Guthlac*, and reveals that, although abbesses are subordinated to bishops in Bede's hierarchical scheme, spiritual leadership was for him so superior in kind that he could countenance even an abbess (and particularly, perhaps, a royal abbess) exercising a guiding influence over the highest secular powers in the land.[99]

Hild and Eangyth, then, in differing ways, represent the exercise of spiritual authority by abbesses – whereas Eangyth's confessorial offices may not have extended beyond her double monastery, Hild's lay ministry reflects Whitby's multi-faceted involvement in the activities of the Northumbrian church. *Theodore's Penitential* does not, of course, preclude women from acting as directors of conscience, provided that they do not formally adjudge penances. Sacramental absolution, on the other hand, can only be given by a priest. The exclusive concern with the lawfulness of women prescribing penance in *Theodore's Penitential* suggests that their exercise of the confessional did not entail absolution. But in this respect, their administration of confession is unlikely to have differed from prevailing practice, since confession was not generally held to be a sacrament until the 12th century, and in the early Roman church absolution was intimated by the laying on of hands or by a prayer, but not by declarative statement.[100] The prevailingly non-sacramental character of confession, then, means that the confessional ministry of an abbess could be regarded merely as an authoritatively sanctioned version of the ministry of all believers. Conceived in the formal terms that Eangyth employs for her role, and accompanied by the assignment of penances, however, the confessional ministry of an abbess would be scarcely distinguishable from that of a priest.[101]

The shortage of priests experienced by the early church in England evidently continued for some time after its re-establishment under Theodore; this doubtless helps to explain the adoption of priestly roles by abbesses and the *Penitential*'s reluctance to preclude them from the exercise of the confessional.[102] But Eangyth's wide-reaching assumption of responsibility for the souls in her care and Hild's extension of her spiritual leadership into a pastoral ministry draw their impetus from the secular status of royal women and their customary

---

[98] *Jonas's Life of Columban*, I.8. McNeill, p. 28, accepts as factual the testimony of the Life of Brendan and of this 7th c. Life, but notes that the Penitential of Columban enjoins confession to a priest. Cf. A.J. Frantzen, *The Literature of Penance in Anglo-Saxon England* (New Brunswick, NJ, 1983), p. 53, concerning *The Life of Brigid* in *The Book of Lismore*: "There is no monastic precedent for a woman's performing the confessor's office, and this story does not mean that women administered the sacrament. Rather, it shows the saint working as an intercessor."

[99] See further fn. 62.

[100] Göller, pp. 125–97, sets out the complexity of this issue; ideas rightly described as sacramental were indubitably associated with penance in the ancient church, but there was no authoritative teaching on the subject.

[101] For Abbess Æbbe's mediation of Wilfrid's sacerdotal power to bind and unbind in her cure of souls (*Life of Wilfrid*, chs. 37–9), see pp. 169–72.

[102] See esp. *Theodore's Penitential*, I.xii.7: "It shall be permitted if necessary that confession be made to God alone. And this [word] 'necessary' is not in some codices." Cf. *Theodore's Penitential*, II.vi.16: "It is also a liberty [*libertas*] of the monastery to adjudge penance to laymen for this is properly a function of the clergy" (McNeill, pp. 195, 205).

participation in the rule of the kingdom – just as the queen is conceived as exercising a protective leadership that parallels that of the king so the role of the abbess parallels that of ecclesiastical office-holders. Hild in particular, dispelling difficulties through wise advice, replicates in the ecclesiastical sphere the role that characterizes the queen as a secular leader. Fundamental to women's participation in the ministry, however, was a willingness to regard them as fellow creatures rather than a distinct and inferior species. *Theodore's Penitential* reveals that monastic women also took part in liturgical celebration and the administration of the mass; most versions of the *Penitential* declare that it is permissible for them to "read the lections and to perform the ministries which pertain to the sacred altar, except those which are the special function of priests and deacons."[103] Theodore, conceivably, found in the office of deaconess a precedent which served to justify, at least in part, the participatory role of English abbesses like Hild; the office of deaconess originated in the Eastern church, and the forms of participation this canon permits equate with the office of deaconess.[104] But a later version of this canon, incorporating a mid 8th century reply of Pope Zacharias to an enquiry of the Gallican clergy, reads: "Women shall not cover the altar with the corporal nor place on the altar the offerings, nor the cup, nor stand among the ordained men in the church, nor sit at a feast among priests."[105] Whereas the earlier canon's conception of ecclesiastical office as the unique prerogative of ordained men still enables women to retain a marginal role in the administration of the mass, the later canon further enhances the elite status of priests by reducing the status of women. As the unique involvement of priests in sacred mysteries elevated them towards divinity, women became simultaneously unholy in their frail carnality and scarcely fit for membership in the body of Christ.

The Boniface Circle: Consolations of Kinship and Community in Christ

Eangyth's letter to Boniface, addressing him as a confidant and kindred spirit, who will identify in perfect understanding with her troubles by the power of love, stands in contrast to monastic women's preclusion from association with male ecclesiastics under the combined pressures of the sacerdotal elitism and generic hostility which is reflected in the later versions of *Theodore's Penitential*. Mystic community in the bonds of the spirit and kinship of flesh and blood, although regarded, in ideal terms, as entirely distinct, merge inextricably in the correspondence of the Boniface circle, and community in Christ is apprehended analogously through secular conceptions of family relation. Boniface's own sense of the church as a family was strong. Involved in a dispute with Rome over the alleged consanguinity of a marriage between a woman and her son's godfather, he affirmed his belief in the church as a family whose relational bonds, created by the sacraments, were entirely supra-natural: "by holy baptism we all

---

103 *Theodore's Penitential*, II.vii.1.
104 For a study of this office, see Davies, 1–11.
105 McNeill, p. 205: cf. MGH *Conc Capit* I, 19 (see Bateson, 163).

become sons and daughters, brothers and sisters of Christ and the Church."[106] But in calling on the English church to pray for the conversion of the Saxons, he located his sense of human fellow-feeling in physical affinity: "Have pity them, for even they themselves are wont to say, 'We are of one blood and one bone."[107] Boniface was presumably aware of the ethnic identity of the English and continental Saxons, but he surely has in mind here the ultimate kinship of all members of the human race, the literal oneness of flesh and blood of all human beings through their common derivation from Adam and Eve.

Like the mystic unity of all believers in the love of Christ, and the conception of the religious orders joined in a common purpose while beset by the troubles afflicting all humanity, the familial conception of Christianity is inclusive, working towards a sense of identity with monastic women and against their alterization: "All who do the will of my Father are my mother and sister," Alcuin quoted, attempting to console the bereaved Abbess Æthelthryth by offering himself as a surrogate for the son that she had lost.[108] Kinship bonds, by their social primacy, readily offered themselves as a matrix for the friendships of monastic men and women; such friendships, in the face of the steady foregrounding of eroticism and the constitution of women as embodiments of sexual temptation, became increasingly unsustainable.

The laments for the loss of male kinsmen which echo in the letters of monastic women in the Boniface circle suggest that the monasteries were more often a refuge from the plight of kinlessness than a locus for the renunciation of earthly ties. The epistolary laments of monastic women echo in naturalistic form the conventional role of women as mourners for the death of male kinsmen in vernacular literature. The literary convention encapsulates the physical vulnerability of kinless women, their particular dependence on family protection.[109] But the grief that inheres in the death of kin is not merely the loss of physical protection. The letters of Eangyth, Ecgburg and Leoba emphasize, not the writers' fears for their safety, but the absence of existential comfort and emotional solidarity that they derived from the presence of family. In asking Boniface to fulfill the role of a surrogate brother they express their confidence that the affectionate care of the absent Boniface, humanly embodying the invisible love of Christ, will fill the void created by the absence of kindred. For Leoba and Ecgburg, however, Christian fraternity and kinship affinity overlap, for both of them are moved to ask Boniface to be a surrogate brother to them on the basis of their connexion with him through kinship relation.

---

[106] Emerton, p. 63; Tangl, 33.

[107] EHD I, 813; Tangl, 46.

[108] Matt. 12.50; Duemmler, 105.

[109] With Hildeburg as mourner for her son and brother in Beowulf, ll. 1114–18, cf. the female laments in the Eddic lays of Guthrun, esp. Guthrúnarkvitha I, ed. Kuhn, I, 202–6. Other examples, and the stereotypicality of female grief in Germanic literature, are surveyed by Renoir, 1975, pp. 224–51. See also U. Schaefer, "Two Women in Need of a Friend: A Comparison of The Wife's Lament and Eangyth's Letter to Boniface" in Germanic Dialects: Linguistic and Philological Investigations, ed. B. Brogyanyi and T. Krömmelbein (Amsterdam, 1986), pp. 491–524. C.E. Fell, "Some Implications of the Boniface Correspondence," ed. Damico and Olsen, pp. 29–43, considers that Christianity's effect was "to encourage a greater emotional openness than had been traditional in a more stoical Germanic ethos," and that women in the Boniface circle should not be regarded as "more emotional or more self-pitying than their male counterparts" (p. 41).

Eangyth's letter reveals implicitly the precarious position of an abbess who was unable to draw on the support of family connexions to protect her monastery against secular powers. Of all the many troubles besetting her rule that she confides to Boniface, her crowning grief is her lack of "friends, connexions and relatives, whether by alliance or blood." Eangyth is a living analogue of the Last Survivor of lyric lament; like the Wanderer and the Seafarer, confronted by the evidence of universal mutability, her mind runs on the coming of the Last Judgment and the kingdom of heaven, when earthly grief will have passed away.[110] Death and the pilgrimage to Rome have claimed all but her widowed daughter and a sister who is old, leaving them no-one to rely on but the son of a brother. But even he is a broken reed. Sunk in gloom because the king holds his family in contempt, he wishes, like Eangyth herself, to put the miseries of his homeland behind him and seek a better place. Eangyth asks Boniface to assist him if he should chance to make his way to the mission. Without the backing of family connexions Eangyth is, implicitly, unable to resist claims for services due to the king and the queen, the bishop and other secular officials. Her difficulties are exacerbated by her brother's fall from favour. This, if it is not the underlying cause of accusations made to the king in an attempt to gain her monastery's land through confiscation, has evident potential for exposing her further to the hostility of the king of which she complains.

For women like Eangyth, lacking the support of either their own kin or their husband's kin, the church represented an alternative form of protection, particularly if they inherited property. It is thus not surprising that a number of early abbesses were widows as Eangyth was. Against the claims of secular powers bishops in particular, specifically charged with the responsibility for protecting the monasteries, did what they could; as the protectors of monastic women struggling to retain their estates, churchmen were often, quite literally, surrogate brothers. Boniface, before he embarked on his mission to the continent, obtained for Abbess Eadburg a written account of the vision of a monk at the Mercian double monastery of Abbess Mildburg, in which the monk had foreseen the eternal damnation of Ceolred of Mercia, a notorious violator of monastic privilege;[111] the circulation of this vision doubtless afforded protection of a kind. Boniface himself was to draw on it for aid, decades later, when he joined forces with seven of his episcopal brethren and wrote to Ceolred's successor Æthelbald.[112] He warned Æthelbald of the eternal dangers awaiting him if he followed Ceolred's footsteps in disregarding customary privilege by taxing the monasteries and seizing their property – his letter, however, is over-ridingly concerned to protect monastic women against Æthelbald's sexual depredations, an endemic hazard of which Eangyth makes no mention. Perhaps she includes it among "those things which can be more easily imagined than described," though it is more likely that Boniface's preoccupation with monastic women's chastity in this late letter reflects his shift to a misogynist conviction that the inherent carnal frailty of women posed a danger that over-rode all other fears on

---

110 See *The Wanderer*, esp. ll. 64ff., *The Seafarer* (ASPR III, 143–7), esp. ll. 48ff.
111 Tangl, 10.
112 Tangl, 73.

their behalf.[113] But, whether against financial or sexual depredations, the episcopal pen, especially when wielded at a distance, was less effective than an
avenging kinsman's sword. Eangyth evidently regards family connexions as the
only conceivable form of protection. Eangyth's problems are compounded, however, by the fact that her bishop, far from affording protection against secular
powers, is joined with them in demanding dues from the monastery.[114]

Despite the implicitly precarious position of Eangyth, she does not present
herself as threatened or ask Boniface to lend practical assistance; her over-riding
emotion is the wearisomeness of the burdens of office, and the plight of kinlessness for her consists in existential isolation. What she asks Boniface to supply is
wise advice and confidential intimacy of a kind that she might otherwise have
found among members of her family – her daughter, she explains, is too young
to share her confidences. Ecgburg, whose letter to Boniface laments the recent
death of her brother, Oshere, does convey a generalized sense of imminent
danger – his removal by a "cruel and bitter death" perhaps conveys that he fell
in battle – but the absence of physical protection is not the essence of her
lament. The departure of Ecgburg's sister, seemingly lost to her forever by her
pilgrimage to Rome, affects her as painfully as the death of her brother. Her
sense of physical identity with the sister from whom she has been severed is
acute: "She with whom I had grown up, whom I adored and who was nursed at
the same mother's breast."

Without the presence of her family, Ecgburg feels herself to be existentially
adrift. Psychologically buffeted by tempests and floundering amidst waves, she
finds in Boniface an anchor to cling to: "Yet I shall always hold your neck
entwined with a sisterly embrace." Secular and devout conceptions of consolation coexist uneasily in her letter. On the one hand, Boniface offers a tangible
link with her dead brother through his former friendship with him, and, by his
intimacy with her near relation, he assumes the aspect of a surrogate brother in
whom she can place her trust: "Since cruel and bitter death has taken from me
one whom I loved beyond all others, my own brother Oshere, I have cherished
you in my affection above almost all other men. . . . Believe then, as God is my
witness, that I hold you in deepest affection, and trust that you are never
unmindful of the affection that you assuredly had for my brother." On the other
hand, Boniface is, as her former teacher, a source of intangible support through
his prayers. As Christ assured his disciples that he remained present with them
in the spirit, "even unto the end of the world,"[115] so Ecgburg appeals to Boniface: "I call to you out of the depths of my heart and from the ends of the earth,

---

[113] Boniface's letter to Æthelbald (746/7), while condemning the king for his sexual depredations among monastic women, also shows a tendency to regard monastic women themselves as
generically frail, in its judgemental strictures on those who give birth to illegitimate children;
this letter (Tangl, 73) is contemporaneous with Boniface's letter to Cuthbert of Canterbury
(Tangl, 78); see further below.
[114] Theodore's 673 synod of Hertford, which ruled that no bishop was to interfere with the
monasteries, nor take anything from them forcibly (HE, IV.5), is an index of the prevalence of
this problem. Tangl's 719x722 dating places Eangyth's letter within the reign of Æthelbald of
Mercia (716–757), but the crimes against the monasteries with which Boniface taxes Æthelbald
(Tangl, 73), although echoing the burden of Eangyth's complaint, were too widespread to
warrant the conclusion that Eangyth's monastery was located in Mercia.
[115] Matt 28.20.

O my blessed master, to set me upon the rock of your prayer." Faith in the sustaining power of Boniface's unseen and omnipresent care requires, nevertheless, the aid of a visible sign: "I beg you earnestly to send me some little remembrance, perhaps a holy relic or at least a few written words, so that I may always have you with me."[116] For Bugga, the affectionate care of the absent Boniface was an efficacious consolation, affording a specific, human embodiment of the unseen and invisible love of the departed Christ; "I am confident," she wrote to him "that no change of earthly conditions can turn me away from the sheltering care of your affection. The power of love grows warm within me, as I perceive that through the support of your prayers I reached the haven of a certain peace."[117] Yet, for all this, she too asks for the consolation of some texts for meditation written in his own hand, and even the consolation that Boniface derived from the copies of devotional books sent from England may have sprung not only from the wisdom they contained but from the fact that they were tangible signs of the affectionate care of the monastic women who were his friends: the copy of the *Epistle of Peter* that he asked Abbess Eadburg to send was to be written in her own hand.[118]

Leoba, writing to Boniface as a young nun, reminded him of his kinship relation to her mother and his former friendship with her father. "I am my parents' only child and I would like to regard you as my brother, for there is no-one in my family in whom I can put my trust as I can in you." Leoba, in contrast to Ecgburg, is not devoid of existential moorings, but merely expresses the wish that the archbishop will hold her in mind, and sends a gift for the purpose of jogging his memory: "I wish to remind you of my lowly self, so that, in spite of the distance that separates us, you may not forget me, but rather be knit more closely to me in the bond of true affection."[119] Leoba asked for Boniface's prayers, and for his interest in her studies, particularly her study of the rules of prosody under Abbess Eadburg, and she sent a four line verse of prayer for his well-being, as a specimen of her budding talent. Leoba begins her letter by reminding Boniface of his friendship with her dead father, and she may seem to be seeking a substitute for paternal care, but, with promising independence and egalitarian spirit, what she says she seeks is a surrogate brother, and "beloved brother" is what she calls him.

Leoba, as kinless woman seeking a male protector in whom she could put her trust, gives the impression of adopting, with no particular emotional commitment, a socially conventional posture. It very probably was. Her request for the interest of Boniface is echoed in a more sophisticated manner by Cena: "I must confess to you dearest friend, that although my bodily eyes see you but seldom, I never cease to look on you with the eyes of the spirit. . . . I beg you by our

[116] Emerton, pp. 34–5; Tangl, 13. Ecgburg is tentatively identified as sister of King Oshere of the Hwicce and as Abbess of Gloucester (Sims-Williams, 1990, pp. 220–9).

[117] Emerton, p. 40; Tangl, 15.

[118] Tangl, 35.

[119] Talbot, 1954, p. 87; Tangl, 29. Leoba was conceivably aware that Boniface had been the teacher of a number of monastic women (see *Life of Boniface*, ch. 2). Like Aldhelm, he was the author of a treatise on grammar (incorporating metrics) which was used in monastic schools (ed. B. Löfstedt and G.J. Gebauer, CCSL 133B [Turnhout, 1980]).

trusted friendship to be loyal to my insignificance, as I have faith in you, and to aid me with your prayers."[120] About the particular friendships of monastic men and women, with their accompanying exchange of gifts and verses, there is a suggestion of a lover-like attachment not quite consistent with the universal extension of *caritas*.[121] The late 8th century council that forbade nuns to write or send *wineleodas* ("lovesongs") evidently thought that monastic women's particular attachments were deeply suspect – although an ecclesiastical council's ability to be profoundly disturbed by metrical prayers of the kind that Leoba sent to Boniface cannot be outruled.[122] Lul sensed a conflict too, but a minor one. Writing to thank an abbess and a nun for having nursed him back to health and for their continuing love of him as a brother in Christ, he sent them each a specimen of his metrical accomplishments, acrostically addressing them both by name, and begging them to keep the poems a secret – the point, I take it, is that Lul feared that his ingenuity would be insufficient to meet the demand that would inevitably grip the entire convent: "I beg you . . . not to show this work to any one without my consent, or to betray the author of it without my permission, that a dangerous crop of envy may not grow, where the concord of true peace should flourish."[123]

To a post-Freudian era, Ecgburg's metaphorical clinging to the neck of Boniface in a sisterly embrace patently invites analysis: though nowhere near so pressingly as the letters of Alcuin to Bishop Arno. In the manner of the bride sorrowing in absence in *Canticles*, Alcuin was, he informed the bishop, "wounded with love," and his wounds remained open until such time as the bishop's countenance shone upon him.[124] Later, Alcuin reciprocated a gift from the bishop by sending two cowls and one white blanket.[125] The innocence of Alcuin's relation to Bishop Arno is held – somewhat shakily – to be vouched for by his letter to a former pupil in which he reproaches him for nameless recidivist behaviour.[126] Alcuin can, alternatively, be merely regarded as having found in *Canticles* a new expressive rhetoric for the emotions he felt for Abbot Æthelheard, whose strength could be expressed only by analogy with kinship affections: "I confess that I have wearied myself to exhaustion with grieving after you and been saddened to tears by your absence. I have not been so exhausted during my whole life abroad by affection for a brother or sister after the flesh as I have by an overwhelming longing for you, my spiritual brother."[127] The nun Berhtgyth, appealing for a visit from her brother, who was, like her, a member of

---

[120] Emerton, p. 173; Tangl, 97.

[121] The friendship of Fortunatus and Radegund, the 6th c. abbess of Poitiers, from which sprang the earliest poetic exchanges between a male and female religious (Radegund's poems do not survive) may have been regarded with some disapprobation. Fortunatus hints at murmurs concerning his friendship with Radegund and her daughter Agnes: see *Opera Poetica*, 11.6: ed. F. Leo, MGH AA 4.1 (Berlin, 1881). A letter to Radegund from Abbess Caesaria of Arles advises her against excessive asceticism but cautions against the dangers of having the company of men too often (Wemple, p. 147).

[122] Capitulary of Charlemagne, 789 (MGH, *Capit Reg Franc*, I, 63).

[123] Kylie, pp. 101–2; Tangl, 98.

[124] Duemmler, 159.

[125] Duemmler, 254. For discussion of Alcuin's poems to Arno, see T. Stehling, trans., *Medieval Latin Poems of Male Love and Friendship* (New York, 1984), pp. xvii–xxxiii.

[126] Duemmler, 294.

[127] Trans. Allott, p. 16; Duemmler, 9.

a religious order, but in another country, also availed herself of the imagery of *Canticles* to express her longing for him: "Sadness has never departed from my soul, nor do I rest in mind through sleep, because love is as strong as death."[128] In the context of the intensity of kinship ties, Ecgburg's figurative clinging in a sisterly embrace to the neck of her brother's friend, Boniface, is perhaps less latent – or at any rate, more latent with incest than elective eroticism – than it at first sight appears.

Monastic friendships between men and women were constituted as analogues of the primary social relation, the ties of kinship. In time the highly developed erotic consciousness promulgated by ecclesiastical councils would take effect in the segregation of the monasteries. Ultimately, *Canticles'* celebration of mystic union, for which the nearest earthly analogue known to Berhtgyth was the union of brother and sister, and for Alcuin male friendship, would attach itself to the postures assumed by Lul when he offered his humble poems with respectful effusions to the altogether superior judgments of his favoured monastic recipients – for whatever the origins of *fine amour*, the monastic friendships such as those of the Boniface circle, flourishing on non-consummation and conscious always of a higher love beyond their immediate object, are surely among them.[129] In the interim, the dominance of kinship as a relational mode enabled the double monasteries to continue, and with them the friendships of monastic men and women.

Eangyth's Journey and Boniface as Spiritual Mentor

The letters of the Boniface circle offer a view of the relations of monastic men and women very different from the official, hierarchical relations that characterize Bede's delineation of the interaction of bishops and abbesses. For the monastic women who sought the help of Boniface in a troubled world, the Holy Spirit was not an abstraction but inhered in specific human relations – for them, the absent Boniface, like the ideal confessor-cum-spiritual guide in Felix's *Life of Guthlac*, was a Christ figure, a universal Comforter, embodying and mediating the invisible spirit of love wherein Christ remains present in the world, able by his *caritas* to identify sympathetically with their troubles. Operating within the familial, egalitarian conception of the church that Boniface himself espouses, they address him not as a priestly Father but a brother in the spirit. But the bonds of fellowship in the unity of the spirit merge with kinship ties, investing the familial metaphors of Christianity with the same emotional potency as social relations. Spiritual community also serves as compensation for the loss of kin, and the understanding comfort and existential support that monastic

---

128 Tangl, 147, cf. Cant 8.6; for other letters of Berhtgyth, see Tangl, 143, 148.
129 P. Dronke, *Women Writers of the Middle Ages* (Cambridge, 1984), pp. 30–5, likens Berhtgyth's verses for her brother to vernacular "women's songs" such as *Wulf and Eadwacer*; see also C. Davidson, "Erotic 'Women's Songs' in Anglo-Saxon England," *Neophilologus* 59 (1975), 451–62.

women seek from Boniface is an expectation formed by their conceptions of the role of kinsmen.

Eangyth, particularly, without friends, relations or family (except for a daughter too young to share her confidences, a sister, by implication, too old, and a nephew preoccupied with his own troubles), in approaching Boniface as trusted confidant and sympathetic advisor, casts him in a role which, in secular society, was held by "friendly kinsmen." Eangyth sought the advice of Boniface on a pilgrimage that she wished to make to Rome with her daughter, who was, like Eangyth, a widow and a nun – for Eangyth, at least, it was a one-way pilgrimage, since her desire to relinquish the burden of ruling a monastery beset by difficulties is made apparent to Boniface, and her reference to her advanced age suggests that, like Abbot Ceolfrith of Wearmouth and King Cædwalla of Wessex, she hoped to find her last resting place among the saints at Rome.[130] Departure on a journey, in the vernacular literature, is the focus of conflicting emotions. Though exiles and solitary wanderers are, in their severance from homeland and kindred, defined by vernacular literature as the epitome of human misery, vernacular literature also presents joyful voyagers and heroic adventurers for whom the journey is a gateway to fame and fortune;[131] the ambivalence of the journey motif in vernacular literature reflects not merely tensions between fear of the unknown and adventurous curiosity, but tensions between individualist aspiration on the one hand, embeddedness in community and corporate identity on the other.

Entry to a monastery – conceived as voluntary self-exile – severed the individual from kindred and homeland; in the context of a society in which identity consisted of membership in a kin group, such a severance was truly a journey into new terrain. The actual heroic dimensions of early female monasticism are thus defined, not by Aldhelm's depictions of the nuns of Barking locked in hand to hand combat with the deadly sins, but in his image of them as journeyers – like a swarm of bees, the nuns of Barking have followed the call of their Leader, and, abandoning the secure comfort of their homeland, have travelled into foreign parts.[132] The sailor's wife in *Maxims I*, loyally awaiting her husband's homecoming, like the woman in *Wulf and Eadwacer* who sits weeping while Wulf wanders wide, are images of women whose lot it is to sit and wait,[133] but

---

[130] See *HE*, V.7; *Historia Abbatum Auctore Anonymo*, ch. 21: ed. Plummer, 1896, I, 388–404 (subsequently referred to as *Life of Ceolfrith*).
[131] In *Widsith* (ASPR III, 149–53), the scop rejoices in the material rewards of the peripatetic life; see also Beowulf's willing journey to win fame and fortune at Hrothgar's court (*Beowulf*, ll. 210–28; cf. Hygelac's apprehension, ll. 1987–98). Scholarship stresses the figural dimensions of exile and journeying in the OE lyric-elegies; the same themes and attitudes are expressed in contexts which do not prompt an allegorical reading, making it feasible to regard the lyric-elegies, at a literal level, as culturally indicative.
[132] *De Virginitate*, ch. 6.
[133] *Maxims I*, ll. 93–9; *Wulf and Eadwacer*, ll. 9–10. Cf. the woman in *The Wife's Lament*, who speaks as one who must sit and weep, but recalls earlier journeys in search of her absent mate, and *The Husband's Message*, which calls the woman to take ship and share the good fortune that the man to whom she has sworn vows has won in another land. *Maxims I*'s approving portrait of the sailor's wife reveals that, already, the woman who wanders is associated with sexual promiscuity; but this passage, like *Maxims I*, ll. 63–6, is not a condemnation of female frailty but a warning against the acquisition of an ill-reputation.

Elene[134] and Thryth[135] are, in their different ways, heroic voyagers, and monastic women were well-represented among those who made the pilgrimage to Rome.[136] Ecgburg's lament for her sister Withburg, incarcerated in Rome,[137] suggests the extreme difficulty that Withburg must have experienced in detaching herself from incorporation in the family group:

> And when at the same time my dearest sister vanished from my sight – a new wound and a new grief; she with whom I had grown up, whom I adored and who was nursed at the same mother's breast – Christ be my witness, everywhere was grief and terror and the dread of death. Gladly would I have died if it had so pleased God.

Predominately, Eangyth's projected pilgrimage to Rome, like her brother's intention of joining the continental mission, appears in her letter as an escape from the plight of kinlessness. But there is also a flicker of curiosity, and a desire to take part in one of the major adventures of her era when she speaks of her desire to visit "the mistress of the world," as so many of her friends and relations have done. In her impulse to take council before setting out, Eangyth is paralleled by St Willibald, later Bishop of Eichstadt, whose journeys to Rome and the Holy Land are recorded by Hygeburg; unaffected by the world-denying idealism that universally afflicts later hagiographers, Hygeburg does not conceal the fact that Willibald, though moved by devotion, was also eager to travel to foreign parts and find out all about them. Hygeburg's account of Willibald reveals, as clearly as the Boniface correspondence, the persistent strength of kinship ties among those who had, in theory, renounced them for the new, spiritual, relationships postulated by community in Christ. Despite the fact that Willibald had spent his life in the monastery to which he had been vowed in his infancy, it was not to his abbot that he went for advice and permission when he decided to "brave the perils of the sea." Instead, Willibald went immediately to his father and opened his heart to him, telling him the secrets he had concealed from others. The account of Willibald also illustrates the tensions between Christian individualism and Anglo-Saxon quasi-tribal identity. For despite the fact that Willibald had decided to be an exile for Christ and forsake his country, parents, and relatives, he urged his father to accompany him to Rome, and, in

---

134 See *Elene*, esp. ll. 225–75.

135 See *Beowulf*, ll. 1931–62. Thryth as journeyer is, in fact, representative of aristocratic women given in marriage, since they normally travelled considerable distances to the bridegroom's court (see, e.g., the account of Eanfled of Kent's perilous journey to Northumbria, *HE*, III.15). For women, marriage had the aspect of a heroic enterprise, and in having gained renown following a sea-voyage, Thryth is not only a foil to virtuous queen Hygd, but parallels the transformation of the hero through his exploit across the sea (cf. *Beowulf*, ll. 2183–9). Female travellers included the East Anglian and Kentish women who travelled to the Frankish monasteries "to be wedded to the heavenly bridegroom" (*HE*, III.8), as well as Anglo-Saxon nuns like Leoba and Hygeburg who joined the mission to the continent.

136 So Boniface believed (Tangl, 78); see also fns. 142, 161. Queens also travelled to Rome; see fn. 155.

137 Ecgburg probably means that Withburg had become an enclosed anchorite, although her sister may have been the same Withburg whose brother travelled to Rome because he feared she had been imprisoned there; see W.J. Moore, *The Saxon Pilgrims to Rome and the Schola Saxonum* (Fribourg, 1937), pp. 46–54.

the event, Willibald became an exile for Christ in the company of his father, his brother, and a band of friends and relations.[138] If, then, Eangyth seems to have a tenuous grasp on the authority of the individual conscience in asking Boniface to endorse her conviction of the rightness of her pilgrimage to Rome, she is impeded not only by the supreme authority claimed for ecclesiastical law but by her membership of a society in which the conception of individuals was not strong; conceivably, individualist self-conception in the Anglo-Saxon world was chiefly attained by those who, like Eangyth, had no surviving family group to which they belonged.

The specific point on which Eangyth sought Boniface's advice concerning her journey to Rome with her daughter was an objection that called for the understanding of a fellow member of the church: "We know how many there are who scoff at this wish and deprecate this desire, and support their view by adducing what the canons of the synods enjoin, that wherever anyone has settled and taken a vow, there shall he remain and there serve God." Relative to her time, the weight that Eangyth gives to this objection seems over-scrupulous. Bede reports that, in the late 7th century, Ine of Wessex set a fashion for the pilgrimage to Rome that was followed by all classes of society:

> After he had ruled over the West Saxons for thirty-seven years, he left his kingdom to younger men and went to the threshold of the apostles, while Gregory was pope, to spend some of his time upon earth as a pilgrim in the neighbourhood of the holy places, so that he might be thought worthy to receive a greater welcome from the saints in heaven. At this time many Englishmen, both nobles and commons, layfolk and clergy, men and women, were eager to do the same thing.[139]

The monastic women who travelled to Rome throughout the 8th century, were evidently no more deterred by canon laws and monastic rules enjoining stability than their monastic brothers were:[140] the abbess whom Ælffled of Whitby sped on her way to Rome at the time that Eangyth was writing had been held back from fulfilling a lifetime ambition only because Ælffled had needed her assistance.[141] It is very probably in consideration of canon law, however, that Bede, whose orthodoxy was undoubtedly scrupulous, gives the impression that it was members of the laity and clergy who were stirred to follow in Ine's footsteps. Synodical pronouncements seeking to enforce the claustration of women in the second half of the 8th century – significantly not an issue for Eangyth – did not

[138] *The Hodoeporicon of St Willibald by Huneberc of Heidenheim*, trans. Talbot, pp. 153–177; *Vita Willibaldi Episcopi Echstetensis*, ed. O. Holder-Egger, MGH SS 15.1 (Hannover, 1887), 86–106, chs. 2, 3. (Hygeburg of Heidenheim's work is hereafter referred to as *Life of Willibald*.) Hild, too, deciding to be an exile for Christ, set out for the Frankish monastery where her sister was resident (HE, IV.23); see further pp. 255–6. Cf. Boniface, whose entry to a monastery was opposed by his father and was made possible by his death (*Life of Boniface*, chs. 1, 5).

[139] C&M, p. 473; HE, V.7.

[140] See, e.g., Council of Hertford, (HE, IV.5); *Rule of Benedict*, chs. 58, 66, 67. Benedict Biscop spent so much time in Rome that he appointed a proxy to run the Wearmouth monastery (*History of the Abbots*, ch. 7).

[141] See Tangl, 8.

effectively debar them from making the pilgrimage to Rome either.[142] The opposition Eangyth encountered presumably came from within her monastery: she states that her former abbess was acquainted with her wish, but elaborates no further. It is not inconceivable that a bishop who joined with secular powers in claiming what was due to him was also capable of claiming a right of jurisdiction over the abbess's movements, although Eangyth does not appear to consider herself answerable to any one but herself for her decision.[143]

Eangyth's request for the advice of Boniface may be regarded simply as a deeply internalized need for ecclesiastical sanction – a monastery which appears to have been using the *Rule of Benedict* is likely to have been orthodox in its attitudes to canon law.[144] But this is to overlook the fact that Eangyth's approach to Boniface is, in itself, an expression of her refusal to regard canon law as the highest form of authority. In effect, her letter asserts her determination to accept the opinion of someone she can trust to identify completely with her own point of view. In approaching Boniface for the confirmatory assurance of a friend, she locates her validation outside the official structures of ecclesiastical authority. In her final, highly cryptic, dismissal of those who cite canon law, she allies Boniface with her in opposition to outward conformity to the letter of the law as the measure of rectitude. In choosing him as advisor, she affirms her conviction that the heart disposed in charity is the ultimate judge of action: "We have scant faith in those who 'glory in appearances and not in heart,'[145] but faith in your love, your charity in God and your goodness." Or as St Paul also said: "Unto the pure all things are pure."[146]

Eangyth's letter represents an exercise in the judgment of the individual conscience against the claims of ecclesiastical authority, which Gregory the Great adumbrated in the *Libellus Responsionum* as the essence of the law of the New Testament.[147] Eangyth's description of her exercise of the confessional is unusual in its concern to respond to individual distinctiveness – her office entails "ministering to many minds and various dispositions." Gregory's principle of accommodating teaching to different classes and conditions of people[148] was widely current as an axiom, but it is reflected in penitential handbooks chiefly in the instructions to the confessor to bear in mind the generic category

---

[142] Schulenburg, pp. 56–8, lists "at least a dozen separate pieces of legislation from c. 750–850 [which] require strict unbroken active claustration for women religious," including the 796/7 Council of Friuli, which prohibited abbesses and nuns from leaving their monasteries on the pretext of a pilgrimage to Rome or to other holy places. But Alcuin, writing c. 800 to Abbess Æthelburg, voiced no such objections, merely advising her not to blame herself if she was unable to fulfil her vow of pilgrimage, and to give the money she would have spent on travel to the poor (Duemmler, 300).

[143] This is in contrast with continental developments in the second half of the 8th c. outlined by Schulenburg (see fn. 142) who shows that strict enclosure deprived abbesses of autonomy, placing them under the authority of their bishops, and forbidding them to leave their monasteries without episcopal permission.

[144] Familiarity with parts of the *Rule of Benedict* does not necessarily prove first-hand knowledge of the Rule *in toto*; Wearmouth followed a rule compiled by Benedict Biscop from the observances of 17 continental monasteries he had visited (*History of the Abbots*, ch. 11).

[145] 2 Cor. 5.12.

[146] Titus 1.15.

[147] HE, I.27.

[148] See *Regula Pastoralis*, III.1–36.

of penitents in determining the severity of penances, particularly their social class and physical constitution.[149] Eangyth again appears to be echoing the *Rule of Benedict*, which follows *Regula Pastoralis* in requiring abbots to take into account differences in natural disposition when they correct the failings of those who are in their charge.[150] Her reflection on the canonical injunction of stability is similarly an affirmation of individual distinctiveness, which she opposes to the claims of monolithic conformity: "For we all live in different ways, and God's purposes are unknown . . . and his sacred will and desire in these things is hidden." God wills to each individual a different destiny.[151] Eangyth's motives for departure to Rome are, as I have indicated, humanly mixed. But the pilgrimage to Rome was an established form of devout vocation, particularly for those who had long been distracted from contemplation by the cares of office;[152] it was no less a means of serving God than the continued observance of a vow of monastic stability. And as the will of God is hidden, the individual, implicitly, may have as much knowledge of it as anyone else and, even, an inarguable conviction that her own inclinations are in perfect accord with it.

But, instead, Eangyth trusts that the best course of action for her and her daughter will be revealed to Boniface through his prayers. Finally, Eangyth's certainty of her knowledge of the will of God is not sufficient to act upon without objective verification. Her letter nevertheless demonstrates the assimilation of the potentialities of the construct of individualism as a limitation on the claims of ecclesiastical authority. Remarkably, Eangyth's role as an administrator of ecclesiastical law through her exercise of the confessional has engendered, not just an unusually scrupulous regards for canonical injunctions, but a critical view of the absolute and over-riding authority claimed by ecclesiastical law. Just as her conception of ministering to distinctive individuals reflects the theology of confession, so too familiarity with confessional emphasis on the essential distinction between intention and action is reflected in her ability to dismiss those who would over-ride the exercise of her individual judgment by citing canon law as "glorying in appearances and not in heart."

Boniface's reply to Eangyth does not survive, but his reply to an evidently similar request for advice from Abbess Bugga, dated some years after his episcopal consecration in 722, reveals that Eangyth's confidence in him was not misplaced. Boniface disavows the possession of superior judgment and refers the decision to Bugga's own, undoubted, knowledge of the will of God: "Be it known to you, dearest sister, that in regard to the matter on which you have sought my advice I cannot presume, on my own responsibility, to either forbid your pilgrimage or to encourage it. . . . Do what God's grace shall inspire you to do." Boniface was, in fact, positively in favour of Bugga travelling to Rome. Like Eangyth, he was of the opinion that the essential issue was how best to find the circumstances in which to pursue a contemplative vocation. He was no less

---

[149] See, for instance, the preamble to one of the Penitentials ascribed to Bede, ed. Albers, 399–41.
[150] See *Rule of Benedict*, ch. 2; see also chs. 6, 24, 30.
[151] See 1 Cor. 12.
[152] See, e.g., *Life of Ceolfrith*, ch. 21.

encouraging to the fulfilment of individual capacities when he approved Leoba's irregular acceptance of a pupil who was not a postulant, assuring her that whatever she saw fit to do to increase the young woman's merits had his consent.[153] Boniface sympathized with Bugga that, despite having set aside her responsibilities as an abbess in order to withdraw to an anchorage, she found herself still under the necessity of dealing with the demands of secular authorities. He did not, however, wish to pre-empt her decision by insisting that making a pilgrimage to Rome was the obviously right thing for her to do: "It appears to me that if, through the interference of seculars, you cannot find freedom and peace of mind in your native land, you should try (provided you have the will and the power to do so) to find freedom for contemplation by making a pilgrimage abroad."[154] He had also written on her behalf to an English nun named Withburg who, Boniface assured Bugga, had found in Rome the tranquility that she had long sought in vain. Her help is promised, although the tranquility to be found in Rome was evidently relative to the troubled state of England: Withburg advised that it would be best for Bugga to wait until the Saracen attack had died down.

Twenty years or so later, Boniface was exercised by an entirely different kind of danger for women travelling to Rome. He wrote to apprise the Archbishop of Canterbury of the statutes passed under his direction at the council of Soissons, and he added a suggestion for improving the reputation of the English church:

> I will not conceal from Your Grace, that all the servants of God here who are especially versed in scripture and strong in the fear of God are agreed that it would be well and favourable for the honour and purity of your church, and provide a certain shield against vice, if your synod and your princes would forbid matrons and veiled women to make these frequent journeys back and forth to Rome. A great part of them perish and few keep their virtue. There are very few towns in Lombardy or Frankland or Gaul in which there is not a courtesan or a harlot of English stock. It is a scandal and a disgrace to your whole church.

Boniface's perception of women in this letter – a class so incapable of moral judgment that only the imposition of ecclesiastical constraint would serve to prevent them from becoming moral castaways and an embarrassment to the male ecclesiastics who constitute the church – is a far cry from the conception of community in Christ that informs his correspondence. Betraying his solidarity with monastic women as sisters and fellow soldiers of Christ, Boniface emphasizes his sense of identity with the Archbishop of Canterbury by virtue of the unique ecclesiastical authority they possessed: "Our ministry is in one and the same cause," he assured the Archbishop, "and an equal oversight of churches and people is given to us . . . on account of the pallium entrusted to us."[155]

---

153 Tangl, 96.
154 Talbot, 1954, pp. 83–4; Tangl, 27. Variously dated, 725x738; Boniface was invested with the pallium in 732, but it was some years before he was formally installed as Archbishop.
155 Emerton, pp. 136, 140; Tangl, 78. There is perhaps a popular echo of this in *Life of Alfred*, ch. 15, which relates that Eadburg of Wessex ended her life as a woman of ill-repute on the route to Rome.

A decade earlier, Boniface had embroiled himself in an argument with Rome over lawful degrees of consanguinity, and had adduced the traditions of the English church in support of his position.[156] By the time he wrote to the Archbishop of Canterbury and urged him to take control of the English church and bring it into line with the standards of orthodoxy that he was attempting to impose on the continent, Boniface had identified so entirely with the authority of Rome that he was engaged in establishing, that he had come to regard the English as scandalously deviant – not only was the licentious conduct of English women a public disgrace; the drunkenness of English priests was equalled only by the pagans, and compelling monks to work on royal buildings was unheard of anywhere except in England.

Boniface's apprehension of rampant female sexuality at large and needing to be brought under control heralds a legislative movement towards the enclosure of monastic women on the continent.[157] The transmission of continental orthodoxy to England, slowed down by the onset of the Viking invasions, gave to the church of the late Anglo-Saxon period a more markedly misogynist character; the elite construction of male ecclesiastical authority in the work of Bede suggests, however, a parallel development towards the enhancement of episcopal power and dignity and a concomitant depression in the status of monastic women. But it would be wrong to conclude that Boniface's letter to Canterbury rather than his correspondence with monastic women represents his real and effective attitude to them. In the same year that he wrote to Archbishop Cuthbert, or very close to it, Boniface met with an English abbess who was on a pilgrimage to Rome, and there, as her brother the king of Kent reminded him, they frequently visited the shrines of the apostle together.[158] His instruction that Leoba was to share his grave at the Fulda monastery when she died, although evidently an embarrassment to the Fulda monastery by the time of her death,[159] reveals that the alterizing derogation of women that informed his rulings at Soissons and his letter to Canterbury had at least not altered his view of Leoba as a fellow soldier of Christ.[160] The disjunction that existed between the public pronouncements of ecclesiastical legislators and the private relationships of individuals could also exist within the mind of an ecclesiastical legislator.[161]

---

[156] See Tangl, 32, 33, 34, 54.
[157] See Schulenburg, 51–86. Cf. fn. 133.
[158] Tangl, 105. In this case, "Bugga" can be identified with reasonable certainty as the Abbess of Thanet; see fn. 81.
[159] *Life of Leoba*, ch. 17; see further pp. 283–8.
[160] See also fn. 113 above for Tangl, 73.
[161] A letter from a deacon, Gemmulus, informs Boniface that he is taking care of a party of monastic women who have arrived in Rome with recommendations from him (Tangl, 62). As this is dated 745, it is uncertain whether Boniface was motivated by concern for the women or a desire to ensure that they were kept under restraint.

5

The Advice of Women and
Eddius's *Life of Wilfrid*

Bishops versus Royal Women

When Bishop Wilfrid first left home as a lad of fourteen, he gathered together
an armed retinue and went to seek service with Queen Eanfled. She, however,
being impressed by his looks and intelligence, appears to have decided that he
was better suited to the church than to the life of a warrior, and sent him off to
Lindisfarne to look after a former retainer who had retired to the monastery in
his declining years.[1] In this fortuitous fashion, Wilfrid's quest for fame and
fortune took an ecclesiastical turn, and his biography records his attempts to
establish his episcopal position as equal to a king's in rank and wealth, and
supreme in authority. Wilfrid's aspirations make themselves felt early in the Life,
in the account of his first meeting with King Alhfrith. The superiority of Wilfrid
was so overwhelmingly evident to Alhfrith that, when Wilfrid preached to him
on the perfect accord that exists between the body and the soul, Alhfrith
prostrated himself at his feet;[2] and this gratifying demonstration of royal subjugation to spiritual headship is echoed in Bede's *History* by King Oswine, who
kneels at the feet of Bishop Aidan to ask his forgiveness, and by King Sigeberht
when, returning from feasting with an excommunicated kinsman, he is confronted with outraged episcopal authority in the person of Bishop Cedd.[3] At the
time of his first meeting with Alhfrith, Wilfrid, though-indubitably destined for
a bishopric, had not even been admitted to holy orders; Alhfrith himself,
however, was only a youthful sub-king, and elevation to the priesthood was
sufficient to bestow on Wilfrid the status appropriate to an intimate companion
and spiritual mentor of the king.[4]

There is of course no reason why kings and bishops should not, on occasions,
have been on intimate friendly terms, but the hagiographical presentation of
these friendships is patently a polemical projection of a wistful ideal of close and
harmonious relations between secular and ecclesiastical authorities, in which
the relative balance of power that actually obtained is turned on its head.[5]

---

[1] B. Colgrave, ed. and trans., *The Life of Bishop Wilfrid by Eddius Stephanus* (Cambridge, 1927),
ch. 2. Subsequent references are to *Life of Wilfrid* (dated 710x720), unless otherwise stated;
translation throughout is from Colgrave.
[2] Ch. 7.
[3] *HE*, III.14, 22.
[4] Ch. 9.
[5] See esp. chs. 41, 42, 44, 48, 59.

Much the same holds true of the depiction of bishops as the friendly mentors of abbesses and queens. In this role, however, bishops were seemingly less successful than they were with kings, and their relations with queens and abbesses are marked by competitive strains.

The source of this conflict is to be found in the particular nature of the friendship with kings that ecclesiastics envisaged. The projected alliance between the episcopal and royal throne, with the bishop as senior partner, was a version of the joint rule that kings exercised at times in conjunction with a younger kinsman, and particularly when a king's warrior days were past – thus it is that the aged Hrothgar in *Beowulf* sits beside his young kinsman, Hrothulf, on the dais.[6] For Alcuin the golden age of Northumbria had come to pass when Bishop Egbert of York wore the pallium and his brother Eadberht adorned the royal throne; for in those days, two brothers ruled the land, helping each other as kinsmen should.[7] Such brotherly harmony in rule was also a secular ideal, and Alcuin's celebration of a unity in the peace of Christ that succeeded where the unaided bonds of kinship were apt to fail, recalls *Widsith*'s acclamation of a notable, though limited, triumph: "Hrothulf and Hrothgar, nephew and uncle, kept peace together for a very long while, after they had driven off the tribe of the Wicingas."[8] *Beowulf* puts it more ominously, seemingly with an eye to Hrothulf's precipitous seizure of the throne for himself: "There those two worthy men sat, nephew and uncle; at that time the loving bond was still intact and each was true to the other."[9] But a more intimate sharer of the royal throne was the queen.

The queen, Asser asserts, was everywhere but in Wessex the sharer of the king's throne.[10] Queen Edith's eleventh century eulogist confirms the traditional nature of this arrangement: in accordance with law and custom, he explains, a throne at the king's side always stood ready for her.[11] Whether or not we take Asser's narrative at face value, it clearly establishes that throne-sharing, like the title of queen – which was also denied to the king's wife in Wessex – was not an empty ceremonial form. Wessex had eschewed queens, King Alfred gave Asser to understand, since the days when Brihtric of Wessex married Eadburg; like Alfred's own wife, Eadburg was a Mercian, the daughter of Wessex's powerful enemy, King Offa, and Eadburg had turned out to be a murderous tyrant just like her father. The overt point at issue in this story is the power of the queen – specifically, it conveys fear of the untrammelled power of a foreign queen – and the throne-sharing to which the Wessex court objected was an emblematic expression of a queen's participation in her husband's reign.[12] The queen's role as joint ruler and throne-sharer is closely linked with her role as adviser. Tacitus

---

6 *Beowulf*, ll. 1163–5 (see also ll. 2196–9, 2490–508); cf. Sigeberht and Ecgric of East Anglia, HE, III.18.
7 *Song of York*, ll. 1277–84.
8 *Widsith*, ll. 45–9.
9 *Beowulf*, ll. 1163–5.
10 See *Life of Alfred*, chs. 13–14.
11 *Life of King Edward*, p. 42; see also pp. 3–4.
12 P. Stafford, "The King's Wife in Wessex 800–1066," *P&P* 91 (1981), 3–27, regards the story of Eadburg as supporting the successional practices that brought Alfred to the throne, powerful queens being apt to back their sons against the king's brother.

claimed that the Germanic peoples thought highly of the advice of women,[13] and it figures in *Maxims I* as an essential aspect of the queen's joint rulership: "A king must procure a queen with payment, with goblets and with rings. Both must be pre-eminently liberal with gifts. In the man the warlike arts must burgeon and the woman must excel as one cherished among her people, be buoyant of mood, keep confidences, be open-heartedly generous with horses and treasure; in deliberation over the mead and in the presence of the troops of companions, she must always and everywhere greet first the chief of those princes and instantly offer the cup to her lord's hand, and she must know what is prudent for them both [lit. "know what advice to give him"] as rulers of the hall."[14]

The union of the royal pair is conceived here as joint possession and overlordship, just as it is in *The Husband's Message*. The lyric message to the "daughter of a prince," asking her to take ship and join the man who awaits her in accordance with the vows they once spoke, is a call to share once more the treasure and overlordship that he has won – as once they held a city, inhabited one country, may God grant that they two together may hereafter distribute treasure to the warrior band.[15] Marital unity in *Maxims I* similarly entails identity of role. The lady shares what is unanimously regarded as the chief virtue of a lord, liberality to retainers. Like all leader-figures of the period, she offers a version of "counsel and consolation," secular notions of advice and cheer blending easily with the guidance and comfort offered by ecclesiastical mentors.[16] There is a significant fissure in *Maxims I*, however, a division of spheres between the lord's exercise of martial skills on the battle field and the lady's exercise of social skills in the hall. Hers is a parallel lordship within a more restricted sphere, where it interlocks with the lord's. Her role is to duplicate and strengthen the warrior bond between the lord and his retainers by creating her own form of *comitatus*. In effect, her role as overlord is to serve his ultimate headship, since her ceremonial office, by the homage that she pays with the offer of the cup, is to assert his pre-eminence over all who are present at the taking of counsel in the hall – and surely over her also. But if a hierarchical construct of marriage as the union of head and body lurks beneath this, the organic union is fully complete – for *Maxims I*, the final word is that the royal couple are rulers *together*.[17]

The role of Wealhtheow in *Beowulf* follows the configurations of the ideal of the royal wife in *Maxims I*. Wealhtheow is significantly displaced from the public and political life of Heorot, for she is not present among the councillors about the king who formally receive the hero-guest[18] – perhaps a sign that the

[13] *Germania*, ch. 8. See further pp. 190–9.
[14] Bradley, p. 348; *Maxims I*, ll. 81–92 ("ond him ræd witan").
[15] *The Husband's Message*, ll. 13–25; see pp. 49–50.
[16] See further pp. 116–19.
[17] "Boldagendum bæm ætsomne" (l. 92). For an extended study of the socio-political implications of this motif, see M.J. Enright, "Lady with a Mead-Cup: Ritual, Group Cohesion and Hierarchy in the Germanic Warband," FS 22 (1988), 170–203.
[18] See *Beowulf*, ll. 356–490.

poem did, in fact, take its final form in the late Old English period.[19] But within the hall – once the hall is constituted as the site of festivity – Wealhtheow exercises a leadership that parallels and interlocks with Hrothgar's, her postures towards the hero, of welcome and of treasure-giving, on each occasion mirroring the king's. She is the joint possessor of wealth, for her gifts, like Hrothgar's, are ancestral treasures of the kingdom.[20] Her perambulations about the hall, distributing festive cheer with the cup, are the graphic embodiment of her role as peaceweaver, the binding of the body of retainers in the hall to the lord on the throne.[21] As she circulates the cup, she dispenses advice, exhorting Beowulf to gain fame by heroic deeds, urging Hrothgar to be generous, reminding Hrothulf of a kinsman's obligations of loyalty. Her advice, invariably an encouragement to pursue the path of honour, is at the same time explicitly concerned with her sons' inheritance of the kingdom. The queen's involvement in determining the succession was to become a point of conflict between queens and bishops; but Queen Emma's clerical encomiast evidently considered it to her credit that she made it a condition of her marriage to Cnut that her son by him should inherit the throne, because she had heard that Cnut had a concubine.[22] In Wealhtheow's involvement in the determination of the succession there is, *as such*, evidently nothing untoward. But the poem demarcates distinct official and festive spheres, which do not exist for *Maxims I*, where mead-drinking is synonymous with taking counsel. Because of this (and for other reasons), it is impossible to tell whether Wealhtheow's advice on the future disposition of the kingdom in the course of the feast is entirely ideal conduct, or whether, in giving her advice, she exploits her role as hostess in a subtly improper, perhaps even divisive, fashion. For the stereotypes of women with which Germanic literary tradition operates – though originating independently of the Ave/Eva matrix, and distinctive in the ideal of the aristocratic woman as peaceweaver – are also formulated as inversions and perversions of the various roles of the ideal woman, including her role as mistress of the feast. Noticeably, the *Beowulf* poet's ideal foil to the inverted peaceweaver, Thryth, is not Wealhtheow, but the Geatish queen, Hygd – whose offer to Beowulf of the throne and treasure-hoard of the fallen king nevertheless endorses, *in principle*, the rectitude of Wealhtheow's involvement in determining the succession of the throne that she shares.[23]

---

[19] *Beowulf* used, most commonly, to be dated to the late 7th or 8th c.; see Introduction, fn. 12.
[20] See *Beowulf*, ll. 1216–18; cf. Hrothgar's treasure giving, ll. 1020–49. (But whereas Wealhtheow says that the accoutrements she gives are *theodgestreona*, Hrothgar is described as *hordweard*.) So, too, the scop praises the generous gift giving of Eormanric and his wife, Ealhild: see *Widsith*, ll. 88–108, 1–8.
[21] For Wealhtheow's two appearances at the feast, see *Beowulf*, ll. 612–41; 1162–231.
[22] *Encomium*, II.16. For an overview of royal women's involvement in the succession, Frankish and English, see P. Stafford, *Queens, Concubines, and Dowagers: The King's Wife in the Early Middle Ages* (Athens, Ga, 1983), pp. 143–74. See further fn. 38.
[23] See *Beowulf*, ll. 1926–62; 2369–79. Beowulf's refusal of Hygd's offer does not undercut its propriety; nor does it necessarily imply that Wealhtheow's attempt to promote the accession of her young sons represents irresponsible attachment to her offspring at the expense of the protection of the kingdom. The salient point of comparison is not the behaviour of the queens but the behaviour of Beowulf and Hrothulf (also a king's nephew), the foreshadowed treachery of Hrothulf towards the sons of Hrothgar and Wealhtheow highlighting Beowulf's ideal conduct in choosing to act as regent for his cousin. But Wealhtheow's link with Grendel's mother

Wealhtheow's last words assert the interlocking nature of overlordship, the incorporation of her rule in Hrothgar's: " 'Here every man is true to the other, gentle of disposition and loyal to his lord. The thanes are obedient, and the people are entirely at the ready: the men of the court, having drunk to it, will do as I bid.' "[24] There are tensions here, for Wealhtheow could be said to be exercising a form of rival lordship. As Hrothgar multiplies potential candidates for the throne by adopting Beowulf as his son, she multiplies supporters for her sons, of whose claims to the succession she evidently considers Hrothgar insufficiently mindful.[25] Hrothgar's nephew Hrothulf is obliquely exhorted to remember the loyalty that he owes, not merely to Hrothgar but to her as well, on account of past favours – for Wealhtheow's emphasis on conjugal union is marked: " 'I expect that he will repay our sons with beneficence if he remembers all that we two have previously done for him.' "[26] Beowulf's support she attempts to gain by present favours and the promise of favours to come: " 'Be kindly disposed towards these boys in giving them good counsels. I shall keep your reward for this in mind.' "[27] Wealhtheow's advice and treasure are not applied to shoring up the reign of the old and waning king but to consolidating the position of the young and future kings. In the first of her appearances, her office with the cup completed, she asserts her joint identity with Hrothgar as ruler, by taking up her seat beside him. On this second appearance, she merely "went to her seat".[28] Presumably the same seat as before – and yet, perhaps not. Unity this time is less than complete. And, symptomatically, the dais about Hrothgar is rather crowded on this occasion, for Hrothulf is already occupying a seat beside the king, and at the king's feet sits his official, the *thyle* Unferth, whose ill-reputation as a slayer of his kinsmen gives further point to Wealhtheow's raising of the doubt that Hrothulf's loyalty to her sons is entirely reliable.

---

through maternal attachment is inescapably suggestive (see fns. 30, 46). In general, our interpretation of her depends on whether we regard the poem as a self-contained work, or whether the placing of Wealhtheow – including her relationship to Grendel's mother – was controlled for AS audiences by knowledge of a tradition that they shared with the poet, lost to us, concerning the precise nature of the events whereby Heorot met its appointed doom (ll. 81–5) and what part, if any, Wealhtheow played in that. E.g., as Wealhtheow rewards Beowulf with a torque (ll. 1192–201) the narrator informs us that Hygelac was wearing this same torque when he was killed in battle (ll. 1202–9, cf. Beowulf's presentation of the torque to Hygd, ll. 2172–6), so that, potentially, she has the aspect of a distributor of death. If the narrator's comparison of the torque to the Brisinga treasure (see Klaeber, pp. 177–9) was the key to recognition of a connexion between these events, which legend of the Brisinga treasure did he and his audience know?

24 Bradley, p. 444; *Beowulf*, ll. 1228–31.
25 Hrothgar's statement that he will henceforth cherish Beowulf as a son (ll. 945–7) *could* have a number of different meanings; Wealhtheow would seem to have good reason for regarding it as threatening the succession of her sons (ll. 1175–80); Beowulf's dying speeches reveal that bestowal of a king's armour designates succession to the kingdom (ll. 2729–32, 2813–15), and the armour that Hrothgar gives Beowulf is the armour that King Heorogar, the brother whom Hrothgar succeeded, chose *not* to give to his own son. Hrothgar, it transpires, made a point of imparting this to Beowulf when he gave him the armour (ll. 2155–62).
26 Bradley, p. 443; *Beowulf*, ll. 1184–7 ("uncran eaferan . . . hwæt wit to willan . . .").
27 Bradley, p. 444; *Beowulf*, ll. 1219–20.
28 *Beowulf*, l. 1232; cf. ll. 640–1.

What bishops like Wilfrid coveted, in their friendships with kings, then, most closely resembled an elder brother's throne-sharing with a younger kinsman. But it was not greatly different from the position of joint ruler held by the queen; and it was no less fraught with potential for the displacement of the queen than throne-sharing by kinsmen appears to be in *Beowulf*. Despite the fact that Eddius accuses Queen Jurmenburg of jealous envy in securing the downfall of Bishop Wilfrid,[29] a counterclaim could with justice have been lodged. Nearness to the throne was not, in itself, at issue; but for the role of adviser to the king, inextricably embedded in the office of the queen and secular ideals of aristocratic women, bishops and queens were inevitably in competition. The insistent categorization of all women as types of either Eve or Mary that characterizes the high middle ages is not deeply ingrained even in the later Old English period.[30] But images of Eve are beginning to take shape in the earliest hagiographical literature, as a form of polemic in the power struggles of queens and bishops. Images of Eve grounded in the view that the fall consisted in following the advice of a woman have, of course, a basis in patristic commentary, but in patristic views of the original and continuing corruption caused by women, the weight of emphasis falls on the seductive temptations of the flesh. In developing a polemical typology of Eve, Anglo-Saxon ecclesiastics took their cue from indigenous roles and attributes of aristocratic women, and particularly from existent inversions and anti-types of the ideal. The patristic typology of Eve, fusing with these, assumed culturally recognizable forms.

The peaceweaver, as presented in *Beowulf*, was a woman given in marriage in order to reconcile traditional enemies; her role was to inspire in her husband and his people an affection for herself which extended also to her people.[31] In this role, then, the woman given in marriage is a pivotal relational force, extending the bonds of friendly kinship from one clan to another. Wealhtheow, making her way through the hall with the cup, graphically embodies the tie-binding role of the peaceweaver. Here, as in *Maxims I*, it is not unity between the two peoples that is foregrounded, but union between the company in the hall and the king. But the hall itself is, presumably, conceived as a microcosmic gathering together of the two nations. In Beowulf's prophecy of the failure of the marriage of Freawaru and Ingeld to effect the hoped-for peace between the two kingdoms, a resurgence of the blood feud is provoked by the presence in the hall of the bride's retinue of kinsmen wearing the arms won in battle against the bridegroom's people. So too in the Finnsburg lay, fighting between Hildeburg's Danish retinue and her husband's Frisian followers first breaks out because the Frisian ruler is felt to be insufficiently generous to the Danes, and the attempted

---

[29] Ch. 24.

[30] *Beowulf* itself may have taken shape in the late OE period (see fn. 19), in which case it presents striking evidence of the absence of a firmly established iconography of Eve and Mary as the model for female representations. Cf. Chance, esp. pp. 95–108. For a study of Wealhtheow in relation to Germanic tradition, particularly the Valkyrie figure, see Damico, 1984, esp. pp. 3–16, 58–86.

[31] It is among the misfortunes of the peaceweaver that the obverse also holds true – when one of Freawaru's Danes kills one of her husband's Frisians, Ingeld's love for his Danish wife will cool (see *Beowulf*, ll. 2057–66); see further pp. 228–32.

resolution to this conflict – separate halls for the Frisians and Danes – embodies a breach of the unity of the two peoples that cannot be healed.[32]

Community wrought by a woman through the extension of kinship ties, and confirmed by her circulation of the hall-cup, cannot have been a prospect pleasing to ecclesiastics. For them, feasting in the hall was, in all its aspects, a diabolic opponent of the mass,[33] and the office of the woman as cup-bearer is altogether too like, and yet unlike, the office of the priestly celebrant. This may account for the hagiographic recurrence of miracles of healing in which a woman is cured by the saint, and having received from him a healing cup, offers him the cup of welcome in homage to his powers. The model for this group of miracles is the healing of Peter's mother-in-law, but the hagiographic miracles differ from their scriptural model in presenting the saint as a priestly celebrant whose ministrations have triumphed over the fatal propensities of the hostess of the profane feast; as Bede exclaims of the reeve's wife healed by Cuthbert: "It was a fair sight to see how she who had escaped the cup of death by the bishop's blessing was the first of all in that eminent man's household to offer him the cup of refreshment."[34] It is consistent with the antagonistic relationship of the priestly celebrant to the woman cup-bearer as creator of secular community that Eve in the Anglo-Saxon period is not an erotic tempter with an apple, but the woman with the poisoned cup.[35] For *Guthlac B*, the fall was accomplished by "the bitter drink which Eve the young bride gave and served up to Adam of old: it harmed them both within that precious home" – though, to be sure, this has the appearance not so much of positive censure as regret for an inexperienced bride's culinary mistake.[36] Aldhelm borrows his image of Eve in *De Virginitate* from the Apocalypse; but whereas the Whore of Babylon who holds the cup of iniquity is herself "drunk with the blood of the saints," for Aldhelm a woman with a cup is inevitably the hostess of a feast, "offering the lethal drink of the brothel in a golden chalice."[37]

It is, accordingly, difficult to tell which of the rumours of homicidal Anglo-Saxon queens dealing out death with the wine are authentic, for the Anglo-Norman chroniclers who are the chief promulgators of such rumours appear particularly prone to fill out the gaps in their information with inventions

---

[32] *Beowulf*, ll. 2032–69; 1080–106.

[33] See esp. Alcuin's "What has Ingeld to do with Christ" diatribe (Duemmler, 124).

[34] Colgrave, pp. 253–5; *Bede's Cuthbert*, ch. 29. See also *Bede's Cuthbert*, ch. 15; *Life of Wilfrid*, ch. 37; *HE*, V.3, 4. Cf. Luke 4.38–9. For discussion see H. Magennis, "Water-Wine Miracles in Anglo-Saxon Saints' Lives," *English Language Notes* 23 (1986), 7–9.

[35] For the typological and exegetical associations of the fatal draught, and the pervasive occurrence of the *poculum mortis* in OE, see H. Magennis, "The Cup as Symbol and Metaphor in Old English Literature," *Speculum* 60 (1985), 517–36.

[36] See *Guthlac B* (ASPR III, 72–88), ll. 865–71, 980–5; trans. Bradley, p. 271. Sometimes the devil is depicted as cup-bearer at the feast, as in the devil's speech in *Juliana*, ll. 483–90: "Some I have led on by my counsels and brought them into discord, so that suddenly, drunk with beer, they renewed old grievances; I have served them strife from out of the goblet so that by resorting to swords within the wine hall, being stricken with wounds, they released their souls to flit doomed away from their body" (Bradley, p. 314).

[37] L&H, p. 73; *De Virginitate*, ch. 17 (Rev. 17.3–6). Of particular interest is the Crucifixion scene carved on the 10th c. Gosforth cross; Eve/Mary, on the *left* hand of Christ, holds up a drinking horn. See R.N. Bailey and R. Cramp, ed., *The Corpus of Anglo-Saxon Stone Sculpture* (Oxford, 1988), II, 102–3 (no. 304).

modeled on Anglo-Saxon motifs, and the more anti-feminist the motifs were, one suspects, the greater their appeal for the Anglo-Norman chroniclers.[38] But even within the pre-Conquest period itself, the spectre of the woman with the poison cup was a useful means of raising suspicion against aristocratic women, and their admission to councils held over the mead-drinking. The image of the woman with the poison cup underlies the account of Eadburg that Asser gives in explanation of why the king's wife in Wessex was not accorded a position of equivalence on the throne. Eadburg, the story runs, secured the destruction of the king's favourites by denouncing them to him; if she could not gain his agreement to depriving them of life or possessions, she poisoned them. Finally, in attempting to poison a young man who was a particular favourite of the king, Eadburg, like Eve, inadvertently poisoned her husband.[39] Even more evidently than Thryth in *Beowulf*, who has men killed and cast into prison for daring to look at her, Eadburg is an inverted peaceweaver, whose distribution of poison perverts the role of mistress of the feast, since the destruction of the king's favourites runs directly counter to the ideal of the royal wife as tie-binder and consolidator of support for her husband's reign.

The most comprehensive inversion of the Germanic ideal of the peaceweaver is offered by Guthrun in the 9th or 10th century Icelandic lay, *Atlakvitha*.[40] Guthrun, left without kinsmen through the execution of her brothers by her husband Atli, can bring about vengeance for their death only by taking the role of male avenger upon herself. In order to conceal the design of her revenge, Guthrun must hold back the tears which may acceptably be shed by women,

[38] E.g., the post-Conquest claims that Ælfthryth assassinated her step-son, Edward, in order to place on the throne her own son; see C. Fell ed., *Edward King and Martyr* (Leeds, 1971), pp. xi–xvii; see further ch. 6, fn. 84. C. Fell, "Edward King and Martyr and the Anglo-Saxon Hagiographic Tradition," in *Ethelred the Unready*, ed. D. Hill (Oxford, 1978), pp. 1–13, discusses Ælfthryth as a wicked step-mother stereotype. The late 11th c. *Passio S Edwardi*, the earliest version to attribute Edward's death to Ælfthryth, relates that she offered the mounted Edward a poisoned cup while her minions stabbed him in the back (for the offer of the cup of welcome to the mounted guest as a traditional part of the woman's role as hostess, see *Bede's Cuthbert*, chs. 15, 29). S.J. Ridyard, p. 163, finds "no early evidence that Edward's murder resulted from a plot within the royal family itself"; cf. D.J.V. Fisher, "The Anti-monastic Reaction in the Reign of Edward the Martyr," *Cambridge Journal of History* 10 (1950–2), 254–70. In William of Malmesbury's account of Ælfthryth, the woman cup-bearer as Eve merges with Eve as the erotic tempter (*Gesta Regum*, ed. Stubbs, I, 183). Queen Edith's responsibility for the murder of a thane called Gospatric during the Christmas festivities at the royal court, in order to further the interests of her brother Tostig, looks probable: *Chronicon ex Chronicis*, ed. B. Thorpe, EHS (London, 1848), I, 145, 223. The monstrous depiction of 6th c. Frankish queens surely owes something to ecclesiastical conceptions of female evil. Fredegund, notorious for her assassinations in Gregory's *History of the Franks* is also said to have poisoned a stirrup-cup (VIII.31): trans. O.M. Dalton (2 vols., Oxford, 1927). Woman as hostess and cup-bearer is not uniquely Germanic: C.M. Bowra, *Heroic Poetry* (New York, 1966), pp. 480–93, discusses it as an epic phenomenon.

[39] *Life of Alfred*, ch. 14; cf. *The Ecclesiastical History of Orderic Vitalis*, ed. M. Chibnall (Oxford, 1969), II, 123, which relates that Mabel, wife of Roger Montgomery, attempted to poison a rival of her husband by inviting him to a feast at which the food and drink were poisoned, but inadvertently killed her husband's only brother instead; she then employed a servant who succeeded in poisoning her husband's rival and two of his associates.

[40] *Atlakvitha*, sts. 34–44. For discussion of Guthrun's role, see Dronke, pp. 15–16, 27–9. The complete Poetic Edda is edited by Kuhn, 1968. Dronke edits, with translation, from which I quote: *Hamthismál* (2nd half 9th c.); *Atlakvitha* (9/10th c.); *Guthrúnarhvot* (late 12th c.); *Atlamál* (12th c.).

who are the licensed mourners of the heroic world; and in this emotional suppression Guthrun achieves a triumph over her female nature fit to rank with the heroic silence in which her brothers undergo execution. It is not poison that Guthrun feeds to her unwitting husband but the carcasses of their young sons whom she has slain, and it is death that she distributes to the retinue as mistress of the feast with the cup. Feverishly pacing the hall, circulating the cup until the moment comes when the drunken Atli can be stabbed in mid embrace, and his wine-fuddled retinue are powerless to escape when she sets fire to the hall, Guthrun recalls the Valkyrie women who weave destruction and war.[41] As unweeping woman she recalls the three female fates, the Norns, who proverbially do not weep, and the revenge she has in mind for Atli's retinue is her own private version of *Ragnarok*, the apocalyptic conflagration that has been known to the Norns since the beginning of the world.[42]

In the image of Eve as the woman with the poison cup, the ecclesiastical conception of archetypal female evil fuses with the Terrible Female stereotype of Germanic tradition, the anti-peaceweaver, who perverts her role to become a weaver of destruction and war.[43] Guthrun as a destroyer of men, however, is not a representative of original female evil – she is the hero of a characteristically Germanic tragedy, trapped in a conflict of loyalties and compelled to act against her nature, rather as the cross in *The Dream of the Rood* is torn up from its roots, transformed from living tree to instrument of death, and compelled to cooperate in the execution of its Lord.[44] What Asser is relating, on the other hand, *is* a myth of origins, an ontological explanation of the unfitness of women to occupy a position of power equivalent to that of men: "The elders of the land maintain that this disputed and indeed infamous custom originated on account of a certain grasping and wicked queen . . . who did everything she could against her lord and the whole people, so that not only did she earn hatred for herself, leading to her expulsion from the queen's throne, but she also brought the same foul stigma on all the queens who came after her. For as a result of her very great wickedness, all the inhabitants of the land swore that they would never permit any king to reign over them who during his lifetime invited the queen to sit beside him on the royal throne."[45] In Asser's report of the tale he was told by King Alfred, we appear to have an early and seminal instance of the drawing of an indigenous literary stereotype within the orbit of ecclesiastical modes of

---

41 See *Helgakvitha Hundingsbana I*, sts. 1–6, for a conflation of the Valkyrie as weavers of war with the Norns as weavers of fate.

42 See *Atlakvitha*, st. 16; Dronke, p. 27, n. 2, explains that "as inexorable judges of men the Norns are presumably without pity. To make them weep would be to achieve a virtual impossibility"; thus, when Guthrun set fire to the hall, "the Huns' children wept, save only Guthrun, who never wept for her brothers, fierce as bears, and the beloved sons, young, untried by life, whom she bore to Atli" (st. 39).

43 The most frequently depicted female cup-bearers are the Valkyrie, who carry the ale-horn to the "chosen heroes" on the field of battle (see *Grímnismál*, st. 36). In *Skáldskaparmál*, st. 17, Valfreyja, "mistress of the slain," pours ale at the feast of the gods; *Edda Snorra Sturlusonar*, ed. G. Jónsson (Copenhagen, 1931). See J. Grimm, *Teutonic Mythology*, trans. J.S. Stallybrass (London, 1883), I, 420; for pictorial illustrations, see H.R.E. Davidson, *Pagan Scandinavia* (New York, 1976), pp. 124, 130, 63. I would not identify the inverted peaceweaver so consistently with the Valkyrie as Damico, 1984, esp. pp. 18–19, 41–57.

44 *Dream of the Rood*, ll. 28–56.

45 Trans. Lapidge and Keynes, p. 71; *Life of Alfred*, ch. 14.

thought. To regard Asser's condemnation of the denial of queenly status to the wife of the king of Wessex as ironic cover for an actual intention of disseminating misogynist polemic seems to me altogether too ingenious; what his account illustrates is that, in antagonism to the power of queens, secular and ecclesiastical culture found a point of contact. Though my emphasis here falls on the conflict of queens and bishops, bishops were not their only competitors for the ear of the king, and it is worth observing that Grendel's mother, suggestively parallel with Wealhtheow in her devotion to what is due to her son, does not snatch a warrior in his prime to devour at leisure, but an old comrade of Hrothgar's fighting days, his privy councillor and adviser.[46]

Though the peaceweaver given in marriage to reconcile parties to a blood-feud is a vernacular literary motif, silence regarding this role in hagiographical literature does not prove it to have been a figment of the poetic imagination. Bede was familiar with it, for it underlies his account of Theodore's intervention in the wars between the Northumbrians and the Mercians, who had been united by the marriage of Osthryth of Northumbria to Æthelred of Mercia. Bede's report of this event reveals further reasons why the peaceweaver was not a popular image with clerics:

> In the ninth year of his reign, King Ecgfrith fought a battle near the River Trent against king Æthelred of the Mercians, in which Ecgfrith's brother Ælfwine was killed. The latter was a young man of about eighteen, who was much loved in both provinces since Æthelred had married his sister Osthryth. This gave every indication of causing fiercer strife and more lasting hatred between the two warlike kings and peoples, until Archbishop Theodore, the beloved of God, enlisting God's help, smothered the flames of this awful peril by his wholesome advice. As a result, peace was restored between the kings and people, and in lieu of further bloodshed, the customary compensation was paid to King Ecgfrith for his brother's death. The peace thus made was maintained between these kings and their peoples for many years.[47]

Vernacular depictions of peaceweavers suggest that the woman who was given in marriage fulfilled her purpose by inspiring affection (it being essential, as *Maxims I* points out, for a queen to be well-liked), and that she was aided in her quest for popularity by liberal dispensations from her treasure-store and her mead-cup. As Bede's account of this outbreak of hostilities shows, the advisory role of the queen that figures in the definition of the ideal in *Maxims I* was also an inseparable aspect of peaceweaving. When hostility between the Mercians and the Northumbrians was exacerbated by the killing of the Northumbrian king's brother by the Mercians, an influential voice was needed to counsel the Mercians to offer compensation for his death, and to persuade the Northumbrians to accept it. In the absence of an archbishop, the woman given in

---

[46] *Beowulf*, ll. 1323–8. A Jungian analysis views Grendel's mother as the "evil latent in women's function . . . . the obverse of the women we meet in the two banqueting scenes": see J. Helterman, "*Beowulf*: The Archetype Enters History," *ELH* 35 (1968), 13–14.

[47] Sherley-Price, p. 243; *HE*, IV.21.

marriage to make peace between traditional enemies was an obvious candidate to attempt reconciliation.[48] Not directly involved in the fighting herself, she had friends on both sides of the conflict to whom she could appeal, and a vested interest in preventing further bloodshed. Vernacular literature's employment of the unsuccessful peaceweaver as a tragic motif, mourner for the dead on both sides in a renewed outbreak of fighting between her husband's people and her own, highlights one potential consequence of the peaceweaver's position: doubtless she did at times assume the aspect of a helpless victim of unrestrainable male violence.[49] But as an acknowledged good adviser with affective influence in both camps, the peaceweaver also had the aspect of advocate and ambassador for two nations.[50]

As advisers and creators of social harmony, aristocratic peaceweavers were, by indigenous definition, wise, and the natural allies of wise men: "Common cause must the wise achieve with the wise. Their minds will be alike. They will always resolve disputes; they will preach peace when discontents have once disturbed it. Counselling belongs with wisdom, justice with the wise."[51] Bishops, however, were not only in conflict with queens for the role of adviser to kings. Rightly or wrongly they believed that they had a superior claim as peacemakers. For the peace of Christ transcended the ties of kinship. Kinship ties, capable of generating endlessly perpetuating hostilities between kin groups, were also the basis of intense attachments that competed with community in Christ. Kinship ties were worldly, created by mortal flesh and blood; but community in Christ was eternal, and born of the spirit.[52]

Such devaluation of kinship bonds held far-reaching and unfortunate implications for the position of the queen. Wealhtheow's social prominence in Heorot rests upon the pivotal position of a married woman as tie binder in a society in which kinship dominates as a social relation. The political power of women depended on the emotional potency of kinship relations.[53] The social displacement attendant on the attrition of those bonds is reflected in later medieval literary portraits of the queen at the feast. Whereas Wealhtheow holds the floor in Heorot, dispensing advice and the hall-cup, Guenevere in *Sir Gawain and the Green Knight* sits silent on the dais.[54] When relations are cemented by oaths between warriors that bind them in the fellowship of Christ, the role of the queen's wife cannot be other than decorative; it is, at most, emblematic of her nebulously harmonious influence and an inspiration to knightly pursuit of the good, the beautiful and the true.

---

[48] For the general willingness of parties to a blood-feud to seek arbitration, see J.M. Wallace-Hadrill, *The Long-Haired Kings and Other Studies in Frankish History* (Oxford, 1962), pp. 12–47.
[49] See Hansen, 109–17.
[50] As advocate, the peaceweaver blends easily with the Virgin. Fell, 1986, p. 104, remarks of the description of the Virgin as *mundbore* and *thingestre*: "Neither of these words could have been invented only to be used of Mary."
[51] Bradley, p. 346; *Maxims I*, ll. 18–23.
[52] See further pp. 38–40, 228–32, 277–8, 293.
[53] See J.A. McNamara and S. Wemple, "The Power of Women through the Family in Medieval Europe," in *Clio's Consciousness Raised*, ed. M.S. Hartmann and L.W. Banner (New York, 1974). Kliman, 32–49, advances the view that women ceased to be peaceweavers and became anchorites, on the dubious grounds that war was less prevalent in the 13th c.
[54] N. Davis, ed., *Sir Gawain and the Green Knight*, 2nd rev. edn. (Oxford, 1967), ll. 74–84.

Osthryth, in Bede's account of the outbreak of hostilities between Northumbria and Mercia, can be regarded as a failed peaceweaver, whose efforts to forge peace proved tragically inadequate to the force of male vengeance and aggression. But she is perhaps, by implication, more in the manner of an anti-peaceweaver, one whose advice was not wholesome, tending to promote further violence and bloodshed instead of peace by desiring vengeance for her slain brother.[55] This seems quite possible. Bede reports elsewhere that Osthryth placed the relics of her uncle, the Northumbrian king Oswald, in a Mercian monastery at Lindsey, despite the Mercian monks' protestations that they had no particular desire to possess the bones of their former Northumbrian overlord, since they had not much cared for him during his lifetime; and if Osthryth's pride in her Northumbrian kin was characteristically accompanied by such disregard of Mercian sensitivities, it is not difficult to understand why she eventually met her death at the hands of her "own" Mercian people.[56] Either way, Osthryth was obviously a negligible force of good influence compared to Theodore. Bede gives us no portrait of a Christian queen as peaceweaver in his *History* – indeed, Eanfled's request to her brother for assistance on behalf of Wilfrid's pilgrimage to Rome is the *History*'s sole allusion to women's use of influence through kinship ties.[57] What Bede gives us instead is the failure of an attempt at peace through an extension of the ties of flesh and blood wrought by the marriage of woman; and what transcends that failure is the lasting success of Theodore, the peace of Christ in the bonds of the spirit, wrought by the inspired wisdom of an archbishop.

Abbesses were, more often than not, royal women who had transferred their rule to a smaller kingdom. An abbess without powerful family backing was reliant on ecclesiastical protection – if she could get it – against the incursions of secular powers.[58] But an abbess with surviving royal connexions continued to be a power in the land, and as capable of assisting bishops as a reigning queen who was well-disposed to the church.[59] Lul's flattering protestations of allegiance and homage to the Abbess Cyniburg at the double monastery of which he had been a member illustrate clearly the replication of secular rule in a monastic context. As Lul was writing to ask the abbess to ensure that two slaves that he had freed before leaving England were not prevented from leaving the country to join him in Germany, it is evident that the scope of the abbess Cyniburg's powers extended far beyond her monastery: "If we were actually present before you on bended knees and with floods of tears, we trust that our request would be granted; so now, in our absence, we humbly beg the same

[55] Cf. Guthrun as the destroyer of her sons by inciting them to take vengeance for the murder of her daughter (*Guthrúnarhvot*, sts. 1–8, *Hamthismál*, sts. 1–10) and Brynhild's instigation of a "chain of woes" by compelling her husband Gunnarr to murder Sigurd, the friend of Gunnarr and the husband of his sister Guthrun (*Sigurtharkvitha en Skamma*, sts. 6–19).

[56] See *HE*, III.11; V.24. For Osthryth's family solidarity with her brother Ecgfrith in his conflict with Wilfrid, see ch. 40.

[57] *HE*, V.19.

[58] See further pp. 139–40.

[59] With Eanfled's use of influence to obtain a monastic endowment for Bishop Trumhere (*HE*, III.24), cf. the assistance granted by Eanfled and Ælffled at Whitby to Trumwine, the refugee bishop (*HE*, IV.26); see further pp. 226–7.

favour of you," he wrote, on behalf of himself and his two companions. "We also wish it known to your care and your wisdom that if any one of the three of us should visit Britain, we should not seek to put ourselves in obedience to the government of any-one else, but only in subjection to your benevolence, for in you we have the most complete confidence."[60]

For abbesses accustomed to royal throne-sharing, partnership with bishops was a natural expectation, and all the more so in the case of an abbess whose particular prestige within a diocese elevated her to an eminence comparable with that of a bishop. Leoba, for instance, assumed the responsibility for over-seeing women's religious communities which was normally held by a bishop, because she was the pioneer founder of monasticism in Germany;[61] Ælffled, the successor of Hild of Whitby, who founded a number of Northumbrian monas-teries, is among the early abbesses who appear to have occupied a similar position of quasi-episcopal eminence.[62] In these circumstances, pressure towards participation in sacerdotal powers was inevitable. The canonical prohibition of women's administration of penance in *Theodore's Penitential*, I have suggested earlier, is a response to monastic women's assumption of some forms of pastoral ministry under the impetus of their customary high level of social participation, in which they were presumably assisted by a shortage of ordinands.[63] Their participation in liturgical celebration is evidenced by Aldhelm's description of the dedication of Abbess Bugga's church, where lectors, both male and female, read from the sacred books.[64] *Theodore's Penitential* also deals with women's participation in the administration of the mass.

The various versions of *Theodore's Penitential* register impulses both towards and against the inclusion of women as ministrants at the sacred feast. In some manuscripts, monastic women are expressly permitted "to read the lection and to perform the ministries which appertain to the confession of the sacred altar, except those which are the special functions of priests and deacons." But in other versions, women are forbidden to participate in the sacramental mysteries, and are sharply excluded as a class from association with men who are cel-ebrants of the sacred feast: "Women shall not cover the altar with the corporal, nor place on the altar the offerings, nor the cup, nor stand among ordained men in the church, nor sit at the feast among priests."[65] The prohibitive versions of the Penitential derive from the 747 reply of Zacharias to an enquiry of the Gallican clergy, which prohibited women from reading the lessons at a public mass, and decreed that they were not to serve at the altar or carry out any of the offices performed by men. As the overall historical development was towards the exclusion of women from the mysteries, the versions of the Penitential that prohibit female administration of the mass, like those which contain the unam-

---

[60] Trans. Fell, 1990, p. 241 (and, in full, by Emerton, pp. 77–8); Tangl, 49.

[61] *Life of Leoba*, ch. 18.

[62] See further ch. 6, pp. 179–85.

[63] *Theodore's Penitential*, II.vii.2; see further pp. 134–7. Cf. Cogitosus's Life of Brigid, trans. Bateson, 165: "she called a great man from his solitary life to govern the church with her in episcopal dignity, that nothing of sacerdotal order should be wanting in her churches, and for the churches of the many provinces that adhered to her."

[64] *Carm Eccles*, 3. Monks and nuns in double monasteries commonly held services together; see Bateson, 137–64.

[65] McNeill, p. 205; *Theodore's Penitential*, II.vii.1 (see Finsterwalder, p. 322).

biguous prohibition of women's adjudgment of penances, are fairly certainly
later in date. The *Penitential of Pseudo-Egbert* in the late Anglo-Saxon period,
affirming that "ignorant and impure" women are not to touch the sacred objects
on Christ's altar, nor the sacred books which are handled by ordained men,
"because St Paul has expressly prohibited it,"[66] marks the forward movement of
the constitution of male clergy as an elite caste.

As the Marian associations of the abbess imply, they also shared in more
nebulous and extensive ways in the status and spiritual mana of bishops as the
representatives of Christ. When Wilfrid died, Eddius reports, his body was
placed on a cloak. Tatberht, whom Bishop Wilfrid had appointed to succeed
him as abbot, had the cloak delivered to the abbess Cynethryth, with a message
asking her to keep it for him just as it was until he required it. As the cloak was
somewhat soiled, however, the abbess ordered it to be washed, and a nun who
plunged her arm into the water in which it was placed was immediately healed,
in the manner of the woman in the gospel who was healed when she touched
the hem of Jesus's garment.[67] The abbess as ruler of a double monastery, I have
suggested, could be emblematically construed as Mary, the bereaved mother and
widowed bride of Christ, whom he entrusted to the care of his favourite disciple
John, regarded by the Celtic church as the true apostolic successor: "Behold thy
mother."[68] This figurative construction underlies Eddius's account. For Wilfrid's
appointed successor was also his kinsman;[69] Cynethryth, who is described in this
episode as "the abbess of Bishop Wilfrid," sounds to have been the abbess of a
double monastery with which Wilfrid's monks were connected, or perhaps an
abbess of particular eminence with whom he was associated, in the manner of
Leoba and Boniface on the continent.[70]

Cynethryth functions in this episode as a Marian typological equivalent of
the Church. The cloak on which the body of Wilfrid lay is, of course, an
allusion to the (seamless) robe that Christ wore on his ascent to Calvary, which
signifies the mystical church. As the Church is the repository and perpetual
channel of divine grace, Cynethryth is the guardian of the miraculous cloak of
Wilfrid-Christ, the mantle inherited by his appointed successor. The allegorical
coupling of abbess and bishop as Christ and Mary affirms their partnership as
spiritual heads of the church. This role Tatberht evidently intended the abbess
to hold in a purely nominal and symbolic sense – Cynethryth was merely to act
as the keeper of the mantle. Her employment of the cloak for the performance
of a miracle of healing – although it is fortuitous and unwitting, accomplished

---

66 OE *Penitential*, III.12. Halitgar's Penitential, from which the OE is translated, clearly knows
that women are ministering at the altar or, possibly, that they are being encouraged to do so (see
Raith, p. 42, notes); the OE does not acknowledge the existence of an actual practice. Like the
prohibitive versions of *Theodore's Penitential*, Halitgar's echoes Zacharias's 747 reply to the
Gallican clergy (see Bateson, 1899, 163). OE *Confessional* omits *Theodore's Penitential*, II.vii.1–2;
but it follows *Theodore's Penitential*, II.vii.4, in allowing women to make offerings as a concession
to regional variation on the basis of Greek precedent (Spindler, p. 189).

67 Ch. 66.

68 John 19.26–7. See further p. 110.

69 Chs. 63–5. Abbot Tatberht, the dedicatee of this Life (Preface, p. 2), must be the source of
this episode, and much else, since Wilfrid related his life-story to him shortly before his death
(ch. 65).

70 See further pp. 289–97.

entirely through the numinous powers of Wilfrid and in no way through her own – is illicit in as much as it contravenes Tatberht's instructions. The conflict which marks the possession of numinous powers here is the corollary of the pressures towards women's participation in the sacerdotal ministry which are being resisted in *Theodore's Penitential*.

The competitive strains that manifest themselves in the relation of bishops and abbesses, then, reflect the transposition to a monastic setting of antagonisms to royal women operative in the secular sphere, which find expression in conflict concerning abbesses' participation in the status and powers of priests and bishops. In the *Life of Wilfrid*, Cynethryth's action passes without a sign of reproach – for Eddius, it appears, the entry of royal women to monasteries is in itself a sufficient neutralization of their powers. But the typology of Eve also functions polemically in the conflict between abbesses and churchmen. Bede, silent on the power of queens in his *History*, expresses a hostility to Abbess Ælffled far more corrosive than Eddius's polemical attack on Queen Jurmenburg.[71] The conversion of the queen's powers to ecclesiastical purposes was on the agenda of the Benedictine Reform movement.[72] If the power of royal women in the age of Bede was too firmly entrenched in the secular sphere to be successfully combatted, it was at least clear that they had little in the way of a traditional claim to participation in the ecclesiastical sphere.

Eddius's *Life of Wilfrid*

Royal women, admired for their wisdom and ideally conceived as advisers to kings, figure in the *Life of Wilfrid* only in so far as their advice affects the fortunes of the episcopal protagonist. Their use of influence, either for or against the interests of Wilfrid, is the basis of the sharp moral dichotomy that marks the presentation of women in this work and reflects the competitive conflicts generated in the relations of bishops and royal women.

Wilfrid's relation with Æthelthryth is the only celebrated instance of a bishop's successful establishment of himself as the friendly mentor of a reigning queen. Bede's *History*, however, does report that Bishop Paulinus accompanied Æthelburg of Kent as *comes*, in order to protect her and her companions from corruption through association with the heathen when she was given in marriage to the pagan king, Edwin of Northumbria. Paulinus in this account offers an ecclesiastical permutation of the retinue of warrior kinsmen who accompanied the woman given in marriage as a peaceweaver, in order to protect her from the danger that might await her at her husband's court – the presence of the bride's protective retinue, as *Beowulf* reveals, had a high potentiality for destroying domestic harmony, and the same conceivably held true of the ecclesiastical

---

[71] See further ch. 6, pp. 199–207.
[72] *Regularis Concordia*, p. 2.

comes.[73] Bede claims to have had it on the authority of Wilfrid himself that
Æthelthryth's husband Ecgfrith offered him lands and much wealth if he could
persuade the queen to consummate the marriage, because he knew that there
was no man that she held in higher regard than Wilfrid.[74] Identified as the
confidant of the king, though more particularly of the queen, Wilfrid assumes
an apparently pivotal position in the royal marriage, which is given more
extensive ramification in the Life. Eddius conveys, somewhat enigmatically,
that the royal pair's acceptance of the bishop's friendly guidance maintained
harmony between them and ensured peace in the kingdom and victory for the
king, but when the king fell out with the bishop, the absence of his good
influence was felt, for the queen left him for a monastery, and the king brought
ruin on himself and an end to the nation's prosperity.[75]

It is a more plausible thesis that Wilfrid's position at court depended on his
friendship with Æthelthryth, and that she was the actual linchpin of the
triangular relationship Eddius describes. But whereas the woman given as peaceweaver created a harmonious social unity, extending outward from her union in
marriage, the marriage of Ecgfrith and Æthelthryth, as depicted by Eddius, is
held together (albeit not intimately) in the unity of the spirit through the peace
of Christ by the presence of Bishop Wilfrid, whose influence is reflected in the
nation at large. In a similar fashion, Bede's *History*, in suggesting a connexion
between the royal couple's adherence to different liturgical calendars for the
celebration of Easter and the outbreak of factional fighting among Celtic and
Roman adherents in the kingdom at large, attributes the preservation of harmony to the omniscient influence of Bishop Aidan.[76] Wilfrid, according to
Eddius, also took to himself the queen's role in shoring up the success of the
king's reign – by following his wise guidance the king gained victory and
extended his territories. Eddius gives passing acknowledgement, as he opens his
account, to the joint nature of the rule exercised by the royal couple, a state of
affairs that evidently obtained in Mercia and Wessex as well: "Now in those
days, the pious King Ecgfrith and his most blessed Queen Æthelthryth (whose
body, still remaining uncorrupted after death, shows that it was unstained
before, while alive) were both obedient to Bishop Wilfrid in all things, and
there ensued, by the aid of God, peace and joy among the people, fruitful years
and victory over their foes."[77] But in his subsequent account – irrespective of
the accuracy of his version of power relations at the Northumbrian court in the
time of Æthelthryth – the potential for the queen's displacement through the
friendship of bishops and kings is evident. Whereas Bede's account suggests that
Ecgfrith might have had cause to feel that the Bishop had alienated his wife's
affections, what Eddius conveys is that the effective ruler of Northumbria was
Wilfrid, who in consequence of the strained relations between the king and
queen, appropriated her position as chief adviser.

[73] HE, II.9; cf. Queen Bertha and Bishop Liudhard, HE, I.25. With Paulinus as protective *comes*
at the death of Edwin in HE, II.20, cf. *Beowulf*, ll. 1146–59; cf. the return of Hildeburg to her
people after the defeat of her husband.
[74] HE, IV.19.
[75] Ch. 19.
[76] HE, III.25.
[77] Colgrave, p. 41; ch. 19: see also ch. 40.

Wilfrid was markedly unsuccessful in influencing Ecgfrith after his marriage to Jurmenburg, which in itself suggests that the attitude of queens towards bishops was more critical to their position than either Eddius or Bede care to admit. Jurmenburg, fulfilling her appropriate role of supporter of her husband's reign and spur to the enhancement of his renown, urged Ecgfrith to appropriate Wilfrid's wealth and armed followers, and to rid himself of a subject whose power evidently rivalled the king's own: "She eloquently described to him all the temporal glories of St Wilfrid, his riches, the number of his monasteries, the greatness of his buildings, his countless army of followers arrayed in royal vestments and arms."[78] Joint rule, in the case of Ecgfrith and his second wife, is affirmed by the insistent plurality of Eddius's account. Wilfrid was banished and deprived of his see – for as powerful secular rulers, Ecgfrith and Jurmenburg had no difficulty in suborning other ecclesiastics to their purposes; Archbishop Theodore was persuaded – by a substantial bribe, according to Eddius – to consecrate three men as bishops in place of Wilfrid while he was absent from the country. And as Ecgfrith's sister was the queen of Mercia, and Jurmenburg's sister was the queen of Wessex, a monstrous regiment of women prevented the exiled bishop from taking up residence in three kingdoms.[79]

Jurmenburg's triumph is marked by Eddius's stigmatization of her as a satanic daughter of Eve, fit to bear comparison with the murderous Jezebel in her persecution of the prophets of God – though the unacknowledged point of contact is not Jurmenburg's slaughter of the prophets but her conspiracy against Naboth to gain the vineyard that the king coveted:[80] "The tempter, 'like a roaring lion,' to quote the Apostle Peter, prowled round the sheepfold of God, seeking an entrance, always on the watch by day and by night and eagerly desiring to overthrow the bravest soldier first, in order that the fearful ones may be more easily overcome. So, taking his usual weapons he sought the weaker vessel, the woman, by whom he has constantly defiled the whole world. . . . Forthwith this sorceress shot poisoned arrows of speech from her quiver into the heart of the king, as the wicked Jezebel did when she slew the prophets of the Lord and persecuted Elijah."[81] As a latter day manifestation of original female corruption, Jurmenburg is not a seductive tempter, but an evil adviser who gains her influential dominance by the eloquence of her words. The self-perpetuating evil that has afflicted the world since time began, as presented in *Maxims I*, is not sex but violence.[82] Like the inverted peaceweavers who represent the defini-

---

[78] Colgrave, p. 49; ch. 24. Cf. ch. 21: "Men of noble birth gave him their sons to be instructed, so that, if they chose, they might devote themselves to the service of God; or that if they preferred, he might give them into the king's charge as warriors when they were grown up" (Colgrave, p. 45). Wilfrid was also making gifts of unparalleled generosity to clerics as well as laymen.

[79] Ch. 40; this episode belongs to the second phase of Wilfrid's exile, following his return from Rome (see chs. 25–39). For studies of the troubled career of Wilfrid, see D.P. Kirby, "Northumbria in the Time of Wilfrid," and D.H. Farmer, "Saint Wilfrid," in *Saint Wilfrid at Hexham*, ed. Kirby, 1974, pp. 1–59. For another account of his relations with women, see J. Nicholson, "*Feminae Gloriosae*: Women in the Age of Bede," in *Medieval Women: Essays Presented to Rosalind Hill*, ed. D. Baker (Oxford, 1978), pp. 15–29.

[80] 1 (3) Kgs. 18.4, 19.2–14, 21.1–29.

[81] Colgrave, p. 49; ch. 24.

[82] *Maxims I*, ll. 192–200.

tion of woman as the source of harm in vernacular literature – such as Thryth in *Beowulf* and Brynhild and Guthrun in the Eddic lays – Jurmenburg is a species of warrior woman, with a touch of the poisoned cup about her ministrations.[83] But her closest counterpart is Asser's Eadburg of Wessex, who deprives the king's favourites of possessions or life by denouncing them to him – in stirring up strife between the king and his former friend, Jurmenburg is a destroyer of men who deviates from the ideal of her womanly role as tie-binder and consolidator of support for her husband's reign. Herself the weapon of the devil in his war against the episcopal champion of the Church Militant, Jurmenburg flaunts her victory by wearing Wilfrid's reliquary as she makes her royal progress in her chariot, as the triumphant Philistines paraded the Ark of the Covenant from city to city. Accused of jealous envy of Wilfrid's power and wealth, Jurmenburg is also an enemy of God's own Church (synonymous here with the Church of Rome);[84] but the crux of the conflict between the queen and God's chosen churchmen is her role as intimate adviser to the king – Jurmenburg's words are arrows that find their mark in the king's heart.

As evil councillor and destroyer of men, the pagan queen Jurmenburg is also in contrast with the pious queen who was the patron of Wilfrid's youth, Oswiu's wife Eanfled, under whose protective guidance Wilfrid sought service when the cruelty of his step-mother drove him to leave home. More precisely, Wilfrid sought to serve God under her "counsel and protection,"[85] but the armed and mounted band he gathered to take with him (seemingly required to manifest Wilfrid's sense of his own importance, even at this early age) reveal his intention to seek service at the court. Queen Eanfled, then, was a leader in her own right, with an independent retinue in which service could be sought. Wilfrid's favourable reception, on account of his handsome appearance and quick wits, in his quest for service with the queen, is an interesting prefiguration of later *Frauendienst*. This, and Eanfled's recommendation that he should enter the Lindisfarne monastery as the servant of Oswiu's retired retainer, despite his armed retinue, is in line with the association of royal women with the arts of peace and the social *comitatus* of the hall, discernible in *Maxims I* and more evident in *Beowulf*, where the murderous Thryth and the troll-wife, Grendel's

---

[83] "Iamiamque de faretra sua venenatas sagittas venifica in cor regis, quasi impiisima Gezabel prophetas Dei occidens et Heliam persequens, per auditum verborum emisit" (Colgrave, p. 48). The comparison with Jezebel is generated by the consistently OT conception of Eddius's Life (and Wilfrid's own life; see Mayr-Harting, 1972, pp. 139–41); she is not associated with lust until her death (2 [4] Kgs. 9.21–37), and it is from this episode that she is developed as a type of the Whore of Babylon (Rev. 2.20–3). The cup offered by the Valkyrie (fn. 43) is also associated with runic charms and magic, including love charms (see *Sigrdrifomál*, st. 1–8), but Eddius does not point us in that direction. Cf. the hostility between the wife and mother-in-law of Eadwig and Bishop Dunstan in the late AS period, fn. 125.

[84] See ch. 34. Wilfrid had brought back from Rome many relics and papal letters of support; Jurmenburg's wearing of the reliquary thus represents a defiant flouting of the power of Rome paralleling Ecgfrith's spurning of the papal letters. Jurmenburg's pagan/Antichrist role here is consistent with typology of both OT (1 [3] Kgs. 16.30–3) and NT (Rev. 2.20–3). Jurmenburg's triumphal chariot reappears in *Bede's Cuthbert*, ch. 27, as a means of escape from the scene of Ecgfrith's military defeat.

[85] Ch. 2 ("consilio et munimine"). Wilfrid's secular intentions are also suggested by the fact that he came with recommendations from noblemen concerning his abilities as a courtly servitor.

mother, mark the divorcement of women from an ethos of male violence in the poet's conception of the ideal.[86] Eanfled, in short, deflecting Wilfrid from warrior *comitatus* to monastic community, is herself re-orientated, and becomes, first and foremost, not a leader of armed men, but a queen who uses her influence on behalf of the servants of God.[87] She is thus more clearly distinguished as a reigning queen from the warrior queen Jurmenburg, and from Queen Balthild – another destroyer of men, and a Jezebel who used her power to persecute God's prophets on the continent in real earnest, for Wilfrid only narrowly escaped death at the hands of her minions.[88]

Were it not for the saving grace that Wilfrid had already decided to serve God before he presented himself to Eanfled, Eanfled would be recognizable in this episode as a queenly counterpart of the abbess Hild, whose advice to Cædmon to abandon the secular life for monastic orders represents the only instance of conversion brought about by a woman in early hagiography.[89] But, in fostering the ecclesiastical career of Wilfrid, Eanfled is in some manner a begetter of spiritual sons for the church, and appropriately assumes the role of a spiritual or surrogate mother to Wilfrid in her protective care of him. Wilfrid forms a number of adoptive relationships during the course of his life; for Wilfrid, in leaving his unhappy homelife behind him to pursue more illustrious connexions, had taken to heart the gospel injunction to forsake natural ties for community in the spirit. As he explained to Bishop Dalfinus who later adopted him as a son: "Everyone that has forsaken father or mother shall receive an hundred fold and shall inherit eternal life."[90] In setting out on his pilgrimage to Rome, Wilfrid sought the advice of his earliest spiritual father, the retired retainer he served at Lindisfarne, who took council with Eanfled. Eanfled continued to serve his interests in a maternal fashion, by fitting him out in an honourable fashion for the journey. She asked her own kinsman, the king of Kent, to assist Wilfrid in his plans, and Wilfrid thus sallied forth like Jacob, equipped with the blessing of his spiritual parents.[91]

The precise counterfoil of the wicked queen Jurmenburg, however, is the monastic adviser Abbess Æbbe, "a very wise and holy woman." By her advice to King Ecgfrith, she undoes the harm that was accomplished by the advice of Jurmenburg – though not entirely. When Wilfrid returns to Northumbria bearing letters from Rome in support of his case, Æbbe succeeds in securing his release from prison and the return of his reliquary, but she is unable to achieve his reinstatement to his see.[92] Wilfrid's reinstatement to his bishopric, and the restoration of his property, was finally accomplished towards the end of his life through the advice of the abbess Ælffled. Ælffled, having been present at the death bed of Ecgfrith's successor Aldfrith, testified at the synod of Nidd

---

[86] See further pp. 86–91.
[87] See *HE*, III.24, for Eanfled's part in the endowment of monasteries.
[88] See ch. 6; cf. *HE*, V.19. Bede implies that Balthild ordered the bishop's summary execution whereas Eddius seems to be thinking of a judicial death sentence; see further fn. 111.
[89] For entry to the monastic life as a form of conversion, see ch. 8, fn. 100.
[90] Matt. 19.29. See chs. 4, 6; cf. ch. 2.
[91] Ch. 3: the "father" with whom Eanfled consults is the monk Cudda whom she sent Wilfrid to serve. Eanfled's maternal role is further affirmed by the allusion to Samuel and Eli in ch. 2; cf. 1 Sam. (1 Kgs.) 1.22–8, 2.19.
[92] Ch. 39.

convened by the Archbishop of Canterbury that it was the king's dying wish that Wilfrid should be reinstated. Eddius's highest praise is, accordingly, bestowed on Ælffled: she was "always the comforter and best councillor of the whole province."[93] Ælffled's reputation as a "councillor and comforter," I suggest in the next chapter, may refer to her use of private influence as the spiritual adviser of King Aldfrith. But Ælffled was evidently a leader among men – seemingly the sole woman present at the gathering of the Northumbrian leaders of church and state – and she is an adviser in the public sphere in as much as she rises at the synod of Nidd to repeat the words that Aldfrith spoke on his death bed.

Abbess Æbbe, on the other hand, is a private adviser to the king. But, as the popularity of friendship between bishops and kings indicates, the private confidant of kings was in a strong position to influence public affairs. Abbess Æbbe's advice to King Ecgfrith when Jurmenburg suddenly contracted a fatal illness illustrates well the overlapping of private, informal, advice with influence on public events. Alcuin's correspondence with kings suggests that one established version of the spiritual mentor's combination of consolation and advice was to extend sympathy to the afflicted, while affirming at the same time that the affliction was a sign of the need to mend the error of former ways, in the hope that affliction might produce a receptivity to guidance that was otherwise lacking.[94] Æbbe's advice to Ecgfrith evinces the same strategy.

Eddius relates that when Æbbe discovered that the queen had been suddenly struck down with acute paralysis of her limbs while she and the king were staying at the Coldingham monastery during a royal progress, she made her way immediately to the king. Jurmenburg's bondage in sickness, her speech implies, is a direct consequence of the outrage that has been perpetrated against Wilfrid's episcopal power to bind and unbind by shutting him up in prison. And this outrage, she intimates, has been compounded by the queen's attempt to appropriate Wilfrid's supernatural powers to herself by wearing his reliquary about her neck. Æbbe thus advises the king to release the bishop from prison and return his relics to him in order that the queen may be released from death. But her advice goes beyond the immediate catastrophe, for she urges the king to at least allow Wilfrid to leave the country unmolested with his companions, and intimates that it would be as well if he restored Wilfrid to his episcopal throne:

'And now my son, obey the instructions of your mother; break his bonds, send back to him by faithful messenger those holy relics of which he has been robbed, which the queen took from his neck and carried about from town to town like the ark of God, to her own destruction. And if you will not have him back as bishop (which would be best of all), then send him away free and let him depart with his friends and go wherever he will, away from your kingdom. Then, according to my belief you will remain alive and the queen will recover, but, if you refuse to do this, God is my witness that you will not be unpunished.' Thereupon the king obeyed the chaste

93 Colgrave, p. 129; see chs. 59, 60.
94 See Duemmler, esp. 197, 198.

matron, released our holy bishop and allowed him to depart freely with his relics, in company with all his friends; and the queen was healed.[95]

Hild, adviser of kings, princes and others who sought her aid when they were in difficulties, was called "mother" by all who knew her.[96] Æbbe, who addresses her nephew as a spiritual son is, similarly, an abbatical Mother whose advice to the laity is an extension of her maternal role. Clearly, she reproves the king for his treatment of Wilfrid in her opening words. But she delivers her speech in tears. Her tears, it is true, are somewhat ambivalent. Although they may signify to the modern reader only an emotional appeal by a helpless woman, wisdom traditionally encompassed prophecy as well as prudent advice, and tears were also a sign of prescience of impending doom.[97] In Bishop Cedd's words to Sigeberht, when he discovered that the king had ignored his ban of excommunication on his kinsmen and gone to feast at their house, prophetic statement is scarcely distinguishable from the power of cursing: "The bishop . . . touching the king with the staff in his hand, exercised his pontifical authority and said: 'I tell you that, since you have refused to avoid the house of a man who is lost and damned, this very house will be the place of your death.' "[98] When Wilfrid saw the courtiers smirking over his defeat as he departed from the court of Ecgfrith and Jurmenburg, he availed himself more liberally and overtly of an extension of the episcopal power of cursing bestowed on Peter with the keys: "On this day twelvemonth, you who now laugh at my condemnation through malice, shall then weep bitterly over your own confusion."[99] In Æbbe's advice to the king, the tears that affirm her prophetic glimpse of impending grief accompany an oblique warning delivered with the intention of prevailing on Ecgfrith to save himself and the queen from disaster. In her advice to Ecgfrith, then, Æbbe is a monastic salvatrix, whose ambivalently tearful speech, tactfully unassertive in its recommendations for Wilfrid's reinstatement, and concerned to secure the safe deliverance of all the parties involved, is in evident contrast with the verbal arrows of Jurmenburg urging Ecgfrith to self-aggrandizement by the destruction of Wilfrid.

Deliverer of Wilfrid from the bondage of prison, Æbbe is also the healer of Jurmenburg from the bonds of sickness, whereby Wilfrid's outraged power of the keys avenges itself, despite Jurmenburg's triumphant rejoicing in her superior worldly power by flaunting her theft of his reliquary. Wilfrid's immaterial potency was at its highest peak during this period of bodily misfortune, for no fetters could serve to confine him in prison.[100] And when the sheriff's wife took ill, and the sheriff confessed to the sin of having been a party to the wrongful persecution of Wilfrid, Wilfrid performed a Peter's mother-in-law variety of

95 Colgrave, p. 79; ch. 29.
96 *HE*, IV.23.
97 See further pp. 190–9.
98 Sherley-Price, p. 180; *HE*, III.22.
99 Colgrave, p. 51; ch. 24. Eddius finds fulfilment of this in the death of Ecgfrith's brother, Ælfwine, in a battle against the Mercians (cf. *HE* IV.21). But the attempt to link Ecgfrith's death and defeat at the hands of the Picts is continued; Eddius remarks that Ecgfrith won no further victories from that day until his death.
100 Ch. 38.

miracle, and unbound the afflicted limbs and tongue of the sheriff's wife.[101] Wilfrid is thus firmly established as the source and origin of miraculous and sacerdotal powers to unbind, and a grateful woman renders due homage to him by her ministrations. By a meaningful coincidence, the sheriff's wife also became an abbess, who took the name of Æbbe in religion, and was wont to recall her episcopal saviour in floods of tears. The time scheme makes it scarcely feasible for Eddius to explicitly identify the sheriff's wife with Ecgfrith's aunt, the abbess of Coldingham, but the sheriff's wife serves nevertheless as a surrogate for the abbess, a paradigmatic demonstration that Wilfrid's abbatical rescuer is in reality indebted to his beneficence, a mere agent and intermediary of the numinous powers of her episcopal superior.

In her instrumental involvement in the miracle of Jurmenburg's healing, Æbbe is connected with Cynethryth, "the abbess of Wilfrid," who is the inadvertent agent of a miraculous cure after his death through the power of the cloak on which his body lay – for there are few exceptions to the rule that women perform miracles only through the power of the relics of male saints.[102] The allegorical coupling of abbess and bishop with Christ and Mary in this episode, I have suggested, gives expression to their partnership as heads of the church, and is redolent with implications for abbesses' participation in the sacerdotal ministry as well as the numinous powers of bishops; a participation subject to severe constraint, as Tatberht demonstrates by his intention to retain exclusive use of the mantle imbued with Wilfrid's spiritual powers. Æbbe's role as a confessorial Mother in Christ – effecting the unbinding of Jurmenburg and employing a species of episcopal curse to turn Ecgfrith from the error of his ways and avert divine judgment – is of particular interest in the light of canonical testimony to conflict concerning the extent to which women could act as confessors. The emphatic establishment of Wilfrid as the font of Æbbe's powers, her obvious devotion to his cause and the extremity of his situation, bespeaks the same jealous possessiveness of supernatural powers as Tatberht's instruction regarding the cloak, but the episode evinces nevertheless a certain willingness to countenance female participation in the sacred mysteries in exceptional circumstances.

Wilfrid was evidently active, at least towards the end of his life, in promoting a cult of Mary with which he had become acquainted in Rome. As Wilfrid was returning from Rome, Eddius says, a vision befell him when his followers thought that he was dead, and, with much weeping, they appealed for the help of God. In Wilfrid's vision, the archangel Michael appeared to him, and informed him that Mary, moved by the lamentations of his followers, had interceded in order to gain for him another four years of life and the return of his possessions on his return home. The archangel taxed Wilfrid with the fact that, although Mary was interceding for him, none of the churches he had built had been dedicated in honour of Mary, and he instructed Wilfrid to remedy this past failure.[103] In Mary, then, the advice of good women finds archetypal

---

[101] Ch. 37.
[102] See further pp. 296–7.
[103] Ch. 56. Wilfrid subsequently sent gifts to the churches in Rome, including St Mary Maggiore (ch. 63); see further fn. 107. Wilfrid had spent some months with Pope Sergius, who was

expression – not only does she intercede in heaven for the continuation of Wilfrid's life and his eternal salvation, she also brings about the restoration of his confiscated property. Ælffled, Eddius's last and best royal woman adviser, thus appears to be the Life's culminating representative of Mary, since it is her testimony at the synod of Nidd that persuades the assembled company to reinstate Wilfrid and return his possessions to him. The sole woman present at a council of the realm convened by the Archbishop of Canterbury, she is an earthly reflection, though a pale one, of Mary at the court of heaven, who, by one reading of *Judgement Day II*, "leads mighty councillors, the sentinels of the skies."[104] The tearful appeals for merciful intercession which appear to have figured in the cult of Mary that Wilfrid fostered towards the end of his life may have struck his Anglo-Saxon contemporaries as alien, considering that warrior-heroic ideals of conduct generally tend to unflinching stoicism. But its currency may account for Lul's epistolary weeping on bended knees in his request for the assistance of Abbess Cyniburg[105] – for while Lul's assumed posture is unstartling to the reader habituated to later medieval romances, whose aristocratic heroines have derived from their Marian archetype the unfailing attribute of mercy to all who mourn, it is in striking contrast to the Eddic lay of *Atlamal*, where Hogni's contempt is absolute for the slave who begs in tears that his life may be spared.[106]

The Roman strain of devotion to Mary that Wilfrid brought back with him appears to have been distinctive in that the focus of devotion was not Mary as mother, but as virgin bride. Eddius, earlier in the Life, describes Wilfrid's erection of the church at Ripon that he dedicated to St Peter; over this account, the archangel's instruction that Wilfrid should henceforth honour Mary through his church building casts a retrospective glow. Eddius's account of the church that Wilfrid dedicated to St Peter is redolent with the imagery of Christ's mystical marriage with his virgin bride, who is, inextricably, both Mary herself and the Church that she symbolizes:

> There grew up in our Bishop, the friend of the eternal Bridegroom, a love which ever increased in ardor for the virgin Bride espoused to one husband and born of charity the mother of all goodness. He adorned her fairly with the rules of discipline as with flowers of virtue, making her chaste and modest, continent, temperate and submissive, and clothed her in garments of many hues. In the words of the prophet, 'The king's daughter is all glorious within.' For as Moses built an earthly tabernacle made with hands, of divers varied colours according to the pattern shown by God in the mount, to stir up the faith of the people of Israel for the worship of God, so the blessed Bishop Wilfrid wondrously adorned the bridal chamber of the true Bridegroom and Bride with gold and silver and varied purples, in the

---

noted for his devotion to Mary; see M. Clayton, *The Cult of the Virgin Mary in Anglo-Saxon England* (Cambridge, 1990), p. 92.

[104] Cf. T.D. Hill, "The Kingdom of the Father, Son, and Counsellor: *Judgement Day II*, 290–300," *N&Q* NS 32 (1985), 7–8.

[105] Tangl, 49 (739x41).

[106] *Atlamál*, st. 60–2.

sight of the multitudes who believed in their hearts and made confession of their faith.[107]

The devotion to Mary that informs the 9th century Prologue to the *Law of Adomnan*, by contrast, is based on reverence for women as the source of life, and suggestive of the cult of the Earth Mother: "Thou shalt establish a law in Ireland and Britain for the sake of the mother of each one, because a mother has borne each one, and for the sake of Mary, mother of Jesus Christ through whom all are. . . . For the sin is great when any one slays the mother and sister of Christ's mother and the mother of Christ, and her who carries the spindle and who clothes every one."[108] Aldhelm's *De Virginitate*, of course, celebrates the perpetual virginity of Mary; but, as Aldhelm is engaged in diplomatically balancing the claims of physical virginity against purity of mind, the virginity of Mary is celebrated without anything like the full force of Aldhelm's rhetorical effusion.[109]

The early Anglo-Saxon abbesses, to whom Marian associations attach, were frequently widows: like bishops, they forwarded the advance of the Church by the building of churches, which they not uncommonly dedicated to Mary. For early Anglo-Saxon abbesses, identification with Mary in her aspect as mother was a good deal more appropriate.[110] But the attraction for Wilfrid of a Marian cult offering an ideal of royal womanhood as modest, submissive and amenable to ecclesiastical discipline is not far to seek, given his experiences with Jurmenburg as well as a murderous continental queen.[111] His seminal contribution to the cult of the perpetual virginity and miraculously uncorrupted body of Æthelthryth – notably submissive to the influence of Bishop Wilfrid and the authority of her husband, according to the account Bede says he obtained from

---

[107] Colgrave, p. 35; ch. 17. Cf. *HE*, V.19, and *Song of York*, ll. 632–45; neither of these accounts of Wilfrid's vision mentions the archangel's instruction regarding the dedication of churches to Mary, nor do they suggest further association with her cult. But a church in Wilfrid's Hexham monastery of St Andrew was dedicated to her: 7th and 8th c. church dedications are listed by Levison, 1946, pp. 259–65, esp. 263. Only dedications to Peter are more frequent in this period than dedications to Mary (18 confirmed): of these, at least five were churches built by women.

[108] *Law of Adomnan*, trans. McNeill, pp. 135–6. Various cults of the Earth-Mother Goddess had currency in pre-Christian Western Europe. Eckenstein, pp. 1–44, argues the case for a connexion between Mother Goddess cults, the cult of Mary and the cult of holy women in the early church, encouraged by Pope Sergius.

[109] *De Virginitate*, ch. 40. Nor does Aldhelm hymn the virginity of Mary in *Carm Eccles* 3, on the church built by Abbess Bugga and dedicated to St Mary. *Carm Eccles* 2 contains the same echoes of *Canticles* as *De Virginitate*, and lauds Mary's motherhood.

[110] Abbesses in the 7th and early 8th c. who are known to have been widows or formerly married women are as follows: Æthelthryth, Seaxburg, Eanfled, Hereburg, Hereswith (at Chelles), and Jurmenburg (mentioned by Bede); Æthelburg, Domne Eafe and Eormenhild (Mildrith Legend, see further p. 72); Cuthburg (ASC, 718); Eangyth (Tangl, 14). Hild is believed to have been a widow: see further p. 213. Jurmenburg can be presumed to have become an abbess after serving her novitiate at her sister's monastery. Osyth, 7th c. founder at Chich, is said to have been the wife of Sigehere of Essex (see Bethell, 75–127). Cynethryth, Offa's widow, who became the abbess of Cookham (see further pp. 000), illustrates the continued existence of widowed abbesses into the late 8th c. (Other identifications are less certain; for the likelihood that Eadburg and Eafe of Gloucester were, respectively, the divorced wife of Wulfhere of Mercia and the widow of Æthelwald of Sussex, see Sims-Williams, 1990, p. 123.)

[111] J. Nelson, "Queens as Jezebels: The Careers of Brunhild and Balthild in Merovingian History," ed. D. Baker, pp. 31–57, shows that there has been a confusion of identities.

Wilfrid – points to a similar interest in the cultivation of an ideal of royally virginal femininity.[112]

The unexpected paucity of Marian reference in the vernacular *Dream of the Rood* gives the impression that Marian devotion did not strike root in the heroic world; liturgical practice perhaps shows otherwise.[113] Wilfrid's evident involvement in the fostering of a cult of Mary suggests that the polarized presentation of royal women in Eddius's Life signals the existence, even at this early date, of an impulse to schematic categorization of all women as types of either Mary or Eve.[114] But despite Wilfrid's devotion to Æthelthryth's perpetual virginity, the conception of Wilfrid's salvatrix, Abbess Æbbe, is essentially maternal, and the virginity of Ælffled, to which her father vowed her in infancy, is merely incidental to Eddius's praise.[115] The polarization of women about the figure of Wilfrid, as protective mothers who rescue men from the destructive toils of tyrannical tempters, and restore to them their lost Eden, is irresistibly explicable as a psychological pattern with its roots in Wilfrid's childhood. For Jurmenburg, in instigating her husband's banishment of Wilfrid, is the echo of his stepmother, whose harsh cruelty drove him out of his father's house; so too is Balthild, whose malice robbed him of his adopted father, Bishop Dalfinus, and forced him, eager though he naturally was to share the bishop's martyrdom, to try his luck in another land. Just so Queen Eanfled, the nurturing mother by adoption, under whose council and protection he went to seek refuge, looks forward to the intercessory ministrations of her daughter, Abbess Ælffled, and to his salvatrix, Abbess Æbbe. But surely Eanfled looks backward as well, to a nostalgic dream of the lost and idolized woman, Wilfrid's own "most pious" mother, whose final fulfilment is to be found in the vision of Mary as his heavenly protector and giver of life.[116]

But the Life's presentation of female advisers is of more general significance in its polemical bearing on the relations of bishops and royal women. Overall, Eddius hints at far more in the way of power and influence possessed by royal

---

[112] *HE*, IV.19.

[113] *Dream of the Rood*, ll. 93–5, links the Cross and Mary as elect instruments of salvation. But she is absent from the Passion (ll. 57–77) and the controlling metaphor encourages a reading of the Deposition and Burial as the actions of a warrior band; and although the Invention is alluded to, Helena is not named. However, the Visitation and Annunciation, together with the traces of a scene variously interpreted as the Nativity or Adoration of the Magi, appear on the early 8th c. Ruthwell Cross, which is runically inscribed with passages from this section of the poem, and Cuthbert's coffin (late 7th c.) includes the Madonna and Child in its iconographical scheme; these and other early AS visual representations are surveyed by Clayton, 1990, pp. 142–57. M. Clayton, "Feasts of the Virgin in the Liturgy of the Anglo-Saxon Church," *ASE* 13 (1984), 209–33 (and, more recently, Clayton, 1990, esp. pp. 25–89), argues that feasts in honour of Mary were introduced rather slowly and that they had not been firmly established by the mid 8th c.; on the other hand, there is unusually marked liturgical devotion to Mary (by monastics) in the late OE period.

[114] Eddius's schematization may also be prompted by the use of structural parallelism and character pairing in vernacular literary tradition, pervasive in *Beowulf* and the Eddic lays; see fn. 30.

[115] Ch. 59 describes her as abbess, wise virgin and daughter of a king; *HE*, III.24.

[116] Every saint is an artifact of his hagiographer, but few have had as much opportunity as Wilfrid to influence the hagiographer's views. Eddius had been a follower of Wilfrid, and presumably used Wilfrid's own account; see fn. 69.

women, whether as queens or abbesses, than Bede does in his *History*. Eanfled, who serves the interests of her servant Wilfrid in the Life, is still visibly a ruler with her own retinue. In Bede's account she has been much more effectively subordinated to ecclesiastical authority and interests. Bede makes a more edifying story out of Wilfrid's career by having him simply decide to enter a monastery at the age of fourteen – but the effect of this is to excise the bishop's youthful career in the service of a queen, a state of affairs not in conformity with Bede's views on the hierarchical superiority of bishops. Gone too is the seminal direction to the monastery given by Eanfled when she sent Wilfrid to Lindisfarne to act as servant to the monk Cudda, as well as her consultation with Cudda over Wilfrid's visit to Rome; her power to intervene in the affairs of the Lindisfarne monastery has also been curtailed. As Bede relates it, Wilfrid obtained the approval of the Lindisfarne monks for his pilgrimage to Rome, and then went to tell Queen Eanfled, "because she knew him and because it was through her council and at her request that he had been admitted to the monastery."[117] Even in the account of the obedient Queen Æthelthryth, in the *Life of Wilfrid*, there is a residual trace of her joint rulership with the king. Bede gives no hint of throne-sharing by any of the few queens he mentions – the only powerful queenly adviser in his work, mentioned merely in passing, and unnamed, is a pagan, the wife of Redwald, who persuades her baptized husband to apostatize; her closest counterpart is the wife of Sebbi, also unnamed, who withholds her consent when he wishes to renounce his kingdom for a monastery.[118]

More comprehensively for Bede than for Eddius, power and politically influential advice are not attributes of Christian queens, or abbesses either. Eddius's evaluation of royal women depends on whether they help or hinder the fortunes of Wilfrid. This evaluative schematization does not quite coincide with their monastic or secular status – for there are pious queenly counterfoils to Jurmenburg and Balthild, and Eddius also mentions that Abbess Hild joined with Theodore in sending letters to Rome opposing Wilfrid's reinstatement to his bishopric.[119] Nor does moral evaluation depend on whether their use of influence is discreetly private – for whereas Jurmenburg advises as an intimate of the king, Ælffled holds in the ecclesiastical sphere the position of official councillor that queens held in the secular sphere. But the effective influence of the wicked pagan queen Jurmenburg is far greater than that of the pious queens Æthelthryth and Eanfled, and exceeds that of her monastic counterfoil Æbbe; Ælffled, admitted to the councils of the leaders of church and state but limited to the role of truthful witness to the king's dying wishes, scarcely compares with her as a power in the land. And in Eddius's adumbration of the magical transformation of Jurmenburg in later life, his underlying hostility to the power of queens, and his ultimate preference for the submergence of their power in ecclesiastical power, are plainly revealed: Jurmenburg "was at that time tortured with envy through the persuasions of the devil, although, after the death of the

---

117 C&M, p. 519; *HE*, V.19: cf. *Life of Wilfrid*, ch. 2. On the question of whether Bede drew on Eddius's Life, see D.P. Kirby, "Bede, Eddius Stephanus and the Life of Wilfrid," *EHR* 98 (1983), 101–14.

118 *HE*, II.12; IV.11.

119 Ch. 54. Hild does not appear to fit this scheme; see ch. 6, fn. 23.

king, from being a she-wolf she was changed into a lamb of God, a perfect abbess and a excellent mother of the community."[120] In the monasteries, royal women were less of a threat; and more liberal in their benefactions too – Wilfrid's Life reports that nearly all of the abbots and abbess made over their possessions to him by vow, and either retained them in his name during their lifetime or named him as heir in their wills.[121] The conversion of royal wives into brides of the lamb did not render them entirely modest, temperate, submissive and adorned with the flowers of virtue but, in the *Life of Wilfrid*, the insubordinate potentialities of abbesses are within episcopal control, and insignificant beside the challenge to the episcopal adviser presented by queens.

As an enemy of Wilfrid, Jurmenburg is also depicted by Eddius as an enemy of the Church itself. Like Redwald's pagan wife in Bede's *History*, she invites the conclusion that queens, with a few devout exceptions, were actively hostile to the conversion. Wilfrid's very considerable talent for provoking personal hostility may have been a self-sufficient cause of Jurmenburg's enmity; conversely, purely secular considerations of policy – Wilfrid's lavish displays of power, for instance – may have determined her attitude to him, just as Redwald's wife appears to have had sound political reasons for her opposition to his conversion.[122] But there were many reasons why royal women might have been hostile to the conversion – *Theodore's Penitential* reveals some of them.[123] Against the rising power of bishops, powerful queens had most to lose. In their conflict with queens for the ear of the king, bishops had an imposing polemical weapon in the theology of original female corruption and its redemption in the Marian idealization of womanhood.

In the Benedictine Reform movement, the position of paramount abbess passed to the queen. *Regularis Concordia* states that, when King Edgar, like a Good Shepherd, had rescued the monasteries from their marauding enemies, he wisely established his queen, Ælfthryth, as the protector and guardian of the convents.[124] By the elevation of the queen to a quasi-sacerdotal role with which the king, as Christ's representative, had been endowed since the arrival of Christianity, her powers of influence were consecrated to ecclesiastical purposes.[125] To the queen, in her role as protector of the nunneries and consort of the Christ-King, passed the identification with Mary that had attached to the early abbesses, the focus shifting from the Universal Mother to the Heavenly

---

[120] Colgrave, p. 49; ch. 24. Bede reports that Jurmenburg received the veil from Cuthbert at her sister's monastery in Carlisle (*Bede's Cuthbert*, chs. 27, 28).

[121] See ch. 21. Wilfrid received land at Hexham from Æthelthryth (ch. 22) at about the time she took the veil from him at Coldingham; see Roper, pp. 169–71.

[122] *HE*, II.12; see further, pp. 232–4.

[123] See further pp. 62–5.

[124] *Regularis Concordia*, p. 2.

[125] For discussion, see M.A. Meyer, "Women and the Tenth Century English Monastic Reform," *RB* 87 (1977), 34–61. See Author B's Life of Dunstan, ch. 21, for a conflict which is parallel to that of Jurmenburg and Wilfrid: ed. W. Stubbs, *Memorials of St Dunstan* (London, 1874), pp. 3–52. Author B's Life (c. 1000) relates that, while Eadwig's coronation was being celebrated, the king himself was lasciviously disporting himself in a side room with a woman who subsequently became his wife, and her designing mother, and had to be dragged back to his throne by Dunstan, whose later downfall and exile are blamed on the hostility of these two women.

Queen.[126] The ideological shift in the conception of the queen is marked by the contrast between the *Beowulf* poet's depiction of Wealhtheow, a queen in the heroic mode, and the self-effacing portrait of Queen Edith in the *Life of King Edward*, who looks forward to the ideal woman of chivalric romance. Wealhtheow advises on the disposition of the kingdom and affirms her position as joint ruler of the hall by taking up her seat beside the king. The Marian idealization of the queen renders Edith so modestly submissive that "although by custom and law a royal throne was always prepared for her at the king's side, she preferred, except in church and at the royal table, to sit at his feet."[127] As a peaceweaver in the Marian mode, Edith exerts, in theory, the pervasive good influence that bishops like Theodore and Wilfrid achieved by the power of the spirit: "Through her advice, peace laps the kingdom round, and keeps mankind from breaking pacts of peace."[128] In practice, the ideal of submissively modest Marian womanhood ensures that Edith's fame as an adviser consists in the fact that "by God's grace she shone above all in counsel, if she were heard."[129] For the conversion of queens and the conversion of the queen's role to ecclesiastical purposes, Eddius's description of the magical transformation of Jurmenburg from a ravening she-wolf to an exemplary lamb of God is fraught with implication.

[126] The identification of the queen with the Queen of Heaven, fully embodied in Turgot's early 12th c. Life of Margaret of Scotland, is embryonically evident in the portrayal of Emma in the *Encomium* and Edith in *Life of King Edward*; see further pp. 208–12, 218–19, 298–9.

[127] Barlow, *Life of King Edward*, p. 42.

[128] Barlow, *Life of King Edward*, p. 15.

[129] Barlow, *Life of King Edward*, p. 54.

6

A Beautiful Friendship Ruined:
Bede's Revisionist Writing of Ælffled
in the Life of Cuthbert

Ælffled, whose participation at the synod of Nidd is related in Eddius's *Life of Wilfrid*, is representative of the political influence of abbesses with powerful family connexions, a class conspicuously absent in Bede's *History* – and not surprisingly, in view of his handling of Ælffled in his revision of the Anonymous Lindisfarne *Life of Cuthbert*.[1] Ælffled, Hild's niece, and successor as Abbess of Whitby, was the daughter of Oswiu of Northumbria and Eanfled of Kent, and the sister of Ecgfrith, who succeeded to the Northumbrian throne after the death of their father Oswiu. She was also related, though more distantly, to Ecgfrith's successor, Aldfrith,[2] and retained some form of connexion with the court at the time of the synod of Nidd (706), when Aldfrith's son, Osred, had been installed on the throne. In the Anonymous *Life of Cuthbert*, she appears as a friend of Bishop Cuthbert, and Eddius's *Life of Wilfrid* mentions that Archbishop Theodore wrote to her when he negotiated for Wilfrid's return to Northumbria. Despite Bede's presentation of bishops as the superior mentors of royal abbesses, their favour and influence could be as significantly useful to bishops as that of queens. Though Eddius gives the impression that, as brides of the Lamb, the powers of royal women were safely under episcopal control, Bede's rewriting of Ælffled's role in the *Life of Cuthbert* reflects, in its considerable hostility to her as an intimate of the bishop-saint, sharp competitive strains concerning women's participation in the ecclesiastical sphere. Eddius's depiction of Ælffled, though moderated by his own stereotyping constructs, gives a glimpse of the actualities of the prestige of particularly eminent royal abbesses, against which Bede's revision of the Anonymous *Life of Cuthbert* is directed.

---

[1] Bede omits Ælffled from his summary of Cuthbert's Life (HE, IV.27–32), and from his account of Wilfrid (HE, V.19). Reference is made to the Anonymous Lindisfarne Life and Bede's prose Life, in B. Colgrave, ed. and trans., *Two Lives of Saint Cuthbert: A Life by an Anonymous Monk of Lindisfarne and Bede's Prose Life* (Cambridge, 1940). Translation throughout is from Colgrave. For Bede's metrical Life, see fns. 44, 106.
[2] Aldfrith was the illegitimate son of Oswiu (*Bede's Cuthbert*, ch. 24).

Ælffled and *The Life of Wilfrid*

Of the royal women who figure as advisers in Eddius's *Life of Wilfrid*, Abbess Ælffled of Whitby calls forth his highest praise: she was "always the comforter and best councillor of the whole province."[3] Whereas Ælffled's aunt, Abbess Æbbe, is a spiritual mentor who advises King Ecgfrith in private,[4] Ælffled is a councillor in the public sphere at the synod of Nidd. The synod met for the express purpose of determining whether or not Wilfrid should be reinstated to the bishopric from which he had – again – been banished, this time by King Aldfrith.[5] Ælffled and Abbess Æthelburg had been present at Aldfrith's deathbed,[6] and Ælffled was able to testify that it had been the king's dying wish to make peace with Wilfrid. Indeed, she went further than this, according to Eddius. The version of the king's last words that Eddius says many could vouch for merely affirms the king's desire for a personal reconciliation; but the speech he attributes to Ælffled at the synod of Nidd – in line with Eddius's own preoccupations with ecclesiastical authority – affirms the king's concern to implement the Apostolic See's judgment in favour of Wilfrid which he had previously spurned.[7] As Ælffled's testimony was instrumental in the restoration of Wilfrid to his bishopric and his possessions, which even his devoted supporter Æbbe had been unable to accomplish, the reason for Eddius's enthusiastic praise is not far to seek.

Although Eddius gives the impression that Ælffled's presence at Nidd depended on a particular and unusual circumstance, the presence of abbesses at councils of the realm does not appear to have been an exceptional occurrence.[8] But Ælffled, if we are to believe Bede, was more privileged than Hild was at the synod that she and her community attended in 664, even though it was held at her own monastery. While one can well believe that Wilfrid's oratorical dedication to the correct dating of Easter may have made it difficult for any else to speak at the synod of Whitby, the silence imposed on Hild in Bede's narrative is scarcely credible.[9] It is a possible implication of Eddius's account that the choice

---

[3] Colgrave, p. 129; *Life of Wilfrid*, ch. 60.

[4] *Life of Wilfrid*, ch. 39.

[5] *Life of Wilfrid*, chs. 46–9.

[6] *Life of Wilfrid*, ch. 59.

[7] *Life of Wilfrid*, ch. 59: " 'If by God's will I die, in the name of God I bid my heir, whoever it may be who shall succeed me in the kingdom, to make peace and a settlement with Bishop Wilfrid for the good of my soul and his own.' " Cf. *Life of Wilfrid*, ch. 60: " 'If I live, I will fulfill all the decrees of the Apostolic See concerning the blessed Bishop Wilfrid which I once refused to obey. But, if I die, I bid my heir, my son, in the name of the Lord, that he fulfill for the good of my soul the Apostolic Judgement concerning Bishop Wilfrid' " (Colgrave, pp. 127, 131–3). See fn. 16.

[8] Synods were not clearly distinct from councils of ecclesiastical and secular leaders. Five abbesses were present at a council at which Wihtred and Queen Werburg (696x716) granted privileges to the churches and monasteries of Kent (Birch, 91). Abbesses attended the synod of Winchester (970), when segregated monasticism was usual; see *Regularis Concordia*, pp. 2–3, and D. Knowles, *The Monastic Order in England*, 2nd edn. (Cambridge, 1963), p. 42.

[9] *Life of Wilfrid*, ch. 10: "Abbots, priests and men of all ranks and orders of the Church gathered in a monastery called Whitby, in the presence of the holy mother and most pious nun

of Whitby for the Roman-Celtic factional debate was a tribute to Hild's powers of conciliation, but she was evidently not a non-participant in ecclesiastical politics; Eddius reveals that, after Wilfrid was exiled from Northumbria by Ecgfrith, Hild and Archbishop Theodore sent letters to Rome in which they put their case against his reinstatement.[10]

Despite the fact that Ælffled's report of the king's dying wish was the critical deciding factor at the synod of Nidd, she achieves no central position in the proceedings, and her role as a unifying link between court and ecclesiastical circles is only barely discernible. She is a highly anomalous and somewhat marginal figure; the account perhaps owes as much to Eddius's evident preference for the dissociation of women from power as to the actual configurations of the debate. For although the secular councillors at Nidd immediately declare their support for the king's dying wish once Ælffled has voiced it, the bishops remain unreconciled and separate for further discussion among themselves. They finally agree to the reinstatement of Wilfrid after consulting sometimes with the archbishop and at other times with Ælffled. Her influence is operative, then, in committee rather than in a public forum, and takes effect only in conjunction with the peacemaking efforts of the archbishop.

Eddius's account of the role of Ælffled at the synod of Nidd contains the merest hint of what must have been a very eminent and influential position. Her high visibility in the political life of Northumbria is suggested by the fact that she is the only abbess in early Anglo-Saxon hagiography who approaches, even remotely, the freedom of movement and involvement in public affairs of Leoba. Leoba was a frequent and highly regarded visitor at the court of Charlemagne, and was consulted by bishops when she met with them at ecclesiastical councils, because of her reputation for learning. Quasi-episcopal in character too is Leoba's overall supervision of women's religious houses. Leoba's hagiographer is at pains to present Leoba's active involvement beyond the confines of her monastery as exceptional, purely contingent on Leoba's unique status as the missionary founder of female monasticism in Germany.[11] The publicly influential position of Ælffled represents a continuity with the pioneering era, and the wider sphere of action open to abbesses in an age of unenclosed monasteries. Her position as Hild's successor at one of the largest and most important monastic centres in the north doubtless contributed to her high prestige.[12] But in the account of the synod of Nidd Ælffled is cut off from the bishop's party and aligned with the secular leaders, and there can be little doubt that her

Hild, as well as the kings and two bishops" (Colgrave, p. 21). Bede's account, on the other hand, implies that Whitby was identified with the Celtic cause (HE, III.25).

[10] *Life of Wilfrid*, ch. 54. Connexion between Hild's pro-Celtic stance at Whitby (664) and her alliance with Theodore against Wilfrid (c. 678) inevitably suggests itself; Plummer, 1896, II, 190, thought personal incompatibility alone might explain her actions. It may also be relevant that, through Theodore's 679 division of Wilfrid's see, Hild's pupil, Bosa, became Bishop of York, into which see Whitby fell, but was subsequently removed to make way for Wilfrid.

[11] See ch. 9, pp. 271–82.

[12] For Hild as a pioneer founder, see pp. 249–50, 253–8; cf. the report of Æthelthryth and her escort travelling about East Anglia visiting women's religious houses, *Liber Eliensis*, I.13, ed. E.O. Blake, RHS Camden 3rd ser. 92 (London, 1962). Bede implies that Ælffled's prestige and rule over a great many religious derived from her virginal state (*Bede's Cuthbert*, ch. 23).

family connexions with successive Northumbrian rulers provided a stronger underpinning to her influence.[13]

Ælffled's presence at the death-bed of Aldfrith indicates familiar, and indeed intimate, access to court circles. Her appearances in the Anonymous *Life of Cuthbert* and Eddius's *Life of Wilfrid* are redolent with suggestions of the kind of involvement in the transmission of the throne and in ecclesiastical appointments that brought queens in the later Anglo-Saxon period into conflict with bishops.[14] The Anonymous *Life of Cuthbert* reports a meeting between her and Cuthbert on Coquet Island, in which she asks the saint to prophecy how long her childless brother has to live and who will follow him on the throne. She also enquires about Cuthbert's intentions concerning the bishopric of Lindisfarne, which she knows her brother is about to offer him.[15] Her access to confidential information concerning the disposition of inheritance at the highest level is also an aspect of her attendance on Aldfrith at the time of his death, since she is a witness, *inter alia*, to his last wishes concerning his successor – whatever they may have been, for the two versions of Aldfrith's death-bed speech Eddius gives are no more in agreement on this point than they are on the form in which Aldfrith expressed his desire to be reconciled with Wilfrid. The version of Aldfrith's last wishes which, Eddius claims, was widely attested, has him refer only to "my heir, whoever it may be who shall succeed me in the kingdom." But what Ælffled affirms at the synod of Nidd is that Aldfrith designated his son as his successor. Regardless of what Aldfrith did or did not say, it is clear that attendance at a king's death-bed had a highly significant political dimension in terms of the legitimization of the succession, and that royal women admitted to this position were well-placed to exercise an influence on the succession by their version of the dying king's last wishes. Judging by the *Life of King Edward*, any claim that Harold Godwinson had to be regarded as Edward's designated successor depended chiefly on the fact that his sister Edith was present at the king's death-bed in the role of wifely mourner.[16]

---

[13] Hagiographic insistence on the relative insignificance of the worldly status of ecclesiastical office holders effectively affirms the reverse, and the reputation for holiness Bede accords Ælffled in *Bede's Cuthbert*, ch. 23, is thus the due portion of a renowned royal abbess, not a mark of personal regard: she "increased the nobility of a royal pedigree with the much more potent nobility of the highest virtue" (Colgrave, p. 231). See also Æbbe (ch. 10) and Verca (ch. 35). Cf. *Life of Wilfrid*, ch. 59: "an abbess and most prudent virgin who is indeed the daughter of a king" (Colgrave, p. 129). Like *Bede's Cuthbert*, ch. 23, HE, III.24 emphasizes Ælffled's royal status as well as her virginity; HE, IV.26 suggests that, after the death of Oswiu, when Eanfled joined Hild and Ælffled at Whitby, its prestige was enhanced by its development as a royal mausoleum.

[14] See further below and fns. 82, 84; see also pp. 154–5.

[15] *Anon Cuthbert*, III.6; *Bede's Cuthbert*, ch. 24.

[16] Eddius's report of two different versions of Aldfrith's last wishes (fn. 7) has far-reaching implications for an oral culture's conception of reliable testimony. Aldfrith was succeeded by Eadwulf, who was quickly overthrown by supporters of Aldfrith's 8 year old son, Osred. Given Osred's minority, the version of Aldfrith's speech which avoids nominating a successor is plausible (*Life of Wilfrid*, ch. 59), and Ælffled's version, which has the king specify his son as his heir, might be Eddius's rewriting; but if Ælffled wished to retain influence at court, she had reason to support the succession of her kinsman's son. Cf. Edward the Confessor's alleged death-bed designation of Harold, *Life of King Edward*, p. 79. Edith, at whose instigation the author wrote (pp. 59–60; see fn. 78 below) had most to gain from the succession of her brother,

Ælffled's appearances in these two contemporary lives,[17] then, indicate her active involvement in both royal and ecclesiastical politics, but suggest that she was more strongly identified with the affairs of the court. Perhaps she was. Leading ecclesiastics were in the habit of acting as secular councillors. The practice was condemned by synods, but the Anonymous *Life of Ceolfrith* reports without embarrassment that Benedict of Wearmouth found it necessary to appoint a surrogate abbot to run his monastery for him, because he was so frequently summoned to give the king the benefit of his wisdom and good advice that he had insufficient time for the monastery's affairs.[18] Ælffled's letter to a continental abbess asking her to assist a sister abbess making her way to Rome, explains that the traveller, "our dear and faithful daughter," had long desired to visit Rome, "but has been kept back by us until now because we needed her, and in order that the souls entrusted to her might profit."[19] Ælffled's controlling interest in another abbess's movements are explicable if we assume that, like Benedict, Ælffled was in such demand at court for her advice that she had appointed a proxy to take care of the management of Whitby.[20]

Eddius's description of Ælffled as "the comforter and best councillor of the whole province" apparently defines her role as a leading councillor at the synodical gathering under Archbishop Berhtwold as the supporter of Wilfrid, in which role she enacts Wilfrid's earlier vision of Mary as merciful intercessor in the councils of heaven on behalf of the restoration of his possessions.[21] Leadership through counsel and consolation was also the office of the confessor and intimate spiritual mentor.[22] In this role too, Ælffled appears, by implication, to have been active in her influence on Wilfrid's behalf.

Towards the end of his life, Archbishop Theodore laid aside his hostility to Wilfrid, and attempted to secure his reinstatement in Northumbria. Theodore evidently regarded Ælffled as one of Wilfrid's foremost ranking enemies, whose favour needed to be won if Wilfrid was to be allowed to return to his see. For he wrote to Ælffled as well as to King Aldfrith, urging her to make peace with the bishop. Theodore's approach to Ælffled is consistent with his having earlier allied himself against Wilfrid with her predecessor Hild, whose opposition to Wilfrid had presumably been shared by the Whitby community.[23] In addition to

and is the most likely source of this report – she was among the few present at Edward's death bed (cf. Barlow, p. 76, fn. 6). See also Abbess Ecgburg, fn. 109 below.

[17] *Anon Cuthbert* is dated 699x705; *Life of Wilfrid*, 710x720. Ælffled died c. 714.

[18] *Life of Ceolfrith*, ch. 12; cf. the orthodox censorship of this in *History of the Abbots*, ch. 7. Legates in 787 prohibited bishops from giving judgment in secular councils, citing 2 Tim. 2.4 (H&S, III, 452).

[19] Tangl, 8.

[20] Æthelburg, who was present with Ælffled at Aldfrith's death, may have been her proxy. Æthelburg is identified as Abbess of Hackness on the strength of a Hackness memorial cross bearing this name (D.H. Haigh, "On the Monasteries of S Heiu and S Hild," *Yorkshire Archaeological and Topographical Journal* 3 [1875], 370), and the name appears immediately below Ælffled's in the *Liber Vitae Ecclesiae Dunelmensis*: ed. J. Stevenson, Surtees Soc. 13 (London, 1841). Simultaneous visions of Hild's soul at Whitby and Hackness imply that they were twin foundations in the manner of Wearmouth and Jarrow (*HE*, IV.23).

[21] *Life of Wilfrid*, ch. 56.

[22] See pp. 116–19.

[23] *Life of Wilfrid*, chs. 43, 54; see fns. 9, 10. Eddius's uncharacteristic praise of an opponent of

this, Ælffled was as well-placed to act as an intermediary between the church and the court in private negotiations as she was in public councils. Eddius, however, merely says that Aldfrith invited Wilfrid to resume his see in accordance with the archbishop's command.[24] Aldfrith, in any case, had only recently come to the throne and had had no previous dealings with Wilfrid. Subsequent disagreements between them came to a head after the death of Theodore, obliging Wilfrid once more to set out for Rome.[25] His visionary intimation that Mary had already been at work securing success for his cause against the time of his arrival in England may obliquely convey that Ælffled had made attempts to persuade the king to return to the harmonious accord that the archbishop had urged upon them both. Aldfrith was not, in fact, positively ill-disposed to the delegation that Wilfrid sent to him when he arrived back from Rome, but was adamant in his refusal to grant him an audience.[26] Like Theodore, Aldfrith found that a charitable disposition towards Wilfrid came only with the prospect of eternal separation from him.

Eddius, characteristically, attributed this change of heart to the king's realization that his fatal illness had befallen him in just retribution for his affront to Wilfrid's god-given power to bind and unbind.[27] But it is difficult to avoid drawing a connexion between Aldfrith's dying wish for reconciliation and the presence of Ælffled and Abbess Æthelburg at his bedside.[28] Ælffled was a life-long protege of her aunt Hild,[29] and the dying wish of the abbess Hild was that the nuns of Whitby should "maintain the gospel peace among themselves and towards all others." The death-bed scene of Whitby's most famous son, the poet Cædmon, echoes the spirit of Hild's last wish. For when Cædmon knew his end was approaching, he held the communion wafer in his hands, "and asked if they were all charitably disposed towards him, and had no complaint nor any quarrel nor grudge against him. They answered that they were all in charity with him, and without the slightest feeling of anger; then they asked him in turn whether he was charitably disposed towards them. He answered at once; 'My sons, I am in charity with all the servants of God.' "[30] Ælffled reflects the Whitby tradition of piety in her letter asking for the help of the abbess Adola, when she appeals to community in Christ: "I pray for your warm affection, for the Lord has said: 'This is my command, that you love one another.' "[31]

Hild, to whom rulers and their subjects alike went for advice when they were in difficulties, demonstrates the merging of royal women's role as advisers to kings with the abbess's role as spiritual mentor that ran parallel to the

Wilfrid suggests that, like Theodore, Hild relented towards Wilfrid before her death: "His adversaries were present, having come hither from Theodore of hallowed memory . . . and from the abbess Hild, of pious memory, in order to accuse him" (Colgrave, p. 117). In Eanfled, who was at Whitby by 686–7 (*HE*, IV.26), Wilfrid had a possible supporter (*Life of Wilfrid*, chs. 2–3).
[24] *Life of Wilfrid*, ch. 44.
[25] *Life of Wilfrid*, ch. 46–7.
[26] *Life of Wilfrid*, ch. 58.
[27] *Life of Wilfrid*, ch. 59.
[28] See Eckenstein, pp. 105–6.
[29] Having been vowed to virginity in infancy by her father, she entered Hild's Hartlepool monastery and later moved with her to Whitby (*HE*, III.24).
[30] C&M, p. 421; *HE*, IV.23, 24 (cf. John 14.27).
[31] Tangl, 8.

confessional ministry of bishops.[32] Eddius's account of the abbess Æbbe reveals the way in which private advice to kings and influence on public affairs could merge inextricably – Wilfrid's bid for intimate friendships with kings testifies to the richly influential potentialities of the position.[33] Ælffled's presence at the death-bed of Aldfrith, and her subsequent report of his dying wish at the synod of Nidd, can be most readily understood as Ælffled's finally successful attempt, in her capacity as spiritual adviser to the king, to bring about the general reconciliation with Wilfrid that Theodore had desired. There can be little doubt that Eddius's account of Ælffled's role at the synod of Nidd significantly under-represents her actual degree of prestige and influence. Given that he has presented her as the mere mouth-piece of oral tradition on this occasion, his description of her as "always the comforter and best councillor of the whole province" might more appropriately serve as praise for her as a private and quasi-confessorial adviser than as commendation of her membership of the councils of the realm.

Bede's *Life of Cuthbert* (1)

In the Anonymous *Life of Cuthbert*, Ælffled appears as the confidential intimate of Bishop Cuthbert. Their relationship is almost unique in representing a form of the "soul friendship" that figures elsewhere in the presentation of friendships between monastic men and those of bishops and kings,[34] although Felix's *Life of Guthlac* offers a more extended analogue in the relation of the hermit saint and his sister Pega.[35] In the Anonymous Life, Ælffled is the confidential sharer of Cuthbert's secret mysteries, to whom he imparts his prophetic knowledge of the future. Of underlying significance for this revelation of secrets is the fact that he also reveals to her the future course of his life and his impending death, and bids her tell no-one of his prophecy.[36] Saints as visionary seers, and confessors to whom all hearts are open, are privy to the hidden mysteries of the universe and

---

[32] HE, IV.23.

[33] *Life of Wilfrid*, ch. 39.

[34] "Soul friend" translates the OIrish *anmchara*, "confessor." I use the term more generally for relationships of particular spiritual affinity which in some way transcend death and/or absence. They sometimes overlap with confessorial relationships: e.g., Oswine and Aidan (HE, III.14); Wilfrid and Alhfrith (*Life of Wilfrid*, ch. 7); Cuthbert and Hereberht in *Bede's Cuthbert*, ch. 28 (cf. *Anon Cuthbert*, IV.9). Relations between monastic women also have elements of soul friendship; see Torhtgyth (who foresees the death of Abbess Æthelburg, who, in turn, communicates posthumously to Torhtgyth the time of her death), and the crippled nun who holds posthumous communication with Æthelburg and dies twelve days after her (HE, IV.9). Cf. the visions of Hild's ascending soul seen by a Whitby nun who "dearly loved Hild" (conceivably Ælffled), and Begu at Hackness (HE, IV.23). Such visions were possibly connected with succession to office; e.g., Cuthbert's vision of the ascending soul of Bishop Aidan (*Anon Cuthbert*, I.5); see fn. 37.

[35] *Life of Guthlac*, chs. 50–1, 53.

[36] *Anon Cuthbert*, III.6, IV.8; cf. I.3.

the secret thoughts of many; but the saint's revelation of his own secrets marks the recipient as a particular friend.[37]

Ælffled, in being made privy to Cuthbert's future knowledge of his death, stands close, in her relationship with him, to his friend the hermit Hereberht. Hereberht and Cuthbert are particularly striking as soul friends, for, intimately bound together in life and in death, they look forward to later romantic lovers like Tristan and Iseult, whose spiritual affinity in life, transcending carnality and physical separation, finds expression in sharing a common death as the gateway to union beyond the grave. The Anonymous Life says that Hereberht, an *alter ego* of Cuthbert in his dedication to the eremitical life, frequently sought out the saint to talk with him, and describes a meeting in which Cuthbert revealed his own impending death. Hereberht begged Cuthbert not to leave him behind in the world to mourn his loss, but to pray to God that he might enter the kingdom of heaven with him. Cuthbert did so, and, in the fullness of time, the bishop and the anchorite died at the very same hour, and now reign together with Christ.[38]

"Greater love hath no man than this, that a man lay down his life for his friends."[39] Bede has destroyed the terms of this friendship, though not as radically as he has destroyed Cuthbert's friendship with Ælffled. As a monastic transmutation of the warrior loyalties that render dying together on the battlefield the culminating expression of physical inseparability in life,[40] the friendship of Cuthbert and Hereberht in the Anonymous Life is somewhat heterodox in its implications of vicarious salvation.[41] Bede's insistence on the episcopal saint's superior detachment from human emotions and the human condition also dictates that the devotion of a friend cannot be allowed to stand as a sufficient reason for participation in Cuthbert's death and translation to the joys of heaven. Bede therefore visits upon Hereberht a long racking illness of his own invention, which he attributes to the mercy of God. This enables Bede to explain, at least to his own satisfaction, why Hereberht was able to share in the death and eternal joy of the episcopal saint. Although Hereberht had previously

[37] Secrecy especially surrounds a saint's possession of supernatural and prophetic powers (Matt. 17.9); see Colgrave, 1940, pp. 319–20. Revelation of impending death and life's knowledge sometimes marks the recipient as heir to the office and/or powers of the dying man; cf. Wilfrid's narration of his life story to his kinsman and successor, "as if he foresaw his death" (*Life of Wilfrid*, chs. 63–5), and the aged Hrothgar's "sermon" to his adopted son (*Beowulf*, ll. 946–56, 1700–84). Boisil, whom Cuthbert succeeded as prior, revealed to him his impending death and spent his last week alive studying the gospel of John with him. This parallels apostolic succession; but Boisil also prophesies Cuthbert's entire future, including his episcopal office (*Bede's Cuthbert*, ch. 8). For Pega and Leoba as the soul friends of saints, see ch. 9, pp. 289–97.
[38] *Anon Cuthbert*, IV.9.
[39] John 15.13.
[40] Woolf, 1976, 63–81, argues against obligation to die beside the slain lord as an authentic AS custom; but there is testimony to physical inseparability through thick and thin as the definition of loyal comradeship (e.g., Aldhelm to the Abbots of Wilfrid [*Epist* 12]), and dying together in battle is, *in extremis*, an expression of this. Bede's account of the friendship of the two English noblemen dying of the plague in Ireland (*HE*, III.27), like *Anon Cuthbert's* account of the friendship of Cuthbert and Hereberht, represents a transmutation of physical inseparability on life's journeys to the journey beyond death; OE *gesitha* and *gefara* (Lat *comes*) encapsulate the synonymity of comradeship and journeying.
[41] Vicarious salvation is also implicit in Guthlac's soul-friend relation with his sister, Pega (*Life of Guthlac*, ch. 50).

lagged behind Cuthbert in merit, he was made equal to his intercessor by suffering, and therefore was *worthy* to depart this life with him at the same time and be received into the same eternal bliss. Consistent with this change is Bede's transformation of the mutual friendship of Cuthbert and Hereberht into an officially ecclesiastical and hierarchical relation. In Bede's revision of Cuthbert's Life, we are evidently meant to understand that Cuthbert's willingness to socialize with the hermit is an exercise of his confessorial office. The meetings have now become annual visits that Hereberht makes to take counsel about his eternal salvation,[42] and when he pleads for the eternal continuation of his companionship with Cuthbert, he explains, dutifully: " 'You know I have always sought to live in accordance with the commands of your mouth, and whatever I have done amiss through ignorance and weakness, I have taken equal care to correct in accordance with your judgment and will.' "[43]

Bede rewrote the Anonymous *Life of Cuthbert* for the edification of the Lindisfarne bishop and monks in accordance with his own pedagogic and hagiographical tastes; Cuthbert has been transformed into Bede's idea of an exemplary bishop, offered first and foremost to Eadfrith of Lindisfarne as a predecessor worthy of his imitation.[44] In Bede's rewriting, Ælffled is no longer the soul friend of Cuthbert, sharing the saint's revelation of his impending death only with Hereberht, and she is no longer uniquely admitted to the knowledge that he cannot avoid accepting the bishopric to which he is destined. A royal abbess's privileged knowledge of an ecclesiastical nominee's intentions was no more acceptable to Bede than the involvement of queens in ecclesiastical appointments was to later reformers. Cuthbert's life-secrets, by Bede's additions, repose centrally with his monastic brothers. He adds an episode in which the prior of Melrose, as he is dying, reveals to the youthful Cuthbert the whole future course of his life, and foretells his elevation to a bishopric, and Cuthbert occasionally hints to the Lindisfarne monks of the impending honour that he would fain avoid.[45]

One of the episodes Bede adds to the Anonymous Life, however, relates to the friendship of Ælffled and Cuthbert. It testifies to the miracle-working powers of the saint, which were of far greater didactic significance to Bede than they had been to the Anonymous Lindisfarne hagiographer, who appears to have felt that the sanctity of Cuthbert was sufficiently evident without his needing to make the most of every marvellous circumstance that had ever been

[42] *Dialogue of Egbert* (H&S, III, 413) claims that annual confession became customary in England from the time of Theodore.
[43] Colgrave, p. 251; *Bede's Cuthbert*, ch. 28.
[44] Bede had already written a metrical Life for Wearmouth (ed. W. Jaager, *Bedas metrische Vita Sancti Cuthberti*, Palaestra 198 [Leipzig, 1935]) also based on the Anonymous Life; see fn. 106. For his prose Life (721) as a model for Eadfrith, see ch. 4, pp. 120–30. Bede's account suggests that Eadfrith, in commissioning a new Life, was combating what he regarded as a deviant preference for *Anon Cuthbert's* portrait of the saint among some sections of the Lindisfarne community (see fn. 121). For other views of the *rationale* of the three early Lives, see M. Lapidge, "Bede's Metrical *Vita S Cuthbert*"; W. Berschin, "*Opus deliberatum ac perfectum*: Why Did the Venerable Bede Write a Second Prose Life of St Cuthbert?" ed. Bonner et al., pp. 77–93, 94–102.
[45] See esp. *Bede's Cuthbert*, chs. 8, 22.

reported of him.[46] Bede, presumably, was under an obligation to incorporate the additional information given to him by Herefrith of Lindisfarne, who had heard the story involving Ælffled from the abbess herself.[47] As told by Bede, the episode reveals the saint's god-like immanence, for when Ælffled was incurably ill, she longed for something belonging to him, in the belief that it would cure her. And although Cuthbert in his solitary hermitage was (symptomatically) "far removed from mankind," Ælffled immediately received by messenger a girdle which cured her own illness as well as the pain of one of her nuns when Ælffled tied the girdle about her.[48]

Though Bede carefully preserves Cuthbert's superior detachment from human emotions by referring only to the deep affection of Ælffled for Cuthbert, Cuthbert's psychic knowledge of Ælffled's thoughts is consistent with the intimacy transcending mortal limits that characterizes a mutual spiritual bond. The episode has a parallel in Columba's intimation of the plight of a woman anchorite who was well-known to him. Adomnan's *Life of Columba* reports that the saint sent a messenger to Maugin, because he sensed that she had fallen in the night on the way back from her oratory, and was repeatedly calling his name in the hope that she might get help from God through him.[49] Gifts of clothing among members of religious orders, particularly the Boniface circle, were also present reminders of absent friends and tangible extensions of affection; Cuthbert's sending of his girdle to Ælffled has, naturalistically regarded, the appearance of a memento of his friendship.

But a bishop's gift of clothing to an abbess who shares a particular relationship with him, and performs a miracle of healing through his powers, can have figurative significance. Cuthbert's bestowal of his girdle on Ælffled in the closing years of his life calls to mind Tatberht sending to Abbess Cynethryth the miracle-working cloak on which Bishop Wilfrid had lain in death. The episode, I have suggested, points to the association of the abbess with Mary as a type of the Church, the repository and guardian of the power to work miracles through the continued presence of the departed Christ-bishop.[50] In the *Life of Leoba*, Archbishop Boniface bestows his hood on Leoba as he goes to meet his death, and the partnership of abbess and bishop, like the relation of the hermit Guthlac and his anchorite sister, is conceived as a form of soul friendship, in which the female partner, as inheritor of the saint's spiritual charisma, is allegorically equated with Mary-Ecclesia.[51] This allegorical coupling of bishop and abbess with Christ and Mary, figuring their union as heads of the church, carries implications of a (restricted) identity in numinous powers and sacerdotal office.

Ælffled's soul friendship with Cuthbert in the Anonymous Life is given no discernible Marian dimension, but the potential symbolic significance of the gift from Cuthbert that enables Ælffled to mediate Cuthbert's miraculous

[46] See ch. 4, fn. 47.
[47] Herefrith, according to Bede's Prologue, was allowed to oversee *Bede's Cuthbert* in draft form because he had known the saint intimately. For Bede's inclusion of Abbess Verca, see fn. 122.
[48] *Bede's Cuthbert*, ch. 23.
[49] *Life of Columba*, II.5; cf. II.40. Columba also foretold the number of years Maugin would live.
[50] *Life of Wilfrid*, ch. 66; see pp. 164–5, 171–2.
[51] See pp. 289–97.

healing powers is interestingly consistent with her participation in his prophetic faculty in the Anonymous Life.[52] On the evidence of Bede's rewriting of the meetings of Ælffled and Cuthbert, Bede would have had no wish to give expression to the allegorical dimensions of the friendships of abbesses and bishops, even if he was familiar with them.[53] For Bede, bishops are the hierarchical superiors and pedagogic supervisors of abbesses. Like his version of the visit of Cuthbert to Abbess Æbbe and to the female religious Censwith, Bede's account of the meetings of Ælffled and Cuthbert is characterized by scrupulous justification. The effect of his alterations is to efface the original indications of familiar social relations between a bishop and a member of the opposite sex, and to reconstitute the meetings as purposively official visits on Cuthbert's part. To some extent, Bede's revisions reflect his rigidly orthodox views on the claustration of monastic women, manifest in his account of scandalous conduct at the Coldingham double monastery.[54] But clearly operative too are Bede's hierarchical and dehumanizing notions of episcopal sanctity. It was a sufficient explanation for the author of the Anonymous Life that Cuthbert frequently visited the devout woman, Censwith, because she had fostered him since he was eight years old and he looked on her as his mother. It was also a sufficient explanation of Cuthbert's presence at the Coldingham monastery that he went there at the invitation of Abbess Æbbe.[55] But as Bede's saint is far above the affectional ties that influence mere mortals, it is necessary to explain that Censwith happened to be on Cuthbert's itinerary one day as he was making his missionary rounds, and it would appear that mere filial piety would not have been enough to gain Censwith the favour of his dutifully frequent visits had it not been for the fact that he knew she was given to good works.[56] It is also necessary for Bede to explain that Æbbe was honoured for her piety, as well as being the sister of King Oswiu, and that she asked Cuthbert to visit her monastery in order to favour them with his exhortations. As Bede has so clearly established the devout and social credentials of the abbess as well as the call of episcopal duty (notwithstanding that subsequent events at Coldingham may suggest that his exhortations were wasted), it is easy to see why Cuthbert could not deny the request that the handmaiden of God made in all charity of heart.[57]

In contrast to the more humane, egalitarian concepts of sanctity that placed the emphasis on Christ-like humility and identity with the suffering human condition, Bede's foregrounding of the transcendent and supra-natural aspects of sanctity goes hand in hand with his insistence on the superior dignity of male ecclesiastics.[58] His rewriting of the episodes involving Cuthbert and Ælffled develops further the implications of his stance. The intimate friendship of Ælffled and Cuthbert gives way under the combined pressure of Bede's anti-

---

[52] For the subsequent disappearance of the girdle, see p. 126.
[53] For the suggestion that the origins are Celtic, see p. 110.
[54] HE, IV.25.
[55] Anon Cuthbert, II.7; II.3.
[56] Bede's Cuthbert, ch. 14; however, the report that Cuthbert chanced, during his pastoral perambulations, to hear of the illness of a nun he healed (ch. 30), derives from Anon Cuthbert, IV.3.
[57] Bede's Cuthbert, ch. 10.
[58] See pp. 120–30.

feminist bias and his elitist alterization of episcopal saints. The meetings function as a demonstration that participation in the divine mysteries is the exclusive prerogative of a clerical elite, from which women are very properly barred.

The Power of Prescience: Knowing Women and All-knowing Bishops

The conflict between bishops and abbesses manifest in Bede's rewriting of the association of Cuthbert and Ælffled touches ultimately on the participation of women in the administration of the sacraments. But the particular focus of hostility is women's possession of prophetic powers. In Felix's portrait of the hermit saint Guthlac, the prophetic faculty is inseparable from the spiritual guide's council and consolation – Guthlac is able to advise the unhappy exile, Æthelbald of Mercia, to take heart and be patient, because he knows for certain that providence will restore his kingdom to him in the fullness of time.[59] In Germanic literature too, wisdom – particularly an attribute of women and old men – is similarly compounded of the ability to give good advice and insight into the future, in which circumspection and prescience merge.[60] Tacitus's much-quoted remark on Germanic reverence for women marks the connexion. The continental Germans did not hesitate to seek the advice of women, Tacitus explains, because they believed that the spirit of prophecy resided in them.[61] In ecclesiastical circles, however, the prophetic faculty ranked highly among the gifts that God bestowed upon his (predominately episcopal) saints, and royal women, whether as queens or abbesses, could scarcely be permitted to share it with them.[62]

The depiction of the fall in the 9th century Old English poem, Genesis B, reflects the intimate association of prophecy and advice in its presentation of Eve. Eve urges Adam to retain the favour of God by carrying out the instructions of the Satanic visitor, whom she takes to be an angelic messenger; and she backs her encouragement by appealing to her visionary prescience. She is filled with the prophetic spirit by eating the fruit, and has a vision of the joys of

---

[59] Life of Guthlac, ch. 49.

[60] The attribution of a combination of "wisdom and acumen" to women in OI and OE literature has been most widely canvassed by Damico, 1984 (see also Damico, 1980, 149–67), who perhaps overestimates the extent to which these attributions relate to residual conceptions of the Valkyrie.

[61] Germania, ch. 8. A.L. Meaney, "The Ides of the Cotton Gnomic Poem," MÆ 48 (1979), 23–39, suggests that the prophetic connotations of ides and its WGnic cognates were modified by Christian influence: cf. Damico, 1980, 149–67. See Fell, 1986, pp. 30–2, for the survival of the concept in OE heahrune, and M. Brie, "Über die ags. Bezeichnung des Wortes Zauberer," Englische Studien 41 (1909), 20–7. See further fn. 95.

[62] Dialogues, II.12–14, defines prophecy as the knowledge of God's secrets possessed by those who are one with him in spirit: Grégoire le Grand: Dialogues, ed. A. de Vogüé (3 vols., Paris, 1978–80). There are a few mild instances of female prescience in Bede's History (see fn. 34); Æthelthryth alone (HE, IV.19) is credited with the gift of prophecy; see p. 253.

heaven, which she attributes to divine origin: "Who could give me such discernment if God, the ruler of Heaven, had not sent it directly to me?"[63] Leaving aside the disagreement that exists among modern readers concerning the extent to which the *Genesis B* poet regards Eve as *culpably* deceived, there is no doubt that Eve *is* deceived.[64] Her identification of the origins of the messenger is as erroneous as her belief that her vision is a direct gift from God, which confirms that eating the fruit accords with his commands. As a councillor to her husband who has his best interests at heart, she carries out the office ideally prescribed for aristocratic women in *Maxims I*; but her advice is ruinous to the whole race because, all unknown to her, a fundamental flaw inheres in women's much-vaunted powers of discernment. Eve in *Genesis B*, then, functions as a discrediting exemplar of the advisory role and powers of aristocratic women in a form that was recognizable to secular society.[65] The poem represents a further stage of polemical development from the bid for exclusive ecclesiastical possession of prophetic powers that is reflected in Bede's rewriting of the Anonymous *Life of Cuthbert*. Before considering his revision, however, it is useful to glance briefly at some of the general configurations of the dispute for possession of prophetic powers.

Particularly characteristic of the wise is a tendency to gloomy intimations of mortality and impending disaster. Thus, the Old Icelandic wisdom poem, the *Hávamál*, opines that it is best not to be too wise, for the wise are not happy: "Everyone should be moderately wise, never excessively so. He who does not foresee his fate has a mind most free from care."[66] Amidst the revelry of the hall in *Beowulf*, the old man and the woman who rule over Heorot are less than entirely happy. Wealhtheow, seeming to sense the dark shadows of Heorot's circumambient doom, turns her mind to the future disposition of the kingdom with wise circumspection. As she hands Hrothgar the cup of festive cheer, she strikes a sombre note of mortality: " 'Make use, while you may, of Heorot's many guerdons, and when you are constrained to go forth to face the decree of Providence, leave the people and the realm to your kinsmen.' "[67] The aged King

---

[63] *Genesis B*, ll. 655–83.
[64] Relevant studies include: J.M. Evans, "*Genesis B* and Its Background," *RES* NS 14 (1963), 1–16, 113–23; R. Woolf, "The Fall of Man in *Genesis B* and the *Mystère d'Adam*," in *Studies in Old English Literature in Honor of Arthur G. Brodeur*, ed. S.B. Greenfield (Eugene, 1963), pp. 187–99; J.F. Vickery, "The Vision of Eve in *Genesis B*," *Speculum* 44 (1969), 86–102; R.E. Finnegan, "Eve and 'Vincible Ignorance' in *Genesis B*," *Texas Studies in Literature and Language* 18 (1976), 329–39.
[65] See *Maxims I*, ll. 81–92.
[66] Clarke, p. 57; *Hávamál*, st. 56. Cf. *Solomon and Saturn II*, ll. 426–64; *Precepts*, ll. 55–8. The conjunction of wisdom, age and gloomy foreknowledge is epitomised by *The Wanderer*. Female prophets in the poetic Edda are generally mythical (e.g., the seer in *Voluspá* who speaks the prophecies of *Ragnarok*); but intimations of doom are not confined to them. With Odin's request for the advice of his wife before he embarks on a journey, *Vafthrúthnismál* (sts. 1–4), cf. *Atlamál* (sts. 9–26), where Hogni ignores the forebodings of his wife before the journey that leads to his death. Cf. the fears of Æthelberht's mother concerning the journey that ends in his murder at Offa's court, in the 11/12th c. *Passio Athelberti*, ed. M.R. James, "Two Lives of St Ethelbert, King and Martyr," *EHR* 32 (1917), 236–44.
[67] Bradley, pp. 442–3; see *Beowulf*, ll. 1169–80.

Hrothgar takes up the harp to entertain the company with the music of joy and ends with lamentation for his vanished youth and his strength in battle.[68] And as he parts from Beowulf, his tears foretell his imminent death, for, "being old and very wise, two things might be expected, the second more strongly – that they would not see one another again."[69]

So too, Guthrun's mother in the Eddic lays weeps prophetically when the cup of oblivion she offers Guthrun to drown the memory of her many sorrows fails to take effect, because she foresees the destruction of the race that Guthrun's vengeance will bring.[70] Hildeburg, in the Beowulf scop's lay of Finnsburg, in her role as mourner for her son and her brother, slain fighting on opposite sides, is thus not merely a tragic victim of the renewal of hostilities between her own people and her husband's that she is powerless to prevent. She is also an unwitting prefiguration of the further slaughter that will arise from the vengeance taken for her brother's death.[71] The Geatish woman who mourns at the pyre of Beowulf echoes her on a vaster scale. She is a symbol of the grief of the nation, which is earlier prophesied by the messenger, and which she also foresees: times of misery, a multitude of violent deaths, humiliation and captivity.[72] For the death of kings spells misery, as Alcuin remarked in a letter to England.[73]

The unhappy women in Beowulf demonstrate that the queen's involvement in the determination of the king's successor is an aspect of her wisely circumspect concern for the future of the kingdom, closely bound up with her prescient knowledge that the death of the king will have disastrous consequences both for her and for the nation. Beowulf's ideal queen, Hygd, is much more closely involved in the determination of the succession than Wealhtheow. In the world of Beowulf, the death of the king is an automatic provocation to attack from the nation's traditional enemies. So, when the king of the Geats falls in battle, Hygd urges Beowulf to take the throne, because she regards her son as too young to serve as a protector of the nation; herself a widow, she is a representative emblem of the nation bereft of its leader.[74] Seaxburg of Kent, too, in the Lambeth "Mildrith Fragment," demonstrates that the queen's determination of the succession and her prescient intimations of impending national disaster are both aspects of her circumspect care for the welfare of the kingdom. Seaxburg, it is said, foresaw the arrival of an invading pagan army;

[68] Beowulf, ll. 2105–14.
[69] Swanton, p. 123; Beowulf, ll. 1873–6.
[70] Guthrúnarkvitha II, sts. 21–34.
[71] For the lay of Finnsburg, see Beowulf, ll. 1068–159. The unweeping women of the poetic Edda, and those who laugh when there is cause for grief, are, by ironic allusion to the convention of the weeping woman as herald of disaster, a yet more ominous prefiguration; Guthrun, famous for her unwomanly tearlessness (Guthrúnarkvitha I), expresses her grief for her brothers' murder in the manner of a warrior, by destroying her husband and all his people (Atlakvitha, sts. 29–39, 44).
[72] Beowulf, ll. 3137–55; cf. ll. 2910–3030. Cf. Frigg's tears for Valhalla's woe at the death of Balder, which prefigure the gods' apocalyptic defeat (Voluspá, sts. 33, 53).
[73] Duemmler, 116. For Alcuin's letters of condolences to royal women on the assassination of Æthelred of Northumbria, see Duemmler, 102, 103, 105, 106.
[74] Beowulf, ll. 2367–79.

realizing that the nation had need of a warrior-protector, it seems, she betook herself to a monastery and entrusted the kingdom to her son, for whom she had been acting as regent.[75]

Beowulf, though preserving the literary heritage of an earlier era, possibly took the form in which it survives in the late Anglo-Saxon period. In its portrait of queens engaged in determining the succession, *Beowulf* bears a provocative relation to the *Encomium Emmae* and the *Life of King Edward*. Both directly and covertly, these two 11th century works, commissioned by the last two Anglo-Saxon queens, express their active interest in the succession.[76] Queen Emma, in the *Encomium*, specifies her son's inheritance of the throne as the condition of her marriage to Cnut.[77] The portrait of Queen Edith has been more thoroughly overtaken by Marian idealization of the queen; the *Life's* intended bearing on the future of the kingdom is far more concealed, and Edith herself more thoroughly self-effacing than Emma.[78] The *Life* echoes, though, the traditional image of the mourning woman as prophet of doom. When Edith's brothers quarrel among themselves and with King Edward, the king himself goes into a fatal decline. Edith weeps in prophetic intimation of the death of the king and the ensuing destruction of the nation: "She plainly showed her foreboding of future evils by her tears. And when she wept inconsolably, the whole palace went into mourning. For when misfortunes had attacked them in the past, she had always stood as a defense, and had both repelled all the hostile forces with her powerful counsels and also cheered the king and his retinue."[79] Her tears in this scene find immediate fulfilment in the final scenes of the *Life*, when she appears as mourner at Edward's death bed.[80] But she is still prophetic of an even greater calamity, the defeat of the nation at Hastings, where her brother Harold fell with his army because, in the under-

---

[75] "Lambeth Fragment," ed. and trans. O. Cockayne, *Leechdoms, Wortcunning, and Starcraft of Early England* (London, 1866), III, 430–2.

[76] The precise political considerations underlying Emma's commissioning of the *Encomium* remain elusive; its celebration of the joint rule of Emma's sons as the crowning achievement of her influence (see Prologue, pp. 6–8, and III.10–14) is evidently purposive, at very least a means of shoring up the *status quo*. Edith's commissioning of the *Life of King Edward* is arguable; see fn. 78.

[77] *Encomium*, II.16. With this exception, Harthacanute's succession is depicted as a a triumph for Emma's nebulous good influence; cf. ASC (CE), 1035–7, which suggests that she offered armed resistance to Harald while she was acting as regent for her son.

[78] Barlow concludes that *Life of King Edward* was started late in 1065 (p. xxvii) and revised in 1067 (p. xxviii); gauging its political intentions is complicated by the author's accommodations to rapidly changing political conditions. Acceptance of his claim to serve Edith (see esp. pp. 59–60), depends on one's interpretation of the intended polemical purpose of the hagiographical account of Edward in Bk. II (the *general* thrust of Bk. I is unquestionably to establish the desirability of England's continuance under the descendants of Earl Godwine, including Edith, p. 6); I regard it as an attempt to advance the widowed Edith as a fitting subject for the protection of the Norman ecclesiastical hierarchy. On her Marian characterization, see pp. 209–12.

[79] Trans. Barlow, *Life of King Edward*, p. 54.

[80] *Life of King Edward*, pp. 79–80; the scene is echoed in the Bayeux Tapestry. In this conflict between queen and bishop, the author's loyalties lie with the queen. She and others present understand Edward's prophecy of the destruction of the kingdom; but Archbishop Stigand dismisses it as senile rambling, thus bearing out the irresponsible oblivion of wrath to come on the part of churchmen, against which both the king and queen had warned them (pp. 76–8).

standing of the Life, his fatal quarrel with his brother, that first provoked the ominous tears of the queen, left him without sufficient force of arms in time of need.[81]

Thus Ælffled, in her direful appeal to Cuthbert to prophesy who will inherit the throne from her childless brother, manifests, in the Anonymous Life, a quasi-prescient concern with the kingdom's succession which attaches to the role of the queen as a protective leader of her people. Ælffled's concern with the royal succession is extended to her involvement in the episcopal succession, since she also asks Cuthbert if he will accept the bishopric that Ecgfrith wishes him to take. As an abbatical Mother and spiritual leader, Ælffled's partnership with the Christ-bishop is the ecclesiastical analogue of the joint rule of the queen and king, her involvement with the episcopal succession representing a transference to the ecclesiastical sphere of royal women's participation in the transmission of the throne.

Like the involvement of royal women in ecclesiastical appointments, their influence on the succession to the throne was a point of conflict with bishops.[82] God was the true king-maker, and his will was known to his bishops. According to the late 12th century Life of Oswald, when King Edgar died, Archbishop Dunstan moved swiftly to install Æthelred's step-brother, Edward, as his successor.[83] Sharp instruments were found to dispose of Edward in order to replace him with Æthelred, and according to the late 11th century Passio of the murdered Edward, it was Æthelred's mother who found them. Whether or not Æthelred's mother did actually instigate her step-son's murder, ecclesiastical influence is evident in the polemical shaping of this and a number of post-Conquest accounts, which depict her as an Eve-like tempter and destroyer of men, treacherously offering a cup of wine to her step-son as her assassin drives in his sword.[84]

---

[81] Life of King Edward, p. lxiii, 15–17, 37–40. See also the breast-beating nurse who interprets the dream of the infant king Cenhelm as a prophecy of his murder in the 11th c. Passio Kenelmi (I refer to the transcript of P.A. Hayward, "The Kenelm Legend in Context: A Study of the Hagiography of the Eleventh Century," unpub. MA diss., Auckland, 1990, pp. 234–59; also ed. R. von Antropoff, "Die Entwicklung der Kenelm-Legende," Inaugural Dissertation, Bonn, 1965). Cf. the prophetic dream of the weeping Leofrun, mother of Æthelbert, Passio Athelberti, ch. 5.

[82] See J.T. Schulenburg, "Female Sanctity, Public and Private, 500–1100," in Women and Power in the Middle Ages, ed. M. Erler and M. Kowaleski (Athens, Ga, 1988), pp. 102–25; for a very explicit continental example of clerical hostility to queens' involvement in ecclesiastical appointments, see Notker's Life of Charlemagne: ed. H.F. Haefele, Notker der Stammler: Taten Kaiser Karls des Grossen (Bern, 1962).

[83] Byrhtferth's late 10th c. Life of Oswald says only that the election of Edward was accompanied by widespread dissension which neither ecclesiastical nor secular leaders could allay: ed. J. Raine, The Historians of the Church of York and its Archbishops, RS 71 (London, 1879), I, 448.

[84] See Passio Edwardi, ed. Fell, 1971, pp. 4–5. In Byrhtferth's Life of Oswald, Æthelred's mother is, at most, obliquely implicated in what is described as an insurrection by Æthelred's thanes; Edward is said to have visited his brother when he was staying with wicked nobles at the estate of his mother, and he is murdered in imitation of Christ betrayed by the kiss of Judas (ed. Raine, I, 448–55). In William of Malmesbury's Gesta Regum, ed. Stubbs, I, 183, the iconography of Eve has become so inextricably linked with the temptations of the flesh that Æthelred's mother

But the prophetic faculty which inheres about the queen's concern with the future of the kingdom was also a contentious issue. When Ælffled in the Anonymous *Life of Cuthbert* weeps at Cuthbert's prophecy that the king has only a year to live, she figures woman as prophetic mourner for the griefs of the nation. Her brother Ecgfrith fell in battle with his army when they were defeated in a campaign against the Picts, and when Cuthbert intimates to Ælffled that the king has only a year to live, Ælffled weeps bitter tears, "and the fall of the members of the royal house by a cruel hand and a hostile sword a year afterwards renewed all the bitterness for her and for many others."[85] Such tearful intimations of disaster are not only the resort of women and old men. Warriors who are powerless to avert disaster by force of arms may also weep – as, for instance, when Gunnarr departs from his court predicting the destruction of his race that will follow if he fails to return from Atli's realm.[86] Clerics and bishops, destined for a near-monopoly on the prophetic faculty, also prefigure doom by shedding tears. In Bede's account of the events at Coldingham, the monk Adomnan bursts into tears outside the walls, because he has been informed in a vision that the wrath of God is about to fall on the monastery as a punishment for its iniquities.[87] Bishop Aidan weeping at the feast echoes a traditional inversion of a popular Germanic theme; for him, as for Hrothgar when he takes up the harp, the joys of the hall are abruptly turned to sorrow.[88] For when he sits down to rejoice at the feast with King Oswine, he is struck with a tearful foreboding of the king's death, which is also an intimation of his own imminent death.[89] Only when indigenous modes of prophetic insight have been fully replaced by ecclesiastical conceptions of divinely inspired prophecy does the gloomy foreboding of disaster by which Germanic tradition defined women and old men as wise become such a thing as might trouble a woman. In the 12th century *Life of Christina of Markyate* there are still traces of the weeping woman as doleful seer, but, by the time her Life was written, intimations of disaster had ceased to have value in defining prophetic status: Christina "became fearful of everything, as the habit of women is."[90]

So, too, the power of cursing, with which Æbbe's tears of impending judgment upon King Ecgfrith merge in the *Life of Wilfrid* is, at a pragmatic level of analysis, the refuge of those without power – and even warriors, in the extremity of defeat, resort to this, for Offa curses Godric and his brothers, on the battlefield of Maldon, for having caused the rest of the army to take flight.[91] But in an

---

leans enticingly towards him as she offers a cup. See further ch. 5, pp. 157–60. Æthelred's mother was, additionally, accused of killing Abbot Brihtnoth of Ely (*Liber Eliensis*, II.56).

[85] Colgrave, p. 105; *Anon Cuthbert*, III.6.

[86] *Atlakvitha*, st. 12; cf. st. 39. See also *Andreas* (ASPR II, 3–51), ll. 1522–55.

[87] HE, IV.25.

[88] The feast turned to mourning has biblical analogues (e.g., Dan. 5.1–9); but see, e.g., *Atlakvitha*, sts. 12, 34–43.

[89] See HE, III.14; see further below.

[90] *Life of Christina of Markyate*, p. 69. For a late survival of women's tears as a dire omen (of divine retribution), see Coventry Shearmen and Tailors Play, ll. 870–6: ed. H. Craig, *Two Coventry Corpus Christi Plays*, EETS ES 87 (2nd edn. London, 1957).

[91] *The Battle of Maldon*, ll. 242–3; see also ll. 315–16.

era when "everybody was a magician"[92] the attribution of uncanny powers was not, as such, a strategy for the alterist marginalization of their possessors. Bishops, canonically denied the use of arms, and frequently without support for their temporal edicts, relied heavily on the power of cursing: the story of how Columba, when he was a young deacon, brought about through his curse the instant death of a man who speared to death a woman who had sought his protection, graphically illustrates the employment of immaterial power by the physically powerless.[93] As vengeance came increasingly to seem un-Christian, and the invocation of God's vengeance not lightly to be undertaken by members of the laity,[94] bishops, in their power of excommunication, became the chief exponents of the curse. In a non-materialist ethos the accredited possession of uncanny powers was a powerful tool. The relative sparsity of evidence of Anglo-Saxon belief in the uncanny powers of women in the predominately clerical literature of the period is, accordingly, not a reliable index of the degree to which that belief was held.[95]

The political potentialities of prophecies of the king's death are evident in Bede's account of conflict between King Sigeberht and Bishop Cedd, whose prophecy of the death of the king for having feasted at the house of an excommunicated kinsman is scarcely distinguishable from a curse.[96] Benedict's revelation of his foreknowledge of the time of King Totila's death – held by some to be the source of episcopal prophecies of the death of kings in early hagiography – clearly serves a corrective function, causing the king to modify his cruelly tyrannical behaviour by the contemplation of his own mortality.[97] Royal women's tears of impending doom such as Ælffled sheds were also capable of functioning as a political tool; and conceivably they did in this instance. The foreboding anxiety concerning Ecgfrith's future that Ælffled evinces in her meeting with Cuthbert at Coquet Island is a reflection of more general apprehension created by Ecgfrith's actions at the time of this meeting. The previous year he had launched an unprovoked attack on Ireland, bringing down upon himself the curses of the Irish; he also attacked the Scots, again without provocation, despite the pleas of the Abbot of Iona. His disastrous campaign

[92] L. Thorndike, *Studies in the History of Magic* (New York, 1904), p. 29.
[93] *Life of Columba*, II.25; in II.33, Columba prophesies the death of a magician who refuses to free a female slave.
[94] HE, IV.26, referring to the curses that the Irish called down on Ecgfrith after his unprovoked attack on them, recalls 1 Cor. 6.10, to the effect that those who curse will not inherit the kingdom of heaven, but their cursing may be effective all the same.
[95] Cf. Fell, 1986, p. 32, who finds philological evidence for the survival of the concept of prophetic women but believes that "Anglo-Saxons in general" did not regard women as having prophetic faculties. Churchmen, however, throughout the period denounced women who engaged in various "supernatural" practices, including divination (see esp. Ælfric, *De Auguriis*, ed. Skeat, I, 372–5); for these denunciations see Meaney, 1989, pp. 9–40; J. Crawford, "Evidence for Witchcraft in Anglo-Saxon England," *MÆ* 32 (1963), 99–116. Meaney, esp. "Ælfric and Idolatry," *Journal of Religious History* 13 (1984), 119–35, argues that these ecclesiastical denunciations referred to actual contemporary practices. F.C. Robinson, "The Prescient Woman in Old English Literature," in *Philologia Anglica*, ed. K. Oshitari et al. (Tokyo, 1988), pp. 241–50, has not been sighted.
[96] HE, III.22.
[97] *Dialogues*, II.14.

against the Picts was carried out against the advice of many, including Cuthbert himself.[98]

The Anonymous Life's association of Cuthbert with a prophecy of Ecgfrith's death, and his subsequent intimation of the moment of the king's fall, may owe its presence simply to the belief (presumably Celtic in origin) that the high priest had a clairvoyant connexion with the king by virtue of their intimacy and shared life-line.[99] Bishop Aidan, in foretelling the death of King Oswine, appears to share with him a form of soul friendship similar to that of Cuthbert and the hermit Hereberht. In character Aidan and Oswine are united in their extreme humility – for it is when Oswine kneels to apologize for having taken exception to the fact that Aidan had given away to a beggar the royal horse that Oswine had given him, that Aidan is provoked to the mournful foreboding that a humble king does not live long. His intimation of Oswine's death is thus an intimation of his own death also, for he died eleven days after the king was assassinated. In the Anonymous *Life of Cuthbert*, the fate of bishop and king is similarly linked and suggestive of a shared life-line – Ælffled's inquiries concerning the succession of the kingdom are coupled with an inquiry concerning his own succession to the bishopric, and elicit Cuthbert's prophecy of the imminence of his own death.

The underlying significance of the report in the Anonymous Life of Cuthbert's foreknowledge of the king's death may be, however, that Cuthbert prophesied that Ecgfrith would shortly meet his death, in the hope that belief in his clairvoyant power would prevent Ecgfrith from attacking the Picts. The murder, enslavement and flight of the English in and near Pictish territory that followed Ecgfrith's defeat – including the forced withdrawal of Bishop Trumwine and his monks – could be foreseen without the aid of clairvoyance, and Bede's report of these matters clearly defines a motive for Cuthbert's opposition to Ecgfrith's extension of his campaigns to the north.[100] In these terms the linking of Ælffled with Cuthbert's prophecy is suggestive, representing perhaps an alliance with him in an attempt to dissuade Ecgfrith from fighting the Picts, in which her utilization of royal women's prophetic faculty for divining the doom of the king and kingdom paralleled the methods of Cuthbert.

Eddius, for his part, evidently wished to create the impression that the origins of Ecgfrith's defeat by the Picts lay in his falling out with Bishop Wilfrid at the time of his separation from Æthelthryth – for had not Wilfrid ensured for Ecgfrith an earlier victory over the Picts in the days when he took his advice? When Wilfrid saw the courtiers smirking over his banishment by Ecgfrith and Jurmenburg, he prophesied that they would be weeping within a year; as a prophecy of the king's death, this was premature, but Eddius, finding fulfilment of Wilfrid's prophecy in the grief of the court for the death of Ecgfrith's brother while he was fighting the Mercians, has the satisfaction of pointing out that

[98] HE, IV.26.
[99] For the view that the meeting of Ælffled and Cuthbert has affinities with Celtic mantic literature, see H.M. and N.K. Chadwick, *The Growth of Literature* (Cambridge, 1932), I, 472. Columba has numerous prophetic insights connecting him with kings, not all of them dire (*Life of Columba*, I.7–15).
[100] HE, IV.26.

Ecgfrith won no further victories from that day.[101] Unexpectedly, Eddius does not press his view of the origins of Ecgfrith's final downfall in his report of his battle against the Picts. But though the curse-*cum*-prophecy of disaster awaiting Ecgfrith delivered by Wilfrid's agent, Abbess Æbbe, serves an immediately corrective purpose in impelling Ecgfrith to release Wilfrid from prison, Æbbe's advice on the reinstatement of Wilfrid, as it is unheeded by Ecgfrith, remains available as a rationale for his ultimately disastrous end.[102] In her foreboding tears for the safety of her nephew Ecgfrith in this episode, Abbess Æbbe functions as the instrument of her friend Wilfrid. Eddius thus presents a partnership of prophetic royal woman and spurned episcopal adviser curiously reminiscent of the Anonymous Life's linking of the prophetic weeping of Ecgfrith's sister Ælffled with Bishop Cuthbert's prophecy of the king's death. It is, in short, tempting to speculate that only widespread knowledge of the dire intimations of Cuthbert and his unsuccessful attempts to prevent the attack on the Picts have inhibited Eddius from pressing the claim that the fall of Ecgfrith was the retributive consequence of his rejection of the councils of Wilfrid.

The Anonymous Life's account of Cuthbert's prophecy to Abbess Ælffled of the king's death, then, links together the prophetic powers of an aged ecclesiastic and a woman religious, in an episode whose origins may lie in their actual alliance as advisers in an attempt to restrain Ecgfrith's use of military force. In their shared status as non-combatants in a warrior world, woman and churchman had the basis for a common cause: what, unfortunately, is more clearly and fully documented is the bid for political influence in which ecclesiastics and royal women were in conflict. Adomnan, weeping outside the walls for God's impending judgment on Coldingham, probably owes more to the Old Testament prophets than to Germanic tradition. But in the light of Bede's antagonism to royal women's prophetic powers, his accounts of an ecclesiastic announcing his prophetic knowledge of impending disaster to an unwitting woman have the appearance of establishing ecclesiastics as superior to women in the matter of gloomy foreboding. Whereas Adomnan, who was merely a visitor to Coldingham, had been fully informed by a visionary messenger of the iniquities which took place at night in the privacy of the monastic cells, the abbess herself was entirely ignorant of anything untoward. And Adomnan himself keeps his prophetic knowledge a secret from her until his tears betray him because, he says, he did not wish to cause her distress. But through his superior knowledge of the future he is able to offer her consolation: "Let it be some comfort to you that this calamity will not happen in your own lifetime."

Similar in kind is Bede's embellishment of the account in the Anonymous Life of Cuthbert's intimation of the defeat of King Ecgfrith's army when he was fighting the Picts. During this battle, Cuthbert went to visit the queen, who had accompanied the king as far as Carlisle, and was awaiting the outcome of the battle there. It is not clear in the Anonymous Life whether Jurmenburg was present when Cuthbert made his sudden announcement that the battle had been decided.[103] But in Bede's account, Cuthbert makes a special point of going

---

[101] See *Life of Wilfrid*, ch. 24, cf. chs. 19, 20.

[102] *Life of Wilfrid*, ch. 39.

[103] *Anon Cuthbert*, IV.8.

to the queen in order to advise her to flee to safety in her chariot, and promises to follow as an escort once he has discharged his episcopal duties. Considering that it was the role of queens to be gloomily prescient on behalf of the nation, and that they had particular personal reasons for developing a clairvoyant sensitivity to the fate of the king, Bede's development of this episode has the appearance of scoring a deliberate point.

Like Bede's account of the prophet Adomnan and his depiction of Cuthbert as the omniscient rescuer of Queen Jurmenburg, the Anonymous Life's account of Ælffled's request to Cuthbert for a prophecy on the death of King Ecgfrith, and his successor's name, can be regarded as a rhetorical affirmation of the primacy of the prophetic powers of ecclesiastics. In the Anonymous Life, however, Ælffled and Cuthbert are soul friends, fellow spirits who are connected by their prescient faculties, and thus more in the nature of equals. In Bede's revision, to which I now turn, the encounters between Cuthbert and Ælffled clearly do serve the polemical purpose of affirming ecclesiastical supremacy, and Ælffled ceases to be the episcopal saint's kindred spirit. Bede does honour the virgin holiness of Ælffled, as he honours all those of saintly memory, but in dramatizing her meetings with Cuthbert, he is guided by his conceptions of royal abbesses as a class.[104]

Bede's *Life of Cuthbert* (2)

Although the encounters of Cuthbert and Ælffled in the Anonymous Life contribute to the validation of the saint's prophetic powers, they are much more irregular, from an orthodox point of view, than the saint's visits to Censwith and Abbess Æbbe, and require far more careful manipulation by Bede. Of the first meeting, the Anonymous Life merely says that Ælffled asked Cuthbert to meet her on Coquet Island, and her intention to discover the life-expectancy and successor of her royal brother is undisguised.[105] Bede's abbesses, however, are not permitted to summon episcopal saints to assignations on remote islands for the purpose of conjuring out of them information on subjects so frivolously irrelevant to the devotional life as the political future of Northumbria. Like King Oswiu's sister, King Ecgfrith's sister, under the guiding hand of Bede, knows her place, and respectfully requests Cuthbert to visit her on Coquet Island, where, it seems, there was a famous community of monks. Ælffled, in Bede's version, at first concealed her real purpose by asking for instruction on more appropriate matters – for it was in the midst of his answers to a number of enquiries that, evidently unable to contain herself, she broke in with her appeal for a prophecy on the future of the kingdom. But although this was of prime importance to Ælffled, to Cuthbert it was a mere worldly distraction from his pursuit of the life of the spirit, for "when he had expounded to her these and many other things about which she asked, and had given her instruction about such things as she

104 For Bede's tributes to Ælffled's virginity, see fn. 13; see also ch. 8, fn. 20.
105 *Anon Cuthbert*, III.6.

needed, he returned to his island and monastery, and industriously continued the life of solitude as he had begun it."[106]

There is perhaps a submerged suggestion in the Anonymous Life's account of the meeting at Coquet Island that the saint, somewhat in the manner of an Arabian *djinn*, has been summoned up by the abbess, and required to place his prophetic insight at her service by answering three questions, because she has the power to invoke the assistance of forces mightier than his own: "The handmaiden of God on bended knees began to ask him many things and finally she adjured him boldly by the name of our Lord Jesus Christ and by the nine orders of angels and the persons of all the saints, and asked him concerning the length of life of her brother King Ecgfrith. Now the man of God, being solemnly adjured and fearing the Lord, began to speak in an indirect way about the brevity of man's life and added these words: 'O handmaiden of the Lord, is it not but a short time though a man were to live twelve months?' " Notwithstanding the compulsion under which Ælffled puts Cuthbert in her urgent desire to know the future disposition of the kingdom, she is to a degree a fellow spirit in her association with uncanny powers and prescient intimations. She is the alert interpreter of the soothsayer's enigmatic brevities, who immediately realizes his meaning; and he "bore with her patiently" when she needed to enquire further into his particularly dark response to her question concerning Ecgfrith's heir. And when she realizes that the king will die within the year, she becomes herself a prophetic figure, whose tears, as I have indicated, are an ominous portent of impending disaster for the kingdom: "She wept bitter tears, and the fall of the members of the royal house by a cruel hand and a hostile sword a year afterwards renewed all the bitterness for her and for many others."

In Bede's account, the gnomic obliquity by which the seer relays the still dim and shapeless configuration of events not yet born has given way to an articulate flow of didactic exhortation. Bede had spent his years as the master of the Wearmouth monastic school to good purpose, and Cuthbert's superior condescension is evident as, in this version, he is at pains to correct the foolish misapprehensions under which Ælffled labours: " 'It is wonderful that you, a wise woman, and learned in the Holy Scriptures, should be willing to speak of the term of human life as if it were long, when the psalmist says that "our years are reckoned as a spider's web," and when Solomon warns . . .,' " and so on. She is wrong again when she enquires about Ecgfrith's heir: " 'Do not say that there is no heir. . . .' " Ælffled, in short, is no match for Cuthbert either as a seer or a scriptural scholar. To him the future is an open book, and the meaning of his prophecies is so plain that Ælffled has no need to tax her intuitive understanding. And whereas Cuthbert in the Anonymous Life adds many more prophetic words before he sails away, including the prophecy of his death two years after his acceptance of the bishopric of Lindisfarne, in Bede's account he answers her questions and gives her necessary advice, before returning to the

---

[106] Colgrave, p. 239; *Bede's Cuthbert*, ch. 24. I refer only to Bede's prose Life. In his metrical Life (see fn. 44), the depiction of Ælffled is less derogatory, but Bede had already conceived the saint's meetings with her as illustrative of his indifference to worldly enticements; see *PL* 94, 586, 589. Translations of *Bede's Cuthbert*, chs. 24 and 34, and *Anon Cuthbert*, III.6 and IV.10, in this section are from Colgrave, 1940, pp. 103–5, 127–9, 235–9, 261–5.

contemplative solitude that Ælffled has interrupted with her worldly preoccupations.

It is consistent with Bede's exclusion of Ælffled from the role of co-sharer with Cuthbert in insight into the mysteries that she also ceases to be a portentous figure of the kingdom's grief. Though Bede himself dated the decline of Northumbria from the fall of Ecgfrith,[107] Ælffled's tears are mere emotional self-expression, testifying to the binding force of Cuthbert's knowledge of the future: "When she heard this, she shed tears and wept over these dire prophecies." The Anonymous Life assumes that Ælffled's dependence on the friendship of the king is the underlying cause of the urgency with which she coerces Cuthbert – Cuthbert understands this with instinctive sympathy.[108] But whereas Cuthbert in the Anonymous Life reassures Ælffled that she will find the future king "to be a brother no less than the other one," Bede decorously turns the answer inside out: "he will have a successor whom you will embrace with as much sisterly affection as if he were Ecgfrith himself." The rationale of Ælffled's enquiries having thus disappeared, the way is open for a different interpretation. Her desire to know the future is mere inquisitive prying into events that a beneficent providence conceals from ordinary mortals' gaze, and her curiosity – characteristic of her sex – satisfies itself by making dangerously free use of the name of God. For when she first adjures Cuthbert by the name of the King of Heaven and his Angels, he is frightened by her invocation of such powers, but still does not wish to reveal the secret into which she enquires. And when he prophesies the death of her brother, her emotional outburst does not long deter her from pressing her enquiries: "She shed tears and wept over these dire prophecies; but drying her eyes, once again with womanly daring [rursus audacia feminea], she adjured him by the Divine Majesty to tell her whom her brother would have as heir to the kingdom."

No less striking is the form that Bede has given to Ælffled's enquiry into Cuthbert's intentions regarding the bishopric that she knew the king wished to offer him. The Anonymous Life does not give the text of her question. The author merely relates that she asked if the matter would be settled as Ecgfrith wished and how long Cuthbert would retain the bishopric. The author's assumptions of motive are less clear here – perhaps she is merely enquiring on behalf of her brother, or perhaps, like the enquiry concerning the king's successor, it implies her reliance on a well-disposed episcopal incumbent for the security of her world – the rightful incumbent of the vacant see of Hexham, had anyone been disposed to heed the 679 decision of Pope Agatho, was Wilfrid.[109] Ælffled's enquiry in Bede is a highly accomplished little speech, guilefully indirect in soliciting the information she wants, and flatteringly insinuating in its prompting to accept the fame and fortune that is held out to him: "How the

---

107 See HE, IV.26.
108 Cf. Anon Cuthbert, II.8.
109 Life of Wilfrid, ch. 32. Cf. the echo of this episode in Life of Guthlac, ch. 48, where Abbess Ecgburg, daughter of King Aldwulf, sends a messenger asking the hermit-saint Guthlac to prophesy the successor to his hermitage, and elicits the reply that he is "still among the pagans"; she thus serves to legitimate the anchorite Cissa's inheritance of Guthlac's hermitage. Felix's reworking of this episode suggests that he was aware of Ælffled's role as witness to the king's designation of his successor (see fn. 16).

hearts of mortal men differ in their several purposes! Some rejoice in the riches they have gained, others who love riches always lack them. You despise the glory of the world, although it is offered, and although you may attain to a bishopric, than which nothing is higher among mortal men, yet will you prefer the fastness of your desert place to that rank?" The Abbess of Whitby would seem to have compromised her integrity a good deal in acquiring the skills of court diplomacy. Like Eve in *Genesis B*, she is eloquent in her encouragement towards greater glory. And it is, surely, to a comparison with Eve that Bede intends to direct his readers by this portrait of female inquisitiveness and insidious temptation to worldly honour. Cuthbert, replying with exemplary humility and submission to the will of God, evades a direct answer to her question. As Bede concludes the chapter with an account of Cuthbert's appointment which carefully relegates Ecgfrith to a supporting role in an ecclesiastically controlled procedure[110] and as Bede has ensured by his additions that knowledge of Cuthbert's episcopal destiny is not the prerogative of Ælffled, but is instead well-established among the Lindisfarne monks, Cuthbert's evasion is unsurprising.[111] Nor does Cuthbert impart to Ælffled, except in the most carefully disguised form, the prophecy of his death which, in the Anonymous Life, identifies Ælffled as a soul friend in the manner of the hermit Hereberht: "If God has determined to subject me to so great a burden, I believe that after a short time he will set me free, and perhaps, after not more than two years, he will send me back to my accustomed rest and solitude."

Ælffled's inappropriate female prying into the mysteries shared by God and his ecclesiastical appointees is much more marked in Bede's account of her feasting with Cuthbert not long before his death. So too is her association with Eve. The Anonymous Life's casual scene setting for the second meeting is an even more troublesome prospect than Cuthbert summoned from contemplative solitude at Ælffled's behest: Ælffled sat feasting with Cuthbert, and presumably at his invitation, since the feast took place in Cuthbert's diocese.[112] Feasting was condemned, both by ecclesiastical moralists and ecclesiastical councils, and regarded as the vice to which monastic orders were particularly prone. In his letter to Bishop Egbert of York, Bede included gluttony and gastronomic overindulgence among the monastic abuses which he wished to see reformed by an exercise of synodical authority. But it was an area in which episcopal role models were sadly lacking, for it was rumoured, Bede informed Egbert, that

---

110 Cf. *Anon Cuthbert*, IV.1.

111 See *Bede's Cuthbert*, ch. 8; in this addition of Bede's, Cuthbert attributes his reluctance to accept a bishopric to fear of being ensnared by worldly temptations if he allows himself to be lured from his contemplative sanctuary.

112 *Anon Cuthbert*, IV.10; this episode, located at Ovington, is part of the visit to Carlisle sequence. Bede shifts this episode towards the end of the Life, making it part of Cuthbert's valedictory visitation, and alters the setting, implicitly, to Whitby-Hackness. But in relating Cuthbert's visit to Carlisle, Bede says he dedicated a church there, and has him tell a story of how, persuaded to forsake his eremitic contemplation to celebrate a feast with the Lindisfarne monks, he was seized with intimations of doom, fulfilled in the outbreak of plague at the monastery (*Bede's Cuthbert*, ch. 27). In other words, Bede has moved what he knew to be a feast celebrating a church dedication in the Carlisle area at which Ælffled was present, and has inserted in its place another feasting episode, modelled on the same lines.

certain bishops surrounded themselves with men given to laughter, jests, tales, gluttony and drunkenness, who fed the stomach with feasts rather than the soul with heavenly sacrifice.[113] For moralists generally, the secular feast is the anti-type of the mass; it is a diabolic inversion of the communion,[114] or, as Bede depicts it his *Life of Cuthbert*, a locus of carnality. *Theodore's Penitential*, prohibit-ing women from ministering at the altar, rules that they are not to stand among ordained men in the church nor to sit at a feast among priests.[115] If community in Christ could not avail to unite ecclesiastical congregations, how much more unseemly the proximity of a bishop and an abbess at a secular feast?

Bede carefully provides official justification for Cuthbert's presence at a feast with Ælffled. The moral onus of the feast has, implicitly, been shifted to Ælffled by moving the scene to an estate belonging to her monastery. Again, it is Ælffled who has requested the interview because she wishes to speak with Cuthbert. Cuthbert, however, has not gone out of his way to be socially oblig-ing, but is, again, carrying out his official ministry. Knowing that his death was imminent, he happened to be making a valedictory visit of his diocese to exhort the faithful, though he was, naturally, eager to return to his contemplative solitude. And furthermore he was visiting Ælffled's monastic estate in order to dedicate a church.[116]

In the Anonymous Life Cuthbert has an involuntary premonition at the feast. Like Bishop Aidan, who wept, foreseeing King Oswine's death when he sat down to eat with him, Cuthbert in the Anonymous Life is a holy wiseman for whom the scene of joy is transformed to grief by a sudden, gloomy intimation of mortality.[117] Ælffled, as in the earlier meeting, instantly catches the direction of Cuthbert's mind, and enquires, privately and unpressingly, into the cause of his disturbance: "She saw the man of God in a trance and seized with ecstasy, and the knife which he had in his hand dropped and fell on the table. Then unheard by the others, she humbly asked him what it was that had been revealed to him. He answered: 'I saw the soul of a servant of God from your household being carried to heaven in the hands of angels and being set amid the choir of angels, saints, and martyrs.' When she asked his name, he replied: 'You will name him to me tomorrow when I am celebrating mass.' "

Ælffled's role in this episode of the Anonymous Life is to co-operate with Cuthbert in bringing to fulfilment the partial knowledge of the future that she shares with him. Learning that a servant had been killed by falling from a tree, she hastens to the church where Cuthbert is saying mass, and arrives at precisely the right moment to participate harmoniously in his liturgical celebration by giving the response.[118] For as he intoned "Remember Lord thy servants," she

---

113 H&S, III, 314–26; see also the account of Coldingham, HE, IV.25.

114 See esp. Alcuin's "What has Ingeld to do with Christ?" letter (Duemmler, 124).

115 *Theodore's Penitential*, II.vii.1.

116 Bede gives the impression that the feast marked the dedication of a monastic church under Ælffled's rule, yet the story hinges on her fortuitous attendance at the mass Cuthbert celebrated; see fn. 112.

117 Cf. the feasting addition in *Bede's Cuthbert*, ch. 27; see fn. 112.

118 See Colgrave, 1940, p. 336; "Memento, Domine, famulorum," where commemoration of the living is made, is a scribal error for the commemoration of the faithful departed, "Memento etiam, Domine."

announced to him the dead servant's name. For Ælffled, the episode is a private confirmation of her knowledge of Cuthbert's gift of prophecy, and she divines by sudden insight that Cuthbert's intimation of a severed life-line signifies that his own death is close at hand: "She came breathlessly into the church and declared the name of the brother, who was called Hadwald, realizing not only that in this matter there was in him a spirit of prophecy, but also perceiving in all things his apostolic foresight whereby he also clearly foretold his own death in many ways."

Bede, on the other hand, is at considerable pains to dissociate Cuthbert from the scene of carnality in which the Lindisfarne Life has placed him. His prophetic insight is no longer spontaneous; Bede's Cuthbert, ever mindful of his own sanctity, "turned his mind from the carnal meal to contemplate spiritual things." Cuthbert, then, demonstrates his elevated superiority to ordinary mortals by his deliberately willed detachment from worldly matters. And since not one vestige of the singular and edifying gifts that God has bestowed on Cuthbert must escape the reader's attention, Cuthbert's trance is spectacularly heightened: "The limbs of his body relaxed and lost their function, the colour of his face changed, and his eyes were fixed against their wont as if in amazement, while the knife which he was holding fell to the table." Far from immediately recognizing the significance of this histrionic performance, the Abbess Ælffled fails to even notice it. Cuthbert's priest must call her attention to it and explain its meaning. He also underlines the elite and exclusive insight that Cuthbert possesses: " 'Ask the bishop what he has seen; for I know that not without cause has his trembling hand loosed the knife, and his countenance changed; but he has seen something spiritual which the rest of us have not been able to see.' " The Abbess Ælffled, then, is not a co-sharer of Cuthbert's prophetic knowledge; she is a mere woman, who cannot directly approach the sacred mysteries, but must have them intermediated by the priestly caste.

Whereas Cuthbert in the Anonymous Life imparts directly and immediately to Ælffled as much as it is given to him to see, Bede's superior and all-knowing bishop has no desire to share his secret with her at all. His patronizing evasion therefore forces Ælffled to ply him with questions, in order that she may plainly demonstrate the insatiable prying curiosity that is latent in her earlier meeting with Cuthbert. With this, the shared confidentiality of Ælffled's relation with Cuthbert disappears too. For, ignoring the reverential awe of the priest, who leans over her and whispers in her ear, Ælffled throws all discretion to the winds and hectors Cuthbert aloud: "She immediately turned to him and said: 'I beseech you, my lord bishop, tell me what you have just seen; for not for nothing did your hand relax and loose the knife it held.' He attempted to hide the fact that he had seen anything secret, and answered jestingly: 'Can I eat all day? I must rest sometimes.' But when she adjured him and importuned him more earnestly to reveal his vision, he said: 'I have seen the soul of a certain holy man being carried by the hands of angels to the joy of the heavenly kingdom.' Again she said: 'From what place was it taken?' He answered: 'From your monastery.' Then she enquired after his name. He said: 'You will tell me his name when I am celebrating mass tomorrow.' "

Bede's identification of the feast with worldly carnality helps to crystallize Ælffled's identification as a type of Eve. The established social role of women as hostesses at the feast lent itself readily to ecclesiastical construction of woman as Eve, particularly in the image of the woman with the poison cup.[119] But, in more general ways too, the role of woman as hostess underpins identification with the carnality of Eve. This equation underlies the officiously hospitable village woman that Bede introduces into an episode that occurs near the beginning of the Anonymous Life. In the Anonymous Life, Cuthbert's concern with food is that of a man who has experienced acute deprivation in his early life,[120] an aspect of the saint to which Bede, for all his theoretical idealization of apostolic poverty, is entirely oblivious. Whereas it is difficult to imagine that Cuthbert, as portrayed in the Anonymous Life, would reject an offer of food while travelling in sparsely populated parts, for Bede the village woman is typical of a species with whom bishops are obliged to mingle by their pastoral ministry. She is temptation incarnate, and persists in her efforts to force food upon Cuthbert, despite his explanation that he is fasting; and on a Friday too, "a day on which most of the faithful are accustomed to protract their fast until the ninth hour."[121]

Cuthbert's attempt to deflect Ælffled with the enquiry "Can I eat all day?" is a shrewd hit, identifying Ælffled as hostess of the profane, convivial feast. Her association with worldly and carnal considerations is consistent with her irreverent prying into visionary mysteries, of which she is as ignorant as she is oblivious of Cuthbert's intimation of earthly mortality. The feast over which she presides is opposed to the communion of the saints to which Cuthbert has turned his thoughts. It is an inversion of the temporal manifestation of the communion of saints, the mass itself, administered by male ecclesiastics like Cuthbert's reverent priest who, having taken over Ælffled's position as the intimate of the saint in Bede's version, intermediates between her and the holy of holies.

The sacramental critique of this feast is carried forward into the immediately following chapter, which is one of Bede's additions to the Life. Cuthbert's visit to Ælffled is replicated in a visit to the monastery of Abbess Verca, where Cuthbert, offered wine or beer to quench his thirst, calls for a drink of water, which he turns into wine.[122] Participation in the worldly and carnal banquet of

---

[119] See pp. 156–60. Cf. the two "Peter's mother-in-law" healing miracles in *Bede's Cuthbert*, ch. 15, 29; both are from *Anon Cuthbert*, II.8 and IV.3. This type of miracle, in which a woman, given a healing drink by the saint, ministers to him with a cup, thereby doing homage to the sacerdotal power by which he has taken from her the cup of death, is particularly well-adapted to the definition of the woman cup-bearer as an inversion of the priestly ministrant.

[120] See esp. his miraculous survival in *Anon Cuthbert*, I.7; in II.5, an eagle appears with a fish in response to the saint's concern with finding food; in *Bede's Cuthbert*, ch. 12, Cuthbert's enquiry is merely to test his companion, and the eagle becomes a female servant (*ministra*).

[121] Colgrave, p. 169; *Bede's Cuthbert*, ch. 5: cf. *Anon Cuthbert*, I.6. Bede is probably recalling *Dialogues*, II.13, where a travelling monk is tempted to break his fast by a devil in male disguise. Cf. *Anon Cuthbert*, II.2, which states (in accordance with the Columban rule which was at that time in use at Lindisfarne) that monastic travellers were allowed to eat at the third hour (see fn. 44).

[122] *Bede's Cuthbert*, ch. 35. Abbess Verca appears only in Bede's prose Life; Cuthbert's desire to be buried in a linen sheet Verca had given him was presumably a Lindisfarne tradition. Like Cuthbert's story of a feast at the Carlisle dedication (see fn. 112), the feast with Verca is a narrative gemination – I suspect that Bede has fictionalized the setting of this incident on the basis of *Anon Cuthbert*, IV.18, which mentions a water-wine miracle associated with Cuthbert, in order to give a figural explanation for Cuthbert's burial in the grave-cloth given by Verca (see

Ælffled is, as it were, cancelled out by Cuthbert's transcendence of the earthly feast by an actualization of its spiritual analogue; in the last resort, his valedictory feasting with the faithful can be regarded as an imitation of the conviviality of Christ at the Last Supper whereby he instituted the mass. So too, Cuthbert's disturbing intimacy with Ælffled is set aside by the honour bestowed on the monastery of Abbess Verca, in a miracle which, recalling the wedding feast at Cana (also a type of the mass) when Christ turned water into wine at the desire of his mother, implicitly suggests that Abbess Verca is a Marian exorcism of Ælffled's Eve.[123] The episode serves as a rationale for Cuthbert's instruction that his body is to be wrapped in the linen cloth given to him by Abbess Verca.[124] Notwithstanding, the abbess and her nuns are not witnesses to the miracle of transubstantiation. Anonymous persons having brought the cup of water, the communion instituted by Cuthbert is the communion of male ecclesiastics, embracing his own priest, the priest of Verca's monastery and a monk who was standing nearby.

Bede's exclusion of Ælffled from the partnership in the sacerdotal mysteries that she has in the Anonymous Life (albeit a junior partnership) culminates in her announcement of the name of the dead servant during the church service. Just as her inquiries into Cuthbert's prophetic knowledge are an intrusion into matters which do not rightly concern her, so her appearance while Cuthbert is saying mass is not timed to coincide harmoniously with his liturgical celebration. Despite the fact that the friendship of Cuthbert and Ælffled has been rigorously transformed to a hierarchical relation in which Cuthbert's over-riding superiority is everywhere apparent, it remains still for Bede to put Ælffled definitively in her place. Accordingly, she is revealed in her true colours, as a foolish woman who intrudes herself upon the attention of a bishop exercising his sacerdotal office. Ælffled precipitates herself disruptively into the orderly liturgical celebration, under the impression that she has something to tell him that he does not already know: "She immediately went to the bishop, who was then dedicating the church; with woman-like astonishment [stupore femineo], as if she were announcing something new and doubtful, she said: 'I pray you, my lord bishop, remember at mass my Hadwald' – for that was the man's name – 'who died yesterday through falling from a tree.' " Consistently, Ælffled is no longer the witting fulfilment of Cuthbert's prophecy, but the oblivious instru-

fn. 124); he is remarkably evasive about the identity of the first-hand witness he claims for this episode. Nothing is known of Verca; Bede locates her monastery on the Tyne (cf. *Bede's Cuthbert*, ch. 3); unlike Whitby, then, it was in Cuthbert's diocese.

[123] See John 2.1–11. The marriage of Cana was celebrated on 6th January; Cuthbert died 20th March.

[124] *Bede's Cuthbert*, ch. 37. Abbess Verca as provider of the shroud is presumably intended to continue the Marian allusion, perhaps reflecting the kind of Marian cult represented by the Prologue to the *Law of Adomnan*, which promotes reverence for Mary as "she who carries the spindle and clothes everyone" (McNeill, p. 136). Cuthbert's instructions for his burial are echoed in *Life of Guthlac*, chs. 48, 50–1, where the saint's burial rites are carried out by Pega, his sister and soul friend. One would expect, from the friendship of Ælffled and Cuthbert in *Anon Cuthbert*, that Ælffled would provide his shroud. An 1104 Durham inventory records a linen grave cloth in which Ælffled wrapped Cuthbert's body (see Haigh, 375, who deduces that Ælffled was present at the translation). If this is an authentic tradition, Bede's focusing on the grave clothes provided by Verca represents a further attempt to diffuse the particularity of Cuthbert's friendship with Ælffled.

ment of his superior foresight. The summary conclusion shifts from her private realization of his prophetic powers and impending death to the public and general recognition of the god-like superiority of Cuthbert. And particularly his superiority to Ælffled, whose actions he has correctly foreseen. She is a species of comic butt in the story, an unwitting spectacle of female stupefaction for the edification of a knowing audience: "Then it was clear to all how manifold was the spirit of prophecy in the breast of the holy man – who could not only see the secret removal of a soul in the present, but could also foresee what would be told to him by others in the future."

Bede's constitution of female alterity serves as the basis of exclusion from participation in divine mysteries, theologically justified by the submerged identification of the abbess as a type of Eve. The construction of women as Eve functions in Bede's *Life of Cuthbert* as it does in Eddius's *Life of Wilfrid*. It is a polemical tool in the conflict between churchmen and royal women, whether as queens or abbesses, whose employment testifies, not to royal women's absence of status, but to their power and prestige. That Bede indulged in this form of polemic in a work composed for a monastic audience, but made no use of it in the *History* – intended for a wider audience, and dedicated to the Northumbrian king – suggests that the misogynist undermining of royal women that was cultivated in ecclesiastical circles was not well-received in secular society. With the secular power of royal women, monks as well as bishops were engaged in unequal struggle: Osthryth's insistence on lodging the relics of King Oswald in the Lindsey monastery in spite of the monks' protests, mentioned in the *History*, is a case in point.[125] Bede's devotion to the elite, hierarchical status of bishops is abundantly plain in his letter to Egbert of York.[126] On the pages of a monastic hagiography designed for the Bishop of Lindisfarne and his monks, royal women's bid for position in the ecclesiastical sphere – including their influence on ecclesiastical appointments – could be more successfully combatted. Bede, in his severance of Ælffled from union with Cuthbert, represents a stage in the exclusive ecclesiastical appropriation of the prophetic faculties traditionally attributed to women, an advance in the direction of *Genesis B* and its depiction of the innately erroneous perversion of women's powers of discernment.[127] In his implicit analogy of the communion feast, he reflects a conflict over participation in the sacerdotal ministry that is manifest also in *Theodore's Penitential*, whose canons indicate that the exclusion of women lagged some way behind the state of affairs that Bede, in his determined handling of Ælffled, adumbrated as ideal.[128]

---

[125] See HE, III.11. Land grants to monasteries attested by queens (see, e.g., fn. 8) are indices of their influence in monastic affairs; see pp. 212–14.

[126] H&S, III, 314–26.

[127] *Bede's Cuthbert* was well-attuned to subsequent developments at Durham, where Cuthbert's relics were lodged. Women were prohibited from approaching his shrine on the grounds of his alleged misogyny; Simeon of Durham, HDE (ed. Arnold, I, 59) claims that the Coldingham scandal (HE, IV.25) led Cuthbert to outlaw women from his Lindisfarne church. Ward, 1982, pp. 1, 233, refers the origins of this to late 11th c. propaganda for the return of monastic rule at Durham.

[128] *Theodore's Penitential*, II.vii.1–4. See pp. 134–7.

7

Queen Converters and the Conversion of the Queen: Bede's *Ecclesiastical History* and the Royal Marriage

The Royal Marriage as *Signum*

The conversionary church's concern with the regulation of marriage, I have suggested, does not represent a purely regulatory impulse, but evinces an attempt to establish an approximate social actualization of the mystic union of the body of believers in the headship of Christ.[1] The royal marriage was, inevitably, the primary focus for the theology of marriage, for the marriage of the king, as Christ's earthly representative, was uniquely suited to emblematize the mystical marriage of Christ and the Church. Ecclesiastical interest in the figural potential of the royal marriage is clearly manifest only in the late Anglo-Saxon period, although there are signs that the royal marriage may already have been linked with the union of Christ and the Church by the time that Asser was writing in the late 9th century. Like the first phase of the conversion, the Benedictine Reform – its effective second phase – was placed under royal patronage and protection. This time, however, the queen was formally co-opted.[2] According to the Prologue to *Regularis Concordia* (c. 970), when King Edgar, like a Good Shepherd, had rescued the religious orders from the jaws of wolves, "he saw to it wisely that his queen, Ælfthryth, should be the protectress and fearless guardian of the communities of nuns, so that, himself helping the monks and his consort helping the women, there should be no cause for any breath of scandal."[3] Edgar's relations with monastic women caused more than a breath of scandal[4], and a possible reading of this eulogy of Edgar is that ecclesiastics were in hopes that Ælfthryth would be particularly vigilant in protecting the convents against the unwelcome attentions of her husband. Ostensibly, however, the queen, cast as a kind of paramount abbess, was endowed with a role parallel to the quasi-sacerdotal position that the king had been accorded

[1] See further pp. 47–50.
[2] Meyer, 34–61, shows that Benedictine reformers benefited from the support of royal women from the 940s onwards.
[3] Symons, *Regularis Concordia*, p. 2.
[4] Edgar's pursuit of Wulfhild during her Wilton novitiate, aided by the Abbess of Wherwell, is related in Goscelin's Life (ed. Esposito), chs. 2–3.

from the outset.[5] The parallel guardianship by king and queen that *Regularis Concordia* envisages for the church, aligned on the segregation of the monasteries, recalls *Maxims I*'s delineation of the royal couple's joint rulership within gender-demarcated spheres, military and social.[6] In the vernacular account of Edgar's restoration of the monasteries, the projected hieratic union assumes a more evidently hierarchical form: Edgar was "ever enquiring about the welfare of the monks, and he kindly exhorted the queen to take thought for the nuns in the same way, following his example."[7]

The identification of the queen consort with Mary, in her aspect of Queen of Heaven, was a natural concomitant of this hieratic construction of the royal marriage. One of the earliest illustrations of Mary as Queen of Heaven appears in the *Benedictional* of Æthelwold, who is generally held to have been the author of the Prologue to *Regularis Concordia*.[8] Copies of a coronation *ordo* that includes provision for the consecration of the queen appear in England from the late 10th or early 11th century onwards. These may have their origin, as Stafford believes, in ecclesiastical backing for the consecration of Ælfthryth when Edgar had himself crowned for a second time in 973.[9] Although there is no certain evidence of any Anglo-Saxon queen having been ritually installed on the throne, the combination of circumstances which all point in the direction of Ælfthryth's consecration make it difficult to believe that it did not take place.[10] At very least, the copying of an *ordo* for the consecration of both queen and king suggests a programmatic interest in promoting a figural conception of the royal marriage and equating it with the union of Christ and Mary-*Ecclesia* in the late Anglo-Saxon period.

Regularis Concordia's ideal conception of the royal couple as protectors of the church is embodied in the earliest Life of Edward the Confessor, completed shortly after the conquest, and dedicated to Edith his queen. The Life depicts Edith and Edward united in their care of the monasteries, he labouring over the monastery church at Westminster, she rebuilding the church of her *alma mater*, the nunnery at Wilton. Wilton above all merited her assistance, the author

---

[5] See *HE*, I.32. G.H. Williams, *The Norman Anonymous of AD 1100* (Cambridge, Mass., 1951), p. 162, suggested that Bede "may well be one of the sources of the theory of the royal and sacerdotal *christi*."

[6] *Maxims I*, ll. 81–92.

[7] *Edgar's Establishment of the Monasteries*, ed. Whitelock, I, 150.

[8] Winchester under Æthelwold was seminal to the development of the iconography of Mary as Queen of Heaven; see R. Deshman, "*Christus rex et magi reges*: Kingship and Christology in Ottonian and Anglo-Saxon Art," *FS* 10 (1976), 367–405. Clayton, 1984, 209–34, shows that two new feasts in her honour were introduced in the 1030s at Winchester, although there is evidence of a flourishing cult from the late 7th to the early 9th c., as well as in the second half of the 10th and in the 11th c. (see also Clayton, 1990).

[9] Stafford, 1983, pp. 129–32, regards Æthelwold as the motivating force in the coronation of Ælfthryth; see also fn. 10 below. She is the first 10th c. queen to witness charters as *regina* (Birch, 1216), although 10th c. queens, from the time of Eadgifu, widow of Edward the Elder, had appeared high in the witness lists (Campbell, 1949, pp. 62–5).

[10] *Lanalet Pontifical*, ed. H.B.S. Doble (London, 1937), pp. 41–2, 59–63 (late 10th or early 11th c.), contains a coronation *ordo* for a queen; *Egbert's Pontifical*, c. 1000, contains only an *ordo* for a king. It used to be said that there was no evidence for the consecration of any AS queen except Judith. J. Nelson, however, who has radically altered earlier views of the AS coronation *ordo*, argues that Ælfthryth was consecrated: see esp. "The Second English *Ordo*," *Politics and Ritual in Early Medieval Europe* (London, 1986), pp. 371–4. See further fns. 41, 49.

explains, because it had taken such pains to teach her the virtues that fitted her to be the queen of the English; as the Benedictine reformers had endowed the queen with the role of Mother Superior of all England, the *Life of King Edward* marks the development of an ideal of the queen that is formed in the same matrix as the ideal of a nun. Edith's author is mindful of her responsibility for all of the convents under her care: "Nowhere did she believe alms better bestowed than where the weaker sex, less skilled in building, more deeply felt the pinch of poverty, and was less able by its own efforts to drive it away."[11] Edith is accorded no role in the political life of the kingdom beyond the extension of a nebulous peaceful influence and the provision of good advice which, though praised in the highest terms, is significantly unheeded; but, together with the officiating bishop, Edith presides over the dedication of the Wilton church, where once the abbess, who was the builder of monastery churches in the pre-Viking age, would have appeared as the partner of the bishop.[12] Obliquely, the Life's hymn to Mary-*Ecclesia* which celebrates the dedication of Edith's church contributes also to the Marian idealization of Edith; like Mary-*Ecclesia*, the childless Edith, knowing neither the joys nor sorrows of carnal motherhood, is, by her construction of the monastery church, a peerless mother of spiritual progeny.[13]

Edith's part in the royal pair's joint exercise of parental responsibility for the church is further extended by the author when, intending to convey that the Norman defeat of the English was a fitting retribution for their iniquities, he explains that the king and queen had frequently admonished the errors of churchmen that Rome had condemned.[14] The extent to which the reality of Edith conformed to the author's idealization is difficult to gauge, but if the annals of St Richier are to be believed, her public assumption of the role of co-hierarch appears to have offended the sensibilities of their abbot when he visited the English court; he is said to have rebuked Edith when she followed her husband in offering him the kiss of peace.[15] Edith is reported as having duly taken this rebuke to heart; discrepancy between the actualities of the status of Anglo-Saxon queens and the expectations of the ecclesiastics who accompanied the Norman conquerers possibly helped to precipitate the tensions that appear in the portrait of Edith in the *Life of King Edward*, for the author is thought to have begun writing shortly before the death of Edward the Confessor and to have completed a revised version of his Life some time after the Conquest.[16]

Edith's eulogist gives the impression of not knowing quite where to put Edith. Prompted to build the church at Wilton by the good example of Edward, Edith shows her mettle as a soldier of Christ. Vying with Edward for the completion of the work – a contest which was pleasing to God and not disagreeable to them – Edith succeeds in finishing her church before his is complete; on the other

[11] F. Barlow, ed. and trans., *Life of King Edward who Rests at Westminster* (London, 1962), p. 47. It was probably begun 1065 and completed 1067 (Barlow, p. xxv).

[12] See further pp. 259–60; ch. 5, fns. 107, 109.

[13] See Barlow, p. 48.

[14] Barlow, p. 77.

[15] *Chronique de l'abbaye de Saint Riquier*, IV.22: ed. F. Lot (Paris, 1894), p. 237. Hariulf says that Edith, though initially displeased, later ordered the English bishops and abbots to follow suit; see fn. 42 below.

[16] See fns. 11, 42.

hand, Edith's was more modestly planned. A similar awkwardness appears when the author describes the generosity of the royal pair. Whereas the ideal king and queen are defined by *Maxims I* as generous distributors of treasure to the retinue, the ideal king and queen, ecclesiastically conceived, are united in their open-handed distribution of alms: "His royal consort did not restrain him in those good works in which he prepared to lead the way, and often enough seemed even to lead the way herself. For while he would give now and then, she was prodigal: but aimed her bounty to such good purpose as to consider the honour of the king himself."[17] The *Life of King Edward* has the appearance of grafting a more recently fashionable ideal of queenly virtue, already emerging in the *Encomium Emmae's* presentation of its modestly self-effacing heroine,[18] on to the earlier, heroic-age, conception of the queen as a leader of men, whose over-lordship ran parallel to her husband's. But an underlying resolution to the tensions in the portrait of Edith – her simultaneous appearance as the leader and inferior subordinate of Edward – is to be found in the author's attempt to portray the royal marriage as an organic union in which Edith transcends herself by following Edward's example, even as the Church is raised up to perfection by its incorporation in Christ, while yet remaining, as body, ultimately submerged in the headship of the Christ-King.[19]

Edith's eulogist certainly knew where to put her when he began the work, for he projects a celebration of Edith as throne-sharer, promising a portrait of a queen who "thrives at Edward's imperial side." And he describes the royal marriage, not as the union of head and body, but as a conjunction of kindred souls – Edith is Edward's other half; they are "one person dwelling in a double form."[20] But in the course of the narrative, the image of Edith as throne-sharer undergoes a radical shift: "Although by custom and law a royal throne was always prepared for her at the king's side, she preferred, except in church and at the royal table, to sit at his feet, unless perchance he should reach out his hand to her, or with a gesture of the hand invite or command her to sit next to him."[21] Edith has found her level – for it is at the feet of the king she is to be found for the whole of Book II's hagiographical account of the Christ-King's death; figuring Mary as mourner at the foot of the cross, she simultaneously pays tribute to Edward's headship.[22] Publicly, then, Edith adopts the status of equal that is hers by law and custom – for, constant in her service to Edward's lordship, she is ever mindful of the ceremonial shows that Edward's exalted office requires. But privately she acknowledges her analogical status as the bride of Christ, whose salvation is accomplished by her raising up through Edward. In her reverential modesty in abnegating a position that all the world holds right-fully hers – in her private knowledge of her true position – Edith is, for the author, an example to all women: "She was, I say, a woman to be placed before

---

17 Barlow, p. 42.
18 See further pp. 89–90, 193.
19 Eph. 5.22–33.
20 Barlow, pp. 3–4.
21 Barlow, p. 42.
22 Barlow, pp. 76, 79. Edward commends Edith and the kingdom to his successor Harold (as his "domina et soror"). Edward could scarcely call his wife "mother," and describes her as a beloved daughter who has always stood close by his side; Mary is the daughter (and sister) of Christ. Considerations of Edith's ability to inherit may also be involved here.

all noble matrons and persons of royal and imperial ranks as a model of virtue and integrity for maintaining both the practices of Christian virtue and worldly dignity."[23] Disseminated through romance fiction, the ideal of womanly virtue embodied in the Life's portrait of Edith was in actuality destined to become the model for aristocratic women.

The royal marriage, then, was a focus for the nexus of allegorical equations deriving from Canticles, and a channel for the figurative construction of every marriage as the microcosmic incorporation of the Marian body of the Church into the headship of Christ. By a more pernicious twist, the metaphorical conception shifted from the union of head and body to the union of body and soul. Whereas the union of head and body, though innately hierarchical, is a union of two entities sharing the same substance, who, by their common identity of flesh are capable of achieving oneness of spirit, the union of body and soul is a marriage of opposites, requiring a much more forceful subjugation of the lower nature to the higher to effect union; and although the female partner in a soul-body union may be identified with the soul, and rule over her husband-body in the manner of Mary, Queen of Heaven, the well-known danger of this form of figural equation is its liability to be flipped over, leaving the wife underneath as Eve-body. The allegorization of the royal marriage, in short, as a focal channel for establishing the figurative construction of marital union, opened the way for the establishment of a distinct female otherness, and the persistent perception of women as types of either Mary or Eve.

The late Anglo-Saxon ecclesiastical cult of the queen as Marian consort of the king and co-protector of the church builds upon the queen's customary role as sharer of the throne, with which the author of the Life of King Edward was evidently familiar. But it also represents the continuation of a long tradition of involvement with the monasteries on the part of reigning queens.[24] There is reason to believe that, even before the time of Bede, the royal couple exercised a joint secular lordship over the monasteries they endowed, which reflected their joint rule over the kingdom at large. The late 8th and 9th century Mercian queens' participation in the rule of the kingdom is reflected in royal charters granting land to the monasteries, or to the church, in which the queen as well as the king appears on the witness list.[25] Kentish charters attested by both the king and the queen date from the reign of Wihtred, in the late 7th century; charters granting land to the monasteries are witnessed by Wihtred as well as by

[23] Barlow, p. 42. Cf. fn. 162.
[24] See Meyer, 34–61.
[25] The following royal couples appear in witness lists; all of the women listed are styled regina (but do not invariably witness with their husbands): Cynethryth and Offa (Birch, 197, 204, 207, 213, 214, 216, 234, 236, 239, 240, 245, 247, 248, 251, 252, 259); Ælfthryth and Cenwulf (Birch, 326, 335, 339, 343, 346, 348, 350, 351, 356, 357, 358); Berhtwulf and Sæthryth (Birch, 428, 430, 432, 433, 434, 435, 436, 443, 450, 453, 454); Burgred and Æthelswith (Birch, 487, 488, 489, 492, 503, 509, 513, 514, 522, 524, 537); Offa and Cyneswith (Birch 222); Wiglaf and Cynethryth (Birch, 400, 461); Cenwulf and Cynegyth (Birch, 296); Burgred and Æthelthryth (Birch, 535). Two charters (796) are attested by Ecgfrith and Cynethryth regina, presumably his mother (Birch, 280, 281). Not all of the charters involve grants of land to the church. Æthelfled, Lady of Mercia, is listed with her husband, Ealdorman Æthelred (Birch, 547, 559, 561, 574, 579, 603, 607, 608); she is not styled regina.

two successive wives of Wihtred, Cynegyth and Æthelburg, both of whom are styled *regina*.[26] In an early 8th century Wessex charter (725), Ine and his wife Æthelburg jointly grant land to Glastonbury;[27] charters attested by their successors, Æthelheard and *regina Fridogitha*,[28] confirm that Asser was correct in his belief that refusal to accord the status of queen to the wife of Alfred represented a departure from a widespread custom that had once been current in Wessex itself.[29]

The land grants witnessed by Wihtred and two of his queens are inextricably connected with royal overlordship of the monasteries of Kent. In return for royal protection and remission of dues, the early Kentish monasteries pledged "honour and obedience" to the throne.[30] The appearance of Queen Werburg as joint witness to Wihtred's reciprocal agreement with the monasteries strongly suggests that she was regarded as joint ruler of the Kentish monasteries, and the same is likely to have held true of Cynegyth and Æthelburg. Joint overlordship of the monasteries in the early 8th century is also indicated in the letter of Abbess Eangyth which complains of the financial exactions of both the king and the queen – her monastery is most likely to have been in Wessex.[31] Cynethryth and Offa certainly exercised a joint lordship over the monasteries that fell within the territories ruled by Mercia in the late 8th century; they were both named in a papal privilege of Hadrian I that granted control of all the monasteries they had built or acquired which had been dedicated to St Peter; Cynethryth retained possession of the extensive lands of the Cookham monastery after Offa's death.[32]

There are, unfortunately, no Northumbrian charters from the age of Bede, but a letter from Alhred and Osgifu of Northumbria to Bishop Lul, dated 773, which asks for his prayers for themselves and their friends and relations, assures Lul that prayers are offered for him in all the monasteries under their protection.[33] In view of Bede's complaint to Bishop Egbert concerning family monasteries, it would be surprising if early Northumbrian kings and queens were not joint overlords of the monasteries, since Bede's complaint implies a high degree of social participation on the part of Anglo-Saxon women; as Bede understood it, many laymen had set up monasteries for themselves with the intention of evading taxes and military service, and established others for their wives, whom they installed as abbesses.[34] Eanfled, who is said in the *History* to have persuaded her husband Oswiu to grant land to found a monastery by way of expiation for

---

[26] Wihtred and Æthelburg are joint donors in Birch, 96, and appear in the witness list of Birch, 90, 97, 98; Wihtred and Cynegyth are joint donors in Birch, 86.

[27] Birch, 143.

[28] Birch, 147, 158. Birch, 132, a 714 grant by Nunna of the South Saxons, is witnessed by Æthelstan and Æthelthryth *regina*.

[29] *Life of Alfred*, trans. S. Keynes and M. Lapidge, *Alfred the Great* (Harmondsworth, 1983), pp. 67–110; ed. W. Stevenson, *Asser's Life of King Alfred*, 2nd edn. by D. Whitelock (Oxford, 1959), chs. 13–14. See further fn. 40.

[30] See Birch, 91, 92, 95.

[31] Tangl, 14; but Boniface's circle extended well beyond his Wessex homeland.

[32] Cynethryth held Cookham as abbess, and was involved in protracted land disputes with the archbishop; see N. Brooks, *The Early History of the Church of Canterbury* (Leicester, 1984), pp. 116, 131, 184.

[33] Tangl, 121.

[34] H&S, III, 320–1.

his murder of King Oswine, and who, according Eddius, sent Wilfrid to the Lindisfarne monastery to look after a former retainer who had become a monk there, is likely to have shared with her husband a much more extensive controlling interest in the affairs of the monasteries.[35] So, too, is Oswiu's daughter Osthryth who, despite the monks' objections, lodged the relics of her uncle Oswald in the Bardney monastery; the monastery, Bede relates, had been greatly enriched by Osthryth and her husband, Æthelred of Mercia.[36] There is every reason to believe that Bede would have no wish to publicize secular overlordship of the monasteries in any form. Benedictine reformers held it responsible for the earlier demise of monasticism,[37] and *Regularis Concordia*, in proclaiming the royal pair the guardians of the monasteries, clearly aims to retain king and queen in their long-standing role as protectors and patrons, while endeavouring to obviate their concomitant tendency to regard the monasteries as their own property by casting them in a quasi-sacerdotal role, whereby they become, like bishops, stewards of property that belongs to God alone, and owe their supremacy over the monasteries to the sanction of the church. But Bede found no obstacle to reporting kings' patronage of the church. Had he been as willing to report the part played by queens we would have had a more representative reflection of the position of early queens than the one that the *History* gives us; his reference to Osthryth and Æthelred's founding of Bardney is his sole allusion to queens' partnership with their husbands; not even the land which Wilfrid was given by Æthelthryth receives a mention in the *History*.[38]

In elevating the queen to a Marian protector of the nunneries, bishops of the late Anglo-Saxon reform period could also be said to have finally found a solution to the problem presented by the queen, deflecting to the service of the nunneries the power with which bishops were apt to find themselves in conflict in their attempts to govern the king. Asser's much-quoted remarks on the position of the queen in Wessex suggest that a hieratic conception of the royal marriage was already being assayed in the 9th century. It is a surprise to find King Alfred's episcopal mentor apparently championing the queen's equal partnership in the royal marriage against the misogyny of the Wessex court. In Wessex, Asser explains, the queen had not been permitted to share the throne or bear the title of queen since the days when Eadburg dealt out death to the retinue and accidentally poisoned the king.[39] Asser would seem to have been offered a myth of origins concerning the dangers of women wielding power whose force any cleric could appreciate, but he is still outraged: Wessex refusal to countenance the queen's sharing of the throne is a perverse and detestable custom, and contrary to the practice of all Germanic peoples.

Asser's interest in queens was not such as to prompt him to give us so much as

---

[35] See *Life of Wilfrid*, ch. 2: HE, III.24.
[36] HE, III.11.
[37] See *Regularis Concordia*, p. 7; *Edgar's Establishment of the Monasteries*, ed. Whitelock, I, 153–4.
[38] *Life of Wilfrid*, ch. 22; cf. HE, IV.19.
[39] *Life of Alfred*, chs. 13–14. Stafford, 1981, 3–27, regards the story of Eadburg as a justification of the successional practices that brought Alfred to the throne (downgrading the queen's status reduced her power to back her son against the king's brother); Asser's disapproval cannot be accounted for in these terms.

a thumb-nail sketch of Alfred's wife, and as he offers no countervailing rationale for queenly status, his account effectively serves to publicize Alfred's justification for the reduction of the king's wife from her customarily high position.[40] But Asser's *Life of Alfred* as a whole gives no encouragement to the view that his handling of the story of Eadburg is the work of a sophisticated ironist. His apparent endorsement of the high status of queens is explicable if he regarded throne-sharing and the title of queen, not as outward signs of the queen's equivalence in power, but as a *signum* of the raising of the Church-bride to union with the Christ king. At least some degree of continental influence underlies the figural conception of the royal marriage promoted by reformers in the late Anglo-Saxon period,[41] as well as its development in the post-Conquest *Life of King Edward* (which is attributed to one of the Flemish ecclesiastics who settled in England during the reign of Edward the Confessor).[42] Asser's stance may also reflect continental influence; Alfred's reforms were accomplished with the assistance of Frankish ecclesiastics,[43] and his father had contracted an alliance with a Frankish princess, Judith, who was consecrated at the insistence of the Frankish court when she was given in marriage to Æthelwulf in 856. Judith's father is likely to have been motivated at least in part by a determination to ensure that a daughter of his was accorded full honour by the Wessex court,[44] but the extension of the sacramentalization of royal power to the king's wife also reflects the development by Frankish ecclesiastics of a sacramental conception of the royal marriage union.[45] Recent scholarship, however, points to the existence of seemingly indigenous queen-making rituals in mid 9th century Mercia, which could conceivably have been already current when Eadburg of Mercia married Brihtric of Wessex in 789,[46] and the attitudes of

---

[40] *Life of Alfred*, ch. 29, does not even name Alfred's Mercian wife, but gives her mother's name as Eadburg (i.e., the same as the notorious Mercian queen of Asser's story). According to Asser, the Wessex court, despite its objection to queens, did not object to Æthelwulf sharing the throne with his consecrated Frankish queen, Judith. Judith subsequently married Æthelwulf's son, Æthelbald, and witnesses charters with him as Judith *regina* (Birch, 495, 500). Two charters are attested by Brihtric of Wessex and his wife, Eadburg, who is styled *regina* in both (Birch, 279, 282). Alfred's wife (Ealhswith) attests only one charter, in the reign of his successor, Edward, as *mater regis*; Edward's wife also attests, as Ælffled *conjux regis* (Birch, 589; sic). From the time of Brihtric's wife Eadburg in the late 8th c., then, until the late 10th c. when Ælfthryth received the backing of clerical reformers (fn. 9), Judith was the only Wessex royal wife to have been styled *regina*, with one striking exception; in a charter dated 868, the year of Alfred's marriage to a Mercian wife (*Life of Alfred*, ch. 29) his brother, King Æthelred, appears in the witness list with Wulfthryth *regina* (Birch, 520): Wulfthryth's name looks Mercian.

[41] Nelson (see fn. 46) dismisses the earlier argument that Dunstan's exile in Gent had a formative influence on the coronation *ordo* itself.

[42] Barlow, pp. xli–lix, 91–109, favours the authorship of Goscelin, who arrived in England from St Bertin c. 1058.

[43] See *Life of Alfred*, ch. 78.

[44] See P. Stafford, "Charles the Bald, Judith and England," in *Charles the Bald: Court and Kingdom*, ed. M. Gibson et al. (Oxford, 1981), pp. 137–51.

[45] Wallace-Hadrill, 1983, pp. 403–11, observes that Hincmar, who drafted the *ordo* for Judith, regarded marriage as "a *signum* of the great and true mystery of Christ's incorporation in the Church," and that his *Epistula de nuptiis Stephanii* was "moving to a sacramental definition of marriage without quite getting there," p. 410.

[46] See J.L. Nelson, "The Earliest Surviving Royal *Ordo*: Some Liturgical and Historical Aspects," *Authority and Power: Studies in Medieval Law and Government*, ed. B. Tierney and P. Linehan (Cambridge, 1980), pp. 29–48, esp. p. 39, n. 51; see further fn. 61.

Asser and the Wessex court may well, in their different ways, have been shaped by their awareness of Mercian practices that enhanced the status of queens by endowing them with charismatic prestige.

Offa, the father of Eadburg, was one of the most powerful rulers of Mercia, which held the overlordship of Wessex until the closing decade of the reign of Alfred's grandfather (that is, until about 827).[47] The anointing of Offa's son and heir, carried out during the lifetime of Offa and at his instruction, some two years before Eadburg's marriage to Brihtric, is the first recorded consecration of an English king.[48] Offa was in contact with the court of Charlemagne; but although he was generally held to have been influenced by Frankish practices, it is now argued that the consecration of kings in Mercia may pre-date the sacring of Offa's son, and that a West Saxon fixed rite for kings may have already existed when Eadburg's Wessex husband came to the throne.[49] Cynethryth, the wife of Offa, who is described as *regina* in the charters she attests with her husband,[50] was powerful enough to acquire notoriety in later ages, if not in her own time; she is the only Anglo-Saxon queen to have had coins struck in her name.[51]

Alcuin of York, who spent much of his life at the court of Charlemagne and was involved in the diplomatic effort to restore friendly relations between Charlemagne and Offa, wrote to Ecgfrith, the son whom Offa had designated as his heir, urging him to follow the example of his parents, to learn authority from his father and piety from his mother, from him how to rule the kingdom with justice, from her how to how to have pity on suffering, and true Christian devotion from both of them.[52] Alcuin's letter is of interest for its conception of the royal union as a figural exemplar, and offers a glimpse of Mercian contact with the direction in which ecclesiastical thinking about the royal marriage was tending at the court of Charlemagne. Marriage, in Alcuin's understanding, essentially consists of the union of binary opposites, and his equation of the royal pair with the attributes of justice and mercy which are mystically united in the perfect reign of Christ, well illustrates the way in which the theology of marriage works towards the creation of distinctively male and female identities, and by its identification of the queen with merciful compassion looks forward to the Marian idealization of queens. Alcuin's letters to the Northumbrian court reveal that, although he thought it worth cultivating cordial relations with Cynethryth, he did not acknowledge her as a power in the land. Greetings to her, enclosed in one letter to Offa, salute her as the lady of the royal household

---

47 ASC (A), 836, reports that Offa helped Brihtric to drive into exile Alfred's grandfather, Ecgberht, because Brihtric had married his daughter (see ASC, 787); Ecgberht succeeded on the death of Brihtric (ASC 800), subsequently conquering Mercia and becoming the eighth Bretwalda (ASC, 827).

48 ASC (A), 785; 787 is the accepted dating among modern scholars.

49 J.L. Nelson, "Inauguration Rituals," ed. Sawyer and Woods, p. 52, suggested that the novelty may have lain in pre-mortem succession rather than the hallowing of Offa's son as such; Nelson, 1980, pp. 29–48, argues for "an English fixed rite [for kings] dating from the first half of the 9th century *at the latest*, [and] the search for origins could take us back a century or more before that," p. 41 (her italics).

50 See fn. 25.

51 See Fell, 1986, pp. 90–1.

52 Duemmler, 61.

and express the hope that she will continue to rejoice in being the mother of Offa's son; in another, Alcuin regrets that he has been too busy with the king's business to enclose a hortatory letter to the queen.[53] For Alcuin, then, Cynethryth was the partner of Offa only in so far she was as the mother of his son. Even supposing, however, that Alcuin had in fact met Cynethryth, it would be unwise to deduce anything about her character or her position at court from these letters; in a letter to Ealdorman Osbert, Alcuin exhorted him to urge the Mercians to keep the laws that Offa had established, but he also interpreted the untimely death of Offa's son and heir as just retribution for the fact that Offa had shed so much blood to secure the kingdom for him.[54]

Offa's wife Cynethryth was not the only Mercian queen who is described in the witness lists of charters as *regina*; her three successors are given the same title.[55] Just as Asser's tale of Eadburg reflects the Wessex court's antagonism to Mercian overlordship and its extension through the marriage alliances contracted by Mercian queens, the Life of Æthelberht of East Anglia, which depicts Cynethryth as the instigator of his murder, no doubt reflects ecclesiastical prejudices against power wielded by queens but may also have its origins in the East Anglian court's resentment of Mercian power and the Mercian queens who were its agents.[56] Nor was Eadburg the only woman of the Mercian royal house to figure in Wessex legend as the killer of one of its kings. The eleventh century Life of the martyred boy-king Cenhelm claims that his sister Cwenthryth had him murdered because she wanted to rule the kingdom. Cwenthryth was the daughter of Offa's immediate successor, Cenwulf of Mercia (796–823), and memory of the power she wielded in Wessex may have contributed to the depiction of her in this life.[57] Whereas Mercian royal women like Eadburg had consolidated their family's rule by their marriage alliances, Cwenthryth was the agent of Mercian overlordship not by her alliance in marriage but by her direct control of the double monasteries; she was simultaneously the abbess of Minster-in-Thanet, in Kent, and of Winchcombe, the Wessex monastery which promulgated the cult of Cenhelm in the 11th century. Both of these double monasteries played an important part in the Mercian administration, and were centres for the collection of royal taxes.[58] In Kent, Cwenthryth served as an effective counterweight to the power of the Archbishop, with whom she was engaged in protracted disputes over the lands and the lordship of Thanet and Lyminge, in which she was backed first by her father and then by her father's brother, who succeeded him on the Mercian throne.[59]

[53] Duemmler, 101 ("dominam et dispensatricem domus regiae"), cf. Duemmler, 62 ("domnam reginam").
[54] Duemmler, 122.
[55] See fn. 25.
[56] *Passio Athelberti*, ch. 6.
[57] In the Douce 368 version of *Passio Kenelmi*, 11th c., Queen Edith, from whom the author claims to have got his information, offers a virtuous contrast to wickedly ambitious Cwenthryth.
[58] For the importance of the double monasteries to the Mercian overlords of Kent, see Brooks, pp. 174–206. For Winchcombe, founded by Offa and added to by Cenwulf, see Levison, 1946, pp. 31–2, 249–59.
[59] For an account of these disputes, and the related disputes of Abbess Selethryth and Archbishop Wulfred, see Brooks, pp. 190–7. Cwenthryth's role as a Mercian counterweight to the growing power of Wulfred is somewhat obscured by Brooks's conviction that archbishops who

In Mercia, then, the title of queen appears to have been the corollary of royal women's substantial participation in the power held by their family. Asser and the Wessex court are likely to have been familiar with the status of Mercian queens, not merely because of the former subordination of Wessex to Mercia, but also because one of the women who bore the title of queen in Mercia was Alfred's sister Æthelswith, who was given in marriage by their father Æthelwulf in 853 to Burgred of Mercia, after Burgred won a victory against the Welsh with Æthelwulf's assistance.[60] Æthelswith is the first English queen to be described in a manner which suggests that she was ritually enthroned.[61] Given the low status of royal wives in Wessex in the time of Alfred, the queen-making rituals bestowed on Æthelswith are much more likely to represent established Mercian custom than Wessex practice; the sacring of Offa's son may thus reflect not only the antiquity of king-making rituals but also preoccupation with the sacramentalization of royal power that extended to the coronation of Offa's wife Cynethryth and his daughter Eadburg.[62]

Despite the fact that papal letters to the early queens of Northumbria and Kent urged them to effect the conversion of their husbands and thereby speed the kingdom's acceptance of the faith, Bede offers no portrait of a queen converter. Not until the early 12th century, when the allegorization of the royal marriage had firmly established the queen's figurative identification with Mary-Ecclesia, is an Anglo-Saxon queen celebrated as the converter of her people – although Margaret of Scotland is an Anglo-Saxon queen only by virtue of her kinship to Edward the Confessor, and strictly speaking the Scots were not converted from paganism but brought to accept orthodox Roman customs. Turgot's Life of Margaret was written at the request of Margaret's daughter Mathilda, the wife of Henry I.[63] Margaret, in Turgot's Life, civilizes the barbarous Scots and her adoring husband, who follows her advice in everything.[64] Dying even before the news of Malcolm's death reaches her, she evidently figures the soul, who prompts her husband-body to the understanding of heavenly things.[65] But her omniscient good influence extends into ecclesiastical affairs, clearly establishing this "precious pearl in God's sight," whose chamber is filled with sacred vessels and

opposed secular lordship were laudable crusaders endeavouring to maintain the religious life of the monasteries; see J. Crick, "Church, Land and Local Nobility in Early Ninth-Century Kent: The Case of Ealdorman Oswulf," *Historical Research* 61 (1988), 251–69. Thryth, *Beowulf*, ll. 1931–62, conceivably reflects the circulation of legends concerning Cynethryth and Cwenthryth.

[60] ASC, 853.
[61] In Birch, 524 (869), Æthelswith appears as "pari coronata stemma regali," which "could imply a consecration-rite for her, paralleling her husband's" (Nelson, 1980, p. 39, n. 51); see also Stafford, 1981, pp. 137–51.
[62] See Stafford, 1983, p. 128, who argues that formal establishment of a royal wife's primacy improved her son's chances of succeeding.
[63] See *Vita Margaritae Scotorum Reginae*, Prologue: *Pinkerton's Lives of the Scottish Saints*, rev. edn. W.M. Metcalfe (Paisley, 1889), II, 159–82 (subsequently cited as *Life of Margaret*). A late 11th c. addition to the entry for 1067 in the D version of ASC (perhaps destined for the Scottish court), parallels the Life's portrait of Margaret.
[64] *Life of Margaret*, ch. 8.
[65] *Life of Margaret*, chs. 26–32.

whose prayer book is constantly in her hand,[66] as the earthly representative of Mary and a symbol of Holy Church. Whereas the *Life of King Edward* merely depicts Edith, in her role of Marian protector of the church, as having joined with Edward to warn ecclesiastics of the need to eradicate abuses in the church, Margaret plays a leading role in the establishment of religious orthodoxy throughout Scotland by her wise and learned advice to men of the church.[67]

Cynewulf's *Elene*, however, in its portrait of the Emperor Constantine's mother marching out with her army to bully the Jews into revealing the location of the True Cross,[68] conceivably reflects awareness within the 9th century Mercian church that queens, as well as kings, were possessed of power, including power over the monasteries, that could be co-opted for the protection and patronage of the church, and that iconographic enhancement was a necessary part of this strategy. Rulers like King Alfred's daughter Æthelfled, who was responsible for Mercia's defence against the Danes in the late 9th and early 10th century, and who retained the leadership of Mercia and its military campaigns after her husband's death, would certainly seem to have lent themselves more readily to the typology of the Church Militant than they did to Marian idealization as mediators of the peace that passes understanding.[69] The proliferation of versions of the Elene legend in the late Anglo-Saxon period, then, perhaps represents the survival of an earlier, distinctively heroic-age, cult of the queen – under the influence of an emerging conception of Mary as the epitome of feminine virtue, Elene assumes, in the later vernacular versions of her legend, the softer lineaments of a romance heroine.[70] Eleventh and twelfth century queens undoubtedly collaborated in their own Marian idealization; like ritual consecration it added, in the short term, to their prestige.[71] In the long term, there was a high price to be paid for basking in the reflected glory of the Queen of Heaven, and Edith's concomitant shift from throne-sharer to foot-sitter in the *Life of King Edward*, held out as an example for the imitation of all women, marks its extent.

Queens, then, appear to have been joint rulers and partners in the royal over-lordship of the monasteries both before and during the lifetime of Bede. They traditionally held the title of queen which Asser associated with throne-sharing, and charters signed by queens confirm the view that the ceremonial forms which Alfred's court refused to bestow on the queen were outward signs of an actual share in rule. Asser may have been familiar with the sacramental and figural conceptions of the royal marriage through the influence of continental clerics, with which the Mercian court also had some form of contact. Bede's

---

66 *Life of Margaret*, ch. 7, 17.
67 *Life of Margaret*, chs. 10–16; cf. Barlow, p. 77.
68 See *Elene*, ll. 276–1235.
69 The belief that Helena was of British origin may have assisted the popularity of her cult; see A.J. Ugolnik, "The Royal Icon: A Structural and Thematic Study of Cynewulf's *Elene*," *DAI* 37 (1976) 342–3A (Brown University). For the Lady of Mercia, see pp. 86–8.
70 For OE Elene legends, see p. 92.
71 See Stafford, 1983, pp. 135–52. Endorsement of their Marian image is implied by Emma's commissioning of the *Encomium* and Mathilda's request for the Life of her mother, and I would accept at face value the claim of *Life of King Edward*, (see esp. Barlow, p. 59), to be written at the request of Edith; see further ch. 6, fn. 78.

History reveals that the idea of the royal marriage as a *signum* of mystic union was, even at this early date, current in embryo – his allusions to the theology of marriage fairly certainly derive from his Canterbury source, although an exegetical commentary on *Canticles* is among his works.[72] But it has clearly failed to take effect in any conception of the queen as the king's partner in the patronage and protection of the church. In Bede's overall representation of the conversion, the influence of reigning queens is conspicuous by its absence.

The near-invisibility of the influence of reigning queens in Bede's *History* can only mean that the attention of the church in the early 8th century was still focused on the conversion of the king and that it had, as yet, no blue-print for the role of the queen as the king's partner in his protection and patronage of the church, although queens, like kings, could serve as examples for the imitation of their subjects. The Marian idealization of the queen depends upon the establishment of the royal marriage as a figure of Christ's union with the church. Although the Marian iconography of *Life of Wilfrid* encompasses Queen Eanfled, it is focused upon the abbess as the partner of the bishop. The slowness with which the royal marriage took on emblematic signification, I want to suggest, is at least in part attributable to the culturally alien conception of marriage union on which it rests. The absence of queen converters in Bede's *History* is very probably an accurate representation of historical actuality. The Marian idealization of the queen as spiritual councillor and all-pervasive influence for good in the *Life of King Edward* and the *Encomium Emmae*, however, is an effective transmutation of the vernacular ideal of the queen as peaceweaver and adviser,[73] and Bede appears to be entirely unacquainted with any form of ideal or stereotype of an influential queen. Given that the *History's* exemplary queen is Æthelthryth, who withdraws to a monastery under the guiding influence of Bishop Wilfrid,[74] it may also be true that Bede preferred to give the impression that the episcopal capture of the queen had already taken place, and that – Redwald's intransigently pagan wife apart – queens had effaced themselves from the public stage and betaken themselves to piety, leaving the advancement of the church, very properly, to the influence of bishops and kings.

Papal Letters to Queens

As Edwin of Northumbria procrastinated over baptism, Pope Boniface wrote to him and also to his wife. Æthelburg was the daughter of Æthelberht, the Kentish king whom Augustine had converted, and a sister of Eadbald, the reigning king of Kent. Pope Boniface urged her to bear in mind her Christian duty to proselytize in and out of season, and he pointed out her singular good fortune in having been granted the opportunity to kindle the spark of true religion in her husband so that his subjects might more swiftly see the light.

[72] *In Cantica Canticorum*, ed. D. Hurst, CCSL 119B (Turnhout, 1983), 167–375. HE, Preface, p. 2, acknowledges Albinus of Canterbury as the work's chief source.
[73] See esp. *Encomium*, II.16; Barlow, pp. 15, 53–4.
[74] HE IV.19.

Boniface included with his letter a gift of a silver mirror and a gold and ivory comb – more appropriate, one would have thought, to a request for Æthelburg's interest in a negotiation between secular powers than an exhortation from her spiritual father. The immaterial inducement he offered Æthelburg, however, was the fullness of marital union. To Edwin he offered rather more intellectual incentives, together with a chance to put himself on an equal footing with the powerful king of Kent. He mentioned Edwin's marriage to a Christian queen, without suggesting, however, that marriage to the Kentish king's sister might influence his desire to be at one with the king of Kent in his religion.[75]

The king and queen of Northumbria were already one flesh to the extent of having produced a daughter, the infant Eanfled whom Edwin was persuaded to allow Paulinus to baptize in thanksgiving for his wife's safe delivery, while cannily suggesting that his own baptism might follow if Paulinus could secure for him a victory in Wessex.[76] But for Pope Boniface there could be no true union here, and certainly not hereafter, without the obliteration of the married couple's religious differences: "For the scripture says: 'The two shall become one flesh.' But how can it be called a true unity between you, so long as he remains alienated from the daylight of your faith by the barrier of a dark and lamentable error?" Christ answered the Pharisees' enquiry into the eternal continuance of marriages by saying that there was no marrying nor giving in marriage in heaven,[77] but, whatever Pope Boniface took that to mean, it did not preclude him from holding out to Æthelburg the further attraction of a marital union that would outlast its own mortality: "Let it be your constant prayer that God of his mercy will bless and enlighten the king, so that you, who are united in one flesh by the ties of bodily affection, may after this fleeting life remain united for ever in the bond of the faith." [78]

Boniface follows his predecessors in regarding the king as the linchpin of the conversion. But his letter to Æthelburg envisages an even more critical role for the queen, as the power behind the throne. In offering her the vicarious achievement of the conversion of Northumbria through the agency of her husband, Boniface clearly regarded it as inconceivable that she should play any overt and public part in the conversion of the nation at large; though, in the event, she and Edwin both travelled with Paulinus to the royal residence at Yeavering to witness the mass baptisms that crowned Paulinus's success with the king.[79] But, in the domestic ministry to which the Pope called Æthelburg, he adjured her to assume an overt and active role, to secure Edwin's conversion not merely by her prayers and the example of her own life, but by constant teaching and exhortation, in order to fulfill the words of St Paul, "the unbeliever is saved by the believing wife."[80] Boniface urged Æthelburg to instruct the king in the commandments, to pour into his mind her knowledge of the mysteries of the eternal reward, and to inflame his heart by teaching him of the Holy Spirit.

Pope Boniface's letter echoes, with a difference, the persuasions that Gregory

---

[75] HE, II.10.
[76] HE, II.9.
[77] Mark 12.25.
[78] Trans. Sherley-Price, p. 121; HE, II.11.
[79] HE, II.14.
[80] 1 Cor. 7.14.

the Great had earlier brought to bear, shortly after the arrival of Augustine's mission, when he wrote to Æthelburg's mother, the queen of Kent, who was a Christianized Frankish princess.[81] Both papal letters fairly certainly spring from a recollection of the encouragement given by Bertha's ancestor Clothild to the conversion of her husband Clovis.[82] Gregory urged Bertha to play an active part in terms that recall the role of heroic womanhood as the spur to warrior achievement and the pursuit of renown. He too was in hopes that the queen would confirm her husband in the faith by constant exhortation and inflame him to the conversion of his subjects. But Gregory was in communication with Bertha's aunt, the powerful Frankish queen Brunhild,[83] and his approach was more attuned to Germanic cultural values than Boniface's – whereas Boniface tempted Æthelburg with the fullness of marital union, Gregory offered Bertha an international reputation and a share in the imperial glory that he had exhorted her husband to gain.[84] Bertha's virtues, he assured her, were already known to the Romans and to Constantinople, and, as Æthelberht was urged to achieve the surpassing fame of a Constantine by conquering England for Christ, Bertha was offered as a model the mother of Constantine, the ever-memorable Helena, who had kindled the hearts of the Romans to the faith by her instrumental role in the cult of the True Cross.

Æthelberht of Kent's marriage to a Frankish princess undoubtedly served as a useful entree for Augustine's mission – the Franks, for instance, provided it with safe passage as well as interpreters.[85] Gregory's letter to Bertha's brother, the Frankish king, in which he remarks that the English desire to be converted, but the local priests hang back, has been construed, though not very plausibly, as meaning that encouragement from Bertha underlay the arrival of the mission.[86] Æthelberht's reception of the mission was cautious, though not hostile; having been informed by messengers of its purpose, he ordered the party to stay on an island until he decided what steps to take, but provided it with necessities in the interim.[87] In Kent, as in Northumbria, providence had prepared the ground for the missionaries – Bede attributes Æthelberht's hospitality to the fact that he was already acquainted with the Christian religion by his wife's practice of it. This looks like a pious gloss on his disposition to look with tolerable favour on a party claiming connexion with his wife through acquaintance with her kin, for Æthelberht's acquaintance with his wife's religion does not appear, elsewhere in Bede's account, to have given him any very favourable impression. He suspected

---

[81] H&S, III, 17–18.
[82] Although J.A. McNamara, "Living Sermons: Consecrated Women and the Conversion of Gaul," ed. Nichols and Shanks, II, 24–5, describes Clothild as "the first link of a chain of queens who secured the conversions of both pagan and Arian monarchs in succeeding centuries," they appear, at most, to be have been credited with preparing the ground for bishops; Gregory says that Clothild's attempts to convert Clovis angered him, but having achieved a victory by appealing to Clothild's God, he was converted by a bishop she had summoned (*History of the Franks*, II.28–31). See fn. 156.
[83] H&S, III, 10–11, 13; Gregory asked Brunhild to assist the Augustinian mission.
[84] HE, I.32.
[85] Wallace-Hadrill, *Early Germanic Kingship in England and on the Continent* (Oxford, 1971), p. 25, and I.N. Wood, *The Merovingian North Sea* (Alingsas, 1983), pp. 12–17, 58–9, discuss the marriage within the context of a possible Frankish hegemony over the south of England.
[86] H&S, III, 10.
[87] HE, I.25.

the missionaries of being likely to practice dangerous magic, and insisted on holding a meeting with them out of doors in order to minimize their powers. And in the account of Æthelberht's meeting with the missionaries, Bede attributes to him a complete ignorance of Christian belief: Æthelberht replies that their words and promises are "new and doubtful." Bede's account of Æthelberht's reception of the mission is in keeping with the failure to proselytize implied in Gregory's letter to Bertha; Augustine's arrival, he urged her, was a fitting moment to repair past neglect.[88]

In Northumbria the royal marriage was even more critical in gaining access for the Roman church, and Bede notes its instrumentality. But in Northumbria also the marriage alliance was merely a providential occasion, providing an opening for the conversionary zeal of Paulinus, who accompanied the bride to Northumbria.[89] Kent's initial reply to Edwin's request for Æthelburg's hand is in no way concerned with the implications for Æthelburg of marriage with a pagan king at the opposite end of England. Edwin was told that it was not permissible for a Christian woman to be given in marriage to a pagan husband, lest the Christian faith and sacraments be profaned by her association with a king who was wholly ignorant of the worship of the true God. The guiding hand here is obviously ecclesiastical, revealing the same concern with the theological fullness of marital union as Pope Boniface's letter to Æthelburg.[90] The marital union of flesh is intimately connected, by virtue of allegorical signification, with the mystic marriage of the communicating believer with Christ. The connexion is, indeed, so intimate that the mystical union itself is felt to be defiled by marriage between a communicant with the body of Christ and an unbaptized pagan; the point seems to be that a Christian woman's corporeal union with a pagan is a form of communion with pagan gods.

The church at Canterbury can scarcely have been so blinded by its own marital theology as to fail to see the opportunities for expansion that Edwin's request opened up.[91] The underlying intention of the reply was surely to secure Edwin's conversion as a condition of the alliance he sought; an attempt by Canterbury to negotiate a politically-motivated conversion would, however, make less edifying reading than the high-minded preoccupation with theological absolutes that Bede's report offers. Edwin evidently grasped what was expected of him, and offered a compromise – he expressed his willingness to convert if his advisers agreed, and undertook to place no obstacles in the way of missionary endeavour. He also offered a promise that took account of the position of Æthelburg, for he gave assurance that she and her retinue would be free to practice their own religion. The agreement to compromise is consistent with the relative power of Northumbria and Kent, both of which stood to gain

---

88 See fn. 104.

89 HE, II.9. Canterbury's consecration of Paulinus reveals expectation of the creation of a northern see.

90 The congruence of Canterbury's initial response and Pope Boniface's letter to Æthelburg can be explained as the retrospective influence of Paulinus on the official history of Canterbury: the papal letters to the Northumbrian royal pair were transmitted through him, and he later returned to Canterbury. See Wallace-Hadrill, 1988, pp. 60–8.

91 See fn. 90. Not even *Theodore's Penitential*, thought to have taken its final form at Canterbury some 20 years after Bede wrote HE, prohibits marriage between a pagan and a Christian; it does permit divorce from a wife who refuses to convert; see fn. 140.

from an alliance.[92] Paulinus, who travelled with Æthelburg as *comes*, represents an interesting variation of the bishop as queen's mentor. His role as protector against the dangerous religious contamination of her husband and his people is a transmutation of the part played by the protective retinue of warrior kinsmen who accompanied Hildeburg in the Finnsburg lay, when she was given as peace-weaver to the traditional enemies of the Danes[93] – an arrangement, as the ensuing bloodshed at Finnsburg shows, that had a high potential for destroying domestic harmony.[94] For Paulinus, the royal marriage of a pagan and a Christian carried with it, not the possibility but the absolute necessity for effecting the mystic union of the nation with Christ – though the reflection that, until such time as Edwin converted, Æthelburg herself was coupled with a multiplicity of pagan gods, conceivably fueled the urgency: Paulinus travelled north, "outwardly bringing her to her marriage according to the flesh. But more truly his whole heart was set on calling the nation to whom he was coming to the knowledge of the truth: his desire was, to present it, in the words of the apostle, as a pure virgin to be espoused to one husband, even Christ." [95] Marital union here, then, is resonant with higher significance, as the royal marriage assumes an inextricable relationship to the union of the nation with God. [96]

The all important royal soul was finally landed in Paulinus' net when he discovered (but from whom?) that the king's hesitation sprang from a vision during his years of exile, and he lost no time in identifying himself as the apparition by whose power Edwin had gained his kingdom, and to whose authority, in a future, earthly manifestation, Edwin had pledged his obedience.[97] Edwin, gripped by the inner conflicts generated by the arrival of the new religion, is said to have spent much time in solitary brooding.[98] Even after Paulinus had announced himself as the fulfilment of Edwin's vision, Edwin still insisted that he could not change his religion without the advice of his councillors.[99] But despite the urgent exhortations of Pope Boniface to Æthelburg, there is not the slightest suggestion that, during the lengthy process of Edwin's conversion, he received the advice, or the instruction, of his wife.

Æthelburg was not the only woman of the Kentish royal house whose marriage to a pagan had, at very least, the potential for introducing Christian mission-

---

[92] At the time Æthelburg's brother gave her in marriage, Kent had lost the *imperium* to Redwald of East Anglia (*HE*, II.5).

[93] For this exceptional use of *comes*, see H.R. Loyn, "Gesiths and Thegns in Anglo-Saxon England from the Seventh to the Tenth Century," *EHR* 70 (1955), 534. Not all members of the royal bride's retinue were warriors; cf. Queen Ealhild's *scop* escort, *Widsith*, ll. 5–9, 88–108. Eanfled's retinue included a Kentish priest (*HE*, III.25). The members of Æthelthryth of East Anglia's retinue, which included a steward and the thane Imma, appear to have become "lordless men" when she separated from Ecgfrith (*HE*, IV.3, 22). For Bertha's bishop escort, see fn. 156.

[94] *Beowulf*, ll. 1068–159; 2024–69.

[95] C&M, p. 165 (2 Cor. 11.2).

[96] As Wallace-Hadrill, 1988, p. 87, remarks, "this presupposes some fusion of the concepts of national and spiritual identity." Bede was familiar (see fn. 72) with the originally Judaic interpretation of *Canticles* as God's love of the nation.

[97] *HE*, II.12.

[98] *HE*, II.9.

[99] *HE*, II.13.

aries into unconverted regions. Mercia, for instance, is said to have converted in the reign of Wulfhere, the son of the pagan king Penda, and the wife of Wulfhere was Eormenhild of Kent, a niece of Æthelthryth and the daughter of Seaxburg, whom she subsequently joined at the Ely monastery.[100] Æthelburg's cousin, Domne Eafe, was also given in marriage to one of Penda of Mercia's sons; according to Minster-in-Sheppey traditions, Domne Eafe and Merewalh of Mercia subsequently separated because both of them wanted to pursue a monastic life.[101] Bede mentions none of these alliances, despite the fact that Albinus of Canterbury provided him with the bulk of his documentary sources.[102] The queen was no more active in Sussex, it appears; Bede mentions the fact that both the king of Sussex and his Wessex-born queen had already been baptized before Bishop Wilfrid arrived, but neither of them had exerted themselves to deliver their people from the penalty of certain damnation.[103]

Bede reproduced Boniface's letter in his History, and he appears to have known Gregory's letter to Bertha, even though – whether by design or accident – he did not include it among the correspondence of Gregory that he copied into the History.[104] But his account of the conversion, in which the influence of Christian queens is barely discernible, has evidently not taken its cue from the encouragement of Popes. The part played by the few royal women he mentions in his History is virtually limited to entering the religious life in monasteries occasionally of their own founding.[105] Even Æthelthryth, whom Alcuin represents as setting her husband afire with her own chaste love of God,[106] casts no conversionary glow in any direction in Bede's account. Osthryth, who discovers the miraculous relics of King Oswald on the battlefield and subsequently lodges them in the Bardney monastery, possibly represents the extent to which Bede was prepared to adopt papal ideals of female piety, since Osthryth's role in the cult of the martyred Oswald offers a point of contact with Helena's finding of the True Cross.[107]

---

[100] With HE, III.24, cf. Cockayne, III, 430: "Eormenhild, daughter of Eorcenberht and Seaxburg, was given to Wulfhere, son of Penda, king of the Mercians, for his queen; and in their days the people of Mercia received baptism."

[101] See Cockayne, III, 422–4.

[102] HE, Preface, pp. 2–4. The description of Sæberht, under whom Essex converted, as the son of Æthelberht's sister, Ricula (HE, II.3) has no apparent implication of female instrumentality in the spread of the church.

[103] HE, IV.13; cf. Life of Wilfrid, ch. 41. Resentment of Mercia plausibly accounts for the royal couple's tepid attitude to Christianity (Wallace-Hadrill, 1988, p. 152).

[104] The argument that Æthelberht was either sympathetic to Christianity or had already been baptized before Augustine arrived (see Mayr-Harting, 1972, pp. 266–9), opens up the possibility that Bertha played a significant role in Æthelberht's conversion. Brechter, 1941, argued that Bede deliberately omitted this letter because it conflicts with his claim for Æthelberht's virtually instantaneous conversion by the Augustinian mission; but its encouragement to the active involvement of queens might also have been a reason for Bede's omission. Markus, 1963, 16–30, claims that Bede did not know of this letter.

[105] He does report that Plectrude, wife of the Frankish mayor of the palace, requested her husband to endow a monastery for the missionary bishop, Swithberht (HE, V.11). Nicholson, pp. 15–29, extrapolates from the History and early English hagiography a convincing picture of the influential position of royal women.

[106] Song of York, ll. 756–63.

[107] HE, III.11.

Eanfled conceivably did exert herself, by using her influence behind the scenes to secure the triumph of the Roman cause at the synod of Whitby, where her husband, Oswiu of Northumbria, came round to the position held by her former protege, Bishop Wilfrid.[108] Shortly after the synod of Whitby, Pope Vitalian sent Eanfled, not exhortations, but commendations of her pious zeal and good deeds blossoming in the sight of God, together with an ornamental cross made from the fetters of Peter and Paul and a golden key.[109] Pope Vitalian's gift alludes to the power of the keys held by Peter's successors at Rome and, for Oswiu, this was the decisive factor in the Whitby debate, notwithstanding the mesmeric fascination that the dating of Easter purportedly exercised over the minds of the ecclesiastics who took part. One way or another, then, Eanfled had been piously zealous on behalf of the church of Rome, but her role in the History barely extends beyond persuading Oswiu to found a monastery as a form of wergild for his murder of his brother, who was also her cousin.[110] Eanfled is not, as she is in the Life of Wilfrid, a ruler to whom Wilfrid went with his armed retinue to seek service under the council and consolation of her leadership, and who hovers on the verge of being a female converter of men in directing him from the secular to the monastic life. She is merely a pious queen with a limited amount of influence in the monasteries. The Life of Wilfrid's report that Eanfled sent Wilfrid off to Lindisfarne to look after an elderly retainer who had become a monk there suggests, as I have indicated, that she and Oswiu regarded themselves as the effective owners of the Northumbrian monasteries they endowed. Bede's version of the role of Eanfled is that Wilfrid had made up his mind to be a monk at the age of fourteen and, encouraged by his father, made his way to Lindisfarne; only later does Bede mention, as an incidental explanation of why Wilfrid went to tell Eanfled of his intention to visit Rome, that it was through her council and at her request that he had been admitted to Lindisfarne. Nor does Eanfled, in Bede's narration, discuss Wilfrid's plan with the Lindisfarne monk he had served – for, here, Wilfrid's plan has already been endorsed by the Lindisfarne community – and, instead of sending him off with all honour accompanied by her messengers bearing commendations to her Kentish royal kinsman, she merely asks the Kentish king to assist Wilfrid with his pilgrimage because she approves of its piety.[111]

Queens in Bede's History, then, in contrast to kings, are not active as proselytizers, either in public or private, and there is barely a trace of their use of political power and influence on behalf of the church or churchmen. The near-invisibility of queens in Bede's History is not merely unexpected in the light of papal encouragement to participate in the advance of the church. It is also in striking contrast to the vernacular image of the queen as adviser and joint ruler, which is echoed in Eddius's Life of Wilfrid.[112] The conclusion to be drawn is not, I think, that the vernacular and hagiographic images of powerful queens are purely fictitious, whereas Bede's History – more precisely his Ecclesiastical History – is an authentic reflection of their social position. Bertha's

108 HE, III.25.
109 HE, III.29. The letter is addressed to Oswiu.
110 HE, III.24.
111 With Life of Wilfrid, ch. 2, cf. HE, V.19.
112 See pp. 152–5.

failure to proselytize is confirmed by Gregory's letter, and I want later to suggest reasons why queens were unlikely to have made a concerted effort to convert their husbands or their husbands' kingdoms, at the heart of which lies a conception of the royal marriage quite different from the monolithic union entailed by the marital theology of Pope Boniface. But the inhibitions on active proselytizing did not preclude queens from becoming patrons of the church by using their influence on its behalf. Some forms of influence – Eanfled's instrumentality in preparing the way for Oswiu's endorsement of the Roman cause, for instance – are inherently likely to have been invisible to chroniclers. Bede's handling of Eanfled's role in the career of Wilfrid, however, suggests that the contribution that reigning queens made to the growth of the church, like the contribution of monastic women, has been deliberately suppressed in the History because Bede was hostile to female influence, particularly in ecclesiastical matters.

Peada of Mercia's Wife

For Bede, the conversion was the work of bishops and kings. His deliberate polemical bias is evident in his handling of the conversion of Peada of Mercia, who asked for the hand of Alhfled, the daughter of Oswiu of Northumbria. Oswiu appears in the History as the most active of Bede's converting kings; his successes included Sigeberht of the East Saxons, with whom he had many brotherly talks about the futility of idol worship and the glory of God.[113] Oswiu's devout exertions coincided with an extension of Northumbrian hegemony. Whereas Canterbury appears to have attempted only to secure the conversion of Edwin himself as the condition of the marriage alliance he sought, Oswiu required the baptism of Peada and all his people.[114] Peada converted with all his leading men, and brought four priests from Northumbria to baptize the Mercian populace. The episode thus confirms that marriage alliance *was* an instrument for the spread of Christianity, in cases where two unequal powers were involved. For Peada's acceptance of the religious customs of Northumbria as a condition of a marriage alliance with the Northumbrian king's daughter is consistent with his status as a Mercian underking, and marks him as a client of Oswiu.[115]

The outcome was the assassination of Peada, followed by a rebellion against Oswiu's overlordship. The initial conversion of Mercia by Oswiu's priests was evidently a superficial illusion, since Bede subsequently tells us that after the accession of Wulfhere, the Mercians, free under their own king, willingly gave

[113] HE, III.22.
[114] HE, III.21. Oswiu's successor, Oswald, having conquered Wessex (HE, III.6), sponsored the king's baptism and married his daughter (HE, III.7). In this case, the woman confirms relationship with a superior power. Such marriages (see also fns. 150, 151) now appear to be a form of hostage taking, but the literary conception of the woman's role as a consolidator of friendly relations is not necessarily an idealizing fiction; Bede, too, regards Oswald's marriage, like his baptismal sponsorship, as a means of forging a familial bond between the two kings.
[115] Peada was given south Mercia when Oswiu killed his father and took the Mercian throne (HE, III.24).

allegiance to Christ the true king.[116] As for Peada, Bede is emphatic that his wife played no part in his conversion; for Peada, once he had been instructed in the faith, said that he would gladly become a Christian even if he were refused the princess. How little good influence she could have exercised can be deduced from Bede's report of a rumour that Peada was assassinated by his wife. Bede is evidently at pains to affirm the authenticity of Peada's conversion; but what is at stake in his reporting of the episode is not simply the ideal of conversion by means of interior conviction.[117] Peada, Bede explains, was persuaded to accept the faith by his kinsman and friend, King Oswiu's son Alhfrith, who had married Peada's sister Cyneburg, a daughter of King Penda. It is unusual for Bede to adduce human influence once piety has been established as a paramount motive. The inference of the episode is plain. Male friendship bonds are an appropriate conversionary channel; conversion undertaken for the sake of a woman is not.

Bede is probably at one with social actuality in conveying the relative strengths of male comradeship and marital relationship as emotional ties exerting a persuasive influence on conduct. This helps to explain why Pope Boniface's urgent exhortations to Æthelburg largely failed to take root as a model of queenly behaviour. Pope Boniface himself, indeed, for all his theological idealism of marital union, did not imagine that marriage to Æthelburg was likely to carry much weight with Edwin, but referred him instead to the sterling example of Christian kingship offered by her brother. But for Æthelburg too, full and perfect marriage union is unlikely to have had the paramount importance that Pope Boniface assumed, compared with her own kinship ties. And the underlying basis of Bede's construction of Peada's conversion, albeit submerged, is in fact the influence of a married woman as the forger of male relational ties. Although Bede might be taken to mean that a pre-existing friendship between Alhfrith and Peada had been further cemented by Alhfrith's marriage to Peada's sister, Alhfrith was not a blood-relative of Peada. Alhfrith was a friendly kinsman of Peada *because* he was the husband of Peada's sister. Irrespective of the truth or otherwise of the narrative strategy by which Peada's conversion becomes a conversion of the heart instead of a political convenience, the conversion in England was more likely to spread, not through influence brought to bear within marriage, but through the kinship ties created by the marriage alliances that women contracted.

Bede's foregrounding of male comradeship bonds as a channel of influence and his submergence of female instrumentality in the creation of those bonds is surprising. It is surprising too that Eanfled, in requesting assistance for Wilfrid from the Kentish king, is the only woman in the *History* to draw on ties of kinship for the benefit of the church. For the traditional role of the woman given in marriage as peaceweaver to cement the reconciliation of feuding kingdoms highlights her position as a pivotal unifying force through the emotional sway that she exercises through her relationships. Bound to her own people by ties of affection, she extends these ties to her husband's people through her

---

[116] *HE* III.24; cf. fn. 100.
[117] See further pp. 17–19.

marriage to him, by which whole groups become friendly-kinsmen, as, individually, Alhfrith and Peada were friendly-kinsmen through the marriage of Cyneburg. Because love for the queen is inseparable from love of her people, Beowulf prophesies that, when fighting between Danes and Finn's men breaks out in the hall, the king's love for Freawaru will cool.[118] The peaceweaver's perambulations about the hall with the mead-cup at the feast graphically embody her unifying role. To love her is to love her people; for her sake her own people will regard her husband's people as kindred – for it is essential for a queen, as Maxims I asserts, to be loved.[119] A variety of non-fictional sources affirm women as the affective motive of male action by their creation of ties of friendship. Æthelberht II of Kent, for instance, was in hopes that Archbishop Boniface would extend his friendship to him on account of his friendship with Æthelberht's sister; on the basis on this connexion, he was also moved to hope that Boniface would send him a pair of really superior German hawks.[120] Bede himself mentions that King Hlothere of Kent paid the ransom of a thane who came to him for help because he had once served in the retinue of Æthelthryth, and Hlothere was Æthelthryth's nephew.[121] Eddius offers an instance of married women's politically unifying influence in his explanation of how Wilfrid, having been banished from Northumbria, was also outlawed in Mercia and Wessex because the queen of Mercia was Ecgfrith's sister, and Jurmenburg's sister was the wife of the Wessex king.[122]

It is perhaps true that female relational influence did not register very powerfully even in secular modes of reportage because, men being perceived as the significant active protagonists in warrior society, the emphasis fell on the influence of male comradeship bonds on action, rather than on the influence of the female agent of their formation. Leoba, in her letter requesting the friendly interest of Boniface, mentions his kinship with her mother, but appeals to him more particularly on the strength of his friendship with her father.[123] It is also true that to Bede, and to hagiographers generally, kinship affection is, as a motive, inferior to devout altruism, and bonds of kinship oppositional to fellowship in Christ – it was a pagan king, Penda, who waged war on Cenwealh, the as yet unconverted king of Wessex, because Cenwealh had divorced Penda's sister.[124] Eddius, though not wishing to conceal the fact that Eanfled, as Wilfrid's adoptive mother in Christ, enlisted the help of her kinsman on his behalf, still cannot allow that kinship ties are a sufficient motive for good works, and explains that the king of Kent was also moved to help because of his admiration

---

[118] See Beowulf, ll. 2063–6.

[119] Maxims I, l. 85: leof mid hyre leodum, "beloved among her people."

[120] Tangl, 105. Æthelbald of Mercia (716–57), as overlord of Kent, claims his relationship to Mildrith, daughter of Domne Eafe, the wife of Merewalh of Mercia (see fn. 100), as the reason for his generosity to Thanet (Birch, 177). Cf. the dedication to Edith, Barlow, p. 59: "it was through love of her you loved her kin and all near her."

[121] HE, IV.22.

[122] Life of Wilfrid, ch. 40. Jurmenburg's sister may have been Seaxburg, who ruled in her own right as the widow of Cenwealh of Wessex (ASC, 672); both names were borne by women of the Kentish royal house.

[123] Tangl, 29.

[124] HE, III.7.

for Wilfrid's singular piety.[125] It is, accordingly, difficult to distinguish devaluation of kinship ties generally from unforthcomingness on specifically female influence, but the net effect is to conceal from view a significant aspect of women's political influence generally and their contribution to the growth of the church in particular.

Peaceweavers

Ecclesiastical hostility to the peaceweaver's pivotal position in the formation of community through kinship bonds is manifest, however, in the employment of her cup-bearing and advisory roles as the basis for creating an iconography of Eve.[126] Bede, as I have remarked in an earlier chapter, was familiar with the peaceweaving role of royal women, for it is the underlying point of reference in his account of Theodore's part in the outbreak of hostilities between Mercia and Northumbria:

> In the ninth year of his reign, King Ecgfrith fought a battle near the River Trent against king Ethelred of the Mercians, in which Ecgfrith's brother Elfwin was killed. The latter was a young man of about eighteen, who was much loved in both provinces since Ethelred had married his sister Osthryth. This gave every indication of causing fiercer strife and more lasting hatred between the two warlike kings and peoples, until Archbishop Theodore, the beloved of God, enlisting God's help, smothered the flames of this awful peril by his wholesome advice. As a result, peace was restored between the kings and people, and in lieu of further bloodshed, the customary compensation was paid to King Ecgfrith for his brother's death. The peace thus made was maintained between these kings and their peoples for many years.[127]

Offering nothing more than the modest efforts of Eanfled to represent queenly advice in the service of the church, Bede glances at the royal woman as peaceweaver only in order to celebrate the superior peace-making of a man of God. Osthryth, in Bede's account, may be regarded as a tragically unsuccessful peaceweaver, whose efforts to forge peace have proved inadequate to the force of male vengeance and aggression. But she is, by implication, more in the manner of an inverted peaceweaver, one whose advice was not wholesome, tending to promote further violence and bloodshed instead of peace. For the role of adviser to kings and peacemakers, I have suggested, bishops and queens were rivals; in place of the failed attempt at peace through an extension of ties of flesh and blood wrought by the marriage of a woman, Bede gives us the lasting peace of Christ in the bonds of the spirit wrought by the inspired wisdom of an archbishop.

[125] *Life of Wilfrid*, ch. 3.
[126] See pp. 156–60.
[127] Sherley-Price, p. 243; HE, IV.21.

The royal peaceweaver's role as influential adviser and pivot in the forging of political unity through the extension of ties of kinship appears, at first sight, to have a high potential for the spread of conversionary influence. As presented by William of Malmesbury, in his 12th century chronicle, that potential was actualized. The queen as converter and councillor to spiritual good was so well-established as a stereotype by William's time that he employed it in rewriting Bede's *History*. He regales us, for example, with the inspiring example that the queen of Wessex furnished for her husband, Ine, who invariably deferred to her advice. Defiling the feast-hall with dung, and constantly exhorting him with her teachings, she proved to him the mutability of earthly joy and converted him to higher things. So too, in his fictionalized account of the conversion of Northumbria, Æthelburg, among other proofs of conjugal affection, continually instructed Edwin in the faith. And so successful was she that the two kingdoms, bound by ties of blood, were also united in friendship and became one in their customs.[128]

William's narrative reveals the effects of allegorization of the royal marriage. His stereotype of the pious queen, transmuted from an adviser to a spiritual councillor, is historically dependent on the identification of the queen with Mary, Queen of Heaven, whose union with the Christ-King figures the union of the body of the Church under the headship of Christ. In their union with pagan or unregenerate kings, however, Marian spiritual councillors assume identity with the soul, pointing the body to higher things – William's depiction of Anglo-Saxon queens in this stock role appears to derive from direct familiarity with Turgot's *Life of Margaret*.[129] The peaceweaver's creation of unity through the extension of ties of kinship has been similarly transmuted in accordance with the queen's identification with Mary-*Ecclesia*, and merges with the unity in the peace of Christ that Archbishop Theodore effected when he transcended the failure of kinship ties created by Osthryth's marriage. This transmutation of the peaceweaver to Marian salvatrix, towards which Bede points in his devaluation of kinship bonds as the basis of community, is already evident in the 11th century eulogies of the last two Anglo-Saxon queens, the *Encomium Emmae* and the *Life of King Edward*, where the influence of the Benedictine Reform's idealization of the queen is discernible. Emma and Edith are still lauded, according to tradition, for their good advice,[130] but their advice lacks concrete embodiment and the queens are marginalized to near invisibility by the narrative. Under the influence of the Marian idealization of the queen, queens – in a perfect, hagiographical world, at any rate – are no longer politically effective as good advisers by their command of relational ties, and merely exert an all-pervasive, but self-effacing, influence for good.

---

[128] *Gesta Regum*, ed. Stubbs, I, 35, 49–50; some versions omit the latter episode.
[129] William's account of Mathilda, *Gesta Regum*, ed. Stubbs, II, 493–5, is heavily influenced by Turgot's Life of her mother. Roger of Wendover offers an example of an AS queen-converter possibly drawn from lost northern annals (trans. Whitelock, *EHD*, I, 283). He relates that Æthelstan's sister, Eadgyth, married Sihtric, a Danish king of Northumbria, who converted for love of her, but subsequently renounced her and lapsed into paganism; as Eadgyth had preserved her virginity, she entered the Polesworth nunnery.
[130] See Barlow, pp. 15, 54; *Encomium*, III.7.

William's account of the conversion of Northumbria effectively implements the exhortations of Pope Boniface to Æthelburg to secure the more speedy conversion of the kingdom through the conversion of her husband. Unity of belief within marriage, through William's Marian transmutation of the peace-weaver, obliterates differences on an even greater scale than Pope Boniface's letter to Æthelburg envisaged, by uniting the two kingdoms in the bonds of the spirit. His account is patently an anachronistic fiction, dependent upon the elaborated developments of the equation of the royal marriage with the mystical marriage of Christ and his Church, which post-date Bede. But, in its own terms, the queen's position as throne-sharer and peaceweaver, traditionally respected for her good advice, does seem to be latent with potential for the exercise of significant conversionary influence on the part of royal women who married pagan kings. The episode in which Redwald's pagan wife figures suggests that there were sound pragmatic reasons why royal brides did not actively proselytize, inherently related to the conception of royal marriages as the alliance of two kingdoms.

Redwald's Wife

Bede relates that Redwald of East Anglia was baptized while he was visiting Kent, but when he returned home he was led astray by his wife and evil councillors and "perverted from the sincerity of his faith."[131] Redwald's wife, however, is not morally unambiguous in the manner of Bishop Wilfrid's antagonist, Queen Jurmenburg. She also figures in the History's account of Edwin's lucky escape from the East Anglian court, where he had taken refuge from his enemy, the Northumbrian king. It was when Edwin learnt that the Northumbrian king had bribed Redwald to either kill him or surrender him to the Northumbrian envoys that he had the vision which made him so reluctant to convert, and which Paulinus turned to good use when he persuaded Edwin that he was the incarnation of the spirit-guide to whom Edwin had promised obedience when next they met. As Edwin brooded over the plot against his life, he was visited by an apparition who promised to secure his escape from death at Redwald's hands, and assured him that he would recover his throne from his enemies. In return for this aid, the spirit-guide required Edwin to promise that he would in future follow his advice, and he laid his hands on Edwin's head in token of the sign by which Edwin would recognize him when he reappeared to him. Bede subsequently relates that it was Redwald's wife who saved Edwin's life, by advising Redwald not to kill Edwin as the Northumbrian king commanded him, saying that it was unworthy in a great king to sell his best friend in the hour of need for gold, and worse still to sacrifice his royal honour, the most valuable of all possessions, for the love of money. Redwald took the advice of his wife, and not only refused to surrender Edwin to the Northumbrian king, but gathered an army against him and restored Edwin to his throne.[132]

---

[131] C&M, p. 191; HE, II.15.
[132] HE, II.12.

The story of Edwin's escape was a popular tradition. The Whitby author of the *Life of Gregory* clearly felt that the traditional story was somewhat intractable to ecclesiastical interpretation, but that it was too well-known to be omitted.[133] In Bede's account, the spirit-guide's prophecy to Edwin of his safety and restoration to the Northumbrian throne is fulfilled in actuality through the influence brought to bear by Redwald's wife. Their connexion suggests rather strongly that Edwin's vision was problematical because it established that Edwin's reluctance to convert sprang from his belief that he owed the recovery of his fortunes to pagan gods whose aid had been enlisted on his behalf by Redwald's wife.[134] In itself, however, the advice of Redwald's wife in this episode is impeccably good – and it is worth observing that, unlike her objections to the king's change of religion, which link her with his official councillors, this advice is given privately. In secular terms, she fulfills an approved role, as the promoter of her husband's honour.[135] Bede may not have recalled her subsequent role in the apostasy of Redwald – or perhaps he felt that her advice demonstrated that to accept a bribe for killing a king (reminiscent of Judas's betrayal) was an act so iniquitous that even a pagan woman would condemn it.[136]

Redwald's wife's response to her husband's conversion suggests a much more fundamental opposition to Christianity than the conflict with Jurmenburg generated by the ambitious personality of Bishop Wilfrid. This, coupled with the fact that Eanfled is the only reigning queen in Bede's *History* to lend her aid to the support of the church, invites the inference that reigning queens were, by and large, either lukewarm or antagonistic to the new religion. It is a plausible inference, although I think it more likely that Bede's scanty reportage gives a misleading impression. That the only influential queen adviser in the *History* is a pagan who "perverts her husband from the sincerity of his faith," whose closest counterpart is the wife of Sebbi who thwarted her husband's desire to enter a monastery by her refusal to agree to a separation,[137] suggests very strongly that political power and influence formed no part of Bede's conception of a Christian queen, and that he incorporated these two instances of female influentiality into his narrative because they served to confirm lapsarian dogma, that the advice of women is inimical to salvation. Both women, we may note, are partially effaced in Bede's record by their namelessness.

The close link between Redwald's wife and Edwin's uncanny visitant may well mean that she was a serious devotee of the old religion. And powerful queens had any number of good reasons to regard the new religion as a threat to their position;[138] not least of these, perhaps, was its destabilizing effect on the marriages of its converts. The missionary church was evidently disposed to bring pressure to bear to dissolve consanguineous marriages.[139] It was also likely to

---

[133] *Life of Gregory*, ch. 16, omits much, including Redwald's wife.

[134] It is tempting to surmise that Edwin sought refuge at Redwald's court because he was related to Redwald's wife.

[135] See further pp. 101, 154.

[136] See fn. 5.

[137] *HE*, IV.11; perhaps Sebbi's assumption that she, too, would give up the throne for a monastery was the stumbling-block. Nicholson, pp. 15–29, suggests that she was motivated by concern for defence of the kingdom.

[138] See ch. 1, esp. pp. 35–40; ch. 2, esp. pp. 62–5.

[139] *HE* I.27.

intervene in the marriage of a baptized king whose wife refused to follow suit; the *Penitential of Theodore* was later to rule that a pagan wife who resisted all attempts to convert her should be renounced[140] and Bede's Canterbury sources for the marriage of Edwin and Æthelburg suggest that the missionary church was also liable to encourage a converted king to replace his pagan wife with a Christian one. There is, nevertheless, a purely pragmatic political explanation offering for the advice that Redwald's wife gave him after he was baptized. Redwald had been baptized while he was visiting the court of Æthelberht of Kent. As the account of Peada's conversion shows, adoption of the customs of a foreign king was associated with acceptance of his overlordship. East Anglia was within the Kentish hegemony during the reign of Æthelberht, but Redwald succeeded Æthelberht as Bretwalda and, even during the lifetime of Æthelberht, East Anglia was gaining dominance.[141] East Anglia under Redwald, then, had no need to court the favour of the Kentish king. Redwald's wife, as queen and participant in the rule of East Anglia, had a vested interest in its power and prestige – although Bede presents her, when she saves the life of Edwin, as concerned for the honour of her husband, in that episode, too, she dissuades Redwald from doing the bidding of another ruler, and she urges that Redwald is too great a king to stoop to the murder of Edwin. Furthermore, kings who converted at the prompting of another king and attempted to carry their people with them were apt to be assassinated by their leading subjects and replaced by a pagan. Among them was Redwald's successor, his son Eorpwold, who was baptized, together with his subjects, at the instigation of Edwin of Northumbria,[142] to whom the supreme power once held by Redwald had passed. Redwald's court, however, did not require the king to abandon his adherence to Christianity altogether. Bede says that he had an altar dedicated to Christ placed in the temple beside an altar dedicated to the pagan gods; what Redwald's wife and councillors prevented was the overthrow of existing religious customs in favour of the king's new religion.

The Royal Marriage as Alliance

The fate of unseasonably converted kings makes it unlikely that queens, even devoutly Christian queens, were active in the conversion of their husbands and their husbands' people in the manner of William of Malmesbury's anachronistic fiction. The king's change of religion, as Bede's kings occasionally intimate, required the agreement of his council;[143] for the king and his people to accept the customs of his wife and her people was tantamount to accepting their

---

[140] *Theodore's Penitential*, II.xii.19; it also rules that children of an unbaptized wife who has been renounced cannot inherit (II.iii.2).

[141] HE, II.5; see Wallace-Hadrill, 1988, pp. 220–2.

[142] Eorpwold was killed by a pagan called Ricberht (HE, II.15); see also the murder of Sigeberht of Essex, who was baptized at the instigation of Oswiu (HE, III.22). The conversion of Redwald's son, Sigeberht, also ended in disaster (HE, III.18).

[143] See Æthelberht of Kent, HE, I.25; Edwin of Northumbria, HE, II.13.

overlordship, particularly if the queen's family was the more powerful of the two kingdoms allied by marriage. What underlies the hostility to the queen as throne-sharer in Asser's account of Wessex in the time of Alfred is a particular hostility to foreign queens. Eadburg, who was blamed for giving queens an ill reputation, was a Mercian and by her murderous plots against the Wessex retinue and the accidental poisoning of King Brihtric, the story runs, she showed herself to be a tyrant just like her father, the extremely powerful King Offa.[144]

The *Anglo-Saxon Chronicle* reveals that Brihtric owed his throne to Offa of Mercia; they joined forces to exile Ecgberht of Wessex who, after the death of Brihtric, returned to found the Wessex dynasty of which Alfred himself was a member. Brihtric's marriage to Offa's daughter Eadburg set the seal on this unequal alliance.[145] Ecgberht's military successes shifted the balance of power in Wessex's favour.[146] From the time of Alfred's father, it was Wessex which was endeavouring to control Mercia through the marriage alliances of royal women; as Æthelwulf of Wessex gave his daughter Æthelswith in marriage to Burgred of Mercia, Alfred's daughter Æthelfled was later given in marriage to Ealdorman Æthelred and became the Lady of Mercia. Alfred further consolidated ties with Mercia by marrying a woman of the Mercian royal house.[147] The currency of the Eadburg legend at the Wessex court suggests continuing fear of a resurgence of Mercian power and mistrust born of its tendency to make a separate peace with the Danes when its Wessex ally was bent on fighting them.[148] Whereas Alfred's sister Æthelswith regularly signs charters with her husband as *regina* of Mercia and is thought to have been ceremonially consecrated,[149] Alfred's Mercian wife was not in a position to object to the Wessex's court's refusal to grant her the title of *cwen* and a share of the throne.

Women like Alfred's Mercian wife may appear, from a modern perspective, to have been in the nature of hostages for the good behaviour of their people;[150] it might be more accurate to accept the vernacular conception of their role, as weavers of peace between nations, as a different but no less authentic construction of social reality. The unsuccessful peaceweaver of tragic lay, mourning the dead on both sides in a resurgence of hostilities that she has not been able to prevent, is not, in any case, emblematically representative of the powerlessness

---

[144] *Life of Alfred*, chs. 13–14; with Asser's report that Eadburg accidentally poisoned the king while attempting to assassinate a young man who was his favourite, cf. ASC, 800, "in this year King Brihtric and Ealdorman Worr died."

[145] See ASC, 787, 836; see also fn. 47.

[146] ASC, 827.

[147] *Life of Alfred*, ch. 29.

[148] Burgred asked Alfred and Æthelred of Wessex for help fighting the Danes, but the Mercians instead made peace with them (ASC, 868). Burgred was eventually driven out by the Danes and replaced by a Mercian puppet king (ASC, 874). So too, presumably, was Burgred's wife, Æthelswith of Wessex; like the notorious Eadburg, she died at Pavia (ASC, 888).

[149] See fns. 61, 25.

[150] The Finnsburg lay (*Beowulf*, ll. 1068–1159), which culminates in the Danes bearing off the treasure of Finn and the sister they had given him in marriage, lends itself to the construction that Hildeburg herself is a precious possession of her male kinsmen, reluctantly made available to an enemy and recovered with alacrity, although it is not clear whether the Danes or the Frisians are to be regarded as the more powerful of the two kingdoms; see fn. 114.

of Anglo-Saxon queens.[151] Queens like Eadburg who had, in their own family, a backing more powerful than their husbands could command were in an entirely different position. What queens in the position of Eadburg evidently appeared to be aiming for – and in some cases surely were – was not joint rule of their husband's kingdom as sharer of his throne, but rule in their own right (although Alfred's daughter Æthelfled, the Lady of Mercia, demonstrates that a woman who achieved rule of another kingdom in her own right did not always bring it more firmly under the control of her family; she appears rather to have established for herself an autonomous kingdom which her brother Edward regarded as threatening to his interests when he became king of Wessex).[152]

To kill the king was a risky move, unless the queen was sure of her hold on the kingdom. Eadburg escaped lightly with a sentence of exile – an accident, they said.[153] Peada of Mercia also, it was rumoured, was assassinated by his Northumbrian wife. It is a plausible rumour, since the dominance of Mercia's powerful Northumbrian neighbour had already been established by Peada's acceptance of a marriage contract that required Peada and his people to adopt the religious customs of the bride's family. His assassination, Bede reports, was followed by three years of direct rule from Northumbria until the Mercians rebelled. Osthryth of Northumbria, conversely, another of the daughters of Oswiu whose marriage consolidated relations with Mercia, was killed by her "own" people, the Mercian chieftains.[154] Elsewhere Bede recounts an episode involving her insistence on lodging, in the Mercian monastery that she and her husband endowed, the bones of her Northumbrian uncle Oswald, defeated and slain by Penda himself, the most notoriously pagan of the Mercian kings. Osthryth's promotion of the cult of Oswald could not help but keep alive the memory of his death at the hands of a Mercian king; however gratifying to her pride in her Northumbrian family, it seems ill-calculated to help lay old feuds to rest, and appears to confirm the impression that, when Northumbrian passions ran high over the Mercian army's killing of Osthryth's Northumbrian brother, Osthryth did not exert herself on behalf of the Mercians. If the account of her lodgement of Oswald's remains in the Bardney monastery is characteristic of Osthryth in its high-handed insensitivity to Mercian independence

---

[151] J. Luecke, "The Unique Experience of Anglo-Saxon Nuns," ed. Nichols and Shank, II, 58, makes a similar point: "Because of the strength of kinship ties, women were not so vulnerable in the role of wife-ambassador to a pagan hostile tribe as we might assume." Cf. Kliman, 32–49; Hansen, 109–117, regards the female mourners in OE poetry as symbols of the "underlying weakness of woman's moral and social powers in the face of the irrepressible evils of man and his society," and considers that they become "a poetic voice for all lonely and innocent victims of fate" (113, 117). A much more complex view is presented by J. Hill, "Þæt wæs geomuru Ides! A Female Stereotype Examined," ed. Damico and Olsen, pp. 235–47.

[152] See further ch. 3, fn. 71.

[153] Regicide was declared an impious crime by papal legates about the time of Eadburg's marriage to Brihtric, and Alfred, Int. 49, echoes them in declaring regicide an offence for which no monetary compensation can atone. Eadburg's return to her Mercian homeland after Brihtric's murder might seem, realistically, a more plausible outcome; but by the time Brihtric died (ASC, 800), Offa's throne had passed to a different branch of the Mercian royal family. Cf. Thryth in Beowulf, ll. 1931–62, whose execution of members of her father's retinue involves no legal penalty, although she is effectively exiled by being sent by her father to become the wife of Offa of Mercia.

[154] HE, V.24.

sentiments – for the Mercian monks, having resented Oswald as an alien overlord in his lifetime, were equally resistant to having his bones foisted upon them after his death – it is not difficult to imagine why Osthryth might have met a violent death at the hands of the Mercian nobles later on in life, when the power of Northumbria was diminished and the throne had passed out of the hands of her immediate family.[155]

In the light of this, Bede's allusions to marriage agreements involving the bride's freedom to practice her own religion are of particular interest. Bertha's Frankish parents, innocent of any attempt to secure Æthelberht of Kent's conversion, and apparently unhampered by objection to union with a pagan, gave Bertha in marriage on condition that she be allowed to hold and practice her faith unhindered, and sent Bishop Liudhard with her for support.[156] Edwin's compromise offered the same terms for Æthelburg and her retinue – he gave an assurance that he would allow them all to live and worship in accordance with Christian custom and belief.[157] Such agreements, it has been suggested, were not traditional practice, but generated by Christianity's uniquely exclusive claims. The marriage agreements surviving from the late Old English period, however, are clearly not ecclesiastical in inspiration – they represent a secular conception of marriage as a social contract, and express concern on the part of the bride's parents to secure her financial position and future protection.[158] That it was Edwin who volunteered the condition rather suggests that he was operating in terms of a tradition of contracts, and, even, a tradition of guaranteeing freedom for the bride and her retinue to practice their own customs.

Eanfled, without apparent benefit of a marriage agreement, continued to observe the Roman practices of her Kentish family after her marriage to Oswiu of Northumbria; like her mother before her, she had brought to Northumbria a retinue that included a priest from her Kentish homeland.[159] We may have in this proof of unusual strong-mindedness on the part of Eanfled.[160] But as Kent, at this time, though not the equal of Northumbria in power, was its foremost ally,[161] Eanfled may merely have been exercising a freedom to adhere to her own family customs that was normal in the political circumstances in which her marriage was contracted. For if a king's acceptance of the customs of his bride's family marked his kingdom's acceptance of her family's overlordship, was not obligatory acceptance by the bride of the customs of her husband's people tantamount to her people's submergence in the overlordship of her husband? Eanfled's adherence to her own religious customs is consistent with the *Life of Wilfrid*'s depiction of her as a ruler in her own right with an independent retinue

---

[155] See HE, IV.26.
[156] HE I.25. For possible connexion with Frankish hegemony, see fn. 85; McNamara, p. 35, n. 2, regards Bertha and her bishop as part of "a conversion strategy" involving a "self-conscious pairing of bishops and queens."
[157] HE, II.9.
[158] See esp. the provision that entitles the bride's family to pay her fines if her husband takes her to a district under the jurisdiction of a different lord, in Be wifmannes beweddunge (975x1030), Liebermann, I, 442–4.
[159] HE, III.25.
[160] Colgrave, 1968, p. 39, deduces that Eanfled was "clearly a woman of strong character."
[161] See HE, IV.1.

in which Wilfrid sought service with his armed band, and with Eddius's assumption that, in Mercia and Wessex, as well as in Northumbria, the royal couple were partners in rule. It is, in other words, consistent with the custom of throne-sharing by the royal pair, which Asser claimed to be universal among the Germanic peoples.

The custom of throne-sharing reflects marriage alliances conceived, not as the submergence of one nation in the dominance of another, but an alliance between two equal and independent powers. The guarantee of the bride's freedom to practice her own customs is not only an assurance to her family of her position as an equal power, but serves simultaneously as an acknowledgement of their autonomous status. It is one interpretation of the literary prominence of unsuccessful peaceweavers that the policy of attempting to end traditional hostilities by marriage alliances was prone to fail because the bride, more attached to her own kin than to her husband,[162] failed to assimilate with his people. Medieval clergymen were largely of the opinion that harmonious accord was achieved by the submergence of the identity of the wife in the headship of the husband, just as peace would fall upon the earth when the nations submitted themselves in perfect obedience and were incorporated in the reign of Christ the king – in the interim, national subjection to the unitary headship of Christ's secular representative would go a long way towards speeding up the culminating establishment of the peace that passed understanding. Rosenthal, in attributing the seeming unsuccess of the Germanic peaceweaver to her tendency to retain identity with her own kin instead of identifying herself with her husband's kin, appears to be of much the same mind as medieval clergymen in his belief in subordination to patriarchal headship as a pre-condition of ideal harmony.[163]

The queen's identification with her own people, if they were politically dominant, had the potential for upsetting the balance of power between throne-sharers and, in extreme cases, toppling the king altogether. But assimilation of the queen into the king's people – in effect, submergence of her power in his rule – is inimical to the position of the queen as peaceweaver. Her traditional role as a pivot of unity rested on her ability to mediate amity through her identification with both her husband's people and her own in the event of conflict, and required a sufficient degree of independent power to enable her to act as the advocate of her own people.[164] For though peaceweaving assumes, even in *Beowulf*, a somewhat mystical form,[165] Theodore's intervention in the hostilities of Mercia and Northumbria demonstrates that persuasive advice to

---

[162] For a late example of a queen who identified with the her family rather than her husband, see K.E. Cutler, "Edith, Queen of England, 1045–1066," *Mediaeval Studies* 35 (1973), 222–31, who argues that she consistently advanced the interests of her own family.

[163] J.T. Rosenthal, "Marriage and the Blood Feud in 'Heroic' Europe," *British Journal of Sociology* 17 (1966), 133–44.

[164] Fell, 1986, p. 104, notes that *thingestre* ("female advocate"), and the feminine form *mundbore* ("protector"), occur only once, in a prayer for the Virgin's intercession, "yet neither of these words could have been invented only to be used of Mary, they must have already been part of the Old English vocabulary."

[165] Freawaru's peaceweaving is located in the love she inspires in her husband, Wealhtheow's in her ministrations with the hall cup, and, more pragmatically, in her role as treasure-giver (*Beowulf*, ll. 1168–231; 2016–66).

both parties to a feud was an essential aspect of peacemaking, and the woman given in marriage, having connexions with her husband's people and her own, was uniquely well-placed to urge an offer of compensation by one side and its acceptance by the other.

For Bede, as for Pope Boniface and Paulinus, true marital unity consisted in the obliteration of differences, and the existence of plurality of custom in the marriage of Eanfled and Oswiu was a situation that could not be suffered to continue: "It is said that in those days it sometimes happened that Easter was celebrated twice in the same year, so that the king had finished the fast and was keeping Holy Sunday, while the queen and her attendants were still in Lent and observing Palm Sunday."[166] The absence of marital concordance in this matter was the microcosmic resonance of a wider conflict – not the outbreak of fighting in the mead-hall between the retinues, but disagreement amongst Celtic and Roman churchmen in which passions ran high. Bede's association of marital and national disharmony looks like a further adversion to the association of the royal marriage with the mystic marriage of Christ and the church, which figures in the account of the reflections of Paulinus when he heads for the pagan north with Æthelburg – here too, Bede may be extrapolating from the marital theology of his Canterbury sources or recalling exegetical commentary on *Canticles*.

Gregory the Great was a proponent of unity amid variety, accepting that local divergences in outward and visible observances did not in themselves constitute actual disunity as long as there prevailed a unity of the spirit.[167] For Bede, and for many, particularly the proponents of the Roman cause at Whitby, the differences between the outward observances of the Celtic and Roman churches, the style of the tonsure as well as the date of Easter – tending to overshadow the question of allegiance to the heirs of either Peter or John – were differences which needed to be definitively obliterated. Members of the Roman church were apt to suspect, and probably with justice, that the Celts' stubborn loyalty to their own customs was a vehicle for expressing their disinclination to be united in spirit with the Romans;[168] though another way of putting this is that the Celts might have found it easier to attain unity of the spirit with the Romans if Roman conceptions of unity had headed in the direction indicated by Gregory and enfolded independent separatism in an encompassingly tolerant embrace. The most charitable way of making sense of Bede's preoccupation with the date of Easter is that differences of outward observances were, in his theology, simply irreconcilable with his understanding of visible conformity as the only possible witness to the mystic union of the Church in Christ. As it is given to Oswiu to observe at Whitby, it was fitting that "all who served the one God should observe one rule of life and not differ in the celebration of the heavenly sacraments, seeing that they all hoped for one kingdom of heaven."[169]

---

166 C&M, p. 297; HE, III.25.
167 HE, I.27; for discussion see Meyvaert, 1963, 141–62.
168 See esp. Aldhelm, *Epist* 4.
169 C&M, p. 299; HE, III.25. As Meyvaert, 1964, p. 17, remarks: "If Bede and his contemporaries could have consulted Gregory on the question of the tonsure and on the issue of conform-

The triumph of the Roman party at Whitby was the triumph of universal hegemony. The obliteration of the regional differences of custom between the kingdoms of Kent and Northumbria, which William of Malmesbury attributed to the spiritually consecrated peaceweaving of Edwin's wife Æthelburg, are presented by Bede – predictably – as the work of bishops and kings. The outcome, as it happens, represented the dominance of the Kentish customs of the queen's family over the indigenous customs of the king and his people. Eanfled, as I have indicated, was well-placed to assist in the success of the Roman cause, and appearances favour the view that she did. But despite Bede's concern for the absence of true marital unity revealed in the divergent religious observances of Eanfled and Oswiu, and notwithstanding the fact that Pope Boniface had sanctioned domestic advocacy of religious conformity on the part of a royal bride, there is no suggestion that Oswiu took part in convening the synod of Whitby because he was disturbed to find himself in less than perfect communion with his wife. He acts upon rumours of the widespread disenchantment with Christianity engendered by schism, and the absence of unity in the royal marriage is not a self-sufficient emblem of a divided nation but is linked with the absence of unity between Oswiu and Alhfrith, his fellow ruler and eldest son.

The vernacular wisdom poems, more monotheistic than precisely Christian, are, in their different ways, struck with admiration and puzzlement by the variety and multiplicity of the creation, and not overwhelmed by its ultimate convergence in the unitary power of God.[170] It is the conclusion of wisdom that nonconformity is in keeping with the ordinance of God: "He gives us understanding, our various temperaments and our many languages. There are many islands, far and wide, containing many species of life. The Ruler, almighty God, established these broad lands for the human race, with just as many customs as there are people."[171] God made a world by taking all sorts, and "as many customs as there are people," is one of the few proverbs whose Anglo-Saxon ethnicity is unquestioned.[172] Abbess Eangyth grounded her claims to an independent conscience on the individualist extension of this: "for we all live in different ways."[173] Indeed, individualist divergence is also among Maxims I's collection of empirical observations: "There are as many opinions as there are men on earth, everyone has a mind of his own."[174] The speaker of the Celtic party at Whitby, Bishop Colman, began by assuming a natural right to follow the customs, hallowed by his ancestors, that he was taught by his superiors in Scotland. Unmoved by the information that the Celtic inhabitants of two tiny islands were out of step with the rest of the known world, Bishop Colman grounded his resistance to ideological totalitarianism on unshakeable loyalty to his own

---

ity with Roman practice on a wider scale they would probably have received an answer which would have caused them some surprise."

[170] See esp. Fortunes of Men, esp. ll. 64–6, 93–6; Gifts of Men, esp. ll. 1–29, 97–109 (ASPR III, 137–40, 154–6).

[171] Shippey, p. 65; Maxims I, ll. 12–18.

[172] See W.W. Skeat, Early English Proverbs (Oxford, 1910), p. 158.

[173] Tangl, 14.

[174] Shippey, p. 73; Maxims I, ll. 167–8.

regional traditions: "And as I have no doubt that they were saints, I shall never cease to follow their way of life, their customs, and their teaching."[175] No-one with a taste for heroic poetry will fail to side with the venerable Colman, and he took the path of exile, defeated but unbowed; the battlefield and the long-term future belonged to Wilfrid, in the prime of his young puppyhood.

The apparent absence of resistance to missionary activity in England suggests an ethos of pluralistic religious tolerance consistent with Maxims I's respect for the diversity of regional custom; it is consistent too with a lack of proselytizing zeal on the part of many kings as well as queens. The assurance of the bride's freedom to practice her own religion that Edwin of Northumbria volunteered is not testimony to the exclusive claims of Christianity but to indigenous willingness to co-exist with foreign mores. Colman's defence of his individual freedom in terms of his traditional cultural identity offers a further dimension to contractual assurances of the bride's freedom to practice her own customs as a simultaneous guarantee of respect for her independent status and that of her people.

Colman's position is echoed again in Bede's account of the role of Aidan at the time when Oswiu and Eanfled followed different liturgical calendars. The peacemaker at the Northumbrian court was, naturally, Bishop Aidan and not Queen Eanfled, but the nature of his peacemaking is of interest for its implications for the royal peaceweaver's adherence to her own customs. Aidan's preservation of unity amid diversity depended on inspiring universal affection which, notably, transcended divergence in customs – he was "rightly loved by all," even by those who differed from his opinion on Easter, and was as much esteemed by Roman bishops as he was by the generality. Notable too is the further reason why the Roman Northumbrians agreed to disagree with Aidan: it was recognized that he was bound to retain the customs of those who sent him.[176] Foreign queens who wanted to rule the kingdom were hateful because they were foreign; a foreign queen who was merely loyal to the customs of those who had sent her might still manage, like Aidan, to carry out the role appointed to her in Maxims I, and be "loved by all."

Redwald's solution to the refusal of his wife and councillors to share his religion was that "he had in the same temple an altar for the holy sacrifice of Christ side by side with an altar on which victims were offered to devils."[177] The East Anglian court's religious syncretism represents a different kind of conversion from the one intended by Gregory the Great when he instructed Augustine to consecrate the temples instead of destroying them.[178] What was to Bede an image of irreconcilably competing claims in which the superiority of Christianity was unquestionable can also be regarded as the proximate conjunction of a perceived resemblance. As Bede defines the particular nature of the resemblance, no modern reader (much less a medieval one) could place an equal value on the two religions, but Redwald's accommodation emblematizes an

---

[175] C&M, p. 305; HE, III.25.
[176] HE, III.25.
[177] C&M, p. 190. The diminutive arula is regarded as contemptuous (Whitelock, 1972, 2–3).
[178] HE, I.30.

intention to do so.[179] The royal pair's joint throne in the mead-hall in *Beowulf*, the altars placed side by side in the East Anglian temple, embody an impulse to the creation of unity, not through the subordination of differences to a hierarchical head, but through the alliance of distinct and polar entities.

[179] Wallace-Hadrill, 1988, p. 76, similarly thinks it "possible that the dual-purpose temple was the brave effort of a defeated Christian at a serious form of religious syncretism; but Bede does not give Redwald the benefit of the doubt." Redwald (probably the king commemorated at Sutton Hoo) was not unique in keeping his options open; see J. Campbell, *The Anglo-Saxons*, (Oxford, 1982), pp. 32–3, 48.

8

Rewriting Female Lives:
Hild of Whitby and Monastic Women
in Bede's *Ecclesiastical History*

Introduction

Precluded from sharing in the active ministry – officially, at least – monastic women could nevertheless gain prestige by the cultivation of learning. For Aldhelm, the nuns of Barking whom he urged on to greater efforts in their scholarly quest of God and his works were fellow soldiers of Christ: that his willingness to praise their learned accomplishments was assisted by a traditional respect for the wisdom of women is an attractive speculation.[1] It was a willingness that Bede did not share. My purpose is to suggest that Bede's account of monastic women in the *History*,[2] like his rewriting of the role of Ælffled in the *Life of Cuthbert*, is an artifact of his own bias. The predominately ecclesiastical sources of the middle ages do not, in any straightforward way, serve to reveal the actual position of women; nor is an author as learned and orthodox as Bede – one of the few Anglo-Saxons of his time who had had the opportunity to immerse himself thoroughly in the patristic literature of Rome – typically representative of ecclesiastical attitudes to women in his own time.

Boniface, writing from the missionary front to monastic women in England, with heart-felt thanks for their gifts and prayers and urgent requests for copies of books, testifies to monastic women's contribution to the advance of the Church Militant in a familiar supporting role.[3] But some took a more active part. His kinswoman Leoba joined him at the mission and became a founder of monasticism in Germany. For Boniface Leoba was a comrade-in-arms in the service of the same lord. Rudolph of Fulda reports that, when Boniface went to meet his death, he left instructions that Leoba was to be buried in his tomb when she died, so that, as they had served God with the same zeal and sincerity, they might together await the resurrection.[4] The nature of the missionary partnership this implies is revealed when Rudolph remarks that Boniface wanted monasteries to be established so that people would be attracted to the church by

---

[1] For Barking as a learned centre, see pp. 75–82. See also Aldhelm's letter to Sigegyth (*Epist* 8).
[2] Translation throughout is from B. Colgrave and R.A.B. Mynors, ed. and trans., *Bede's Ecclesiastical History of the English People* (Oxford, 1969), cited as C&M.
[3] See Tangl, 27, 30, 35, 65, 94.
[4] *Life of Leoba*, ch. 17.

the communities of monks and nuns.[5] The establishment of monasteries was not, self-containedly, to the greater glory of God; they were conversionary and pastoral centres, engaged in the same work as the perambulatory bishops and priests.

Rudolph's early 9th century Life pays tribute to Leoba's prodigious scholarship. So great was her fame for learning and wisdom, he informs us, that bishops discussed spiritual matters and ecclesiastical discipline with her.[6] But what prevents Rudolph from giving an account of monastic women's participation in the conversion is that it entailed interaction with the laity. Religious communities that were to attract people to the church needed to be openly accessible to the laity and to move freely in the world about them. As presented by Rudolph, Leoba attracted converts by performing miracles. Whether or not the English mission to the continent did gain adherents by miracles rather than teaching, miracle working as a conversionary method clearly avoids any semblance of conflict with Paul's decisive prohibition of women preachers: "But I suffer not a woman to teach, nor to usurp authority over the man, but to be in silence."[7] In the course of reporting Leoba's miracles, Rudolph enables us to glimpse the close involvement of monasteries with lay society – Leoba, for instance, miraculously protected the villagers when they sought refuge in the monastery church during a terrifying storm.[8] There is, perhaps, also a deeply submerged implication that the nuns were responsible for the baptism of infants during Leoba's lifetime;[9] the administration of baptism was certainly central to the role of the double monasteries in Kent.[10] The influential benefits of Leoba's contact with secular society are clearly evident – Rudolph tells us that Leoba was on intimate visiting terms with the court, and that she was highly regarded by noblemen, who put forward their daughters as monastic postulants. To a high degree, however, Rudolph's account is constrained by his consciousness that Germany's pioneer founder of monasticism was far from exemplary in terms of the rigidly segregated and enclosed monasticism demanded by the more ortho-

---

[5] *Life of Leoba*, ch. 10.

[6] *Life of Leoba*, ch. 18.

[7] 1 Tim. 2.12; 1 Cor. 14.34–5.

[8] *Life of Leoba*, ch. 14.

[9] *Life of Leoba*, ch. 12, reports that villagers, thinking the nuns had drowned an illegitimate child, jeered at them for being mothers and priests, baptizing those to whom they gave birth; Bateson, 185–6, regards this as evidence that the nuns assumed sacerdotal roles such as the administration of baptism because there were insufficient priests. For other intimations, see ch. 9, pp. 280, 290, 297 fn. 136.

[10] Brooks, 1984, pp. 187–97, argues that 11th c. payment of chrism-money by former Kentish double monasteries was a "relic of an age when the Kentish 'monasteries' were true baptismal churches, taking a dominant role in the pastoral work of the diocese" (p. 189). I agree with Godfrey, pp. 344–9, insofar as he regards double monasteries as conversionary centres, but am unable to follow his argument that this explains the existence of male-female communities. To accept that nuns baptized is to accept (as I do) that they effectively shared sacerdotal powers; it thus seems odd that Godfrey, p. 346, implies that AS society countenanced baptism by women but balked at preaching, particularly as the distinction between preaching and proselytizing (permitted even to lay women) can be very fine (see fn. 136). Non-ordained persons were evidently baptizing in the early church (*Theodore's Penitential*, I.ix.11, excommunicates and permanently excludes such persons from orders). For the slightness of the evidence that it was the male communities at double monasteries who engaged in pastoral work, see ch. 3, fn. 99. For the ministry of Frankish women, see Wemple, 1981, 127–47.

dox thinkers of his own time, and to which Rudolph himself is polemically committed.[11]

Bede's aversion to mixed religious communities is evident in his report of scandalous conduct by the monks and nuns at the double monastery of Coldingham.[12] His inclusion of the Coldingham episode is all the more marked considering that his *History* gives an account of only four other communities of monastic women, one of which is Frankish.[13] In his account of Barking and Faremoutiers, Bede makes a point of stating that the monks and nuns were separately housed; whereas Hildelith of Barking appears to have taken the eternal view of union after death, Bede reports the miraculous origins of the nuns' separate burial ground.[14] At Ely, he relates, the monks and nuns were stationed on opposite sides of the shrine for the translation of Æthelthryth. Bede's insistence on the rigidly segregated character of double monasteries, coupled with his report of a scandal at Coldingham, seems as consciously polemical as Rudolph's portrait of the Wimbourne double monastery where Leoba spent her youth – twin fortresses for men and women, geographically proximate, but in every other respect conforming to 9th century monachistic orthodoxy.[15]

In Bede's account of Coldingham, however, the culminating debauchery is not the union, carnal or otherwise, of monastic men and women, but monastic women's involvement with secular society. The Coldingham nuns certainly attracted the laity, but the means and the ends were entirely out of keeping with their calling, we are told: they spent their time weaving elaborate garments in which to adorn themselves like brides, and cultivated relationships with laymen. Bede's relatively greater commitment to the enclosure of female religious is demonstrated by the fact that it is not uncommon to find monks roaming at large in the pages of the *History*, even as far as Rome. The pilgrimage to Rome was no less popular among monastic women.[16] But the only woman who leaves the confines of her monastery in the *History* is Abbess Æthelhild, whose contact with secular society is dictated by her role as witness to the sanctity of King Oswald when his niece, Queen Osthryth, strikes resistance to her promotion of his cult. Æthelhild visits the queen, while she is staying at a nearby monastery, in order to report the supernatural light she has seen shining above Oswald's relics. Aided by a relic of Oswald given to her by the queen, Æthelhild is also the only woman in the *History* to perform a miracle. Unlike Leoba's conversionary miracles, however, Æthelhild's miracle of healing is not performed before a lay audience, but in the privacy of her own monastery. It takes place when she is urgently summoned during the night to attend a male visitor to the monastery who has been taken ill; he is, of course, lodged in the monks' quarters, whose architectural distinctness Bede carefully establishes, and Æthelhild is no less

---

[11] *Life of Leoba*, ch. 16–18; see further ch. 9, pp. 271–82.

[12] *HE*, IV.25; see pp. 101–2.

[13] Barking (*HE*, IV.6–10); Ely (*HE*, IV.19); Whitby (*HE*, IV.23–4); Faremoutiers (*HE*, III.8). There is incidental reference to Hild's foundation of Hackness and refoundation of Hartlepool (originally founded by Heiu), to the Lindsey monastery of Æthelhild (*HE*, III.11), and to Abbess Heriburg at Watton (*HE*, V.3).

[14] See ch. 3, pp. 111–12.

[15] *Life of Leoba*, ch. 2.

[16] See ch. 4, pp. 146–7, 149.

carefully provided with an accompanying priest and another nun when she goes to attend the visitor.[17] Only one other miracle that Bede mentions in his accounts of women religious involves the presence of the laity on monastic precincts, and it takes place at night in the Barking burial ground without the knowledge of the abbess and her nuns.[18]

Bede's account of Whitby under Hild is the closest approach his History makes to intimating that monastic women contributed, directly and indirectly, to the conversion in England. The depiction of monastic women in the History is not a representation of their actual role in the conversion period; it approximates to the invisibility that it was thought proper for them to assume in accordance with canon law, once the resurgence of the church under Theodore had rendered their assistance in converting the laity less critically necessary. The orthodox censorship of writers such as Bede and Rudolph – their rewriting of the past in terms of a present presumed to be in ideal conformity with canonical requirements – exerts its own pressures to conformity, by establishing strict enclosure as normative.[19] At the same time, it suppressed alternative models of female sanctity. The omissions and discernible suppression in Bede's account of female monasticism, however, go beyond the requirements of orthodox censorship.

Hagiography and Bede's History

There are, however, constraints on Bede's portrait of Hild that need to be taken account of, over and above the derogatory attitude to monastic women manifest in his handling of Ælfflæd in the rewriting of the Life of Cuthbert – for the admiration that some readers have seen reflected in Bede's portrait of Hild is to a high degree their own.[20] One of these constraints is Bede's conception of sanctity in general, and female sanctity in particular. Conceivably, the writing of female saints' lives constituted an unprecedented literary foregrounding of women, for the narrative marginalization of monastic women in Bede's History is paralleled in epic form by Beowulf.[21] The 11th century eulogists writing for Queen Emma and Queen Edith claim to be celebrating them through praise of

---

[17] HE, III.11.

[18] HE, IV.10.

[19] Patristic literature and early monastic rules requiring segregation and strict enclosure, especially of women, and the movement to strict enclosure and segregation in continental canons from the 8th c. on, culminating in the 787 prohibition of double monasteries, are surveyed by Schulenburg, 51–86. Bede probably knew that Theodore (Theodore's Penitential, II.vi.8) had pronounced them unorthodox.

[20] See, e.g., Colgrave, 1968, p. 38: "Bede evidently looked upon her with a deep respect." Not all of the founders of the English church portrayed in the History had established, or more than local, status as saints in Bede's time.

[21] Elene, Juliana and Judith may owe something to the influence of lost OE lays resembling the Eddic lays of Guthrun; but even Guthrun fails to achieve the narrative centrality of female saints.

their male relatives.[22] Æthelweard, in the late 10th century chronicle of the deeds of his Wessex ancestors that he wrote for his kinswoman, Abbess Mathilda of Essen, betrays his sense that the abbess might be more interested in the marriage alliances of Wessex women than "so many wars and slayings of men," but nevertheless offers her less information about women than the *Anglo-Saxon Chronicle* on which he drew.[23] Attitudes to women shifted in the late Anglo-Saxon period under the influence of the Benedictine Reform. But in early Wessex, too, women's reputation appears to have derived primarily from the deeds of their kinsmen; fulsome as Aldhelm is in praising the nuns of Barking for their learning, his poem in honour of the church that Abbess Bugga built scarcely mentions Bugga at all, and the deeds of her father, the Wessex king Centwine, together with the achievements of his successor, receive as much attention as the church itself.[24] Hrothgar, commending Beowulf on his triumphant defeat of Grendel's mother, exclaims: "Whoever the woman was who gave birth to such a son among men may well say, if she is yet living, that eternal Providence showed favour to her."[25] The androcentricity of Bede's presentation of Hild, whose fame is to a high degree adumbrated through the fame of Whitby's spiritual sons, may therefore be regarded as culturally determined; warrior reputation was itself somewhat vicarious,[26] and Bede also regards the learnedness of Abbot Albinus as a substantial enhancement of the fame of his teacher Theodore.[27] Roman saints' Lives, however, provided both an authoritative precedent and a variety of models for foregrounding women, and the model congenial to Bede's taste was the persecuted virgin.[28]

Early abbesses tended to be widows or separated women.[29] Æthelthryth, however, although not a fully orthodox bride of the Lord, had at least valiantly preserved her virginity through the two marriages she contracted. Her claims to sanctity, materially assisted by the patronage of Bishop Wilfrid, and possibly also by Ely's familiarity with Roman conventions of hagiography, were given a decisive boost by Bede. Her miraculous incorruptibility in death, manifesting the purity of her life, is a family trait she shares with her equally virginal kinswomen at Faremoutiers whom the *History* also celebrates.[30] But she is

---

[22] See *Encomium*, esp. pp. 4–8; *Life of King Edward*, esp. pp. 2–5.

[23] *The Chronicle of Æthelweard*, ed. and trans. A. Campbell (London, 1962); see pp. 1–2.

[24] *Carm Eccles*, 3. But cf. the scop's eulogy of Queen Ealhild, *Widsith*, ll. 97–108; there may have been regional differences.

[25] See *Beowulf*, ll. 942–6.

[26] See *Germania*, ch. 14; cf. *Beowulf*, ll. 2131–51.

[27] *HE*, V.20; *Life of Leoba*, ch. 3, refers Leoba's merits to her teacher, Abbess Tette.

[28] Bede's hymn to Æthelthryth (*HE*, IV.20) compares her with 6 virgin martyrs; all of whom, except Euphemia (see Plummer, II, 241–2), are included in Bede's martyrology: *Édition practique des martyrologes de Bède, de l'anonyme lyonnais et de Florus*, ed. J. DuBuis and G. Renaud (Paris, 1976). But Bede's martyrology (like Aldhelm's in *De Virginitate*) offers a variety of models, such as Constantina, converter of women, and the learned Eustochium.

[29] See pp. 50–61, 71–2, 80–1, ch. 5, fn. 110.

[30] See *HE*, IV.19–20; III.8. As the Faremoutiers Lives of Æthelthryth's kinswomen used by Bede may have reached him *via* Ely, the similarities between the Lives of Æthelthryth and her kinswomen could derive from direct literary influence. *Vita S Balthildis*, ed. B. Krusch, MGH SRM 2 (Hannover, 1888), 482–508, written *c*. 680, by a nun at Chelles (a notable literary centre, closely connected with Faremoutiers), also has parallels with the Æthelthryth's Life: see R. Folz, "Tradition hagiographique et culte de Sainte Bathilde, reine des Francs," *Acad. des*

unique in the report of posthumous miracles at her tomb, *de rigueur* in the classic Life.[31] She alone resembled Bede's idea of female sanctity, and he awarded her the accolade of an acrostic hymn of his own devising.

Hild, on the other hand, was merely a widow, though Bede is too decorous to say so outright; for Paul had not only given his *imprimatur* to virginity, but opposed the admission to the religious life of widows under sixty.[32] Further, the sources Bede chose to use for his account of Hild – generally thought to have been a lost Whitby Life – do not appear to have offered him much material for the construction of a Life according to his own mental set. His conceptions of sanctity in general are egregiously individualistic and supra-human. The ethos of Whitby is unlikely to have been conducive to the production of a self-aggrandizing Life of its founder, trumpeting abroad her deeds and virtues. It was even less likely to have contrived a miraculous cast to them. The Whitby *Life of Gregory*, written some twenty years after Hild's death, adheres to the same tradition of conversion by interior conviction that Bede's Canterbury sources identified with Pope Gregory and his English mission. The Whitby *Life of Gregory* would have affirmed roundly – if its author had not preferred to concede peaceably that there was much to be said on both sides – that it is not visible displays of supernatural powers that make a saint, but the imitation of Christ's love and humility. It is only unbelievers who require a sign, the author points out. For their conversion God may grant miracles; but to rely on miracles perverts the work of teaching and the obligation to live as an exemplar of the virtues of Christ.[33]

In its apostolic mission, Whitby seems to have lived by the author's faith in teaching and example for converting the laity. Bede's sources reported nothing that could be construed as miraculous – nothing, at any rate, that he considered suitable for inclusion – except for one or two visions of Hild's soul ascending at death and the story of Cædmon's divinely inspired poetic gift.[34] It is not just modern literary scholars' interest in Old English poetic technique that makes the story of Cædmon the most striking feature of Bede's account of Whitby under Hild. The miracle is of a kind that the Whitby author would have approved, consisting as it does of the inward and invisible operation of grace leading to the conversion of Cædmon's way of life. But in contrast to the account of Hild, the story of Cædmon is a self-contained, tightly focused little *Vita*, full of dramatic incident, to which the narrative art of Bede has con-

Inscriptions et Belles-Lettres (1975), 369–84. For Bishop Wilfrid as a possible channel of Gaulish influence at Ely, see P. Wormald, "Bede and Benedict Biscop," ed. Bonner, p. 144.

[31] Only the odour of sanctity is present at the translation of Eorcengota; the miracles associated with her, which Bede elects not to relate, were evidently not posthumous.

[32] As Fell, 1981, pp. 76–99, points out, neither Bede nor contemporary sources describe Hild as *virgo*, and her intended self-exile is consistent with widowhood. Fell suggests marriage to a pagan as the explanation of Bede's reticence. I am unable to agree that Bede "can have had no prejudices against married women entering the religious life" (see 1 Tim. 5.9–14 and *Theodore's Penitential*, II.iii.7, discussed pp. 57, 80); he mentions Heriburg's wish to be succeeded by her daughter, and the former marriages of Seaxburg and Hereswith, but does not otherwise specify the circumstances of the women religious not described as virgins.

[33] *Life of Gregory*, chs. 3–8.

[34] Only one of the two visions of Hild's soul reported by Bede appears in OE *Bede*, ed. Miller, pp. 338–42. C.L. Wrenn, "The Poetry of Caedmon," PBA 32 (1946), 277–95, suggested that the translator had access to other traditions.

tributed to an undefinable extent. In foregrounding Cædmon, Bede could be said – up to a point – to have done his best by Hild according to his own lights, since Cædmon's divine inspiration lends to her, by geographic proximity, something like the kind of testimony to sanctity for the edification of future generations that Bede felt to be required.[35]

In his predilection for the persecuted virgin model of female sanctity, Bede was at one with the Benedictine reformers of the late Anglo-Saxon period. If Ælfric knew of indigenous female saints other than those mentioned by Bede, he appears to have regarded them as too unorthodox or too insignificant to merit a Life from him. But such was the influential authority of Bede that Æthelthryth assumed for Ælfric the status of a national saint worthy to rank with Cuthbert and King Edmund, and he included her Life among the Roman female saints in his vernacular collection.[36] Hild was not entirely overlooked: she fairly certainly owes her place in the OE Martyrology to Bede[37] and his History and the Alfredian translation of it carried a memory of her into the 12th century and beyond which might otherwise have been lost – at least to the literary tradition of hagiography – in the Viking raids.[38]

But although the general biographical configurations of the account of Hild distinguish her as a pioneer founder of monasticism, she is presented as a conventionally pious and orthodox abbess. There are only the faintest indications that her activities might have differed from those of an abbess living in an age of segregated and enclosed monasticism; as if to counterbalance these, Bede emphasizes her rigorous imposition of strict conformity to a monastic rule of life in the monasteries she founded. Beside the River Wear she "lived the monastic life with a small band of companions;" at Hartlepool she "at once set about establishing a Rule of life in all respects like that which she had been taught. . . . When she had ruled over the monastery for some years, wholly occupied in establishing a Rule of life there, it happened that she undertook either to found or to set in order a monastery at a place called Streanæshalch, a task imposed upon her which she carried out with great industry. She established the same

---

[35] Bede's unease with miracles seems to me less marked than that of his modern admirers; see further pp. 120–30. He did not believe that miracles in themselves made a saint (Ward, 1976, pp. 70–6); as testimony to sanctity, he does not appear to have regarded them as dispensable. See fn. 20.

[36] *Ælfric's Lives of Saints*, ed. Skeat, I, 332. AS female saints are better represented in the liturgical calendars than they are in Ælfric's Lives (written for laymen, but said to comprise saints whose feasts are celebrated by monks); see, e.g., F. Wormald, ed., *English Kalendars before AD 1100* (London 1934), esp. pp. 1–13. Bede was responsible for establishing Æthelthryth in the learned-literary tradition; the prominence of her cult proper is to a degree independent of hagiographic promotion. Her relics were owned by the Ely monks, following Ely's 970 refoundation by Ælfric's mentor, Bishop Æthelwold. Ælfric's reference to Æthelthryth's uncorrupted sister (Withburg), translated to Ely by Abbot Brihtnoth in 974 (*Liber Eliensis*, II.53), indicates his familiarity with the contemporary cult. For the benefits accruing to the 10th c. promoters of this cult, see Ridyard, pp. 181–96. See further pp. 65–74.

[37] See OE *Martyrology*, 17 November; Hild appears only in an 11th c. copy of this 9th c. compilation. J.E. Cross argues that OE *Martyrology* was independently based on a lost Life: "A Lost Life of Hilda of Whitby: The Evidence of the Old English Martyrology," in *The Early Middle Ages*, ed. W.H. Snyder and P.E. Szarmach (Binghamton, NY, 1982), pp. 21–43.

[38] Fell, 1981, 76–99, surveys the distribution and later development of Hild's cult, including liturgical commemoration: "Her real fame was largely in her own generation, and after that in her own locality," p. 94.

Rule of life as in the other monastery." Of the bishops of the Celtic church in whose traditions of piety Whitby was founded, Bede recorded some memorable and vivifying details – Aidan, for instance, from whom Hild took the veil, reproached by Oswine for having given away to a beggar his gift of a horse and its royal trappings, enquired: " 'Surely this son of a mare is not dearer to you than that child of God?' "[39] Of Hild's death, Bede reports: "About cockcrow she received the viaticum of the holy communion, and, summoning the hand-maidens of Christ who were in the monastery, she urged them to maintain the gospel peace among themselves and towards all others; even while she was still exhorting them, she joyfully saw death approach or rather, to use the words of the Lord, she 'passed from death into life.' " She was called Mother by all who knew her, and above all she taught the virtues of peace and charity.[40] These details alone give life to the piety of Hild.

Bede's History, then, bequeathed barely an inkling of women religious whose scope of action was wider than the permitted bounds of enclosure, or of virtues other than devout conformity to the monastic rule. Hild is a prototype for abbesses in an age of enclosed monasticism, whose Lives, written by their female communities, generally held so little interest for the world beyond their monas-teries that they failed to gain sufficient currency to ensure their preservation; unless the relics chanced to pass into the possession of monks – then a cleric like Goscelin would be employed to mould them closer to the Roman virgins and deck them in all the colours of his rhetoric.[41] Endowed with sufficient authoritative prestige and substantive detail of her piety, there was a faint chance that Hild might have provided an indigenous model of female sanctity that consisted not of the sensational preservation of virginity attended by miraculous events, but in personal sanctity, along the lines of the Whitby author's imitation of the love and humility of Christ. Bede, however, did not launch into an acrostic hymn in praise of Hild, and his History was not calcu-lated to lodge in the mainstream of learned hagiographical writings a model of female sanctity that could compete in prestige with Lives dedicated to the preservation of virginity, which, in their cumulative effect, were unfortunately apt to encourage the view that it was for this that Christ had died.

[39] C&M, p. 259; HE III.14.

[40] C&M, pp. 407–13; HE IV.23.

[41] Goscelin's late 11th c. Lives of AS female saints (10 in all, according to Talbot, 1955, 13), are the earliest surviving. As early AS monastic women were, in terms of education, as capable of writing Latin Lives as their continental counterparts (see fn. 30) and the AS missionary nun, Hygeburg, who wrote the Lives of Willibald and Wynnebald (ed. Holder-Egger, 86–106), at least some of the lost Lives used by Goscelin must have been written by women; for lost Lives of Mildrith, see fn. 82. Mildrith's relics were translated to St Augustine's, for which Goscelin's Life was written, and the relics of Æthelthryth and Seaxburg were owned by the monks of Ely (see fn. 36); for lost early Lives of Æthelthryth and her female relatives, see Ridyard, pp. 50–61. Cults of post-Viking age abbesses also depended on the vested interests of male ecclesiastics; e.g., the relics of Eadburg of Winchester, whose early 12th c. Life was written by Osbert of Clare, were owned by the monks of Pershore (see Ridyard, pp. 16–37). Monastic women in the late OE period were generally less educated, but Goscelin reports that Wilton was founded as a learned centre by Edgar for his daughter, Edith, and it is difficult to believe that sources he used for his Life of Edith, whose connexion with the AS monarchy presumably accounts for Bishop Hermann's commissioning of this Life (see Ridyard, pp. 140–75), did not include Lives by Wilton nuns.

Bede's limitations as a historian of female monasticism are, obviously, not clearly distinguishable from those of his sources, which may well have concealed from him the scale of female monasticism in England – Albinus of Canterbury, for instance, who provided Bede with much of his information, might not have thought that the religious communities in Kent founded by women were worth mentioning, however eminently connected their founders were.[42] It is also conceivable that, by the time Bede wrote in 731, double monasteries such as Whitby were less involved with lay society than they had formerly been, and that their monastic schools were no longer serving the purpose of training priests. Bede's sources, perhaps, did not make clear the scope of activities of the early double monasteries – such as the existence of a monastic school among the nuns at Barking – and their authors may have already suppressed indications of conversionary involvement with the laity in the interests of maintaining the appearance of monastic enclosure according to the Benedictine and other monastic rules in use.[43] Bede, then, might not have been solely responsible for depicting the early abbesses of double monasteries as nothing other than pious and orthodox guardians of their female communities, and for conveying the impression that visions of ascending souls and communication with the departed were the primary occupations of monastic women. On the other hand, for the history of Northumbria, Bede drew upon his personal knowledge and oral report. If Bede's written sources were insufficiently forthcoming about Hild and her Northumbrian counterparts, there can have been no shortage of available oral traditions that met Bede's criteria for reliability. There was John of Beverley, for instance, one of the bishops who had been educated at Whitby under Hild. Bede had had the opportunity to talk to him and those who knew him, for Bede had been ordained by John.[44] Above all, there was Hild's niece Ælffled, who had spent most of her life at Hild's monasteries, and who succeeded her as abbess of Whitby. Ælffled, though dead by the time Bede wrote his History, was within living memory. Ælffled had been in direct contact with the Lindisfarne monks, for the Lindisfarne author of the Life of Cuthbert got some of his information at first-hand from her; so too did Herefrith of Lindisfarne, who provided Bede with additional material for his revision of Cuthbert's Life during the time that he stayed at Bede's monastery.[45] But despite the fact that Ælffled is hailed by Eddius as the best advisor in the province, and was evidently publicly visible by virtue of her involvement in the affairs of bishops and kings,[46] there is no Life of Ælffled in the History. The History merely mentions incidentally that her father Oswiu vowed her to virginity in her infancy, and adds the information that she entered Hild's monastery at

---

[42] Three of the five abbesses named in a Kentish charter (696x716), Birch, 91, figured in early versions of the Mildrith Legend (see fn. 82). For English monastic women's houses, 7–8th c., see Eckenstein, pp. 79–117; Bateson, 168–83.

[43] See HE, Preface, pp. 4–6: Bede, naturally, names only male ecclesiastics as his sources, although his written sources for double monasteries could have been written by women; see fns. 80, 82, 41, 30. Bede knew of Aldhelm's De Virginitate (HE, V.18), perhaps not at first hand.

[44] HE, V.24.

[45] See Anon Cuthbert, IV.10; Bede's Cuthbert, ch. 23, and Prologue, p. 144. (Hild died 680, Ælffled c. 714.)

[46] Life of Wilfrid, ch. 60.

Hartlepool, and afterwards became first a pupil and then a teacher of the regular monastic life at Whitby, until she departed at the age of about sixty to the wedding-feast and the embrace of her heavenly bridegroom. In the abridged version of the *Life of Cuthbert* that Bede included in the *History*, her part has been excised. Given that the hostility that marks Bede's treatment of Ælffled in the *Life of Cuthbert* appears to be generic rather than personal,[47] it is tempting to regard his omission of Ælffled from the *History's* account of Cuthbert as typifying his overall handling of his sources.

Relative to his age, Bede was unusually concerned with the rectitude of doctrine and conduct; Eddius, for instance, who records Wilfrid's claim to have been the first to introduce the *Rule of Benedict* to Northumbria,[48] reports without embarrassment episodes that reveal Wilfrid's own flagrant transgressions of its prescriptions. The Anonymous *Life of Cuthbert* depicts a saint far less constrained by propriety than Bede's. Bede's scrupulous justifications for Cuthbert's encounters with women religious in his revision of the Anonymous Life show how thoroughly his own mental filters could act as a check upon his sources. The limitations on his depiction of Whitby as monastic school are not merely those generated by a desire to preserve the appearance of segregated and enclosed monasticism. The very consistency of this attempt, coupled with the consistency with which he avoids associating female religious with learning, suggests that the *History* is Bede's consciously contrived expression of his own views of what was appropriate for monastic women. His reputation as a sober and reliable chronicler of the conversion period rests on the fact that his *History* is the only surviving account of most of the events he relates. His sobriety is unquestionable; his reliability is not.[49]

---

[47] See *HE*, III.24, cf. IV.27–32. A broader organizing principle is not outruled; D.P. Kirby, "Bede's Native Sources for the *Historia Ecclesiastica*," *BJRL* 48 (1965–6), 355, suggests that Bede did not wish to say much about his own degenerate times.

[48] *Life of Wilfrid*, ch. 47.

[49] The plain meaning of Bede's much-discussed claim to have written "true history" (*HE*, Preface, p. 6) is that responsibility for any factual inaccuracies rests with his sources (R. Ray, "Bede's *Vera Lex Historiae*," *Speculum* 55 [1980], 1–21). But it does not follow that he reproduced them with literal fidelity. In regarding *HE* as Bede's interpretive construct of the interpretive constructs of his oral and written sources, I am in broad agreement with Jones, 1947, pp. 74–9, 85, that the truth that Bede presents is not the truth of factual objectivity (insofar as there is such a thing). Bede's account is "selective and purposeful," as Wallace-Hadrill, 1976, remarked, and the conclusion he draws concerning the miracle-stories holds good for the whole: "Bede was no forger, but he does bring the same high religious sense to his history – I mean, his history as opposed to the facts out of which it is constructed. What this signifies for the historian could be further explored" (pp. 375, 379). Opinions differ on the nature of his purposeful selectivity and the extent to which it enables us to distinguish "facts" from Bede's interpretation; for the view that the purposes guiding Bede's selection are artistic, see D.K. Fry, "The Art of Bede II: The Reliable Narrator as Persona," ed. Snyder and Szarmach, pp. 63–82.

Hild of Whitby (1)

Hild's life, Bede relates, fulfilled a visionary dream of her mother when her husband was poisoned in exile at the court of a British king. Sensing his loss in a dream, she searched about for him and instead discovered under her clothing a precious necklace; as she looked at it closely, it emitted such a brilliant light that all England was lit by its splendor. The vision of the saint's mother was to become a hagiographic convention. Except in this motif, which owes its currency to Gabriel's annunciation to the mother of Christ, hagiographic attribution of prophetic faculties to women is rare. Royal women's possession of prescient powers, I have suggested, was disputed by ecclesiastics, for whom the gift of prophecy was a mark of considerable sanctity. Æthelthryth is not the only woman religious in the History with foreknowledge of impending death, but to her alone is the spirit of prophecy explicitly attributed, although not very vigorously: "some say" that she possessed it.[50]

The closest analogue to the dream of Hild's mother in the Lives of Roman saints known to the early English church is a dream of a formerly married monk, where the jewel signifies the virginity of his daughter which he urges her to preserve by entering a monastery.[51] Breguswith's dream looks like a plausible psychic intimation of the death of her husband and the consolation for her loss in the child she was carrying. As interpreted, the dream prefigured Hild's future, both as a shining example to her community and also as the bringer of salvation and amendment to many who lived at a distance and heard the inspiring story of her industry and goodness.[52] The vision of the saint's mother in this Life, then, is not merely a generalized sign of saintly destiny, but signifies election to a conversionary role. In the earliest Lives of English saints, only Wilfrid is surrounded at birth by portents of his future evangelical role.[53] Not unexpectedly, evidence of divine sanction for a conversionary role appears to have been required chiefly by female saints; Leoba's missionary role on the continent is similarly validated by visions in Rudolph's Life.[54]

The Old English Martyrology's version of Breguswith's dream has her bring forth a jewel that illumined the whole land, which is interpreted simply as a betokening of the fame of Hild's sanctity. This might confirm the view that the

---

[50] HE, IV.19. Cf. Eorcengota (HE, III.8); Torhtgyth, who foresees Abbess Æthelburg's death and her own; and an unnamed Barking nun (HE, IV.9). See further pp. 190–9.

[51] See Fortunatus's Life of Hilary of Poitiers, ed. B. Krusch, MGH AA 4.2 (Hannover, 1885), 1–11.

[52] But whose interpretation of the dream does Bede give? Dream interpretation, often associated with the pre-natal vision of the saint's mother, is another area in which female prescience figures in hagiography; for female dream interpreters in Life of Leoba, ch. 6, see p. 278. Cf. the early Lives of Æthelwold: Wulfstan (ch. 2) says the saint's mother sought interpretation of her pre-natal dream from an abbess, whereas Ælfric (ch. 2) offers his own retrospective deductions ("we can easily interpret these dreams"): ed. M. Winterbottom, Three Lives of English Saints (Toronto, 1972).

[53] Life of Wilfrid, ch. 1. In Life of Columba, III.1, the saint's mother in her pre-natal dream is given an embroidered robe by an angel, who then takes it back, explaining that such an honour cannot long be hers.

[54] Life of Leoba, chs. 6, 8.

compiler drew independently on a lost Life of Hild,[55] but it is equally possible
that he had failed to register the implication of Hild as a bringer of light to the
pagan darkness in Bede's account. It is easy to overlook, for a displacement of
agency has already occurred in the interpretation of Breguswith's dream that
Bede gives – salvation flows to many living at a distance, not directly from Hild
herself, but by oral report of her merits. The channels by which Hild's renown
reached beyond her monastery to the outside world are not noticeably marked
in Bede's account. Even within the confines of her monastery, the means by
which Hild exerted an influence are somewhat nebulous. Virtue spread by oral
report, action at a distance, the mysterious influence of goodness without discernible human agency – such things, in their kinship to the Holy Spirit, are as
dear to monastic chroniclers as the lover, inspired to adoration by renown of the
unseen much-sung lady, is dear to the medieval romancer. It is, as a general
proposition, very possible that early chroniclers, measured by modern concep-
tual modes, had a weak analytical grasp of cause and effect. Mysterious agency,
however, usually proves on inspection to obviate an explanation that the monastic chronicler had reasons for wishing to avoid.

Bede does offer a point of contact between Hild and the outside world in his
terse allusion to her role as lay adviser: "So great was her prudence that not only
ordinary people, but kings and princes sometimes sought and received her
counsel when in difficulties."[56] The foregrounding of kings and princes – generally acceptable as monastic guests, and easily understood as relatives of Hild –
obscures perception of that openness of the monastery to the world at large
which Hild's role as lay adviser would necessarily have entailed. The impression
this remark creates is misleading if it merely conjures up a picture of a motherly
interest in village problems or advice on the politics of the court. Hild is likely
to have been acting as a spiritual guide and confessor to the laity in the manner
of women famed for holiness in the Irish church. As a purely secular advisor
sought out by the laity, Hild is far from the ideal of monastic life, especially
female life, as withdrawal from the world; on the other hand, Bede is likely to
have been more rather than less opposed to the exercise of the confessional by
women than is the Penitential of Theodore.[57] Whether as secular or spiritual
adviser, Hild's involvement with the laity is problematic for Bede. It is thus not
surprising that he pays lip-service in this equivocal fashion to the wise advice for
which Hild was remembered, and passes quickly on to other matters, even
though one would expect Hild's fame among the laity to have been preserved in
reports of specific occasions when her advice had brought comfort to those "in
difficulties" – for the cure of souls and the cure of sickness are inextricably
connected, and hagiographers are normally apt to include such successes as
testimony to the saint's miraculous power to heal.

Bede's reference to the kings and princes who visited Hild is his only intimation of the political involvement of royal abbesses, since private advice to kings
shades imperceptibly into public affairs – as the Life of Wilfrid reveals in its

---

[55] See fn. 37.

[56] HE IV.23: "Tantae autem erat ipsa prudentiae, ut non solum mediocres quique in necessi-
tatibus suis sed etiam reges ac principes nonnumquam ab ea consilium quaererent et inuenirent"
(C&M, p. 408).

[57] Theodore's Penitential, II.vii.2. See further ch. 4, pp. 127–9, 134–7.

account of Abbess Æbbe, when the illness that seizes Queen Jurmenburg while she and Ecgfrith are staying at the monastery provides Æbbe with an occasion for urging the king to release Wilfrid from prison and give back his confiscated land and his episcopal see.[58] Ælffled, whose involvement in royal and episcopal politics is discernible in the Lives of Wilfrid and Cuthbert, as I have remarked, figures in the *History* only in the account of how her father King Oswiu vowed her to a monastery in her infancy, together with a tribute to her virginity in a notice of her death. In Bede's account of the synod that was held at Hild's monastery when Wilfrid routed the adherents of the Celtic church, Hild herself is seen and not heard; of the letters that she and Theodore subsequently sent to Rome opposing Wilfrid's reinstatement to his Northumbrian see, Bede seemingly knows nothing.[59]

Heiu, the first woman in the north to take the veil from Aidan, went to live in the township of Tadcaster, shortly after founding the monastery at Hartlepool that Hild took over. This sounds more like a shift in operations than the complete failure of the enterprise – and it is not without interest that Heiu appears to have sought closer contacts with a lay community. But whatever the reason for Heiu's move, Aidan's request to Hild, already on her way to a monastery in Gaul, to return instead to her homeland and found a monastery there, suggests that he was in rather urgent need of monastic founders.[60] Women monastic founders were slow to emerge in the south, and Kentish and East Anglian women continued to travel to Gaul for some time after Hild had founded her monasteries in the north.[61] Hild's embarkation upon the religious life illustrates well the operation of kinship ties in the growth and development of early monasticism. Though her projected journey to Chelles is hailed, in accordance with the prevailing ideal of monasticism, as a form of exile for Christ, Chelles was in the nature of a home away from home, for Hild was on her way to join her sister who was already a nun there.[62] Exile for Christ, whether the goal was a local monastery or a destination overseas, was not infrequently undertaken by those who were reduced to a state of kinlessness; although, as the letter of Abbess Eangyth to Boniface demonstrates, kinlessness could be both the cause and the effect of broader political misfortunes involving the loss of royal favour.[63] The degree of relationship in which Hild's family stood to successive Northumbrian kings was fraught with more risks than benefits: if not for Hild herself, certainly for the men who belonged to the same branch of the Deiran royal house as she; if any one of them was still alive when Hild set

---

[58] See *Life of Wilfrid*, ch. 39.
[59] HE, III.25; cf. *Life of Wilfrid*, ch. 54.
[60] "It seems to have been part of Aidan's plan to establish monasteries for women such as he had been familiar with in Ireland, where they had existed in some numbers in the sixth century" (Colgrave, 1968, p. 33). Hunter Blair, 1985, pp. 30–2, who attributes the Whitby double monastery to Gaulish influence, doubts that Heiu's monastery and Hartlepool were double; cf. Bateson, 149–63. See further ch. 3, fn. 96.
[61] HE, III.8. Æthelthryth's monastery was among the earliest in the south, contemporary with Barking and Dereham.
[62] Wallace-Hadrill, 1988, p. 232, points out that Chelles was not founded or refounded until at least 660; he suggests confusion with Jouarre.
[63] Tangl, 14.

out, he bore a charmed life. The political circumstances in which Hild went to seek assistance for her journey overseas from the East Anglian royal family into which her sister had married are not evident in the *History*, but in setting out with the intention of joining her sister – perhaps at the onset of widowhood or the death of her mother – Hild has the appearance not so much of an exile from kin as of a refugee from kinlessness, seeking community with one of the last survivors of her family.[64]

In the idealistic gloss that Bede puts upon Hild's move, however, she was "inspired by the example" of her monastic sister. Hild herself was a shining example to her mother, and was later joined at Hartlepool by her niece Ælffled, who in turn was joined at Whitby by her widowed mother Eanfled. To Aidan – arrived some fifteen years earlier from Iona to re-establish the church in Northumbria – Hild can have been no less important in her potential for attracting other members of the nobility to the monastic life than Æthelthryth appeared to be in the eyes of Bishop Wilfrid and Bede, but in the case of Hild, the social embedding of the attraction is more evident. Of noble blood though Hild was, she was not a member of the immediate family of a reigning king, and her role as founder of Whitby appears to have been easily eclipsed by the more illustrious connections of Ælffled who, however disparagingly treated by Bede in his *Life of Cuthbert*, was at least an authentic bride of the Lord: Ælffled was buried at Whitby together with her father Oswiu, her mother Eanfled, her mother's father Edwin, and many other nobles.[65]

As Bede has not brought into focus Hild's seminal role for the development of monasticism – both mixed and female – it is a conclusion we must draw for ourselves that one of the ways in which her monasteries at Hartlepool and Whitby contributed to the growth of the church was by educating other Northumbrian abbesses. Rudolph of Fulda, at much the same temporal distance from events that he was reporting as Bede was, had no difficulty in observing causality in the pioneering work of Leoba; her disciples "made such progress in her teaching that many of them afterwards became the superiors of others, so that there was hardly a convent of nuns in that part which had not one of her

---

[64] Hild belonged to the same branch of the Deiran royal family as Edwin; her father was presumably assassinated by Æthelfrith, who exiled Edwin and conspired against his life (*HE*, II.12). Edwin subsequently defeated Æthelfrith, driving out Æthelfrith's sons, Oswald and Oswiu, who regained the throne after a battle that destroyed Edwin's supporters (for the death of three of Edwin's sons, see *HE*, II.20); under Oswald the kingdom of Deira reverted to descendants of Edwin's uncle, one later assassinated by Oswiu (*HE*, III.14). The fact that Hild was baptized with Edwin, and her sister's marriage to an East Anglian king, might mean that, under Edwin, Hild's family were in favour (*HE*, IV.23; cf. II.14, II.9). Would such favour have continued under Oswald (633–41) and Oswiu (641–71), particularly if Hild's sons, real or potential, represented a dynastic threat? Oswiu's wife, Eanfled, however, was Edwin's daughter; but if Oswiu's placing of the daughter he vowed to God in Hild's monastery (*HE*, III.24) was a sign of favour (perhaps there were no other houses for women), it is curious that Hild appears not to have received land when Oswiu endowed 12 monasteries (see fn. 83). The absence of endowments from Oswiu, her year in East Anglia (overly long for one bent on serving Christ with her sister in Gaul), and the fact that she appears to have had no lands of her own (see fn. 83), could be connected; i.e., a possible explanation of Hild's departure from Northumbria is that confiscation of her lands by hostile Northumbrian kings c. 647 caused her to seek refuge with her sister's relations.

[65] *HE*, III.24.

disciples as abbess."[66] But, apart from the accession at Whitby of Hild's pupil Ælfflæd, and the establishment of a Whitby offshoot at Hackness, the lines of growth and development from the work of Hild are at best dimly discernible. One of Hild's monasteries seems an obvious place for the novitiate of Oswiu's sister, Æbbe of Coldingham, for instance; Coldingham, in its turn, is a not implausible place of origin for the refugee community of nuns mentioned in the *Life of Cuthbert*, who appear to have been part of the missionary extension into Pictish territory which was imperilled by Ecgfrith's unsuccessful campaign.[67]

What is clearly implicit, however, is the indirect contribution to the conversion at large that Whitby made in educating priests and bishops: Bede reports that Hild required those under her rule to find time to make a thorough study of the scriptures and apply themselves to good works, to such effect that many were found fit for holy orders and the service of the altar, and five men from Whitby became bishops in later life.[68] If those under the direction of Hild were required to study the scriptures, they needed someone to teach them – to teach them, in the first instance, how to read, and, as the copies of the scriptures available in Northumbria at the time can scarcely have been in any other language, to teach them to read Latin.[69] It seems natural to deduce that it was Hild who taught the bishops and priests who came from Whitby, and, indeed, that she was a learned woman in the manner of the nuns at Barking for whom Aldhelm wrote *De Virginitate*.[70] But were it not for *De Virginitate* and the correspondence of the Boniface circle, we would be largely dependent for our knowledge of early Anglo-Saxon nuns' high educational achievements on indirect evidence such as book ownership.[71] It is not for her learning that Hild is celebrated by Bede. What Aidan and other devout men admired was "her innate wisdom and her devotion to the service of God."[72] This, precisely, is not a tribute to her scholarship and learning. Bede, for whom Hæddi was "a good, just man, whose life and teaching as a bishop depended more on his innate love of virtue than on what he learned by books,"[73] was no less conscious of the

---

[66] Talbot, p. 214; *Life of Leoba*, ch. 11.

[67] See *Bede's Cuthbert*, ch. 30.

[68] "Tantum lectioni diuinarum scripturarum suos uacare subditos, tantum operibus iustitiae se exercere faciebat, ut facillime uiderentur ibidem qui ecclesiasticum gradum, hoc est altaris officium, apte subirent plurimi posse repperiri" (C&M, p. 408).

[69] Hunter Blair, 1985, p. 24; "There is no evidence of any vernacular translations from the seventh century."

[70] Modern scholars have generally taken their cue from Bede; Fell, 1981, p. 95, remarks Hild's evident concern with education, but regards the extent of her own literacy as doubtful (cf. the evidence of monastic women's educational achievements, Fell, 1986, pp. 109–28); Godfrey, p. 345, says some monastic women "were engaged in teaching, though they do not give the impression of being a highly scholarly group"; Hunter Blair, 1985, pp. 29–30, concludes that Whitby was the pre-eminent northern centre of learning in Hild's time, but limits her role to "a vision" of Whitby as a place where men were to be trained for orders (p. 26); in *The World of Bede* (London, 1970), pp. 148–51, he concludes that Whitby was "probably more a place of educational training than of profound scholarship." Bodden, p. 45, takes Bede to confirm the view that "religious education of women did not include the intensive study of the scriptures that was prescribed for the clergy."

[71] See, e.g., P. Sims-Williams, "Cuthswith, Seventh Century Abbess of Inkberrow, near Worcester, and the Würzburg Manuscript of Jerome on Ecclesiastes," ASE 5 (1976), 1–21.

[72] See fn. 96.

[73] C&M, p. 513; HE, V.18.

distinction between nature and nurture than Lul, who praised a young nun for being "illumined not only by the outer brilliance of learning but by the inner light of divine wisdom."[74]

Barking, Ely and Faremoutiers

Bede's reference to study by those who were under Hild's direction, from whence emerged men fit to be priests and bishops, is the nearest he comes to hinting that study was an occupation of female religious. His account of Barking, like his account of Ely and the East Anglian nuns at Faremoutiers, consists of reported supernatural events, strange lights in the sky and intimations of impending death. In naming Faremoutiers (Brie) among the Gaulish double monasteries to which East Anglian and Kentish women travelled in the early days, Bede indicates that he may have been aware of their status as centres of learning, since he reports that daughters were sent by their parents to be taught and to be wedded to the heavenly bridegroom.[75] Chelles in particular, also named by Bede, where Hild was headed to join her sister, was celebrated for its monastic school under Abbess Bertila. Such was her fame for learning among English royalty, according to her Life, that she was asked to send over men and women whom she had taught so that they could found monasteries there and teach. The indications are that there was at least one continental abbess in England in 675;[76] the Life of Bertila also mentions that the teachers she sent brought with them many books.[77] If it is true that Hild's double monasteries were founded on Gaulish models, there is further reason to believe that she too became a learned teacher of men and women; although there were also learned women in the Irish church.[78]

The monastic school at Barking may also have owed its origins to one of the Gaulish double monasteries. But the only recipient of an education at Barking in Bede's account is a three year old boy who, in consideration of his youth, was looked after and taught in the nun's quarters.[79] Hildelith, the abbess of Barking effusively hailed as a learned monastic teacher by Aldhelm in De Virginitate, like her predecessor Æthelburg, the founder of Barking, is notable only for her prudent foresightfulness and circumspect provision for her charges' needs; maternal shepherds both, they are the watchful protectors of their flock as Æbbe of Coldingham so evidently was not. When the plague struck at Barking, Æthelburg took counsel with her nuns on the siting of a burial ground. At Ely too, Æthelthryth is said to have prophesied the coming of the plague; a less practical guardian than Æthelburg, she foretold the number of deaths it would

---

[74] Kylie, p. 99; Tangl, 98.
[75] HE, III.8.
[76] See Sims-Williams, 1975, 1–10.
[77] Vita Bertilae, ch. 6. The fame of Bertila's monastic school at Chelles was contemporaneous with Hild's rule at Whitby, but post-dates Hild's intention to join her sister; see fn. 62.
[78] See fn. 60; for women in the Irish church, see Bateson, 165–8.
[79] HE, IV.8.

cause, including her own. Still locked in a triumphant struggle against the flesh, Æthelthryth figures as an exemplary ascetic, her pedagogy limited to moralizing on the tumor in her throat and its aptness as retribution for the jewels that she once wore.

Bede indicates that, for Faremoutiers, he is making selective use of a written source that came from the monastery itself, and the same probably held true of the Barking *Libellus* he used, as well as his source for Whitby – in itself capable of bringing into consciousness the learned activities of these monasteries, one would have thought.[80] Obliquely, his accounts hint at another significant activity of early abbesses which forwarded the conversion, their erection of churches. At very least the churches they built maintained a presence for Christianity; at many double monasteries the church is likely to have served as the parish church, as Leoba's church did on the continent – for Rudolph feels no compulsion to explain that the villagers' presence in the monastery church during a storm was exceptional. Bede's indications of building activities are few, however. At Faremoutiers, Æthelburg's death interrupted the building of the church she had begun; at Barking, Hildelith removed the bones of male and female religious to a single shrine in the process of her building extensions. Seaxburg, celebrated in the traditions of Minster-in-Sheppey for the thirty years of building that went into the church she erected for the monastery there,[81] appears in Bede's account only as yet another devotee to the cult of Æthelthryth. But Seaxburg is accorded responsibility for Æthelthryth's translation, and it was on her instructions that the monks of Ely discovered a marble coffin that Providence had obviously intended for this purpose; her testimony to the uncorrupted state of her sister's body, however, was evidently regarded as less substantive than the medical opinion of the male physician whose unsuccessful operation on Æthelthryth's throat appears to have precipitated her death.

A different kind of commemoration of monastic women is offered by two of the vernacular "Mildrith Fragments": they survive in mid- to late 11th century copies, but it is possible that the texts from which these fragments descend were written by monastic women.[82] Employing the conventions of dynastic

---

[80] Historical chronicles were on the Barking curriculum (*De Virginitate*, ch. 4), and the Barking *Libellus*, which included information on King Sebbi and Bishop Eorcenwold (see Kirby, 1965–6, 360), was more chronicle than hagiography; it circulated widely (*HE*, IV.7), but vernacular chronicle is generally held to have originated with Alfred. Bede, though he evidently made use of Wilfrid's oral testimony, may have had a written Life for Ely; see fn. 30.

[81] "Lambeth Fragment" (Cockayne, III, 430–2), also mentions Eadburg of Thanet's church building.

[82] The respective foundation stories of Thanet and Sheppey in "S Mildryth" and "Lambeth Fragment" (ed. Cockayne, III, 422–8, 430–2, and more recently, by M.J. Swanton, "A Fragmentary Life of St Mildred and Other Kentish Royal Saints," *Archaeologia Cantiana* 91 [1975], 15–27) effectively assert these two monasteries' traditional title to their lands. Rollason, 1981, esp. pp. 34–6, concludes that the earliest texts containing the story of Domne Eafe's foundation originated at Thanet in the time of Eadburg. Although Thanet and Sheppey were double monasteries, we are not bound to assume that these texts were written by monks; Eadburg's identification with the learned abbess of that name with whom Boniface and Lul corresponded is not secure (P. Sims-Williams, "An Unpublished Seventh- or Eighth-century Anglo-Latin Letter in Boulogne-sur-Mer MS 74 (82)," *MÆ* 48 [1979], 22, n. 119), but Eadburg's predecessor, Mildrith, having been educated at Chelles (Rollason, 1981, pp. 74–8), was capable of transmitting its traditions of scholarship (see fn. 30 above). The relationship of the vernacular "Mildrith

genealogy, the two fragments commemorate the respective monastic founders of Thanet and Sheppey, Domne Eafe and Seaxburg, and focus on the means by which they gained possession of their monasteries' lands; S. *Mildryth* relates how Domne Eafe tricked the king into giving her the whole of Thanet as wergild for the murder of her brothers, and Seaxburg is said to have bought the lands of Sheppey from her son when she resigned the kingdom to him. Bede, on the other hand, is not alive to the heroic dimensions of the monastic founders' enterprise. The source of the land on which Æthelthryth and Hild established their monasteries does not emerge in his account – possibly both widows made use of dowry lands.[83] The origins of Barking are not left in doubt, however; it was founded by Æthelburg's brother, Bishop Eorcenwold, who built one monastery for himself and one for Æthelburg.[84] Further, Eorcenwold had already established an orthodox rule of life at both monasteries. Æthelburg's role, then, was merely to carry on her brother's work in a manner worthy of his exalted station by becoming (despite the fact that Barking was a double monastery) the mother and mentor (*nutrix*) of women, assisted by the mistress of the novices in maintaining observance of the monastic rule.[85]

In their dire foreboding of impending peril to their monastic communities, Bede's abbesses offer a monastic analogue to royal women's wise prescience of disaster threatening the kingdom.[86] The intimations of approaching death and visions of ascending souls, which are particularly prevalent in the account of Barking, were authorized by Roman Lives, such as the Life of Benedict in Gregory's *Dialogues*, and could be regarded as bestowing considerable spiritual *cachet*.[87] Because martyrdom in the forms available under the more zealously persecuting Roman emperors was, by and large, denied to Anglo-Saxons, it was necessary to make the most of the opportunities for being "made perfect by suffering" that were afforded by lengthy and incapacitating illnesses.[88] But when all is said and done, Bede's accounts of the Barking, Ely and Faremoutiers, consisting of a handful of details overridingly concerned with death, burial and disease, give no very encouraging impression of the preoccupations of monastic women. Given that the details selected are supernatural manifestations which

---

Fragments" (preserved in 11th c. manuscripts) to the texts composed in Eadburg's lifetime is undetermined. Rollason suggests (pp. 29–31) that they originated in the late OE period at the monasteries whose foundation stories they relate; since Kentish double monasteries destroyed in the 9th c. Viking raids were refounded, if at all, as female houses (Brooks, pp. 200–5), the vernacular fragments might also have been written by women.

[83] *Liber Eliensis*, I.15, claims that Æthelthryth received Ely as dowry from her first husband. Contrary to expectations, as Fell, 1981, p. 85, points out, Bede does not explicitly state the source of *any* of Hild's foundations; Fell concludes that Hartlepool and Whitby were refoundations. Alternatively, Bede may have omitted to mention that Hild used the dowry lands or matrimonial inheritance that a widow of royal family normally possessed; see further fn. 64.

[84] A dubious charter of King "Suidfrid" (Birch, 87) includes Barking in a grant to Eorcenwold; but grants to Barking monastery by Æthelred (Birch, 81) and Cædwalla (Birch, 82) name Æthelburg as the beneficiary. For other examples of 7th c. charters which grant land specifically to a monastic woman, see Birch, 27, 35, 40, 42, 44, 57, 78, 81, 85, 86, 88, 96.

[85] *HE*, IV.6.

[86] See pp. 190–9.

[87] See *Dialogues*, II.33, 35, 37.

[88] 2 Cor. 12.9. With Torhtgyth (*HE*, IV.9) and Æthelthryth (*HE*, IV.19), cf. the unnamed Barking nun (*HE*, IV.9).

involve no breach of female claustration, we are not bound to conclude that Bede is faithfully reflecting the emphasis of his sources, much less that the *History* gives an accurate reflection of the actual preoccupations of monastic women at these three establishments.[89]

Hild of Whitby (2)

Bede continues to the present day to exert an authoritative influence on the construction of history; though, as I read his *History*, it is his firm commitment to the appearance of propriety, in one way or another, running through the whole, which pervasively but unobtrusively leads us to believe that what he offers is not his own interpretive construction of facts but a generally unbiased factual account. Medieval monastic chroniclers are not alone in their transcendence of instrumentality. A recent study of Whitby deduces – chiefly from its hosting of the synod and the story of the poet Cædmon – that Whitby during the lifetime of Hild was "the pre-eminent centre of learning in Anglo-Saxon England," and that it made a unique contribution to the church at a time when its fortunes were at their nadir, particularly as the priests and bishops it trained were in desperately short supply.[90] As Bede barely presents Whitby as a centre of learning at all, his failure to tell us who did the teaching at Whitby is the less marked. The deduction that Whitby was a pre-eminent centre of learning under Hild would seem to raise the question in a very acute form; but as Bede was content to suggest that the men of Whitby studying the scriptures were self-sufficiently guided by divine light, "Whitby as a Centre of Learning" does not address the question either. In Bede's ambiguous statement, Hild's contribution to education is limited to that of an educational administrator, who "compelled those under her direction to make a thorough study of the scriptures." In "Whitby as a Centre of Learning," the part played by Hild, taking its cue from the nebulous exercise of influence that characterizes Bede's portrayal, is entirely visionary: "It was a great part of Hild's vision that she saw Whitby not as a community of men and women withdrawn from the world, but as a place where men were to be trained for the minor and the major orders of the clergy."[91] By a displacement more radical than that of the *Old English Martyrology*, the jewel shedding light in the darkness has become, not Hild herself, nor the fame of her

---

[89] The vision of the monk at Abbess Mildburg's monastery, which Boniface obtained for Abbess Eadburg from Hildelith of Barking (Tangl, 10), represents a different kind of eschatological interest (again, not confined to female religious); for its political usefulness, see p. 139. Plummer, 1896, II, 218, concluded from the style of Bede's Barking account that he "worked up the materials in his own way." D.K. Fry, "Bede Fortunate in his Translator: The Barking Nuns," in *Studies in Earlier Old English Prose*, ed. P. Szarmach (Albany, 1985), pp. 345–62, considers that Bede gave artistic unity to "a series of unspectacular and diffuse miracle stories" (p. 356) by "complicated diction involving light and fearful confinement" (p. 346), but does not enquire into the psychological implications of this.

[90] Hunter Blair, 1985, pp. 1–32, esp. p. 30.

[91] Hunter Blair, 1985, p. 26.

sanctity, but the Whitby monastery preserving the light of learning in the church's darkest hour.[92]

Though Bede is the reverse of forthcoming in telling us that Hild required those under her direction to study the scriptures, there is no discernible means by which Whitby could have produced men equipped for holy orders unless Hild herself taught them; the undoubted force of personality that Bede conveys by his emphasis on her implementation of an orthodox rule of life seems scarcely adequate on its own.[93] Presumably she was equipped by Aidan with the education needed to found a monastic school during the year she spent with a small band of companions on the River Wear on her return to Northumbria. But throughout England the establishment and running of monastic schools must have required a good deal more travel and interaction between monastic men and women than is permitted to surface. Boniface's earliest hagiographer reveals that women travelled to hear him teach while he was in England. As the information is in conflict with the principle of strict enclosure, he goes on to explain that the nuns were unable to attend Boniface's lectures on a regular basis, but were inspired by his wisdom and charity to study the sacred texts and meditate on their mysteries:[94] like Bede, Boniface's hagiographer would have found the invention of radio a blessed relief. Bede was cognizant of episcopal visits to women's religious houses for instructional purposes, since he used them as an explanation of Cuthbert's stay at the Coldingham monastery, though moral exhortation appears to be what Bede had in mind.[95] He also reports that Aidan and other devout men visited Hild at her Hartlepool monastery; but the meaning that he wishes this to carry is that Hild, in a manner reminiscent of Æthelburg of Barking, implemented regular observance of the monastic rule under episcopal guidance. At Hartlepool, Hild "at once set about establishing a Rule of life in all respects like that which she had been taught by many learned men; for Bishop Aidan and other devout men who knew her visited her frequently and instructed her assiduously."[96]

Hild's fame for learning, then, like her salvatory influence, is associative and vicarious, consisting of her monastery's production, by vaguely mysterious means, of priests and bishops, her indirect outreach receiving a notable extension in the much-travelled Oftfor, first of the pilgrims to Rome. The clerical sons of Whitby, though a woman spurs them on, are not born of her teaching, but are made fit for ordination by their own humanly unaided study of the scriptures. The story of Cædmon is the culminating expression of the same phenomenon. The generative agency of what is, for the modern reader,

---

[92] Hunter Blair, 1985, p. 30.

[93] See fn. 68. Cf. OE Bede: "Ond heo swa swiðe leornunge godcundra gewreota 7 sothfæstnisse weorcum hire undertheodde dyde to bigongenne . . ." (p. 334).

[94] Life of Boniface, ch. 2.

[95] Bede's Cuthbert, ch. 10. Symeon, HDE, ed. Arnold, I, 199, says Cuthbert established a monastery for women at Carlisle and founded schools there (cf. Bede's Cuthbert, chs. 27, 28).

[96] "Praelata autem regimini monasterii illius famula Christi Hild, mox hoc regulari uita per omnia, prout a doctis uiris discere poterat, ordinare curabat. Nam et episcopus Aidan et quique nouerant eam religiosi, pro insita ei sapientia et amore diuini famulatus, sedulo eam uisitare, obnixe amare, diligenter erudire solebant" (C&M, pp. 406–8).

Whitby's most famous son, is clearly supernatural, an angelic visitation which inspires Cædmon, a servant on the monastic estate, to the composition of his first poem and the first Christian poem in the vernacular. It is a story of origins, alluding *inter alia* to the birth of Christ in a stable and the annunciation to the shepherds, and as these events portend Christ's particular identification with the lowly, to whom he first revealed his presence on earth, the miracle accords well with the ethos evoked by the Whitby hagiographer's celebration of Gregory's imitation of the humility of Christ. The nativity dimensions of this episode presumably connect it with Hild as universal Mother, since abbesses elsewhere appear to have attracted Marian associations.[97]

The story of Cædmon is also about conversion. Cædmon, who is himself the medium for the conversion of native poetic technique to Christian purposes, subsequently converts to the monastic life and goes on to turn all the events of sacred history into vernacular verse. These verses, by their circulation, moved others to follow suit – they inspired many to contempt of the world and the longing for heavenly things, Bede reports. Whitby's role as a centre for the conversion of the laity, then, is displaced from the account of its origins under Hild to the *Vita* of Cædmon, and communicated only in oblique, emblematic form through his story. Cædmon, in effect, is the transposed fulfilment of the prophecy of Hild as the bringer of salvation to many living at a distance.

Hild has been credited with foresight in recognizing the potential of Cædmon as a lay teaching medium and fostering his talents,[98] and we are surely right to regard her as the motivating force of Whitby's achievements. But, as described, her part is that of the handmaidens of God through all ages, to be "delighted that God had given such grace to the man." That she does not come to a decision on Cædmon's poetic gifts on her own, but has him repeat his verses before learned men so that a decision can be reached by common consent as to their quality and origin, we may take, if we wish, as a reflection of the corporate and communal values that are evoked in the account of her death.[99] It is Hild, though, who advises Cædmon to renounce the secular life and become a monk. By this, she becomes – though in a purely secondary sense – the only woman in the contemporary annals of the conversion of England to have converted anyone;[100] abbatical mothers are the nurturers of spiritual progeny, it seems, but bishops like Wilfrid, steadfastly forsaking the prospect of earthly heirs, are their only begetters.[101] With the reception of Cædmon into her monastery, Hild's part ends. It is not she who teaches him the scriptural stories he turns into verse. Like the incarnation itself, Cædmon's poetic gift is

---

[97] See p. 110.

[98] See Fell, 1986, pp. 113–14. Hunter Blair, 1985, p. 25, is after Bede ("Hild's monastery and the men of learning" perceived the conversionary uses of Cædmon's gift).

[99] *HE* IV.24: "Veniensque mane ad uilicum, qui sibi praeerat, quid doni percepisset indicauit, atque ad abbatissam perductus iussus est, multis doctioribus uiris praesentibus, indicare somnium et dicere carmen, ut uniuersorum iudicio quid uel unde esset quod referebat probaretur" (C&M, p. 416). Cf. *Rule of Benedict*, ch. 2; the final decision always rests with the abbot, but all monks should be consulted on matters of importance.

[100] But cf. Eanfled in *Life of Wilfrid*, ch. 2; for queen converters of pagan husbands, see ch. 7, fn. 129, pp. 220–7. Renunciation of the world for the monastic life was a recognized form of "converting" (*Theodore's Penitential*, II.xiv.8).

[101] See *Life of Wilfrid*, ch. 4; *History of the Abbots*, ch. 1.

conceived free of human taint: "He did not learn the art of poetry from men nor through a man," and it follows – though not according to the terms of incarnational theology – that he did not receive the substance of his poems through a woman. Hild, on Cædmon's incorporation into the community of brothers, "ordered that he should be instructed in the whole course of sacred history."[102] Somewhat awkwardly – in unison perhaps – the learned men, summoned by Hild to give judgment when Cædmon's gift first came to light, contrived to fulfill the role of teachers: "they then read to him a passage of sacred history or doctrine, bidding him make a song out of it in metrical form."[103]

For the rest, Hild is an abbess of the same conventional stamp as Hildelith of Barking, an indefatigable ruler who taught regular observance of the monastic rule well into an advanced and vigorous old age – a leader in the heroic mould then, transposed to the ideal of Christian fortitude, soldiering on despite the weakness of the flesh. Renowned for her piety and devotion, she set an example to her flock by her noble sufferance of her last illness – this, then, is the extent of Hild's instruction of her community. She taught the cultivation of righteousness, mercy, purity and other virtues, but above all she taught peace and charity. Dying, she summoned her community – her female community – and, in imitation of Christ, urged them to keep the gospel peace among themselves and others.[104] Community of the spirit is matched by economic collectivism; after the example of the primitive church, no-one at Whitby was rich or needy, because everything was held in common and nothing was regarded as personal property. This is certainly a contrast to the individualistic vying in the spiritual life that characterizes Aldhelm's work for the soldiers of Christ at Barking. It is also in contrast with the essentially individualistic portrait of Æthelthryth's achievements that is generated by the Roman models of heroic virgin martyrs.

Contrary to the impression Bede creates, that all monasteries were following a single orthodox rule of life, the rule that Hild espoused, as a protege of Aidan, is extremely unlikely to have been the *Rule of Benedict*, even after the triumph of the Roman cause under Wilfrid, who credited himself with having introduced its use in the north of England.[105] But the *Rule of Benedict* is directed towards a return to the spirit of the primitive church, particularly in its insistence on the communal ownership of property.[106] There is a case to be made that Bede's portrait of Whitby represents another aspect of his orthodox normalization of

---

[102] HE, IV.24: "Vnde mox abbatissa amplexata gratiam Dei in uiro, saecularem illum habitum relinquere et monachicum suscipere propositum docuit; susceptumque in monasterium cum omnibus suis fratrum cohorti adsociauit, iussitque illum seriem sacrae historiae doceri" (C&M, p. 420).

[103] HE, IV.24: "Visumque est omnibus caelestem ei a Domino concessam esse gratiam, exponebantque illi quendam sacrae historiae siue doctrinae sermonem, praecipientes eum, si posset, hunc in modulationem carminis transferre" (C&M, pp. 416–18).

[104] John 14.27.

[105] See *Life of Wilfrid*, chs. 14, 47. Opinions differ on the extent to which *Rule of Benedict* was known and/or followed in the early AS period; Wormald, 1976, pp. 141–6, concludes that "very little of what we can find out about Monkwearmouth-Jarrow is actually incompatible with the Benedictine Rule."

[106] *Rule of Benedict*, esp. chs. 2, 33–4, 59, requires that all things be held in common.

the past – that his account of Whitby, in other words, embodies in ideal form the spirit of the primitive church to which the *Rule of Benedict* pointed a return. On the other hand, although Bede gives the impression that the dating of Easter, on which the Celtic church was in error, was an unwritten tenet of the Creed, he was nevertheless willing to give its adherents credit where credit was due.[107] He consistently attributes to Celtic bishops the simplicity of life and peaceful accord with all humanity held to characterize the primitive church; particularly Hild's teacher Aidan, whose willingness to make peace in an argument with King Oswine is echoed in Bede's explanation that it was Aidan who, until his death, maintained accord between the Roman and Celtic factions in the controversy surrounding the date of Easter.[108] Bede's appreciation of the Celtic bishops, like his portrait of Whitby, is probably mediated through the ideals of the *Rule of Benedict*, but the consistency of his characterization suggests that he found a certain coherence of values in his sources, and his account of Whitby under Hild also seems likely to have taken its cue from the sources he was using.[109] Like the story of Cædmon, the account of Whitby is in keeping with the egalitarian ideals of the author of the Whitby *Life of Gregory*, and it is born out by Ælffled, who echoes Hild's dying speech in her appeal to community of the spirit in requesting the help of a continental abbess for an English abbess making the pilgrimage to Rome: "For the Lord has said: 'This is my commandment, that you love one another.' "[110]

Although Bede, in depicting holy men and women of the early Northumbrian church, is likely to have intended to show, not a specifically Celtic form of sanctity, but a timeless ideal of Christian virtue that was less commonly to be found in his own degenerate age,[111] his handling of Whitby as a monastic school is undoubtedly shaped by his preconceptions concerning the Celtic church. Possessed of the true spirit of the primitive church he could allow that it was. But Bede was the master of the monastic school at Wearmouth, the heir to the learning and the literary treasures of Rome brought back by three successive abbots, one of them his own teacher Ceolfrith,[112] and the Celtic church's ideas on the date of Easter were the product of an entrenched tradition of scholarship that was provincial and outmoded.[113] Bede dates the arrival of learning in

---

[107] As the account of Aidan in HE, III.17, shows, Bede is struggling, against his inclinations, to be faithful to the testimony to Aidan's virtues that his sources affirmed. Bede was not unique in the importance he attached to the dating of Easter, nor was the issue entirely academic; see J. Campbell, "Bede," in *Latin Historians*, ed. T.A. Dorey (London, 1966), pp. 180–1.

[108] HE, III.14, 25.

[109] Cf. *Song of York*, ll. 865–72, not derived from Bede, which stresses dedication to collective ownership in its portrait of Hild's pupil, Bishop Bosa. Although the death-bed speeches of Hild and Cædmon appear "conventional," hagiographic holy dying takes a variety of forms.

[110] Tangl, 8.

[111] Thacker, 1983, pp. 144–6. See also ch. 4, pp. 129–30.

[112] *Homily* I.13, CCSL 122, 92–3; *History of the Abbots*, chs. 4, 6, 11, 15, 18.

[113] Eddius's portrait offers no reason to believe that Wilfrid spoke at Whitby "with his customary humility" (*Life of Wilfrid*, ch. 10), but the arrogance with which he holds forth as an authority on the dating of Easter (HE, III.25) persuades me that he is a mouthpiece for Bede's expertise (cf. the brevity of the arguments in *Life of Wilfrid*, ch. 10, which also confirms the impression that Oswiu, for one, would have given a very different account of this synod); Wilfrid the dramatic *persona* was not constrained by charitable toleration as Bede the historical

England from the coming of Theodore and Hadrian, a decade or so before Hild's death.[114] Theodore established a school at Canterbury to which many travelled to study under him, including Northumbrians such as Hild's former pupil Oftfor, who was "anxious to reach greater heights." To Theodore, the school at Wearmouth, and perhaps even the curriculum taught by Bede, owed its inspiration.[115] As well as sacred and secular literature, astronomy, metrics, and, of course, computistical methods for calculating the correct date of Easter, Theodore taught both Latin *and* Greek, and it is the addition of Greek that constitutes true distinction of learning for Bede. Just as Hild is merely praised for innate wisdom and devout love of God, Bede is less than fulsome in his praise of Whitby's leading male luminaries. They were, all of them, "men of singular merit and holiness," although Tatfrith, bishop-elect of the Hwicce, contrived to be "a most energetic and learned man of great ability."[116] Abbot Albinus, on the other hand, pupil and successor of Theodore – now there was a *real* scholar, worthy to rank with Bede himself, "so well trained in the study of the scriptures that he had no small knowledge of the Greek language, and he knew Latin as well as his native tongue."[117]

The sum of Whitby's learned endeavours, according to Bede, was study of the scriptures, issuing in vernacular poetry. At Barking, where the nuns energetically plumbed the depths of the divine oracles of the ancient prophets and explored wisely the fourfold text of the evangelical story, the curriculum taught by Abbess Hildelith included patristic commentaries, histories and chronicles, grammar and metrics. Barking, however, was in touch with the new learning brought by Theodore, if only by virtue of its association with Aldhelm.[118] Aldhelm could scarcely have praised it so highly had it been otherwise. He was overtly scornful of the learning of Ireland from which Northumbria derived its earliest educational traditions. So, it is thought, did Aldhelm himself.[119] But Aldhelm had studied at Canterbury, and his denigration of Irish learning is compounded of partisan prejudices: once the Greek and Latin scholarship of Theodore and Hadrian had put England on the map – and considering that Theodore could beat anyone in a fight on the date of Easter – Aldhelm could see no further need for Englishmen in search of learning to travel to Ireland, which for impenetrable reasons he also regarded as morally dangerous.[120]

narrator was. For the debate on the status of Bede's account of Whitby, see Wallace-Hadrill, 1981, pp. 124–9.

[114] See HE, IV.2.

[115] See Wallace-Hadrill, 1988, p. 138. The foundation of Wearmouth was closely associated with Theodore (*History of the Abbots*, ch. 3). Bede is generally held to have been a pupil of Ceolfrith (see HE, V.24), who studied at Theodore's Canterbury school (*Life of Ceolfrith*, ch. 3). John of Beverley's reference to Theodore's teaching (see below) could mean that some were taught by Theodore when he visited Northumbria.

[116] C&M, pp. 409, 411; HE, IV.23.

[117] C&M, p. 531; HE, V.20. See also HE, V.8, 23; HE; IV.2; *History of the Abbots*, ch. 3. For Bede's knowledge of Greek, see A.C. Dionisotti, "On Bede, Grammars and Greek," RB 92 (1982), 111–41.

[118] *De Virginitate*, ch. 4. See ch. 3, p. 79.

[119] L&H, pp. 6–7, 146–7, cast doubt on the tradition that Aldhelm's early education was Irish. Bede's early teachers included Trumberht (the only teacher he names, see fn. 115), who was trained by a Celtic bishop (HE IV.3).

[120] See *Epist* 2, 3, 5.

For Whitby, the elite cultivation of knowledge of God through learning may well have been less important than holiness of life.[121] The story of Cædmon recalls Gregory's reminder that simple shepherds were the archetypal *pastores*. Felix, in the *Life of Guthlac* – another priest educated at a double monastery, possibly by the abbess herself[122] – also cites Gregory in positioning himself against the kind of self-advertising rhetoric that was cultivated by the school of Canterbury: the kingdom of God does not consist in the eloquence of language but in constancy of faith, he urges, and salvation was not preached to the world by orators but by fishermen.[123] But although the learned tradition that Whitby derived from Ireland was (arguably) less broad than the curriculum Theodore introduced, it was more varied and a great deal stronger than Bede's portrait of pious simplicity suggests.[124]

Seminally important though the establishment of indigenous educational centres was at the time when Aidan and Hild recognized their need, they were altogether eclipsed by the exotic import brought by Theodore. As Bede reports it, Wilfrid's winning arguments at the synod of Whitby derived their prestige from the fact that Wilfrid had been to Rome and therefore knew better than any of the adherents of the Celtic church; confined to two islands at the ends of the earth, they could not even grasp that they were out of step with the rest of the world.[125] Hild had stayed home; so did Hild's nuns and all their English sisters after them, if they were anything like as mindful as Bede of what was expected of them. The indications are that Hild's clerical progeny were no more forthcoming in praise of her learning than Bede, after the arrival of Theodore. Bede, later in the *History*, presents a scene in which John of Beverley is found rebuking an abbess who has begged him to heal her daughter. But the dialogue is so consistent with Bede's rewriting, in his revision of the Anonymous Life, of Ælffled's interviews with Cuthbert, that it may be Bede's own invention. In the retort of John of Beverley, the superior authority of a bishop, backed by the technical expertise of the new learning, opposes the uneducated meddlesomeness of a female religious. The issue, we should note, is the correct calculation of the appropriate times for bloodletting, and therefore involves computistical studies, a subject on which Bede was the leading authority of his era: "You have acted foolishly and ignorantly to carry out blood-letting on the fourth day of the moon," John of Beverley informs the abbess; "I remember how Archbishop Theodore of blessed memory used to say that it was very dangerous

---

[121] For the view that holiness of life was more important to the Celtic church than doctrine and discipline, see J. Kelly, "Pelagius, Pelagianism and the Early Irish Church," *Medievalia* 4 (1978), 116.

[122] Guthlac entered the monastery of Abbess Ælfthryth at Repton (*Life of Guthlac*, ch. 20). An abbess holding a book (identified as "Æbbe") is depicted at his tonsuring in the 12th c. *Guthlac Roll*.

[123] *Life of Guthlac*, Prologue, pp. 60–2; see also note, p. 174. Colgrave, 1968, p. 55, finds the Whitby author's Latin much inferior to Bede's, and concludes from its style and range of borrowing that neither the teaching of rhetoric at Whitby, nor its library, was of high standard (p. 37). Viking destruction of Whitby inhibits assessment of the quality of its library, but archeological finds confirm the existence of a scriptorium; see Hunter Blair, 1985, p. 30.

[124] In particular, the existence of classical learning in 7th c. Ireland is debated; see L&H, p. 197.

[125] See fn. 113.

to bleed a patient when the moon is waxing and the Ocean tide flowing. And what can I do for the girl if she is at the point of death?"[126] Hild's pupil – and the bishop who ordained Bede – appears to have travelled a long way.

After Theodore arrived, Bede reports, there was no shortage of teachers – people eagerly sought the new-found joys of the kingdom of heaven and all who wished for instruction in the reading of the scriptures found teachers ready at hand.[127] The effect cannot have been instantaneous, but in the long term the monastic schools of abbesses like Hild were not needed for the training of priests and bishops. Once there were enough clerics for the purposes of evangelization, there was no reason why women's religious communities should not withdraw in a canonical fashion behind their walls. Their access to the new learning and the wider world thus reduced, their prestige could only diminish.

At the time Bede wrote his *History*, double monasteries in Wessex were still educating priests and monks who joined the continental mission.[128] At roughly the same time, too, Leoba was learning how to compose Latin verse from her teacher, Abbess Eadburg.[129] In Northumbria, endowed with a monastic school run by Bede himself, double monasteries like Whitby might have ceased to serve the purpose of training men when he came to write the *History* towards the end of his life. Indeed, if we take seriously the implication of his *Life of Cuthbert*, the double monastery at Whitby had already been dissolved in the time of Ælffled, for he describes her as ruling over a sizeable company of women.[130] But the tradition of the learned nun outlasted the immediate needs of the conversion period.[131] Despite Rudolph's commitment to enclosed monasticism, his celebration of the prodigious learning of Leoba was intended as an exemplary model for the imitation of the German nun for whom Leoba's Life was written in the early 9th century. For Alcuin at the court of Charlemagne towards the end of the eighth century, no less than for Aldhelm at its beginning, learning as the means to know God was still the essence of the religious life, and study and church building the twin occupations of monastic women; his Latin correspondence with women religious in the north of England points to the

126 C&M, p. 461; *HE*, V.3.

127 *HE*, IV.2.

128 One of these was Lul, later Bishop of Mainz; see Tangl, 49, 70, 98.

129 See Tangl, 29. The learned centres that housed Boniface's women correspondents have not, as such, been studied (although Sims-Williams, 1990, esp. chs. 5–8, gives particular attention to some of the monastic women associated with Boniface); identification, particularly of the women addressed as "Bugga" and "Eadburg," is problematic (see further ch. 9, fn. 24). Boniface's requests to monastic women for copies of books (see fn. 3) indicate the existence of scriptoria, which are the mark of an establishment both learned and wealthy. The occasional quotations from the classics in the letters of women in the Boniface circle (esp. Tangl, 13, 14) might derive either from their grammatical studies or from a broader study of secular literature (see Sims-Williams, 1990, 215–21).

130 *Bede's Cuthbert*, ch. 23.

131 See Byrne, 1932. Information on monastic centres of learning in England between the mid 8th and late 10th c. is scanty; learning generally may have been in decline even before the Viking invasions; see H. Gneuss, "King Alfred and the History of Anglo-Saxon Libraries," in *Modes of Interpretation in Old English Literature: Essays in Honour of Stanley B. Greenfield*, ed. P.R. Brown et al. (Toronto, 1986), pp. 29–49; J. Morrish, "King Alfred's Letter as a Source on Learning in England," ed. Szarmach, 1983, pp. 87–108.

continuity of the tradition in England.[132] If Bede had contrived to discover, in the oral and written sources that he drew on for his *History*, nothing which gave the impression that double monasteries such as Whitby and Barking were much occupied with study, like his own monastery at Wearmouth, he was still not wholly unacquainted with the fact. In Bede, as in Boniface, public stance and private transaction are not wholly congruent. Bede wrote a learned exegetical commentary on *Habakkuk*, which mystically describes the passion, incarnation, resurrection and ascension, as well as the faith of the nations and the perfidy of the Jews, wherein it seems that the prophet in his lamentation views the deplorable condition of the present era; and Bede states that he wrote this exegetical commentary at the request of "a beloved sister in Christ."[133]

To a degree, Bede's low opinion of the standard of learning generally before the coming of Theodore accounts for his unadmiring and deeply submerged presentation of Whitby as a monastic school. But his failure to associate Hild with learning, and his reduction of her role as a teacher to one of instructor in moral piety to the women in her monastery, is not an inevitable concomitant of that low opinion. Bede can countenance – though only just – a royal abbess as a ruler of monks, perhaps because the power of Northumbrian queens was a part of the unshakeable order of his world; the same power was evidently held by East Anglian queens, for in Seaxburg despatching the Ely monks to find a stone coffin for Æthelthryth there is a faint echo of her earlier role of supervisor of works as a queen in her own right.[134] Hild is permitted to "compel men under her direction" to study the scriptures and to order Cædmon to be instructed in salvation history, even though it did not come naturally to Bede, as it did to the vernacular translator, to say that Hild ordered the learned teachers to assemble to hear Cædmon's song, and that *she* received Cædmon into the community.[135] But it is cumulatively difficult to avoid the conclusion that he evades presenting Hild as a *teacher* of men – men, moreover, who, like Bede himself, had been found worthy of the honour of ordination, and even bishoprics – not because Hild as a teacher conflicts with his desire to present a portrait of effectively segregated monasticism, but because Bede found such an assumption of authority as insufferable as did Paul;[136] Hild implementing regular monastic

---

[132] Alcuin repeatedly encouraged Charlemagne's sister, Gisla, and daughter, Rodtruda, to pursue learning (see esp. Duemmler, 15); he dedicated to them his commentary on John (Duemmler, 195, 196, 213, 214), and assured Nathaniel, master of the palace school, that they were worthy of his instruction (Duemmler, 262). He corresponded with Æthelburg of Fladbury, daughter of Offa of Mercia (Duemmler, 36, 102, 103, 300) and Æthelthryth, mother of Æthelred of Northumbria (Duemmler, 79, 105, 106). See also Duemmler, 68.

[133] *In Habacuc*, ed. J.E. Hudson, CCSL 119B (Turnhout, 1983), 370–409.

[134] See Cockayne, III, 430.

[135] Cf. HE, IV.23, "atque ad abbatissam perductus iussus est, multis doctioribus uiris praesentibus, indicare somnium et dicere carmen. . . . susceptumque in monasterium cum omnibus suis fratrum cohorti adsociauit, iussitque illum seriem sacrae historiae doceri" (C&M, pp. 416–18); OE *Bede*, "Tha heht heo gesomnian ealle tha gelæredestan men 7 tha leorneras: 7 him ondweardum het secgan thæt swefn. . . . Ond heo hine in thæt mynster onfeng mid his godum, 7 hine getheodde to gesomnunge thara Godes theowa; and heht him læran thæt getæl thæs halgan stæres 7 spelles" (p. 344).

[136] That Bede "even envisaged women preachers" (Thacker, 1983, p. 131) is true in the sense that a verse of Ezra he was interpreting ("et in ipsis cantores atque cantrices ducanti," Ezra 2.65) brought women to his consciousness (elsewhere, he gives no indication of having realized that

observances under the direction of Aidan and other clerics thus appears as a countervailing assertion of the proper position for monastic women in their relations with ecclesiastics. His failure to depict Hild as a teacher of scriptural study to the monastic women in her community is explicable only as a reflection of the view that learning is a male province, piety and orthodoxy the proper sphere of women. Ælffled, Hild's lifelong protege, reveals the limitations of Bede's account. Ælffled's Latin, like that of the Whitby *Life of Gregory* which was written during her rule – quite possibly by a nun[137] – has not escaped the censure of modern scholars; but she was well enough instructed to write a letter which suggests the literary influence of Aldhelm.[138] She appears to have followed in Hild's footsteps as a teacher at Whitby. Consistently, what Bede says is that she became first a pupil and then a teacher "of life under the Rule," although his unexpected use of *magistra* might suggest that he had reason to believe that Ælffled's teaching entailed more than pious and obedient conformity to the monastic Rules thoughtfully provided by male ecclesiastics.[139]

Lul, who – at least in his private correspondence – praised monastic women for their learning and as teachers, had been educated at a double monastery.[140] Bede had not. Born on the monastic lands of Wearmouth and Jarrow, entrusted to its abbots at the age of seven, he spent the rest of his life amongst its exclusively male community;[141] there, thanks to the many journeys Benedict Biscop had undertaken to Rome, Bede abounded "in all the repasts of salutary knowledge" and could "rest within the monastery walls and serve Christ with carefree liberty."[142] Bede's attitudes to monastic women, like his extreme sensitivity to narrative events involving contact between male and female religious, bespeak a lack of first-hand acquaintance, and he thus epitomizes, finally, the manner in which the enclosure of female religious that he espouses works as much to the detriment of their historical reputation as it did to their actual position.

his extension of the role of *pastores* and *sacerdotes* to those outside the ordained hierarchy could, logically, be held to include women), but the female auxiliaries envisaged appear to be lay proselytizers: "It is good indeed that to the male cantors are joined female cantors on account of their sex, whereby are found very many people who, not only by their life but by their words, inflame the hearts of their neighbours, not only by living but indeed by preaching, and assist the labour of those building the temple of the Lord as though by the pleasing quality of their holy voices." See *In Ezram*, ed. D. Hurst, CCSL 119A (Turnhout, 1969), 257.

[137] Hunter Blair, 1985, p. 30, n. 150, notes that nothing in the text excludes the possibility that the author was a woman. Its non-authoritative handling of the role of miracles and polemical interest in the plight of widows (ch. 29) are suggestive.

[138] Tangl, 8; see Colgrave, 1968, p. 40.

[139] *HE*, III.24. This term (used by Bede for Theodore, *HE*, IV.2) is the one Leoba uses for her abbess-teacher (Tangl, 29).

[140] See Tangl, 98, 49.

[141] *HE*, V.24.

[142] *Homily* I.13, CCSL 122, 93.

9

Rudolph of Fulda's *Life of Leoba*: an Elegy for the Double Monastery

Leoba's Life

Long ago and far away. . . . In this appropriately fairy-tale fashion, Rudolph of Fulda opens his *Life of Leoba* with a description of the double monastery at Wimbourne where Leoba was a nun before she left England to join her kinsman, Archbishop Boniface, at the mission in Germany:

> In the island of Britain, which is inhabited by the English nation, there is a place called Wimbourne. . . . In olden times the kings of that nation had built two monasteries in the place, one for men, the other for women, both surrounded by strong and lofty walls and provided with all the necessities that prudence could devise. From the beginning of the foundation the rule firmly laid down for both was that no entrance should be allowed to a person of the other sex. No woman was permitted to go into the men's community, nor was any man allowed into the women's except in the case of priests who had to celebrate mass in their churches; even so, immediately after the function was ended the priest had to withdraw. Any woman who wished to renounce the world and entered the cloister did so on the understanding that she would never leave it. She could only come out if there was a reasonable cause and some great advantage accrued to the monastery.[1]

Written at the behest of his abbot, Hrabanus Maurus, shortly before the translation of Leoba's remains in 837 or 838,[2] Rudolph's Life was composed for a female religious called Hadamout, in order that she might read with pleasure and imitate with profit.[3] The pedagogic stance that Rudolph assumes, adopted with increasing confidence by male religious in their dealings with their female counterparts in the ensuing centuries, testifies eloquently to assumptions of relative status and educational achievements. Entirely without Aldhelm's effusive courtliness of manner and flatteringly respectful admiration, Rudolph is

---

[1] Trans. C.H. Talbot, *The Anglo-Saxon Missionaries in Germany* (London, 1954), pp. 205–26. *Vita Leobae Abbatissae Biscofesheimensis Auctore Rudolfo Fuldensi*, ed. G. Waitz, MGH SS 15.1 (Hannover, 1887), 118–31, ch. 2. Subsequent references are to *Life of Leoba* unless otherwise stated.
[2] Waitz, p. 118, dates it to 836.
[3] Ch. 1.

nevertheless gravely polite to the reader of his Latin Life. Scholarship continued to flourish in women's religious houses at the time that Rudolph wrote[4] (making it difficult to believe that none of the extant Lives of Leoba known to him were written by the women she taught), and Rudolph does not engage in overt didacticism; nor – despite his polemical dedication to monastic segregation and orthodox claustration – does he in any way disparage women as a class or suggest that he himself regards them as the embodiment of carnal temptation.

Rudolph states that he derived his information from venerable men who wrote down what they had heard from four nuns who were closely associated with Leoba, and especially from a priest called Mago, who was on friendly terms with them and learnt much about her life during his visits to them.[5] Mago, naturally, is said to have visited the four nuns in his official capacity, but even this form of words implies rather more first-hand contact between male and female religious than Rudolph is prepared to countenance, either at the double monastery at Wimbourne where Leoba served her novitiate, or at his own single-sex monastery at Fulda, which – by an entirely meaningful coincidence – had also been off limits to members of the opposite sex from the very moment of its inception. As the orthodoxy of Rudolph's time required priests to withdraw from convents the moment they had said mass, so at the Wimbourne double monastery, according to Rudolph, priests were not permitted to linger on, talking to the nuns, after the service[6] – as Mago must have done at the Bischofsheim convent. Wihtberht, a priest from Glastonbury, who wrote back to England on his arrival at the mission, asking his abbot and the Glastonbury monks to send word of his safe arrival to "his Mother, Tette" and the Wimbourne sorority, can scarcely have developed his friendly relations with Abbess Tette and her nuns under the conditions that Rudolph describes – and neither could Boniface.[7] Rudolph's account of Wimbourne is generally accepted as a historically accurate description of the form of organization assumed by the double monasteries in 7th and 8th century England. In the light of the overall didactic intention of Rudolph's work, his account of Wimbourne can be regarded as certain evidence only of the movement towards strict enclosure of religious, particularly female religious, at the time he was writing,[8] and the associated fears of contact between monastic men and women that brought an end to the double monasteries; and with them died the egalitarian comradeship of the pioneering era.

---

[4] Eckenstein, pp. 134–83, surveys German monastic women.
[5] Ch. 1.
[6] The 787 Second Council of Nice which forbade the foundation of double monasteries also restricted entry to women's houses by priests and monks (Bateson, 163). The emphasis on stout walls in the description of Wimbourne, ch. 2, recalls the 9th c. *Regula Monacharum*, ch. 17 (PL 30, 391–426); its provisions for strict enclosure also require priests who serve female houses to leave immediately after saying mass. In these circumstances, Rudolph's dedication of his Life to Hadamout calls for an explanation; see fn. 88.
[7] See Tangl, 101. Boniface was the friend of a number of monastic women (see pp. 130–3, 137–50); for Tette, see fn. 24.
[8] For the "proliferation of sex-specific canons stipulating rigorous unbroken claustration for nuns" from the mid 8th to mid 9th c., see Schulenburg, 51–86, esp. 56–8.

Aldhelm's *De Virginitate* foreshadows a division in the ranks of the monastic soldiers of Christ, the eventual severance of women from the monastic brotherhood, when they ceased to be sisters and became instead daughters of Eve, whose sexual frailty was rendered no less threatening by their vocation as brides of Christ. Rudolph's Life enacts the fulfilment of this separation. Boniface's dying wish was to be buried in the same grave as Leoba at the monastery church of Fulda, because she had been his comrade-at-arms in the service of Christ.[9] Rudolph rewrites Leoba's role as a partner in Boniface's missionary labours, refashioning her life in order that it may serve as an exemplar for monastic women in an age of segregated enclosure. Implicitly and explicitly, Rudolph's Life justifies Fulda's failure to carry out its founder's desire to affirm in death the solidarity he had felt with Leoba in life. Rudolph's portrait of the double monastery at Wimbourne, as an enclosed and segregated institution conforming to 9th century canon law, establishes the ideological basis of Fulda's severance of those whom God had joined in his service, and is also a blueprint for the future history of monasticism.

The disappearance of the double monasteries in England – ultimately doomed from the moment Theodore arrived[10] – is obscured from view by the arrival of the Vikings. They were perhaps not so much regulated out of existence as allowed to perish in the invasion.[11] When Alfred set about restoring monasticism, he drew on the assistance of orthodox continental ecclesiastics, and the monasteries he founded were single-sex establishments.[12] Rudolph is at pains to promulgate the view that orthodoxy in this matter had prevailed in Germany from the very beginning. Because Boniface wanted the first communities of monks and nuns that he established to be organized in accordance with the Benedictine Rule, Rudolph claims, he chose two suitable superiors, Sturm and Leoba. Sturm was sent to study at Monte Cassino, where (according to tradition) the *Rule of Benedict* originated, and became the first abbot of the monks of Fulda. Leoba, according to Rudolph, was released by her abbess at Wimbourne at the express desire of Boniface, and took charge of a community at Bischofsheim that he had founded exclusively for women.[13]

There was, however, at least one double monastery established by Anglo-

---

[9] Ch. 17.

[10] See *Theodore's Penitential*, II.vi.8.

[11] Eadmer's Life of Oswald, ch. 17 (ed. Raine, II, 20), suggests that "when Oswald reformed Winchcombe and six other monasteries in his diocese [in the late 10th c.], there may have been a survival of some kind of double monasteries" (Levison, 1946, p. 257, n. 3). Winchcombe's status as a double monastery is confirmed by an 897 charter; see Sims-Williams, 1990, p. 120, n. 26, who also points out that a 901 witness list reveals that Much Wenlock was still a double monastery at that date. The survival of double monasteries may have been one of the abuses with which the Archbishop of Reims taxed Alfred c. 890 (Whitelock, I, 12–13). See further fn. 150.

[12] See *Life of Alfred*, chs. 92–8; Alfred's daughter, Ælfgifu, became abbess of the women's house he founded at Shaftesbury. Diminished enthusiasm for monasticism, as well as Viking destruction, was responsible for the disappearance of monasteries from the early 9th c. onwards (*Life of Alfred*, ch. 93).

[13] Chs. 10, 11.

Saxons in Germany in the 8th century, at Heidenheim[14]. Founded by Willibald, later Bishop of Eichstadt, Heidenheim was ruled first by his brother Wynnebald and then by their sister Waldburg; Boniface is said to have encouraged its foundation.[15] Heidenheim was more relaxed about fraternization than Wimbourne as portrayed by Rudolph: the nun Hygeburg based her account of Willibald's travels on the report that she, and others, heard from Willibald himself when he visited her monastery in the company of two deacons. The Latinity of the women at the Heidenheim monastery was evidently well thought of; Hygeburg's humility *topos*, ominously, protests her inadequacy to the task in hand on the grounds that she is a mere weak woman, but her *Hodoeporicon* is written for the priests, deacons, abbots and brothers of the diocese[16] – an impressive phenomenon that again calls into question Rudolph's negative testimony concerning Lives of Leoba written by monastic women, and further compels the conclusion that the lack of early female saints Lives written by women is not a reflection of the general level of their literary skill; rather, even if female religious did not believe that an abbess worthy of written commemoration was, by definition, one whose Life was written by a man, interest in the Lives written by women was insufficient to generate enough copies to ensure their survival. Rudolph's work is a classic female Life in so far as it owes its existence to the fact that Leoba's relics were in the possession of a male community,[17] but Hadamout was exceptionally fortunate that Rudolph's idea of an exemplar suitable for female edification is dedicated to the pursuit of learning instead of virginity preserved.

Rudolph's description of Wimbourne as the site of Leoba's early life strategically locates her in a dim and distant past. She had been dead for less than fifty years when Rudolph wrote – in Bede's scheme of things, long enough to place her within the Golden Age, yet not so long as to have rendered her entirely remote. Like the monastic women of the conversion period in England whom Bede (sporadically) included in his *History*, Leoba's life was distinctly unexemplary: inherently it could not be brought into entire conformity with the requirements of strict enclosure. Rudolph's solution is to emphasize her legendary and uniquely privileged status – her virtues, not her actions, are offered as a model for imitation. And as Germany's own founder of female monasticism was so at odds with the orthodoxy of his time, Rudolph presents her spiritual descendants with a fount and origin no less impeccable than Monte Cassino in his reconstructed portrait of Wimbourne. Leoba herself is thus established as impeccably trained, and the traces of unorthodoxy that linger on in her life merely appear as

---

[14] Bateson, 183–8, considered that a number of religious houses in Germany, 8th–11th c., were double monasteries. Hilpisch, p. 50, claims that Heidenheim was the only double monastery in 8th c. Germany. Heidenheim is said to have fallen into decay after Waldburg's death in the late 8th c.; her 9th c. Life intimates that her authority was resisted by her monks: see *Ex Wolfhardi Haserensis Miraculis S Waldburgis Monheimensibus*, ed. O. Holder-Egger, MGH SS 15.1 (Hannover, 1887) 535–55, ch. 10 (subsequently cited as *Life of Waldburg*).

[15] *Life of Waldburg*, I.1; *Vita Wynnebaldi Abbatis Heidenheimensis*, ed. O. Holder-Egger, MGH SS, 15.1 (Hannover, 1887), 106–17, ch. 13.

[16] Trans. Talbot, 1954, 153–77; *Vita Willibaldi Episcopi Eichstetensis*, ed. O. Holder-Egger, MGH SS 15.1 (Hannover, 1887), 86–106, esp. 86–7. Cited as *Life of Willibald*.

[17] See fn. 62.

the aberrations of a pioneering era. To a greater extent than Bede, Rudolph's strategies enable him to leave unconcealed the fact that current orthodoxy had no universal or timeless sanction, but by his overall normalization of the portrait of Leoba, Rudolph, like Bede in his account of Abbess Hild, suppresses an alternative model of female sanctity, and reduces the effective scope of the devout life to actions consistent with strict segregation and enclosure.

Over these two segregated fortresses of common pursuit at Wimbourne ruled Abbess Tette, chiefly notable and esteemed, in the manner of Bede's abbesses, for the maintenance of monastic discipline. The ideal is somewhat undercut by Rudolph's inclusion of a story concerning a Wimbourne prioress who had been such a strict disciplinarian that the nuns took their revenge by stamping on her grave, with such maledictory force that it subsided six inches in token of her damnation;[18] like Tette, Rudolph is in favour of merciful forgiveness, though it was evidently not yet so ideally desirable in women as to make it impossible to retell the story. So concerned was Tette to sequester her charges from the company of men, Rudolph reports, that she denied entry even to bishops.[19] As the 970 charter agreed to by English monks and nuns includes the proviso that those having spiritual authority over nuns should not behave as worldly tyrants but exercise their power only to ensure conformity to the monastic rule,[20] there are other ways of construing Tette's ban on the visitations of bishops. Their administrative attentions had not been welcome at Wimbourne in the days of its founder Cuthburg, either; Aldhelm's charter guaranteeing free elections to all the communities in his see specifically affirms Wimbourne's right to choose its own abbess[21] – and it is worth recalling, since Rudolph does not, that Cuthburg, in Roman terms, was a distinctly heterodox abbess, having embarked on the monastic life after separating from her husband, Aldfrith of Northumbria, and that, according to the *Anglo-Saxon Chronicle*, it was she who founded Wimbourne, not the Wessex kings who were her brothers.[22]

As the power of bishops gained ascendancy, abbesses lost to them the autonomous control of their houses; formally precluded from dealing with the world at large, their sphere of influence diminished radically, and the status of women's communities with it.[23] Rudolph's description of Tette transacting the affairs of the monastery through a window defines a means by which abbesses, despite pressures to remain invisible, could retain control of their monasteries' affairs and a degree of external influence. But Rudolph is surely reconciling truth with didactic purposes by describing a practice that Tette adopted only towards the end of her life, at an age when abbots and abbesses, including Leoba herself, not uncommonly became anchorites.[24]

---

[18] Ch. 4.
[19] Ch. 3.
[20] *Regularis Concordia*, pp. 4–5.
[21] Charter 5 (Ehwald, 514–16).
[22] ASC, 718: Cuthburg was the sister of Ine and Ingeld of Wessex. Tette, also described as a king's sister (ch. 3), cannot be identified with Cuthburg (see fn. 24), because Rudolph states that a number of abbesses ruled at Wimbourne before Tette.
[23] See Schulenburg, 73–9; cf. fn. 143.
[24] The elderly abbess Boniface addresses as "Bugga," Tangl, 94, appears to have retired to an anchorage; she may have been the former abbess of Leoba. Leoba's letter gives the name of her teacher as Abbess Eadburg (Tangl, 29). Because Rudolph calls the Abbess of Wimbourne

Despite Tette's alleged care to keep her charges sequestered from the world, Leoba's fame, mysteriously, burst forth; such was her reputation for learning and holiness, spread far and wide by report, Rudolph explains, that Boniface wrote and asked Tette to send her to him.[25] Hagiography such as Rudolph's, with its tale of a male and female religious, physically separated in life and united only in death, finding eternal recompense for their separation in an otherworldly union, cannot but have contributed to the development of the rarified platonic passions of secular lovers in romance literature; and when, at the end of the Malory's *Morte Darthur*, Lancelot betakes himself to a monastery in order that he may remain united with Guenevere by sharing the devout vocation for which she has rejected him, romantic love can be said to have found its culminating apotheosis at the site of one of its origins.[26] Rudolph's evocation of Boniface's desire for a far-distant maiden known only by repute as a paragon of virtue, and called to his side by messengers bearing letters, is another of the Life's quasi-romance elements. Rudolph is probably recalling the ambassadorial quest of Old Testament kings for a suitably worthy bride and its New Testament fulfilment in Christ's choice of Mary, the foremost of all women, as his mother and bride. The *Encomium Emmae*, in its account of how the messengers dispatched by Cnut to find a bride fit for him, knew by the pre-eminent reputation of Emma that she alone was worthy to be his queen, illustrates the motif's transitional passage from hagiography to romance.[27] But secular loves and secular literature were not invariably the borrowers. Just as Alcuin condemns the recitation of heroic lays in the monasteries,[28] Rudolph disapproves of conventual interest in "girlish romances" – Hadamout is obliquely encouraged to pay no heed to them by the information that Leoba wasted no time on such idle entertainments[29] – and it is tempting to suppose that Rudolph's Life, avowing its intention to please by giving edification, is offered as a devout substitute for "girlish romances," and that his portrait of Boniface and Leoba, united in

"Tette," it has been assumed that Leoba's teacher must have been Eadburg of Thanet. This hypothesis, which receives no support from Rudolph's Life, is unnecessary, and rests on the dubious identification of Boniface's correspondent "Bugga" with Eadburg of Thanet, on the grounds that Eadburg of Thanet is referred to as "Bugga" by her brother, Æthelberht of Kent, in a letter to Boniface (Tangl, 105); "Bugga" was a common hypocorism for female names containing -*burg* (Fell, 1986, p. 111). Presumably, Abbess Eadburg was Cuthburg's successor at Wimbourne. Æthelburg of Kent was known as "Tate" (*HE*, II.9); hence "Tette" might have been the familiar name by which Abbess Eadburg of Wimbourne was known to Leoba and others (e.g., Wihtberht, in Tangl, 101). It is not impossible that the woman called "Tette" by the Wimbourne community was called "Bugga" by Boniface (although not all of his letters to "Bugga" and "Eadburg" are necessarily intended for one and the same woman). Cf. Colgrave, 1956, p. 177, who accepts the identification of Tette in Rudolph's Life with Cuthburg, the founder abbess of Wimbourne; see fn. 22.

[25] Ch. 10.

[26] *Le Morte Darthur*, ed. E. Vinaver (London, 1954), VIII.5.

[27] *Encomium*, II.16. See also the *exemplum* of Christ the Lover-Knight wooing the maiden-soul by messengers in *Ancrene Wisse*, Pt. 7 (ed. Dobson, pp. 284–7).

[28] "What has Ingeld to do with Christ?" (Duemmler, 124).

[29] Ch. 7 ("inanibus iuvencularum fabulis," p. 124).

heaven though denied a common grave by the monks of Fulda, is a conscious echo of the other-world unions that figured in secular lays.[30]

No letter of request from Boniface to Abbess Tette is extant.[31] But the mystery of Boniface's acquaintance with Leoba's reputation is solved by a letter that she wrote to him as a young nun, drawing herself to his notice, and asking him, on the strength of his ties of kinship with her mother and his former friendship with her father, to stand to her in the role of surrogate brother: "I am my parents' only child, and, though I am not worthy of so great a privilege, I would like to regard you as my brother, for there is no other man in my family in whom I can put my trust as I can in you."[32] She sent with her letter a gift for Boniface, in the hope that the memory of her would remain present and the bond of their love remain firm for ever. Though the ideal of entry to the religious life is exile from kindred and homeland, it was for many, like Leoba, also a refuge from kinlessness. At the continental mission, as well as in the English monasteries, community in Christ was substantially based on the kinship network and, in leaving her homeland behind her to join a kinsman at the mission, Leoba is representative of the significant role that kinship attraction played in the growth of the early church.[33] But as erotic love is the profane rival of *caritas* for the post 12th century world, for heroic age hagiographers kinship is oppositional to unity in the bonds of the spirit.

Rudolph, in seeking to present Boniface and Leoba as exemplary in their transcendence of kinship attachment, implicitly testifies to its motivating force. Boniface greeted Leoba with warm respect and placed her in charge of the monastery he had founded, Rudolph assures us, not so much because she was related to him as because he knew that one so wise and holy would benefit many by her teaching and example.[34] If Leoba never gave a thought to her homeland and relatives that she had left behind,[35] she achieved a triumph of *contemptus mundi* to which Boniface did not aspire – "I hope, my dear son," he wrote to his former pupil, Abbot Duddo, "that you remember the saying of a certain wise man, 'hold fast to your old friend,' and forget not in old age the friendship we began in our youth and have preserved till now"[36] – and we can better gauge the nature of his feelings for Leoba from his letter to his old friend Abbess Bugga in England than we can from Rudolph's *Life*. Assuring Bugga that "soldiers of Christ of both sexes" have triumphed over tribulations, Boniface confided his regret that they had long been separated, and wrote to offer his sympathy and encouragement because he had never forgotten her kindness to him and their long-standing friendship.[37] Nor did Boniface imagine that exile for Christ obliterated thoughts of the English homeland at a stroke. The report of his departure from Leoba recognizes that their friendship has sustained them

[30] The union of lovers beyond death which figures as a motif in post-12th c. romance presumably had embryonic existence in heroic age legends (see, e.g., *Helgakvitha Hjorvarthzsonar*, sts. 39–50, *Sigurtharkvitha en Scamma* and *Heilreith Brynhildar*, ed. Kuhn, I, 140–9, 207–18, 219–22).
[31] See fn. 24. A general appeal for the assistance of the English church survives (Tangl, 46).
[32] Talbot, 1954, p. 87; Tangl, 29.
[33] See ch. 4, esp. pp. 138–43.
[34] Ch. 10.
[35] Ch. 11.
[36] Trans. Emerton, p. 63; Tangl, 34.
[37] Tangl, 94.

in their work as exiles for Christ, for, knowing that his death is imminent, Boniface repeatedly appeals to Leoba not to abandon her adopted homeland; giving her his cowl as a visible sign of his continued presence, he evinces a sympathetic understanding that, in having lost his presence, she might feel herself to have lost all that sustained her in the sacrifice of her homeland.[38] For the full implications of this, it needs to be remembered that the consolations Boniface and his correspondents offer to others are the consolations for which they themselves feel a need. Boniface's message to Tette, Rudolph relates, solicited Leoba as a comfort to him in exile and a helper in the mission with which he had been charged,[39] and Boniface's letters to Bischofsheim asking for Leoba's intercessory prayers affirm his sense of their shared hardships and mutual dependence.[40]

Tette is reported as displeased by Leoba's departure. As Rudolph has none of Bede's polemical dedication to the establishment of hierarchy, Tette's consent is not attributed to her obedience to a bishop's request; indeed, it is noteworthy that Rudolph accepts that an abbess has the authority to give consent in this instance, since canon law of his own time required the abbess to obtain the permission of her own bishop if a nun wished to leave her monastery for any reason.[41] Tette accepts what she regards as a fulfilment of the will of providence, and visionary signs that Leoba is predestined by God to play a part in the mission serve to reconcile her effective breach of claustration with the high standards of orthodoxy that Rudolph has set for Wimbourne. The pre-natal dream of Leoba's mother, in which she draws from her bosom a merrily ringing church bell, even more than the dream of Hild's mother in which she discovers under her clothing a jewel that radiates light in the darkness,[42] suggests that the daughter to be born is destined to an evangelic role. But the dream is instead interpreted as a prophecy of a girl child who must be offered to the church.[43] Leoba's own dream, however, is interpreted as destining her to an evangelical role. Her vision, in its general physiological resemblance to her mother's dream, recalls the hagiographic theme of renunciation of natural progeny for the begetting of spiritual offspring.[44] Leoba dreams of a seemingly unending purple thread issuing from her mouth, which she draws forth little by little, until exhaustion overcomes her, "as if from her very bowels," and winds into a ball.[45] The elderly nun who provides the interpretation explains that the dream is a prophecy that Leoba's teaching and good example will bring benefits to many in far-off lands, and the purple thread – suggestive of the advice of royal women in their role as metaphoric weavers of peace – signifies the wise councils for which she will be famed.

Boniface envisaged that the monastic communities would participate in the conversion of the laity and so aid the growth of the church – Boniface built

[38] Ch. 17.
[39] Ch. 10; see fn. 132.
[40] Tangl, 66, 67; see ch. 4, pp. 131–2.
[41] See Schulenburg, 56–8.
[42] HE, IV.23; see ch. 8, pp. 253, 261–3.
[43] Ch. 6.
[44] See esp. Life of Wilfrid, ch. 4.
[45] Ch. 8.

monasteries as well as churches, Rudolph explains, because he believed that people would be drawn to the church not only by the beauty of its religion but also by the communities of monks and nuns.[46] But the fulfilment of this role entailed precisely the free interaction between female monastic communities and the world at large that Rudolph is at such pains to discourage. He therefore foregrounds the normative aspects of Leoba's life, concentrating on her devotion to the contemplative life and the virtuous example that she set for her community.[47] For Rudolph study of the scriptures is still central to the ideal of the devout life for monastic women. The secular literature that was on the curriculum at Barking was evidently not favoured by Rudolph; on the other hand, Leoba's studies are broadened to include the church fathers, the decrees of councils and the whole of ecclesiastical law. Rudolph's approval doubtless reflects his assumption that knowledge of the canons would automatically guarantee conformity to them, but the positive benefits of the cultivation of learning among female religious are revealed when Rudolph explains that Leoba was admitted to the councils of bishops, and even consulted on their regulation of female religious, it would seem: because of Leoba's fame for wisdom and learning, bishops often discussed scriptural matters and ecclesiastical discipline with her.[48]

But in Germany as in England, the participation of monastic women was less crucial once the initial period of missionary activity had won for the church a degree of security, and the effect of strict enclosure was to secure their exclusion from the mainstream of the church's activities. If the monastic school of Leoba contributed to the conversion, as Whitby did, by educating priests, Rudolph, officially at any rate, knows nothing of it. Nor does he mention scriptoria, although as monastic women in England assisted the mission by copying books it is likely that those who joined the mission performed the same service[49] – presuming that they were not wholly occupied with day to day survival, for Rudolph's explanation that Leoba was industrious in manual labour because she had learnt that "whoever will not work should not eat"[50] suggests that conditions had been as hard at Bischofsheim as they were in the early days of Fulda, when the monks were unable to produce enough food for themselves.[51] Leoba's prodigious learnedness and ceaseless study is implicitly recommended to Hadamout as a model for imitation; but it is symptomatic of the diminished usefulness of learned monastic women in the eyes of the post-missionary church that, learned as Leoba herself is, Rudolph (like Bede, the master of his monastic school) evinces little interest in her role as monastic teacher, and foregrounds the example she set by her virtuous manner of life. Unlike Bede in his account of Hild, Rudolph acknowledges the seminal contribution to the spread of monasticism made by Leoba's teaching – but although the many women trained by her who later became abbesses are commended for their thorough-going orthodoxy, there is no suggestion that they perpetuated a tradition of scholarship. In

---

[46] Ch. 10.
[47] Chs. 7, 11.
[48] Ch. 18.
[49] See Tangl, 15, 30, 35.
[50] Ch. 7; 2 Thess. 3.10.
[51] See ch. 17; cf. Tangl, 93, 67.

presenting Leoba's visionary dream as a sign of grace that crowns all her other endeavours, Rudolph points in the direction of a shift in the conception of the religious life that would prove less productive of abbesses so famed for wisdom and learning that bishops would seek their advice.[52]

Rudolph's retrospective imposition of orthodoxy largely conceals the contribution of female religious communities like those at Bischofsheim, but his Life of Leoba reveals more than Bede's History of the participatory roles of a mission-ary-age abbess. Most evidently Leoba holds a quasi-episcopal position in her supervisory oversight of the monasteries that she founded. Episcopal in character, too, is her inclusion in counsels on ecclesiastical discipline,[53] and her familiar access to the court where, in the manner of Bishop Wilfrid, her close friendship with the queen enables her to exert an influence on secular affairs.[54] In all these roles she evinces an independent self determination and the freedom to leave her monastery and mingle with secular society that canon law, during her lifetime, progressively prohibited: subordinating abbesses to the authority of bishops, it required them, as well as the members of their communities, to have episcopal permission for their movements. Though Rudolph has not assimilated to his thinking this ultimate consequence of the rigid claustration of monastic women, it is a sign of changing times that when Leoba retires to an anchorage towards the end of her life, she is guided by the advice of Boniface's successor, Bishop Lul.[55] But for all Leoba's freedom of movement and participation in the affairs of the church, the Life – despite the early vision that validates her as an evangelist, and despite Rudolph's eulogy of her as a learned teacher of nuns – divulges nothing which suggests that she was active in teaching the laity; nor is she, after the fashion of Abbess Hild, sought out for her advice by all ranks of lay society.[56] Like Whitby under Hild, however, Bischofsheim evidently was actively engaged in conversion, for Rudolph states that miracles performed by Leoba inspired devotion among the laity and attracted other women to the monastic life.[57] Rudolph's report of the villagers' jibes – that the nuns drowned their illegitimate children, thus acting as mothers and priests – also suggests that, when the services of a priest were lacking, Leoba and her nuns may have carried out lay baptisms because there was a shortage of priests; Rudolph's story contextually defines this role as no more appropriate for monastic women than motherhood.[58]

---

[52] The disappearance of the abbess-advisor is more marked in England than in Germany. Hildegard von Bingen, most notably, sustained in the 12th c. the politically influential role held by early Anglo-Saxon abbesses like Leoba, Ælffled and Hild (although even Hildegard's influence depended on her prophetic powers as well as her exceptional learnedness). Hild's closest parallel in 12th c. English hagiography is Christina of Markyate, credited with the gift of prophecy but not remembered as a learned woman, who was the friend and influential advisor of Abbot Geoffrey of St. Albans (Life of Christina of Markyate, chs. 55–86).

[53] Ch. 18.

[54] Chs. 18, 20.

[55] Ch. 19.

[56] HE, IV.23.

[57] Chs. 13, 16.

[58] For the ministry of monastic women and lay baptism, see ch. 8, fn. 10; Boniface was exercised by the problem of insufficient priests for the baptism of infants (Tangl, 91). The priest, Torhthat,

Whether or not the mission to Germany relied on supernatural signs, instead of the teaching and example preferred by monasteries like Whitby,[59] miracles were essential as a validation of sanctity to Rudolph, and the miracles he reports afford a glimpse of the extent to which missionary-age monasteries were, necessarily, involved with lay society: Leoba's miraculous protection of the villagers in a storm, as Rudolph himself points out, became known to many only because it was performed in public. Rudolph is careful, though, in his choice of miracles involving the laity; in each case, Leoba's interaction with the laity is not of her seeking, but fortuitously occasioned by an act of God. Her miracle of healing is, similarly, a special emergency, involving her only in a visit to one of her nuns who was dying and had therefore been permitted to return to her home.[60]

To a high degree, hagiographic "miracles" are pure artifacts of journalism. Rudolph's account of the "miraculous" way in which Leoba saved her monastery and the nearby village when a fire broke out is a case in point: she poured into the river some salt that had been blessed by Boniface, and then instructed the villagers to draw the water from it and put out the fire.[61] The talent for showmanship we are witnessing here was not necessarily Leoba's, and one way of explaining the fact that abbess-saints throughout the middle ages rarely made a significant impact unless their Lives were written by a male ecclesiastic[62] – though impossible to substantiate – is that women religious (increasingly the only permissible witnesses to the deeds of a female saint) were less adept at contriving a miraculous cast to their actions than were their male counterparts.

In miraculously assuaging the dangers of both fire and storm, Leoba appears as the leader and protector of the villagers and the monastic community. In contrast to the Marian idealization of the closing scene of the Life, the storm episode links Leoba with the Marian typology of warrior culture, with Our Lady of Victories, who has "bruised the head of the serpent."[63] For as the villagers, terrified by the storm, huddle in the church, and lightning and thunderbolts provoke a fresh wave of panic, Leoba is called upon to validate the villagers' trust in her and to intercede for the safety of them all: "Beloved, all the hopes of these people lie in you; you are their only support," her kinswoman Thecla urges her. "Arise, and pray to the Mother of God, your mistress, for us, that by her intercession we may be delivered from this fearful storm."[64] Leoba's response is not to plead on her knees in the fashion of later medieval devotees invoking the intercession of an all-merciful mistress and heavenly queen, but to fling herself

---

although described as a long-time devoted servant of Leoba, appears only as the companion of her retreat from the world (ch. 21).

[59] Willibald, with few exceptions, reports that Boniface converted by preaching and example. Miracles figure prominently in *Life of Waldburg*; IV.6 reports that Hildegard, daughter of King Ludovic, was attracted to the Heidenheim monastery by the miracles performed there. For Whitby, see pp. 125–7, 248–9.

[60] Ch. 15; cf. *Life of Waldburg*, I.3, where Waldburg leaves her monastery to cure the dying daughter of a local noble.

[61] Ch. 13. See fn. 136.

[62] For Goscelin's contribution to the post-Conquest cult of AS female saints, see ch. 2, fn. 101, ch. 8, fn. 41.

[63] The prophecy that the seed of Eve will vanquish the serpent (Gen. 3.15; see also Ps. 91.13 [90.13]), though more commonly regarded as fulfilled in Christ, is also associated with Mary as victrix. See fn. 66.

[64] Talbot, pp. 219–20; ch. 14.

into battle against the storm. "As if challenged to a contest," she flung off the cloak she was wearing,[65] and standing on the threshold, she made the sign of the cross, opposing the fury of the elements with the name of God. Leoba is a different kind of soldier of Christ from the overwhelming majority of female saints, of whom Æthelthryth, as constructed by Bede, is typical.[66] Whereas their heroic struggles against the powers of darkness, psychomachic and actual, are a matter of individualist self-defence, and reflect the conviction of male ecclesiastics that female sanctity consists chiefly, if not exclusively, in the preservation of virginity, Leoba is a saviour of her people who parallels secular battle-leaders like the Lady of Mercia.[67] She is a type of the Church Militant, triumphantly championing her people against the pagan gods whose destructive power is expressed in the storm.[68] The Mary that Leoba serves inspires, not the cultivation of distinctively female virtues, but the courage to resist.

The openness of monastic communities to public view, however, was double-edged, potentially as capable of exposing them to lay criticism as of inspiring a desire to embrace the same faith. Leoba is also the protector and saviour of her nuns against the villagers in miraculously identifying the true culprit when the villagers accuse the nuns of scandalous misconduct.[69] Rudolph reports that, when a village woman drowned her illegitimate child one night in the river that flowed through the monastery, the villagers immediately denounced the nuns, and sarcastic wit flowed at their expense: "How admirable is the life of nuns, who beneath their veils give birth to children and exercise at one and the same time the function of mothers and priests, baptizing those to whom they have given birth."[70] Suspicion immediately fell on any nun away from the community at the time, and as it chanced, Agatha was absent: although, Rudolph explains hastily, she had full permission for her absence, and was visiting her parents on urgent business. Entirely uninfluenced himself by the construction of women as frailty incarnate, Rudolph implicitly locates the need for stricter claustration of monastic women, not in their generic liability to succumb to temptation, but in their liability to become the innocent victims of secular scandal-mongers. In this he retains the world view of male ecclesiastics in the embattled missionary church, for whom the enemy was without; danger, for men in the early church, did not inhere in the women who were their fellow soldiers of Christ, but in the hostility and scorn of the largely unconverted world that they inhabited. Whether or not it was true that secular society was generally prone to point an accusing finger at the communities of female celibates in their midst, the moral of Rudolph's Life is as unmistakable in this miracle story as it is in his account of Leoba's *alma mater* at Wimbourne.[71]

[65] Cf. the depiction of Christ ascending the cross as a young warrior stripping himself for battle in *Dream of the Rood*, l. 37.

[66] Bede's hymn to Æthelthryth (HE, IV.20) describes her preservation of her virginity as a triumphant defeat of the foe who conquered Eve.

[67] MR, 910–18.

[68] For the Church's response to "magic of the heavens," including storm raisers, see V.I.J. Flint, *The Rise of Magic in Early Medieval Europe* (Princeton, 1991), pp. 87–193.

[69] Ch. 12.

[70] Talbot, p. 217; ch. 12.

[71] Some scandal such as Rudolph reports may have come to the notice of Boniface, who, condemning Æthelbald of Mercia for ravishing monastic women (Tangl, 73), states that the offence is compounded because they are driven to commit infanticide.

Leoba and Boniface: Union and Division

(1) The last wishes of Boniface

When Boniface, full of years, set out to meet the martyrdom awaiting him in Frisia, Rudolph relates, he summoned Lul, his auxiliary bishop and designated successor, and instructed him to carry to its completion the work he had begun. Above all, Boniface urged Lul to finish building the monastery he had established at Fulda, and commanded him to have his body taken there for burial. Then he sent for Leoba and urged her too to carry on with her missionary labours, and begged her not to abandon the country of her adoption. Commending her to the care of Lul and the senior monks of Fulda, who were also present, Boniface "reaffirmed his wish that after his death her bones should be placed next to his in the tomb, so that they who had served God during their lifetime with equal sincerity and zeal should await together the day of resurrection."[72] And begging her again not to leave her adopted land, he left with her his cowl.

Rudolph's opening portrait of the double monastery at Wimbourne is a portrait of union in absence, of male and female religious physically divided, but one in spirit, united in a life of devotion governed by the same monastic rule. This ideal of union in absence defines the direction of Rudolph's presentation of the relation of Leoba and Boniface, which has been no less radically rewritten than her role as a missionary-age abbess and founder of monasticism. Boniface's express desire to lie beside Leoba in the grave because they had served God equally, on the other hand, implies not union in absence but a desire for continued close proximity, for the perpetuation beyond death of their close partnership in life. His fear that, after his death, she might return to England, affirms his recognition that his own physical presence was an irreplaceable support, and the cowl he gives to sustain her in her work among strangers in an alien land, is a concrete token of the invisible continuity of his former, physically present, support. Physical inseparability is the essence of the warrior-heroic ideal of comradeship – to share the same death, to lie side by side on the battle-field, is the culminating expression of life-long indivisibility in the journey through life.[73] For Christianity, death is liminal, but the monastic friendships that are modeled on warrior comradeship still look to an eternal perpetuation of physical proximity in life through identity in death. In Bede's account of how Ecgberht and his friend Æthelhun travelled to Ireland where both men fell victim to the plague, Æthelhun, discovering that Ecgberht had prayed that God would spare his life, laments his severance from his travelling companion in the journey to the next world.[74] For Cuthbert's hermit friend, too,

---

[72] Talbot, p. 222; ch. 17. "Suaeque voluntatis esse affirmans, ut post obitum eius corpus illius ad ossa sua in eodem sepulchro poneretur, quatenus pariter diem resurrectionis exspectarent, qui pari voto ac studio in vita sua Christo servierant" (p. 129).
[73] *The Battle of Maldon*, ll. 288–94; see further, pp. 48–50, ch. 6, fn. 40.
[74] HE, III.27.

who persuades the saint to pray for a postponement of the hour of his death, union in death is the gateway to union in the next life.[75]

The relation of Leoba and Boniface, defined as central by Boniface's departing speech, is drastically marginalized in Rudolph's account. By implication, they met only on the two occasions that Rudolph mentions; that is, when Boniface greeted her on her arrival at the mission, and when he summoned her in the presence of Lul and others, in order to announce his impending death in Frisia and to make known his last wishes. The two or three surviving letters from Boniface to Leoba – confirming his conception of her as a comrade in the service of the same lord – point to a far greater degree of direct contact between them.[76] Boniface's dying wish is, in any case, innately at odds with Rudolph's presentation of their relationship – two meetings, twenty or more years apart, is scarcely a convincing basis for Boniface's choice of Leoba as the sharer of his grave. The relationship of Leoba and Boniface in Rudolph's Life is reminiscent of the account of Benedict and his sister Scholastica in Gregory's Dialogues. Like Boniface, Benedict placed the women's religious house he had founded under the rule of his kinswoman. Demonstrating scrupulous adherence to the Rule ascribed to him, Benedict is said to have met with his sister only once a year, and their meetings involved no breach of segregation, since they took place at a house near the gateway of her monastery. At their last meeting, Gregory relates, Scholastica, foreseeing her own death, tried to persuade her brother to stay with her overnight; but as Benedict refused, because it was contrary to his own Rule, Scholastica petitioned God – successfully – to detain him by sending a storm. On the following day, Benedict saw from afar her soul ascending to heaven in the form of a dove, and sent his monks to fetch her body so that she could be buried with him in the grave he had prepared for himself at his monastery. And so it came about, Gregory concludes, that as their souls were always one in life, their bodies continued together in the tomb.[77]

Rudolph's report of Boniface's last wishes is not substantiated by two closely associated Lives which are of an earlier date, Willibald's Life of Boniface and the Life of Sturm, written by Eigil, who succeeded Sturm as abbot of Fulda. Willibald, like Rudolph, relates that Boniface announced his impending death and last wishes before he departed for Frisia. But in Willibald's Life, Boniface summons only Lul to him, and he gives instructions only for the burial of his own body at Fulda.[78] Eigil's Life contains no parallel to this episode – it merely asserts that, on his visits to Fulda, Boniface had repeatedly pointed out the place where he wanted to buried, and the Fulda monks had no doubt that he wished to be buried there.[79] Eigil's silence concerning Boniface's final reaffirmation of his wish to be buried at Fulda might seem to be all the more telling in view of the fact that Eigil reveals that Fulda's possession of Boniface's relics was

[75] Anon Cuthbert, IV.9.
[76] Tangl, 67, 96, 66; see ch. 4, pp. 131–2.
[77] Dialogues, II.33–4.
[78] Life of Boniface, trans. Talbot, pp. 25–62; Vita S Bonifatii Archiepiscopi Auctore Willibaldo Presbytero, ch. 6: ed. G.H. Pertz, MGH SS 2 (Hannover, 1829), 331–53, ch. 11 (more recently ed. and trans. R. Rau, Bonifatii Epistulae, Willibaldi Vita Bonifatii [Darmstadt, 1968], not sighted).
[79] Life of Sturm, trans. Talbot, pp. 181–202; Eigilis Vita S Sturmi Abbatis Fuldensis, ed. G.H. Pertz, MGH SS, 2, 365–77, ch. 15.

contested. Eigil, in other words, has not incorporated Willibald's testimony to Boniface's dying wish to be buried at Fulda, even though it constitutes absolute validation of Fulda's right to possess his relics. The conclusion to be drawn from these two Lives, however, is not that Rudolph's report of Boniface's instructions for his burial is apocryphal,[80] a mere hagiographic fiction prompted by Gregory's *Dialogues*.

Leoba is not merely absent from Willibald and Eigil's account of Boniface's instructions for his burial – their silence on her existence is total. Willibald, for his part, contrives to report that Boniface's missionary fame attracted many holy and learned persons to his aid without so much as mentioning Leoba or, indeed, the presence of any English missionary nuns.[81] Yet Willibald was writing less than thirteen years after the death of Boniface – during the lifetime of Leoba, then, and long before her withdrawal to an anchorage could have dimmed the memory of her.[82] What he does tell us is that – by a process of osmosis as satisfying to faith in the operation of the Holy Spirit as it was to orthodox expectations of female religious – the English nuns taught by Boniface were inspired from afar by his wisdom and charity to diligent study of the scriptures.[83] The propriety of this account was not necessarily dictated by Willibald's own perception of female religious. Willibald was chosen to write Boniface's Life by Lul and the Archbishop of Würzburg,[84] and Lul's letter to Abbess Switha, informing her that he had excommunicated her and the two nuns she had allowed to return to their families without his consent, reveals that, although Lul suspected Abbess Switha would be no more likely to accept orders from him on this occasion than she had been in the past, enforcement of female enclosure was an aspect of Lul's intention to subordinate abbesses to his episcopal authority.[85]

Orthodox censorship evidently operates in the *Life of Boniface*, then, as it does in the *Life of Leoba* and in English sources like Bede's *History*, to give women's contribution to the conversion the invisibility which, it was felt, monastic women should themselves assume. It is a salutary reminder of the limitations of the surviving documentation of the early church that we would have had no reason at all to suppose that Leoba had played a significant part in the mission had it not been for the fact that Fulda's possession of Leoba's relics occasioned an account of her life by one of the Fulda monks.[86] For, in the event,

---

[80] Levison, 1946, p. 76, n. 2, discerned borrowings in Rudolph's Life from *Life of Boniface*, Athanasius's *Vita Antonii*, Jerome's *Vita Hilarionis*, Paulinus's *Vita Ambrosii*, Constantius's Life of Germanus of Auxerre, and the *Actus Silvestri* as well as Gregory's *Dialogues*. I am in broad agreement that "not all the statements in the work can be accepted at face value."

[81] *Life of Boniface*, ch. 6.

[82] Boniface was martyred in 754; Leoba's obit is recorded in the Fulda Annals for 780. Willibald's Life can be dated to the period 763x769 by its dedication to Archbishop Megingoz of Würzburg.

[83] *Life of Boniface*, ch. 2.

[84] *Life of Boniface*, Prologue, pp. 333–4.

[85] Tangl, 128. Cf. G. Huyghe, *La clôture des moniales des origines à la fin du XIIIme siècle* (Roubaix, 1944), p. 39, who assumes that Lul's letter proves that the Rule was still well enough observed for the bishop to believe so harsh a sanction would be effective.

[86] Leoba appears in an 11th c. Life of Lul; Boniface's parting speech commends her for having taken charge of the monastery he founded for her and attracting many women to the monastic life. See *Vita Lulli Archiepiscopi Moguntini Auctore Lamberto Hersfeldensis*, ed. O. Holder-Egger,

as Rudolph's Life explains, Leoba was buried at Fulda – not, however, in the same tomb as Boniface, but beside an altar that Boniface had built and dedicated.[87] Eigil's *Life of Sturm*, which pre-dates Rudolph's Life by some twenty years, as I have remarked, preserves the same total silence on the subject of Leoba as Willibald's *Life of Boniface*. Yet Eigil wrote his *Life of Sturm* – Leoba's male counterpart as a monastic founder selected by Boniface – at the request of a nun called Angildruth.[88] Leoba would surely have been of at least passing interest to Angildruth; her monastery is more than likely to have been founded by either Leoba or one of the women she taught. Abbot Eigil of Fulda was unquestionably well aware of the existence of Leoba; Rudolph reports that he had Leoba's remains moved from the altar that Boniface built to a shrine in the western porch.[89] He was probably present too for her original burial beside the altar during the abbacy of Sturm, since he describes himself as a faithful disciple of Sturm.

Eigil's overall reticence is, presumably, also attributable, in part, to orthodox censorship. But just as Rudolph's Life throws into high relief Eigil's failure to include the scene in which Boniface reaffirms his wish to be buried at Fulda before he embarks on his journey to Frisia, so Eigil's Life gives an additional dimension of significance to the form this scene assumes in the *Life of Boniface* that Willibald wrote for Bishop Lul. According to Eigil, when Boniface's body had been transported as far as Mainz – where Lul, as Boniface's successor, was to have his episcopal seat – Lul issued orders forbidding the body to be carried on to Fulda.[90] As Lul is the sole witness to Boniface's announcement of his impending death in Willibald's Life, and is specifically entrusted with the burial of Boniface's body at Fulda, Willibald can scarcely be expected to confirm this claim; his report that Lul was engaged in private consultation at the royal palace when the body arrived in Mainz is, nevertheless, suggestively consistent with Eigil's statement that, when Boniface's remains were carried into Mainz, a

---

MGH SS, 15.1, 132–48, ch. 6. The author's familiarity with Rudolph's Life (Holder-Egger, p. 133) accounts for its inclusion. Leoba is not present here for Boniface's final speech, but, in Lambert's version, Boniface concludes with a request that Leoba be buried in his tomb so that their names may continue undivided after death; it is given to Boniface to explain that, although he has always averted his eyes from all other women, Leoba occupies a unique place in his affections because of her exemplary purity. Lambert also adds an explanation of Lul's guiding role in Leoba's retirement to an anchorage at Schornsheim; he wished to minimize the trouble of carrying her corpse to Fulda (ch. 20). Concerning her burial, Lambert states that his only certain knowledge is that she was buried at Fulda, but not in the same tomb as Boniface.
[87] Ch. 21.
[88] *Life of Sturm*, ch. 1. It is conjectured that Angildruth was at Bischofsheim or Kizzingen (Duemmler, p. 556). Notwithstanding the rubric, Duemmler considers that *Life of Sturm* was written 779x814, before Eigil became abbot. Like Rudolph's dedication of his Life to Hadamout (see fn. 6), Eigil's dedication of his Life to a nun whose spiritual superiority he had long recognized seems to indicate greater fraternization with monastic women on the part of the Fulda monks than Rudolph allows for. Neither woman is addressed as an abbess or a kinswoman, and the style of address does not suggest that they had court connexions; one 12th c. copy of *Life of Leoba* refers to "venerabili virgini Hademute" (Waitz, p. 131). Fulda appears to have had links with a convent at Milz founded by one of Leoba's nuns; the abbess willed the foundation to the Abbot of Fulda in 783, stating that the nuns should choose their abbess with the advice of their spiritual masters, the priests of Fulda (Bateson, 187).
[89] Ch. 21.
[90] *Life of Sturm*, ch. 15.

messenger came from the palace with orders that the body was to stay in the city, if that should prove to be the will of the saint.

Over and above the affront to orthodox sensibilities offered by Boniface's desire to perpetuate his union with Leoba in the grave, the financial benefits of possessing the body of a famous martyr who would attract pilgrims were an important consideration; and especially to a monastery as impoverished as Fulda was at the time of Boniface's death.[91] At Utrecht too, Eigil claims, the populace tried to detain the saint's body because they wanted to retain his protection; at Mainz, clergy and laity were united on the point that it was unfitting to remove Boniface's body from his episcopal see.[92] Such general considerations may also have weighed with Lul; but Lul had more specific and personal reasons for detaining Boniface's body at Mainz in the hope that, notwithstanding Boniface's own express wishes, no miraculous sign would eventuate which showed that the martyred saint was opposed to being buried in his episcopal see.[93] Lul was the successor on whose appointment Boniface himself had insisted, uncanonically and to the annoyance of Rome which, not unnaturally, attached considerable importance to its own prerogative in determining the episcopal succession.[94] The persistent tendency of ecclesiastical office-holders to appoint their own successors – despite repeated canonical prohibitions – reflects the importance that Germanic culture attached to the transfer of inheritance,[95] and in the hagiographical conventions that Willibald is employing to portray Lul as Boniface's successor, I want later to suggest, the saint's appointment of his successor is redolent with suggestions of direct inheritance of his nebulous powers – an informal parallel, in effect, to the formal transference of the apostolic power to bind and unbind that was accomplished by episcopal consecration.

For Lul himself – a prime source of information for the Life of Boniface and one of its two dedicatees – something in the nature of inheritance of Boniface's spiritual charisma, or a desire to consolidate his role as Boniface's chosen successor, may have been involved in his attempt to retain possession of the saint's mortal remains. There was also a deeply personal dimension to the choice of a successor. Willibald describes Lul in terms that echo the warrior comitatus ideal of loyalty to the leader through thick and thin, in life and in death; like the kinsman whom Bishop Wilfrid appointed to succeed him as abbot,[96] Lul was Boniface's comes, the companion of his journeying, who shared both his joys and his sorrows.[97] A letter written by Lul expresses his pride in his close relation

---

[91] Rudolph's explanation that Boniface urged Lul to look after the Fulda monks because they were entirely without revenue echoes the concern Boniface expresses in a letter seeking support for the succession of Lul (Tangl, 93).

[92] Life of Sturm, ch. 15.

[93] Lul was out-manoeuvred by a deacon who testified to a dream in which Boniface demanded to be carried to Fulda.

[94] See Tangl, 50, 93; Life of Boniface, ch. 8.

[95] See, e.g., Bede's Letter to Egbert, H&S, III, 318–20; Life of Wilfrid, chs. 64, 65; Life of Ceolfrith, chs. 2–3. Bede's insistence on Wearmouth's scrupulously orthodox appointment of abbots, in accordance with the Rule of Benedict (chs. 2, 58), glosses over the fact that Benedict Biscop's appointees were his kinsmen (History of the Abbots, chs. 7, 11).

[96] Life of Wilfrid, chs. 64, 65.

[97] Life of Boniface, ch. 10; see fn. 132.

to Boniface.[98] All in all, Boniface's choice of Leoba as the partner in his life's labours with whom he wanted to share a grave at Fulda was not something that Lul would have wanted to perpetuate. Despite the fact that there were many who could have written Boniface's Life from first-hand experience, Lul and the Archbishop of Würzburg entrusted the task to a priest who had never met him[99] – possibly he had not arrived on the continent until after the death of Boniface.

Rudolph cannot have invented Boniface's instruction that Leoba was to be buried in his tomb; it is so entirely at odds with his own rigidly orthodox position on monastic segregation. And Leoba's burial at the church of Fulda, evidently an embarrassment to the monastery, is explicable only in the terms Rudolph offers. Eigil's silence in the *Life of Sturm* is one of the manifestations of that embarrassment. But whereas Eigil could avoid mentioning that Leoba was included in Boniface's instructions for his burial by referring Fulda's right to possess his relics to the conversations Boniface had with various monks when he visited the monastery, Rudolph, writing a Life of Leoba for a nun – perhaps even a Bischofsheim nun – could not suppress information that was so central and so widely known, and has instead found a neutralizing, quasi-mythological form for presenting the friendship of Leoba and Boniface. Unable to cast aspersions on Fulda's founder saint by simply declaring his last wishes uncanonical,[100] Rudolph is obliged to explain that when Leoba died (some twenty five years after Boniface) Fulda felt such reverence for its saint that the monks were afraid to open his tomb, so they compromised with his instructions by burying Leoba at the altar Boniface had dedicated; not the union Boniface had requested, he admits, but still enabling their remains to lie in close proximity.[101] Abbot Eigil, it seems, was less constrained by reverence than his predecessor. Eigil did not go quite so far as to exclude Leoba's tomb from the church altogether, but he did the next best thing, and seized the opportunity offered by his rebuilding project to relegate her remains to the least hallowed end of the church. As the stages of Leoba's translation are the correlative of a developing conception of monastic women as inalienably and dangerously other, the configurations of Abbot Eigil's reorganized church may be taken as graphically emblematic of the position of monastic women in the church as a whole. It remained only for Eigil's successor, Hrabanus Maurus, to remove Leoba's remains from the precincts; and Rudolph's Life, written at his instructions shortly before this translation, signals the imminent fulfilment of Hrabanus's intention to decree monastic segregation absolute. Hrabanus moved Leoba's relics to the most eminent of the churches that he built, but consigned them to a reliquary in the crypt, placed behind an altar dedicated to the Mother of God and the female virgins of Christ.[102]

---

[98] Tangl, 98.

[99] *Life of Boniface*, Prologue, pp. 333–4.

[100] See D.S. Bailey, *The Man-Woman Relation in Christian Thought* (London, 1959), p. 70. Bateson, 137–98, shows that burial of monks and nuns in the same cemetery was usual at double monasteries; for Barking, see ch. 3, pp. 111–12.

[101] Chs. 21, 23; Leoba's own priest (see fn. 58) is said to have performed the burial.

[102] Rudolph recorded the translation of Leoba in *Rudolfi Miracula Sanctorum in Fuldenses Ecclesias Translatorum*, ed. G. Waitz, MGH SS 15.1, 328–41, ch. 14. Fulda's possession of Leoba's relics was problematic only because of the circumstances by which they obtained them; male communities who acquired possession of the relics of holy women were generally the creators of their cults (see ch. 8, fn. 41). Leoba was only one of a great number of saints, female and male,

(2) Kindred souls: Leoba and Boniface and Felix's *Life of Guthlac*

The kindred-soul relation of Benedict and Scholastica provides the justifying authorization and the model for the hagiographic presentation of the friendships of male and female religious: as their souls were always one in life, Gregory explains, their bodies continued together in the tomb.[103] Boniface, in instructing that his kinswoman and missionary partner was to be buried in his tomb, may have had in mind Gregory's account of the spiritual affinity of Benedict and his sister that found its culminating expression in their burial in the same tomb. But his desire to be buried with Leoba so that, having served God during their lifetime with equal devotion, they could await together the day of resurrection, is metaphorically grounded in a conception of their relation as the comradeship of fellow soldiers in Christ, whose union in death is the continuation of inseparable association in life. For Rudolph it was highly fortuitous that Benedict's Life offered a precedent for a request that, by the time Leoba died, was fraught with disturbing implications, since he is committed to affirming the *Rule of Benedict* as the foundation on which German monasticism was erected.[104] Rudolph thus presents Boniface and Leoba, not as monastic comrades whose union in death perpetuates their union in life, but as kindred souls who, in the manner of Benedict and Scholastica, were united by a spiritual bond that transcended physical severance. But even the meetings of Benedict and Scholastica – which are intended, by their infrequency, to reflect the monastic ideal of the renunciation of earthly ties as enshrined in the *Rule of Benedict* – take place once a year, and their union in the grave is a fitting outward sign of the affinity that bound them by virtue of their holy lives. Rudolph allows Boniface and Leoba to meet only when she arrives at the mission and when he departs to his death; Boniface's wish to be buried with Leoba thus has the appearance, in the context Rudolph creates, of a final conjunction in death of bodies that were separated in life. And when Leoba died, the senior monks at Fulda, "afraid to open the tomb of the blessed martyr," evidently could not bring themselves to sanction a posthumous consummation when orthodoxy forbade even the geographic proximity of male and female monasteries.

Divided in life by Rudolph and denied intimate conjunction in death by the monks of Fulda, the union of Leoba and Boniface is infinitely deferred. They achieve their apotheosis at the end of the Life in the vision of a man who is reported to have been miraculously healed at Fulda.[105] Rudolph relates that, after the man had prayed at the shrine of Leoba, which by that time had been moved into the western porch of the church, he went to pray at the tomb of Boniface, and there he saw a vision of a venerable old man, vested in a bishop's

whom Hrabanus translated to the churches he built; a brief notice of her in Hrabanus's Martyrology is drawn from Rudolph's Life (Waitz, p. 120).

103 *Dialogues*, II.34.

104 Frankish church reformers in the second half of the 8th c. aimed to impose the *Rule of Benedict* on all monasteries and to eliminate all other Rules. Levison, 1946, pp. 103–5, considers that its position on the Continent had been strengthened by Anglo-Saxon missionaries who came from Benedictine houses.

105 The Annals of Fulda, for which Rudolph himself was responsible from 838, contain no mention of this or any other posthumous miracles attributed to Leoba (Waitz, p. 118).

stole, who was accompanied by a young woman in nun's habit. In the man's vision, the young woman took him by the hand and lifted him up and presented him to the bishop for his blessing. When the bishop made the sign of the cross on the man's breast, an inky-black bird like a raven flew out of his bosom, restoring him to health. And so, Rudolph concludes, although Boniface and Leoba do not share a tomb, they nevertheless lie in one place, and show the same compassion to those who seek their intercession as they showed on earth to those who suffer.[106]

The eternal union that rewards Boniface and Leoba at the end of the Life, then, serves as a form of compensation to the reader for the frustration of earthly wishes, further affirming union in the spirit as a transcendent reality that prevails despite physical separation. Yet this is not a posthumous, eschatological union, but the eternal replication of their union in life. Obliquely, the vision of Leoba expresses her role as an evangelizer and partner of Boniface's missionary work, on which Rudolph has preserved such a discrete silence throughout the Life. Leoba, in the vision, is a salvatrix who leads men to the blessing of the church; specifically, she functions as the suffering visionary's baptismal sponsor, initiating him into spiritual health as she leads him by the hand and raises him up to receive the bishop's sacramental exorcism of his sins.[107] Leoba and Boniface, as abbess and bishop united as protective nurturers in the cure of souls, are spiritual parents, an image that Hygeburg evoked with homely picturesqueness in her account of Bishop Willibald: "Willibald and Mother Church, like a hen that cherishes her offspring beneath her wings, won over many adoptive sons to the Lord, protecting them continually with the shield of his kindliness."[108] The depiction of Leoba in the vision, perpetually youthful, interceding for the mercy of Boniface, the aged Father, is in striking contrast with the earlier evocation of her as Lady of Victories who champions her people against the wrath of the heavens, and points to the incipient development of a less heroic, more sentimental cult of the Virgin, in which she is envisaged, not as Mother, but as the eternal feminine.

Rudolph's depiction of the relationship of Leoba and Boniface in his Life is not directly modeled on the account of Benedict and his sister in Gregory's *Dialogues*. It derives from the hagiographical elaboration of kindred soul relationships between men and women, and the connexion of these relationships with the partnership of bishops and abbesses who, as heads of the church, symbolize the union of Christ and Mary-*Ecclesia*. These conventions are represented in English hagiography by Eddius's *Life of Wilfrid* and Felix's *Life of Guthlac*. Continental conventions probably developed independently, but Willibald was an English priest, and Rudolph is also likely to have been familiar with English hagiography, since the Anglo-Saxon mission transmitted to the continent the devotional texts that were in use in English monasteries. Felix's *Life of Guthlac* is among the English works that may have been known in areas where Anglo-Saxon missionaries were active: it survives in continental copies, and is

---

[106] Ch. 23.

[107] For an instance of the employment of rebaptism in miracles of healing, see HE, V.6.

[108] Talbot, p. 176; *Life of Willibald*, ch. 6. Hygeburg's "Mother Church" might be a figurative allusion to her abbess, Waldburg, the sister of Willibald; see fn. 14.

dedicated to an East Anglian king who was in correspondence with Boniface.[109] Rudolph's *Life of Leoba* resembles the *Life of Guthlac* in its presentation of a kindred-soul relation that ultimately figures the mystic church. Together with Eddius's *Life of Wilfrid*, the *Life of Guthlac* casts light on the scene in which Boniface announces his impending death, an announcement which is made to Lul alone in Willibald's Life but to both Lul and Leoba in Rudolph's Life, and in the presence of the senior monks of Fulda.

The kindred soul relations in the Lives of Wilfrid and Guthlac are intimately bound up with the possession of supernatural power and charisma, particularly through inheritance. Christ entrusted his disciples with his teachings and warned them of his impending death; at his departure he bade them spread his teachings throughout the nations, and, promising them his continued presence in the spirit, he left with them his peace. The disciples Christ chose, then, are his heirs, and the privileged recipients of the foreknowledge of his death to whom he communicates his departing instructions. But at the cross there remained only Mary and his beloved disciple John, who, in the eyes of the Celtic church, was more truly the apostolic successor of Christ than Peter, through whom the Church of Rome claimed inheritance of the power of the keys.[110] To John, as his surrogate, Christ commended the care of his mother and widowed bride, whose presence in this scene is exegetically related to her status as a type of the church: "When Jesus therefore saw his mother, and the disciple standing by, whom he loved, he saith unto his mother, 'Woman behold thy son!' Then saith he to the disciple, 'Behold thy mother!' And from that hour that disciple took her unto his own home."[111] As a bishop is Christ's successor and earthly representative, so an abbess may emblematize Christ's bride and widowed mother. As ruler of a double monastery, I have suggested, the abbess was iconographically connected with Mary, in the care of Christ's spiritual sons. As the special friend of a bishop – particularly if she was, like Leoba, especially eminent and uniquely privileged as an intimate – an abbess could figure Mary-*Ecclesia*. The equation of bishop and abbess with Christ and Mary, united as Mother and Father of the Church, gives figurative expression to their working partnership and approximately equal status as heads of the church. It entails the abbess's participation in the bishop's spiritual charisma, which hagiography expresses as the ability of an abbess to perform miracles through the episcopal saint's power. It also hints, darkly, at abbesses' participation in the sacerdotal offices of bishops, such as the administration of confession.[112]

Hagiography presents, in imitation of Christ, ecclesiastical office-holders who reveal in confidence to their successors the approach of their death, and entrust to them their last wishes and spiritual inheritance.[113] In Eddius's *Life of Wilfrid* secular practices of designating an heir and executor blend with ecclesiastical

---

[109] See Tangl, 81; for continental manuscripts of *Life of Guthlac* and identification of Boniface's correspondent with its dedicatee, see Colgrave, 1956, pp. 16, 34–44.

[110] See *HE*, III.25. The sole presence of Mary the Mother is traditional (cf. John 19.25).

[111] John 19.26–7.

[112] See ch. 6, pp. 188–90.

[113] With Wilfrid's nomination of his successors (see below), cf. *Bede's Cuthbert*, ch. 8. Boisil, whom Cuthbert succeeded as Prior of Melrose, reveals to him his impending death; he also spends the last week of his life studying the gospel of St John with Cuthbert, and foretells the future course of Cuthbert's life.

conceptions of apostolic succession which involve the transference of spiritual charisma. Entirely untroubled by the fact that the *Rule of Benedict* requires an abbot to be elected by consent of the whole community and forbids abbots to appoint their own kinsmen as their successors,[114] Eddius relates that Bishop Wilfrid appointed his kinsman Tatberht to succeed him as the abbot of Ripon. Tatberht's position as heir to Wilfrid's abbacy is confirmed by the confidential revelations Wilfrid imparts to him shortly before his death. As the aged King Hrothgar bestows on his adopted son Beowulf the sum of his life's experience,[115] Wilfrid, "as though he foresaw his death," told to Tatberht the story of his life as they were riding along one day. Wilfrid bestowed on his successor, then, his spiritual inheritance as a sign that his end was at hand. At the same time he charged Tatberht with his instructions regarding the distribution of his earthly inheritance – he recounted to him all the lands in various localities that he had previously given to abbots or now willed to give.[116]

When Wilfrid died, Eddius relates, Tatberht sent the cloak on which his body had lain to "the abbess of our holy bishop, Cynethryth by name." Tatberht instructed the abbess to keep the soiled cloak for him, just as it was, until he required it. Disregarding his instruction, however, Abbess Cynethryth washed it, and a nun who plunged her arm into the water was miraculously healed in the manner of the woman who touched the hem of Jesus's robe. As the robe taken from the crucified Christ is exegetically interpreted as the Church in its mystical sense, the mantle of Christ's saint fittingly descends upon his chosen abbatical successor. Cynethryth's role in this episode is explicable in terms of a figurative identification with Mary and Mother Church, repository of the mysteries and channel of miraculous grace, wherein Christ, though physically absent, remains perpetually present with her in the spirit. Wilfrid's devoted supporter Abbess Æbbe is permitted to exercise a version of the power to bind and unbind – but only as an intermediary of Bishop Wilfrid; the pressures towards exclusion of women from the sacerdotal ministry manifested in *Theodore's Penitential* surface more markedly in Tatberht's instructions regarding the bishop's cloak.[117] The Marian partners of Guthlac and Boniface are more fully and directly endowed with spiritual inheritance by the Christ-saint.

Felix's depiction of St Guthlac's sister Pega as his kindred soul and a type of Mary-*Ecclesia* may reflect his familiarity with an allegorical interpretation of *Canticles* as a mystic union (or "soul union") of Christ and his sister.[118] Exegesis of *Canticles* inevitably enhanced the figurative construction of Mary and the church as the Bride of Christ; as the marital-erotic relationship rose to prominence as the metaphoric vehicle of mystic union, Christ's relation to Mary and the Church was less commonly conceived in terms other than nuptial. But, as

---

114 *Rule of Benedict*, chs. 2, 58.
115 *Beowulf*, ll. 946–56, 1698–1784.
116 *Life of Wilfrid*, chs. 64, 65. Wilfrid's episcopal successor was Acca, to whom, with Tatberht, Eddius's Life is dedicated. Acca is endowed with tokens of his succession in *Life of Wilfrid*, ch. 56; Wilfrid reveals to him alone the vision which portends his death four years later. For other spiritual heirs in English hagiography, see ch. 6, fns. 34, 37.
117 See *Life of Wilfrid*, chs. 39, 66; *Theodore's Penitential*, II.vii.1–4.
118 For Bede's exegetical commentary on *Canticles*, see CCSL 119B, 175–375.

Aldhelm reminded the nuns of Barking, by her shared descent from God the Father, Mary was also a sister of Christ,[119] and in *Canticles* the woman whom exegesis equates with Mary and the church is addressed by her Christ-lover as "sister" as well as "spouse."[120] Felix, however, was an assiduous borrower of hagiographical motifs; seemingly, he wished to endow his hermit saint with the signs that distinguished episcopal saints in the Lives known to him.[121] Felix's allegorical casting of the relation of Pega and her brother, then, is possibly influenced by exegesis of *Canticles*, but may also have been prompted by his understanding of the abbess-bishop relation as a motif in episcopal saints Lives. The woman most closely linked with Felix's hermit saint, however, was his sister – for although Benedict and Scholastica doubtless provided the authorizing precedent for Felix's depiction of an affinity between brother and sister, Felix's report that Pega inherited her brother's anchorage presumably represents the factual explanation for her introduction into the Life.

Like Rudolph, Felix has transmuted a male-female kinship of flesh and blood into the kinship of souls, purged and spiritualized through absence; here too, polemical idealization of the ascetic renunciation of natural kinship ties has the simultaneous effect of affirming the strength of those ties. Guthlac's sister Pega is not mentioned until he announces his impending death to his servant. Guthlac, foreseeing his death, designates his sister as the person to whom his servant is to take the news of his death. "After my spirit has left this poor body," he instructs his servant, "go to my sister and tell her that I have in this life avoided her presence so that in eternity we may see one another in the presence of our Father amid eternal joys."[122] Because Guthlac has sacrificed the earthly joy of his sister's presence, he looks forward at death to the compensation of eternal union with her, in which they will share the heavenly reward that his sacrifice has won. Guthlac's words are an echo of Matthew 19.29: "And every one that hath forsaken houses, or brethren, or sisters, or father, or mother, or wife, or children, or lands, for my name's sake, shall receive a hundredfold, and shall inherit everlasting life."[123] The eternal reward promised those who forsake kindred has been interpreted in Guthlac's dying wishes, not as a heavenly reward that is transcendentally distinct from earthly joy, but as the eternal restoration of the earthly good that was sacrificed – testimony to the emotional potency of kinship relations could scarcely go further than Guthlac's conception of eternal joy as union with his sister.[124]

Pega's reception of the news of Guthlac's death both affirms her close affinity

119 *De Virginitate*, ch. 40.

120 See esp. S. of S. 4.9–12.

121 E.g., Abbess Ecgburg in *Life of Guthlac*, ch. 48, mirrors Ælffled's request to Cuthbert for a prophecy of the king's successor, and Guthlac's request to be buried in the shroud she gave him (ch. 50) recalls Abbess Verca as the donor of Cuthbert's burial shroud: see *Bede's Cuthbert*, chs. 24, 37. See further ch. 6, fns. 109, 122, 124.

122 Colgrave, p. 155; *Life of Guthlac*, ch. 50.

123 Matt. 19.29 was a popular hagiographic text: see, e.g., *History of the Abbots*, ch. 1; *Life of Wilfrid*, ch. 4.

124 Pega is the only Anglo-Saxon female saint commemorated in OE *Martyrology* not found in HE. She owes her place to the Mercian compiler's familiarity with the cult of her brother, being remembered as the sister of Guthlac, and for the miraculous cure found in *Life of Guthlac*, ch. 53 (see Kotzor, II, 282).

as kindred soul and points towards her identification as Marian mourner for the departed Christ in the closing scenes of the Life. Sharing her brother's sufferings in death as, though absent, she has shared them in life by his physical severance from her, Pega falls to the ground in a death-like trance when she learns of Guthlac's death, for like Mary, whose identification with Christ's sufferings on the cross is prophesied by Simeon ("a sword shall pierce through thy own soul also").[125] Like Tatberht, Pega is surrounded by signs that mark her as a chosen heir of the saint. By proxy, she is the uniquely privileged recipient of the news of Guthlac's death and the confidential knowledge of his life. More specifically, she is the heir to the saint's mystery: Guthlac bids his confidential messenger to reveal to her alone the knowledge of the prophetic and visionary powers and their invisible, secret source. But, by analogy with Mary and John at the foot of the cross, who together figure the Church, Pega, as a repository of the super-natural knowledge left by the departing Christ-saint, is linked with a male anchorite who has more direct and intimate insight into the mysteries than she: "Keep these words of mine," Guthlac exhorts his messenger "and tell them to no-one except to Pega or Ecgberht if ever you should happen to converse with him, for he alone will know that such things have happened to me."[126] Guth-lac's designation of Pega as the one who is to carry out his burial rites, in accordance with the instructions he gives his messenger, assists her typological identification with Mother Church, and may be an additional sign that marks Pega as his heir.[127]

Inheritor of Guthlac's mystery, and projected co-sharer of the eternal joy that he has won, Pega is also the heir to Guthlac's hermitage; strictly speaking, she is the regent until the coming of Guthlac's appointed successor who, in accord-ance with Guthlac's prophecy to Abbess Eadburg, was "still among the pagans" at the time of his death.[128] But Pega, at the end of the Life, is the effective heir of her brother's micro-kingdom; she takes possession of the fenland island that he won by his victorious conquest against the demons who inhabited it when he first took up his abode – anchorages, more acceptably than monastic lands, could be treated as family property.[129] In accordance with Guthlac's instructions,

[125] Life of Guthlac, ch. 50; cf. Luke 2.35.

[126] Colgrave, p. 157; Life of Guthlac, ch. 50. Ecgburg and Ecgberht are confused in ch. 51, the attribution of the gift of the burial shroud to "Ecgberht anachorita" clearly being a scribal error (cf. ch. 48), but the original mention of the anchorite Ecgberht in Guthlac's instruction to the messenger presumably is not.

[127] In Carmen de Hastingae Proelio, William the Conqueror insists on burying the body of Harold Godwinson himself, and assumes the name of king beside the howe: ed. and trans. C. Morton and H. Muntz (Oxford, 1972), pp. 38–9. P.E. Schramm, A History of the English Coronation, trans. L.G. Wickham-Legg (Oxford 1937), pp. 4, 38, regards this as an appeal to "that pre-Christian magic by which a king took his stand on the tumulus of his predecessor."

[128] Life of Guthlac, ch. 48. Inheritance of Guthlac's shrine is a significant issue in the Life; Beccel, the servant who conveys Guthlac's revelations to Pega, attempted to kill Guthlac to gain his hermitage (ch. 35). Abbess Ecgburg as recipient of Guthlac's prophecy serves to validate possession of the hermitage by Cissa, who occupied it in Felix's time.

[129] Alcuin's Prologue to the Life of his kinsman Willibrord mentions his inheritance of the hermitage built by the saint's father (ed. W. Levison, MGH SRM 7, 81–141). Cf. Christina of Markyate's inheritance, as adopted daughter, of the hermitage of the male anchorite with whom she shared a cell for many years (Life of Christina of Markyate, pp. 20–2). Felix is presumably implying that, even before the death of Guthlac, Pega was already an anchorite, and thus united

she takes charge of his burial rites, and later is the witness to the uncorruption of his body when she supervises his translation to the shrine that has been built for it. She gives permission for a man who is blind to be brought to Guthlac's shrine, and, with the aid of a relic of Guthlac – a piece of salt that he had blessed – she miraculously restores the pilgrim's sight.[130] Pega, then, is a type of Mary-*Ecclesia*; repository of Guthlac's mysteries and mediator of his miraculous healing power, she is like Mary a mourner at the tomb and witness to a miracle of incorruption, and a type of the church in her role as guardian of the shrine and the administrator of the Christ-saint's cult.

Rudolph's culminating portrait of Leoba and Boniface – kindred souls divided in life who, united eternally, achieve identification with the heavenly *Ecclesia* that they figure on earth by their partnership as abbess and bishop – is the fulfilment of the scene of Boniface's departure. In Willibald's *Life of Boniface*, Boniface's designated episcopal successor Lul is the inseparable companion and kindred soul of the saint. When Boniface departs, wittingly, to the martyrdom awaiting him in Frisia, Lul is the uniquely privileged recipient of the Christ-saint's revelation of his impending death. Their spiritual affinity is affirmed by Lul's putatively uncanny arrival in Mainz at the very same moment as Boniface's body.[131] Lul's commission to carry out Boniface's instructions for his burial, assimilated to the convention of confidential intimacy in the saint's revelation of his death to his kindred soul, becomes a clear sign of his role as the appointed heir – not only is he instructed to take the body to Fulda but, sharing the saint's prophetic foreknowledge of his death, he is also privately entrusted with the task of ensuring that Boniface's shroud is packed to accompany him on his journey to Frisia. Charged with the continuation of the evangelical mission and the church building that Boniface has set on foot, entrusted by Boniface with the care of the souls that he had already won for Christ, Lul is unquestionably the apostolic successor. In Rudolph's account, Lul retains the configurations of apostolic successor, but loses his uniquely privileged status as kindred soul – as he must – when Boniface also summons Leoba to inform her of his imminent death, instructs her too to carry on with the mission she has begun, and reaffirms his desire to be united with her in death.[132]

On the one hand, Boniface's words to Leoba elaborate the heroic conception of her as comrade-in-arms; he urges her to go forward unflinchingly, undeterred

---

with him in absence. Post-Conquest tradition concerning Pega reflects the advance of stereotypes harking back to Eve – Henry of Avranches claimed that she lived with Guthlac on the island in the early stages of his hermit career, but when the devil assumed her appearance in order to persuade Guthlac to break his vow never to take food before sunset, he sent her away from the island in order to prevent such diabolical impersonations, and never saw her again (Colgrave, 1956, p. 24).

130 *Life of Guthlac*, chs. 51, 53. See further fn. 136.

131 *Life of Boniface*, ch. 12.

132 Ch. 17. With Willibald's description of Lul as the companion of his journeying, sharing his sufferings and consolations in *Life of Boniface*, ch. 10 ("comes peregrinationis eius erat, et testis utrubique passionis et consolationis," p. 348), cf. Boniface's request for the presence of Leoba, ch. 10, "ad solatium suae peregrinationis atque ad auxilium legationis sibi iniunctae transmitteret ei Leobam virginem," p. 125). Levison, 1946, p. 76, n. 2, considers that Willibald's *Life of Boniface* was among Rudolph's sources.

by physical weakness. On the other hand, she is commended to Lul and the senior monks at Fulda, who are to care for her with reverence and respect: thus placed in the protective keeping of Boniface's spiritual son and his monastic brothers, Leoba assumes the aspect of the widowed bride and mother of Christ. Lul, a distinctly Petrine successor in the *Life of Boniface* – appointed and consecrated by Boniface himself – has become Johanine; his protection of the abbess, summoned with him to witness the departing words of the saint, figures the care of the Church that Boniface has entrusted to him. In the context of this recollection of Mary and John at the foot of the cross, Boniface's concern for the future of Leoba takes on the colour of allegory. The ongoing apostolic mission to which Boniface's reported speech urges her, her continuing role as the partner and female counterpart of his episcopal successor, are neatly assimilated to her symbolic status as Mary-*Ecclesia*, the Church as Mother.

Fulda appears, at least in Rudolph's Life, to have been no more willingly mindful of this parting instruction than of Boniface's intentions concerning his burial. Lul, for his part, was not unaccustomed to the role of protector of the monastic daughters of Mary with which Rudolph's Life endows him, though the letter he wrote to Leoba prior to the death of Boniface is without the effusive courtly homage of incipient *Frauendienst* that characterizes his offers of service to the extremely powerful Abbess Cyniburg who taught him at the double monastery he had left behind in England.[133] His letter to Leoba is not without interest for the light it casts on Rudolph's valorization of absence – just as Boniface regretted that his desire for exile in the service of Christ made it impossible for him to offer in person his consolations for the troubles that beset his old friend Abbess Bugga,[134] Lul assumes that his physical presence is the appropriate expression of his spiritual affinity with Leoba and his concern for her: "Although for a long time we have been kept apart in the body," he assured her, "you must not believe that our true kinship in the Lord has been given over to contempt or forgetfulness. Nor must you suppose that I am at all weary with your affairs, but only, as you should know, occupied by the crafty wiles of the devil and worn out by the cunning assaults of his ministers . . . . Should anything be wanting that you need, tell me of it through the deacon Gundwin, who is to return here."[135]

In striking contrast with Tatberht's possessive handling of the mantle of Wilfrid, Boniface at his departure bestows his visible token of perpetual presence, not on his appointed episcopal successor, but on Leoba; yet, as Felix's Life shows, this is not without allegorical aptness. The personal significance with which Boniface's gift of the cowl is potentially charged – a part of himself that he leaves to sustain her in the continuation of her labours in an alien land – is thus distanced by the typological construction of the scene. The cowl does not function in any overt way in the Life as the perpetual source of miraculous grace reposing in Leoba as Mother Church. Leoba, like Pega, employs for the performance of a miracle a gift of rock salt blessed by the departed saint, which

---

133 Tangl, 49; see also Lul's offers of service to Abbess Eadburg, Tangl, 70.
134 Tangl, 94.
135 Kylie, p. 107; Tangl, 100.

she always kept by her.[136] How great Leoba's own stature – or, what is the same thing, how willing her hagiographer to grant her supernatural gifts – is revealed by the fact that she is unique in early hagiography as a female saint who performs a miracle of healing with the aid of one of her own familiar possessions, the small spoon she habitually used at meals.[137]

Thus imaged in the role of Maria-*Ecclesia*, Leoba, in seeking proximity to the grave of Boniface in her visits to Fulda "to pray in the church," can be regarded, like Guthlac's sister Pega, as a symbol of the Church in its aspect of perpetual mourner for the martyred dead. In life as in death, Leoba's presence in the exclusively male precincts of Fulda lays a heavy burden of explanation on Rudolph: "The following regulations, however, were observed when she came there. Her disciples and companions were left behind in a nearby cell and she entered the monastery always in daylight, with one nun older than the rest; and after she had finished her prayers and held a conversation with the brethren, she returned towards nightfall to her disciples whom she had left behind in the cell." Whether or not it is strictly true that Leoba's visits to the Fulda monastery were "a privilege never granted before or since to any woman," whether, indeed, her visits to the Fulda monastery were, in actuality, solely for the purpose of praying at Boniface's tomb (for Rudolph concedes that she took the opportunity to talk with the monks) her presence at Fulda after the death of Boniface, like her burial in the monastery church, is explicable only in the terms that Rudolph offers: permission was only granted for her visits, he claims, "for the simple reason that the holy martyr St Boniface had commended her to the seniors of the monastery and because he had ordered her remains to be buried there."[138]

(3) Conclusion: Leoba and Queen Hildegard as kindred souls

Despite Rudolph's successful neutralization of Boniface's dying wish, his anxieties concerning the relation of Boniface and Leoba continue to manifest themselves in the inclusion of an extended account of Leoba's friendship with Queen Hildegard. Reticent in the extreme on Leoba's kindred-soul relation with Boniface, Rudolph offers instead a portrait of her spiritual affinity with Charlemagne's second wife.[139] By this strategic transference, Leoba's attachment to Boniface – and the focus of the reader's attention – is redirected into a relationship between Leoba and a member of her own sex; the demands of canonical segregation have finally been satisfied. Like Bishop Wilfrid in his relation with King Alhfrith,[140] Leoba is the intimate friend and spiritual mentor

---

[136] Ch. 13. The thaumaturgic usefulness of rock salt whose natural curative powers had been enhanced by a saint's blessing probably accounts for its possession by women in the these two Lives. English monastic women, as well as men, evidently studied the healing arts, since incense, pepper and cinnamon, which Lul sent to Anglo-Saxon abbesses (Tangl, 49, 70), were pharmaceutical ingredients. But salt was also used in the preparation of holy water for baptism.
[137] Ch. 15.
[138] Talbot, p. 223; ch. 19.
[139] Chs. 18, 20. The posthumous communication and visions of souls ascending at death in Bede's accounts of Barking and Whitby (*HE*, IV.8, 9, 19) possibly reflect "soul unions" between monastic women; see further ch. 6, fn. 34.
[140] *Life of Wilfrid*, chs. 7, 9; see further pp. 151–2.

of Queen Hildegard, who loved Leoba "as her own soul," and would have liked her to remain always by her side so that she might progress in the spiritual life and profit by her words and example. But here, too, earthly union is denied in hope of heavenly reward, the soul friendship rendered exemplary by being spiritualized through absence. Leoba, particularly detesting life at court, renounces the world altogether by becoming an anchorite, and answers a final summons from the queen only with considerable reluctance. Even on discovering that the "most precious half of her soul" has summoned her to announce her impending death, Leoba refuses to remain beside the queen for her last few days on earth, and stays only to make her speech of farewell. Recognizing that the death of one to whom she is so closely bound in the spirit spells her own end, Leoba returns to her anchorage, immediately sickens, and dies a few days later.[141]

The polemical intentions of this soul-friendship are as transparent as they are in the hagiographic depiction of bishops as the soul-friends of kings; such friendships project an interest in fostering closer relations between the throne and the church. Boniface could commend Leoba to the care of senior monks at Fulda, but female religious could not expect the same assistance from their spiritual brothers under segregated monasticism, and Rudolph's shifting of attention to Leoba's union with Hildegard is an implicit encouragement to seek instead the protective patronage of the queen. Alcuin's letter to Abbess Æthelburg, which relays a gift from Luitgard, the wife of Charlemagne, and urges the abbess to cultivate her friendship, points in the same direction.[142] Under the stricter segregation and enclosure of the English monasteries envisaged by Regularis Concordia, restrictions on abbesses' dealings with the world at large produced an enhancement in the role of the queen at the further expense of abbesses' autonomous rule. Regularis Concordia, instructing abbesses to seek assistance from no other secular but the queen,[143] formally endowed her with the position of protective patron of the convents and Mother of the Church; to the queen, effectively, passed the role of paramount abbess of all England. The depth of Regularis Concordia's preoccupation with gender division is evident from its extension into the royal marriage, and the segregated patronage that it envisages – King Edgar helping the monks and Queen Ælfthryth protecting the nuns in order to avoid even a hint of scandal[144] – is graphically imaged at the great Easter gathering described in the Life of Oswald, where Ælfthryth eats in one room with the nuns and Edgar and the monks in another.[145] It is a con-

---

141 Cf. Bishop Aidan, who foresaw the death of his soul friend King Oswine and died twelve days after him (HE, III.14); see further p. 197.

142 Duemmler, 102 (conceivably connected with Alcuin's attempts to make peace between Charlemagne and Offa of Mercia, the abbess's father). Waldburg's Life also links her with royal women; see fn. 59.

143 Regularis Concordia, p. 7. Regularis Concordia allows abbesses to seek the assistance of the queen, and permits the invitation of secular notables to the monastery; it is less concerned to subordinate abbesses to the control of bishops than is the continental legislation of the latter half of the 9th c. analyzed by Schulenburg, 51–86. For queens' patronage of the monasteries in the late AS period, see Meyer, 34–61.

144 Regularis Concordia, p. 2.

145 Vita Oswaldi Auctore Anonymo, ed. Raine, I, 425. Knowles, 1963, p. 42, suggests that the Easter gathering described here was actually the occasion of the Winchester Council which led to the composition of Regularis Concordia.

comitant of this shift that, in the hagiography of the late Old English period, the female friend of an episcopal saint is a queen rather than an abbess.[146]

Rudolph's redirection of a friendship between male and female monastic comrades into the monosexual union of queen and abbess is, then, no less emblematic of historical developments than his reconstructed portrait of the double monastery at Wimbourne. But the warmth of Leoba's farewell to the queen is in striking contrast with the high degree of rarification postulated by Rudolph's spiritual union in absence, and exceeds the requirements of the rhetorical and polemical purposes that this friendship serves: "Embracing her friend rather more affectionately than usual, she kissed her on the mouth, the forehead and the eyes and took leave of her with these words: 'Farewell for evermore, my dearly beloved lady and sister; farewell, most precious half of my soul. May Christ our Creator and Redeemer grant that we shall meet again without shame on the day of judgement. Never more on earth shall we enjoy each other's presence.' "[147] To make speculation overt, Rudolph appears to me to have not simply relocated Leoba's kindred-soul relation with Boniface, but to have reassigned the words that he spoke to her – Leoba's farewell speech to the queen, in other words, is explicable as the words that tradition ascribed to Boniface himself when he parted from Leoba. The speech of farewell, it may be noted, is not directed to union in heaven as the reward of earthly separation; it is a lament for the severance of earthly union that hopes for its renewal in eternity.

There were, as Rudolph intimates, a number of existing Lives of Leoba. More pervasively, her fame circulated by oral report. Rudolph affirms that there were "several men still living who can vouch for the facts mentioned in the documents, since they heard them from their predecessors, and can add some others worthy of remembrance." But the four nuns at Bischofsheim who had been closely associated with Leoba cannot have passed on her life history only to the venerable men whom Rudolph mentions as the authors of the existing Lives – it was surely handed down also to the Bischofsheim community, and spread to other monasteries by the abbesses whom Leoba had taught.[148] Above all, there was the unedited, first-hand report from Mago of Fulda – dead only five years since – of what the nuns at Bischofsheim had told him. But Mago's record, in the opinion of Rudolph, gave quite the wrong impression – as he is at pains to explain:

He was careful to make short notes of everything he heard, but, unfortunately, what he left was almost unintelligible, because, whilst he was trying to be brief and succinct, he expressed things in such a way as to leave the

---

[146] Ælfric's *Life of Æthelwold*, ch. 7 (ed. Winterbottom, 1972, pp. 15–29), relates that Eadgifu, King Eadred's mother, prevailed on Æthelwold to remain in England and secured the Abingdon monastery for him by using her influence with the king: Meyer, 34–61, assigns her an important supporting role in the successes of the Benedictine reformers. Whereas episcopal saints like Cuthbert are said to have paid friendly visits to monastic women, Ælfwynn, whom Dunstan visits in Author B's Life of Dunstan, ch. 12, is described as a noblewoman.

[147] Talbot, p. 224; ch. 20. "Vale in aeternum, domina et soror dilectissima! vale, animae meae portio pretiosa! Christus creator et redemptor noster tribuat, ut nos in die iudicii sine confusione videamus! Ceterum in hac luce mutuo numquam ab hac die fruemur aspectu" (p. 130).

[148] See fn. 86.

facts open to misunderstanding and provide no basis for certainty. This happened, in my opinion, because in his eagerness to take down every detail before it escaped his memory he wrote the facts down in a kind of shorthand and hoped that during his leisure he could put them in order and make the book more easy for people to understand. The reason why he left everything in such disorder, jotted down on odd pieces of parchment, was that he died quite suddenly and had no time to carry out his purpose."[149]

Hrabanus Maurus, in instructing Rudolph to compose a new Life, appears to have been of the same opinion concerning Mago's account. Rudolph's Life, written no more than a year before Hrabanus moved to implement the final solution to the problematic presence of Leoba, serves the purpose of providing an authoritative re-interpretation of awkward and well-known facts – most evidently, the instructions Boniface gave for his burial fell into this category, but so also, I suspect, did his last words to Leoba. Rudolph's work is, wittingly, an announcement that the pioneering era of monasticism was over. In England, as on the continent, there are signs of residual survival of the double monastery organization into the 10th century;[150] there were a few attempted revivals, most notably by the Gilbertine order, founded in England in the mid 12th century. But in the main, male and female religious would henceforward pursue their common goal in absence behind their identically strong and lofty walls. Inasmuch as the monasteries were the seminal site for the construction of generic alterity, the undying lament of the woman in *Wulf and Eadwacer* will serve with particular aptness as an elegy for the double monastery: "Wulf is on one island, I am on another . . . unalike are we."[151]

[149] Talbot, pp. 205–6; ch. 1.
[150] For the continued existence of double monasteries in England and on the continent, see fns. 11, 14. For the resurgence of the double monastery organization, see S.K. Elkins, "All Ages, Every Condition, and Both Sexes: The Emergence of a Gilbertine Identity," and P.S. Gold, "Male/Female Cooperation: The Example of Fontevrault," ed. Nichols and Shank, I, 151–68, 169–82. Although Fontevrault and the Gilbertine foundations formally included men and women, they were not in actuality a single community. Gilbert laid down that the canons were only to have access to the women when they were dying, and also required the presence of witnesses (Elkins, 171); at Fontevrault too, contact between men and women was strictly limited and the women were engaged solely in psalm singing and contemplation, physical and spiritual labours being assigned only to men (Gold, 152). The organizational inclusion of male communities in these later foundations, then, does not signify an attitude to monastic women that differed significantly from that which underlay the establishment of segregated monasteries, and the conditions governing the lives of female religious were not altered by their formal unification with male communities.
[151] See *Wulf and Eadwacer*, ll. 4–8.

Works Cited

Primary Sources

Allott, S., trans. *Alcuin of York*. York, 1974.

Anderson, A.O, and M.O. Anderson, ed. and trans. *Adomnán's Life of Columba*. Rev. edn. Oxford, 1991.

Antropoff, R. von, ed. *Die Entwicklung der Kenelm-Legende*. Inaugural Dissertation. Bonn, 1965.

Arnold, T., ed. *Symeonis Monachi Opera Omnia*. RS 75. 2 vols. London, 1882–5.

Assmann, B., ed. *Angelsächsische Homilien und Heiligenleben*. Bib ags Prosa 3. Kassel, 1889.

Barlow, F., ed. *The Life of King Edward who Rests at Westminster*. London, 1962.

Bately, J.M., ed. *The Anglo-Saxon Chronicle: MS A*. Anglo-Saxon Chronicle Collaborative Edition 3. Cambridge, 1986.

Benson, L.D., ed. *The Riverside Chaucer*. Oxford, 1988.

Bieler, L., ed. and trans. *The Irish Penitentials*. With an Appendix by D.A. Binchy. Scriptores Latini Hiberniae 5. Dublin, 1963.

Birch, W. de G., ed. *Cartularium Saxonicum*. 3 vols. London, 1885–93.

Blake, E.O., ed. *Liber Eliensis*. RHS Camden 3rd ser. 92. London, 1962.

Bodden, M.C., ed. and trans. *The Old English Finding of the True Cross*. Cambridge, 1987.

Boretius, A., et al. *MGH Legum II Capitularia Regum Francorum I*. Hannover, 1883.

Bradley, S.A.J., trans. *Anglo-Saxon Poetry*. London, 1982.

Campbell, A., ed. and trans. *Encomium Emmae Reginae*. RHS Camden 3rd ser. 72. London, 1949.

Campbell, A., ed. and trans. *The Chronicle of Æthelweard*. London, 1962.

Chibnall, M., ed. and trans. *The Ecclesiastical History of Orderic Vitalis*. Vol. II. Oxford, 1969.

Clark, C., ed. *The Peterborough Chronicle, 1070–1154*. 2nd edn. Oxford, 1970.

Clarke, D.E.M., ed. and trans. *The Hávamál*. Cambridge, 1923.

Cockayne, O., ed. and trans. "Lambeth Fragment" and "S. Mildryth." In *Leechdoms, Wortcunning and Starcraft of Early England*. London, 1866. Vol. III, 422–33.

Colgrave, B., ed. and trans. *The Life of Bishop Wilfrid by Eddius Stephanus*. Cambridge, 1927.

Colgrave B., ed. and trans. *Two Lives of Saint Cuthbert: A Life by an Anonymous Monk of Lindisfarne and Bede's Prose Life*. Cambridge, 1940.

Colgrave, B., ed. and trans. *Felix's Life of Saint Guthlac*. Cambridge, 1956.

Colgrave, B., ed. and trans. *The Earliest Life of Gregory the Great by an Anonymous Monk of Whitby*. Lawrence, Ka, 1968.

Colgrave, B. and R.A.B. Mynors, ed. and trans. *Bede's Ecclesiastical History of the English People*. Oxford, 1969.

Craig, H., ed. *Two Coventry Corpus Christi Plays*. EETS ES 87. 2nd edn. London, 1957.

Crawford, S.J., ed. *The Old English Version of the Heptateuch*. EETS OS 160. London, 1922.

Cyprian. *De Habitu Virginum. PL* 4, 335–64.

Dalton, O.M., trans. *The History of the Franks by Gregory of Tours*. 2 vols. Oxford, 1927.

Davis, N., ed. *Sir Gawain and the Green Knight*. 2nd rev. edn. Oxford, 1967.

Deferrari, R.J., ed. and trans. *St Basil: The Letters*. Loeb Classical Library. 4 vols. London, 1926–34.

Doble, G.H., ed. *Pontificale Lanaletense*. HBS 74. London, 1937.

Dobson, E.J., ed. *The English Text of the Ancrene Riwle*. EETS OS 267. London, 1972.

Dronke, U., ed. and trans. *The Poetic Edda*. Oxford, 1969.

DuBuis, J., and G. Renaud, ed. *Édition practique des martyrologes de Bède, de l'anonyme lyonnais et de Florus*. Paris, 1976.

Duemmler, E., ed. *Epistolae Karolini Aevi II. MGH Epist* 4. Berlin, 1895.

Ehwald, R., ed. *Aldhelmi Opera. MGH AA* 15. Berlin, 1919.

Emerton, E., trans. *The Letters of Saint Boniface*. New York, 1940.

Esposito, M., ed. "La Vie de Sainte Vulfhilde par Goscelin de Cantorbéry." *AB* 32 (1913), 10–26.

Evagrius. *Vita Beati Antonii Abbatis Auctore Sancto Athanasio. PL* 73, 125–94.

Fell, C., ed. *Edward King and Martyr*. Leeds, 1971.

Finsterwalder, P.W., ed. *Die Canones Theodori Cantuariensis und ihre Überlieferungsformen*. Weimar, 1929.

Fowler, R., ed. "A Late OE Handbook for the Use of a Confessor." *Anglia* 83 (1965), 1–34.

Fraipont, J., ed. *Bedae Venerabilis Opera, Pars IV, Opera Rhythmica*. CCSL 122. Turnhout, 1955.

Godman, P., ed. and trans. *Alcuin: The Bishops, Kings, and Saints of York*. Oxford, 1982.

Gregory the Great. *Regula Pastoralis. PL* 77, 12–130.

Gregory the Great. *Moralia in Job. PL* 75, 499–1162.

Haddan, A.W., and W. Stubbs, ed. *Councils and Ecclesiastical Documents Relating to Great Britain and Ireland*. 3 vols. Oxford, 1869–71.

Haefele, H.F., ed. *Notker der Stammler: Taten Kaiser Karls des Grossen*. SRG NS 12. Berlin, 1962.

Hall, G.D.G., ed. and trans. *The Treatise on the Laws and Customs of the Realm of England Commonly Called Glanvill*. London, 1965.

Harmer, F.E., ed. and trans. *Select English Historical Documents of the Ninth and Tenth Century*. Cambridge, 1914.

Harmer, F.E., ed. and trans. *Anglo-Saxon Writs*. Manchester, 1952.

Hecht, H., ed. *Bischofs Wærferth von Worcester Übersetzung der Dialoge Gregors des Grossen*. Bib ags Prosa 5. Leipzig, 1900.

Holder-Egger, O., ed. *Ex Wolfhardi Haserensis Miraculis S Waldburgis Monheimensibus. MGH SS* 15.1. Hannover, 1887, 535–55.

Holder-Egger, O., ed. *Vita Lulli Archiepiscopi Moguntini Auctore Lamberto Hersfeldensi.* MGH SS 15.1. Hannover, 1887, 132–48.

Holder-Egger, O., ed. *Vita Willibaldi Episcopi Eichstetensis.* MGH SS 15.1. Hannover, 1887, 86–106.

Holder-Egger, O., ed. *Vita Wynnebaldi Abbatis Heidenheimensis.* MGH SS. 15.1. Hannover, 1887, 106–17.

Holtzmann, R., ed. *Die Chronik des Bischofs Thietmar von Merseburg und ihre korveier Überarbeitung.* MGH SRG NS 9. 2nd edn. Berlin, 1955.

Horstman, C., ed. *Nova Legenda Anglie, as Collected by John of Tynmouth, John Capgrave and Others.* 2 vols. Oxford, 1901.

Hudson, J.E., ed. Bede, *In Habacuc.* CCSL 119B. Turnhout, 1983, 370–409.

Hugh of St Victor. *De Sacramentis Christianae Fidei.* PL 176, 173–618.

Hurst, D., ed. *Bedae Venerabilis Opera, pars III, Opera Homiletica.* CCSL 122. Turnhout, 1955.

Hurst, D., ed. Bede, *In Ezram et Neemiam.* CCSL 119A. Turnhout, 1969, 237–392.

Hurst, D., ed. Bede, *In Cantica Canticorum.* CCSL 119B. Turnhout, 1983, 167–375.

Jaager, W., ed. *Bedas metrische Vita Sancti Cuthberti.* Palaestra 198. Leipzig, 1935.

James, M.R., ed. "Two Lives of St Ethelbert, King and Martyr." EHR 32 (1917), 214–44.

Jonas of Orleans. *De Institutione Laicali.* PL 106, 122–278.

Jónsson, G., ed. *Edda Snorra Sturlusonar.* Copenhagen, 1931.

Jost, K., ed. *Die "Institutes of Polity, Civil and Ecclesiastical".* Bern, 1959.

Keynes, S., and M. Lapidge, trans. *Alfred the Great: Asser's "Life of King Alfred" and Other Contemporary Sources.* Harmondsworth, 1983.

Klaeber, F., ed. *Beowulf and the Fight at Finnsburg.* 3rd edn. Boston, 1950.

Kotzor, G., ed. *Das altenglische Martyrologium.* Bayerische Akademie der Wissenschaften, Phil.-Hist. Klasse Abhandlungen, NF 88.1, 2. 2 vols. München, 1981.

Krapp, G.P., and E.V.K. Dobbie, ed. *Anglo-Saxon Poetic Records.* 6 vols. New York, 1931–42.

Krusch, B., ed. *Venanti Fortunati Vita S Hilarii.* MGH AA 4.2. Hannover, 1885, 1–11.

Krusch, B., ed. *Vita S Balthildis.* MGH SRM 2. Hannover, 1888, 482–508.

Krusch, B., ed. *Vita S Geretrudis.* MGH SRM 2. Hannover, 1888, 453–74.

Krusch, B., ed. *Vita Eligii Episcopi Noviomagensis.* MGH SRM 4. Hannover, 1902, 663–742.

Krusch, B., ed. *Vitae Columbani Abbatis Disciplorumque Eius.* MGH SRG in usum scholarum. Hannover, 1905.

Kuhn, H., ed. *Edda: Die Lieder des Codex Regius nebst verwandten Denkmälern.* 4th rev. edn. 2 vols. Heidelberg, 1962.

Kylie, E., trans. *The English Correspondence of Saint Boniface.* London, 1911.

Lapidge, M., and M. Herren, trans. *Aldhelm: The Prose Works.* Cambridge, 1979.

Lapidge, M., and J.L. Rosier, trans. *Aldhelm: The Poetic Works.* With an Appendix by N. Wright. Cambridge, 1985.

Leo, F., ed. *Venanti Fortunati Opera Poetica.* MGH AA 4.1. Berlin, 1881.

Levison, W., ed. *Vita Bertilae Abbatissae Calensis.* MGH SRM 6. Hannover, 1913, 95–109.

Levison, W., ed. *Vita Willibrodi Archiepiscopi Traiectensis Auctore Alcuino*. MGH SRM 7. Hannover, 1920, 81–141.

Liebermann, F., ed. *Die Gesetze der Angelsachsen*. 3 vols. Halle, 1903–16.

Löfstedt, B., and G.J. Gebauer, ed. *Bonifatii (Vynfreth) Ars Grammatica*. CCSL 133B. Turnhout, 1980.

Lot, F., ed. *Chronique de l'abbaye de Saint Riquier*. Paris, 1894.

Mattingly, H., trans. *Tacitus on Britain and Germany*. Harmondsworth, 1948.

McNeill, J.T., and H.M. Gamer, trans. *Medieval Handbooks of Penance*. New York, 1938.

Metcalfe, W.M., ed. *Vita Margaritae Scotorum Reginae*. In *Pinkerton's Lives of the Scottish Saints*. Rev. edn., Paisley, 1889. II, 159–82.

Meyer, K., ed. *Cáin Adamnáin: An Old-Irish Treatise on the Law of Adamnan*. Oxford, 1905.

Miller, T., ed. and trans. *The Old English Version of Bede's Ecclesiastical History of the English People*. EETS OS 95, 96, 110, 111. London, 1890–8.

Morris, R., ed. *Legends of the Holy Rood*. EETS OS 46. London, 1871.

Morton, C., and H. Muntz, ed. *Carmen de Hastingae Proelio of Guy, Bishop of Amiens*. Oxford, 1972.

Napier, A.S., ed. *History of the Holy Rood Tree*. EETS OS 103. London, 1894.

Pertz, G.H., ed. *Vita S Bonifatii Archiepiscopi Auctore Willibaldo Presbytero*. MGH SS 2. Hannover, 1829, 331–53.

Pertz, G.H., ed. *Eigilis Vita S Sturmi Abbatis Fuldensis*. MGH SS 2. Hannover, 1829, 365–77.

Plummer, C., ed. *Venerabilis Baedae Opera Historica*. 2 vols. Oxford, 1896.

Plummer, C., ed. *Vitae Sanctorum Hiberniae*. 2 vols. Oxford, 1910.

Pseudo-Jerome. *Regula Monacharum*. PL 30, 391–426.

Raine, J. *The Historians of the Church of York and its Archbishops*. RS 71. 3 vols. London, 1879.

Rau, R., ed. and trans. *Bonifatii Epistulae, Willibaldi Vita Bonifatii*. Darmstadt, 1968. (Not sighted.)

Raith, J., ed. *Die altenglische Version des Halitgar'schen Bussbuches (sog. Pseudo-Ecgberti)*. Bib ags Prosa 13. Hamburg, 1933.

Robertson, A.J., ed. and trans. *Anglo-Saxon Charters*. 2nd edn. Cambridge, 1956.

Robinson, R.P., ed. *The Germania of Tacitus*. Middletown, Ct., 1935.

Schoell, R., and G. Kroll, ed. *Corpus Juris Civilis III: Novellae*. Berlin, 1963.

Sherley-Price, L., trans. *Bede: A History of the English Church and People*. Rev. edn. by R.E. Latham. Harmondsworth, 1984.

Shippey, T.A., ed. and trans. *Poems of Wisdom and Learning in Old English*. Cambridge, 1976.

Skeat, W.W., ed. and trans. *Ælfric's Lives of Saints*. EETS OS 76, 82, 94, 114. London, 1881–1900.

Spindler, R., ed. *Das altenglische Bussbuch (sog. Confessionale Pseudo-Egberti)*. Leipzig, 1934.

Stehling, T., trans. *Medieval Latin Poems of Male Love and Friendship*. New York, 1984.

Stevenson, J., ed. *Liber Vitae Ecclesiae Dunelmensis*. Surtees Soc. 13. London, 1841.

Stevenson, W.H., ed. *Asser's Life of King Alfred*. 2nd edn., rev. D. Whitelock. Oxford, 1959.

Stokes, W., ed. and trans. *The Martyrology of OEngus the Culdee*. HBS 29. London, 1905.

Stubbs, W., ed. *Memorials of Saint Dunstan*. RS 63. London, 1874.

Stubbs, W., ed. *Willelmi Malmsbiriensis Monachi De Gestis Regum Anglorum*. RS 90. 2 vols. London, 1887–9.

Sveinsson, E.O., ed. *Brennu-Njáls Saga. Islenzk Fomrit 12*. Reykjavik, 1954.

Swanton, M.J., ed. and trans. "A Fragmentary Life of St Mildred and Other Kentish Royal Saints." *Archaeologia Cantiana* 91 (1975), 15–27.

Swanton, M.J., ed. and trans. *Beowulf*. Manchester, 1978.

Sweet, H., ed. *King Alfred's West-Saxon Version of Gregory's Pastoral Care*. EETS OS 45, 50. London, 1871.

Symons, T., ed. and trans. *Regularis Concordia*. London, 1953.

Talbot, C.H., trans. *The Anglo-Saxon Missionaries in Germany*. London, 1954.

Talbot, C.H., ed. "The *Liber Confortatorius* of Goscelin of Saint Bertin." *Studia Anselmiana* 37 (1955), 1–117.

Talbot, C.H., ed. and trans. *The Life of Christina of Markyate*. Oxford, 1959.

Talbot, C.H., ed. Aelred of Rievaulx, *De Institutione Inclusarum*. CCCM I. Turnhout, 1971, 637–82.

Tangl, M., ed. *Die Briefe des heiligen Bonifatius und Lullus*. 2nd edn. MGH ES I. Berlin, 1955.

Thorpe, B., ed. *Florentii Wigorniensis Monachi Chronicon ex Chronicis*. 2 vols. London, 1848.

Taylor, S., ed. *The Anglo-Saxon Chronicle: MS B*. Anglo-Saxon Chronicle Collaborative Edition 4. Cambridge, 1983.

Vinaver, E., ed. *Malory: Le Morte Darthur*. London, 1954.

Vogüé, A. de, ed. *La Règle de Saint Benoît*. Paris, 1972.

Vogüé, A. de, ed. *Grégoire le Grand: Dialogues*. 3 vols. Paris, 1978–80.

Waitz, G., ed. *Rudolfi Miracula Sanctorum in Fuldenses Ecclesias Translatorum*. MGH SS 15.1. Hannover, 1887, 328–41.

Waitz, G., ed. *Vita Leobae Abbatissae Biscofesheimensis Auctore Rudolfo Fuldensi*. MGH SS 15.1. Hannover, 1887, 118–31.

Webb, J.F., and D.H. Farmer, trans. *The Age of Bede*. Rev. edn. Harmondsworth, 1983.

Werminghoff A., ed. *MGH Legum III Concilia II*. Hannover, 1906.

Whitelock D., ed. *English Historical Documents: c. 500–1042*. English Historical Documents 1. 2nd edn. London, 1979.

Whitelock, D., et al., ed. *Councils & Synods, with Other Documents Relating to the English Church*. Vol. I (Part 1 871–1066). Oxford 1981.

Wilmart, A., ed. "La Légende de Sainte Édithe en prose et vers par le moine Goscelin." *AB* 56 (1938), 5–101, 265–307.

Windeatt, B.A., trans. *The Book of Margery Kempe*. Harmondsworth, 1985.

Winterbottom, M., ed. *Three Lives of English Saints*. Toronto, 1972.

Wormald, F., ed. *English Kalendars before AD 1100*. HBS 72. London, 1934.

Secondary Studies

Albers, B. "Wann sind die Beda-Egbert'schen Bussbücher verfasst worden, und wer ist ihr Verfasser?" *Archiv für Katholisches Kirchenrecht* 81 (1901), 393–420.

Atkinson, C.W. " 'Precious Balsam in a Fragile Glass': The Ideology of Virginity in the Later Middle Ages." *Journal of Family History* 8 (1983), 131–43.

Bailey, D.S. *The Man-Woman Relation in Christian Thought.* London, 1959.

Bailey, R.N. and R. Cramp, ed. *The Corpus of Anglo-Saxon Stone Sculpture.* Vol. II. Oxford, 1988.

Bandel, B. "The English Chroniclers' Attitude toward Women." *Journal of the History of Ideas* 16 (1955), 113–18.

Bateson, M. "Origin and Early History of Double Monasteries." *TRHS* NS 13 (1899), 137–98.

Berschin, W. "*Opus deliberatum ac perfectum*: Why Did the Venerable Bede Write a Second Prose Life of St Cuthbert?" In *St Cuthbert, His Cult and His Community to AD 1200.* Ed. G. Bonner et al. Cambridge, 1989, pp. 94–102.

Bethell, D. "The Lives of St Osyth of Essex and St Osyth of Aylesbury." *AB* 88 (1970), 75–127.

Borresen, K.E. *Subordination and Equivalence: The Nature and Role of Women in Augustine and Thomas Aquinas.* Trans. C.H. Talbot. Washington, 1981.

Bowra, C.M. *Heroic Poetry.* New York, 1966.

Brechter, S. *Die Quellen zur Angelsachsenmission Gregors des Grossen.* Münster in Westfalen, 1941.

Brie, M. "Über die ags. Bezeichnung des Wortes Zauberer." *Englische Studien* 41 (1909), 20–7.

Brooks, N. *The Early History of the Church of Canterbury.* Leicester, 1984.

Brown, P. *The Making of Late Antiquity.* Cambridge, Mass., 1978.

Browne, G.F. *The Importance of Women in Anglo-Saxon Times, and Other Addresses.* London, 1919.

Buckstaff, F. "Married Women's Property in Anglo-Saxon and Anglo-Norman Law and the Origin of the Common Law Dower." *Annals of the American Academy of Political and Social Science* 4 (1893), 233–64.

Bugge, J. *Virginitas: An Essay in the History of a Medieval Ideal.* The Hague, 1975.

Byrne, M. *The Tradition of the Nun in Medieval England.* Washington, 1932.

Campbell, J. "Bede." In *Latin Historians.* Ed. T.A. Dorey. London, 1966, pp. 159–90.

Campbell, J., et al. *The Anglo-Saxons.* Oxford, 1982.

Chadwick, H.M., and N.K. Chadwick. *The Growth of Literature.* Vol. I. Cambridge, 1932.

Chadwick, O. *John Cassian: A Study in Primitive Monasticism.* 2nd edn. Cambridge, 1968.

Chance, J. *Woman as Hero in Old English Literature.* Syracuse, NY, 1986.

Chase, C., ed. *The Dating of Beowulf.* Toronto, 1981.

Clayton, M. "Feasts of the Virgin in the Liturgy of the Anglo-Saxon Church." *ASE* 13 (1984), 209–33.

Clayton, M. *The Cult of the Virgin Mary in Anglo-Saxon England.* Cambridge 1990.

Clover, C.J. "The Politics of Scarcity: Notes on the Sex Ratio in Early Scandinavia." In *New Readings on Women in Old English Literature*. Ed. H. Damico and A.H. Olsen. Bloomington, 1990, pp. 100–36.

Clunies Ross, M. "Concubinage in Anglo-Saxon England." *P&P* 108 (1985), 3–34.

Crick, J. "Church, Land and Local Nobility in Early Ninth-Century Kent: The Case of Ealdorman Oswulf." *Historical Research* 61 (1988), 251–69.

Cross J.E. "A Lost Life of Hilda of Whitby: The Evidence of the *Old English Martyrology*." In *The Early Middle Ages*. Acta 6. Ed. W.H. Snyder and P.E. Szarmach. Binghamton, NY, 1982 for 1979, pp. 21–43.

Cutler, K.E. "Edith, Queen of England, 1045–1066." *Mediaeval Studies* 35 (1973), 222–31.

Damico, H. "The Valkyrie Reflex in Old English Literature." *Allegorica* 5 (1980), 149–67.

Damico, H. *Beowulf's Wealhtheow and the Valkyrie Tradition*. Madison, Wis., 1984.

Damico, H., and A.H. Olsen, ed. *New Readings on Women in Old English Literature*. Bloomington, 1990.

Davidson, C. "Erotic 'Women's Songs' in Anglo-Saxon England." *Neophilologus* 59 (1975), 451–62.

Davidson, H.R.E. *Pagan Scandinavia*. New York, 1976.

Davies, J.G. "Deacons, Deaconesses and Minor Orders in the Patristic Period." *JEH* 14 (1963), 1–11.

Deanesly, M. "English and Gallic Minsters." *TRHS* 4th ser. 23 (1941), 25–69.

Delling, G. *Paulus' Stellung zu Frau und Ehe*. Stuttgart, 1931.

Deshman, R. "*Christus rex et magi reges*: Kingship and Christology in Ottonian and Anglo-Saxon Art." *FS* 10 (1976), 367–405.

Dietrich, S.C. "An Introduction to Women in Anglo-Saxon Society (c 600–1066)." In *The Women of England from Anglo-Saxon Times to the Present*. Ed. B. Kanner. Hamden, Conn., 1979, pp. 32–56.

Dionisotti, A.C. "On Bede, Grammars and Greek." *RB* 92 (1982), 111–41.

Dodds, E.R. *Pagan and Christian in an Age of Anxiety*. New York, 1970.

Dronke, P. *Women Writers of the Middle Ages*. Cambridge, 1984.

Eckenstein, L. *Women Under Monasticism*. Cambridge, 1896.

Elkins, S.K. "All Ages, Every Condition, and Both Sexes: The Emergence of a Gilbertine Identity." In *Medieval Religious Women*. Ed. J.A. Nichols and L.T. Shank. Kalamazoo, 1984. Vol. I, *Distant Echoes*, pp. 169–82.

Enright, M.J. "Lady with a Mead-Cup: Ritual, Group Cohesion and Hierarchy in the Germanic Warband." *FS* 22 (1988), 170–203.

Evans, J.M. "*Genesis B* and Its Background." *RES NS* 14 (1963), 1–16, 113–23.

Farmer, D.H. "Saint Wilfrid." In *Saint Wilfrid at Hexham*. Ed. D.P. Kirby. Newcastle upon Tyne, 1974, pp. 35–59.

Fell, C.E. "Edward King and Martyr and the Anglo-Saxon Hagiographic Tradition." In *Ethelred the Unready*. Ed. D. Hill. Oxford, 1978, pp. 1–13.

Fell, C.E. "Hild, Abbess of Streonæshalch." In *Hagiography and Medieval Literature: A Symposium*. Ed. H. Bekker-Nielsen et al. Odense, 1981, pp. 76–99.

Fell, C.E. "A *friwif locbore* Revisited." *ASE* 13 (1984), 157–65.

Fell, C.E. "Some Implications of the Boniface Correspondence." In *New Read-*

ings on Women in Old English Literature. Ed. H. Damico and A.H. Olsen. Bloomington, 1990, pp. 29–43.

Fell, C., et al. *Women in Anglo-Saxon England and the Impact of 1066.* Paperback edn. Oxford, 1986.

Finberg, H.P.R. *The Early Charters of the West Midlands.* 2nd edn. Leicester, 1972.

Finnegan, R.E. "Eve and 'Vincible Ignorance' in *Genesis B.*" *Texas Studies in Literature and Language* 18 (1976), 329–39.

Fisher, D.J.V. "The Anti-monastic Reaction in the Reign of Edward the Martyr." *Cambridge Journal of History* 10 (1950–2), 254–70.

Flint, V.I.J. *The Rise of Magic in Early Medieval Europe.* Princeton, 1991.

Folz, R. "Tradition hagiographique et culte de Sainte Bathilde, reine des Francs." *Académie des Inscriptions et Belles-Lettres* (1975), 369–84.

Foucault, M. *The History of Sexuality, I: An Introduction.* Trans. R. Hurley. New York, 1978.

Foucault, M. "Afterword." In H.L. Dreyfus and P. Rabinow. *Michel Foucault: Beyond Structuralism and Hermeneutics.* Chicago, 1983.

Frantzen, A.J. *The Literature of Penance in Anglo-Saxon England.* New Brunswick, NJ, 1983.

Frantzen, A.J. "The Tradition of Penitentials in Anglo-Saxon England." *ASE* 11 (1983), 23–56.

Frantzen, A. J. "The Penitentials Attributed to Bede." *Speculum* 58 (1983), 573–97.

Fry, D.K. "The Art of Bede: Edwin's Council." In *Saints, Scholars and Heroes.* Ed. M.H. King and W.M. Stevens. Collegeville, Minn., 1979. Vol. I, 191–207.

Fry, D.K. "The Art of Bede II: The Reliable Narrator as Persona." In *The Early Middle Ages.* Acta 6. Ed. W. Snyder and P.E. Szarmach. Binghamton, NY, 1982 for 1979, pp. 63–82.

Fry, D.K. "Bede Fortunate in his Translator: The Barking Nuns." In *Studies in Earlier Old English Prose.* Ed. P.E. Szarmach. Albany, NY, 1985, pp. 345–62.

Gneuss, H. "King Alfred and the History of Anglo-Saxon Libraries." In *Modes of Interpretation in Old English Literature: Essays in Honour of Stanley B. Greenfield.* Ed. P.R. Brown et al. Toronto, 1986, pp. 29–49.

Godfrey, J. "The Double Monastery in Early English History." *Ampleforth Journal* 79 (1974), 19–32.

Godfrey, J. "The Place of the Double Monastery in the Anglo-Saxon Minster System." In *Famulus Christi: Essays in Commemoration of the Thirteenth Centenary of the Birth of the Venerable Bede.* Ed. G. Bonner. London, 1976, pp. 344–50.

Godman, P. "The Anglo-Latin *Opus Geminatum*: From Aldhelm to Alcuin." *MÆ* 50 (1981), 215–29.

Göller, E. *Papsttum und Bussgewalt in spätrömischer und frühmittelalterlicher Zeit.* Freiburg im Breisgau, 1933.

Gold, P.S. "Male/Female Cooperation: The Example of Fontevrault." In *Medieval Religious Women.* Ed. J.A. Nichols and L.T. Shank. Kalamazoo, 1984. Vol. I, *Distant Echoes*, pp. 151–68.

Gougaud, L. "*Mulier Consortia*: Etude sur le Syneisaktisme chez les ascetes Celtiques." *Ériu* 9 (1921), 147–56.

Gougaud, L. *Christianity in Celtic Lands.* Trans. M. Joynt. London, 1932.

Grimm, J. *Teutonic Mythology*. Trans. J.S. Stallybrass. 4 vols. London, 1880–8.

Haigh, D.H. "On the Monasteries of S Heiu and S Hild." *Yorkshire Archaeological and Topographical Journal* 3 (1875), 349–91.

Hansen, E.T. "Women in Old English Poetry Reconsidered." *Michigan Academician* 9 (1976), 109–17.

Hayward, P.A. "The Kenelm Legend in Context: A Study of the Hagiography of the Eleventh Century." Unpub. MA dissertation, Auckland University, 1990.

Hazeltine, H.D. *Zur Geschichte der Eheschliessung nach angelsächsischen Recht*. Berlin, 1905.

Helterman, J. "*Beowulf*: The Archetype Enters History." *ELH* 35 (1968), 1–20.

Herlihy, D. "Life Expectancies for Women." In *The Role of Women in the Middle Ages*. Ed. R.T. Morewedge. Albany, NY, 1975, pp. 1–22.

Hermann, J.P. *Allegories of War: Language and Violence in Old English Poetry*. Ann Arbor, 1989.

Hill, J. "*Þæt wæs geomuru ides!* A Female Stereotype Examined." In *New Readings on Women in Old English Literature*. Ed. H. Damico and A.H. Olsen. Bloomington, 1990, pp. 235–47.

Hill, R. "Marriage in Seventh-Century England." In *Saints, Scholars, and Heroes*. Ed. M.H. King and W.M. Stevens. Collegeville, Minn., 1979. Vol. I, 67–75.

Hill, T.D. "The Kingdom of the Father, Son, and Counsellor: *Judgement Day II*, 290–300." *Notes and Queries* NS 32 (1985), 7–8.

Hilpisch, S. *Die Doppelklöster: Entstehung und Organisation*. Munster, 1928.

Hunter Blair, P. *The World of Bede*. London 1970.

Hunter Blair, P. "Whitby as a Centre of Learning in the Seventh Century." In *Learning and Literature in Anglo-Saxon England: Studies Presented to Peter Clemoes*. Ed. M. Lapidge and H. Gneuss. Cambridge, 1985, pp. 3–32.

Huyghe, G. *La clôture des moniales des origines à la fin du XIIIme siècle*. Roubaix, 1944.

Jones, C.W. *Saints' Lives and Chronicles in Early England*. Ithaca, NY, 1947.

Kelly, J.F. "Pelagius, Pelagianism and the Early Irish Church." *Medievalia* 4 (1978), 99–124.

Kirby, D.P. "Bede's Native Sources for the *Historia Ecclesiastica*." *BJRL* 48 (1965–6), 341–71.

Kirby, D.P. *The Making of Early England*. New York, 1968.

Kirby, D.P. "Northumbria in the Time of Wilfrid." In *Saint Wilfrid at Hexham*. Ed. D.P. Kirby. Newcastle upon Tyne, 1974, pp. 1–34.

Kirby, D.P. "Bede, Eddius Stephanus and the 'Life of Wilfrid'." *EHR* 98 (1983), 101–14.

Kliman, B.W. "Women in Early English Literature: 'Beowulf' to the 'Ancrene Wisse'." *Nottingham Medieval Studies* 21 (1977), 32–49.

Klinck, A.L. " Female Characterization in Old English Poetry and the Growth of Psychological Realism: *Genesis B* and *Christ I*." *Neophilologus* 63 (1979), 597–610.

Klinck, A.L. "Anglo-Saxon Women and the Law." *JMH* 8 (1982), 107–21.

Knowles, D. *The Monastic Order in England*. 2nd edn. Cambridge, 1963.

Kottje, R. "Ehe und Eheverständnis in den vorgratianischen Bussbüchern." In

Love and Marriage in the Twelfth Century. Ed. W. van Hoeck and A. Welken-huysen. Louvain, 1981, pp. 8–40.

Lapidge, M. "A Seventh-Century Insular Latin Debate Poem on Divorce." *Cambridge Medieval Celtic Studies* 10 (1985), 1–23.

Lapidge, M. "Bede's Metrical *Vita S Cuthbert*." In *St Cuthbert, His Cult and His Community to AD 1200*. Ed. G. Bonner et al. Cambridge, 1989, pp. 77–93.

Levison, W. *England and the Continent in the Eighth Century*. London, 1946.

Lewis, C.S. *The Allegory of Love*. New York, 1958.

Loyn, H.R. "Gesiths and Thegns in Anglo-Saxon England from the Seventh to the Tenth Century." *EHR* 70 (1955), 529–49.

Luecke, J. "The Unique Experience of Anglo-Saxon Nuns." In *Medieval Religious Women*. Ed. J.A. Nichols and L.T. Shank. Kalamazoo, 1988. Vol. II, *Peaceweavers*.

Lynch, J. H. *Godparents and Kinship in Early Medieval Europe*. Princeton, 1986.

Magennis, H. "The Cup as Symbol and Metaphor in Old English Literature." *Speculum* 60 (1985), 517–36.

Magennis, H. "Water-Wine Miracles in Anglo-Saxon Saints' Lives." *English Language Notes* 23 (1986), 7–9.

Markus, R.A. "The Chronology of the Gregorian Mission to England: Bede's Narrative and Gregory's Correspondence." *JEH* 14 (1963), 16–30.

Markus, R.A. "Gregory the Great and a Papal Missionary Strategy." In *The Mission of the Church and the Propagation of the Faith*. Studies in Church History 6. Ed. G.J. Cuming. Cambridge, 1970, pp. 29–38.

Markus, R.A. *Saeculum: History and Society in the Theology of St Augustine*. Cambridge, 1970.

Mayr-Harting, H. *The Coming of Christianity to Anglo-Saxon England*. London, 1972.

McNamara, J.A. "Living Sermons: Consecrated Women and the Conversion of Gaul." In *Medieval Religious Women*. Ed. J.A. Nichols and L.T. Shank. Kalamazoo, 1988. Vol. II, *Peaceweavers*.

McNamara, J.A., and S. Wemple. "The Power of Women through the Family in Medieval Europe: 500–1100." In *Clio's Consciousness Raised*. Ed. M.S. Hartmann and L.W. Banner. New York, 1974, pp. 103–18.

Meaney, A.L. "The *Ides* of the Cotton Gnomic Poem." *MÆ* 48 (1979), 23–39.

Meaney, A.L. "Ælfric and Idolatry." *Journal of Religious History* 13 (1984), 119–35.

Meaney, A.L. "Women, Witchcraft and Magic in Anglo-Saxon England." In *Superstition and Popular Medicine in Anglo-Saxon England*, ed. D.G. Scragg. Manchester, 1989, pp. 9–40.

Meyer, M.A. "Women and the Tenth Century English Monastic Reform." *RB* 87 (1977), 34–61.

Meyvaert, P. "Diversity Within Unity: A Gregorian Theme." *Heythrop Journal*, 4 (1963), 141–62.

Meyvaert, P. *Bede and Gregory the Great*. Jarrow, 1964.

Meyvaert, P. "Bede's Text of the *Libellus Responsionum* of Gregory the Great to Augustine of Canterbury." In *England Before the Conquest: Studies in Primary Sources presented to Dorothy Whitelock*. Ed. P. Clemoes and K. Hughes. Cambridge, 1971, pp. 15–33.

Moore, W.J. *The Saxon Pilgrims to Rome and the Schola Saxonum*. D. ès L. dissertation, Faculty of Letters. Fribourg, Switz., 1937.

Morrish, J. "King Alfred's Letter as a Source on Learning in England." In *Studies in Earlier Old English Prose*. Ed. P.E. Szarmach. 1983, pp. 87–108.

Murphy, M. "Vows, Boasts and Taunts, and the Role of Women in Some Medieval Literature." *English Studies* 66 (1985), 105–12.

Nelson, J.L. "Ritual and Reality in Early Medieval *Ordines*." In *The Materials, Sources and Methods of Ecclesiastical History*. Studies in Church History 11. Ed. D. Baker. Oxford, 1975, pp. 41–51.

Nelson, J.L. "Inauguration Rituals." In *Early Medieval Kingship*. Ed. P.H. Sawyer and I.N. Woods. Leeds, 1977, pp. 50–71.

Nelson, J.L. "Queens as Jezebels: The Careers of Brunhild and Balthild in Merovingian History." In *Medieval Women: Essays Presented to Rosalind Hill*. Ed. D Baker. Studies in Church History: Subsidia 1. Oxford, 1978, pp. 31–57.

Nelson, J.L. "The Earliest Surviving Royal Ordo: Some Liturgical and Historical Aspects." In *Authority and Power: Studies in Medieval Law and Government*. Ed. B. Tierney and P. Linehan. Cambridge, 1980, pp. 29–48.

Nelson, J.L. "The Second English Ordo." In *Politics and Ritual in Early Medieval Europe*. London 1986, pp. 361–74.

Nicholson, J. "*Feminae Gloriosae*: Women in the Age of Bede." In *Medieval Women: Essays Presented to Rosalind Hill*. Ed. D. Baker. Studies in Church History: Subsidia 1. Oxford, 1978, pp. 15–29.

Oakley, T.P. *English Penitential Discipline and Anglo-Saxon Law in Their Joint Influence*. New York, 1923.

Olsen, A.H. "Cynewulf's Autonomous Women: A Reconsideration of Elene and Juliana." In *New Readings on Women in Old English Literature*. Ed. H. Damico and A.H. Olsen. Bloomington, 1990, pp. 262–72.

Page, R.I. *Life in Anglo-Saxon England*. London, 1970.

Payer, P.J. *Sex and the Penitentials: The Development of a Sexual Code*. Toronto, 1984.

Pettazzoni, R. "Confession of Sins in the Classics." *HTR* 30 (1937), 1–14.

Ray, R. "Bede's *Vera Lex Historiae*." *Speculum* 55 (1980), 1–21.

Renoir, A. "A Reading Context for *The Wife's Lament*." In *Anglo-Saxon Poetry: Essays in Appreciation for John C. McGalliard*. Ed. L.E. Nicholson and D.W. Frese. Notre Dame, 1975, pp. 224–51.

Renoir, A. "Eve's I.Q. Rating: Two Sexist Views of *Genesis B*." In *New Readings on Women in Old English Literature*. Ed. H. Damico and A.H. Olsen. Bloomington, 1990, pp. 262–72.

Reuther, R.R. *Religion and Sexism*. New York, 1974.

Reynolds, R. "*Virgines subintroductae* in Celtic Christianity." *HTR* 61 (1968), 547–66.

Richards, M.P. and B.J. Stanfield. "Concepts of Anglo-Saxon Women in the Laws." In *New Readings on Women in Old English Literature*. Ed. H. Damico and A.H. Olsen. Bloomington, 1990, pp. 262–72.

Ridyard, S.J. *The Royal Saints of Anglo-Saxon England: A Study of West Saxon and East Anglian Cults*. Cambridge, 1988.

Rigold, S.E. "The 'Double Minsters' of Kent and their Analogies." *Journal of the British Archaeological Association* 3rd ser. 31 (1961), 27–37.

Rivers, T.J. "Widows' Rights in Anglo-Saxon Law." *American Journal of Legal History* 19 (1975), 208–15.

Robinson, F.C. "The Prescient Woman in Old English Literature." In *Philologia Anglica: Essays Presented to Professor Y. Oshio Teresawa on the Occasion of his Sixtieth Birthday.* Ed. K. Oshitari et al. Tokyo, 1988, pp. 241–50.

Roeder, F. *Die Familie bei den Angelsachsen, I: Mann und Frau. Studien zur Englischen Philologie* 4. Halle, 1899.

Rollason, D.W., ed. "Lists of Saints' Resting Places in Anglo-Saxon England." *ASE* 7 (1978), 61–93.

Rollason, D.W. *The Mildrith Legend: A Study in Early Medieval Hagiography in England.* Leicester, 1982.

Rollason, D.W. *Saints and Relics in Anglo-Saxon England.* Oxford, 1989.

Roper, M. "Wilfrid's Landholdings in Northumbria." In *St Wilfrid at Hexham.* Ed. D.P. Kirby. Newcastle upon Tyne, 1974, pp. 61–79, 169–71.

Rosenthal, J.T. "Marriage and the Blood Feud in 'Heroic' Europe." *British Journal of Sociology* 17 (1966), 133–44.

Rosenthal, J.T. *Angles, Angels, and Conquerors: 400–1154.* New York, 1973.

Ryan, J. *Irish Monasticism: Origins and Early Development.* Dublin, 1931.

Scammell, J. "Freedom and Marriage in Medieval England." *EconHR* 2nd ser. 27 (1974), 532–7.

Scammell, J. "Wife-Rents and Merchet." *EconHR* 2nd ser. 29 (1976), 487–90.

Schaefer, U. "Two Women in Need of a Friend: A Comparison of *The Wife's Lament* and Eangyth's Letter to Boniface." In *Germanic Dialects: Linguistic and Philological Investigations.* Ed. B. Brogyanyi and T. Krömmelbein. Amsterdam, 1986, pp. 491–524.

Schneider, C. "Cynewulf's Devaluation of Heroic Tradition in *Juliana*." *ASE* 7 (1978), 107–18.

Schneider, D.B. "Anglo-Saxon Women in the Religious Life: A Study of the Status and Position of Women in an Early Medieval Society." Unpubl. PhD dissertation, Cambridge University, 1985.

Schramm, P.E. *A History of the English Coronation.* Trans. L.G. Wickham-Legg. Oxford, 1937.

Schulenburg, J.T. "Strict Active Enclosure and its Effects on the Female Monastic Experience (ca 500–1100)." In *Medieval Religious Women.* Ed. J.A. Nichols and L.T. Shank. Kalamazoo, 1984. Vol. I, *Distant Echoes*, pp. 51–86.

Schulenburg, J.T. "Female Sanctity, Public and Private, 500–1100." In *Women and Power in the Middle Ages.* Ed. M. Erler and M. Kowaleski. Athens, Ga, 1988, pp. 102–25.

Searle, E. "Freedom and Marriage in Medieval England: An Alternative Hypothesis." *EconHR* 2nd ser. 29 (1976), 482–6.

Sims-Williams, P. "Continental Influence at Bath Monastery in the Seventh Century." *ASE* 4 (1975), 1–10.

Sims-Williams, P. "Cuthswith, Seventh Century Abbess of Inkberrow, near Worcester, and the Würzburg Manuscript of Jerome on Ecclesiastes." *ASE* 5 (1976), 1–21.

Sims-Williams, P. "An Unpublished Seventh- or Eighth-Century Anglo-Latin Letter in Boulogne-sur-Mer MS 74 (82)." *MÆ* 48 (1979), 1–22.

Sims-Williams, P. *Religion and Literature in Western England, 600–800.* Cambridge, 1990.

Skeat, W.W. *Early English Proverbs*. Oxford, 1910.

Southern, R.W. *Western Society and the Church in the Middle Ages*. Harmondsworth, 1970.

Spamer, J.B. "The Marriage Concept in *Wulf and Eadwacer*." *Neophilologus* 62 (1978), 143–4.

Stafford, P. "Charles the Bald, Judith and England." In *Charles the Bald: Court and Kingdom*. Ed. M. Gibson et al. BAR International ser. 101. Oxford, 1981, pp. 137–51.

Stafford, P. "The King's Wife in Wessex 800–1066." *P&P* 91 (1981), 3–27.

Stafford, P. *Queens, Concubines, and Dowagers: The King's Wife in the Early Middle Ages*. Athens, Ga, 1983.

Stancliffe, C. "Kings Who Opted Out." In *Ideal and Reality in Frankish and Anglo-Saxon Society*. Ed. P. Wormald et al. Oxford, 1983, pp. 154–76.

Stancliffe, C. "Cuthbert and the Polarity between Pastor and Solitary." In *St Cuthbert, His Cult and His Community to AD 1200*. Ed. G. Bonner et al. Woodbridge, 1989, pp. 21–44.

Stenton, D.M. *The English Woman in History*. London, 1957.

Stenton, F.M. "The Historical Bearing of Place-Name Studies: The Place of Women in Anglo-Saxon Society." *TRHS* 4th ser. 25 (1943), 1–13.

Stenton, F.M. *Preparatory to Anglo-Saxon England*. Ed. D.M. Stenton. Oxford, 1970.

Stenton, F.M. *Anglo-Saxon England*. 3rd edn. rev. D.M. Stenton and D. Whitelock. Oxford, 1971.

Stuart, H. "The Anglo-Saxon Elf." *Studia Neophilologica* 48 (1976), 313–20.

Thacker, A. "Bede's Ideal of Reform." In *Ideal and Reality in Frankish and Anglo-Saxon Society*. Ed. P. Wormald et al. Oxford, 1983, pp. 130–53.

Thompson, A.T. "Double Monasteries and the Male Element in Nunneries." In *The Ministry of Women: A Report by a Committee Appointed by His Grace the Lord Archbishop of Canterbury*. London, 1919.

Thorndike, L. *Studies in the History of Magic*. New York, 1904.

Thrupp, J. *The Anglo-Saxon Home*. London, 1862.

Turner, S. *History of the Anglo-Saxons*. 3 vols. London, 1799–1805.

Ugolnik, A.J., Jr. "The Royal Icon: A Structural and Thematic Study of Cynewulf's *Elene*." *DAI* 37 (1976) 342–3A (Brown University).

Vickery, J.F. "The Vision of Eve in *Genesis B*." *Speculum* 44 (1969), 86–102.

Wainwright, F.T. "Æthelflæd, Lady of the Mercians." In *The Anglo-Saxons: Studies in Some Aspects of Their History and Culture*. Ed. P. Clemoes. London, 1959, pp. 53–69.

Wallace-Hadrill, J.M. *The Long-Haired Kings and Other Studies in Frankish History*. London, 1962.

Wallace-Hadrill, J.M. *Early Germanic Kingship in England and on the Continent*. Oxford, 1971.

Wallace-Hadrill, J.M. *The Frankish Church*. Oxford, 1983.

Wallace-Hadrill, J.M. *Bede's Ecclesiastical History of the English People: A Historical Commentary*. Oxford, 1988.

Wallace-Hadrill, J.M. "Bede and Plummer." In *Famulus Christi: Essays in Commemoration of the Thirteenth Centenary of the Birth of the Venerable Bede*. Ed. G. Bonner. London, 1976, pp. 366–85.

Ward, B. "Miracles and History: A Reconsideration of the Miracle Stories Used by Bede." In *Famulus Christi: Essays in Commemoration of the Thirteenth Centenary of the Birth of the Venerable Bede*. Ed. G. Bonner. London, 1976, pp. 70–6.

Ward, B. *Miracles and the Medieval Mind*. Oxford, 1982.

Warren, A.K. "The Nun as Anchoress: England 1100–1500." In *Medieval Religious Women*. Ed. J.A. Nichols and L.T. Shank. Kalamazoo, 1984. Vol. I, *Distant Echoes*, pp. 197–212.

Warren, A.K. *Anchorites and their Patrons in Medieval England*. Berkeley, 1985.

Watkins, O.D. *A History of Penance*. 2 vols. London, 1920.

Wemple, S.F. *Women in Frankish Society: Marriage and the Cloister, 500–900*. Philadelphia, 1981.

Whitelock, D. *The Beginnings of English Society*. Harmondsworth, 1952.

Whitelock, D. "The Pre-Viking Church in East Anglia." ASE 1 (1972), 1–22.

Wieland, G. "*Geminus Stilus*: Studies in Anglo-Latin Hagiography." In *Insular Latin Studies*. Ed. M.W. Herren. Toronto, 1981, pp. 113–33.

Williams, E.W. "What's So New about the Sexual Revolution? Some Comments on Anglo-Saxon Attitudes towards Sexuality in Women Based on Four Exeter Book Riddles." *Texas Quarterly* 18 (1975), 46–55.

Williams, G.H. *The Norman Anonymous of AD 1100*. Cambridge, Mass., 1951.

Wood, I.N. *The Merovingian North Sea*. Alingsas, 1983.

Woolf, R. "The Fall of Man in Genesis B and the Mystère d'Adam." In *Studies in Old English Literature in Honor of Arthur G. Brodeur*. Ed. S.B. Greenfield. Eugene, 1963, pp. 187–99.

Woolf, R. "The Ideal of Warriors Dying with Their Lord in the Germania and in The Battle of Maldon." ASE 5 (1976), 63–81.

Wormald, P. "Bede and Benedict Biscop." In *Famulus Christi: Essays in Commemoration of the Thirteenth Centenary of the Birth of the Venerable Bede*. Ed. G. Bonner. London, 1976, pp. 141–69.

Wrenn, C.L. "The Poetry of Caedmon." PBA 32 (1946), 277–95.

Wright, C.E. *The Cultivation of Saga in Anglo-Saxon England*. London, 1939.

Wright, T. *Womankind in Western Europe*. London, 1869.

Young, E. "The Anglo-Saxon Family Law." In *Essays in Anglo-Saxon Law*. Ed. H. Adams. Boston, 1876, pp. 121–82.

INDEX

Abbesses (*see also* Women, monastic):
Adola, 146, 183–4, 265, 270
Æbbe, 257; in *HE*, 101–2, 189, 258;
  Life of Cuthbert: Anon, 199; Bede's,
  129, 189; *Life of Wilfrid*, 169–72,
  175–6, 180, 185, 189, 195, 198,
  254–5, 292; *see also* Coldingham
Æbbe, Sheriff's wife, 172
Ælffled, 12, 126, 163, 251; in *HE*, 59
  fn. 51, 119, 129, 179, 251–2,
  255–6, 270; *Life of Cuthbert*: Anon,
  68, 194–9; Bede's, 13, 126, 165,
  179, 185–90, 199–207, 243, 251–2,
  255, 256, 257, 267, 268; *Life of*
  Wilfrid, 169–70, 173, 175, 176,
  179–85, 251, 255; Letter to Adola,
  146, 183–4, 265, 270; *see also*
  Whitby
Æthelburg of Barking, 111, 258, 260,
  262; *see also* Barking
Æthelburg, Letter from Alcuin, 34,
  97, 298
Æthelburg, companion of Ælffled,
  180, 183 fn. 20, 184
Æthelburg of Faremoutiers, 68, 259
Æthelhild, 245
Æthelthryth, 93, 247–8, 258–61;
  monastic kinswomen, 68, 73, 274;
  see also Queens
Bertila, *Life* of, 78, 258
Bugga, Correspondence with
  Boniface, 34, 131, 141, 148–9, 275
  fn. 24, 277, 296
Bugga, Centwine's daughter, 63, 247
Cuthburg, 72, 78, 81, 275
Cwenthryth, 217
Cynethryth, "Abbess of Wilfrid,"
  164–5, 172, 188, 291–2
Cynethryth, Offa's wife, *see* Queens
Cyniburg, 162–3, 173, 296
Domne Eafe, 72, 225, 260
Eadburg, 259 fn. 82; Leoba's teacher,
  141, 268; Correspondence with
  Boniface, 79, 131, 139, 141

Abbesses *cont.*
Eadburg, *Life of Guthlac*, 294
Eanfled, 256; *see also* Queens
Eangyth, Letter to Boniface, 34, 106,
  132–4, 136–40, 143–8, 213, 240,
  255
Edith, Goscelin's *Life*, 34–5, 43, 99,
  106; William of Malmesbury and,
  35
Fara, Jonas's *Life*, 134–5
Gertrude, 96
Heiu, 255
Hereburg, and John of Beverly, 267–8
Hild, 7, 12, 78, 163, 169, 179, 181; in
  HE, 13, 119, 125–7, 129, 135–7,
  180, 243–70, 275, 279, 280; *Life of*
  Wilfrid, 176, 181, 183–5, 255; her
  mother, 253–4, 256; *see also*
  Whitby
Hildelith, in *De Virginitate*, 75, 78–9,
  83, 258–9, 266; *HE*, 81, 111–12,
  245, 258, 264; *see also* Barking
Jurmenburg, 177–8; *see also* Queens
Leoba, Rudolph's *Life* of, 13, 43, 150,
  163, 164, 188, 243–5, 253, 256–7,
  259, 268, 271–86, 288–91,
  295–300; and Boniface, 13, 150,
  164, 188, 243, 283–6, 288–91,
  295–300; Lives of Boniface and of
  Sturm, 284–8; Correspondence
  with Boniface, 138, 141–2, 149,
  229, 268, 277, 284; Letter from
  Lul, 296
Mathilda, 247
Mildburg, 139; *see also* Much Wenlock
Radegund, 76, 142 fn. 121
Rodtruda, Alcuin Correspondence, 76
Seaxburg, 225, 259, 269; in *Mildrith*
  Fragments, 192–3, 259–60; *see also*
  Queens
Switha, Letter from Lul, 106, 285
Tette, 114, 134, 272, 275–7
Verca, 205–6
Waldburg, 274

Abbesses, ministry and contribution of, 13, 93–6, 114–15, 125–6, 130–7, 163–5, 170–2, 179–85, 203–7, 243–6, 248–70, 278–82, 292 (see also Baptism; Confessors); and bishops; 1, 13, 33, 110, 127–30, 139–40, 162–5, 169–72, 174–8, 181–5, 185–8, 194, 196–207, 275, 278, 284, 289–97; and queens, 177–8, 297–9

Adomnan, Law of, 88–9, 110, 174; Life of Columba, 65–7, 70, 89, 97, 188, 196

Adomnan of Coldingham, 101, 195, 198–9

Adultery, 46–8, 51–6, 59–60, 64–5, 73

Aelred, 76, 97

Albinus, 225, 247, 251, 266

Alcuin, Song of York, 73–4, 152; Life of Willibrord, 76; Correspondence: 34, 39–40, 41, 62, 73, 76, 95, 98, 99, 115–16, 142, 170, 216–17; with English women, 34, 97, 192 fn. 73, 216–17, 268–9, 298; with Charlemagne's kinswomen, 76

Aldebert, Gaulish priest, 124

Aldhelm, 266, 270, 271; De Virginitate: Prose, 12, 13, 14, 75–85, 87, 91, 93, 95, 98–100, 103–10, 157, 174, 243, 247, 257, 258, 264, 273, 293; Metrical, 76, 82, 101; Carm Eccles, 163, 247; Charter, 78, 275; Letter to Abbots of Wilfrid, 48, 85, 86, 91

Alfredian translations, 20

Ancrene Wisse, 96, 107

Anglo-Saxon Chronicle, 86, 87, 88, 247, 275; see also Mercian Register

Anna, widow, 83, 108

Anglo-Norman chronicles, 35, 88, 158

Antony, Evagrian Life of, 120

Asser, Life of King Alfred, 47–8, 50, 208, 213, 218–19, 238; see also Queens, Eadburg

Atlakvitha, see Guthrun, Lays of

Atlamál, see Guthrun, Lays of

Atli, 195

Augustine of Hippo, 81, 84, 106

Ælfric, 43; Life of Æthelthryth, 73–4; Homily on Judith, 92

Æthelfled, Lady of the Mercians, 86–8, 92, 219, 235, 236, 282

Æthelthryth, see Abbesses; Queens

Æthelweard, Chronicle of, 247

Baptism, women and, 244, 280, 290, 297 fn. 136

Bardney, 213, 225, 236

Barking, Libellus, 79, 111–12, 259; monastic school, 43, 78–9, 81–3, 251, 258–9, 266, 279; in HE 109–12, 245–6, 258–61; De Virginitate, 12, 13, 75–7, 78, 83, 91, 93, 98–100, 114, 144, 243, 247, 257, 264, 266, 293; see also Abbesses, Hildelith; Æthelburg

Basil, Canonical Letters, 51–2, 60–1, 63, 80

Bass, 90

Battle of Maldon, 23, 48–50, 93, 195

Be wifmannes beweddunge, 237 fn. 158

Bede, 76, 95, 213; and Penitentials, 22, 121; HE: 6, 12–13, 15–19, 21, 23, 24, 62, 76, 84, 129, 151, 227; queens in, 12–13, 67–74, 90, 160, 162, 165, 166, 167, 176, 177, 218–42, 269; monastic women in, 12–13, 78, 81, 146, 189, 243–70, 274, 275, 280, 285; Life of Cuthbert: 12, 13, 23, 24, 90, 114–15, 120–4, 127–9, 133, 187, 251; women in, 128–9, 157, 205, 257 (see also Æbbe, Ælflled, Censwith, Hildmer's Wife, Jurmenburg, Verca); History of the Abbots, 39, 130; Commentaries: on Ezra, 18 fn. 17; on Habukkuk, 269; Letter to Egbert of York, 6, 95, 96, 120, 121, 128, 202–3, 207, 213

Benedict, 196, 284, 289, 290, 293; Rule of, 43, 91, 130, 134–5, 147, 148, 251, 252, 264–5, 273, 284, 289, 292

Benedict Biscop, 39, 183, 270

Benedictine Reform, 35, 44, 103, 104, 120, 165, 194, 247; and queens, 177–8, 208, 215; see also Regularis Concordia

Beowulf, 6, 87, 90–1, 93, 100, 101, 152, 153, 154, 156, 165, 168, 178, 191–3, 224, 229, 238, 246, 247, 292; women in, see Geatish woman, Grendel's mother, Freawaru, Hildeburg, Hygd, Thryth, Wealhtheow

Bischofsheim, 272, 273, 277, 279, 280, 288, 299

Bishops:
Aidan, 78, 119, 129, 151, 166, 195, 197, 203, 241, 250, 255, 256, 262, 264, 265, 267, 270

Bishops *cont.*
  Augustine of Canterbury, 16–19, 46,
    54, 55, 62, 72, 222, 241; *see also*
    Gregory, *Libellus*
  Æthelwold, *Benedictional* of, 209; and
    queens, 118; *see also Regularis
    Concordia*
  Boniface, 18, 64, 77, 80, 104, 107,
    229, 269; and popes, 16, 20, 27–33,
    133, 150; and Lul, 287–8; and
    monastic women: 11, 12, 33, 97,
    115, 130–3, 137–50, 272, teacher
    of, 43, 79, 132, 262, 285;
    Correspondence: with women, 12,
    27, 77, 79, 115, 130–3, 148–50,
    243, 277 (*see also* Eangyth, Bugga,
    Ecgburg, Eadburg, Cena, Leoba);
    with Canterbury, 149–50; with
    others, 29, 30, 97, 139, 277, 291
    (*see also* Boniface circle); in Eigil's
    Life of Sturm, 284–7; Willibald's
    Life of, 79, 284–8, 295–6; for
    Rudolph's *Life*, *see* Abbesses, Leoba
  Cedd, 49, 151, 196
  Chad, 129
  Colman, 240–1
  Cuthbert, 68, 73, 135; and Ecgfrith,
    197–8; and Hereberht, 186–7;
    misogyny of, 102; friendships with
    women: 102, 127–9, 205–6, 262,
    abbesses, 128–9, 189–90, Ælffled,
    179, 185–90, 194, 197, 199–207,
    Jurmenburg, 198–9; *see also*
    Hildmer's wife, Censwith, Æbbe.
    For *Lives*, *see* Bede; Lindisfarne
  Dalfinus (*recte* count), 169, 175
  Daniel, 18, 24, 131, 133
  Dunstan, 194
  Eadfrith, 121, 187
  Eanbald, 34
  Egbert, *see* Bede, Letter to
  Eorcenwold, 78, 260
  Fulk, 44
  Hæddi, 257
  Headda, 123
  John of Beverly, 251, 267–8
  Lul, 114, 287–8; and Leoba, 288, 296;
    in *Life of Boniface*, 285, 286–8, 291,
    295–6; *Life of Leoba*, 280, 283, 284,
    291, 295–6; Correspondence with
    women, 142–3, 258, 270, 287–8;
    Switha, 106, 285; Cyniburg, 162,

Bishops *cont.*
    173, 296; Osgifu of Northumbria,
    213; Leoba, 296
  Liudhard, and Bertha, 237
  Mellitus, 17
  Nothhelm, 29, 30
  Oftfor, 262, 266
  Paulinus, 90, 165, 221, 223, 224, 232,
    239
  Pehthelm, 30
  Theodore, 19, 24, 120, 246; in HE,
    129–30, and Osthryth, 230, 231–8;
    Life of Wilfrid, 167, 176, and
    Ælffled, 179, 183–5, and Hild,
    176, 181, 183–4, 255; learning
    brought by, 23, 42, 43, 79, 247,
    266–8, 269; *see also* Canterbury
    school; Hertford Council;
    Theodore's Penitential
  Trumwine, 118, 129, 197
  Wilfrid, 63, 201; and women: Sussex
    queen in HE, 225; in Eddius's *Life*,
    165–78, *see also* Eanfled,
    Jurmenburg, Æbbe, Æthelthryth,
    Hild, Ælffled; and cult of Mary,
    172–5; and kings: 151, 182, 184,
    185, 297, Ecgfrith, 197–8; and
    successor, 287, 291–2; Whitby
    synod, 15, 125, 180–1, 241, 255,
    267; *see also* Eddius's *Life* of
  Willibald, 114, 145–6, 274, 290
  Wulfstan, *Institutes of Polity*, 108
Bishops, and abbesses, *see* Abbesses; and
  queens, *see* Queens; as spiritual
  mentors, 118–30, 143–50; and kings,
  118–19, 123–4, 151–2
Boniface circle, 32, 188; correspondence
  of, 8, 12, 50, 113–14, 130–4, 137–50,
  229, 257, 291; *see also* Boniface
Breguswith, mother of Hild, 253–4, 256
Brendan, *Life of*, 135
Bride price, 3 fn. 4, 40, 58 fn. 49, 63
Brides of Christ, 12, 82–109, 177, 245,
  273, 292
Brie, *see* Faremoutiers
Brynhild, 167
Caesarius of Arles, *Rule* of, 91
Canterbury, school, 78, 266, 267
Canticles, 49, 101, 142–3, 212, 239,
  292–3
Carlisle, 86, 95
Cassian, 79

Cáin Adamnáin, see Adomnan
Cædmon, 126, 169, 184, 247–50, 261, 262–4, 265, 267, 269
Cecilia, 71, 73
Celtic church, 15, 18, 23, 53, 110, 125, 129–30, 135, 164, 166, 181, 197, 239–41, 250, 255, 265–7, 291
Cena, see Women, monastic
Censwith, see Women, monastic
Cenhelm, *Life* of, 217
Ceolfrith, 144, 265; *Life* of, 183
Charlemagne, 73, 216, 268; Leoba and, 181; wives, see Queens, Hildegard; Luitgard; kinswomen, see Alcuin, Correspondence
Charm, OE, for a Swarm of Bees, 85
Chelles, 255, 258–61
Chertsey, 110
Christ I, 6
Christina of Markyate, *Life* of, 45, 195
Chrétien, 76
Coldingham, 257, 262; in *HE*, 94, 101–2, 111, 189, 195, 198, 245; in *Life of Wilfrid*, 170, 172, 262; see also Abbesses, Æbbe
Columba, see Adomnan, *Life* of
Columban, 135–6
Confessors, 66–7, 71, 115–50, 185–7; women as, 113, 130–7, 147–8, 179–85, 254
Consanguinity, 16, 20, 27–33, 37–8, 46, 137, 150, 233
Constantina, 109
Constantine, Emperor, 92, 222; see also Helena
Cookham, 213
Coquet, 196, 199–202
Cross, Finding of; see Helena
Cudda of Lindisfarne, 176
Cummean, *Penitential* of, 52 fn. 24
Cwen, title of, 235
Cynewulf, see *Elene*, *Juliana*
Deaconesses, 137
Dialogue of Egbert, 120
Double Monasteries, 5, 11–13, 42–3, 75–81; 93–6, 101–7, 109–12, 114, 119, 134–7, 139, 147–8, 162–4, 189, 217, 242–70, 271–82; 291–3, 299–300; see also Abbesses, ministry and contribution
Dream of the Rood, 159, 175
Dryhthelm, 83; and wife, 61, 65 fn. 79
Eadgisl, priest, 102

Ealhswith, Alfred's wife, see Queens
Ecgberht, in *Life of Guthlac*, 294
Ecgburg, see Women, monastic
Eddic lays, 168, 173, 192 see also Guthrun
Eddius Stephanus, *Life of Wilfrid*, 12, 13, 16–17, 69–71, 95, 100, 103, 117–18, 151, 165–78, 179–85, 226, 229–30, 252, 253, 254–5, 287, 290–2
Edward of New Minister, 45
Egbert of York, in *Song of York*, 142; see also Bede, Letter to
Egbert, Dialogue of, see *Dialogue of Egbert*
Eigil, *Life of Sturm*, 284–8
Elene, 91–2, 99, 145, 219; see also Helena
Ely, 68, 69, 73, 93, 225, 245, 258–60, 269
Encomium Emmae, see Queens, Emma
Eoda, 22
Eosterwine, 130
Eustochium, 109
Eve, 6, 9–11, 36, 100–1, 156–9, 165, 167, 175, 194, 202, 204–7, 212, 230, 273; see also *Genesis B*
Faremoutiers, 96, 134–5, 245; Æthelthryth's kin at, 247, 258–61
Felix, *Life of Guthlac*, 40, 121–4, 132, 133, 135, 136, 143, 185, 190, 267, 290–5, 297
Finnian, *Penitential* of, 52–3, 60
Finnsburg, Lay of, 224
Fortunatus, and Radegund, 76, 142, fn. 121
Franks, 222, 237
Frauendienst, 168, 296
Freawaru, 156, 229
Frisian sailor's wife, see *Maxims*
Gawain and the Green Knight, 161
Geatish woman, 192
Genesis B, 101, 157, 190–1, 202, 207
Germania, 85, 90, 101, 103–4, 153, 190
Gilbertine foundations, 300
Gisla, see Women, monastic
Glanvill's Laws, 50
Glastonbury, 113, 131, 213, 272
Goscelin, 71 fn. 101, 250; *Life of Edith*, see Abbesses
Gregory the Great, 105, 239, 267; and the English mission; 17–19, 21, 55, 124–5, 241, 248; *Dialogues*, 260, 284–5, 289–90; *Libellus Responsionum*,

11, 16, 20–22, 24–8, 30, 31–6, 42, 46, 50, 95, 103, 106, 107, 147; *Moralia*, 17, 77, 79; *Regula Pastoralis*, 17–18, 99, 123–5, 147–8; Letters: to Bertha, 92, 222–3, 225, 227; to Brunhild, 222; see also Whitby, *Life* of
Gregory II, III, see Popes
Grendel's mother, 87, 91, 160, 168–9, 247
Guenevere, 161, 276
Gunnarr, 195
Guthlac, 121–4, 185, 290–5, 297
Guthlac B, 157
Guthrun, 158–9, 191–2; Lays of, 91, 168, 173
Habakkuk, see Bede, Commentary on
Hackness, 257
Hadrian, 22, 72
Hartlepool, 78, 252, 255, 256, 262
Hávamál, 116, 133, 191
Hæsten, 86
Heidenheim, 274
Helena, Empress, Mother of Constantine, 92, 219, 222, 225; Finding of the True Cross, OE legends, 92
Hereberht, and Cuthbert, 186–7
Herefrith of Lindisfarne, 188, 251
Hertford, Council, 46–7, 52, 53, 56, 59, 60, 62, 69
Hewalds, 16
Hexham, 201
Hildeburg, 156, 192, 224
Hildegyth, 92, 101
Hildmer's wife, 128
History of the Abbots, see Bede
Hodoeporicon, Hygeburg's, 145, 274, 290
Homilies: *De Inventione Sanctae Crucis*, 92; On Judith, 92
Hrabanus Maurus, 271, 288, 300
Hrothgar, 152, 154, 155, 191–2, 195, 247, 292
Husband's Message, 49, 153
Hygd, 154, 192
Hygeburg (Huneberc), see Women, monastic
Icelandic literature, 49, 86, 87, 158; see also *Hávamál*; Guthrun
Individualism, 11, 33–4, 84, 100, 145–8, 240–1
Ingeld, 81
Institutes of Polity, 108
Ita, St, 135

Iona, 196, 256
Iseult, 186
Jerome, 127
Jezebel, 167, 169
John, the disciple, 103, 110, 164, 234, 291; gospel of, 76
Jonas, *Life* of Fara, 96
Judith: OT, 87, 98, 105; Ælfric's Homily, 92
Judith, 87, 91
Juliana, 91–2, 97
Judgement Day II, 115, 173
Justinian, 111
Kenelm, see Cenhelm
Kinship, 10–11, 29, 38–40, 42, 113–15, 137–46, 160–2, 227–32, 234–41, 255–6, 277–8, 290–5; see also Consanguinity
Kings:
   Aldfrith, 81, 169–70, and Ælffled, 179–85, 275
   Alfred, 1, 11, 24, 44, 159, 214–16, 218, 219, 235, 273; Laws of, 64 fn. 74, 65 fn. 78, 96; wife of, see Queens, Ealhswith; daughter of, see Æthelfled, Lady of the Mercians; sister of, see Queens, Æthelswith; see also Asser, *Life* of
   Alhfrith, 123, 151, 229, 240, 297
   Alhred, 213
   Anna, daughters of, 68
   Æthelbald, *Life of Guthlac*, 123–4, 132, 190; Boniface Letter to, 97, 139
   Æthelberht of Kent, 222, 234, 237; conversion of, 17–19, 23, 222–3; Laws, 54, 62–5
   Æthelberht, Martyr, *Life* of, 217
   Æthelheard, 213
   Æthelred, 194; woman in the charter of, 87; mother of, see Queens, Ælfthryth
   Æthelred of Northumbria, 98
   Æthelred of Mercia, 160, 213
   Æthelwulf, 215–18, 235
   Brihtric, 152, 206, 235
   Burgred, 218, 235
   Cædwalla, 90, 144
   Centwine, 163, 247
   Cenwealh, 62, 229
   Cenwulf, 217
   Ceolred, 139
   Ceolwulf, and *HE*, 17, 19

Kings *cont.*
Clovis, 222
Cnut, 193, 276; Laws of, 58, 63 fn.
    67, 64 fn. 75, 65 fn. 78
Eadbald, 19, 220
Eadberht, 152
Ecgberht, 235
Ecgfrith, 160, 197–8, 201, 229, 257;
    see also Jurmenburg, Æthelthryth,
    Ælffled, Æbbe
Eadric and Hlothere, Laws of, 54
Edgar, 118, 177, 194, 208–9, 298
Edmund, Martyr, 73, 249
Edward the Confessor, 7, 35, 182,
    209, 210, 215, 218, 220; *Life* of, *see*
    Queens, Edith
Edward, Martyr, *Passio*, 194
Edward of Wessex, 236
Edwin, 17, 90, 165, 220–4, 227–8,
    232–4, 237, 240–1, 256
Eorpwold, 234
Harold Godwinson, 182, 193–4
Hlothere, 229; Laws of, 54
Ine, 81, 87, 146, 213, 231; Laws, 64
Malcolm, 218
Merewalh, 225
Offa, 41, 152, 213, 216–17, 218, 235
Oswald, 162, 207, 214, 225, 236–7,
    245, 256
Oswine, 129, 151, 195, 265
Oswiu, 18, 19, 68, 84, 86, 117, 129,
    168, 179, 189, 199, 213, 226, 227,
    228, 236, 237, 239, 240, 241, 251,
    255, 256, 257
Peada, 19, 227–30, 234, 236; wife of,
    see Queens, Alhfled
Penda, 62, 86, 90, 225, 228, 229, 236
Redwald, 17, 232–4; wife of, *see*
    Queens
Sebbi, 72, 96, 115, 176; wife of, *see*
    Queens
Sigeberht, 40, 151, 196, 227
Wihtred, 212–3; Laws of, 54–5
Wulfhere, 225, 227
Kings, conversion of, 16–19, 220–42
Lady of the Mercians, *see* Æthelfled
Lancelot, 276
Laws, OE, 7, 11, 24, 57–8, 62–5, 80,
    104, 108
Learning, *see* Women, education
Leviticus, 20, 22
Libellus Responsionum, *see* Gregory the
    Great

Lindisfarne, Anonymous *Life of
    Cuthbert*, 251; Bede's revision of:
    Cuthbert, 120–3; his relations with
    Hildmer's wife, Censwith and Æbbe,
    127–9, 189; with Ælffled, 179, 185–6,
    187–90, 191, 199–207, 251–2; with
    village woman, 205–6; with
    Hereberht, 186–7
Lindisfarne, 98, 102, 117, 151, 168, 169,
    176, 187, 200, 202–7, 214, 226, 251
Lindsey, 162, 207
Lombards, 16
Lyminge, 217
Mago, 272, 299–300
Malory, *Morte Darthur*, 276
Margery Kempe, 65
Marriage, 46–74; regulation of, 11–12,
    37–8, 40–2, 46–8, 50–65, 68–9 (*see
    also* Consanguinity); in *Life of
    Columba*, 65–7; in Æthelthryth's Life,
    67–74; as metaphor, 10–11, 36–8,
    40–1, 47–8, 50; and virginity in *De
    Virginitate*, 80–1, 83–4, 107–8; and
    warrior vows, 48–50, 85–6, 93; OE
    agreements, 237; *see also* Royal
    marriage
Martyrology, OE, 71 fn. 101, 249, 253–4,
    261–2; Aldhelm's, 109–10
Mary, 6, 9, 109–12, 156; as mother, 174,
    177; virgin, 173–4; Heavenly Queen,
    177, 209, 212, 231; abbesses and, 110,
    164–5, 172–5, 183–4, 188–9, 206,
    263, 281–2, 290–7; Pega and, 188,
    292–5; queens and, 118, 174–5, 193,
    209–12, 216, 218–19, 220, 231–2,
    276, 298–9; Benedictine reform and,
    177–8, 231; double monasteries and,
    103, 109–10, 164; church
    dedications, 111 fn. 175, 172–3;
    Wilfrid's cult of, 172–5, 220; in *Law
    of Adomnan*, 88–9, 110, 174; *De
    Virginitate*, 83, 109–10, 174
Mathilda, Empress, 87
Maugin, in *Life of Columba*, 188
Maxims, 48, 99, 100, 167, 240–1; Frisian
    sailor's wife, 64, 144; queen, 153–4,
    156, 160, 168, 191, 209, 211, 229,
    241
Melrose, prior, 187; nuns, 257
Mercian Register, 87, 92
Mildrith Legend, 71 fn. 101, 72, 174 fn.
    110, 259 fn. 82, 259–60
Ministry of believers, 131–3

Minster-in-Sheppey, 225, 259–60
Minster-in-Thanet, 72, 217, 260
Monte Cassino, 274
Moralia, *see* Gregory the Great
Much Wenlock, monk's vision, 79, 139
Nidd, synod, 169–70, 173, 179–81, 185
Norman conquest, 2, 4, 7, 35, 210
Norns, 91, 159
Old English Martyrology, *see* Martyrology
Oswald, Lives of, 194, 298
Patrick, *Canons Attributed to*, 52, 58, 60
Paul, St, 8, 37, 46–8, 52, 57, 80, 82, 83, 91, 98, 99, 107–8, 147, 269
Peaceweaving, 153–61, 230–2, 238–41
Peada, wife of, *see* Queens, Alhfled
Pega, in *Life of Guthlac*, 188, 292–5, 297
Penitentials, 115; attributed to Bede, 22; English, 38, 53, 54, 57, 64, 69 fn. 95; *see also* Pseudo-Ecgbert; *Dialogue of Egbert*; Irish, 39, 40, 52–3; *see also* Patrick; Finnian; Cummean; *Theodore's Penitential*
Peter, the disciple, 226, 239, 291
Peter's mother-in-law, miracles, 157, 171, 205 fn. 119
Pilgrimage, women and, 34, 40, 132, 139, 140, 144–50, 183, 184, 245
Poetry; Old English, 5–6, 9, 33–4, 240; *see also Battle of Maldon*; *Beowulf*; *Christ I*; *Dream of the Rood*; *Elene*; *Genesis B*; *Guthlac B*; *Husband's Message*; *Judith*; *Juliana*; *Judgement Day II*; *Maxims*; *Seafarer*; *Solomon and Saturn*; *Waldere*; *Wanderer*; *Widsith*; *Wife's Lament*; *Wulf and Eadwacer*; Charm; Riddles
Popes, Letters to queens, 220–7; Correspondence of Boniface with, 27–33
    Agatho, 201
    Boniface, Letter to Æthelburg, 220–1, 222–5, 227, 228, 232, 239, 240
    Gregory II, III, 27–31
    Vitalian, 22; and Eanfled, 226
    Zacharias, 30–1, 137, 163
Pseudo-Ecgbert, *Penitential* of, 164
Pseudo-Egbert, *Confessional*, 57, 73
Psychomachia, 91
Queens:
    Alhfled, Peada's wife, 227–30, 236
    Ælfthryth, 177, 208–9, 298; mother of Æthelred, 194

Æthelburg, Ine's wife, 87, 213
Æthelburg of Kent, 90, 165; Pope's Letter to, 220–1, 222–3, 233; Marriage to Edwin, 223, 225, 234, 237, 239, 240; and Paulinus, 224; William of Malmesbury and, 231–2
Æthelburg, Wihtred's wife, 213
Æthelswith, Alfred's sister, 218
Æthelthryth, 225; in *HE*, 12, 65, 67–74, 81, 166, 174–5, 220, 225, 229, 245, 247–8, 253, 256, 258–61, 264, 269, 282; *Theodore's Penitential* and, 68–9; *Life of Wilfrid*, 69–71, 165–6, 175–7; Ælfric's *Life*, 73–4; Alcuin and, 73, 225; *see also* Abbesses
Balthild, 169, 175, 176
Bertha, 92, 222–3, 225, 226–7, 237
Brunhild, 222
Clothild, 222
Cyneburg of Mercia, 228, 229
Cynegyth, Wihtred's wife, 213
Cynethryth, Offa's wife, 41, 213, 216–18
Cynewise of Mercia, 86
Eadburg of Wessex, Offa's daughter, 47, 50, 152–3, 158, 159–60, 168, 214–16, 217, 218, 235–6; *see also* Asser
Ealhswith, Alfred's wife, 152, 213, 235
Eanfled, 227; in *HE*, 176, 213–14, 226, 227, 228–30, 233, 237, 239–41, 256; *Life of Wilfrid*, 117–18, 151, 168–9, 175–6, 179, 214, 220, 226, 229–30, 237–8; *see also* Abbesses
Edith, Confessor's wife, 99, 152, 178, 231; and royal marriage, 209–12, 246–7; advice, 117–19, 210, 219; prophecy, 193; succession, 182, 193–4
Emma, *Encomium* of, 89–90, 92, 154, 211, 220, 231, 276; and succession, 193, 246–7
Eormenhild of Kent, 225
Fridogitha, Æthelheard's wife, 213
Hildegard, Charlemagne's wife, 297–9
Judith, Æthelwulf's wife, 215
Jurmenburg, 68, 95; in *Life of Wilfrid*, 70, 99, 100–1, 156, 165, 167–70, 172, 175–8, 229, 232–3, 255; *Life of Cuthbert*, Anon, 86, Bede's

Queens *cont.*
    revision, 90, 198–9; *see also*
        Abbesses
    Luitgard, Charlemagne's wife, 298
    Mathilda, Empress, 87
    Mathilda, Henry I's wife, 218,
    Margaret, Turgot's Life of, 218–19
    Osgifu, Alhred's wife, 213
    Osthryth, 160, 162, 167, 207, 214,
        225, 230–1, 236–7, 245
    Peada's wife, *see* Alhfled
    Redwald's wife, in *HE*, 17, 176, 177,
        220, 232–4
    Seaxburg, 225, 269; *see also* Abbesses
    Sebbi's wife, 61, 72, 96, 233
    Sussex, queen of, and Wilfrid, 225
    Werburg, Wihtred's wife, 213
Queens, 151–78, 208–42; and abbesses,
    177–8, 297–9; and bishops, 151–62,
    165–9, 174–8, 194–5, 207; *see also*
    Royal marriage; Asser; *Beowulf*;
    Maxims
Ragnarok, 159
Redwald's wife, *see* Queens
Regula Pastoralis, *see* Gregory the Great
Regularis Concordia, 118, 177, 208–9,
    214, 275, 298
Riddles, OE, 101
Ripon, 173
Riquier, Chronicle of, 210
Rodtruda, *see* Abbesses
Romances, 173, 178, 186, 219, 276
Royal marriage, 117–18, 152–62, 298–9;
    as *signum*, 208–20, 231; and
    conversion, 220–34; as alliance,
    234–42; theology of, 223–4, 227–8,
    238–9; Æthelthryth, 65–74; *see also*
    Marriage
Royal charters, 212–14, 219
Rudolph, *Life of Leoba*, 13, 107, 134,
    243–5, 246, 256, 259, 268, 271–86,
    288–91, 295–300
Saints Lives, female authorship of, *see*
    Women, education and learning
Sanctity, in Bede and Whitby *Life of
    Gregory*, 120–30, 187–9; female, 12,
    67–74, 109, 127, 246–53, 260, 264,
    274–5, 281–2, 297
Scholastica, and Benedict, 284, 289, 293
Seafarer, 139
Sebbi's wife, *see* Queens
Sermon on the Mount, 16

Sexuality, female, 11, 21–2, 24–6, 35–7,
    41–2, 98, 100–6, 114, 137, 139–40,
    142–3, 149–50, 156, 272–3, 282; *see
    also* Adultery
Sheppey, *see* Minster-in-Sheppey
Simeon of Durham, 102
Soissons, Council, 149–50
Soldiers of Christ, 82–98, 103, 149, 177,
    210–11, 219, 264, 273, 282
Solomon and Saturn, prose, 23, 115
Song of York, *see* Alcuin
Soul friends, 13–14, 116 fn. 13, 123,
    185–8, 197, 199, 202, 289–300
Sturm, Eigil's *Life of*, 273, 284–8
Suttee, 80
Tacitus, *see Germania*
Tatberht, 164, 172, 188, 292
Thanet, *see* Minster-in-Thanet
Theodore's Penitential, 5, 8, 10, 11, 12,
    22–3, 46–8, 51–65, 121, 134, 177;
    'Rite of Women,' 135–7, 163–5, 203,
    207, 254; and consanguinity, 27–8,
    32; and women, 5, 8, 10, 35–6, 50–62,
    65, 233–4; and Æthelthryth, 67–9,
    73; and monastic widows, 80–1; and
    double monasteries, 93, 103, 111, 273
Thryth, 145, 154, 158, 168
Tristan, 186
Turgot, *Life of Margaret*, 218–19, 231
Valkyrie, 85, 91, 159
Virginity, 274, 282; *De Virginitate*, 12,
    57, 80–1, 83–4, 99, 103, 105–10;
    Æthelthryth and, 65–74, 247–50;
    Mary and, 173–5; Ælffled and, 181
    fn. 12, 199, 251–2, 255
Vows: warrior, 48–50, 85–6, and
    monastic friendships, 186, 283–4,
    287–8; widows', 60, 69, 80, 108
War, women and, 84–91; *see also*
    Peaceweaving
Waldere, 92, 101
Wanderer, 115–17, 139
Wealhtheow, 93, 101, 153–6, 160–1,
    178, 191–3
Wearmouth, 130, 200, 265, 266, 270
Wenlock, *see* Much Wenlock
Whitby, 12, 78, 125–7, 135–6, 179,
    183–4, 246, 248–9, 251–2, 264–7,
    279, 280–1; Trumwine at, 119, 129,
    197; *Life of Gregory*, 12, 125–7, 129,
    233, 248, 265, 270; lost *Life of Hild*,
    126, 248, 254, 259; synod, 15, 19,

125, 180, 226, 239–41, 255, 261, 267; see also Cædmon; Abbesses, Ælffled; Eanfled; Hild

Whore of Babylon, 99, 157

Widsith, 152

Wife's Lament, 49–50

Widows, and formerly married monastic women, 12, 56–61, 66–74, 80–2, 84, 106, 108, 110, 139–40, 174 fn. 110, 192, 247–8, 255–6, 260; see also Vows

Wihtberht of Glastonbury, 113, 131, 272

Wihtberht, mission to the Frisians, 15

William of Malmesbury; and Edith of Wilton, 35; and AS queens, 194 fn. 84, 231–2, 234, 240

Willibald, Life of Boniface, 284–8, 290, 295–6

Wilton, 34, 143, 209–10

Wimbourne, 72, 78, 81, 114, 134, 245, 271–5, 277, 282, 283, 299

Winchcombe, 217

Winileodas, 142

Wives: Dryhthelm's, 61, 65 fn. 79; Hildmer's, 128; for wives of Peada, Redwald, Sebbi, etc., see Queens

Women, education and learning of, 12–13, 42–5, 75–83, 106–7, 243–4, 251, 256–70, 271–2, 274, 278–80, 286; letters by, 139–49; saints Lives,

female authorship of, 12–13, 250, 259–60, 270 fn. 137, 272, 274, 281, 299; Hygeburg's Hodoeporicon, 145, 274, 290

Women, monastic:
Agatha, Bischofsheim nun, 282

Angildruth, dedicatee of Eigil's Life of Sturm, 286

Berhtgyth, Correspondence of, 142–3

Cena, Letter to Boniface, 141–2

Censwith, foster-mother of Cuthbert, 129, 189, 199

Ecgburg, Letter to Boniface, 40, 138, 140–3, 145

Gisla, Correspondence with Alcuin, 76

Hadamout, dedicatee of Life of Leoba, 271, 274, 276

Hygeburg, Hodoeporicon, 145, 274, 290

Maugin, in Life of Columba, 188

Pega, and her brother in Life of Guthlac, 188, 292–5, 297

Thecla, missionary nun, 281

Withburg, Ecgburg's sister, AS nun in Rome, 145, 149

Wulf and Eadwacer, 49, 144, 300

Würzburg, Archbishop, 285

Wynnebald of Heidenheim, 274

Lightning Source UK Ltd.
Milton Keynes UK
UKOW01n2207080917

308835UK00003B/229/P